An Improbable War

An Improbable War

*The Outbreak of World War I and
European Political Culture before 1914*

Edited By
Holger Afflerbach
&
David Stevenson

Berghahn Books
New York • Oxford

Published in 2007 by
Berghahn Books
www.berghahnbooks.com

©2007, 2012 Holger Afflerbach and David Stevenson
First paperback edition published in 2012

All rights reserved.
Except for the quotation of short passages
for the purposes of criticism and review, no part of this book
may be reproduced in any form or by any means, electronic or
mechanical, including photocopying, recording, or any information
storage and retrieval system now known or to be invented,
without written permission of the publisher.

Library of Congress Cataloging-in-Publication Data
An improbable war : the outbreak of World War I and European political culture before 1914 / edited by Holger Afflerbach and David Stevenson.
   p. cm.
   Revisions of papers from a conference held Oct. 2004 at Emory University in Atlanta.
   Includes bibliographical references and index.
   ISBN: 978-1-84545-275-9 (hbk.)—ISBN: 978-0-85745-310-5 (pbk.)
   1. World War, 1914–1918—Causes—Congresses. 2. Europe—Politics and government—1871–1918—Congresses. I. Afflerbach, Holger. II. Stevenson, D. (David), 1954–.

D511.I46 2007
940.3′11—dc22   20070007090

British Library Cataloguing in Publication Data
A catalogue record for this book is available from the British Library

Printed in the United States on acid-free paper

ISBN 978-0-85745-310-5 (paperback) ISBN 978-0-85745-596-3 (ebook)

Contents

List of Maps	viii
List of Illustrations	viii
List of Tables	viii
Acknowledgements	xi
Foreword	xii
President Jimmy Carter: A Century of War and Peace	
Introduction	1

Part I: European Statescraft and the Question of War and Peace before 1914

Chapter 1
Stealing Horses to Great Applause: Austria-Hungary's Decision in 1914 in Systemic Perspective   17
Paul W. Schroeder

Chapter 2
Did Norms Matter in Nineteenth-Century International Relations? Progress and Decline in the "Culture of Peace" before World War I   43
Matthias Schulz

Chapter 3
Aggressive and Defensive Aims of Political Elites? Austro-Hungarian Policy in 1914   61
Samuel R. Williamson, Jr.

Chapter 4
The Curious Case of the Kaiser's Disappearing War Guilt: Wilhelm II in July 1914   75
John C. G. Röhl

PART II: THE MILITARY SITUATION BEFORE 1914:
EUROPE BETWEEN HOT AND COLD WAR

CHAPTER 5
Chances and Limits of Armament Control 1898–1914   95
    Jost Dülffer

CHAPTER 6
Was a Peaceful Outcome Thinkable? The Naval Race before 1914   113
    Michael Epkenhans

CHAPTER 7
Was a Peaceful Outcome Thinkable? The European Land Armaments
    Race before 1914   130
    David Stevenson

CHAPTER 8
The German and Austro-Hungarian General Staffs and their Reflections
    on an "Impossible" War   149
    Günther Kronenbitter

PART III: HOPES AND FEARS OF WAR AND PEACE: SUBJECTIVE EXPECTATIONS
AND UNSPOKEN ASSUMPTIONS IN EUROPEAN SOCIETIES BEFORE 1914

CHAPTER 9
The Topos of Improbable War in Europe before 1914   161
    Holger Afflerbach

CHAPTER 10
Unfought Wars: The Effect of Détente before World War I   183
    Friedrich Kießling

CHAPTER 11
"War Enthusiasm?" Public Opinion and the Outbreak of War in 1914   200
    Roger Chickering

CHAPTER 12
Education for War, Peace, and Patriotism in Russia on the Eve of
    World War I   213
    Joshua A. Sanborn

PART IV: CULTURE, GENDER, RELIGIOSITY, AND THE COMING OF WAR

CHAPTER 13
Honor, Gender, and Power: The Politics of Satisfaction in Pre-War Europe   233
    Ute Frevert

CHAPTER 14
International Solidarity in European and North American Protestantism
    before 1914 and after   256
    Hartmut Lehmann

CHAPTER 15
International Relations, Arts, and Culture before 1914   271
    Jessica C. E. Gienow-Hecht

PART V: THE PERSPECTIVE FROM AFAR: THE OUTBREAK OF WAR IN EUROPE
          IN THE EYES OF OTHER CONTINENTS

CHAPTER 16
War as the Savior? Hopes for War and Peace in Ottoman Politics
    before 1914   287
    Mustafa Aksakal

CHAPTER 17
The View from Japan: War and Peace in Europe around 1914   303
    Frederick R. Dickinson

CHAPTER 18
War, Peace, and Commerce: The American Reaction to the Outbreak of
    World War I in Europe   320
    Fraser J. Harbutt

Contributors   335

Selected Bibliography   341

Index of Names   361

LIST OF FIGURES

List of Maps

Map 1.1: The European Powers on 4 August 1914   13
Map 3.1: The Balkans, 1912–1914   63

List of Illustrations

Frontispiece: Alfred Kubin: Alfred Kubin, *Die Kriegsfackel*, 1914,
   Oberösterreichisches Landesmuseum, Linz. © SESAM, Paris, 1998.   ii
Illustration 4.1: Prince Heinrich in Sussex, 26 July 1914   85
Illustration 4.2: Wilhelm II.   89
Illustration 5.1: Punch, 30 May 1896   97
Illustration 6.1: Der Wahre Jakob, 22 June 1909   115
Illustration 11.1: Max Beckmann: *Der Kriegsausbruch*, 1914, Radierung,
   19,8 × 24,8 cm. © SESAM, Paris, 1998.   202
Illustration 16.1: Punch, 4 December 1912   289
Illustration 17.1: Nihon oyobi Nihonjin [Japan and the Japanese],
   15 September 1914, 154   310

List of Tables

Table 6.1 Naval expenditure of the European Powers, 1900–13   127
Table 6.2, 6.3 Cumulative *Dreadnought* Battleship and Battle Cruiser
   Starts: Britain, Germany, and the United States, 1905–14   127–128
Table 7.1 Real Defense Burden (Defense Expenditure/Net National
   Product), 1900–1913   131
Table 7.2 Naval Expenditure of the European Powers, 1900–13   131
Table 7.3 Army Expenditure of the European Powers, 1900–13   132
Table 7.4 Peacetime Effectives of the European Powers, 1904–13   132

Acknowledgements

The book is the outcome of a conference held on the ninetieth anniversary of World War I at Emory University in Atlanta in October 2004. It comprises a carefully revised selection of the contributions made on that occasion. The conference was conceived and organized by Holger Afflerbach, while this volume has been edited and revised through the efforts of Afflerbach and David Stevenson. It is for us not only a duty, but also a great pleasure to thank all the persons and institutions whose help and generosity made the conference and this volume possible.

First, we wish to thank the Graduate School of Arts and Sciences and the History Department of Emory University, who hosted and generously sponsored the conference and the volume. We are also deeply indebted to the DAAD (German Academic Exchange Service), who contributed significant financial support for this conference. We express our gratitude also toward the German, British, French, and Austrian travel funds (DFG, Imperial Fund, the French General Consulate in Atlanta, and Österreichischer Forschungsförderungsfonds) for financing a portion of the airfare for our participants.

We are also thankful to the persons whose substantial support helped us to realize this project. These include Virginia Shadron and Elizabeth Gallu from the Emory Graduate School of Arts and Sciences; Professor James Van Hoorn Melton, Chair (2004), and Rosalyn Page, Office Manager, and many other members of the Emory History Department for their friendliness and continuous support. Chad Fulwider, Joe Renouard, and Nathan Vigil, graduate students in the Department of History at Emory University, helped us with the organization of the conference and to ensure that events ran smoothly. Chad and Joe were also an invaluable help in the editing process. Chad invested much of his time and energy to serve as copyeditor for the volume. Later Holly Jones proofread the entire manuscript. We owe them each our gratitude.

We thank also Dr. Michael Nentwich, Director of the Goethe Institut Atlanta, for his hospitality, as well as for his practical help and sound advice. Professor Roy Bridge read the entire manuscript and made helpful comments on style and contributions. Finally, we thank our publisher, Marion Berghahn, for her friendliness and her professional support.

Holger Afflerbach and David Stevenson

Foreword

A CENTURY OF WAR AND PEACE

Jimmy Carter

The first Nobel Prize for Peace was awarded in 1901, but the century that followed could not be characterized by peace. The explanation for why those pursuing peace did not prevail is explored in this book. It focuses on the origins and causes of the first great war of the century. My own reflections on World War I will focus more on its significance and aftermath. It continues to affect the world, my nation, and me personally.

I was born in 1924, soon after the end of World War I. My father had served as a first lieutenant during the war. I remember as I was growing up in Plains, Georgia, that a number of the men around me were incapacitated and on veterans' pay because they had been afflicted with poison gas on the European battlefields. Luckily, my father was not wounded. Later, after I joined the Navy, I served under perhaps the most famous American World War I veteran, Harry Truman, my commander-in-chief. He made a great, but modest display of his experience in that devastating war.

War has been a very prevalent part of the life and times of people of my generation and those that followed. There has been a close interrelationship between my family and war. I pray that my grandchildren will not have to say the same about their own lives. In my own life, I decided to become a professional military officer during the depression years. Nobody in my father's family had ever had the opportunity to attend college or even to complete their high school education. I aspired to a college where my expenses would be covered. One possibility was West Point, the other was Annapolis. Although my father had been in the Army, my favorite uncle was in the Navy and I chose that branch, serving for eleven years.

This included my college years in the Naval ROTC at Georgia Tech and at the Naval Academy, and my tours on two different battleships and three different submarines. I served during World War II and then the Korean War.

When the Vietnam War began, my oldest son Jack was a student at Georgia Tech. He was exempt from the draft, but he felt it was unfair for the poor and less fortunate to be drafted and sent to Vietnam while he and others were deferred. He volunteered himself and went to Vietnam, serving for three years. In recent years, my immediate family has not served in the military, but there have certainly been plenty of opportunities for other Americans to serve. Since I left the White House, the United States has launched military attacks resulting in anywhere from a few to tens of thousands of deaths in Honduras, Macedonia, Albania, Libya, Nicaragua, Lebanon, Sudan, Grenada, Panama, Kuwait, Somalia, Yugoslavia, Bosnia, Haiti, Croatia, Afghanistan, and Iraq. War remains a prevalent aspect of our lives.

Through my work at The Carter Center, I have been involved in both active and potential military conflicts. In 1994, I became especially involved in conflict resolution efforts. In June of that year, I went to North Korea as a second Korean war was threatening. It was very likely then that if severe sanctions were imposed on the North Korean government and their leader, Kim Il Sung, North Korea would attack South Korea. This was a common belief of both the Chinese, who came to see me, and of the US military commander in Korea, General Gary Luck. In September, when the United States had some twenty thousand troops marshaled to invade Haiti, I visited that country with then-retired General Colin Powell and Georgia Senator Sam Nunn to try, successfully, to prevent military conflict. At the end of that same year, I went to Sarajevo in Bosnia to try to bring reconciliation among the ethnic groups of that country. While there, I visited the site where in June 1914, the Archduke Franz Ferdinand and his wife were assassinated by a nineteen-year-old Bosnian Serb—the event that generated World War I.

Many years later there is still an ongoing debate as to whether the war was an inevitable result of imperialistic powers building up an excessively competitive attitude toward one another or whether it was a tragic comedy of errors that resulted from the assassination of Archduke Franz Ferdinand and his wife. Perhaps the problem was the excessively-binding treaty system that tied the superpowers of those days together, so that when one did enter the war, others were brought into the war as a result of their treaty obligations. The essays in this volume will suggest potential reasons for the beginning of this war, which George Kennan described as the "seminal catastrophe" of the twentieth century.

Nowadays, the ordinary American doesn't hear nearly as much about World War I as when I was a child or even when I was a young officer in the Navy. World War I was a devastating conflict that resulted in approximately 8.6 million deaths on the battlefield. The United States entered late, but we lost over 115,000 soldiers, more than we would lose in Korea and Vietnam combined. For roughly forty-three years before 1914, there had been no major wars in Europe. World War I resulted in the collapse of four major empires: the German Empire, the Austro-Hungarian

Empire, the Russian Empire, and the Ottoman Empire. The Treaty of Versailles, orchestrated by the victors, imposed what many scholars and historians consider to have been oppressive restraints and humiliation upon Germany, which may have resulted in the rise of Hitler and caused, at least indirectly, World War II.

In Russia, the Tsar was overthrown, and the Bolshevik Revolution resulted in the rise of the Soviet Union and communism. When I was president, the Soviet Union presented the major threat to my country and, perhaps, to world peace. For four years I faced the possibility of a third World War caused by the launching of nuclear weaponry either from the Soviet Union or perhaps inadvertently from the United States. Just one nuclear missile submarine over which I had command, with its multiple warheads, could have destroyed every city in the entire Soviet Union with a population of more than 100,000. The Soviets had similar capabilities with which to destroy us. I was constantly concerned about what action I would take if I were notified that the Soviets had launched a nuclear weapon. From their launching sites, the flight time was only twenty-six minutes. I would have had only twenty-six minutes to answer the following: should I let my country be totally destroyed without response or would I destroy the U.S.S.R. in retaliation? I doubt that any leader on earth has ever been confronted with a more serious question than I, my predecessors, and my successors.

All this was a legacy of World War I. So too were the national arrangements in the Near East. The arbitrary division of the Near East or the Middle East, which fell after 1918 into the hands of the French and the British, resulted in the drawing of national boundaries that were quite artificial in nature and has precipitated much of the violence that we still see there today. Iraq is one example of the serious problems caused by these decisions. The disposition of Palestine is another.

In 1962, President John F. Kennedy is said to have told members of his cabinet to read *The Guns of August* by Barbara Tuchman, so they would be better informed about the history of World War I in order to avoid another such disaster in the future. It helped to shape Kennedy's actions that year when nuclear-armed missiles were detected in and on the way to Cuba from the Soviet Union. The Cuban Missile crisis was an event that could very easily have deteriorated into a nuclear confrontation and a nuclear exchange of a massive scale between the United States and the Soviet Union. In 1973, under Richard Nixon, the United States was faced with the escalation of an Arab-Israeli War. Egypt and Syria, supplied by the Soviets, had inflicted serious damage to the Israeli military, but Israel, supplied by the U.S., had counterattacked on both fronts, crossing the Suez Canal and advancing to the road to Damascus. The Soviet Union threatened direct military intervention on behalf of the Arabs. This was the only time in history that nuclear forces on both the Soviet and US sides were put on the highest alert. Had Israel not stopped its advance under pressure from Washington, there could very well have been a nuclear exchange. Later, during my presidency, the Soviets invaded Afghanistan, which I saw as another test of the US-Soviet relationship. We did not resort to nuclear weapons, but there was still a threat to peace in the world. These kinds of events, circumstances, confrontations, or crises that all presidents and world leaders have experienced, have resulted from World War I—not indirectly, but, I think, almost directly.

However, there were also positive developments from the war. The League of Nations was proposed by Woodrow Wilson, and he consequently received the Nobel Peace Prize. Unfortunately, the League did not receive adequate support. Out of World War II came the United Nations, which was a breath of fresh air, hope, and expectation in 1945. Nevertheless, challenges to the integrity, influence, and the authority of the United Nations still exist. Still today, the threat of conflagration is always present.

I continue to be troubled and disturbed by the attractiveness of war. My own belief is that there were strong forces in Europe before 1914 that were prepared for a war. Certain leaders saw war as a way to exert their political influence and perhaps territorial expansion. They thought they could go to war with impunity and win without the danger of loss. We still have that situation. This is a unique time in history in that there is one unchallenged superpower on earth, the United States of America. Our military capability now is at least equal to the combined military of all the other nations in the world. We have the feeling of invulnerability. There is no other nation that can possible challenge us militarily, seemingly giving us a free hand to exert our military strength whenever and wherever we choose. Almost without fear of retaliation, we interceded in former Yugoslavia, relying on high-level aerial bombing and the launching of missiles from a distance. Our pilots and our Navy personnel stayed out of danger. We do not know how many Serbs were killed in those attacks; maybe a few tens of thousands of people died. We could have destroyed Iraq without invading forces as well. On 9/11, however, we learned that the United States is not invulnerable.

There is a great economic advantage to a country that can prevail militarily. There is no question that if we do succeed in Iraq, which is still doubtful, we can control Iraq's oil wells and, to some degree, its political situation. From there we can extend our own hegemony to other places. War can be popular. The unquestioned change in status of a beleaguered president, from a prime minister dealing with budgets, welfare, taxation, and environmental questions, into the commander-in-chief of military forces is a supreme change. It results in a totally predictable and inordinate popularity because it becomes almost improper to criticize a government that professes to be at war. The threat and dangers of conflict and its enticements now perhaps even equal what was extant during the weeks following the assassination of the archduke.

I hope that this collection of essays, as it assesses the causes and the potential retrospective prevention of World War I, can be very helpful in the modern day. We now have an ongoing debate about war in the United States. So far as I know, in the last more than two centuries, we have never had a government that espoused preventive war or preemptive war. Now it is a matter of some macho pride to maintain that the United States, with its superior position on earth, has a right and a duty to take military action. I can go down a list of fifteen or more countries in which we have been involved in military actions quite often with total impunity. So what is the proper role of a superpower in our times? Of a superpower, which is dominant not only militarily, but politically, economically, socially, and culturally? I hope that one of the characteristics of our nation in the future will be to avoid war and to use our tremendous information and strength for peace—not just peace for ourselves, but peace for others as well. I would like to see leaders of countries around the world who are threatened with civil war to naturally think, "Why don't we go to Washington? That's a repository of a deep commitment to peace. We know that America espouses peace and thinks of war as a last resort." I hope we will see that in the future, a superpower has a potential for promoting its own moral and ethical political standards of freedom and democracy. It would be nice if whenever a democracy is in danger, their first thought would be: "Let's go to Washington." I would wish for the same reaction when faced with challenges regarding the environment, basic human rights or civil rights, personal freedoms, or suffering. Those are the characteristics that should be derived from superpower status.

At the beginning of the century, I was invited to make a couple of speeches in Asia and Oslo, Norway. My subject was: "What is the greatest challenge that the world faces in this new millennium?" My decision was to identify the growing chasm between the rich and the poor people on earth. I think that it is indisputable that the chasm is increasingly divisive and is engendering among the poorest and most destitute, forgotten, and ignored peoples on earth a sense of neglect, resentment, and animosity. It may even provide a breeding ground for terrorism among those most susceptible to influence.

My hope is that from this book, one can learn some lessons on how to avoid a future catastrophe. War is a past as well as a present danger. We have to be alert. Because now, with nuclear weaponry at the world's disposal, a death rate of one million or even ten million would be only the beginning.

Introduction

AN IMPROBABLE WAR?
The Outbreak of World War I and European Political Culture Before 1914

Holger Afflerbach and David Stevenson

"Being doubtful is more fruitful than being sure." Ernst von Salomon's aphorism is highly applicable to this volume. It focuses on the balance between underlying and immediate reasons for the outbreak of World War I in the summer of 1914. The essays united here address the fundamental question of whether that war represented a logical—not to say predictable and even inevitable—response to political conditions in Europe before 1914 or rather, constituted a reaction against and a break with them.

It is not our intention here to re-analyze the political decision-making process in 1914. This has been done extensively, minute by minute: Luigi Albertini's three-volume analysis of the July Crisis is still unsurpassed.[1] Modern essay collections, such as those edited by Keith Wilson[2] or by Richard Hamilton and Holger Herwig,[3] provide good summaries of the decision-making process within each national capital. The formidable bulk of publications on this topic has already been surveyed in excellent historiographical overviews.[4] Nor has it been our intention to write a balanced overall synthesis of the literature on the July crisis, such as the classic account by James Joll.[5]

Instead, our volume focuses on a single, but crucial, issue: the degree of probability and inevitability in the outbreak of the conflict. Our contributors—most of whom originally presented papers on the same topic in October of 2004 at a conference organized by Holger Afflerbach at Emory University—were asked to analyze the potential for peace in pre-1914 societies. They investigated whether the international system was so beset by competing nationalisms and imperialisms that armed conflict was 'inevitable' and the Sarajevo assassinations were merely the last straw. Or was this system in fact less pernicious than its posthumous reputation has suggested? Perhaps, in contrast, only the contingent and eminently avoidable mistakes and misperceptions of a very small number of decision makers triggered an unnecessary, anachronistic, and yet devastating catastrophe. This question is fundamental for an evaluation of European culture in the period. To understand World War I as the result of a series of serious professional mistakes by a comparatively small group of diplomats, politicians, and military leaders is profoundly different in its implications from an interpretation of the war as the automatic outcome of the mindset of the European "generation of 1914."[6]

The underlying intention of this volume is to argue in favor of a significant change in historical perspective. To make our intention clear, we present the notion of Europe's enthusiasm for the war as an example. It was a common suggestion among many writers until the early 1990s that Europeans, in the summer of 1914, were filled with suicidal enthusiasm for the incipient conflict. However, Jean-Jacques Becker started to question this assumption in his book on France in 1914,[7] and new research over the last decade has successfully challenged this view. Presently, cutting edge investigation suggests that public opinion in the belligerent countries was highly differentiated by region and by social class.[8] The simple idea of universal European war enthusiasm is no longer tenable.

This book seeks to provoke a corresponding reappraisal of how European "political culture" before 1914 dealt with the question of war and peace. We understand that the theoretical implications of this topic are immense, but we limit ourselves to a brief description of our central interests. The term "political culture" seems broad and vague, and this, to an extent, is unavoidable in the face of the complex phenomena we are dealing with. We have a certain focus on high politics and strategy, because it is evident that the final decisions were made in this realm. Yet although our question is essentially, in our understanding, a political one, we seek to define politics in a broad sense and to investigate its cultural roots. We focus not only on the political and military leaderships, but also more widely and comparatively. And by invoking "culture" we refer not only to "high culture" in the classic meaning of the term, but also to the "mindset" of contemporaries. Our concern is with an ensemble of conventions, interests, customs, expectations, unspoken assumptions, hopes, and fears diffused among the millions of people who shaped the fundamental and distinctive characteristics of the political environment. To this end, our contributors' fields of enquiry include not only the organization and culture of individual states, such as Germany, Austria-Hungary, or Russia, but also pan-European themes such as the roles of honor, gender, religion, and the arts.[9]

We cannot cover every aspect of each society, and we do not claim to be so comprehensive. Nonetheless, we have sought not to lean in the direction of our own assumptions, but to give scholars of varying opinions the opportunity to expound their views. In this volume, eighteen contributors from six countries draw on their fields of special expertise in order to grapple with these issues. The list of authors includes both established historians and rising young researchers. This volume, like the conference that preceded it, has been organized specifically to highlight contrasting opinions and yet also to look for common ground from which we may draw conclusions accepted by all. Despite the diversity of interpretations, each essay is related—in their different ways—to the volume's central theme.

One contributor should be mentioned before all others. We are honored that former US President Jimmy Carter has supplied the foreword. The Nobel Peace Prize winner presents his own, very personal thoughts on the topic, "A Century of War and Peace." Jimmy Carter reflects on the ways in which World War I affected his life and that of his family, the history of his country and, finally, his own policies during his presidency.

The first essay is by Paul Schroeder, Professor Emeritus of History at the University of Illinois, Champaign-Urbana, whose magnum opus, *The Transformation of European Politics*,[10] has been acclaimed as a milestone in the historiography of international relations. He contends that World War I was ultimately the outcome of changes in the unwritten "rules," or norms, of the international system. The ever increasing brutality of those rules placed enormous pressure on some members of the international community, robbed them of breathing space, and ultimately forced them into suicidal action. According to Schroeder, Austria-Hungary might eventually have become a perpetrator, but it was also a victim.[11] His provocative essay challenges scholarly orthodoxy regarding the decisions made in Vienna and seeks to turn conventional wisdom on its head. In contrast with the "improbability" approach, which forms the central theme of this volume, he suggests that war was essentially unavoidable by 1914. Even those who dissent from his conclusions must concede that Schroeder offers a forceful and well-constructed argument full of insights, as well as a powerful indictment of a degenerating international system.

In his chapter, Matthias Schulz counters some of Schroeder's arguments while agreeing with others.[12] Schulz provides an innovative examination of European congressional diplomacy between 1815 and 1914. He contends that even at the end of this period, adequate peace-keeping mechanisms existed, and that the Austro-Serbian crisis could have been resolved by a conference or by a multilateral peace-keeping effort, instead of by forceful and unilateral Austrian action with German support. Schulz blames the powers (and especially Germany) for rejecting any kind of multilateralism, and for doing so more emphatically as 1914 approached. In this respect, his analysis conforms with Paul Schroeder's: as the international system lost its ethical foundation, war became more probable. But on one major point the two disagree: Schroeder sees in Austria-Hungary the great victim of the international system, whereas Schulz characterizes the Habsburg monarchy, from a statistical analysis of the incidence of crises, as the leading fomenter of instability in Europe.

Vienna is also the focus of the contribution by Samuel Williamson.[13] Here we see yet a further viewpoint on the July crisis and on the Habsburg Monarchy's role. Williamson, the leading US expert on Austria-Hungary, analyzes its decision-making process during 1914. While Schroeder and Schulz agree that changes in the underlying ethos of international politics made the Great War probable, Williamson's case study of the Habsburg political elite shows that they had not resolved the question of war against Serbia before the Sarajevo assassinations, and that they had other political priorities. Thus Sarajevo really was the decisive moment: without the murder of Francis Ferdinand and his wife, there would have been no decision for war in Vienna, and therefore no general conflict, notwithstanding the previous history of acute and recurrent Austro-Serb tension. Also crucial for the debate on war guilt (and at odds with Schulz's emphasis) is Williamson's denial that German pressure was decisive: the Habsburg leaders made their own decisions. Williamson's contribution can be understood as a strong argument in favor of the improbability thesis, or at least, against any conclusion that war was inevitable. And yet he also warns the reader, in the light of our contemporary global situation, not to think that our contemporary politicians are wiser than the Austrian government in 1914.

This volume reflects recent trends in historical scholarship by awarding Austria-Hungary due prominence. Naturally, however, the decisions made in Berlin and the public mood in Germany are not neglected. John Röhl, the leading international expert on Wilhelm II, provides a powerful analysis of the German Emperor's political line and his personal goals and responsibility during the July crisis, drawing on some startling new evidence.[14] In a forceful contribution, he argues a case that he has developed through decades of research. Röhl does not accept the "improbability" thesis, which is irrelevant to his own view of how the war began, and even contradicts it. He believes that the German leaders deliberately started the war and traces the roots of the conflict to the German political system and the personality of the German ruler, whom he indicts for his duplicity and recklessness.

The second section of the book deals with military developments in Europe before 1914. Here we expected to find some of the strongest arguments against the improbability thesis.

Jost Dülffer discusses the two Hague peace conferences and their attempts to limit the level of armaments and to outlaw the use of certain weapons. He concludes that these attempts could not change the overriding course of events. Alternatives to the existing European balance-of-power system, with its adjustment mechanisms of arms build-ups and deterrence, had no chance of making headway in an era when every state was keen on keeping control over its own sovereignty, including the right to configure its armed forces in the light of its own strategic planning and perceived security needs. Hence, although the Hague conferences had some successes, their importance was marginal. Nonetheless, they initiated an ongoing process, and a third conference was envisaged for 1915. Had war not intervened, the momentum in favor of arms control and international arbitration might have developed further.

The failure of any agreement for international arms limitation left an open field for armaments competition both at sea and on land. Did the arms race make war probable or inevitable? Two essays are devoted to this question. Michael Epkenhans analyses the Anglo-German naval race, showing how Admiral Alfred von Tirpitz, Secretary of State of the Imperial German Naval Office, overcame all internal resistance to his fleet-building program. Unquestionably, the naval rivalry poisoned Anglo-German relations. Yet on the other hand, Epkenhans contends that by 1914, the most acute phase of the naval race was over, and that the British had won it, not least because Tirpitz and the German navy had run out of money. Although the naval rivalry contributed to the deterioration of the international situation, and especially to Germany's place within it, it did not in itself trigger the outbreak of war.

Similarly, in his discussion of the land armaments race David Stevenson confronts directly the question of whether or not the world war was improbable. He argues that land armaments competition indeed destabilized European international relations, but that the leaders of the powers could have found peaceful solutions to their security predicaments. Earlier arms races had ended without hostilities and the pre-1914 race, although a critical danger to European peace, might have evolved into a non-violent confrontation or "cold" war. Stevenson's "approach goes some way towards meeting the improbability thesis, although with reservations."[15]

The essay by Günther Kronenbitter investigates the war planning of Helmuth von Moltke the Younger and Franz Conrad von Hötzendorf, the Chiefs of the German and Austrian General Staffs. Both men agreed that the impact of a large-scale continental war would have devastating repercussions on European civilization for decades. They also recognized the unpredictability of such a conflict's outcome. Yet precisely because they were trapped by their understanding of national and personal duty, they prepared for a war which they thought would inevitably be a disaster for Europe and their countries. Admittedly, Kronenbitter concludes that neither Moltke nor Conrad had the final say in the question of war and peace; they alone could not start hostilities. Nonetheless, their narrow understanding of military security subjected European peace to an enormous structural burden. The upshot of this section can be summarized as follows: although developments in armaments policy and in strategic planning did serve to endanger peace, they did not so destabilize the international order as to make war unavoidable.

The next group of essays is dedicated to the question of contemporary expectations and "unspoken assumptions." Holger Afflerbach addresses the central theme of the volume by analyzing the expectations about war current among the Europeans of 1914.[16] His basic contention is that if contemporaries had really believed war to be unavoidable, then everyone would have expected after Sarajevo that events would lead quickly to the outbreak of hostilities. But in fact the opposite was true. Afflerbach draws on a vast quantity of sources to show that contemporaries did not believe that a great war was probable and they were completely surprised by its outbreak. The notion that nobody would risk such a devastating catastrophe was all the more widely accepted because of the highly-developed system of deterrence of the day. For that reason Afflerbach denies that European societies—including Germany—expected a cataclysm, despite what important and influential historians such as Wolfgang J. Mommsen, Eric Hobsbawm, and many others have claimed.[17] Afflerbach also discusses the various military leaders who notoriously dreamed of a great European war out of self-indulgent motives, but he suggests that even they believed that such a war was both improbable and liable to be immensely destructive. However, the danger in this situation was that some statesmen were so confident that a great war was impossible that they planned their actions without the necessary caution. The war was, according to Afflerbach, "improbable," because it went against the tides of that time. The actual outbreak of war was even a consequence of misplaced confidence that peace was secure. Here we see a link between the improbability thesis and the onset of hostilities.

Friedrich Kießling pursues a similar line of argument in his analysis of policy makers' conduct during the diplomatic crises of the years leading up to 1914.[18] He insists that in trying to explain the war's origins it is a mistake to focus only on those factors which seemingly led to an escalation of international tensions. He looks instead at efforts to achieve détente and de-escalation in political conflict. Paradoxically, this policy of seeking détente may have been too successful, leading to miscalculations by some of Europe's leading statesmen in the July crisis. Because compromise had been achieved in previous crises and war had repeatedly been averted, the assumption may have been that in 1914, too, conflict could be avoided. The mindset of "improbable war," identified by Afflerbach, or the dangerous faith in détente, posited by Kießling, made key decision makers perilously insouciant. For both Afflerbach and Kießling, the outbreak of war in Europe was a consequence of carelessness caused by overconfidence; comparable to the complacency of the crew of the *Titanic*, who failed to reduce their speed at the moment of danger.

Regarding the long running debate over European "war enthusiasm," Roger Chickering analyzes the popular mood in the summer of 1914, focusing his attention on the middle-sized German town of Freiburg im Breisgau.[19] His essay combines a general survey of the public opinion literature with an interesting case study. He comments, "It would in all events overtax the evidence from the street to conclude that their enthusiasm reflected long-standing or deep-seated popular attitudes about the probability or desirability of war."[20] And he adds further: "The dramatic scenes of the summer of 1914 ought to be understood in the light of their own political and cultural dynamics. They should not be taken as evidence that an inveterate German war enthusiasm made war probable or inevitable."[21] Hence Chickering's contribution also weakens the hypothesis that World War I was unavoidable.

The next essay deals with developments in Russia, again with reference to the question of whether the political culture in this country made the Great War probable or not. The "cultures" of war and peace underlying the political discourses in the Russian society of the day are investigated by Joshua A. Sanborn.[22] His complex argument shows how difficult it is to find clear and simple trends in prewar societies. Sanborn discusses the evidence for growing popular patriotism and militarism in pre-1914 Russia, as in other European countries. Examples include the celebration of the Franco-Russian alliance, government-led centenary commemorations, the abolition of schoolteachers' exemption from conscription, changes to the school curriculum, and the creation of new patriotic societies. On the other hand, he also demonstrates the reservations felt about these developments on the part of pacifists and of authoritarian conservatives, including Nicholas II. Yet he concludes that a particular form of patriotism—a deep concern for Russia's "Great-Power status"—was decisive in hardening policy in the July Crisis and impelled decision makers to opt for a war that no one regarded with enthusiasm and was widely considered to be highly inopportune. On balance, therefore, the developments discussed by Sanborn do not support the "improbability thesis," though his interpretation is a nuanced one and can be read in more than one way.

The essays in the next section turn toward the question of the roles that culture, religion, and gender played in international relations before 1914, as well as to the topic of internationalism and its influence on the question of European peace. Ute Frevert shows in her essay that a gender-related understanding of "honor" in European societies had a distinctive influence on the events of summer 1914.[23] She does not claim that the concepts of honor and the gender roles of the time made war inevitable, but concludes: "This manly posture made attempts to peacefully solve the crisis extremely difficult."

Hartmut Lehmann examines pacifism in the Protestant churches and their inability to act in international solidarity at the critical moment.[24] They were surprised, as was everybody else; they had thought, "our best times lay in front of us,"[25] and had believed in a better future without war. Here we see a link with Jost Dülffer's contribution: Protestant pacifists, like the promoters of disarmament, were too weak to transform the existing political system of balance of power and military deterrence.

Jessica Gienow-Hecht discusses international cultural relations before 1914, taking transatlantic cultural exchanges as an example.[26] She concludes that such exchanges operated in a kind of parallel world; no political catastrophe was foreseen by those engaged in them, and for that reason after 1918 international cultural relations could be resumed with relative ease.

The art milieu, as well as the religious pacifists described by Hartmut Lehmann, did not foresee and did not believe in the possibility of a great armed conflict. Gienow-Hecht concludes about her field of expertise, the relations between art and war: "Whatever politicians may negotiate or say, whatever military leaders may plan, whatever our newspapers report, many believed, art leads a life on its own. While cultural nationalism had been a theme in the nineteenth century and while the two decades prior to World War I witnessed intensive debates around the creation of an American music, there were no signs for cultural pessimism or any hint of the coming catastrophe."[27] Similar observations can be made about the world of finance and industry.[28]

The essays in this section show a reality full of ambiguities: on the one hand, optimism and confidence in the future among evangelical Protestants and among artists; on the other hand, a gender-related and deeply traditional understanding of male honor, which inhibited compromise in times of crisis.

The last three chapters describe the view from afar. Ottoman Turkish politics and their view on Europe are analyzed in the paper by Mustafa Aksakal.[29] He draws on newspapers, political statements, and other publications in order to demonstrate that the Ottoman leaders (not unlike the Austrian ones) felt they were victims of the international system. They actually hoped for war in order to be saved from their difficulties. From their perspective, a *local* war was not only probable, but also desirable. The Young Turks dreamed of a war of liberation and independence, taking the German war of 1870–71 as an example, and they were eager to secure German help for it. Aksakal emphasizes strongly that such a war of liberation was viewed as necessary not only by "hawks" such as Enver Pasha, but throughout the Empire's political elite. Their ultimate goal was to stabilize, with German help, Turkey's international position and to halt its secular decline. This was, at least, the attitude in July and August 1914, when the decisive alliance with Germany was concluded. It should be stressed that Aksakal's essay concentrates on the Turkish perspective, and does not focus on the question of whether *a general* European war was considered probable or improbable before 1914. In fact his evidence suggests that the government in Constantinople neither envisaged nor predicted such a conflict, although when this event occurred it perceived it as a great opportunity.

Fred Dickinson analyzes the reaction in Japan to the war in Europe.[30] His essay shows the surprise felt in Japan when hostilities broke out, as well as the working of a mechanism that we can observe also in post-1918 historiography: the world war was unexpected, but once it had broken out it was with hindsight deemed to have been inevitable. Japanese newspapers and political commentators looked for explanations and found them in the materialistic European culture, in the instability of the balance of power (which they considered to be a unique political phenomenon and characteristically European), and finally by conceiving of the war as a racial struggle. In addition to these general explanations, however,

Japanese commentators tended to see Germany as being primarily responsible for the catastrophe. To these interesting reflections, Dickinson adds another consideration that would be of great importance later in the twentieth century. He identifies a Japanese culture of profiting from turbulence in Europe in order to make opportunistic gains in East Asia: a tendency that the World War I experience reinforced.

Fraser Harbutt examines another perspective from afar: that from the United States. Americans were generally shocked and surprised by the outbreak of conflict. It seemed to them an act of European suicide, which they had not previously considered to be possible or probable. But this perspective quickly changed, and Harbutt highlights the struggle between morality and commercial interest that was central in shaping US public opinion toward the war.[31] Developments during the first few months had already made it likely that American neutrality would be pro-Allied and that the U.S. would eventually intervene against Germany. Nonetheless, American commercial expansion—like Japan's opportunism in Asia—represented a second-stage reaction to the European cataclysm. The initial reaction is more revealing for the general question treated in this volume: in neither country was a great European war expected and in both it came as a total surprise. The view from afar demonstrates again that many contemporary observers both inside and outside Europe did not foresee the conflict and that they considered it a highly improbable event.

How can we summarize the conclusions of this volume? It offers a broad spectrum of viewpoints. Each author acknowledges that the international system before 1914 was endangered by several developments, prominent among which were armaments competition and a single-minded military understanding of national security. But how do they answer our main question: whether such developments made the outbreak of a general war the most likely outcome? On this issue we see differences in interpretation that are difficult to hide. Schroeder and Röhl think that war was probable, not to say unavoidable: Schroeder points to an international system corrupted by imperialism; Röhl to an incompetent and bellicose German government. Frevert underlines the role of gender-related honor in pre-1914 European societies, which made political compromise difficult. Dülffer and Lehmann demonstrate the limited importance of disarmament initiatives and international pacifism, although this did not mean that the existing system, despite its flaws, had to perish in a world war. However, other contributors underline the openness and ambiguity of the pre-war situation. They dwell on the one hand on the danger to peace from developments such as imperialist rivalries and the armaments race, but on the other they also highlight the factors working for peace, such as the widespread aversion from a suicidal great war. They see serious dangers in the situation (albeit disagreeing about the gravity of those dangers), but they deny any kind of inevitability. The essays by Epkenhans and Stevenson fall into this category. Other authors focus on the elites and their decision making in the summer of 1914, in other words, on serious professional mistakes by diplomats and military leaders that led to an eminently avoidable catastrophe. This is the view, for example, of Williamson, who argues that the war was the result of Sarajevo; that without the assassination nothing would have happened because Austria-Hungary's political designs were not directed toward a war of aggression. Afflerbach contends that the international system was far from ideal, but the war ran against the tide of the times, and that pro-war tendencies and international tensions before 1914 have been grossly overestimated in order to explain the catastrophe by "deeper causes" instead of by poor crisis management in the weeks after Sarajevo. Kießling goes in a similar direction. War was possible, of course, but improbable. Furthermore, the essays widen the scope of the debate by broadening out from the usual analysis of the decisions in Berlin and examining the view from centers such as Constantinople and St. Petersburg, as well as invoking cultural factors. Thus, Aksakal focuses on the Turkish leaders' desire for a war, but not for a world war, which lay outside the scope of their ambitions, while Sanborn gives an evaluation of Russian political culture as making more than one outcome possible. That this disastrous conclusion to the era was not the automatic and inevitable result either of European political developments or of underlying trends in European culture, is also underlined by Jessica Gienow-Hecht, as well as by the essays on the "view from afar" by Dickinson and Harbutt.

While most editors of a collected volume would hope for a certain uniformity among the individual contributions, here such uniformity has been attainable only to a certain extent. It is questionable, though, whether complete consensus is really desirable. Unanimity can spell the death of a historical debate. However, it is unlikely that the outbreak of World War I, one of the most complex and influential political events in history, about which tens of thousands of books have been published, will ever be the subject of a simple, unifying interpretation.

Nevertheless, we hope that we can show a tendency, a train of thought, which suggests that World War I marked an abrupt departure from previous trends in European political culture, not their continuation or automatic outcome. Historians who declare, after the event, that World War I (or any other war) was inevitable, and build into any prehistory of a war the path of inevitability, repeat the same mistake, which was called already in 1914 a "monstrous proposition,"[32] over and over again. If this train of thought is persuasive, important revisions of received accounts are needed in order to represent pre-war developments more accurately and to nuance the impression of ever intensifying European great-power antagonisms. In the words of a pre-1914 French schoolbook, "War is not probable, but it is possible."[33]

If World War I was simply the product of intense and irrational nationalist hatreds, the story would be straightforward. Yet if it was not the culmination of deep-seated trends, the message for our own time is more disturbing. Our circumstances are different, but Samuel Williamson warns that our solutions to our current security dilemmas are not necessarily wiser or superior to those favored a century ago. As President Carter warns, the improbable—even if the majority do not want it—can nonetheless occur.

This volume shows—as did the conference that preceded it—that as we near the centenary of World War I, fresh approaches can still stimulate dialogue even about enduring historiographical controversies. We hope the volume will reflect and recapture the atmosphere of lively discussion at the conference and that it will contribute to the ongoing debate on this great seminal catastrophe of the twentieth century.

Notes

1. Luigi Albertini, *The Origins of the War of 1914*, 3 vols., translated and edited by Isabella M.Massey, (London/New York/Toronto, 1952–1957); see also the new edition: Enigma Books, 2005, with a foreword by Samuel Williamson.
2. Keith Wilson, ed., *Decisions for War, 1914* (London, 1995).
3. Richard F. Hamilton and Holger H. Herwig, eds., *The Origins of World War I* (Cambridge, 2003).
4. Keith Wilson, *Forging the Collective Memory: Government and International Historians through Two World Wars* (Providence and Oxford, 1996); Annika Mombauer, *The Origins of the First World War: Controversies and Consensus* (London, 2002); John W. Langdon, *July 1914: the Long Debate, 1918–1990* (New York and Oxford, 1991).
5. James Joll, *The Origins of the First World War*, 2nd ed., (London, 1992.), third edition, revised by Gordon Martel, forthcoming.
6. Robert Wohl, *The Generation of 1914* (Cambridge, MS, 1979).
7. Jean-Jacques Becker, *1914. Comment les Français sont entrés dans la guerre* (Paris, 1977).
8. On this topic, see the contribution of Roger Chickering (chapter 11) in this volume.
9. For a similar pragmatic understanding of the term "culture" see John Keegan, *A History of Warfare* (London, 1993). The title of the German translation of this book is: *Die Kultur des Krieges* (Berlin, 1995).
10. Paul Schroeder: *The Transformation of European Politics* (Oxford and New York, 1994).
11. See p. 17–42.
12. See p. 43–60.
13. See p. 64–74.
14. See p. 75–92.
15. See p. 130.
16. See p. 161–182.
17. Ibid., p. 171.
18. See p. 183–199.
19. See p. 200–212.
20. Ibid., p. 210.
21. Ibid., p. 200.
22. See p. 213–229.

23. See p. 233–255.
24. See p. 256–270.
25. Ibid., p. 261.
26. See p. 271–283.
27. See p. 272.
28. Boris Barth, *Die deutsche Hochfinanz und die Imperialismen: Banken und Aussenpolitik vor 1914* (Stuttgart, 1995).
29. See p. 287–302.
30. See p. 309–319.
31. See p. 320–334.
32. John C. Trautwine, Jr., a civil engineer in Philadelphia, in an open letter from 11 November 1914 to Bethmann Hollweg, in: PA/AA, R 34295. We thank Chad Fulwider for drawing our attention to this quotation.
33. Joll, *Origins*, 220.

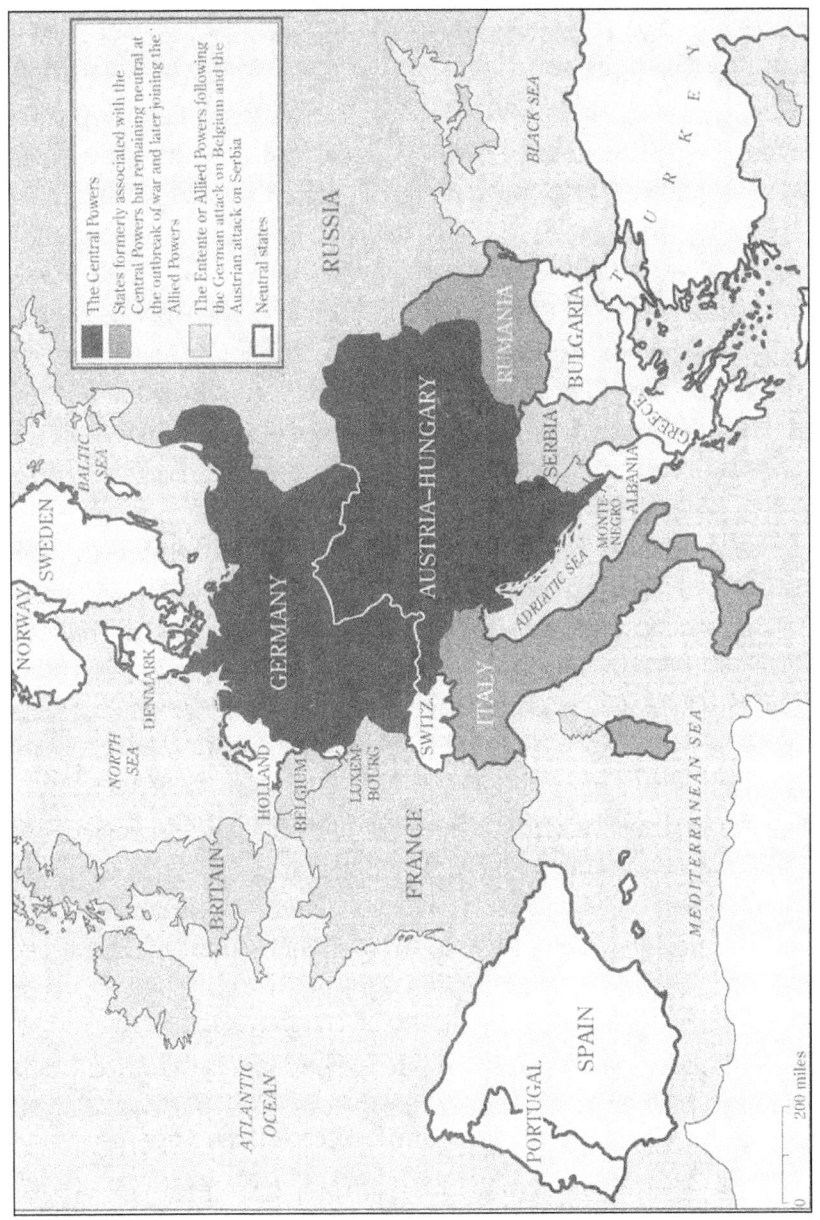

Map I.1: The European Powers on 4 August 1914, from: *Atlas of World War I*, 2/e, by Martin Gilbert, p. 12, Oxford 1994

Part I

European Statescraft and the Question of War and Peace before 1914

Chapter 1

STEALING HORSES TO GREAT APPLAUSE
Austria-Hungary's Decision in 1914 in Systemic Perspective

Paul W. Schroeder

This essay does not present new research or attempt to revise the many recent and earlier accounts of the immediate origins of the war in 1914 and Austria-Hungary's role in it. On these scores, as will be seen, it basically agrees with the reigning view. It instead proposes a reinterpretation of the general causes of the war and the nature of Austria's decision, mainly by using well-known facts from familiar chapters of history, but viewing them and the international system from a different perspective. It therefore emphasizes not what Austria-Hungary did in 1914 and how its actions affected the international system, but rather what happened in the international system in the quarter-century before 1914 and how this affected all the actors, Austria-Hungary in particular.[1] The cryptic reference in the title to stealing horses, as will be seen, applies to the international system rather than to Austria-Hungary.

The reinterpretation must begin with two methodological views or working principles almost universally accepted by international historians. The first is that foreign and domestic policy are inextricably interwoven and interdependent. One cannot analyze the foreign policy of a state or government without factoring in the economic, domestic-political, social, ideological, cultural, and other internal factors that influence it. From these emerge the interests and aims that the government and its leaders seek to protect and advance in its foreign policy. Endorsing this principle does not mean asserting the primacy of domestic politics or subordinating other strategic, military, and diplomatic factors in foreign policy to it, but simply accepting that these elements are interwoven and inseparable. The second working principle is that the central task in international history involves analyzing the foreign policy decision-making process, explaining above all how and why statesmen, governments, and ruling elites made the decisions they did.

These two principles, self-evidently true, seem to apply with particular force to Austria-Hungary before 1914. Nowhere else do domestic conditions, above all the multi national composition of the state and the resultant nationalities conflicts within it, seem more obviously the decisive determinants of foreign policy. In Austria's case, the very distinction between foreign policy and domestic issues and interests proves artificial and unworkable. Every question of domestic politics, constitutional authority, economic interest, and above all national identity turned in some important respect into a foreign policy question directly affecting its security, strategy, alliances, and international prestige. Equally plainly, the question of who actually made and influenced foreign policy decisions in Austria-Hungary and how they did so becomes especially crucial and complicated, given the peculiar constitution of the Dual Monarchy and the way its two autonomous halves worked together, or failed to do so.

Therefore most historians addressing the question, "What led Austria-Hungary to decide and act as it did in 1914?" point to these two areas: the juncture between its foreign policy and its domestic situation, and the workings of its particular foreign policy decision-making process. Most would say that the Austro-Hungarian government decided to act as it did in 1914 because the Monarchy's ruling elite came to believe that the Monarchy's interwoven external and internal problems and challenges, especially those in its South Slav regions and those emanating from Serbia, Rumania, Russia, and Italy, had become unmanageable and intolerable, calling for drastic action to change Austria-Hungary's situation, and that the special nature, composition, and interests of this elite strongly influenced both this conclusion and the choice of a violent rather than peaceful solution.

I agree in general with both this approach and this verdict, so far as they go. Yet these two methods of studying international politics (in this case, Austria-Hungary's decision), i.e., interweaving the interdependent factors of foreign and domestic policy and analyzing the foreign policy decision-making process, important though they are, are not exhaustive or sufficient. The results and conclusions they yield represent at best penultimate truths, and penultimate truths, taken as final, have a way of hiding and obstructing deeper ones, especially in history. A deeper answer to the questions of what caused Austria to choose the policy it did in 1914 and how that choice should be interpreted, I contend, comes not simply from studying Austria's foreign and domestic situation and its decision-making process, vital though this is, but from also looking carefully at the prevailing rules of the European system. When that is done, one sees that in choosing to act as it did, Austria was not breaking those rules or overturning the prevailing system, but finally following it.

So broad an argument obviously has to be presented here in bare-bones fashion, without very much scholarly evidence or detail. It starts therefore with propositions that are widely accepted.

First, Austria-Hungary started the war, deciding in 1914 deliberately to provoke a local war with Serbia, in the knowledge that this risked a general war. Moreover, Vienna, not Berlin, was the main locus of this decision. This latter point is more controversial; many have argued that since Austria could not have acted without Germany and Germany could have stopped Austria but instead after 5 July urged it forward, Germany was therefore the real center of the decision. Furthermore, Germany had its own reasons for wanting at least a major shift in the balance of power and deliberately risking a general war to achieve it. This reasoning is not in the end persuasive, however. Austria made the original decision on its own and demanded rather than requested German support, and did so in the knowledge that Germany by denying it would do unacceptable damage to the alliance and thereby further imperil its own position. The question of German responsibility is really a separate one; the initiative for provoking a local war at the risk of general war came from Vienna and remained there.

Given Austria-Hungary's notorious weakness and vulnerability, this decision in itself seems hard to explain. Other well-known facts make it still stranger. Before 1914, Vienna had repeatedly rejected this course. In the previous decade, it had had numerous opportunities for a local or a general war that in objective military-strategic terms offered much better chances of success. Yet when it took the plunge under unfavorable conditions in 1914, it did so at the urging of some who had actively opposed it earlier.

Austria-Hungary furthermore launched the war with no positive program of war aims. True, no great power government in 1914 had a set of aims for which it was ready or eager to fight, much less deliberately to start a war. Yet they all had given thought to what concrete gains they ought to seek once the Great War that had long been anticipated broke out. Hence, all the other original belligerents, including Serbia, quickly developed concrete war aims programs. So did later entrants—the Ottoman Empire, Italy, Bulgaria, Greece, Rumania, Japan, and China. Even neutral Belgium, brought into the war solely by the German invasion, soon developed extensive plans both for territorial changes in Europe (including claims on the neutral Netherlands going back to 1839) and for colonial gains. Austria-Hungary, however, started the war without such a program, and the program it did develop during the war in regard to Poland and the Balkans was mainly a reaction to military events and Germany's actions rather than a set of concrete aims of its own, intended primarily to preserve Austria-Hungary's status as an independent great power and to avoid becoming a dependent satellite of Germany. The lack of positive war aims is illustrated by the very aim for which it decided on war, eliminating Serbia as a political factor in the Balkans. Even among themselves Austrians could not define precisely what this phrase meant—annexing Serbia, dividing it, reducing it to satellite status, partitioning it with Bulgaria, or something else. The other major objective that other great powers and some lesser ones pursued before and during the war, that of gaining overseas colonies and improving their world position, though present in Austria-Hungary before the war to a lesser degree than in other great powers, almost disappeared once it started.

The obvious reply to these points is that Austria-Hungary's war aim was not to make positive gains, but to eliminate threats. Yet this fact too has remarkable aspects. While opting for war against Serbia, Austria-Hungary neither intended nor expected thereby to eliminate the main military threat it faced, that from Russia, even if the war proved successful. The Monarchy's decision makers, though they did not really expect Russia to accept a local Austro-Serbian war, hoped that Russia would do so and wished, if general war were avoided, to use the crisis to work out a new compromise with Russia over the Balkans and the Ukrainian question.[2] In other words, they expected to continue to have to coexist with Russia as a great power. This differs from the other great powers' expectations. Britain, France, and Russia expected a victorious war to eliminate the main threat to their security by reducing Germany's power, and developed their war plans accordingly. German leaders, at least in their optimistic moments, expected military victory to make Germany dominant on the Continent, ending the threat of encirclement and insecurity. The Russians expected war to end Austria-Hungary's very existence as a major power. Austria, however, did not expect to eliminate Russia as a great power and potential rival. Even the Austrian Chief of Staff Conrad von Hötzendorff, a constant advocate of preventive war, much preferred to target lesser threats, Italy and Serbia, rather than Russia. In opting for a violent solution to their problems, Austrians seem to have accepted the permanence of the Russian threat and hoped to contain it by breaking up the Balkan League, ending the Serbian challenge, restoring Austria's alliance with Rumania, and demonstrating that their alliance with Germany was unbreakable and invincible, so that Russia would go back to their previous mutually restraining relationship, and perhaps even to the old Three-Emperors League.

This unusual Austrian attitude toward its main enemy was more than matched by its strange stance toward its ally Germany, both before and during the war. No other great power was more one-sidedly dependent on its main ally than Austria-Hungary, and none feared that ally as much. While differences, tensions, and suspicions certainly existed among the Entente powers, they did not privately refer to one another, as Austro-Hungarians did to Germany, as "the enemy to the North." No other great power, furthermore, feared as much as Austria-Hungary did that a victory achieved in partnership with this ally might destroy its great power independence as surely as defeat.[3]

Two further facts: first, Austria-Hungary, along with Russia and Italy, had especially powerful reasons to fear that a great war, especially if it were prolonged or unsuccessful, would bring on revolution. Second, Austria more than any other great power had previously endeavored to maintain its position and status and to manage its many international threats and challenges mainly by defending the legal status quo, practicing peaceful diplomacy, seeking international support, and invoking the Concert of Europe to deal with international problems and defend Austrian interests. Provoking even a local war would therefore undermine these international assets and tools and starting a general war would surely destroy them.

Thus, a decision remarkable enough on its face becomes even more baffling on closer examination. The great power with the most to lose and least to gain from war, weaker than any other in terms of its resources in relation to its security needs and challenges, and most inclined by its character, position, and requirements to be conservative, pacific, and risk averse in foreign policy, deliberately started the very war it had been trying to avoid and thus willfully caused its own destruction. It appears, as it has often been described, a case of committing suicide out of fear of death.

A historical comparison may possibly be useful. This was not the first time in the nineteenth century Austria suddenly decided to precipitate a war it had been trying to avoid and thus brought disaster down on its head. One previous instance is obvious. In 1859 Austria, apparently on the point of winning a diplomatic victory in its conflict with Sardinia-Piedmont and Piedmont's ally France, provoked a war by issuing a deliberately unacceptable ultimatum to Sardinia-Piedmont. The result was to isolate Austria, save Sardinia-Piedmont's premier Count Camillo Cavour from defeat and resignation, and bring France, which had seemed about to defect from its alliance, into a war in which Austria was quickly defeated and set on the road to expulsion from Italy. The other instance, less obvious, seems even more suicidal than its decision in 1914. In 1809 Austria decided to go to war with Napoleon and his Empire—this despite the facts that Austria had already suffered disastrous defeat in three previous wars with France, Germany and Italy were wholly in Napoleon's grip, Prussia had recently been crushed and Russia defeated in a war Austria had declined to join, Russia was now Napoleon's ally, and the British, besides being remote from the continental theater, otherwise preoccupied, and unable to help, were basically indifferent to Austria's fate. As a result, Austria suffered another crushing defeat and an even more humiliating peace treaty, and managed to avert the danger that Napoleon would extinguish the dynasty and divide the Austrian empire only at the cost of becoming Napoleon's subservient ally.

This historical comparison seems merely to make the problem of 1914 worse, requiring three apparently inexplicable decisions to be explained instead of one.[4] A historian who looks for common features, however, will quickly find them. Here are some similar attitudes shown by Austria's leaders in the three cases:

1. a perception of an intolerable, growing threat to Austria's great power security and status stemming not from the danger of immediate or direct attack by its enemies, but from the unrelenting pressure of encirclement, isolation, subversion, and exhaustion—death by a thousand cuts;

2. a keen awareness of Austria's internal weaknesses, especially its political, national, financial, and military ones, and a recognition that a war, especially a long war, would heighten the dangers of revolution and the overthrow of the dynasty;

3. a widespread consensus reached on the eve of the decision that Austria's foreign policy in the preceding years, which had been risk averse and directed at avoiding war by conciliation, had not merely failed but had made Austria's position worse;

4. a strong show of resolve by certain political and military leaders, whose optimistic appraisals of Austria's immediate military situation and its chances for success were not accompanied either by adequate military preparations or by clear ideas on how the planned preventive strike and quick victory would produce long-range security and advantages;

5. a similar short-term optimism in regard to the international political constellation—the hope that somehow quick successful action by Austria would break up the opposing alliance or produce allies for itself;

6. finally, a consensus that peaceful remedies were exhausted, leading former opponents of war to join the war party or fall silent.

Yet these parallels, even if they illuminate the background of the decisions and suggest that all three are instances of the familiar strategy of desperate flight forward, do not explain the particular choice in 1914.

Certain inadequate answers have been proffered. One, formerly common and still occasionally encountered, is that it was typical for nineteenth-century Austria to behave thus, reacting too slowly and too late to danger and then plunging ahead in headstrong, obstinate panic. Napoleon said this; Henry Kissinger suggests it.[5] This is not to explain the problem, but to dismiss it. Another answer, earlier alluded to, is that this kind of action is not rare in international politics—many wars arise from attempts by a threatened declining power to reverse its decline through violence. Yet to show that something happens fairly frequently is not to explain why it does, or why the same power should commit the same suicidal blunder three times in a century.

The serious attempts to interpret and explain Austro-Hungarian policy in 1914 divide roughly into two camps, one primarily emphasizing internal factors and motives and the other primarily external ones. To summarize and oversimplify both positions, the first holds that the assassination of Franz Ferdinand coincided with an approaching crisis and breakdown in Austria-Hungary's creaking, semi-paralyzed state machine, and thus served to bring to a climax the spiraling, converging problems that were making the Dual Monarchy progressively more and more ungovernable—the failure of the 1907 electoral reform, the breakdown of parliament in the Austrian half, the necessity of emergency rule, an unsatisfactory turn in a weak economy, the persistent unsolved problem of Austro-Hungarian relations, and above all critical nationalities problems, those with the South Slavs and Rumanians in particular. The decision to provoke a war with Serbia therefore represents a policy of secondary integration and manipulated social imperialism in which a failed, bankrupt leadership and ruling elite sought to save itself, rally its loyal followers, and distract attention from its insoluble internal problems by a flight forward into war. The other view is that the 1914 decision was motivated primarily by traditional foreign policy considerations of security, military strategy, and the determination to remain an independent great power and act as one.

The latter view seems to me more satisfactory. True, Austria-Hungary did face the problems emphasized by the former interpretation and some leaders hoped if it came to war that a successful war would help solve and manage them. Yet these factors, though present, were not decisive in opting for war. The issue is not critical to this essay, however, because the aim is to show that a third reason was more basic than either.

It is interesting that these two lines of explanations (whose differences I have over-sharpened here—there is no reason why they cannot be reconciled) converge tacitly on one point: Austria-Hungary's decision was wrong. Some judge it harshly as driven by class-bound prejudice, arrogance, and a determination to defend entrenched privilege and power. Others are more sympathetic, inclined to see it as a blunder understandable in view of the extreme pressures to which Austria-Hungary was subjected and the narrow choices available to it. Nonetheless, there is considerable agreement that other decisions and options were available, that this decision was a wrong, disastrous one, and that it had horrendous consequences for Austria and Europe. Which of the two labels for Austria-Hungary's decision in 1914, crime or blunder, is more fair and accurate is again not important for this essay, for it argues that the decision in one important sense was neither—that, understood within the context of international history, it was the correct, right decision.

The term "correct" or "right" as used in this context must be carefully defined. It does not mean "morally and legally justifiable." To reach any such conclusion would require delving into legal, philosophical, and ethical issues impossible to deal with here. Nor does "right" here mean "sensible, prudent, representing a rational choice of ends and reasonable correlation of means and ends." One might well argue forcefully that Austria-Hungary's policy was none of these things and point to its results as proof. Yet one could grant this and still contend that Austria-Hungary's decision was right in this respect, that it made a correct, accurate assessment of the nature and direction of the prevailing international system and of Austria-Hungary's position within it, and it recognized that some such course of action as it took in 1914 was the only serious choice left available to it.

This is not the sort of conclusion historians readily embrace. Most, including international historians, are nominalist pragmatic empiricists, suspicious of abstract entities like "the system," fond of historical contingency and averse to any hint of determinism. They work on the reasonable assumption that historical actors face an uncertain, undetermined or under-determined future in which they almost always have alternatives open and real choices to make. The claim therefore that Austria-Hungary did not have viable alternatives in 1914 faces major hurdles both in terms of the facts and evidence needed to back it and in regard to its assault on most historians' working assumptions. To back it up would require two things. The first would be to show that the courses of action proposed as alternative ways by which Austria-Hungary could have met its challenges peacefully, whether these involved internal reforms or a different diplomatic strategy or a combination of both, are at best specious and offered Austria-Hungary no real chance of success, and that its leaders were correct in finally recognizing this. I have tried to defend this position elsewhere and for reasons of time cannot present that case here.[6] The second and more important task, central to this essay, is to show that those who argue for alternative possibilities and courses of action ignore or underrate the international system as a limiting factor and a determinant of outcomes in international politics, and thereby overestimate the possibilities of Austria-Hungary's acting differently and solving or managing its problems largely on its own.

This argument, it must be conceded, cannot be made simply on the basis of objective facts and evidence, but involves certain definitions and assumptions that can at best only be rendered plausible in an essay like this. These are that in international politics the term "system" refers not merely to relationships of power and influence between the actors and the institutions through which power and influence are exerted, but also and importantly to a more intangible set of widely shared assumptions and expectations as to what rules and norms prevail and govern the shared practice of international politics. These "rules of the game" enter significantly into the calculations and decisions leaders and elites make, and constitute an incentives structure by indicating what kind of conduct is likely to have consequences of success or failure, reward, toleration, or punitive sanction. They rest in good part on a political culture always subject to changes, both subtle and violent. Despite an inevitable vagueness and uncertainty, one can detect and define a certain ethos or underlying spirit and code behind them, a governing collective mentality, and note shifts occurring in that reigning ethos, collective mentality, set of reigning assumptions and expectations, and resultant prevailing rules and norms of the game.

This definition of "international system" may be vague and abstract, and I will not try to illustrate it here with historical examples, because the case of Austria-Hungary's decision in 1914 is supposed to do so. But if it is accepted at least provisionally *ex hypothesi*, two further considerations follow. In international politics, domestic factors influence foreign policy decisions, and these decisions aim at certain outcomes, but in an important sense, while actors propose, the system finally disposes, that is, determines the outcomes by limiting the range of options and outcomes possible. That system, moreover, never involves a level playing field with clear rules and an impartial umpire, or a smooth billiard table where the outcome is determined by the mechanical interactions of the balls. The rules are made and changed as the games go on by the players themselves, especially the most powerful and successful ones. The table is thus always rigged. In 1914, I contend, the table was rigged to make Austria-Hungary lose. It was therefore a rational choice, though made too late and executed badly, to attempt something drastic to change the rules and alter the tilt of the table, even at the risk of knocking it over and ending the game.

First a brief statement of how the system was rigged to make Austria lose, followed by an argument to support it. A Spanish proverb says: "Some men steal horses to great applause, while others are hanged for looking over the fence." The proverb can be read as an ironic observation on how unfairly the law, systems of justice, and life in general sometimes work. Here it is offered as an accurate summary of how the European international system actually was working by 1914. Its rules had been so fashioned and bent that certain states could steal horses to great applause while other states were hanged for looking over the fence. This result was not incidental, accidental, or unintended, but regular, structural, and intentional.

The name given to the horse-stealing game was imperialism (or its synonym, "world policy"). The best way briefly to envision the basic difference in the ethos and the attendant rules, norms, and incentives structure of the latter nineteenth century European states system and those of imperialism is to see it as the difference between high-stakes poker played by heavily-armed men out to win but nonetheless aware of conventional limits on their bets and tacitly in agreement on the importance of keeping all essential players in the game, and the board game Monopoly, in which players aim to maximize gains through the elimination of rivals.[7]

The imperialist game, to be sure, had been played for centuries, but in the earlier decades of the pre-war era it remained what it had been most of the previous centuries, a game largely separate from the main game of European international politics, or attached but auxiliary to it. The Anglo-Russian Great Game in Asia and the Anglo-French competition for colonies during much of the nineteenth century illustrate this. They were played chiefly outside Europe, governments were initially less centrally involved in them than individuals, firms, or particular interests, and their stakes were not generally critical in the game of European politics. So long as imperialism remained an ancillary game, it did not destroy or directly undermine the European system and could even help preserve it by offering an outlet for European expansionist energies and material for profitable deals and combinations among various powers. This held true even though the game was always so constituted that some powers could steal more horses than others and some could only stand and look over the fence, since those whose horses were being stolen were non-Europeans and outside the states system.

After 1890, however, this game with its imperialist ethos and rules not only became more ruthlessly competitive and involved higher stakes; it also gradually took over as the main game in European politics itself and increasingly involved stealing horses claimed by other Europeans. This development, emerging clearly about the turn of the century, made the game of European politics more competitive, dangerous, and likely to end in a great war. Even this heightened level of imperialist competition, however, did not of itself necessarily lead to general war. It was in fact sustained for a time without general war, and could have been sustained even longer, simply because of the high barriers holding back a general war between great powers in an age of mass politics, industrialization, major advances in military technology, and huge armies. But the next stage that occurred in the first decade of the twentieth century, partly through natural development and partly by design, heightened the danger by transferring the imperialist game with its special ethos and rules to Europe itself. The contest over imperial prizes abroad was absorbed into, and instrumentalized for, a larger struggle for domination and control of the European system, and with it the world. Even that was not all. From 1907 on, this struggle to control the European balance came to focus, again partly through natural developments and partly by design, on the most explosive part of Europe with its most intractable problems, the Balkan peninsula. It thus targeted Europe's most vulnerable and exposed great power, Austria-Hungary.

This completed the cycle of change in the nature of European politics over several decades. First an imperialist ethos accompanied European politics; then it invaded it and came to pervade it and replace the older one; then the game itself was transferred back to Europe, with control of the European system for security and survival becoming its essential stake; and finally that contest was concentrated on Europe's most dangerous and vulnerable point. This long process, like a poisonous snake circling back upon itself and sinking its fangs into its own tail, made Austria-Hungary's decision in 1914 a rational choice and response to its situation.

This, in brief, is the argument. Much of its particular content is familiar and conventional, but its conclusion is not. One can anticipate certain reactions—that this argument is selective in its use of facts and evidence and unrealistic in its approach to international politics. Moreover, it fails in particular to recognize that European imperialism is as old as the European system and integral to it, that European politics has always been driven by power and interests, not ideals, and that ruthless competition and survival of the fittest rather than normative rules and restraints have always governed it. The argument in addition is moralistic, applying inappropriate moral standards selectively to some actions and certain powers, and biased in favor of Austria and against some other states (Britain, Russia, Serbia).

The less serious charges, those of bias and moralism, can be met quickly. Both strictly speaking are irrelevant—a scholar may be subjectively biased and moralistic (in this case, pro-Habsburg) and still interpret the issues and evidence correctly. In any case, the issue here is not the character of the Habsburg Monarchy, or its alleged historic European mission and whether it was fulfilling or betraying it, or whether it could and should have survived with what results, or any other such questions. The issue here is solely how best to understand the Austro-Hungarian decision in 1914, and whether, as claimed here, this requires above all understanding the prevailing nature and rules of the European system.

As for the charge of moralism, this interpretation does suggest a moral view of the origins of World War I—that it is like a Greek or Shakespearean tragedy. To go beyond that conclusion, to play the blame game further by apportioning blame to particular actors, is useless, distracting, and deceptive, because the game itself was to blame. But this moral judgment also is strictly speaking irrelevant to the question of causation.

A more serious charge is that this account of the changes in international politics and their impact on Austria-Hungary's decision is unrealistic in failing to see that the developments briefly described earlier as perverting and undermining the normal European game and its rules actually represented normal *Realpolitik* and constituted no reason for Austria-Hungary to overthrow the game. The answer, drawing on basic international relations theory, is that the judgment that Austria-Hungary made a correct, rational choice in 1914 under the conditions of the prevailing European system rests theoretically on a conventional realist approach to international politics, which starts with the rational actor model. It assumes that states are the primary actors in international politics, that they can for analytical purposes be considered unitary rational actors, and that they decide and act primarily on the basis of cost-benefit utility analysis. Their calculations therefore must include an appraisal of the incentives or payoff structure of the prevailing international system, and routinely do so. My claim is that over decades the incentives structure of the European international system was so warped by imperialist competition as systematically to reward conduct subversive of stability and peace and to penalize conduct designed to uphold them. I contend further that this process of distortion of the system led to the general crisis situation of 1914 focused on the Balkans and targeting Austria, and that the crisis produced by this process made Austria's decision for preventive war a rational, appropriate one in terms of the prevailing rules and incentives of that system. Such an argument is therefore plainly, in terms of theory, an attempt to describe what happened in strictly realist terms. To refuse to take this factor of the systemic incentives structure into account, instead assuming that the decision must necessarily have been wrong or unjustified because it started a great war with horrendous results and that there must have been a better way for Austria-Hungary to seek its reasonable goals, is to be unrealistic and moralistic.

But theory of course will not get us far; the central question is historical. Did a change in the system such as I have posited occur, or has international politics always been essentially a struggle for power, security, and advantage played with rules and incentives based on a survival of the fittest? The evidence, I hold, shows clearly that until late in the nineteenth century a European system with a different payoff structure prevailed. True, the ethos of the Vienna era and its solidarity order had since the mid century given way to the *Realpolitik* of Napoleon III, Cavour, Bismarck, and others. Yet the system continued on the whole to discourage and penalize attempts to steal horses and to encourage and reward those who stopped at looking over the fence, at least within Europe. Bismarck himself led in restoring and maintaining this system for self-interested reasons. The evidence of this is familiar to historians and too extensive to rehearse—Russia and Britain in 1875 warning Germany off another war with France and France off a war of revenge for Alsace-Lorraine; Bismarck refusing to promise neutrality to Alexander II in a Russo-Austrian war because Germany could not allow either of them to be destroyed; Russia being forced to retreat from its violation of the Budapest Accords in 1878 and Germany trying to build a golden bridge for its retreat; various instances, especially in the Near East, in which ambitious smaller powers willing to start a great fire if they could roast their particular marshmallows in the ashes were controlled. Until about 1890, perhaps somewhat beyond this, the incentives structure of the European system continued to sustain a tolerable level of international relations in which, in general, policies of not stealing horses paid off and vice versa.

The New Imperialism beginning in the early 1870s and escalating thereafter ultimately changed this. In a sense, it was bound to, for imperialism and an international system are intrinsically alien, imperial rule being the logical contradictory of membership in a community of independent, juridically equal units. More important in practical terms was the principle on which New Imperialism came to operate, namely, that those who stole horses deserved to win while those who only looked over the fence deserved to lose out. This principle became an explicit part of international law with the Berlin Congo Conference of 1885, making legal colonial possession a matter of successful theft—finding a territory no other so-called civilized state had taken and appropriating it by effective occupation or the appearance of it.[8]

This had a much greater impact on the ethos of the late nineteenth century system than the imperialism starting in the late fifteenth century, involving major seizures of territory especially in the New World, had had earlier. For most of the fifteenth to the early seventeenth centuries the European system or society of states was only being formed. Not until the early eighteenth century can one detect any serious regulative principle in it (the so-called balance of power); not until the late eighteenth century did the system embrace both western and eastern Europe; even then the rules and norms were almost as rapacious in Europe itself as in the colonial arena. Moreover, only in the late nineteenth century did so many powerful states compete for empire on so broad a scale and in so frantic a manner. Furthermore, an unwritten rule in the Vienna era that lasted into the latter part of the century had erected a certain separation of imperialist activity from European international politics. The imperialist ethos, though applied with drastic effects to lesser breeds without the law, had no great impact on the incentives structure of the European system.

Two developments at the end of the century ended this separation. The first was the virtually universal triumph of the belief that the survival and prosperity of European states in the twentieth century would depend on their success in world policy, i.e., imperialism. This doctrine sharply raised the stakes and tempo of an already heated competition. The second was a series of dramatic events serving to demonstrate that the ethos and tactics of imperialism, hitherto largely confined to the extra-European world, now applied equally to European or Europeanized powers as well, and thus drastically altering the unwritten understandings and incentives structure of the European system.

The best date for marking this sea change is 1898—not, of course, that everything important happened in this calendar year, but that in 1898 many developments began, combined, and jelled to prove that an imperialism already red in tooth and claw abroad would now infect relations between European peoples and states. The British conquest of the Sudan that year in the most glorious and bloody of what Bismarck once called Britain's sporting wars demonstrated the power-political lesson aptly summed up by Hilaire Belloc: "Whatever happens, we have got the Maxim gun, and they have not." A direct aftermath and consequence of this conquest was the Fashoda Crisis, teaching the French government to its astonishment and chagrin that the unwritten rule prevailing in European politics since 1815, that European powers might quarrel over colonial territory but not go to war with each other over it, no longer held. Britain was not only ready to go to war with another European great power over territory in Africa, but also would neither negotiate over that power's claim to the territory nor allow the rival any face-saving compromise. The British resort to *Machtpolitik* was successful. The German Naval Bill of 1898 demonstrated that Germany, pursuing its *Welt- und Machtpolitik*, proposed to challenge British naval supremacy more seriously than anyone had done since the Napoleonic wars. The Second Anglo-Boer War (1899–1902) was clearly foreshadowed already in 1898 by the British government's firm decision to bring de facto independent South African republics of European stock into its Empire by military force if necessary, and its willingness to respond with force to any European interference. In 1898, Théophile Delcassé took over the French Foreign Ministry and immediately began working to transform the Russo-French alliance from a defensive instrument into a general weapon of world policy. One of his first moves was to seek agreements with Russia and Italy on partitioning Austria-Hungary should it collapse, so as to prevent Germany from getting particular portions of it.[9] In 1897–98, European imperialism in China, already underway, escalated sharply from a competition mainly over trade and dominant political influence into a scramble for territorial concessions and naval bases. This touched off a great Chinese revolt, the Boxer Rebellion, leading to further Western intervention and imperialism, and ultimately in 1904 to the Russo-Japanese War.

1898, finally, included the Spanish-Cuban-American War in which the United States defeated Spain and ended Spanish misrule in Cuba only to bring it quickly under its own domination, expand the American empire in the Caribbean and Pacific, and seize the Philippine Islands, provoking an insurrection and war that killed thousands of Filipinos.

In every one of these cases, horse stealing paid off. Breaches of precedent and the use or threat of force never led to any international sanctions or resistance. Concern for how these actions would affect the international system and the relations between its members never served as a deterrent; if anything, it acted in certain instances as a spur to action. The rule was no longer the traditional "*Do ut des*" ("I give so that you give"), and still less "Do to others as you would have them do to you," but "Do to others what they might do to you, but do it first."

The Spanish-American-Cuban War illustrates particularly well how the ascendant ethos of imperialism defeated the declining ethos of European balance and Concert. The centenary observances and discussions of the war in 1998 and publications since have reexamined various effects of the war on Cuba, the Caribbean, Latin America in general, the Philippines, and above all the United States in its rise to world power. One aspect has received little attention: the impact of this disastrous, humiliating war on Spain. Historians of Spain tell us that this war was a major step in the decline and downfall of the Spanish monarchy that led in turn to military dictatorship in the 1920s, the ill-starred Republic of 1931–1936, and civil war and semi-Fascist dictatorship under Franco from 1936 on.[10] International historians know that in the 1880s and 1890s fear of a revolution in Spain and concern about how to prop up the feeble Spanish monarchy and thereby avoid European complications were a persistent if minor theme in European politics. Two small incidents illustrate that concern, and the difference it made in two eras. In the 1880s a dispute arose between Spain and Germany over the Caroline Islands in the Pacific, arousing the public in both countries and leading to republican agitation in Spain. Bismarck could have forced Spain to yield. Considering, however, that to do so would damage Germany's reputation and undermine the feeble Spanish monarchy, endangering European peace, the notoriously hardheaded realist Bismarck proposed settling the issue by Papal arbitration, and, as Bismarck intended, Pope Leo XIII decided in favor of Spain.[11] In April 1898 the Austro-Hungarian foreign minister Count Agenor Goluchowski tried to organize a European Concert mediation of the Spanish-Cuban and Spanish-American conflict so as to prevent a Spanish-American war and help the Spanish monarchy survive. The effort went nowhere. The United States rejected mediation, Spain refused to give way entirely to American demands, Germany and Russia feared jeopardizing their commercial relations with the United States, and Great Britain, concerned over South Africa and actively engaged in appeasing the Americans, wanted nothing to do with it. The British government later claimed credit in Washington for having foiled a continental European attempt to interfere. Imperialism easily trumped European balance and Concert.[12]

The Spanish-Cuban-American War involved Austria-Hungary only in a minor way, to be sure. In general, it had little directly to do with the late-century developments marking the triumph of the imperialist ethos. Preoccupied with its domestic nationality problems and crises, it could not compete seriously in the imperialist scramble for power and territory overseas and was already seen itself as a possible target of partition. Its efforts later to join the scramble for imperialist prizes, largely for prestige reasons, were half-hearted and proved unsuccessful.[13] Nonetheless, Austria-Hungary had a vital role to play in European international politics in the critical years around 1898. In 1897, in agreement with Russia, it began a decade of wary Austro-Russian cooperation in damping down the revolutionary insurrection in Macedonia and the growing rivalry and clashes between various Balkan states and peoples over it, to keep the Balkans on ice and avert an Austro-Russian clash there.[14] Here the ethos of Concert and balance trumped imperialism.

Naturally, Austria-Hungary had particular reasons and interests of its own for promoting peace with Russia and restraining revolt and ethnic conflict in the Balkans at this time, the main ones being a serious domestic crisis with the Czechs and growing problems with Hungary. The question, however, is what kind of incentives and rewards an international system must provide in order for it to survive durably and work effectively to control conflict and promote general stability and peace. The policy Austria-Hungary adopted in the Macedonian question, which it followed fairly faithfully until 1907, when Russia under British pressure and with Italian encouragement abandoned their agreement, involved cooperating with its most dangerous rival in the area of their sharpest historic competition in order to manage a critical problem, keep their rivalry within bounds, and preserve the general peace, even while the Austrians knew that this policy offered their opponent the opportunity to make gains elsewhere that would enhance its overall power. A policy such as this must pay off in some clear benefits for both sides if the rival parties are to continue their cooperation and if the international system and peace are to endure. Russia gained major direct benefits from this Austro-Hungarian stance. With their European and Balkan flanks secure, the Russians were able to concentrate on imperialist expansion in the Far East, and when this venture led them into a disastrous war and revolution, Austria-Hungary's guarantee of neutrality and cooperation paid off still more handsomely in helping the regime survive. Austria-Hungary's payoff for its cooperation in Macedonia then and later consisted, as leading Russians conceived it, in the opportunity to survive a while longer, provided it could do so by its own resources.

This is not to portray Austria-Hungary as a victim, which would be inappropriate and irrelevant. It merely asks, to repeat, how long an international system with the kind of ethos and attendant rules, norms, and incentives that emerged around the turn of the century could be expected to last, or states like Austria-Hungary, even if they depended on it to survive, could be expected to continue sustaining it in the face of adverse payoffs.

1898, of course, marked only the point at which the ascendancy of the politics of imperialism over those of European balance and Concert became clear. It would take far too long here to show how almost every subsequent major event and development in European politics further promoted the triumph of an imperialist ethos and fit into its pattern of perverse, destructive payoffs. The list is a long one: the Second Anglo-Boer War and its outcome; the course of Western imperialism in East Asia culminating in the Russo-Japanese War; the results and aftermath of that war, bringing great gains to Japan, colonial occupation to Korea, new threats to China, revolution to Russia, and immense benefits in various theaters (East Asia, India, Central Asia, Europe, and the high seas) to Britain—an instance in which a state could profit by simply being a silent partner to another's horse stealing; the Anglo-French Entente Cordiale and the accompanying French deals with Italy and Spain on Morocco, designed to exclude Germany; the succeeding French move to gain control of Morocco and isolate Germany, leading to the First Moroccan Crisis and a partial French victory; the Anglo-Russian Convention dividing up Persia and Central Asia, again intended to exclude Germany; the French takeover in Morocco and the Second Moroccan Crisis of 1911; Italy's cynically aggressive attack on the Ottoman Empire in Libya, soon extended, in total disregard of the international consequences and dangers, to the Turkish Straits and the Dodecanese islands; Russia's moves to isolate Austria and control the Balkans through its Balkan League; the Serbian-Bulgarian-Greek offensive alliance, aimed directly against Turkey and indirectly against Austria-Hungary, which Russian diplomacy promoted, and the two Balkan Wars it prompted. All these well-known developments fit the pattern already seen. Those who set out to steal horses, unless stopped by other horse stealers by threat or superior force, were rewarded; those who held back lost out and were punished.

Two major developments do not obviously conform to the pattern—the Anglo-German naval race and the Berlin-to-Baghdad Railway. Even these, however, do not contradict it and basically fit in. The German naval challenge to Britain represented an attempt to better equip Germany better for horse stealing, i.e., for competing with Britain for empire and world position. The German bid failed because Germany faced too many other challenges to concentrate fully on it and the British had the resources and will to defeat it. The Berlin-to-Baghdad Railway scheme ended in an apparently peaceful compromise because Russia and Britain had previously secured the prizes in Persia, Central Asia, and the Ottoman Empire most important to them and decided that it would be too costly and dangerous to exclude Germany from a share of the economic spoils in Anatolia—an instance of the shared horse stealing not uncommon in the New Imperialism.

Without trying to expound and defend this interpretation of the whole period from 1900 to 1914 further here, the central point concerning the ultimate impact of the ethos, collective mentality, and incentives structure of imperialism on the international system in general and on Austria-Hungary in particular, can be illustrated through one major development, the Russo-Japanese War. Russia's policy toward Japan in East Asia from 1895 to 1903 bears a striking similarity in certain respects to Russian policy toward Austria in the Balkans from 1909 to 1914. That is, in both cases Russia did not want a war or desire the physical elimination of its rival. It simply wished to keep its opponent isolated, hold it off, fob it off if necessary with meaningless assurances and agreements, and over time consolidate its hold over the area in dispute until its control became so strong that the opponent would have to recognize and accept it. One difference between the two instances, so far as Russian policy is concerned, is that in East Asia Russia encountered some resistance from outside powers, notably Britain, while in the Balkans it was encouraged and aided by Serbia, France, Britain, Italy, and Rumania.

The difference between the two cases that most affected the respective outcomes, however, lies in the way Russia's opponents, Japan and Austria-Hungary, reacted to Russia's moves. The Japanese government came to understand Russia's policy in East Asia and its ultimate consequences for Japan early on and decided, after much debate and considerable hesitation and division, that Japan must either obtain a satisfactory, reliable agreement with Russia dividing the spoils (essentially Korea for Japan, Manchuria for Russia) or fight. When the Japanese government concluded that it could not obtain the deal it wanted from Russia, well before the possibilities of peaceful negotiation with Russia were formally exhausted, it chose not, as Austria-Hungary did in 1914, merely to take actions to protect its interests at the risk of war (such as occupying Korea), allowing Russia to decide on its response. Instead, it chose all-out, immediate preventive war, attacking Russia suddenly and with all its might. In terms of my metaphor, the Japanese saw that under the current imperialist system it was foolish to look over the fence, see a thief preparing to steal horses one coveted oneself, try to reach agreement on shared theft, and failing this fall back on the hope that the horses would not be stolen after all or that one could simply steal a few oneself without fighting the other thief. The rational though risky course was to attack the other thief first, drive him off, and then steal the horses oneself. And that policy worked.

Contrast this with Austria-Hungary and Germany's reaction to the war, especially to Russia's severe defeat at Japan's hands and the paralyzing Russian Revolution that followed in 1905–06. Recall that many historians (including me) interpret the joint Austro-Hungarian and German decision in 1914 as tantamount to opting for, if not directly starting, a preventive war. Historians also agree (though many ignore its implications, slide over it, or explain it away) that Germany and Austria-Hungary in the previous decade had passed up several better opportunities for preventive war or other drastic actions to improve their position. These arose in 1912–13, 1911, 1908–09, and best of all in 1904–06. At this juncture, with Russia mired in a losing war and revolution, Germany could have used the First Moroccan Crisis to attack France and Austria-Hungary could have acted to punish Serbia for its anti-Habsburg moves in 1903 and force it back into line without having to worry about Russian intervention at all. I do not contend that they had no good reasons, domestic, foreign-political, and strategic, not to do this—they did. My point instead is two-fold: first, that their decision against preventive war at this juncture and later (against prominent advocates of it in both countries) saved the system and preserved general peace, and furthermore, that in 1904–06 they consciously followed a policy precisely the reverse of preventive war, that of helping to prevent the collapse of their main rival.

This is no exaggeration. Austria-Hungary's and Germany's conduct in 1904–06 saved the Tsarist regime. The only way the Russian government could put down the revolution was to scatter its army away from the western front all over European Russia. The only way the premier Count Sergius Witte could persuade Russia's military authorities to do this, who on general principles strongly opposed using the army for police duty and to repress revolution, was to assure them that there was no chance of a German or Austrian attack.[15] Any Austro-German or Austro-Hungarian mobilization or threat on Russia's western front would have sufficed to paralyze this use of the Russian army and bring the regime down.

Once again, Austria-Hungary had particular reasons at this time for not exploiting Russia's desperate situation, above all its own threat of civil war in Hungary. Nonetheless, both German powers courted and supported Russia rather than threatening it and using the crisis to solve their internal problems through secondary integration,[16] and (to repeat) the policy they followed in this crisis is the kind any system needs to preserve peace and the existence of essential actors. In international affairs, results count more than motives and intentions.

The results here, however, demonstrate the adage that in that era, no good deed went unpunished, for the payoff both powers received was entirely negative. Even before the revolution was finally quelled and political order restored, Russia had turned to the Entente powers for vital financial aid and ideological support and friendship, and within months of its survival, the Russian regime had abandoned its decade-long cooperation with Austria in Macedonia and launched its own campaign for reforms in partnership with Britain.[17] Within a year, the Russian foreign minister A. P. Izvolski was complaining bitterly that Austria's proposed railway in the Sanjak of Novi-Bazar (a project that Isvolski admitted Austria-Hungary was entitled by treaty to carry out) represented "a bomb rolled between his legs."[18] To sum up: in 1904–10, Japan stole horses to great applause. Austria-Hungary was hanged despite attempting to help the owner save his horses and repair his fence. It is hard to conceive a better illustration of a perverse international incentives structure.

There is an obvious objection to this line of argument. It appears to disregard one of the most important events and developments of the pre-war era, and one that destroys the portrait of Austria-Hungary as the victim of the imperialist ethos, because it shows Austria-Hungary at this time doing major horse stealing of its own. In 1908, it annexed Bosnia-Herzegovina in violation of the Treaty of Berlin, provoking the Bosnian Crisis of 1908–09. Out of this, historians agree (and I concur), grew fatal developments contributing directly to war in 1914—an even more bitter and incurable Austro-Russian enmity and rivalry, heightened Austro-Serbian tensions, a spiraling land arms race, and a chain of events in the Balkans and Mediterranean that led to the ultimate explosion.

Rather than ignoring the Bosnian Crisis, I was saving it, to present it as evidence for my thesis that the ultimate ground for Austria-Hungary's decision in 1914 and therefore the deeper cause of the war was the triumph of an imperialist ethos and incentives structure over the earlier ethos of balance and Concert in European international politics. In explaining why, I ask your indulgence for recounting how my own views on this subject have changed. It shows, if nothing else, how revisionist views may in time and under examination become more radical rather than moderate.

A central problem for historians of the Bosnian Crisis has always been how to explain why the annexation of Bosnia-Herzegovina, which changed the existing power-political situation hardly at all, had such crucial international effects. Under the Treaty of Berlin of 1878, Austria-Hungary had already occupied and administered the provinces sine die for thirty years, exercising what amounted in practical terms to full, permanent possession and governance and largely transforming the provinces in the process. No one expected the occupation to end; annexation by Austria had long been anticipated and even foreseen in various treaties. A formal transfer of sovereignty to Austria-Hungary from the Ottoman Sultan, who had lost effective control over the provinces long before 1878, would seem in this era of high imperialism, replete with overt land grabs, major conflicts over disputed territory and rights, and not a few violations of treaties, to be an insufficient cause for such huge consequences.

Many historians, to be sure, don't see this as a problem. The annexation had the consequences it did, they argue, for two main reasons: first, because Austria-Hungary's move was ill-planned and ill-prepared, executed badly, and when it encountered trouble pushed through by Austria-Hungary and Germany with ultimative threats to Serbia and Russia that left deep, abiding resentment; and second, because it was inherently an aggressive, imperialist move intended to shift the balance of power in the Balkans and indirectly in Europe in favor of the Dual Alliance. It unquestionably violated the letter of an important international treaty and negated the residual rights of the Ottoman Empire and the nationalist hopes of the Serbs. In particular, it was designed to take advantage of Russia's weakness following its lost war and revolution in order to assert Austro-Hungarian primacy over the whole western half of the Balkans, to check Italian and Serbian pretensions, and to foster an Austro-German economic *Drang nach Osten*.

On the basis of some research on the question, though relying mainly on more thorough work by other scholars, I have earlier argued that this interpretation clashes with too many facts to be persuasive. Most of the points I and others have made are familiar, and some need not be rehearsed here. The important ones, boiled down, are: the crisis arose out of an Austro-Russian bargain initially proposed by the Russian Foreign Minister A. P. Isvolski, freely negotiated and entered into by him, and approved by the Tsar. Isvolski and his second in command Charykov knew well in advance of Austria-Hungary's intention to annex Bosnia-Herzegovina, believed that Russia could not stop it and even had no legal ground to do so, and made the bargain in order to obtain a concession important to Russia. Baron Alois Aehrenthal, the Austro-Hungarian Foreign Minister, though he bargained hard, did so in good faith—more so than his Russian counterpart, who always intended to betray the agreement by later seeking further concessions from Austria-Hungary on top of the agreed quid pro quo. Aehrenthal's main motives for the move, moreover, were domestic-political and defensive rather than power-political and aggressive, and directed against Italy and Serbia but not Russia. From a purely power-political, military, and strategic standpoint, moreover, the annexation marked a retreat from any alleged Austrian *Drang nach Osten* rather than an advance. True, Aehrenthal miscalculated the reactions in the Ottoman Empire, Serbia, and Russia, but Isvolski's miscalculations proved far worse, and he actively lied to cover himself and save his position. It was not Austria-Hungary's or Germany's fault, moreover, but that of France and Great Britain that Russia failed to get its intended payoff. The Russian government, not the Austro-Hungarian one, changed its mind and repudiated the original bargain. As to the charge of treaty violation, the Treaty of Berlin had repeatedly been violated and revised ever since its inception thirty years before, sometimes at the instigation, or with the connivance of the states that now denounced this violation. Russia's asking Britain and France to help uphold the sanctity of international treaties by enforcing the Treaty of Berlin therefore looks a bit like Bluebeard's seeking Don Juan's and Casanova's help in upholding the honor of women and marriage by defending Sadie Thompson.[19]

In other words, my previous argument was essentially that the annexation of Bosnia-Herzegovina was so mild and relatively innocuous an instance of imperialism (indirect informal imperialism, to use the language of Michael Behnen and others) that it should never have caused a crisis at all, but would in a saner international system have been accepted and allowed to succeed.

I still believe this, but no longer consider this the most effective reply to critics or, more important, the best way to understand the real meaning and significance of the Bosnian Crisis for the international system—in particular, how the crisis concretely illustrates the clash between the old European and the new imperialist ethos and incentives structure in international politics. Impressive and invaluable though the detailed research on the crisis by many scholars has been, there is a way in which the intense focus on the immediate story in all its details and close analysis of the moves and countermoves of the various players, examining their respective motives, aims, strategy, and tactics and how these intersected and reacted with each other as the crisis evolved, can make one miss the forest for the trees, overlook what it reveals about the evolution of the European international system. The current dominant tendency is to interpret the decision to annex Bosnia-Herzegovina and to strike a deal with Russia as a move within the ongoing imperialist competition and thus judge it a rash, ill-prepared attempt to make Austria-Hungary once more a serious player in the new imperialist game, a strategy that blew up in Aehrenthal's face because of his own bad planning and execution and Austria-Hungary's weaknesses and vulnerability. This is certainly one tenable way to interpret the evidence; Aehrenthal and the Austro-Hungarian government were unquestionably caught up in that era and spirit and compelled to try to compete within it. But it is important also to understand the Austro-Hungarian move from a broader systemic perspective at the same time. From that perspective, the initiative must be seen as Aehrenthal's attempt to escape the imperialist game and to revive the ethos, rules, and incentives of the Bismarckian era in international politics.

Almost everything about the move and the Austro-Russian bargain fits this interpretation, beginning with Aehrenthal's central foreign policy purpose: to restore good relations with Russia, revive the Three Emperors' League (which Michael Behnen calls Aehrenthal's pet idea ["*Lieblingsidee*"]), and renew Austro-Russian cooperation in the Balkans. Aehrenthal, more pro-Russian than any Austrian foreign minister at least since Count Rechberg in 1864, perhaps in the whole nineteenth century, had in mind a return not to the barely concealed or open Austro-Russian rivalry of the late 1870s and 1880s, but to the wary partnership of the early 1870s, when Austria and Russia buried the hatchet following Germany's unification in order, among other things, to become more independent of Germany—which was another of Aehrenthal's leading aims. The goal of monarchical solidarity against revolution prominent in the 1870s fits equally well. Aehrenthal was certainly more intent on supporting the Tsar's authority than Isvolski, eager to cultivate the conservative-liberals in the Duma and the aristocratic liberals in London and Paris. The bargaining between Aehrenthal and Isvolski in 1908 bears strong similarities to the Austro-Russian bargaining over the Eastern Question in 1876–77. The presuppositions of the bargain reached in 1908, at least on Austria-Hungary's side, were those that Bismarck had then repeatedly urged on both sides without success: that they tacitly divide the Balkans into their respective spheres, cooperate in holding down rebellions, and mutually act in the spirit of *"Do ut des,"* with Austria-Hungary recognizing Russia's special interest in the Straits and Russia recognizing Austrian interests in the western Balkans and the Adriatic. True, the 1908 agreement was asking for trouble in leaving out the other great powers, ignoring Italy's desire to play an active role in Balkan affairs, overriding Ottoman concerns (where, incidentally, Russia's demand for a special status at the Straits represented a far greater threat to the Turks than Austria-Hungary's extinction of the Sultan's purely formal rights in Bosnia-Herzegovina), and paying no attention to Serbian nationalism or the wishes of Bosnia-Herzegovina's inhabitants. But all these traits also characterized the politics of the Bismarckian era, especially in regard to the Balkans, and contributed to its success in warding off general war.

As to the claim that the annexation represented a serious violation of an important international treaty, the main point is not that this charge was overblown and unusually hypocritical in this era of high imperialism, but that it fundamentally mistakes the general nature and purpose of treaties in the Bismarckian era. They were not expected to last forever, but intended to be revised and if necessary cancelled to meet changing needs and circumstances. The operating rule, one of Bismarck's favorite axioms, was *"Pacta sunt servanda rebus sic stantibus,"* ("Pacts must be observed so long as conditions remain the same"). This applied to the entire Treaty of Berlin, consciously devised as a provisional solution to an immediate crisis and subjected to repeated revision by negotiation and unilateral action almost from the day it was concluded. One of the many ironies in the Bosnian Crisis is that Great Britain, which had throughout the 1870s and 1880s done its best to promote and exploit Austro-Russian rivalry for its purposes heedless of the danger for European peace, and had under Gladstone in the early 1880s and Salisbury in 1885 led the charge to revise or overthrow central provisions of the Berlin Treaty, would in 1908 ardently defend that treaty's sanctity against the very change it had advocated a generation earlier.

To heighten the irony further, the provisions of the Berlin Treaty granting Austria-Hungary the right to occupy and administer Bosnia-Herzegovina sine die, violated in 1908, were specifically *intended* to be impermanent. Everyone knew at the time that they were a fig leaf for Austro-Hungarian annexation and expected annexation to follow quickly. The British advocated this, Russia accepted it, Germany and Russia formally recognized Austria-Hungary's right to do it in 1881 and 1884, and no power at that time would have thought of opposing it. If, as claimed, Austria-Hungary in 1908 ignored Ottoman rights, Serbian outcries, and the wishes of Bosnia's inhabitants, it did so far more openly in 1878–81, touching off a serious rebellion, and did so with the approval of the international community.

That last phrase is a key one. For ultimately the Bismarckian system rested on the formal or informal acceptance of treaty revisions by the European family of states as a way of coming to terms with change while avoiding general war, whether the changes came about through negotiation or unilateral acts such as the Russian repudiation of the Black Sea clauses in 1870 or the Bulgarian unification coup in 1885. This understanding about the international community's needing to accept change and those making changes needing to seek its approval was part of the agreement reached at Buchlau in 1908, and Aehrenthal accepted the obligation more genuinely than did Isvolski. Austria-Hungary, like Germany and unlike Britain and France, was ready to support Russia's proposal for a change in the status of the Turkish Straits and to accept a conference like the London Conference of 1871 to sanction its action in Bosnia-Herzegovina, provided the conference would grant it without unacceptable conditions.

This is not intended to portray the ethos, rules, and incentives structure of the Bismarckian age as ideal for meeting international problems and crises, even in that era. They were simply better for general peace and stability than what followed. Still less should Aehrenthal and the Austro-Hungarian government be seen as shining examples of honesty, restraint, and cooperation in a lawless era. Holger Afflerbach's characterization of Austro-Hungarian policy in this era as half-Machiavellian and half-defensive is apt, and can be understood as a natural consequence of the Monarchy's situation and special nature. It was caught in a dangerous, escalating competition in which it was losing and becoming steadily more insecure, and it was therefore strongly tempted to regain ground by the same tactics and strategies others used against it, but at the same time aware that this ruthless Darwinian competition was killing it. Aehrenthal's policy thus resembles the half-piracy, half-legality characteristic of Austrian actions in the 1790s vis-à-vis the Polish question, the French Revolution, the duel with Prussia in Germany, and the wars against France and Napoleon. Austria-Hungary wanted to restore the earlier nineteenth century rules for obvious self-interested reasons; it depended on those rules or something like them for survival. Never throughout its history as a great power since the late seventeenth century had Austria been able to meet its many dangers and threats solely or mainly by its own power. Its security had always depended not only upon powerful allies, but also on international consent—what I have called elsewhere "negative Austrophilia,"[20] meaning thereby not positive support for Austria from other powers or their active willingness to defend it, but at least their grudging, half-contemptuous recognition that whatever its virtues and shortcomings, Austria fulfilled functions in the European system difficult or impossible to replace by anything else and that it therefore needed to be accepted and at least minimally supported and kept alive. That minimal level of support or toleration required systemic restraints at least as durable and powerful as those of the Bismarckian era. The Bosnian Crisis, I contend, arose out of an Austro-Hungarian attempt to revive those restraints and that ethos within that system.

The disastrous outcome of that effort proved that this simply could not be done. The single biggest reason why not is that the Russians simply did not want any durable agreement with Austria-Hungary. Isvolski wanted only a temporary one that he could turn to Russia's advantage, in order to restore Russia's prestige and enhance his own. Other Russians, especially the military and parliamentary leaders, the Prime Minister Peter Stolypin, and Tsar Nicholas, decided that any agreement with Austria-Hungary that offended so-called "public opinion" or appeared to betray the cause of their Slav relatives was out of the question. How much this decision was affected by the Russian fear of Germany and of being drawn into dependence on Germany through rapprochement with Austria-Hungary is more difficult to say. That Italians and Serbs would resist any revival of earlier nineteenth century norms is obvious; so would other small ambitious states. France during this period had no active rivalry with Austria-Hungary and no desire to fight for Russian interests in the Near East, but its fear of Germany, determination to retain Russia as an ally, and desire to break Italy away from the Triple Alliance outweighed everything else. Germany, though it would have liked to revive the Three Emperors' League in order to split the growing coalition against it, would not be restrained by its partners and in the end decided to use the Bosnian Crisis to teach Russia a lesson. As for Britain, throughout the nineteenth century it had almost always opposed any alignment between Germany, Austria, and Russia and tried to break it up. The current German naval threat to Britain and the German threat on land to the continental balance of power, combined with the looming Russian threat to the British Empire, made this policy even more a self-understood necessity. The oft-debated question of which factor weighed more in British policy, its Empire or the continental balance of power, is almost impossible to answer because both concerns fit seamlessly together, and here the question is irrelevant in any case. Alongside these overriding British interests, Austria-Hungary's existence and its European functions did not count—or rather, Austria-Hungary counted only as Germany's ally.

The Bosnian Crisis is significant therefore not simply because more than any other crisis it started Europe's fatal descent into the maelstrom, but even more because it involved the last serious attempt to turn European politics around by reviving its previous spirit and ethos, and the attempt not merely failed miserably but confirmed and accelerated the trend it was meant to reverse. As a result, Austria-Hungary was bound to conclude that it must do something drastic to change a system that was slowly but surely strangling it. In 1914 as in 1809, it waited too long. Not every reckless gamble is irrational; it may be rational to choose one form of death over another—and, as has been observed, Austria-Hungary committed suicide not out of fear of death, but out of fear of the hangman.[21] The hangman was not a particular enemy power, but the international system.

Notes

1. For this reason and given the wide-ranging character of the essay, in which almost every sentence includes a fact or judgment on which a large literature exists, I will keep the footnotes to a minimum, using them only for points that I believe need grounding. On Austria-Hungary's role in the longer-range and immediate origins of the war, essential works include F. R. Bridge, *The Habsburg Monarchy among the Great Powers, 1815–1918* (New York, 1990); Bridge, *Great Britain and Austria-Hungary, 1906–1914: A Diplomatic History* (London, 1972); Samuel R. Williamson Jr., *Austria-Hungary and the Origins of the First World War* (New York, 1991); and Günther Kronenbitter, *Krieg im Frieden. Die Führung der k.u.k. Armee und die Grossmachtpolitik Österreich-Ungarns 1906–1914* (Munich, 2003). Three excellent studies dealing with pre-war Austro-Hungarian policy especially toward its Triple Alliance partners are Michael Behnen, *Rüstung, Bündnis, Sicherheit: Dreibund und informeller Imperialismus, 1900–1908* (Tübingen, 1985); Jürgen Angelow, *Kalkül*

und Prestige: der Zweibund am Vorabend des Ersten Weltkrieges (Cologne, 2000); and Holger Afflerbach, *Der Dreibund: europäische Grossmacht- und Allianzpolitik vor dem Ersten Weltkrieg* (Vienna, 2002). Important essays are in Helmut Rumpler and Jan Paul Niederkorn, eds, *Der "Zweibund" 1879: das deutsch-österreichische Bündnis und die europäische Diplomatie* (Vienna, 1996). On the race in land armaments that contributed heavily to the spiral into war, David Herrmann, *The Arming of Europe and the Making of the First World War* (Princeton, 1996) is good, and David Stevenson, *Armaments and the Coming of War: Europe, 1904–1914* (Oxford, 1996) even better. There are many older and recent accounts of the origins of the war, but the most satisfactory general treatment still seems to me James Joll's *The Origins of the First World War* (London, 1984).
2. John Leslie, "Österreich-Ungarn vor dem Kriegsausbruch," in *Deutschland und Europa in der Neuzeit*, 2 vols., Ralph Melville et al., eds. (Stuttgart, 1988), vol.2, 670–84.
3. Holger Herwig, *The First World War: Germany and Austria-Hungary, 1914–1918* (London, 1997); Gary Shanafelt, *The Secret Enemy: Austria-Hungary and the German Alliance, 1914–1918* (New York, 1985).
4. Geoffrey Wawro finds a fourth instance in the Austro-Prussian War of 1866—"The Habsburg Flucht nach vorne in 1866: Domestic Political Origins of the Austro-Prussian War," *The International History Review* 17, 2 (May 1995), 221–48. The case, however, does not seem to me really comparable to those in 1809, 1859, and 1914.
5. Henry A. Kissinger, *Diplomacy* (New York, 1994), 194–96, 211–12, et passim.
6. Paul W. Schroeder, "Embedded Counterfactuals and World War I as an Unavoidable War," in Paul W. Schroeder, *Systems, Stability and Statecraft: Essays on the International History of Modern Europe*, David Wetzel, Robert Jervis, and Jack S. Levy, eds. (New York, 2004), 157–91.
7. For a good mordant discussion of the imperialist ethos, especially in the relation between great powers and the objects of imperialism, see Gordon Martel, "Afterword: The Imperial Contract—an Ethology of Power," in A. H. Ion and E. J. Herrington, eds., *Great Powers and Little Wars: The Limits of Power* (Westport, CN, 1993), 203–25.
8. Stig Förster et al., eds., *Europe and Africa: The Berlin Congo Conference 1884–1885 and the Onset of Partition* (Oxford, 1989).
9. Christopher Andrew, *Théophile Delcassé and the Making of the Entente Cordiale: a Reappraisal of French Foreign Policy, 1898–1905* (New York, 1968), 126–29.
10. Sebastian Balfour, *The End of the Spanish Empire, 1898–1923* (Oxford, 1997); Balfour, "The Impact of War within Spain: Continuity or Crisis?" in *The Crisis of 1898*, Angel Smith and Emma Davila-Cox, eds. (New York, 1999), 180–94.
11. Hans-Ulrich Wehler, *Bismarck und der Imperialismus* (Cologne, 1969), 400–07.
12. F. R. Bridge, "Great Britain, Austria-Hungary and the European Concert on the Eve of the Spanish-American War," *Mitteilungen des österreichischen Staatsarchivs* 44 (1996), 87–108.
13. F. R. Bridge, "'Tarde venientibus ossa': Austro-Hungarian Colonial Aspirations in Asia Minor 1913–14," *Middle Eastern Studies* 6, 3 (October 1970), 319–30; Wolfdieter Bihl, "Zu den österreichisch-ungarischen Kriegszielen 1914," *Jahrbücher für die Geschichte Osteuropas* XVI, 4 (1968), 505–30.
14. Steven W. Sowards, *Austria's Policy of Macedonian Reform* (Boulder, CO, 1989).
15. William C. Fuller, *Civil-Military Conflict in Russia, 1881–1914* (Princeton, 1985), 129–68, especially 138–39.
16. Given these facts and Austria-Hungary's goal of reviving the Three Emperors' League, Michael Behnen's view (*Rüstung, Bündnis*, 109–13) that the Austro-Russian neutrality agreement of October 1904 represented a victory for Austria-Hungary, clearing the decks for a possible clash with Italy, seems to me strained.
17. While the general story is well known, two points worth noting here are: (1) that Austria-Hungary participated substantially in the French-English loan in 1906, thus helping save the Tsarist regime from having to make further concessions to the Russian liberals and the Duma;

(2) that other powers—Italy, France, and Great Britain—had long worked to break up the Austro-Russian partnership in the Macedonian question or insert themselves into it, even while recognizing that it was good for general peace. See Behnen, *Rüstung, Bündnis*, 368–71; Sowards, *Austria's Policy of Macedonian Reform*, 78–81; Douglas Dakin, "British Sources on the Greek Struggle in Macedonia," *Balkan Studies* 2, 1 (1961), 76–77.

18. Sowards, *Austria's Policy of Macedonian Reform*, 84–87; F. R. Bridge, "Isvolsky, Aehrenthal and the End of the Austro-Russian Entente, 1906–8," *Mitteilungen des Österreichischen Staatsarchivs* 29 (1976), 315–62. Behnen's account (*Rüstung, Bündnis*, 419–37) though very critical of Aehrenthal and Austrian policy, makes clear that if the Sanjak project was a bomb at all, it was rolled between Italy's legs, not Russia's.

19. Sadie Thompson, a prostitute, was the central character in W. Somerset Maugham's well-known short story *Rain*.

20. Paul W. Schroeder, "Comment: The Luck of the House of Habsburg: Military Defeat and Political Survival," *Austrian History Yearbook* 32 (2001), 215–24.

21. Helmut Rumpler, *Eine Chance für Mitteleuropa: bürgerliche Emanzipation und Staatsverfall in der Habsburgermonarchie* (Vienna, 1997), 604.

Chapter 2

DID NORMS MATTER IN NINETEENTH-CENTURY INTERNATIONAL RELATIONS?
Progress and Decline in the "Culture of Peace" before World War I[1]

Matthias Schulz

Accounts of the origins of World War I usually emphasize the increasing tensions, the structural antagonisms arising out of imperial competition and the arms race, nationalistic and bellicose mentalities, the Balkan wars, wounded prestige, the "encirclement" fears among German political and military elites, the "flaws" of decision-makers, as well as the July crisis as a "trigger" for a more or less inevitable chain reaction which, finally, culminated in what was a European catastrophe and the first truly global war. Yet about one hundred years earlier, as a consequence of the Revolutionary and Napoleonic Wars, the Quadruple Alliance against France had made substantial efforts to find mechanisms and structural impediments which would allow international relations to be regulated peacefully, and on the basis of a solid legal foundation. Instead of utilizing primarily dynastic marriages, alliance politics, and military force to gain advantages or resolve conflicts, in the nineteenth century political actors sought to develop behavioral norms, international procedures of collective decision making, and other principles and practices to resolve international problems. Expectations and normative ideas gradually rose to prominence, and, when they were recognized as generally binding, political actors had to deal with them as objective notions and terms of reference.[2] As a consequence the European states system developed the contours of a society of states or, to use a more modern term, an international society. In this international society political decision makers not only had to take into account the preferences of the elite milieu and other domestic forces, but also international procedures, normative ideas, and expectations of other governments about what they considered proper state behavior. The more the web of international norms thickened, the less states could afford to commit serious violations of those expectations without incurring the displeasure of or sanctions by other states.

How deeply was this new "culture of peace" rooted in international norms, how long did it last, and how important was it for international relations? How can we analyze it and determine its significance for the period before World War I? These questions are significant because, if that system and its normative base collapsed very soon after 1815 without being reestablished, or if norms disappeared without new norms being accepted instead, then there was a serious problem with the state of international affairs. In other words: if international anarchy reigned well before 1914, then there were no reliable norms according to which governments could be held accountable. Thus, if all states played the Hobbesian game, "each man is the other man's wolf," then no rules were violated. Yet, at the end of the war, the victors tried to hold accountable those who, from their point of view, caused the war—this was the foundation for the notorious "War-guilt" clause in the Treaty of Versailles, and for German reparations.

The creation of a system of norms, and its operation, can be traced by looking at international treaties, at customary law, and at diplomatic discourse. For these reasons, historians of international relations are well placed to analyze the rise, transformation, and fall of international normative ideas with a view to gaining insights into the "culture" of foreign policy and international systems of distinct eras and spaces.[3] From this perspective, historians who analyze international relations exclusively as an eternal struggle between nations for more economic and military power miss half of the picture. A more comprehensive approach looks at the role of actors and their domestic environment, the distribution of power, as well as the evolution of norms and international institutions in the respective international system.

The purpose of this essay is to move norms and institution building back to the center of the analysis of nineteenth-century international politics. It will try to answer the question of the "probability" of the war of 1914 by analyzing the rise and decline of the nineteenth-century "culture of peace," and by giving new answers as to why it was destroyed before, or with, the outbreak of World War I.

Within this framework of analysis, this chapter will present a historical-sociological analysis of the Concert of Europe and the "culture of peace," which evolved in tandem with it during the nineteenth century. These developments are highly relevant to the debate on the "inevitability" of World War I.[4] The point of departure is Winfried Baumgart's recent statement that there is still "no satisfactory study which combines the theory and practice of the Concert of Europe."[5]

Indeed, although several case studies and narrative overviews have been produced on the Concert, not even the definitions suggested, ranging from an "idea" (Medlicott) to an "international organization" (Stanley Hoffmann), are satisfactory so far.[6] Instead, it is proposed to examine the Concert as an *international institution*, namely a nineteenth-century version of a "security council," whose character and perception evolved with time. Unlike the legal-political term "international organization," the sociological term "institution" requires neither a legal statute nor a permanent secretariat. An institution comprises certain regulative functions exerted within society, has a relatively constant existence, and its human representatives and addressees need to have "internalized" its cultural patterns. International institutions are established to stabilize and develop a normative order, allow for the peaceful adjustment of interests, and provide a framework to "reach and execute decisions that are generally binding."[7] Hence, the regulation of state behavior through institution building in the international arena indicates a non-linear, unsteady, and reversible process of civilization in international society.[8]

In order to examine whether the criteria are met, the chapter will first take stock of the institutional characteristics of the European Concert by systematically identifying cultural patterns, procedures, and actions typical of the Concert. Secondly, it will explore which normative ideas played a role in the decision-making process of the Concert as it evolved over time. Those normative ideas, and certain shifts in what may be called the *normative culture* of international relations, have been identified in a careful process of context-oriented discourse analysis, the end result of which will be presented in a book on nineteenth-century conflict resolution.[9] Finally, the chapter will look briefly at violations of Concert norms by individual state actors, indicate the major reasons for the demise and eventual collapse of the Concert, and mention alternatives discussed and/or operative before World War I. Thus, by the end we will have a fairer view of the "culture of peace" and the machinery available to the governments to avoid armed conflict prior to World War I.

I. Institutional Characteristics of the Concert of Europe

As Sidney Pollard and others have shown, economic interdependence in Europe, and between Europe and other continents, grew at an accelerated pace after the middle of the eighteenth century.[10] This process was severely disturbed by the French Revolution, the associated disruption of public finances, and the collapse of the eighteenth-century European balance of power. Against the background of the Napoleonic Wars, the anti-Napoleonic alliance developed a pattern of intense cooperation after 1813, which was based upon personal encounters between monarchs and foreign ministers, and resulted in a change in the "culture," i.e. the style, methods, and norms, of foreign policy.[11] Out of this spontaneous cooperative practice, and agreements concluded at Chaumont in 1814 and at Paris in 1815, the European Concert of Great Powers arose. At the Congress of Aix-la-Chapelle, the Great Powers invited France to join their circle and agreed upon regular conferences for the preservation of peace. As general principles of conduct, they embraced, at first, only vague notions of justice, unity, and moderation.[12]

The fuzzy terminology used by the governments at the time indicates that they did not know exactly what they had created. While the Austrian foreign minister Prince Metternich imagined a "moral pentarchy"[13]—and the term pentarchy was widely used in the political literature of Germany, Austria, and Russia at the time[14]—his British counterpart Castlereagh reported to Prime Minister Lord Liverpool that they had established a "European Government … giving to the great Powers the efficiency and almost the simplicity of a single state."[15] Only gradually did the term "Concert européen" take hold, and finally prevail in the language of diplomacy. With growing practical experience, the political decision-makers, diplomats, and legal counsellors who took part in the diplomatic discourse developed an understanding of the Concert as an entity and as a device for the protection of peace and security in Europe.[16]

The Concert developed certain cultural patterns for the preservation of peace and for the resolution of conflicts, which replaced the unstable eighteenth-century balance of power with a system of *plurilateral*, institutional cooperation, which managed the European society of states quite successfully.[17] I would argue that this cooperative institutional framework was the major reason why the era from 1815 to the outbreak of World War I was more peaceful in Europe than the eighteenth or twentieth centuries in terms of casualties, frequency, and duration of war.[18] This success is all the more remarkable, since the nineteenth century saw an explosion of technological, economic, social, and political dynamism; and outside Europe, politics was anything but rule-oriented.

The following behavioral and structural norms, procedures, functions, instruments, and patterns of legitimization can be identified as the basic institutional characteristics of the Concert:

1. the Great Powers obliged themselves to cooperate in international affairs that were of a general interest to Europe, and vowed to moderate their ambitions. As a consequence, the behavioral norms for states changed in the long run.[19] The *ius ad bellum* was not abolished, but parties to an international conflict were subjected to the doctrine of *bellum justum* and had to reckon with the other party appealing to the Concert to mediate, or with an unsolicited attempt by the Concert to mediate or even intervene.[20]

2. the Vienna Congress and the establishment of the Concert introduced a new politico-legal hierarchy into the structure of the European states system.[21] The Great Powers created a new status for themselves, which then became a customary norm.[22] This status entailed the option of managing

European affairs collectively whenever conflicts could not be resolved on the bilateral level. This special status has persisted until today and evolved into certain privileges, most obviously a permanent seat and the right to veto decisions in the Security Council of the United Nations. However, neither permanent membership nor the right to veto decisions was granted in the Concert of Europe.

3. Queen Victoria described the functions of the Concert by referring to the Great Powers collectively as "guarantors of treaties, guardians of civilization, defenders of the right, and the real arbiters of the Nations."[23] She understood these functions as a "sacred office," which put responsibilities and duties into the hands of the Great Powers collectively. Accordingly, the Concert mediated conflicts like an international authority. It took hundreds of decisions in European and international affairs collectively, mostly decisions which a single Great Power could not have taken legitimately under the rules of the system. The Concert provided decisions for the governance of the European society of states as a whole, and thereby fulfilled the essential criterion for the term "institution" in its sociological sense.[24]

4. congresses, ambassadorial conferences, and commissions were the ad hoc organs of the Concert for the preservation of peace and the governance of European affairs. These organs provided for the procedural legitimization of decisions and mediation proposals put forward by the Concert. The frequency of the Concert's conference activities varied over the century of its existence,[25] but overall ambassadors' conferences met much more frequently than has been suggested in older research.[26] After 1856, the ambassadors' conference in Constantinople practically became a permanent body.

5. the Concert used numerous legal and coercive instruments to collectively secure peace, e.g. the plurilateral guarantee of a territory, the right to propose a compromise when involved in mediation, similar and collective dispatches, ultimata, naval demonstrations, naval blockades, and military interventions, both by its members collectively and by means of delegation to individual states. In modern terms, the Concert developed some instruments of soft power and hard power that are the basis for any effective collective security mechanism.[27] It legitimized the use of these instruments through the procedures mentioned, and through pronouncements such as conference protocols and collective representations by ambassadors. The protocols, which became more widely used and more detailed until reaching a peak in the second half of the nineteenth century, exemplified the evolving formal, institutional character of the Concert.[28] The British Prime Minister William E. Gladstone described them as "authoritative documents."[29] In the second half of the nineteenth century they were usually published, with some delay,

in treaty collections like the *Martens* or the *LeClerq*. Hence, the protocols were considered as sources of international law.

6. the increasing frequency of mediation by the Concert exerted more pressure upon the parties involved in disputes to compromise or to accept such mediation. A party to a conflict put itself at a disadvantage when it rejected the mediation or made claims that were considered unreasonable by the (other) Great Powers.[30] Usually it could no longer count on the support of the Concert once it had rejected mediation.

These points will suffice to demonstrate the Concert's growing degree of institutionalization in the nineteenth century, which in terms of the frequency of conferences was greatest from 1848 to the 1880s. A high degree of institutionalization, however, does not necessarily mean that the Concert always followed norms in its decision-making process.

II. Normative Ideas in Practice and Discourse

Conflict outcomes are neither exclusively nor automatically determined by power alignments,[31] but mostly by communicative processes, in which legal styles of reasoning, the relative legitimacy of claims made, and incentives to compromise all may play a role. Therefore, conflicts provide a good testing ground for analyzing the contribution made by normative ideas. Which normative ideas figured prominently in diplomatic discourse when the Concert tried to deescalate conflicts or justified intervention? Here we need to take into account the *dynamic development* of legal orders in general, i.e. the transformation of normative ideas in time,[32] as well as the logical inconsistency of pragmatic normative and legal reasoning.[33] As a third variable, we must refer to the different roots and types of conflict.[34] Fourth, it must be admitted that, as Max Weber contended, normative preferences may also reflect interests. Within this essay, this topic can be outlined only in broad strokes.

The Concert was in agreement that whenever a collective or delegated intervention was necessary, it must not be used to acquire territory or gain an unfair advantage, as this would undermine the Concert's legitimacy; nor, to state the obvious, did the Concert embrace any doctrines of collective "preventive" war. As to the question of whether an intervention was justified, the Concert operated with a set of competing criteria, to which the diplomats usually referred. Among these normative ideas, the following figured prominently: the principle of legitimacy, the territorial and/or legal status quo, the balance of power, the principle of nationality and even self-determination, and humanitarian considerations.[35] In other words, conservative and monarchical ideas competed with more liberal, pragmatic, and humanitarian ones. Depending on the type and location of the conflict, the applicability of certain norms in a given case, and the evolution of international culture, different mixes of normative ideas could be found in the discourse of decision makers.

In the first phase of the emerging Concert, an anti-revolutionary consensus shaped by the common experience with the French Revolution defined the Concert's policies. The three conservative Eastern powers, more or less supported by France, held the majority in the conferences taking places from 1820 to 1822, and authorized anti-revolutionary interventions in Naples, Piedmont, and Spain. However, the British government gradually broke away from this consensus, arguing that purely domestic revolts in minor states should not be equated with the threat to international security posed by the French Revolution. The British government rejected the ideological automatism entailed in Metternich's views, and withdrew from the conference system.[36]

The second phase of the Concert, which began with the Monroe Doctrine and ended roughly with the revolutions of 1848, was still characterized by ideological tensions and different policy preferences for dealing with revolutions. However, during this phase, the Concert gradually followed the British preference for a more pragmatic style of communicative conflict resolution, based upon the careful examination of each case and a realistic assessment of things happening on the ground. Essentially, the British governments led by Canning, Aberdeen, and Palmerston forestalled the rise of an anti-revolutionary doctrine in international law. For this purpose, they prevented anti-revolutionary interventions from occurring. Beginning in 1823, Britain's naval supremacy allowed it to protect Latin American independence movements against European interventions. Britain's headstart in industrial development, which reached its widest advantage over the continent around 1840, allowed for the victory of the so-called doctrine of non-intervention.[37] This doctrine allowed for the intervention by the Concert only when a situation represented a true menace for international security, or when a revolt turned into a humanitarian catastrophe. Once the anti-revolutionary automatism was switched off, the foundation for a more pragmatic approach to conflict resolution was laid. Liberated from ideological determinism, the Concert could choose neutrality or intervention on the grounds of more pragmatic considerations. Thus, Britain, France and Russia embarked on a collective intervention in favor of the Greek movement for independence. The Concert powers stayed neutral during the July Revolution, supported Belgian independence in 1830–31, and, following British pressure, refrained from intervention in Spain in 1837.[38]

When the great national struggles and the third phase of the Concert began in 1848–49, national identity and the notion of national, as opposed to monarchical, independence had become widely accepted normative ideas of international life, as long as one's own country suffered no disadvantage. Thus, the Russian Chancellor of State Nesselrode proposed the division of Schleswig according to the principle of nationality in 1849. Yet, this solution failed, because the Germans and the Danes in Schleswig rejected it. The Western powers and Austria supported Polish autonomy from Russia in 1863, but Austria disagreed with Italian pleas for the same status. British governments eyed Italian autonomy favorably, but not the Irish movement. Successive Prussian governments more or less sympathized with the German national movement, but not with the Danish or Polish ones. The normative change that took place in diplomatic discourse was at odds with the territorial order. Following the Crimean War these contradictions within the international order became more apparent.

In the Crimean War, the Concert fulfilled quite successfully its role as a guardian of the balance of power and arbiter of nations.[39] The motives of the Western powers for entry into the war were mixed, but the Concert had clearly condemned the Russian provocation and publicly justified the war of intervention. At the same time, the Crimean War heightened the readiness on the continent to use limited war as means of conflict resolution. This resulted in the temporary delegitimization of the Concert and weakened its authority. On the one hand the Concert held conferences almost permanently from 1852 to 1869 and resolved numerous smaller conflicts in this period—the question of Neuchâtel, the border question in the Danube area, the Greek succession, the Luxemburg question, and the Greek-Ottoman conflict concerning Crete. Moreover, it undertook several humanitarian initiatives such as protesting against the bombardment of Belgrade by the Ottomans, and intervening on behalf of the Christians massacred in Syria in 1861. None the less, it failed to resolve any of the looming national problems of this era: the Polish, German, and Italian questions. While Britain preferred to remain somewhat aloof from European affairs after the Crimean War, Denmark, Piedmont, Prussia, Austria, and France more or less skillfully withdrew themselves from the Concert's mediation and preferred to achieve their particular objectives or to restore their prestige by means of "duel wars," i.e. formally declared wars of honor, which followed the customary rules of warfare. By doing so they undermined the Concert.

Once the German and Italian questions were resolved, the situation was initially stabilized, but soon imperialistic ambitions began to subvert the practice of the Concert. Pragmatic and humanitarian considerations still played a role, but instead of the previous practice of weighing of all claims in a dispute, the normative reasoning within the Concert was weakened; and the principle that the Great Powers should not abuse their competence to manage European affairs was violated. At the Congress of Berlin in 1878, the Concert undid most of Russia's annexations, but allowed Great Britain and Austria to take possession of Cyprus and Bosnia-Herzegovina in the guise of temporary occupations.[40] The Concert achieved its last successes with the independence of Serbia, Bulgaria, Rumania, Montenegro (1878), and Albania (1913), as well as with its mediation between Ottoman Turkey and Greece over Crete in the 1890s. However, growing economic interdependence, the European "standard of civilization," and cooperative efforts to regulate inter-state relations were increasingly jeopardized by the conflicting ambitions of the Great Powers. The system of fixed alliances and an escalating arms race reduced diplomatic flexibility and eventually made the Concert dysfunctional. At the Algeciras Conference on Morocco in 1906 demanded by the German government, the main purpose of the deliberations was to regulate imperialist competition.[41] Although the French had clearly violated the 1880 Madrid convention on Morocco, the *Entente cordiale* and German ill-tempered tactics in 1906 determined an outcome that seemed to underline the isolation of the German government.[42] The London conference in 1912–13 on the Balkan Wars helped to settle the local disputes, but could not prevent the Balkan states from engaging in a second round of fighting.[43]

As to the generation and spreading of norms that were not related to the question of intervention, a few examples might be appropriate to emphasize this function of the Concert. The prohibition of the slave trade at the Vienna Congress, the establishment of administrative bodies for shipping on the Rhine, Danube, Congo, Niger, and the Suez Canal are tied closely to the history of the Concert. The Concert recommended arbitration as an additional means for conflict resolution at the Congress of Paris in 1856 and thus promoted the spread of this legal practice. In 1886, envoys of the Great Powers expressly prohibited aggressive war in the course of collective representations in Athens, Sofia, and Belgrade.[44] This foreshadowed the outlawing of aggression under the Kellogg-Briand-Pact in 1928. At the Africa Conference in Berlin, the signatories obliged themselves to respect human rights and liberties in colonies, thus effectively expanding normative ideas beyond the realm of the *ius publicum europaeum*. Subsequently, those rights were drastically violated, but this declaration nevertheless foreshadows the trend toward universal human rights, taken up again after World War II.[45]

III. Norm Violations and the Demise of the Concert

Norm violations occur in any socio-political order. To understand the demise of the Concert, it is appropriate to look at which actors resisted mediation most frequently, and those who rejected its authority in a grave, destructive manner in the last period of the Concert, from 1878 to 1914. Not each and every violation of norms destroys a normative system. The effect of a violation depends on the gravity, context, and justification (e.g. by reference to a higher principle) of the violation. Since small states alone usually do not cause a major war, it suffices here to sketch the behavior of the Great Powers. Not surprisingly, their behavior and discourse show that different degrees of internalization of international norms existed between the Great Powers.[46]

Despite blunders probably committed in the crisis leading to the Russo-Ottoman war in 1853, the British government did not cause a single war in nineteenth-century

Europe, and clearly stands out as *primus inter pares* as far as its respect for the Concert and the *ius publicum europaeum* is concerned. In Britain, politicians, international lawyers, and monarchs had internalized the Concert norms most deeply. The great historian of the Crimean War, Alexander Kinglake, treated the Concert as a collective actor, equal to an international authority and court of appeal.[47] The international lawyer T. J. Lawrence argued in the 1880s that power and practice had created a customary right for the Great Powers collectively to adjudicate international conflicts, and oblige smaller states to acquiesce in their decisions.[48] Lawrence argued an international authority with real competence was necessary in each legal order, and therefore also in international society. Similarly, John Westlake, one of the leading international lawyers in Britain, stated that practice and conviction had consolidated the legal character of the Concert of Europe.[49] James Lorimer considered that the Concert, as an international organization charged with defining, applying, and executing international law, was incomplete, and he criticized the absence of a statute with guidelines and a controlling body.[50] The growing interdependence of the society of states, according to Lorimer, required an international organization with a written constitution.[51]

France concluded an aggressive alliance with Piedmont in 1858, put the Concert out of operation in 1870 by declaring war on Prussia, and, in 1904, following its colonial bargain with Britain, violated the Madrid convention of 1880 pertaining to Morocco. In 1911, the French intervention in Morocco violated the Convention of Algeçiras. Despite these actions, France otherwise broadly conformed to the norms of the European system. The historian and international lawyer Charles Dupuis, and the lawyer, foreign minister, and Prime Minister Léon Bourgeois were among the most prominent and widely respected proponents of international solidarity in France. They embraced progressive notions about the Concert quite similar to those held by British lawyers.[52]

Russia, on the other hand, violated Polish rights constantly, persistently rejected conferences about Poland, and generally took risks frequently over the Eastern Question and outside Europe.[53] But, since Russia's expansion was largely directed toward Asia, it was not the most dangerous violator of the Concert's rules or of international law.

Surprisingly, Franz-Joseph's Habsburg monarchy rejected mediation by the Concert most frequently. An overextended empire, national and ethnic struggles, and a rigid interpretation of what was required to maintain honor and prestige contributed to this record. After having violated international law with the annexation of Krakow in 1846, the Austrian government delayed and then broke up the Brussels conference that was to mediate the conflict with Piedmont in 1849. In 1850, it rejected a European conference on the German question, in 1859 a conference on Italy, in 1866 a conference on the conflict with Prussia, and in 1908 a conference on the annexation of Bosnia. Finally, it refused to heed Sir Edward Grey's call for a European conference during the July crisis of 1914.[54]

However, the final collapse of the Concert had more to do with the politico-legal culture of the elite of the German Empire before World War I. In the early nineteenth century, some German lawyers had been keenly interested in positive international law, some handbooks were even translated into French and English, and the most important treaty collection of the times was edited in Göttingen by Martens. However, after Germany had been unified by war, and its military and industrial power rose to unexpected heights,[55] the German political elite became preoccupied with military and naval power and afraid of a weakening influence in European politics. They cut themselves off from the advance of Western-style progressive liberalism and international normative culture. As Martti Koskenniemi, a leading international lawyer of the present, points out, German legal culture before 1914 followed a special path, a "Sonderweg."[56] While since the 1880s top universities in Britain, France, and Austria had established chairs exclusively devoted to International Law, no such chair or professorship existed in Germany prior to 1914. At The Hague conferences the German Emperor was represented by law professors Baron Karl von Stengel, who had ridiculed Kant's idea of a League of Nations, and Philipp Zorn, rector of the University of Bonn, who went as far as to deny the existence of international law.[57] Baron Stengel held a view typical of the military establishment and German culture of the time, namely that war was something good, dynamic, and heroic, which had a cleansing effect on society. Without a warrior-like mentality, he claimed, Europe would soon be subjugated by what he called the "yellow race."[58]

At this point, the British crown had already recognized Japan as a member of the Family of Nations, and concluded an alliance with it. Around the same time during the Sino-Japanese war of 1894–95 and the Russo-Japanese war of 1904–05, Japan took great pains to abide by the Geneva conventions for the protection of the wounded, in order to emphasize its status as a civilized nation.[59]

The mentality of the German political and military elite of the day, and its inconsistent operation with international law, were the root cause of grave miscalculations that brought the Concert down. In 1911, Germany's stationing of the warship *Panther* at the port of Agadir violated the Convention of Algeçiras and conflicted with Germany's agreement, made in 1909 in a separate convention with France, to renounce all political influence in Morocco. Had the German government only pointed out the prior French violation of the same convention, it would have had a clear case. But through the Panther affair, Germany put itself in the position of the challenger of the system, as it did in the naval arms race with Britain. During the Balkan Wars, Chancellor Bethmann-Hollweg supported a resolution of the conflict through the Concert, which succeeded in localizing the conflict. So why did the German government fail completely to press its ally Austria to agree to a conference of the European Concert in the July Crisis of 1914? The Concert could have mediated in the conflict with Serbia, and it could have been used to set up an international investigative mission to identify the perpetrators and the circumstances of the assassination of Francis Ferdinand and his spouse. Austria would most certainly have received an indemnity, and Serbia would have been relatively isolated. Even Russia would have had great difficulties in supporting its ally. Second, the German attack on Belgium was probably the most flagrant violation of international law norms in Europe since even before 1815. Not only had Belgium the right and obligation to remain neutral, but also Prussia was among the five Powers that had guaranteed the neutrality and inviolability of Belgium in 1831–39, and was therefore a protector of that nation. The existence of the Schlieffen Plan strengthens the argument that the demise of international law in German political culture had occurred long before 1914. The gravity of this violation of norms, which was completely disproportionate to the assassinations of Sarajevo, was perceived by neighboring countries as a rupture with the concept of "civilization."[60] As a consequence, Britain had to enter the war, and the Concert and a vast portion of the catalogue of international rules and norms such as the gold standard, the most-favored-nation principle, and the Geneva Conventions collapsed.[61] After the war, Germany was not admitted to the League of Nations that replaced the Concert until 1926, because in the eyes of the West it had to redeem its status as a "civilized nation."[62]

IV. Procedures, Norms, and the Outbreak of War

By the late nineteenth century, numerous procedures and norms had been well established which could have prevented the outbreak of World War I, such as international arbitration by a court, mediation by a friendly neutral power, mediation and pressure by the Concert of Europe sitting in conference, even the establishment of a fact-finding and surveillance mission as practiced by the Concert in Syria in 1861. Similar methods could have been applied to manage, and even to resolve, the July Crisis peacefully. Given the existence of such well-developed and sophisticated means to deal with international conflict in the nineteenth century, it was the demise of the "culture of peace," i.e. the declining adherence to procedural and normative rules of international conduct, which paved the way for world war. This decline took place "asymmetrically," that is, to a differing extent in each nation. While the British and French political elite remained relatively attached to the culture of peace, among the German and Austrian political and military elite, the notion of international law and propriety of conduct had declined precipitously for some time. In Germany, this decline accelerated after the founding of the Empire and the consequent dramatic rise in relative power. On a general level, this points to the tragic dilemma faced by the leaders of some of the most powerful nations. While these leaders were in theory best placed to enforce international norms, they were often precisely the ones who despised or disregarded them when they were inconvenient or collided with national ambitions. Instead, they believed they could regulate everything by means of power. Furthermore, these leaders were preoccupied with prestige, and incapable of seeing things in proportion.

Although it did not automatically trigger war, the Serbian government's support of terrorism was without doubt outside the norms of nineteenth-century international politics. Yet, Serbia ironically came out as one of the big winners of the Great War. The Serbian elite, apparently, had never internalized the international legal norms established in nineteenth-century politics. Instead, they had internalized the nationalism which destabilized the society of states throughout the century. Austria's preference for resolving the conflict by a bilateral war, as several powers had attempted in the wars of 1859, 1864, 1866, and 1870, was, in theory, compatible with the "culture of war" as practised in the mid century. But this practice of waging war to preserve one's honor, like in a duel, had fallen in abeyance since the Franco-German War, and since then considerable efforts had been deployed to prevent the recurrence of war, both through Concert mediation and international arbitration.

Nonetheless, by any standards, Germany's choice to turn the limited war into a world war—by preemptively declaring war on Russia, almost a week before Austria had done so, and invading Belgium—was clearly outside any international norms and practices, and void of any legitimacy. Accordingly, from a normative viewpoint, Germany was the main culprit, because its violation of the "culture of peace" was much more severe than Serbia's or Austria-Hungary's; and it was the crucial violation which turned the conflict into a world war that killed approximately 10 million people. Austria-Hungary was culpable as well, because it ran high risks in opting for a bilateral war against Serbia without knowing exactly whether the Serbian government had been involved in the assassination or not; although its government knew that Russia was protecting Serbia. As Franz Joseph's government had taken risks before and frequently rejected Great Power conferences, it should have known that any war could turn out as a calamity. The Habsburg monarchy had learned nothing from previous disasters.

Russia's general mobilization, though clearly a trigger for the expansion of the war, was not by any standard a violation of norms. It was essentially a precaution intended to warn Austria and put pressure on Germany to rein in its ally, not an aggressive act. Considering the heat of the moment in the crisis, it could be considered provocative. Yet, contrary to Bethmann Hollweg's allegations, there was no "necessity" for Germany to declare war, there was only a defensive necessity to mobilize in response. Thus, from a normative standpoint, renewed revisionist tendencies in German historiography about the causes of World War I are to be rejected. In particular, attempts to put some blame on Britain's powerless King for making ambivalent remarks to the German Crown Prince are quite out of proportion, for the German Ambassador in London Prince Lichnowsky had sent enough warnings about the British government's sentiments to Berlin during the July Crisis. Moreover, Britain was the last country to uphold the procedures and norms of the Concert. By suggesting that a conference be held to preserve peace, the Austrian government might conceivably have had an opportunity to score a diplomatic victory without having to risk a catastrophe. It would have been legitimate and in concordance with Concert practice to demand the establishment of an international surveillance commission charged by the European Concert to observe the Serbs' search for those who facilitated the assassination. If the Serbians had produced no results, backtracked, or hampered such a commission, the majority of the powers in the Concert might have given Austria some diplomatic support, whatever that might have amounted to. At least this procedure would have been a proportionate response in line with the nineteenth-century "culture of peace."

Notes

1. This essay is based partly upon my observations in "'Wächter der Zivilisation'? Institutionelle Merkmale und normative Grundlagen des Europäischen Konzerts im 19. Jahrhundert," in *Historische Mitteilungen (HMRG)* 17 (2004), 35–47. Here my purpose is to relate the observations to the origins of World War I.
2. See Evan Luard, *International Society* (New York, 1990), 23.
3. Different approaches and observations in this field have been put forward by the political scientists Terry Nardin, Friedrich Kratochwil, Evan Luard, and Andreas Osiander, as well as by the historian Paul W. Schroeder and Peter Krüger, and myself, see note 1 and Matthias Schulz, "Normen und Netzwerke in der internationalen Geschichte," in *HMRG* 17 (2004), 1–13. For Luard, see note 2; Terry Nardin, *Law, Morality, and the Relations of States* (Princeton, New Jersey, 1983); Friedrich Kratochwil, *Rules, Norms, and Decisions: On the Conditions of Practical and Legal Reasoning in International Relations and Domestic Affairs* (Cambridge, 1995), especially 33–35, 60–69; Andreas Osiander, *The States System of Europe, 1640–1990: Peacemaking and the Conditions of International Stability* (Oxford, 1994); several essays in Peter Krüger and Paul W. Schroeder, *"The Transformation of European Politics, 1763–1848": Episode or Model in Modern History?* (Münster, 2002); Paul W. Schroeder, *The Transformation of European Politics, 1763–1848* (Oxford, 1994).
4. Matthias Schulz, *Das Europäische Konzert der Großmächte als Sicherheitsrat: Normen und Praxis plurilateraler Konfliktlösung, 1815–1852*, post-doctoral dissertation [Habilschrift] Rostock, 2001, 517 p.; book publication envisaged for 2007.
5. Winfried Baumgart, *Europäisches Konzert und nationale Bewegung: Internationale Beziehungen 1830–1878* (Paderborn, 1999), 165. The quotation in the text was my own translation. There are studies presenting annotated documents, diplomatic narratives which usually pay little attention to the Concert as such, analyses from the perspective of one country in a given period, and case studies of individual conflicts in which the Concert was involved, e.g. by René Albrecht-Carrié, Jean-Baptiste Duroselle, Richard Elrod, Winfried Baumgart, Paul Schroeder, William Echard, William Daugherty, and a few others. Yet Baumgart's statement takes all these older studies into account.
6. Compare W. Norton Medlicott, *Bismarck, Gladstone and the Concert of Europe* (London, 1957); Stanley Hoffmann, *Organisations internationales et pouvoirs politiques des Etats* (Paris, 1954), 23–120.

7. For a general discussion of the term "institution", see Gerhard Göhler, "Einleitung: Politische Ideengeschichte—institutionentheoretisch gelesen," in Ders., Kurt Lenk, Herfried Münkler, Manfred Walther, eds., *Politische Institutionen im gesellschaftlichen Umbruch. Ideengeschichtliche Beiträge zur Theorie politischer Institutionen* (Opladen, 1990), 7–20, quoted, 12; and Rainer Lepsius, *Interessen, Ideen und Institutionen* (Opladen, 1990), passim, 61.
8. About the social constraint to "civilize" oneself, and the example of the "chivalry of warriors," see Norbert Elias, *Über den Prozeß der Zivilisation. Soziogenetische und psychogenetische Untersuchungen* (Frankfurt am Main, 1976), vol. 2: *Wandlungen der Gesellschaft: Entwurf zu einer Theorie der Zivilisation*, 312ff, 351–369.
9. See note 4. The sources are protocols and correspondence related to conferences, congresses, and commissions established by the Concert, contemporary legal treatises, and treaty series, e.g. Martens' *Nouveau Récueil général des Traités*, LeClerq's *Récueil des traités de la France*, *The British Digest of International Law* (1860–1914), *Répértoire de la République française en Matière de Droit International Public (1861–87)*, and *La prassi italiana di diritto internazionale* (1887–1918).
10. Cf. Clive Trebilcock, *The Industrialization of the Continental Powers 1780–1914* (London, 1981), 179f.; Robert Latham, "Nineteenth-century lessons" *RIS* 23 (1997), 419–443, 429; see also Sidney Pollard, "Probleme der europäischen Integration im 19. und 20. Jahrhundert," in Helmut Berding, ed., *Wirtschaftliche und politische Integration in Europa im 19. und 20. Jahrhundert* (Göttingen, 1984), 9–33.
11. Schulz, *Das Europäische Konzert*, 39–63.
12. Ibid., 52–54; Wilhelm Grewe, *Epochen der Völkerrechtsgeschichte* (Baden-Baden, 1988), 40.
13. Quoted in Carsten Holbraad, *The Concert of Europe: A Study in German and British International Theory, 1815–1914* (London, 1970), 25; for Metternich's ideas on international order, see Enno Kraehe, ed., *The Metternich Controversy* (New York, 1971).
14. Cf. Schulz, *Das Europäische Konzert*, passim.
15. Castlereagh to Lord Liverpool, 20 Oct, 1818, quoted in René Albrecht-Carrié, *The Concert of Europe 1815–1914* (London, Melbourne, 1968), 43 (Documentary History of Western Civilization); compare Memorandum of the British government on the treaties of 1814 and 1815, presented at the Congress of Aix-la-Chapelle, October 1818, printed in ibid., see p. 42. On another occasion Castlereagh referred to a "union et ... concert pacifique," see Duke of Wellington, *Despatches, Correspondence and Memoranda of Field Marshal Arthur Duke of Wellington*, vol. VII (London, 1867), 168.
16. Such ideas were transfered e.g. by legal literature, diplomatic dispatches, conversations and negotiations, and monarchical correspondence.
17. I prefer to call this "plurilateral" (involving several states) so as to distinguish it from multilateral cooperation (involving many or all states), because the Concert was not open to the participation of all states. The Concert represented a form of cooperation of its own, situated between bilateral and multilateral cooperation. But compare Wolfram Pyta, "Konzert der Mächte und kollektives Sicherheitssystem: Neue Wege zwischenstaatlicher Friedenswahrung in Europa nach dem Wiener Kongreß," in *Jahrbuch des Historischen Kollegs* (Bayerischen Akademie der Wissenschaften: München, 1996), 133–173.
18. Compare Jack S. Levy, *War in the Modern Great Power System, 1494–1975* (Lexington, 1983) 90 and passim.
19. Johann L. Klüber, *Pragmatische Geschichte der nationalen und politischen Wiedergeburt Griechenlands, bis zu dem Regierungsantritt des Königs Otto* (Frankfurt am Main, 1835), x–xiii; ibid., *Europäisches Völkerrecht* (Schotthausen, 1851 (1819)); also published as *Droit de gens moderne de l'Europe*. About Klüber see Martti Koskenniemi, *The Gentle Civilizer of Nations: The Rise and Fall of International Law* (Cambridge, 2002), 21–24.
20. Compare Perry Glenn Lovett, *Justifying War: The Just War Tradition until 1919*, PhD Diss., University of Oklahoma, 1982 (Ann Arbor: University Microfilms International, 1982).

21. "The representatives of the smaller powers," writes James Lorimer about the Congress of Vienna, "might, for the most part, just as well have stayed at home." James Lorimer, *The Institutes of the Law of Nations: A Treatise of the Jural Relations of Separate Political Communities*, 2 vols. (Edinburgh/London, 1883–84), vol. I, 176.
22. Only Spain protested against the introduction of a two-class hierarchy of states. However, its government protested not against the principle, it simply wanted to be counted among the Great Powers and participate in their decision-making body. See Hoffmann, *Organisations internationales*, 25. According to Pyta, the legal quarrel between Spain and Austria about the succession in Italian principalities provided the background for the Spanish position. Pyta, *Konzert der Mächte*, 153.
23. Victoria to Friedrich Wilhelm IV, 17 March 1854, in Arthur C. Benson, Viscount Esher, eds., *The Letters of Queen Victoria, a selection from Her Majesty's correspondence between the years 1837 and 1861, published by authority of His Majesty the king* (London, 1907), vol. III, 18.
24. "Politische Institutionen [sind] ... immer dann historisch zu orten, wenn es um Ordnungsleistungen für ein soziales Ganzes geht," Göhler, *Einleitung*, 14.
25. Most intensive were the years from the Congress of Vienna to 1822, and from 1849 to 1885. The Concert was not destroyed in the Crimean War. Compare for a different point of view Paul W. Schroeder, *Austria, Great Britain and the Crimean War: The Destruction of the European Concert* (Ithaca, London, 1972); Ian Clark, *The Hierarchy of States: Reform and Resistance in the International Order* (Cambridge, 1989), 122ff: Richard B. Elrod, "The Concert of Europe: A Fresh Look at an International System," in *World Politics* 28 (1976), 159–174. Doering-Manteuffel interpretes the year 1856 not as the end of the Concert, but as the end of the Vienna order. This illustrates the different use of terms, but in the limited space allotted to me here, I cannot comment on this any further. Anselm Doering-Manteuffel, *Vom Wiener Kongreß zur Pariser Konferenz. England, die deutsche Frage und das Mächtesystem 1815–1856* (Göttingen, 1991).
26. Instead of twenty six conferences and congresses listed by Charles Webster, I have identified forty three conference series, many of which lasted several months or even years. Charles K. Webster, *The Art and Practice of Diplomacy* (1961), 59, 69.
27. Unilateral interventions are not the subject here. Their political character belongs more in a discussion of imperialism and hegemony theory.
28. The protocols at the Vienna conferences 1854 and 1855 were clearly more differentiated and detailed than those of the Congress of Troppau in 1821. The protocols of the European Commission for Syria (1860–61) comprise 500 pages. See HHStA, PA XII, Türkei 218; GStA PK, III. HA, 2.4.I/7573. Protocols were published, usually several years after the conferences were held, in Georg Friedrich von Martens' "Recueil Général des Traités", and in France in Jules de LeClercq's "Traités de France," so they were considered as sources of international law.
29. Gladstone in the House of Commons, 6 May 1856, in *Hansard's Parliamentary Debates*, 3rd series, CXLII, 101f.
30. Numerous examples in Schulz, *Das Europäische Konzert*.
31. See for selections of case studies of conflicts ibid., and James L. Richardson, *Crisis Diplomacy: The Great Powers since the Mid-Nineteenth Century* (Cambridge, 1994); Jost Dülffer, Martin Kröger, Rolf-Harald Wippich, *Vermiedene Kriege: Deeskalation von Konflikten der Großmächte zwischen Krimkrieg und Erstem Weltkrieg (1856–1914)* (Munich, 1997).
32. Legal orders are not static, but dynamic; compare Kratochwil, p. 2. Historians, ironically, tend to view law as something static.
33. Kratochwil, p. 33–35. Each normative system featured tensions and contradictions (e.g. liberty and equality as norms figuring in discourse on human rights and democracy), and the resolution of cases of normative conflict usually on normative reasoning.
34. Among the types of conflicts were revolutions, religious conflicts, wars of secession and unification.

35. Schulz, *Das Europäische Konzert*, discusses the discourse on norms among individuals like Metternich, Castlereagh, Canning, Droysen, Friedrich Ancillon, Friedrich Wilhelm IV, Alexander I, Nesselrode, Clarendon, Russell, Palmerston, Gladstone, Gortschakow, Bismarck, free traders like Richard Cobden, a few nineteenth-century historians, and international lawyers, etc.
36. Schulz, *Das Europäische Konzert*, 64–80.
37. Ibid., passim, 127–180.
38. Ibid., 81–108.
39. Cf. Winfried Baumgart, *The Crimean War 1853–1856* (London, Sidney, Auckland, 1999), 16, 18.
40. Documents published in Albrecht-Carrie, *Concert of Europe*, 247–281.
41. Ibid., 310–314.
42. Richard Langhorne, *The Collapse of the Concert of Europe: International Politics 1890–1914* (New York, 1981), 91ff.
43. Ibid., 105ff.
44. Stephan Verosta, *Kollektivaktionen der Mächte des Europäischen Konzerts (1886–1914)* (Wien 1988), 27.
45. The universalization of the *ius publicum europaeum* took place very slowly in a complex environment featured by European expansion, European discrimination against non-western peoples through unequal treaties, capitulations, clauses of extraterrioriality, protectorates, and colonization, and resistance and adaptation by the non-western world, which lasted well into the second half of the twentieth-century. See for more Gerrit W. Gong, *The Standard of 'Civilization' in International Society* (Oxford, 1984).
46. Whether a normative system is functional depends on the socialization and internalization of norms by the relevant actors. Educational content, discourse, and compliance with norms are indicators of internalization. Compare Schulz, *Das Europäische Konzert*, 324–447. See also Kratochwil, 67.
47. Alexander W. Kinglake, *The Invasion of the Crimea*, 6 vols, 6th edition, (Edinburgh, 1877) vol. I, 6.
48. T. J. Lawrence, "The Primacy of the Great Powers," in ibid., *Essays on Some Disputed Questions in Modern International Law* (Cambridge, 1884), 191–213, 209.
49. John Westlake, *International Law* vol. I, *Peace*, 2nd edition, (Cambridge, 1910), 321–323; John Westlake, *The Collected Papers of John Westlake on Public International Law*, Part I, Lassa Oppenheim, ed. (Cambridge, 1914), 101.
50. James Lorimer, *The Institutes of the Law of Nations: A Treatise of the Jural Relations of Separate Political Communities*, 2 vols. (Edinburgh, London, 1883–84), vol. I, 57, 175–177.
51. "Most important of all, for practical purposes, is the attempt which is now being made to establish a sort of permanent international executive, by means of the concert of the six great European powers. ... It does not contain an element of self-control, on which even its external action is dependent; it never can be either wiser or stronger than the particular treaty which it professes to execute." Lorimer, *Institutes of the Law of Nations*, vol. I, 57.
52. See Louis Dupuis, *Le principe d'équilibre et le Concert européen* (Paris, 1909); about Léon Bourgeois, see Koskenniemi, *Gentle Civilizer*, 284–291.
53. The author is unfamiliar with Russian legal culture in the decades before World War I. Earlier in the nineteenth century, German international lawyers exerted some influence there.
54. It seems that Berchtold and the Austrian government saw the Concert around 1900 only as a useful instrument to keep Russia in check, and control the Ottoman question.
55. See Paul Kennedy, *Aufstieg und Fall der großen Mächte: Ökonomischer Wandel und militärischer Konflikt von 1500 bis 2000* (Frankfurt, 1991), 370.
56. Koskenniemi, *Gentle Civilizer*, 210f.
57. See Philipp Zorn, *Das Deutsche Reich und die internationale Schiedsgerichtsbarkeit* (Berlin, 1911), 6.

58. Baron Karl von Stengel, *Weltstaat und Friedensproblem* (Berlin, 1909).
59. Cf. Gerrit W. Gong, *The Standard of 'Civilization' in International Society* (Oxford, 1984), 18, 28, 29, 184f.
60. The so-called "standard of civilization" was a notion firmly established in nineteenth-century international law. It comprised the respect for international law and the fulfilment of international obligations. Around the mid-nineteenth century a state was recognized as being "civilized" when it possessed a stable government that was capable of concluding and upholding international treaties, and of protecting the lives, liberties, and property of foreigners on its territory. Later, the standard included free trade and free travel for Europeans, a functioning administration and legal system protecting indigenous people as well as foreigners, respect for international law and the laws of warfare, and the maintenance of diplomatic relations. The development of the standard can be followed in several editions of Henry Wheaton's *Elements of International Law*, published for the first time in 1836 and reissued in several editions until 1944. Compare Gong, *Standard of 'Civilization' in International Society*, especially 14f, 24ff. L. Oppenheim also mentions the recognition by European states as a criterion for gaining the status as a civilized state. L. Oppenheim, *International Law* (London, 1905), 32.
61. Cf. Michael Walzer, *Just and Unjust Wars: A Moral Argument with Historical Illustrations* (New York, 1977), 240f.
62. Compare note 53.

Chapter 3

AGGRESSIVE AND DEFENSIVE AIMS OF POLITICAL ELITES?
Austro-Hungarian Policy in 1914

Samuel R. Williamson, Jr.

On Tuesday, 28 July 1914, Emperor Franz Joseph approved the Habsburg declaration of war against Serbia. He did so at his desk in his beloved summer residence at Bad Ischl, and he did so with a clear appreciation of the risks the war might bring. The declaration represented the culmination of nearly twenty-four months of continuous diplomatic tension for Austria-Hungary and its ruling elite. Four times since the fall of 1912 they had confronted the prospect of war: twice against Serbia, in December 1912 and October 1913, once against Montenegro in May 1913, and, in a case usually ignored, against Russia in the opening months of 1913. What now led the decision makers to war? Was their decision the probable outcome and logical consequence of previous international tensions, or was it the result of a completely new political situation caused by the Sarajevo assassinations? To answer these questions, we must examine more closely the perceptions and expectations of the Austro-Hungarian decision makers before and after Sarajevo.[1]

I

By late spring 1914 the repeated crises had altered the lineup and attitudes of the Habsburg leadership. Among the leaders actively shaping government policy, Franz Joseph remained—after more than six decades—the final arbiter for peace or war.

Though seriously sick in the late spring, the 83-year-old ruler had returned to his proverbial writing desk, a step or two slower but still in charge. Committed to the German alliance if not especially fond of Kaiser Wilhelm II, concerned about Russia, and alarmed about Serbia's longer-term threat, he came increasingly to believe that Vienna might have to act decisively to protect its great power status. To that end he now accepted the need to force Rumania to declare whether or not it was still aligned with the Triple Alliance. If not, then Vienna, in spite of Berlin, would have to approach Bulgaria as a counter-weight in the Balkans, however distasteful that might be. Under no circumstances would Vienna allow its Bosnian-Herzegovinian gain from the Ottoman inheritance to be challenged. For Franz Joseph the question was not one of aggressive or expansionist aims but one of protection and defense.[2]

The monarch's foreign minister, Count Leopold Berchtold, shared those views but with still more rigor and increasing inflexibility. During the war-peace crises, Berchtold had used the threat of military action to wrest a series of diplomatic victories: Serbia blocked from the Adriatic, Albania created, Russia forced to make its Serbian client abandon territory. A policy of "militant diplomacy" had worked, even as its fiscal costs had wrecked the Habsburg budget process.[3]

But by June the aristocratic Berchtold had new worries. Since 1879 the alliance with Germany had been the keystone of Habsburg foreign policy. Italy's participation in the alliance since 1882 had, for the most part, been helpful, as had Rumania's silent membership. But now the alliance appeared increasingly in disarray. Rome, always a troublesome ally, had become more problematic as the two governments competed for control of Albania and Italian claims for the Trentino accelerated. The long secret ties with Rumania were in jeopardy as St. Petersburg's campaign to woo Bucharest gained ground. And then there was the problem of Germany. For Berchtold the German alliance remained essential, but he resented Berlin's failure to understand the gravity of the South Slav issue, its "hot-cold" support during the recent crises, and the imperious tone of the German press about the long-term future of the Monarchy. He recognized that Berlin could veto a major policy decision, such as a local war against Serbia or even an alliance overture to Sofia. But he also knew that Vienna could veto any German move that might threaten war.

But the foreign minister realized, most of all, by mid June that Vienna needed to reshape and restart its diplomatic policy. He wanted to make a final effort to keep Rumania or, failing that, move to enlist Bulgaria in the isolation of Serbia. He also wanted to convince a skeptical Berlin that Russia posed the largest threat to their joint interests. From his perspective, Berchtold wanted a new, more effective defensive posture but knew it would require initiative to achieve. Less aggressive than protective, his policy sought to stabilize the monarchy's Balkan flank.[4]

In the pursuit of this agenda Berchtold now had two important allies: István Tisza and István Burián. Since returning to power in July 1913, Tisza, the Hun-

Map 3.1: The Balkans, 1912–14. From: Francis Roy Bridge and Roger Bullen: *The Great Powers and the European States System 1814–1914*, second edition, Harlow 2005, p. 325 (with friendly permission of Francis Roy Bridge).

garian prime minister, had, unlike his Austrian counterpart, become deeply involved in debates about the formation of the Monarchy's foreign policy. Either he, or Burián, his permanent representative in Vienna, pressed Berchtold with their own policy suggestions. The so-called "imperial Magyars," as John Leslie so aptly described them, valued the alliance with Germany, favored an arrangement with Bulgaria, wanted no more Slavs in the Monarchy, and had even talked of overtures to Russia for a new round of negotiations. They, like Berchtold and Franz Joseph, also considered any potential union of Serbia and Montenegro as completely unacceptable. Moreover, Tisza had coerced the Hungarian government into accepting an increase in the annual recruit quota for the army, so that the Habsburg standing army could be increased for the first time since 1889. From the perspective of Budapest, protection of the status quo, not adventure, constituted the fabric of foreign policy.[5]

Karl Stürgkh, Tisza's Austrian counterpart, and Leon Bilinski, who helped to administer Bosnia-Herzegovina, also supported Berchtold's policy of "militant diplomacy." Nor were they unmindful of the "spill-over" effect of foreign events upon the complex domestic life of Austria-Hungary.[6] Far more aggressive than any of the civilian ministers, or the emperor/king, was General Conrad von Hötzendorf, Chief of the General Staff. While one can speak of defensive, protective stances for the other members of the senior elite, Conrad wanted to pursue an aggressive, expansionist policy. Some would see him as a "defensive realist," others as a blatant militarist. [7]

Appointed chief in 1906, Conrad advocated war with Serbia in 1908, against his Italian ally in late 1911 (for which he was dismissed from his post), and then repeatedly against Serbia and/or Montenegro in 1912–13 after his reappointment in December 1912. For the general, war offered a chance to infuse the aging Monarchy with a new vigor, resolve the South Slav menace and protect Habsburg interests as a great power. He and Prussian General Helmuth von Moltke came to share an increasingly pessimistic view of the growing Russian threat and each talked of a preventive war in a fashion that the administration of President George W. Bush would understand in 2003. At various times, completely disregarding Hungarian opposition to more Slavs in the monarchy, the general advocated a partition of Serbia, the annexation of Serbia, or even its forced incorporation into the Monarchy as an Austro-Hungarian Bavaria. Although he repeated his themes often, he found scant support for them—especially not from Tisza. On the other hand, as the senior general (and backed by War Minister General Alexander Krobatin), he was an influential decision maker.[8]

By mid June 1914 the Habsburg decision-making elite had recognized that the Monarchy was on the defensive; it also realized that it had to seek a new diplomatic alignment in the Balkans or make its old one more effective. Either Rumania had to become a reliable partner or Vienna must turn to Bulgaria as a counterweight against Serbia, however unhappy the Bulgarians made Kaiser Wilhelm. Nor were the elite unaware of increasing German speculation about Vienna's long-term prospects in an age of intensive nationalism. Equally important, the elite appreciated and feared the surging power of Russia.

But there was another decision circle in Vienna: that of the Archduke Franz Ferdinand and his associates. Formally anointed as the heir apparent in 1898, the archduke in 1906 established his own military chancellery; in 1913 Franz Joseph made his nephew the inspector general of the armed forces. Relations between uncle and nephew might be described as correct, formal, and infrequent; but the older man had gradually allowed Franz Ferdinand influence over key appointments, with Conrad one of his first. By 1914 cynics could note that Austria-Hungary had three armies, three governments, and two emperors. For those in the so-called "Belvedere circle" of the archduke, the question each morning, "how is the health of the emperor?" was not academic. In fact, during the emperor's serious illness in the spring of 1914, a train stood ready at the archduke's Bohemian castle for the run to Vienna. At any moment Franz Ferdinand could become the emperor, a prospect that filled the Magyars with dread and many others with apprehension.[9]

If the official, authorized governing circle had concluded that a more active foreign policy was needed and if they did not eschew force, the heir apparent had different views. Save for a brief three-week period in late 1912, Franz Ferdinand had since 1906 favored a cautious, peaceful foreign policy. He did not want an unnecessary war and one that might make his accession to power more difficult. Thus throughout 1913 he had urged against war with Serbia or Montenegro or Russia. His opposition in October 1913 to a confrontation with Belgrade led Berchtold to ignore him altogether. However assessed, Franz Ferdinand constituted a force for peace and restraint; he had no aggressive agenda in the realm of foreign policy. At the same time he remained on good terms with Berchtold and the two spent a weekend together just two weeks before Sarajevo.

Further, the archduke's close friendship with the mercurial Wilhelm II meant that he had a foreign policy importance that became increasingly salient. Like the German ruler, Franz Ferdinand loved the navy, favored the alliance with Rumania, disliked the Bulgarians, and worried about the Russians while loathing the Italians. Unlike the German Kaiser, who liked Tisza, the archduke distrusted the Magyar leader; and, unlike Wilhelm, he recognized the threat posed by the South Slavs. The two men were together only two weeks before Sarajevo, a fact that certainly helps to explain the German's determination to back Vienna in any showdown with Belgrade.[10]

For his part, the archduke worked reasonably well with Foreign Minister Berchtold and the Austrian ministers. On the other hand, a series of incidents with Conrad in 1913 left their relationship tarnished, with the general almost certainly scheduled for replacement after the 1914 maneuvers. Meanwhile, a series of potential ministers in future Franz Ferdinand governments drifted in and out of favor at the Belvedere. But the sheer fact of their presence served as a reminder that there were two sets of power in Vienna, one in the present and one in the imminent future.

The situation in Vienna on the eve of Sarajevo thus permits no easy label of an "aggressive elite." The governing group was reexamining the Monarchy's foreign policy, convinced some changes had to be made to offset the growth of Serbia and the impact of the South Slav movement, both within the Habsburg holdings and in the Balkans more generally. And, of course, there were the complicated maneuvers arising from nationalist frictions inside the Monarchy, frictions between Czechs and Germans in Bohemia and between Magyars and Rumanians in Transylvania. Moreover, members of the elite had already considered a war with Serbia and at least Conrad had talked of military force and imperial ambitions for the future of Austria-Hungary. The others would almost certainly have said that stability and an enhanced international position would have been adequate.

If one had made a summary statement of the Habsburg elite and its agenda on Saturday, 27 June, the following would have been included:

- preserve the multinational Monarchy;
- keep Bosnia-Herzegovina;
- make a final attempt to keep Rumania as a secret ally and, failing that, then approach to Bulgaria;
- keep the alliance with Berlin and remain cautious with Rome;
- maintain an independent Albania;
- remain wary of Russia;
- oppose any union of Serbia and Montenegro even to the point of war;
- monitor Serbian and Russian support of Slavs within Austria-Hungary, including apparent support for various terrorist acts;
- stake a claim for a part of the Ottoman Empire should it collapse;
- survive a transition from Franz Joseph to Franz Ferdinand;
- a preventive war against Serbia, though sometimes under serious consideration, had not been unequivocally accepted as the elite's preferred option, but would remain a strong possibility, even probability.

II

A day later, 28 June, parts of the agenda had been abruptly altered, or so it might appear. The next month saw the governing elite, no longer worried about a transition or a restless heir apparent, prepared to revisit their earlier discussions about using force to resolve the South Slav problem. Their debates revealed an elite less concerned about aggression for possible territorial gain, than about self-preservation, regime change in Belgrade and defense against what they considered state-sponsored terrorism. Or put another way, for the elite an aggressive policy against Serbia became a form of self-preservation and of defensive realism.

The context for their decisions after 28 June, however, requires additional comment. The death of Franz Ferdinand not only provided the ultimate pretext for war, it also made it possible by drastically simplifying the Habsburg decision process. No longer did Berchtold have to worry about a cautious archduke; no longer did Conrad have to worry about being replaced; and no longer did Tisza have to worry about the archduke's enmity. To these structural considerations personal ones also have to be added. The sheer shock of the new situation, the grim death of people with whom they had worked intimately, and the realization that the monarchy's next heir apparent was an untried, unimpressive Karl Franz Joseph, age twenty-six: all influenced the attitudes of the decision of the elite in the first days after Sarajevo. If one worried about the future and believed decisive action might revive sagging Habsburg fortunes, then the pressures for a confrontation with Serbia had dramatically increased.[11]

A second consideration also merits attention: the position of Wilhelm II and Germany. Until the afternoon of 2 July, Vienna expected that the German monarch would attend the funeral of Franz Ferdinand and Sophie. Memoranda were prepared for the expected visit and some decisions about next steps postponed on the assumption that the two rulers would talk. But security fears in Berlin about Wilhelm's safety, possibly coupled with almost no pressure from Vienna for him to come (indeed, some relief that he would not come, thereby calling attention to the unlamented archduke) led to his remaining in Berlin. In practical terms, Wilhelm's failure to come meant that Vienna would now have to sound Berlin in Berlin, hence the celebrated mission of Count Alexander Hoyos, the *chef de cabinet* of the Foreign Ministry. Whether a face-to-face discussion with Wilhelm in Vienna would have altered any dimension of the final decisions in early July remains, of course, a counter-factual whimsy. Yet a clear sign of public coordination between the two powers might have sent a less ambiguous signal to other powers about their joint intentions, rather than the subsequent confused set of signals as Kaiser Wilhelm II sailed off for his annual North Sea cruise.[12]

Linked to the question of the cancelled royal visit is the entire issue of the relationship between Berlin and Vienna. Or, put another way, did Berlin push Vienna to war or did Vienna make its own decisions? All of the key policy makers of the Habsburg elite, save Tisza, had by 1 July concluded that strong action against Serbia had become necessary; the terrorist attacks had now gone too far and Belgrade, even though its role was not exactly clear, had to be punished. These conclusions came before any visit by Victor Nauman or any pressure of any kind from the German ally. Later, as the July days unfolded, there would be clear German impatience, as Vienna seemed to take forever to make its démarche in Belgrade. But while some judge this as pressure, it can also and should be seen as worry that the moment for any successful, localized action against Serbia was slipping away.[13]

On the other hand, had Berlin failed to give the famous "blank check" or had Berlin later made an unequivocal *volte face* about its support of the Habsburg intentions, Vienna would have almost certainly have been stymied and even forced to back away. One possible explanation for Berchtold's precipitate declaration of war on 28 July may have been to thwart any possible German abandonment of its ally; his action certainly made it less likely.

From 29 June and thereafter, Austrian Prime Minister Karl Stürgkh and Common Finance Minister Leon Bilinski favored a military confrontation with Serbia. In this stance they had support, not surprisingly, from War Minister Krobatin and General Conrad. And outside this narrow circle, two very senior diplomats, Prince Gottfried Hohenlohe, scheduled to be the next ambassador to Berlin, and Friedrich Szápáry, the current ambassador to Russia, added their support for a showdown with the troublesome southern neighbor.[14]

For his part a stricken Berchtold initially reacted more cautiously. Of all the ministers, he had with the death of Franz Ferdinand lost his most important ally in his pursuit of an assertive, even militant policy, but without actually going to war. Now Berchtold faced the task of how to respond to a terrorist attack that clearly had—as the investigation in Sarajevo soon demonstrated—ties with some officials of the Serbian government.

But if initially cautious, by 30 June Berchtold had already begun to harden his position. While Conrad wanted (completely unrealistically) to have an immediate attack, the minister demurred, saying that they had to wait for the arrival of Wilhelm II. Nevertheless, the foreign minister gave Franz Joseph and Conrad the clear impression that a showdown was necessary and probably unavoidable.

No one fretted about Berchtold's position more than Tisza. From the start, he resisted the idea of a military confrontation. He disliked the talk of war, worried about Russia's position, and preferred a severe diplomatic humiliation of Serbia. For the first two weeks of July Berchtold and Tisza competed to gain control of Habsburg foreign policy. Each knew that Franz Joseph remained the pivotal figure, each that they had to convince him of their preferred course of action.[15]

For his part the aged monarch leaned toward a more confrontational policy vis-à-vis Serbia. He especially worried about appearing to be weak in the face of the Serbian challenge to the Monarchy's leadership in the Balkans. But he also wanted more information on the assassinations and thought he ought to defer a decision until he could see Wilhelm II. And Tisza worked hard to reinforce the monarch's caution, first when he saw him on 30 June and then in a memorandum he sent the next day that detailed the case for a prudent, careful diplomatic posture.[16]

Still, the veteran ruler told German ambassador Heinrich Tschirschky on 2 July that the Monarchy might have to take action, a step the ambassador (on his own) said that Germany would support.[17] Thus, when the German Kaiser did not come to Vienna, Franz Joseph agreed with Berchtold that they could wait no longer to see if Germany would support them against Serbia and any complications that might flow from such an action. Berchtold knew from bitter experience that Berlin could blow hot and cold; this time he wanted it committed before he moved forward.

This formed the background for Berchtold's decision to send Hoyos, one of the leading zealots for action in the Ballhausplatz, to Berlin. The envoy carried a handwritten note from Franz Joseph, a policy memorandum of late June (slightly revised) arguing for an aggressive foreign policy in the Balkans, and additional instructions (copies of which have never surfaced). In sending Hoyos, Berchtold also strengthened his own position against Tisza, since solid German support would make it harder for the Magyar leader to resist. (This tactic, it should be added, Berchtold would utilize repeatedly once he had the "blank check.")[18]

As these shifts and turns occurred among the familiar senior Habsburg officials, another player injected himself into the circle: General Oskar Potiorek, the Governor General of Bosnia-Herzegovina, and a senior military politician. Indeed, he was senior enough to have been considered by many to deserve the chief's position when Conrad received it in 1906. Now he was the embarrassed general whose security failures had led to the assassinations; indeed, he might well have been a target if Sophie had not been in the car since he was also riding with the royal couple. He now became a vociferous advocate of military action against Serbia. The fact that there had been attacks by Croats and Muslims against Serb shops in Sarajevo and elsewhere in the provinces in anger at the royal deaths gave his reports added urgency. Moreover, he controlled the flow of information gathered about the assassinations. Over the first three weeks of July he filed exhaustive reports (he never believed one paragraph was enough when he could write three pages). These reports went to his nominal superior, Bilinski, to Conrad, and some directly to the military chancellery of Franz Joseph. In them he was not above exaggerating the unrest in the provinces nor did he always send each the same information.[19]

Potiorek's most important contribution to the internal debate came from his forceful injection of domestic (*Innen*) considerations into the policy discussions. To be sure, given the ethnic composition of the Habsburg monarchy, almost any foreign policy issue had a domestic component and vice-versa. In this instance, however, Potiorek stressed the domestic instability caused by Serbia among the Monarchy's South Slavs and the need to end this threat once and for all. In that sense, the Habsburg decision makers, who did worry about the conditions in the imperial provinces, were making a foreign policy decision to go to war at least in part from domestic considerations. Potiorek's continued refrain on this theme thus helped to shape a final Habsburg decision for war, a war in which Potiorek hoped he might rescue his tattered reputation; he failed and would be relieved at the end of 1914 from all commands.

The next breaking point in the Habsburg decision process came on 6–7 July. Already, late on 5 July, Ambassador Ladislaus Szögyény had sent a telegram (drafted by Hoyos) that said the German Kaiser would support any action that Vienna took against Serbia, even though he worried about Russia's reaction; but that the Kaiser had to see Chancellor Bethmann Hollweg late that Sunday before any final decision could be ratified. On the sixth, Bethmann and Undersecretary of State Arthur Zimmermann met with Szögyény and Hoyos, with the two German officials affirming Wilhelm's statement of support for immediate action. The telegrams from Berlin with this news gave Berchtold the tool with which to lever, or attempt to lever, Tisza into agreeing to support a military attack on the terrorist threat posed by Serbia.[20]

A further climatic moment came the next day, 7 July, with a nearly all day session of the Common Ministerial Council. But before that meeting formally opened, Berchtold met with Tisza, Hoyos, and Ambassador Tschirschky to review the situation. The ambassador reaffirmed Germany's support but did not intrude further. The more explosive aspect of this mini-meeting came from Hoyos's disclosure that he and Zimmermann, when he was in Berlin, had discussed the possible partition of Serbia. This news caused a veritable volcanic reaction from Tisza who thoroughly and totally rejected the idea. Indeed, he went further, demanding that Tschirschky inform Berlin that "everything that Count Hoyos said . . . is to be regarded as his own personal opinion. (This limitation refers particularly to the fact that Count Hoyos stated that a complete partition of Serbia was under consideration here.)" A chastened Hoyos did not return to the idea, an idea whose origins remain unclear.[21]

In the ministerial conference Tisza and Berchtold held center stage, one arguing for restraint and diplomacy, the other for confrontation and possible war. With the exception of Tisza, all of the ministers favored an ultimatum and possible military action against Serbia. Three results emerged from the long meeting, which General Conrad and Admiral Karl Kailer, the deputy chief of the naval staff, had joined in the afternoon.[22]

First, there would be no surprise attack, an option rendered all the more impossible given the harvest leave policies which saw Habsburg troops scattered across the Monarchy so that their recall would alert Serbia to an attack. But second, a mere diplomatic victory, comparable to those of 1912–13, was now unacceptable to the group. A broader confrontation had support, with Stürgkh and Bilinski insisting that Vienna had to show everyone that the South Slav ideal had no future, either for those inside the Danubian monarchy or in the rest of the Balkans. Again and again Berchtold insisted, sounding almost like Conrad, "better now than later." At length, in the third result, even with Tisza still dissenting, the council agreed to send an ultimatum and prepare for a military confrontation. For those ministers any war that followed would be defensive and conservative, designed to protect the Habsburg state.[23]

In his review of the military situation Conrad focused on a Serbian campaign, without revealing many details save for the fact that he needed to know by the fifth day whether or not to expect Russian intervention. If Russia did enter, then the Germans would have to help. But he also assured a worried Tisza that any Rumanian incursion into Transylvania could be resisted. Yet, for all of his apparent candor, Conrad remained vague about his arrangements with Moltke and excessively optimistic about Russia allowing the Austrians to attack Serbia. None of the civilians questioned the inconsistencies.[24]

Even as the meeting ended, the Berchtold-Tisza struggle over an actual war continued. The foreign minister traveled to Bad Ischl to brief Franz Joseph on their differences and the ruler sought during the next week to bridge the gap between his foreign minister and his Hungarian premier. In this he received help from Burián who had earlier administered Bosnia-Herzegovina and who believed the provinces had to be defended against Serbian ambition. A friend of Tisza and a leading Magyar political leader, Burián also realized that Franz Joseph had now come to favor a resolution of the Serb problem. To help convince Tisza, the monarch made it clear that he agreed that there should be no talk of any additional territory. Also Burián, the emperor, and Berchtold could point to the strength of German support and new assurances that Rumania would remain neutral. Though what finally tilted the issue for Tisza can be debated, by 14 July, when he traveled again to Vienna, he agreed to a forty-eight hour ultimatum and military confrontation, even as they awaited final reports from the investigation into the assassinations. A day later, on 15 July, Tisza told the Hungarian parliament that states sometimes had to defend their interests, a speech which Belgrade correctly interpreted as signaling trouble ahead.[25]

The next turning point on the road to war came on 19 July. The ministers, along with Conrad, met incognito at Berchtold's private residence. Surprisingly, the group gave little attention to the exact wording of the ultimatum and focused instead upon the question of any future territorial changes. Even at this late date, Tisza threatened to balk unless Berchtold agreed there would be no territorial changes, a point Tisza also insisted might help to appease the Russians. Finally, the group agreed that some minor border changes for strategic reasons might take place but nothing more. Of this arrangement, a cynical Conrad told General Krobatin after the meeting: "We will see. Before the Balkan Wars, the powers also talked of the status quo; after the war no one concerned himself with it."[26]

Two additional observations about this meeting are necessary. At no point did the question of German pressure for action arise. The Habsburgs were making their own decisions about their future. Second, the almost cavalier attitude toward Russia continued, as if Russia posed no threat even though the group had earlier recognized that Russia remained the greater long-term threat. This tactical oversight would ultimately doom the entire adventure.

The rest of the story can be quickly summarized. Two days later, on 21 July, Franz Joseph accepted the ultimatum, even as he found some of the demands "sharp." He knew, as did everyone else, that Serbia would not accept all of the demands, and certainly not the one about a joint commission. Delivered on 23 July, the ultimatum's terms were considered and the answer returned forty-eight hours later. The Austrian envoy deemed the reply unacceptable and immediately broke diplomatic relations.

Three days later Berchtold persuaded the emperor to declare war and later that night the Austrians and the Serbs exchanged gunfire along the Sava River. While various schemes for mediation were advanced, including a "Halt in Belgrade," the Habsburgs moved ahead with their war. When Russia declared general mobilization on 30 July and Germany responded, general war had come to Europe.

III

Why did this group of senior Habsburg statesmen, who had four times before considered war, now take a gambler's chance with the future of the monarchy? First, a form of "group-think" and a unity of views had been achieved around a strong, assertive option. With no Franz Ferdinand present, there was no one and no mechanism to force a reconsideration of the war option or even to slow the momentum, once Tisza agreed. Second, while the Monarchy had had its share of domestic terror attacks, an international one escalated the stakes—even if Vienna did not have all of the evidence linking the Belgrade authorities to the plot. State sponsored terrorism that struck at the Monarchy's heir apparent went beyond the bounds of acceptable international behavior. Nikola Pašić's failure to investigate any Serbian links to the murders and the glee of the Belgrade press over the deaths at Sarajevo provided additional incentive and anger. In a post 9/11 world, Vienna's response possibly becomes more understandable than it would have been for previous generations of historians. Sometimes enough is felt to be enough, whether or not that feeling is wise. Third, the question of domestic stability and the protection of Bosnia-Herzegovina became important refrains. Nor could the group ignore the aggressiveness of recent Russian diplomacy: the Balkan League, the retention of 220,000 extra Russian troops during the First Balkan War along the eastern Habsburg frontier, deliberate Russian efforts to create trouble in Galicia, and St. Petersburg's successful wooing of Rumania from the Triple Alliance. Better check with Russia now, rather than later when Russian military power increases would make any chance of victory impossible.

But like successive governments since, not excluding the United States and Britain in 2003, the Habsburg leadership were never quite clear what a war would achieve. The partition of Serbia was excluded, though by mid August the Habsburg foreign office had begun to work on various schemes for territorial rearrangements in Poland and elsewhere, in the same heady mood that brought forth the "September memorandum" in Berlin.[27] To be sure, the war was supposed to deter the Russians from further intrusions into the Balkans, while showing the South Slavs that the future lay with Vienna, not Belgrade. It was also designed to chasten the Serbs and possibly bring a friendlier regime in the Serb capital. Moreover, considerations of prestige were at stake. Vienna and Budapest had to act like a great power and defend their position in the international system. A successful war might also convince Berlin of the Monarchy's value as an ally. The Habsburg ministers got their war but none of their objectives.

In this instance a discretionary war became a total disaster. Undertaken less for aggressive or imperial purposes, the war sprang rather from a burst of "defensive realism" in an effort to rescue to the Monarchy and keep it intact. Of such illusions are wars made, whether in 1914 or 2003.

Notes

1. On this see Manfried Rauchensteiner, *Der Tod des Doppeladlers: Österreich-Ungarn und der Erste Weltkrieg* (Graz, 1993); Mark Cornwall, ed., *The Last Years of Austria-Hungary: A Multi-National Experiment in Early Twentieth Century Europe*, 2nd ed. rev. (Exeter, 2002); Robin Okey, *The Habsburg Monarchy* (New York, 2001); F. R. Bridge, *The Habsburg Monarchy among the Great Powers, 1815–1918* (New York, 1990); Samuel R. Williamson, Jr., *Austria-Hungary and the Origins of the First World War* (New York, 1991). Also John W. Boyer, *Culture and Political Crisis in Vienna: Christian Socialism in Power, 1897–1918* (Chicago, 1995).
2. Steven Beller, *Francis Joseph* (New York, 1996); Jean-Paul Bled, *Franz Joseph*, Teresa Bridgeman, trans. (Oxford, 1992).
3. Williamson, *Austria-Hungary*, 164–89; John Leslie, "The Antecedents of Austria-Hungary's War Aims: Policies and Policy-Makers in Vienna and Budapest before and during 1914," in *Archiv und Forschung: Das Haus-, Hof- und Staatsarchiv in seiner Bedeutung für die Geschichte Österreichs und Europas*, Elisabeth Springer and Leopold Kammerhold, eds. (Vienna, 1993), 375–94.
4. Williamson, *Austria-Hungary*, 164–8; Bridge, *Habsburg Monarchy*, 329–38; also see Alan Sked, *The Decline and Fall of the Habsburg Monarchy, 1815–1918*, 2nd ed. (Harlow, England, 2001), 244–77. On Berchtold and the Foreign Ministry, see William D. Godsey, Jr., *Aristocratic Redoubt: The Austro-Hungarian Foreign Office on the Eve of the First World War* (West Lafayette, IN, 1999).
5. Leslie, "Antecedents," 323–47; Günther Kronenbitter, *"Krieg im Frieden": Die Führung der k.u.k. Armee und die Grossmachtpolitik Österreichs-Ungarns 1906–1914* (Munich, 2003), 425–8; Gabor Vermes, *István Tisza: The Liberal Vision and Conservative Statecraft of a Magyar Nationalist* (New York, 1985); István Diószegi, *Hungarians in the Ballhausplatz: Studies on the Austro-Hungarian Common Foreign Policy*, Kornél Balás and Mary Boros, trans. (Budapest, 1983).
6. Leslie, "Antecedents," 348–75; Lothar Höbelt, "'Well-tempered Discontent': Austrian Domestic Politics," in *The Last Years of Austria-Hungary*, 47–74; Lothar Höbelt, "Parteien und Fraktionen im Cisleithanischen Reichsrat," in *Die Habsburgermonarchie, 1848–1918*, vol. VII: *Verfassung und Parlamentarismus*, 2 vols., pt. I: *Verfassungsrecht, Verfassungs-Wirklichkeit, Zentrale Repräsentativkörperschaften*, Helmut Rumpler and Peter Urbanitsch, eds. (Vienna, 2000), 975–96.
7. Kronenbitter, *"Krieg im Frieden,"* passim; Leslie, "Antecedents," 310–23; Lawrence Sondhaus, *Franz Conrad von Hötzendorf: Architect of the Apocalypse* (Boston, 2000); Rauchensteiner, *Der Tod des Doppeladlers*, 41–61; Williamson, *Austria-Hungary*, 49–51; Conrad von Hötzendorf, *Private Auf-*

zeichnungen: Erste Veröffentlichen aus den Papieren des k. u.k. Generalstab-Chefs, Kurt Peball, ed. (Vienna, 1977).

8. Kronenbitter, "Krieg im Frieden," 448–54 and "Bundesgenossen? Zur militärpolitischen Kooperation zwischen Berlin und Wien 1912 bis 1914," in Deutschland in den internationalen Beziehungen des 19. und 20. Jahrhunderts, Walther L. Berneckker and Volker Dotterweich, eds. (Munich, 1996), 143–68; Jürgen Angelow, Kalkül und Prestige: Der Zweibund am Vorabend des Ersten Weltkrieges (Cologne, 2000), 434–65.
9. Samuel R. Williamson, Jr., "Influence, Power, and the Policy Process: The Case of Franz Ferdinand, 1906–1914," The Historical Journal 17 (1974), 17–34; Robert A. Kann, Dynasty, Politics and Culture: Selected Essays, Stanley B. Winters, ed. (Boulder, 1991), 103–89.
10. Robert A. Kann, Erzherzog Franz Ferdinand Studien (Vienna, 1976), 47–85.
11. Kronenbitter, "Krieg im Frieden," 455–86; Rauchensteiner, Der Tod des Doppeladlers, 63–121; Williamson, Austria-Hungary, 190–212.
12. Fritz Fischer, Krieg der Illusionen: Die deutsche Politik von 1911 bis 1914 (Düsseldorf, 1969), 686–94; cf. Williamson, Austria-Hungary, 190–97, and Annika Mombauer, Helmuth von Moltke and the Origins of the First World War (Cambridge, Eng., 2001), 182–92. Also see Annika Mombauer and Wilhelm Deist, eds., The Kaiser: New Research on Wilhelm II's Role in Imperial Germany (Cambridge, Eng., 2003) and John C. G. Röhl, "Germany," in Decisions for War, 1914, Keith Wilson, ed. (New York, 1995), 27–54.
13. Williamson, Austria-Hungary, 190–7.
14. The essay by Leslie is valuable for an understanding of the crisis; but also see Conrad von Hötzendorf, Aus meiner Dienstzeit, 1906–1918, vol. IV (Vienna, 1923), 13–168, and Hugo Hantsch, Leopold Graf Berchtold, 2 vols. (Graz, 1963), vo. 2, 557–647.
15. Leslie, "Antecedents," 341–43; Rauchensteiner, Der Tod des Doppeladlers, 67–77; Kronenbitter, "Krieg im Frieden," 465–74.
16. Kann, Dynasty, Politics and Culture, 283–307; Tisza to Franz Joseph, 1 July 1914, in Österreich-Ungarns Aussenpolitik von der bosnischen Krise 1908 bis zum Kriegsausbruch 1914, 9 vols., Ludwig Bittner and Hans Übersberger, eds. (Vienna, 1930), VIII: no. 9978; hereafter ÖU.
17. Tschirschky to Bethmann Hollweg, 2 July (tel.) 1914, in Outbreak of the World War: German Documents Collected by Karl Kautsky, Max Montgelas and Walther Schüking, eds. (New York, 1924), no. 9; hereafter KD.
18. Fritz Fellner, "Die 'Mission Hoyos,'" in Vom Dreibund zum Völkerbund: Studien zur Geschichte der internationalen Beziehungen, 1882–1919, Heidrun Maschl and Brigitte Mazohl-Wallnig, eds. (Vienna, 1994), 112–41. The essay was first published in 1984.
19. Kronenbitter, "Krieg im Frieden," 462–5; Rudolf Jěrabék, Potiorek: General im Schatten von Sarajevo (Graz, 1991), 94–6, 107–9; Leslie, "Antecedents," 368–70; Williamson, Austria-Hungary, 192–4.
20. Szögyény to Berchtold, 5 July (tel.), 6 July (tel.) 1914, ÖU, VIII, nos. 10058, 10076.
21. Tschirschky to Bethmann Hollweg, 7 July (tel.) 1914, KD, no. 18.
22. A partial English translation of the Protocol of the Council of Ministers for Common Affairs, 7 July 1914, can be found in July 1914: The Outbreak of the First World War: Selected Documents, Imanuel Geiss, ed. (New York, 1967), no. 9; the original can be found in ÖU, VIII, no. 10118.
23. Kronenbitter, "Krieg im Frieden," 468–73; Samuel R. Williamson, Jr., "Confrontation with Serbia: The Consequences of Vienna's Failure to Achieve Surprise in July 1914," Mitteilungen des Österreichischen Staatsarchiv 43 (1993), 168–177.
24. Rauchensteiner, Der Tod des Doppeladlers, 74–76. On Conrad and Berchtold during the July Crisis, see Samuel R. Williamson, Jr. and Russ Van Wyk, July 1914: Soldiers, Statesmen, and the Coming of the Great War: A Brief Documentary History (Boston, 2003), 57–72.
25. Leslie, "Antecedents," 341–4, 380–1; Williamson, Austria-Hungary, 200–2; Kronenbitter, "Krieg im Frieden," 472–4.
26. Williamson, Austria-Hungary, 203.
27. Leslie, "Antecedents," 381–94.

Chapter 4

THE CURIOUS CASE OF THE KAISER'S DISAPPEARING WAR GUILT
Wilhelm II in July 1914

John C. G. Röhl

The Great War was the point at which, after many years of tension, Old Europe tore itself apart, the point at which the great empires of the east disintegrated and the Kaiser's Germany, exhausted and humiliated in defeat, descended into chaos. The War in which more than ten million men lost their lives is now seen to have been the "seminal catastrophe of the twentieth-century"—the boiling cauldron out of which sprang the horrors of Bolshevism and Stalinism, fascism, Nazism, and genocide. After decades of bitter and highly charged controversy there is today widespread recognition in Germany too, in the popular media as well as in the scholarly community, that 1914 marked the beginning of what was to become a new Thirty Years' War.[1]

But who brought on this unprecedented cataclysm in July 1914 whose effects are still with us today? If you had asked this question in 1918, the answer would have been obvious to everyone. In Britain, France, and America politicians, the press, and the public bayed for the Kaiser's blood. "Hang the Kaiser!" was a slogan that had reverberated throughout the Allied side, and with it, David Lloyd George swept to victory in the coupon election of 1918. The victorious Powers at Versailles not only saddled Germany in general with responsibility for the war; in article 227 of the Treaty, they accused Kaiser Wilhelm II in person of "a supreme offence against international morality and the sanctity of treaties," demanding his extradition to face an international tribunal composed of one judge each from the USA, Great Britain, France, Italy, and Japan. Whatever the merits of the case against him, there is little doubt that, in the poisoned atmosphere of the time, Wilhelm would have been found guilty. In his exile in The Netherlands, the ex-Emperor lived in constant fear of being extradited or kidnapped. He dyed his hair and grew a beard. He spent many weeks with his head wreathed in bandages, ready to make his escape in a waiting ambulance.[2]

In revolution-torn Germany, this damning view of the Kaiser and of the "rotten" old regime, which he had personified, was initially shared by many. Karl Kautsky, the Marxist ideologue of the powerful Social Democratic party, was put in charge of publishing the thousand diplomatic documents in the German archives that had been generated by the July Crisis of 1914 alone. His four-volume edition appeared in 1919 and is a superb example of meticulous scholarship which is still indispensable today.[3] I shall be drawing heavily on his work in a moment when I come to examine Wilhelm's role in those five fateful weeks. Soon, however, the mood in Germany changed. Once the "war guilt" clause of the Treaty of Versailles was used by the victors to justify the punitive treatment of the fledgling Weimar Republic—the unpayable reparations, the territorial amputations, the confiscation of the colonies, the restrictions on rearmament, and the demilitarization of the Rhineland—it quickly became a matter of vital national interest to deny or disprove the so-called "war guilt lie" of the Allies. Kautsky was marginalized and his four-volume edition swamped by an official publication eventually amounting to more than forty volumes stretching all the way back to 1871.[4] And the part played by the Kaiser in the making of German policy was also minimized. Since the many warlike speeches he had made throughout his reign had been widely reported, since his manipulative correspondence with Tsar Nicholas II had been revealed by the Bolsheviks, and since his notorious marginal comments on thousands of diplomatic reports could not be suppressed altogether, the tactic used was to represent Wilhelm's views as irrelevant to the actual intentions of the official Imperial government.[5] The Kaiser was depicted as having been something of an impotent maverick buffoon. And with time he was airbrushed out of historical accounts of his 30-year reign altogether. Kaiser Wilhelm II could not have been guilty of causing war in 1914 because he had been nothing but a "shadow emperor" without knowledge of, let alone control over, events.

It is tempting to dismiss this interpretation as a cynical ploy designed to regain for Germany the power and prestige it had enjoyed before 1914, and this is indeed what it was. However, there is nevertheless an element of truth in the legend of the Kaiser's innocence of which we should not lose sight. Even sharp critics of German policy in July 1914 such as the ex-Chancellor Prince Bülow and the shipping magnate Albert Ballin were genuinely convinced that Wilhelm's role in causing the catastrophe had been slight. After all, had he not spent most of the crisis month of July on his annual cruise along the Norwegian coast to the Arctic Circle? And had he not, on his return to Berlin, tried to get the Austrians to halt in Belgrade?

On the Allied side, too, the determination to put Wilhelm on trial as a war criminal was less firm than article 227 appeared to suggest. True, the French, British, and Italian delegates favored the idea, with Lloyd George even proposing that the Kaiser be banished to Devil's Island or the Falklands, but the American President Woodrow Wilson thought that trying a monarch would seem excessively vindictive and destabilizing and might even push the German people into the arms of the revolutionaries. Would you, he asked his colleagues at Versailles, "rather have the Kaiser or the Bolsheviks?" In the end a compromise was reached by which article 227 was introduced on the understanding that nothing would be done to enforce it.[6] In other words, the Kaiser need not have bothered with the beard and the bandages. In addition to these tactical considerations, there was some disquiet at Versailles over the paucity of the evidence that the victors actually possessed. Apart from Lichnowsky's famous memorandum, which put the blame for the war squarely on Germany's shoulders but barely mentioned the monarch, and the Belgian King's record of a menacing conversation with Wilhelm in Potsdam in November 1913, there was at that time little by way of a paper trail for the prosecution to go on.

This situation has now changed. A huge amount of research has been carried out not only on the origins of the war but also on the Kaiser's character, his intentions, and his role in German decision making. The commemorative year of 2004 in particular has seen countless publications, conferences, exhibitions, and television documentaries on the war and its origins.[7] In the international historical fraternity, there is something close to consensus that the war came about as a result of the policies pursued by Berlin and Vienna, though the crucial question of what these two governments actually intended to achieve is still a matter of debate.

My aim in focusing on the Kaiser's role in July 1914 is not to cast him as the main mover of events in Berlin. However great his personal power had been at the turn of the century, he was never a dictator of any kind, and in the years after 1908 his overpowering self-confidence had been shaken and his influence had to some extent waned. He now presided over an often-dysfunctional governmental machine that has aptly been characterized as verging on "polycratic chaos." In the July Crisis, as we shall see, there were clearly occasions when he was pushed and bounced and manipulated by others, and equally clearly there were times when he lost his nerve. But he was still German Kaiser, King of Prussia, Supreme War Lord, and commander-in-chief of the Navy, and as such he stood at the very centre of German policy making. From the decision to give Austria-Hungary carte blanche at the beginning of July to the signing of the mobilization order on 1 August and the invasion of Belgium and Luxemburg, Wilhelm had the final say. Everyone involved in the decision-making process was obliged to try to influence him, to pull him onto their side. By focusing on him, then, we should be able to establish not just what his intentions were, but also shed more light on the policies that were being pursued by the other figures involved in the decision-making process in Berlin.

In attempting to determine Wilhelm II's personal responsibility for the catastrophe that ensued, we need to keep the following questions in mind:

1. Who, apart from the Kaiser, was involved in German decision making?

2. What was the Kaiser's understanding of the intentions of these other men? What was he told, and when? To what extent was he complicit in their plans?

3. Crucially, did he favor a *diplomatic* victory of the Central Powers over Russia while accepting the *risk* that the Austro-Serbian conflict could lead to war, or was his *preferred* outcome the launching of a continental war?

4. How did he assess the risk that Britain might enter the war in support of France and Russia, and what effect did this assessment have on his attitude?

5. When and why did his nerve appear to fail? And how serious were his efforts at such times of uncertainty to pull back from the brink?

Unlike the victorious Allies at Versailles in 1919, we now have sufficient evidence to provide firm answers to most of these crucial questions.

The number of people involved in making decisions in Berlin in July 1914 was tiny. The documents enable us to identify as the decision makers, apart from the Kaiser and a handful of men in his immediate entourage, the Reich Chancellor, the Auswärtiges Amt, the General Staff, the Prussian War Ministry, the Reich Navy Office, and the Admiralty Staff, that is to say no more than twenty men and their direct subordinates. As several of these were away from the capital when the crisis began, and others (including the Kaiser) were sent away or asked to stay away to preserve the appearance of normality, the initiative at first lay with Chancellor Theobald von Bethmann Hollweg, Undersecretary of State Alfred Zimmermann, Wilhelm von Stumm, and (a little later) Gottlieb von Jagow in the Wilhelmstrasse. These men collaborated secretly with Count Georg von Waldersee, the Quartermaster-General, who in Moltke's absence was in charge of the General Staff. With the return of Moltke, War Minister Erich von Falkenhayn, and Reich Navy Secretary Alfred von Tirpitz to Berlin on 24 and 25 July, military imperatives came increasingly into conflict with the diplomatic niceties that were of primary concern to the civilians. It was the Kaiser's task, upon his return to Berlin on 27 July, to adjudicate between these rival pressures. He did not fulfill this role very competently, but given the enormity of the responsibility he carried, we should not be surprised that he showed signs of vacillation. Nor should we always take bitter comments made by one frustrated side or the other at face value.

It is vital to stress, however, that the differences between these decision makers were minimal. All of them, including the Kaiser, believed they could see a golden opportunity that was too good to miss. They shared the illusion that, if only matters were handled adroitly so that Russia could be made to seem the aggressor and the German nation would rise to defend the Fatherland, Germany could have war against the Franco-Russian alliance under almost ideal conditions: the army had been enlarged, the widening of the Kiel Canal was due to be completed that very summer, the harvest was almost in, the season ideal for combat, the French army deemed to be in complete disarray, Russia's military hopelessly backward, and its strategic railway program years from completion. Above all, Britain was thought to be so deeply mired in the Irish troubles that the danger of becoming involved in a continental war was assessed as negligible—this grave miscalculation more than any other neutralized the deterrence effect till then implicit in the Triple Entente. And given Britain's probable neutrality, the decision makers in Berlin shared the belief that not only Austria-Hungary, but also Italy, Greece, Turkey, Bulgaria, Rumania, and perhaps even Sweden would join Germany in the showdown with France and Russia. In view of the Habsburg Monarchy's growing decrepitude and the volatility of Italian public opinion, the Generals argued, such a golden opportunity might never present itself again. In the weeks and months before the assassination at Sarajevo on 28 June 1914, they were already on the threshold of a decision for continental war, as Colonel Edward House reported to President Wilson after visiting Berlin at the end of May.[8] Indeed, it is not impossible that some of the Army leaders had wind of the planned outrage before the event.[9]

The Kaiser fully shared this assessment of his Generals. In the eighteen months prior to Sarajevo, he spoke repeatedly of the need for war against Russia and France. As recently as 16 June 1914 he had thundered: "Whoever in Germany still does not believe that Russo-Gaul is working with urgency towards an imminent war against us, and that we must take countermeasures accordingly, deserves to be sent straightaway to the madhouse at Dalldorf!"[10] And he had commanded the Wilhelmstrasse to clarify the attitude that Britain would take.[11]

In assessing the role played by Wilhelm II in July 1914, it is important to distinguish four phases:

1. the eight days between Sarajevo and his departure for Norway on 6 July;

2. the 21 days spent at sea;

3. his four days back in Potsdam between 27 and 31 July; and

4. the final dramatic days in Berlin from 31 July to the invasion of Belgium and Britain's entry into the war four days later.

Phase One

Given his warlike utterances against "Russo-Gaul" of just a few days earlier, the response of the monarch to the news that his friend "Franzi" and his wife had been murdered at Sarajevo was surprisingly muted. He broke off his yachting regatta at Kiel and returned to Potsdam, but for many days, there was no sign of any intention to begin a war. He planned to attend Franz Ferdinand's funeral in Vienna but called off the trip when warned that he too might be assassinated. As late as 3 July he spoke of his intention to visit Romania in the autumn.[12] But that same night he gave the signal that would lead to war. In a marginal comment, he reprimanded his ambassador in Vienna for counseling restraint and demanded unequivocal support for an immediate punitive action by Austria against Serbia. "Now or never," he proclaimed. "The Serbs must be disposed of, *and* that right *soon!*"[13] The toughening of the Kaiser's mood can perhaps be attributed in part to the meeting he had that very evening with the German military attaché in Bucharest, Major Günther Bronsart von Schellendorff,[14] but in truth we still know too little about the influences that were brought to bear on him in these crucial first days.

The Kaiser's comment of 3–4 July proved decisive. It swept aside any lingering doubt there might have been among the decision makers that Wilhelm would authorize German support for Austria in her conflict with Serbia, whatever the consequences. Undersecretary Zimmermann estimated the chances that the Balkan conflict would escalate into a war against Russia at 90 percent.[15] Whether Wilhelm himself foresaw the consequences so clearly is open to question. At times in his statements over the next two days, he appeared to expect and even desire the Austro-Serbian conflict to escalate into continental war, at other times merely to accept that there was a risk that it might. As we shall see, this ambivalence at the heart of German policy was to harden even before the Kaiser's return from his cruise into a determination not to back down, however Russia reacted.

On 5 July, Kaiser Wilhelm received the Austro-Hungarian ambassador Count Szögyény at the Neues Palais in Potsdam. After reading the two documents Szögyény had brought with him, he expressed his delight that Vienna was determined to "eliminate Serbia as a power factor in the Balkans" and again urged speedy action. He promised the Habsburg Monarchy that Germany would support it come what may. "Russia's attitude will no doubt be hostile, but for this he had been for years prepared, and should a war between Austria-Hungary and Russia be unavoidable, we might be convinced that Germany ... would stand at our side."[16]

Later that day Wilhelm summoned the Chancellor and Zimmermann, then War Minister von Falkenhayn, the head of the Military Cabinet Moriz Freiherr von Lyncker, and Generaladjutant Hans von Plessen, and finally the representative of the Admiralty Staff to inform them of the assurances he had given Szögyény over lunch. He asked the Generals whether the army was "prepared for all eventualities," which they confirmed "without reservation."[17] No one objected. Indeed, one gains the impression that agreement on this policy had been reached between the civilian and military leaders even before they were summoned to the Palace.

Before departing for Kiel the next morning, the Kaiser received Admiral von Capelle as the representative of the Reichs-Marine-Amt and then General von

Bertrab as the representative of the General Staff. He expected the crisis to end with a Serbian retreat and an Austrian occupation of the country, he said, and did not think Russia and France would become involved since they were at present "militarily and financially totally unprepared for war," but he nevertheless thought it necessary "to be armed and ready for a different outcome." Wilhelm ordered Capelle secretly to prepare for the mobilization of the Fleet.[18]

Phase Two

With his departure for Norway on 6 July, Phase Two began. Bethmann's purpose in insisting that the Kaiser undertake his cruise as normal was twofold. First, he wished to give the world the impression that Germany had no foreknowledge of the pending Austro-Serbian conflict. And second, he hoped to be free of the monarch's interference over the next few weeks. This was to become the more difficult the closer the moment of truth approached.

That the Kaiser's cruise was an elaborate sham is shown by the fact that the imperial yacht *Hohenzollern*, instead of sailing up to the North Cape as usual, remained anchored off Balholm in the Sognefjord, just one hundred kilometers north of Bergen, for two entire weeks. From there, as members of his entourage informed their families in letters home, the monarch could reach Cuxhaven within twenty two hours or be back in Kiel in under two days.[19]

Far from being out of touch, several dozen dispatches were sent from the Wilhelmstrasse to the *Hoflager* in Balholm. The Kaiser, along with his two Cabinet Chiefs and the Foreign Office representative Count Georg von Wedel, was not only kept fully informed of the aims of Bethmann's policy, but impatiently joined in exerting pressure on the Vienna government to act quickly and decisively. At Bethmann's urging the monarch issued a reprimand to the hotheaded Crown Prince, whose public demands for "war, ... struggle and violence" it was feared might make foreign governments suspicious of Germany's intentions.[20]

While in Balholm, Wilhelm played an active part in trying to secure alliances with Turkey, Bulgaria, Romania, and Greece for the imminent struggle against Russia and ensuring Italy's participation in the war.[21] "The task now is to muster every gun that is prepared ... to fight *for* Austria against the Slavs," he ordered on 23 July.[22] Throughout his so-called cruise his aggression toward Russia and his disdain for France, the "absolute socialistic Sansculotte Republic!" as he called it, remained undiminished.[23] He insisted that the Franco-Russian Alliance had been formed for the purpose of "joint robbery raids upon us!"[24] His hatred of Serbia bubbled constantly to the surface. "These rascals are guilty of agitation and murder and must be humbled. ... Serbia is a band of robbers which must be caught and punished for its crimes!" he declared on 23 July.[25]

There are numerous other indications that Kaiser Wilhelm was complicit in Bethmann's plot and the timetable for war attached to it. On 19 July 1914, four days *before* the Austrian ultimatum to Serbia of which neither he nor the Chancellor was supposed to have any prior knowledge, he suggested that the Auswärtiges Amt secretly inform the directors of Germany's two steamship companies, Hapag and the North German Lloyd, that the ultimatum would be delivered in Belgrade on 23 July. "In view of the unpredictable consequences that might follow perhaps very suddenly it appears to H. M. desirable to alert the two great shipping lines in good time so that they can make their arrangements accordingly," Count Wedel telegraphed from the *Hohenzollern* to Berlin.[26] The Kaiser's concern was not just for the safety of the passengers; the ocean liners were to be pressed into service as auxiliary cruisers.

On that same day, 19 July, Admiral von Müller recorded that His Majesty was "in a state of great excitement about the consequences of the ultimatum which is to be presented by Austria to Serbia on 23rd."[27] When the text of the ultimatum reached the *Hohenzollern*, Wilhelm declared in triumph "Well, that's a vigorous note for a change."[28] He greeted with glee early reports that the Serbs were about to give in without a fight and exulted: "bravo! One would not have believed it of the Viennese! ... The proud Slavs! How hollow the whole so-called Serbian Great Power is proving itself to be; thus it is with all Slav states! Just tread hard on the toes of that rabble!"[29] But we should not take his delight at Serbia's apparent backing down as a sign of relief that there would not now be war against Russia. For on that very same day, 25 July, he gave orders to the Commander of the High Seas Fleet for the bombardment of the Russian naval bases in the Baltic to commence. Admiral von Ingenohl managed to put the Kaiser's orders on hold—for a week.

At this point in time, the Kaiser was clearly more militant than the Chancellor and the Wilhelmstrasse, who were struggling to retain control over the monarch. On 25 July Bethmann wondered aloud what "this puffed up lieutenant" would do with the world once he had conquered it.[30] With the German High Seas Fleet on maneuvers off southern Norway, Bethmann was most anxious not to alarm the Royal Navy, which had assembled off Spithead for a grand review and was not due to disperse until 27 July, but the Kaiser's excitability put this scheme at risk. On the morning of 25 July, Wilhelm gave orders for the Fleet to prepare for an immediate return home. Bethmann's plea to avoid any such move that could alert the British was met with the most insulting comments. Serbia's decision to mobilize, the monarch thundered, "*can* lead to Russia's mobilization, *will* lead to Austria's mobilization! In this case, I must bring together my armed forces on land and sea. ... If and when Russia mobilizes my Fleet must already be in the Baltic, that is why it is sailing home!"[31]

Not only was the Fleet ordered back prematurely, the Kaiser himself now decided to return home. On 25 July, Müller informed him that he, Lyncker, and Wedel all thought the position in Balholm had become untenable. The *Hohenzollern* weighed anchor at six o'clock that evening. On the voyage home, there were still no indications of a more conciliatory mood. Wilhelm continued to insist that there had to be a shift in the balance of power. "Austria must become preponderant in the Balkans ... and at Russia's expense; otherwise there will be no peace."[32] Serbia was "not a state in the European sense, but a band of robbers!"[33] He rejected British, French, and Russian proposals for mediation, and to the Russian Foreign Minister's warning that if Austria invaded Serbia, Russia would declare war against it, Wilhelm responded with the words "na denn zu!"—"well then, let's do it!"[34]

On the voyage home, the Kaiser appeared eager for continental war. His entourage was therefore all the more baffled when on the evening of 26 July he telegraphed the Kaiserin saying he hoped to be able to join her for a holiday at Wilhelmshöhe near Kassel in a few days' time.[35] For the next four days, from 27 to the 31 July, his mood flip-flopped from wild aggression to half-baked attempts at mediation and back again. The key to explaining these mood swings in this third phase is to be found, as I shall show, in Wilhelm's perception of Britain's attitude.

Phase Three

When the *Hohenzollern* docked at Kiel, his warlike mood alarmed not only the civilian statesmen but also the Admirals. The orders he gave to seal off the eastern Baltic were described by Capelle as "pathological" and by Tirpitz as "military nonsense and a political mistake." "Now he is playing soldiers!" the latter cried.[36] Wilhelm was outraged at the Chancellor's plea that he should not to come to Berlin as this might give the impression that Germany wanted war.[37] "This really is the limit, now the man is telling me that I cannot show myself to my people," he complained.[38] His aggressive mood continued throughout his meetings with Bethmann, Moltke, and Admiral Pohl at Potsdam on the afternoon of 27 July. He turned down as premature the Chancellor's request to send the first of several planned telegrams to the Tsar. He ordered Tschirschky to pressure the Austrians into offering compensation to Italy to ensure the latter took part on Germany's side in the coming war. He again rejected a British proposal for an international peace conference. The upshot of the Kaiser's meetings with his advisers is recorded by Müller in the words: Germany would "keep quiet, letting Russia put herself in the wrong, but then not shying away from war."[39] War Minister von Falkenhayn also heard that the decision had been taken to see the thing through, whatever the cost.[40]

At this juncture, the Kaiser blithely assumed that Britain would stay out of the conflict so long as Russia could be made to appear the aggressor. To maintain this illusion, the Chancellor had doctored several of Lichnowsky's telegrams warning of Sir Edward Grey's growing concern.[41] On 27 July, however, the ambassador sent news so alarming that Bethmann saw no way of withholding the dispatch from the Kaiser: Grey, Lichnowsky reported, considered the Serbian reply so compliant that

Austria and Germany would forfeit Britain's sympathy if they failed to enter into negotiations.[42] This telegram was passed on to the Kaiser in the early morning of 28 July and prompted the first wobble in his hard-line stance.[43]

Given the extent of Serbia's compliance, Wilhelm now considered that there was no longer any need for Austria to go to war to achieve its aims. Instead, the nation should occupy Belgrade and the surrounding area as a *Faustpfand* (pledge) until all its demands had been met.[44] The Kaiser had such confidence that this proposal would resolve the crisis that, briefly, he revived his plans for a holiday in Wilhelmshöhe.[45] He became confused when Vienna failed to react to his initiative, complaining on 29 July that for the past four weeks the Austrians had kept him in the dark as to their intentions.[46]

With his nerves on edge, Wilhelm failed to see through the machinations of his own government. As is well known, Bethmann and Stumm passed on the monarch's proposal to Vienna in an almost unrecognizable form, and far too late for it to prevent the Austrian declaration of war on Serbia. What is more, in their instructions to Tschirschky they made it clear that Germany had no wish to hold Austria back.[47] And in any case, under pressure from his Generals, Wilhelm soon changed his mind once more. On the evening of 28 July, Falkenhayn found the Kaiser "confused" and talking as if "now," he no longer wanted war. "I make it clear to him," the hawkish War Minister recorded, "that he no longer has the matter under his control." On the following day, Falkenhayn noted: "H. M.'s mood has flipped again. He believes ... that the ball which has begun to roll cannot now be stopped."[48]

Why? What persuaded the Kaiser to throw the caution he had displayed on 28 July to the winds and revert to his original hard line on 29 July? The explanation is to be found in the letter he received that morning from his brother Prince Heinrich, who, in a mysterious mission which seems in retrospect like a dress rehearsal for Rudolf Hess's infamous flight to Scotland in 1941, had slipped over to London to speak to King George V.[49] As with Hess, we do not know with any certainty who authorized Heinrich's trip, but it is inconceivable that he should have undertaken the mission without his brother's knowledge and blessing. After seeing the King at Buckingham Palace for a few minutes before church on Sunday morning, 26 July 1914, the Prince joined his two sisters Sophie of Greece and Margarethe of Hesse at Maresfield in Sussex, and then returned quickly to Kiel. [see Illustration: Prince Heinrich in Sussex, 26 July 1914]. From there, Heinrich repeated in a letter to his brother the King's assurance that "we shall try all we can to keep out of this and shall remain neutral."[50] In a stroke, Wilhelm was able to ignore Lichnowsky's dire warnings and believe once again that he could have war against Russia and France without fear of British involvement. To a dubious Tirpitz he announced: "I have the word of a King, that is enough for me."[51] In this jubilant mood Wilhelm rejected Heinrich's offer to visit the Tsar in St. Petersburg as "pointless," but kept open the possibility of his making another trip to London.[52]

Illustration 4.1: Prince Heinrich in Sussex, 26 July 1914

He approved the notorious and revealing offer the Chancellor made to the British ambassador that same evening to *restore* France's territorial integrity in Europe *after* the war *provided that* Britain remained neutral.[53] There was not the slightest willingness, even now, though, to back down on the most contentious Anglo-German problem of all. Bethmann's plea that agreement should be sought over the battleship program was roundly rejected by the Kaiser and all the Admirals, and the Chancellor left the meeting with a "very red face."[54]

The celebrated exchange of telegrams between Willy and Nicky—Tsar Nicholas II—in the final days of the July Crisis was a carefully choreographed maneuver designed to place the blame for war on Russia—"to increase Russia's guilt and document it in the eyes of the whole world," as Bethmann reminded his sovereign.[55] The monarch's personal contribution was confined to making stylistic amendments to the text presented to him by his officials. By contrast, Wilhelm's last-minute correspondence with cousin "Georgie" in London was much more direct. When Admirals Müller and Pohl arrived at the Neues Palais for their audience on the morning of 30 July, they were kept waiting because Wilhelm and Heinrich were busy concocting a telegram to the King. Ironically, Pohl had brought with him a telegram that had arrived in the night making clear Grey's view that Britain would not be able to stand idly by in a war between Germany and France. Once again, the Kaiser was devastated, and once again, he flip flopped. "That was the hardest blow of all," Müller recorded. "The Kaiser … was deeply confounded when he read it, but remained outwardly calm." After the meeting Müller noted that "the Kaiser's nerves were on the edge of a breakdown."[56] Bewildered, Wilhelm wrote (in English) on an article in the *Morning Post*: "King George has communicated England's intention to remain neutral to me by Prince Henry. ... On the other hand, ... Sir E. Grey in a private conversation with Prince Lichnowsky, declared, that if Germany made war on France, England would immediately attack Germany with its fleet! Consequently Sir E. Grey says the direct contrary to what his Sovereign communicated to me through my brother and places his King in the position of a double tongued liar vis-à-vis to me." Wilhelm now claimed to be the victim of a dastardly plot by Britain, France, and Russia to destroy him and his country. "The whole war is plainly arranged between England, France and Russia for the annihilation of Germany ... and the Austro-Servian strife is only an excuse to fall upon *us!* God help us in this fight for our existence, brought about by falseness, lies, and poisonous envy!"[57] Numerous crazed and self-pitying diatribes of this nature have survived from this phase of the Crisis. They are not easy to interpret. Certainly they reflect a growing sense of panic at the enormity of what was about to take place, mixed with fury at having so badly miscalculated the reaction of the other Great Powers. But unmistakably these lachrymose expectorations also amounted to an effort on Wilhelm's part to provide himself with a moral alibi by attributing sinister designs to his neighbors in order to justify the attack he himself was planning to launch on them.

Nevertheless, Grey's threat of British intervention did prompt him to make one last attempt to stop the ball from rolling out of control. Just before midnight on 30 July 1914, a telegram arrived from King George to Prince Heinrich welcoming the Kaiser's Halt-in-Belgrade initiative and assuring him of his own determination to do all in his power to avert the catastrophe.[58] Wilhelm immediately ordered his brother to drive to Berlin to inform the Chancellor of the King's telegram, which he said should be forwarded to Vienna. At the same time Bethmann was to inform London that Austria was now ready to forgo all territorial gains at Serbia's expense. Heinrich delivered his message to Bethmann at 1:15 AM and was back at Potsdam at 2:20 in the morning.[59] Four and a half hours later, when the Kaiser awoke, he repeated his order to the Chancellor to present him with the draft of an answer to the King of England and the Tsar of Russia "about the English and Viennese proposals, which are almost identical to mine."[60] Prince Heinrich's midnight dash from Potsdam to the Wilhelmstrasse was the closest the Kaiser came to preventing the war. But Bethmann ignored his instructions. Neither the German nor the Austrian government was ever prepared to accept Kaiser Wilhelm's initiative, but he was never told as much.

Phase Four

By this time, the dogs of war were being unleashed, and the Kaiser was swept along by the force of events. In this fourth and final phase of the Crisis, there was no further sign of hesitation on his part. He still had to mediate between the different factions in Berlin, but he did so in the conviction that victory over Russia and France, and therefore German domination over Europe, lay in his grasp. "The Kaiser is decidedly on the side of Moltke and the War Minister," the Bavarian General von Wenninger reported on 30 July.[61] He was "determined to settle accounts with France" and to do so thoroughly, Wilhelm told the Austrian ambassador on 1 August.[62] To the end, his declared aim was to "liberate the Balkans from Russia for all time!"[63] Upon the outbreak of war against France and Russia, Wilhelm praised the "manly attitude taken by the Reich Chancellor and ... his correct execution of his intentions."[64] The Kaiser was encouraged in this warlike mood by his brother and his six sons, who had gathered around him. "All of them," the Chief of the Civil Cabinet Rudolf von Valentini noted on 30 July, were "terribly warlike."[65] The Kaiserin, too, ensured that the monarch remained resolute.

Moltke and Falkenhayn had been pressing for the declaration of a "state of imminent danger of war," the prelude to mobilization, but Bethmann held back in the hope that Russia would put itself in the wrong. On 30 July, they agreed to wait until noon on the following day, but then to take the irrevocable step to war. To everyone's delight, news of Russia's general mobilization arrived at 11:40 AM on 31 July with just twenty minutes to spare. "Everywhere beaming faces," Wenninger recorded after visiting the War Ministry.[66] Wilhelm gave his consent to the "imminent danger of war" declaration by telephone and moved with his brother and sons from Potsdam to Berlin. That afternoon, at the Schloss, surrounded by his Generals, the Kaiser gave an exposé of the situation which the fiery War Minister described as "worthy of a German Kaiser! Worthy of a Prussian King."[67] He authorized the Chancellor to issue an ultimatum to Russia and France. The speeches he and Bethmann made from the balcony had the desired effect. "The mood [is] brilliant," Müller recorded in his diary. "The government has succeeded very well in making us appear as the attacked."[68] The Kaiser dispatched a telegram to the Emperor Franz Joseph demanding that Austria now ignore the war against Serbia as "completely irrelevant" and fight with its entire strength against Russia.[69] He sent personal letters to the Kings of Italy, Greece, and Romania and to the governments in Sofia and Constantinople demanding that all join the great fight against the common enemy.[70]

Still hoping that the appearance of Russian aggression would serve to keep Britain neutral, Bethmann resisted pressure from the Generals to declare mobilization, but at 4:00 PM on 1 August, he gave way. He, Falkenhayn, Moltke, and Tirpitz were on the point of leaving for the Schloss to persuade the Kaiser to sign the order when the telephone rang and Wilhelm himself demanded that they bring him the mobilization order. An hour later, he signed the document on a table carved from the wood of Nelson's flagship *Victory*. Both he and the War Minister had tears in their eyes, but they were tears of triumph, not of dismay or regret.[71]

The events that followed make up perhaps the most famous scene in the drama of the July Crisis and are largely responsible for the widespread impression that

Kaiser Wilhelm was out of touch with reality. After leaving the Schloss, Moltke and Falkenhayn were recalled to be told that a telegram had arrived from Lichnowsky in London holding out the promise that, if Germany attacked Russia but not France, Britain would not only stay out of the war but also guarantee France's neutrality. To Moltke's horror the Kaiser exclaimed: "So we simply deploy the whole army in the East!"[72] The Chief of General Staff pointed out that he only had one plan, to attack in the West, and that the Army could not simply be turned around to face the other way. Wilhelm responded by saying "your uncle would have given me a different answer," and commanded his Flügeladjutant to halt the invasion of Luxembourg by telephone. Moltke, red and blue in the face, returned to his office in tears, saying, "I want to wage a war against the French and the Russians, but not against such a Kaiser."[73]

However, this version of events is based on Moltke's own account. The many other witnesses to the drama make it clear that the Kaiser's response to the (albeit bizarre) news from London was rational, measured, and "joyfully" shared by everyone else present, from the Reich Chancellor to the War Minister. The Head of the Military Cabinet expressed his delight at the prospect that Germany would have to fight only one enemy instead of three.[74] And when a second telegram arrived from Lichnowsky holding out the promise of British neutrality even if Germany did attack France, the jubilation knew no bounds, as the primary aim behind Berlin's stratagem from the beginning—to unleash continental war without British intervention—had seemingly been attained. "What a fabulous turn of events," wrote Admiral von Müller. "In the adjutants' room we drank a glass of champagne. The Kaiser was in a most jubilant mood."[75]

Later that night, a dispatch arrived from George V explaining that Lichnowsky's telegrams must have been based on a misunderstanding. "Now there's nothing for it but war and my husband and my six sons will be in the thick of it," declared the irate Kaiserin in front of witnesses.[76] Moltke was recalled to the Schloss, where he found the Kaiser "very agitated." "Now do as you please; I don't care either way," the Supreme War Lord told him.[77] And so the world was plunged into the cataclysm from which it has still not recovered.

There *was* one German leader who knew what was afoot and tried to avert the disaster, but it was not the Kaiser. Prince Lichnowsky, who had gone without sleep for several nights in his efforts to find a solution, was beside himself with grief at the outbreak of war. Walter Page, the American ambassador in London, encountered him running about the German embassy in Carlton Terrace like a madman, dressed in his pyjamas in the middle of the afternoon. Princess Lichnowsky, Page reported to President Wilson, had thrown the Kaiser's portrait face down on her desk and shouted: "That is the swine that did this."[78] Harsh words spoken in anger, perhaps, but closer to reflecting Wilhelm's responsibility for the terrible calamity that now befell the world than the widely held view that he was an innocent monarch, unable to understand, let alone control, events.

Illustration 4.2: Wilhelm II

Notes

1. For a recent authoritative survey of the debate, see Annika Mombauer, *The Origins of the First World War: Controversies and Consensus* (London, 2002).
2. Sally Marks, "'My Name is Ozymandias': The Kaiser in Exile," *Central European History*, XVI, 2 (June 1983), 122–70.
3. Karl Kautsky, ed., *Die deutschen Dokumente zum Kriegsausbruch*, 4 vols. (Berlin, 1919), cited below as *Deutsche Dokumente*.
4. Johannes Lepsius, Albrecht Mendelsohn Bartholdy, Friedrich Thimme, eds., *Die Grosse Politik der Europäischen Kabinette 1871–1914*, 40 vols. (Berlin, 1922–27).
5. See for example Lydia Franke, *Die Randbemerkungen Wilhelms II. in den Akten der auswärtigen Politik als historische und psychologische Quelle* (Berlin, 1933). Lydia Franke was forced to emigrate soon after receiving her doctorate, with the result that the second part of her dissertation was never published.
6. On the deliberations at Versailles see Marks, "My Name is Ozymandias," 136–8. Further Manfred F. Boemeke, "Woodrow Wilson's Image of Germany, the War-Guilt Question, and the Treaty of Versailles," in Manfred F. Boemeke, Gerald D. Feldman, and Elisabeth Glaser, eds., *The Treaty of Versailles: A Reassessment after 75 Years* (New York, 1998), 603–14.
7. See in particular Annika Mombauer and Wilhelm Deist, eds., *The Kaiser: New Research on Wilhelm II's Role in Imperial Germany* (Cambridge, 2003); Michael Epkenhans, ed., *Albert Hopman: Das ereignisreiche Leben eines 'Wilhelminers'. Tagebücher, Briefe, Aufzeichnungen 1901 bis 1920*, (Munich, 2004); Holger Afflerbach, ed., *Kaiser Wilhelm II. als Oberster Kriegsherr im Ersten Weltkrieg. Quellen aus der militärischen Umgebung des Kaisers 1914–1918* (Munich, 2005).

8. Edward House to Woodrow Wilson, 29 May and 3 June 1914, *Public Papers of Woodrow Wilson*, vol. 30, 108f and 139f., Princeton, NJ, 1985. Further Edward House, diary entry for 1 June 1914, in Charles Seymour, ed., *The Intimate Papers of Colonel House*, 2 vols. (London, 1926), vol. I, 259–64. See Ragnhild Fiebig-von Hase, "Amerikanische Friedensbemühungen in Europa, 1905–1914," in Norbert Finzsch and Hermann Wellenreuther, eds., *Liberalitas* (Stuttgart, 1992), 312ff.
9. Foreknowledge of the assassination plot can perhaps be inferred from the meeting Quartermaster-General Georg von Waldersee had with the military plenipotentiaries of Bavaria, Saxony, and Württemberg on 16 June 1914. At that meeting he requested them to cease all written reporting until further notice; an officer of the General Staff, he said, was on his way to their respective capitals to explain to the three governments the reasons for this extraordinary step. General von Wenninger to Bavarian Minister of War, 16 June 1914. See John C. G. Röhl, "Germany," in Keith Wilson, ed., *Decisions for War, 1914* (London, 1995), 46. For another interpretation of this source see Stevenson's contribution in this volume, p. 142, 148.
10. Kaiser Wilhelm II, marginal comment of 16 June 1914, *Deutsche Dokumente*, No. 2.
11. Bethmann Hollweg to Lichnowsky, 16 June 1914, *Deutsche Dokumente*, No. 3. See Willibald Gutsche, *Wilhelm II. Der letzte Kaiser des Deutschen Reiches* (Berlin, 1991), 153.
12. Waldersee to Zimmermann, 4 July 1914, Politisches Archiv des Auswärtigen Amtes Berlin, R 996.
13. *Deutsche Dokumente*, No. 7.
14. Waldersee to Zimmermann, 4 July 1914, Politisches Archiv des Auswärtigen Amtes Berlin, R 996.
15. Graf Alexander Hoyos, "Meine Mission nach Berlin," printed in Fritz Fellner, "Die Mission Hoyos," in Wilhelm Alff, ed., *Deutschlands Sonderung von Europa 1862–1945* (Frankfurt am Main, Bern, New York, 1984), 309–16.
16. Szögyény to Berchtold, 5 July 1914, printed in *Österreich-Ungarns Aussenpolitik von der Bosnischen Krise 1908 bis zum Kriegsausbruch 1914. Diplomatische Aktenstücke des Österreichisch-Ungarischen Ministeriums des Äussern*, 8 vols., (Vienna, 1930), vol. 8, No. 10058. See also Bethmann Hollweg to Tschirschky, 6 July 1914, *Deutsche Dokumente*, No. 15.
17. Falkenhayn, statement to the parliamentary committee of enquiry, November 1919, Imanuel Geiss, ed., *Julikrise und Kriegsausbruch 1914*, 2 vols. (Hanover, 1963–4), vol. I, Nos. 23 a and b. Plessen, diary entry for 5 July 1914, ibid., No. 24a. See Afflerbach, *Oberster Kriegsherr*, 641.
18. Hopman to Tirpitz, 6 July 1914, printed in Volker R. Berghahn and Wilhelm Deist, eds., "Kaiserliche Marine und Kriegsausbruch 1914. Neue Dokumente zur Juli-Krise," *Militärgeschichtliche Mitteilungen* 1/1970, No. 1. Hopman, diary entry for 6 July 1914, Epkenhans, *Albert Hopman*, 382–4.
19. Lyncker to his wife, 21 July 1914, Afflerbach, *Oberster Kriegsherr*, 125ff.
20. Bethmann Hollweg to Kaiser Wilhelm II, 20 July 1914, Kaiser Wilhelm II to Crown Prince, 21 July 1914, *Deutsche Dokumente*, Nos. 84 and 105. See Karl Dietrich Erdmann, ed., *Kurt Riezler, Tagebücher, Aufsätze, Dokumente* (Göttingen, 1972), 190.
21. See Jagow to Kaiser Wilhelm II, 23 July 1914 with the Kaiser's marginal comments, *Grosse Politik*, vol. 34/2, No. 14647. Also King Constantine of Greece to his brother-in-law Kaiser Wilhelm II, 27 July 1914, *Deutsche Dokumente*, No. 243.
22. Kaiser Wilhelm II, marginal comments on Wangenheim's report from Constantinople of 22 July 1914, *Deutsche Dokumente*, No. 117.
23. Kaiser Wilhelm II, marginal comments on Pourtalès's report from St. Petersburg of 24 July 1914, *Deutsche Dokumente*, No. 203.
24. Kaiser Wilhelm II, marginal comments of 25 July 1914 on newspaper article, Geheimes Staatsarchiv Berlin, Eberhardt Papers, Rep. 92, No. 18.
25. Kaiser Wilhelm II, marginal comments on Jagow's report of 23 July 1914, *Deutsche Dokumente*, No. 121.

26. Wedel to Jagow, 19 July 1914, *Deutsche Dokumente*, No. 80.
27. Müller, diary entry for 19 July 1914, Bundesarchiv-Militärarchiv Freiburg, Müller Papers. See Walter Görlitz, ed., *Regierte der Kaiser? Kriegstagebücher, Aufzeichnungen und Briefe des Chefs des Marine-Kabinetts Admiral Georg Alexander von Müller 1914–1918* (Göttingen, 1959) 32. John C. G. Röhl, "Admiral von Müller and the Approach of War, 1911–1914," XII, 4 (1969), 668.
28. Görlitz, *Regierte der Kaiser?*, 33.
29. Kaiser Wilhelm II, marginal comment on Griesinger's telegramm from Belgrade of 24 July 1914, *Deutsche Dokumente*, No. 159.
30. Professor Rheindorf's notes on a conversation with Kurt Riezler on 20 May 1931, printed in Bernd-Felix Schulte, *Die Verfälschung der Riezler Tagebücher* (Frankfurt a. M., Bern, New York, 1985), 175.
31. Kaiser Wilhelm II, marginal comments on Bethmann's telegramm of 25 July 1914, *Deutsche Dokumente*, No. 182.
32. Kaiser Wilhelm II, marginal comment on Tschirschky's telegram from Vienna of 24 July 1914, *Deutsche Dokumente*, No. 155.
33. Kaiser Wilhelm II, marginal comments of 26 July 1914 on Lichnowsky's report from London of 24 July 1914, *Deutsche Dokumente*, No. 157.
34. Kaiser Wilhelm II, marginal comments on Pourtalès's report from St. Petersburg of 25 July 1914, *Deutsche Dokumente*, No. 160.
35. Lyncker to his wife, 25–26 July 1914, printed in Afflerbach, *Oberster Kriegsherr*, 129–31.
36. Hopman, diary entry for 27 July 1914, Epkenhans, *Albert Hopman*, 399–401.
37. Bethmann Hollweg to Kaiser Wilhelm II, 26 July 1914, cited in Gutsche, *Wilhelm II*, 164.
38. Müller, diary entry for 27 July 1914; Görlitz, *Regierte der Kaiser?* p. 35.
39. Müller, diary entry for 27 July 1914, Bundesarchiv-Militärarchiv Freiburg, Müller Papers, printed in Röhl, "Müller and the Approach of War," 669. Cf. Görlitz, *Regierte der Kaiser?*, 35f.
40. Holger Afflerbach, *Falkenhayn. Politisches Denken und Handeln im Kaiserreich* (Munich, 1994), 154.
41. Lichnowsky's dispatch of 26 July with the omissions ordered by the Chancellor is printed in *Deutsche Dokumente*, No. 236.
42. Lichnowsky's dispatch of 27 July 1914, *Deutsche Dokumente*, No. 258.
43. Bethmann Hollweg to Kaiser Wilhelm II, 27 July 1914, *Deutsche Dokumente*, No. 283.
44. Kaiser Wilhelm II to Jagow, 28 July 1914, *Deutsche Dokumente*, No. 293.
45. Hopman, diary entry for 28 July 1914, Epkenhans, *Albert Hopman*, 402.
46. Alfred von Tirpitz, *Politische Dokumente. Deutsche Ohnmachtspolitik im Weltkriege* (Hamburg and Berlin, 1926), 2ff.
47. Bethmann Hollweg to Tschirschky, 28 July 1914, *Deutsche Dokumente*, No. 323.
48. Falkenhayn, diary entries for 28 and 29 July 1914, Afflerbach, *Falkenhayn*, 154 and 156.
49. Prince Heinrich of Prussia, diary entry for 24–27 July 1914, Maritim- und Schifffahrtsmuseum, Hamburg.
50. Prince Heinrich of Prussia to Kaiser Wilhelm II, 28 July 1914, *Deutsche Dokumente*, No. 374.
51. Tirpitz, *Ohnmachtspolitik*, 2ff.
52. Prince Heinrich of Prussia, diary entry for 29 July 1914, Maritim- und Schifffahrtsmuseum, Hamburg.
53. Bethmann Hollweg to Goschen, 29 July 1914, *Deutsche Dokumente*, No. 373.
54. Müller, diary entry for 29 July 1914, Bundesarchiv-Militärarchiv Freiburg, Müller Papers; cf. Görlitz, *Regierte der Kaiser?*, 36.
55. Bethmann Hollweg to Kaiser Wilhelm II, 30 July 1914, *Deutsche Dokumente*, No. 407.
56. Müller, diary entry for 30 July 1914, Bundesarchiv-Militärarchiv Freiburg, Müller Papers; cf. Görlitz, *Regierte der Kaiser?*, 37.
57. Kaiser Wilhelm II, marginal comments of 30 July 1914 on an article in the *Morning Post* of 28 July 1914, *Deutsche Dokumente*, No. 402.

58. King George V to Prince Heinrich of Prussia, 30 July 1914, *Deutsche Dokumente*, No. 452.
59. Prince Heinrich of Prussia, diary entry for 30 July 1914, Maritim- und Schifffahrtsmuseum, Hamburg.
60. Kaiser Wilhelm II, marginal comments on Bethmann Hollweg's report of 30 July 1914, *Deutsche Dokumente*, No. 466.
61. Wenninger to Kress von Kressenstein, 30 July 1914, printed in Bernd-Felix Schulte, "Neue Dokumente zu Kriegsausbruch und Kriegsverlauf 1914," *Militärgeschichtliche Mitteilungen*, 25 (1979), 138f.
62. Szögyény to Berchtold, 2 August 1914, Geiss, *Julikrise und Kriegsausbruch*, vol. 2, No. 1063.
63. Kaiser Wilhelm II, marginal comments on the letter from King Constantine of Greece, 2 August 1914, *Deutsche Dokumente*, No. 702.
64. Szögyény to Berchtold, 2 August 1914, Geiss, *Julikrise und Kriegsausbruch*, vol. 2, No. 1063.
65. Valentini, diary entry for 31 July 1914, Bundesarchiv Koblenz, Valentini Papers.
66. Wenninger, diary entry for 31 July 1914, printed in Schulte, "Neue Dokumente zu Kriegsausbruch," 139f.
67. Falkenhayn, diary entry for 31 July 1914, Afflerbach, *Falkenhayn*, 160f.
68. Müller, diary entry for 1 August 1914, Bundesarchiv-Militärarchiv Freiburg, Müller Papers. Cited in Röhl, "Müller and the Approach of War," 670; cf. Görlitz, *Regierte der Kaiser?*, 38.
69. Kaiser Wilhelm II to Kaiser Franz Joseph, 31 July 1914, *Deutsche Dokumente*, No. 503.
70. Kaiser Wilhelm II to King Vittorio Emanuele III of Italy, 31 July 1914, *Deutsche Dokumente*, No. 530; Kaiser Wilhelm II to King Carol of Romania, 31 July 1914, *Deutsche Dokumente*, No. 472; for the correspondence with King Constantine see *Deutsche Dokumente*, Nos. 466 and 702.
71. Falkenhayn, diary entry for 1 August 1914, Bundesarchiv-Militärarchiv Freiburg, W 10/50635. See Afflerbach, *Falkenhayn*, 162; Hans von Zwehl, *Falkenhayn* (Berlin, 1926), 58f.
72. Helmuth von Moltke, *Erinnerungen, Briefe, Dokumente, 1877–1916* (Stuttgart, 1922), 19ff.; Annika Mombauer, *Helmuth von Moltke and the Origins of the First World War* (Cambridge, 2001), 219.
73. Hans von Haeften, "Meine Erlebnisse aus den Mobilmachungstagen 1914," cited in Mombauer, *Moltke*, 223.
74. Lyncker, diary entry for 1 August 1914, Afflerbach, *Oberster Kriegsherr*, 132f.
75. Müller, diary entry for 1 August 1914, Bundesarchiv-Militärarchiv Freiburg; cf. Görlitz, *Regierte der Kaiser?*, 39.
76. General Karl Freiherr von Plettenberg, Erinnerungen, in private hands, Essen.
77. Moltke, *Erinnerungen*, 22f.; Mombauer, *Moltke*, 223f.
78. Page to Wilson, 9 August 1914, *Papers of Woodrow Wilson*, vol. 30, 366ff.

Part II

The Military Situation before 1914: Europe between Hot and Cold War

Chapter 5

CHANCES AND LIMITS OF ARMAMENT CONTROL 1898–1914

Jost Dülffer

"To put an end to these incessant armaments and to seek the means of warding off the calamities which are threatening the whole world—such is the supreme duty which is today imposed on all states."[1] These were the objectives urged in a diplomatic note published by the Russian Foreign Minister, Count Muraviev, on 12/24 August 1898[2]:

> The intellectual and physical strength of the nations, labor and capital, are for the major part diverted from their natural application, and unproductively consumed. Hundreds of millions are devoted to acquiring terrible engines of destruction, which, though today regarded as the last word of science, are destined tomorrow to lose all value in consequence of some fresh discovery in this field. National culture, economic progress, and the production of wealth are either paralyzed or checked in their development. Moreover, in proportion as the armaments of each Power increase, so do they less and less fulfill the object which the Government has set before themselves.

Was there a chance to prevent World War I by armament control? And if so, why was this chance not used successfully? This is the question I try to answer in this chapter.

Before World War I, armaments did indeed play a great role in international politics. They directly threatened the world with conflict and destruction, even if the prime motive for the arms races of the period was, as the Norwegian historian Rolf Hobson has argued, "a cold war strategy, or perhaps a revisionism short of war."[3] Moreover, armaments had a dual quality. As Janus-faced instruments, they had aggressive and defensive functions. It is in this context that we must place the debate about armaments in the period prior to 1914. The Russian note of 1898 did not only mention the diversion of civil expenditure to military purposes and the potential impact on the economy and on social welfare. It also hinted at the ultimate danger, the risk of real, shooting war ("cataclysm"). It is true that at the time, naval and land armaments were still only loosely interconnected, and that air warfare remained at a nascent stage. Although the great powers basically accepted armaments competition as a fact of life, smaller states were involved in it only to a limited extent. And although alliances mattered, statesmen in general did not think of coalitions as vehicles for common military preparation against an opposing coalition—at least before the turn of the century. This changed, however, in the wake of the first Moroccan crisis of 1905-6, after which Anglo-French military staff talks began and, somewhat later, an Anglo-French naval agreement was reached, while in the opposing bloc exchanges between the German and Austro-Hungarian general staffs were renewed. National armament efforts and the emergence of a dangerous polarization between two coalitions were prime reasons for the outbreak of war in 1914.

Despite these factors, it is important to realize that these interconnections that are so clear in hindsight might well have been viewed differently in contemporary assessments. The competition between major powers over armaments can be seen as regional, national, or even multi-national races that served to reinforce the rationale for each involved party and to justify an increase in arms to keep up with one's neighbor or neighbor's ally. Controlling armaments and especially the enormous financial burden of armaments was therefore a dream of many contemporaries. When the British delegate to the Second Hague Peace Conference introduced arms limitation proposals, he praised them in words from Virgil's eclogue:

> Now the last age of the Cumaean prophecies begins
> A great order of the centuries is newly born
> The virgin returns, and also Saturn's reign.[4]

This implies that disarmament was regarded as a vision for a better world.[5]

I. The Hague Conference of 1899

Muraviev's note caused considerable surprise among governments and societies in Europe. Similarly, pacifists were taken aback to see the "wrong" person saying the

Illustration 5.1: Punch, 30 May 1896

right thing. Nonetheless, following extended diplomatic exchanges, two conferences, both called "peace conferences," were held at The Hague; the first one in 1899, the second in 1907. A third one was scheduled for 1915–16, but for obvious reasons did not take place. Regarding armaments, the 1899 conference led only to a declaration of intent or *voeu* (i.e. wish) "that the Governments, taking into consideration the proposals made at the Conference, may examine the possibility of an agreement as to the limitation of armed forces by land and sea, and of war budgets."[6] The second conference ended with a resolution that the limitation of armaments would be "highly desirable."[7] Nothing of real substance was achieved at either gathering. Particularly at the first Hague conference, governments made considerable efforts to evade arms control and disarmament issues. Even so, while armaments were not central to the conference debates, they formed an important part of the agenda.

The fundamental point was that early twentieth-century governments were simply not willing to discuss one of the cornerstones of their sovereignty. Freedom to determine the scale of armaments was considered a self-evident attribute of the nation state—at least for the great powers. The part played by the armaments question in the international debate on peace may well be discussed in connection with the Hague Conferences. Furthermore, the proposals made to limit armaments offer an excellent opportunity to study the general problems of arms limitation in competitive international systems, which also manifested themselves after 1945.

Muraviev's proposal for a conference did not lead immediately to concrete results. But international public debate helped or forced governments to formulate a conference proposal. The program that was eventually adopted centered on codifying the international law of land and sea warfare, and in this domain, the two Hague Conferences obtained their most lasting achievements. Nevertheless, the first four points in a second circular letter sent out by Muraviev on 30 December 1898 (11 January 1899), did address arms limitation. The first point proposed "an understanding not to increase for a fixed period the present effectives of the military and naval forces and at the time not to increase the budgets hereto." This implies that a reduction of these figures might follow in the future. The second point dealt with firearms. The third referred to more powerful explosives, especially if thrown from balloons, and the fourth wanted to forbid the use of "submarine torpedo boats or plungers" and the future "construction of vessels with rams."

On the one hand, these proposals contained some very far reaching and theoretically promising ideas. Yet on the other, they seem somewhat problematic in view of the military situation at the dawn of the twentieth century. In the ensuing debates, several approaches to the practicalities of arms control and disarmament were developed. They can be summarized schematically as: budgetary ceilings, limits on the numbers of soldiers permitted in armies (either at "peacetime strength" or upon mobilization), and ceilings on numbers and sizes of weapons. Possible candidates for restrictions for the third category included battleship size, overall tonnage of battleships/navies, artillery pieces, rifles, combinations of land warfare weapons, and alternative land/naval forces (such as submarines in place of battleships).

At the time, the states involved in the discussions varied widely in their underlying circumstances. The smaller states in western Europe were basically status quo oriented and therefore favored the lowest level of armaments possible. In southeastern Europe, on the other hand, small (and sometimes only semi-sovereign) states such as Bulgaria had major ambitions for further territorial acquisitions, against their neighbors as well as the Ottoman Empire. In Austria-Hungary, the feeling prevailed that the Dual Monarchy lacked even the armaments needed for self-defense. The German Empire was just starting major naval rearmament, thus relatively neglecting the army, which had been the focus of a massive build-up in the previous decade. Great Britain to some extent feared land-based arms limitation, which might enable other states to transfer resources into naval expansion. The United States had just won a war against Spain and regarded its navy as inadequate. In Russia, the military leadership originally had seen some advantage in forbidding the expensive new quick-firing field artillery, with which Austria-Hungary was in the process of re-equipping its army. However, the impression prevails that even the Russian military delegates were unenthusiastic about developing specific plans that could form a real basis for an agreement on arms limitation.

It was only on 23 June 1899, more than a month after the conference, that a commission addressed the general aspects of arms limitation. The Dutch General Den Beer Portuael proclaimed, "let us halt on the edge of the abyss," and spoke against an "increase in armies, fleets, budgets, debts. ... The unlucky gift of a wicked fairy."[8] More important was a Russian proposal which had grown out of earlier unofficial debates, not for disarmament but for an end to the armaments race. Colonel Gilinsky's military proposal centered on three points: a five-year freeze on the numbers of soldiers maintained by each country in the motherland (i.e. excluding the colonies) in time of peace, a much more far reaching proposal to set a maximum peacetime strength, and the maintenance of military budgets at present levels for the next five years. What Gilinsky proposed for armies was adapted by his naval colleague Captain Scheine for the navies: holding naval budgets for three years at the same level, and publishing in the meantime the figures for the tonnages of ships, the numbers of officers and men, and expenditure on coastal fortifications. The first goal of Scheine's plan was to achieve transparency by publishing relevant statistics for existing military strength. This step would create a basis for comparison. Second, the idea of a "holiday" (or a "freeze" as it would later be called) could end arms races in the weapons categories concerned. Baron de Staal, the Russian president of conference, argued, "if we are only able for some years to provide for a certain stability, everything points to the belief that a tendency towards a diminution of military burdens will be able to grow and to develop."[9]

Colonel Groß von Schwarzhoff, the first German military delegate, challenged these notions two days later. As far as is known, he spoke under general instructions from Berlin, but with freedom to determine his own tactics. In part, he opposed the Russian scheme on points of substance. He argued that many other types of data were relevant to military strength, such as public instruction, duration of army service, geographical factors, and elements of infrastructure such as the railway system, fortifications, and other matters. He added that it was not possible, as the Russians proposed, to include troops stationed in the motherland but exclude colonial forces. The other delegates agreed with these arguments. But this meant that a more practical formula was now needed to define peacetime strengths. Moreover, while Groß von Schwarzhoff warned that the Russian proposals would disturb the "European equilibrium," the Russians had intended precisely to consolidate that equilibrium by maintaining the military—and thus to a certain extent also the political—power ratios between the European states. More fundamentally, however, Groß von Schwarzhoff challenged on principle the basic assumption of the Russian manifesto:

> I do not believe that among my honored colleagues there is a single one ready to admit that his sovereign, his Government, is engaged in working for the inevitable ruin, the slow, but sure annihilation of his country.... The German people are not crushed beneath the weight of expenditures and taxes. They are not hanging at the edge of the precipice.... Quite the contrary, public and private wealth is increasing, the general welfare, and standard of life, are rising from year to year.[10]

Compulsory military service, according to Groß, was seen in his country not as a heavy burden but "as a sacred and patriotic duty" essential for the future. In his opinion German society was based on military service, which stabilized the existing order. Of course his speech bore little relation to political realities in Berlin, where armaments debates were always tense struggles over scarce resources, especially as military expenditure accounted for some 60 to 80 percent of the total Reich budget. But Groß was making a programmatic declaration that looked forward to a dynamic future of German greatness and well being. His contribution was unique at The Hague in its offensive and outspoken language, but many of his colleagues from other countries might well have agreed with its substance, and he relieved them of the need to be so forthright themselves. In fact, opposition to the German viewpoint came mainly from representatives of the smaller countries. For example, van Karnebeek of the Netherlands urged that "enormous military expenditures which burden nations may turn into dangerous weapons against the established social order in the different countries." A solution to the armaments question would reduce the danger of domestic political agitation at home. Bulgaria's first delegate argued similarly and with tactical regard to the relative strength of his country's neighbors. In contrast, Léon Bourgeois, the first French delegate, contended merely that the conference should "try to prove to public opinion that we have at least sincerely examined the problem placed before us." Outside the confidential discussions in the conference commissions, in other words, a new public opinion was becoming evident, in which pacifists and publicists played important roles.

In the discussions at The Hague about naval armaments, the Russian proposals for budgetary limitations were countered by the German delegate, Admiral Siegel, with a surprising argument: the German government's hands were tied because the Reichstag had just passed legislation that not only matched the proposals but even surpassed them. For the next few years the German navy's building program (which also largely determined the budget) would be fixed by law. In contrast, the Danish delegate, Bille, feared that nations might not limit their budgets but instead would increase them beyond reasonable measure. According to the Portuguese delegate, naval and colonial budgets were impossible to separate. For these reasons, the question was eventually deferred for further studies by the governments. Meanwhile Captain Alfred Mahan for the United States declared flatly that while he did not want to give any opinion on the European side of the problem, "[t]he military and naval armaments of the United States are at present so small, relatively to the extent of territory and to the number of the population, as well as in comparison with those of other nations, that their size can entail no additional burden of expense upon the latter, nor can even form a subject for profitable mutual discussion."[11] Eventually, Auguste Beernaert, the Belgian president of the armaments commission who officially tried to support all proposals, cabled to his capital that indeed no one seriously wanted disarmament.[12]

These general debates about arms limitation were transcended by a more specialized discussion in the two sub-commissions for land and naval armaments. "Should we waive the right to use any new improvement in the art of war and forbid the adoption in armies and navies of any new firearms and new explosives as well as of more powerful powders than those now adopted both for guns and cannon?" asked Beernaert as president at the beginning of the debates.[13] In particular, the Russian Colonel Gilinsky argued that rifles in all armies had reached an equivalent quality and he suggested an agreement not to introduce machine guns, which would help to limit costs. The debate on this question had two main facets. One of them concerned definitions of technical progress. The Russian delegate proposed to use the weight of the gun, the maximum caliber, the weight of the bullets, the initial velocity, and the rapidity of shots per minute. Implicitly all speakers were critical of these proposals, and military officers discussed in detail why such criteria could not work. All these factors were interdependent and a limitation in one category would provoke an increase in another one. New kinds of explosives might not only be more effective, but also be cheaper, argued the US delegate. Another point was made that not all rifles in present-day armies were in fact of the same quality. In the naval sub-commission similar arguments were considered, especially concerning the relationship between artillery and plate armor. The second debate in the sub-commissions was more abstract and addressed the possibility of improving existing military devices while not introducing completely new ones. However, it might be cheaper to develop a new weapon than to improve old ones, ran one counter argument. The relative advantages of incremental improvement versus more radical innovation could not be defined. And finally, the question of verification was discussed: e.g. new rifles might be collected in arsenals. The argument that mutual trust between the parties was essential failed to convince all sides; secrecy being one of the principal characteristics of armaments developments during this period. The idea that public opinion could be a means of verification was unconvincing, especially when brought forward by the delegate of autocratic Russia. That states' sovereignty could be limited in any way by something so elusive as public opinion seemed absurd at the time, and not only to military officers.

It is unclear how the issue of warships with rams came to appear on the Russian agenda. It was agreed that ships could have a stem to withstand a shock, and all existing armor should be maintained. Smaller states, it was argued, could nevertheless defend their coasts with rams quite cheaply. Thus, the debate about this somewhat antiquated weapon was adjourned. But the conference discussed three other war instruments that might be important in the future. The fact that there should have been a debate about the future significance of electricity and chemistry in warfare was remarkable in itself, although this too was easily adjourned because the impact was not yet discernible. The opposite argument that precisely for this reason, a general military prohibition could have far reaching consequences for world developments, failed to come into consideration.

The Hague Conference of 1899 agreed on the following three points:

1. "Asphyxiating" gases were consistently viewed as a specialized form of munitions. This point addressed one of the most important means of future warfare, especially in World War I. But here again, unforeseeable developments served to discredit the whole approach. While the problem was resolved at the conference by declaring that all ammunition on detonating produced some gas that might be noxious, the insertion of the word "intentionally" (as opposed to an incidental use), forced further discussion of the question. Alfred Mahan argued that using asphyxiating gas might not be more cruel than using torpedoes, which might throw "four or five hundred men into the sea to be choked by water, with scarcely the remotest chance of escape."[14] Others argued that land warfare was different in this respect. Evidently, the potential use of gas as an instrument for mass destruction was not yet considered at all, although there was a hint that gases might afflict civilians as well as military personnel. But the possibility that gas might not only disable but also kill opponents, gained some attention. Nevertheless, because the development of such a gas in the next few years was unlikely, all the governments except that of the United States agreed to a five-year moratorium on such weapons.

2. That Great Britain accepted this was partly because of a related question: that of "dum-dum" bullets. The (unratified) St. Petersburg Convention on

land warfare signed in 1874 had concluded that the aim of warfare was not primarily to kill soldiers, but to prevent them from fighting. This precedent set a standard for the Hague debates. Some officers were vehemently critical of all such limitations. Sir John Fisher's dictum—"humanizing warfare? You could as well speak of humanizing hell!"—was characteristic of this attitude. Similar views were widely shared especially by the US officers, while others did not need to be so outspoken. The British general Sir John Ardagh could speak about British experiences at the battle of Omdurman only three years earlier. Flattened projectiles belonged to standard British equipment in colonial warfare. "In civilized war a soldier penetrated by a small projectile if wounded, withdraws to the ambulance, and does not advance any further. It is very different with a savage. Even though pierced two or three times, he does not cease to march forward, does not call upon the hospital attendants, but continues on, and before anyone has time to explain to him that he is flagrantly violating the decisions of the Hague Conference, he cuts off your head."[15] This mixture of racist arguments with invocation of military necessities should have proved the absurdity of the whole debate, but in this case, the reliance upon the mood of public opinion offered a convenient excuse for not reaching more precise agreements. This prevailed during the conference.

3. A third question regarded throwing projectiles out of balloons. As currently used, according to the American delegate Captain Crozier, balloons were neither effective nor humane as instruments of warfare. But with future developments in technology they might become more easily navigable (dirigible balloons) and thus might increase the duration of combat and consequently the evils and costs of warfare. Thus, aerial warfare, one of the most effective and menacing combat instruments of the next several decades, was already being discussed, but—as it remained impractical for the time being—was not considered to be a real problem.

As the outcome of these proceedings three declarations on the non-use of certain categories of weapon were indeed signed. (A declaration was situated at the lowest rank of diplomatic instruments, carrying less authority than conventions and resolutions.) By the first declaration the signatories agreed "to forbid [for the next five years] the discharge of projectiles and explosives from balloons or by other new methods of similar nature." The second and third declarations were concluded with no time limit, although they could also be denounced. By their terms, the signatories were obliged "to abstain from the use of projectiles the sole object of which is the diffusion of asphyxiating gases" and "to abstain from the use of bullets which expand or flatten easily in the human body, such as bullets with a hard envelope which does not entirely cover the core or is pierced with incisions."[16] The British delegation filed its vehement opposition to the dum-dum declaration and thus was not bound by it, as was the case for all the other governments that did not sign.

The results of the arms limitation and disarmament debates at the first Hague Conference were to some extent predictable. Immediately after the conference, it was argued that there had been a "hopeless technical tangle and mathematical snarl."[17] This was true, but it was a symptom of the implicit decision of all the great powers, including Russia, not to embark on anything like real arms limitation and not to restrict the sovereignty of their states in a future war. The debates took place in an international environment in which great power conflict seemed relatively remote, after the Franco-British crisis over the Sudan had been overcome in spring 1899 and before the Boer War had broken out. But some respect had been paid to the prestige of the Russian Tsar and the role of Russia as a great power on the one hand, and on the other to the expectations that had been created on the part of public opinion in many states. Thus, at least a basic and theoretical discussion about the most fruitful means of dealing with the costly problem of armaments had taken place, which also set standards for further debates up to the end of the twentieth century.

II. Changes in the International System

During the five or six years following the conclusion of the first Hague Peace Conference in July 1899, the international situation changed rapidly. Three new features stood out. First, international politics gradually took on the character of a bipolar system. Of course, the Dual and Triple Alliances had existed since 1879–82 and the Russo-French Alliance since 1891–94; but now the former Anglo-French antagonism was muted by the public conclusion of the "Entente Cordiale" in April 1904. Together with the accompanying secret colonial agreements and the first secret military staff discussions of 1905–06, it demonstrated a willingness for closer cooperation in European affairs. It was supplemented by an Anglo-Russian Entente in 1907, a mainly Asian arrangement that also entailed a tendency toward diplomatic cooperation in Europe. "Encirclement" became a contemporary assessment on the German side.

The second new feature was that real wars took place, not only colonial conflicts such as Britain's "Boer War" in South Africa or the German colonial campaigns in South-West Africa or East Africa, but a major war involving great powers, between Japan and Russia, which ended with some unexpected, and even sensational, results. The power with the numerically largest army on Earth not only lost its Asian and European fleets, but also suffered military defeat at the hands of a smaller country. It was predictable that the Russian government would try to make up the ground lost due to the war and due to the 1905 revolution at home. A dynamic Russian rearmament program, with all its international consequences, could now be expected.

The third development was that a competition in armaments had also started at sea. Especially in Britain, the German naval challenge that followed the naval laws of 1898 and 1900 was accepted and countered by an acceleration of battleship building as well as by a qualitative leap through the introduction of "Dreadnought" capital ships, which in effect restarted the naval race from zero. Not only did armaments matter as a factor in international politics, but also the new big ships proved to be a good scale by which admirals and politicians could measure the powers' naval strength.

III. Preparations for the Second Hague Conference

The increasing international polarization and new armaments initiatives by some powers demanded reactions by others. These reactions could be diplomatic (e.g. the ententes) and/or military. When US President Theodore Roosevelt called for a new worldwide peace congress in October 1904, such an appeal during wartime was easily stalled. A year later, however, the Russian Ambassador to Washington, with an almost impolite directness, again asserted Russia's right to give birth to a new conference at The Hague. Neither these impulses for a new "peace conference" in principle had anything do with disarmament or arms control, but were aimed mainly at codifying the laws of sea and land warfare as well as establishing rules for international arbitration. Nevertheless, armaments questions would again be placed on the agenda.

In Britain, after the resignation of the Unionist Prime Minister, Arthur James Balfour, the Liberals won an impressive electoral victory in 1906. Alongside Liberal Imperialists such as the new Foreign Secretary, Sir Edward Grey, the Chancellor of the Exchequer, Herbert Asquith, and the Secretary for War, Richard Burdon Haldane, the Liberal party contained important pacifist-internationalist tendencies that called for reduced spending on armaments. The money should be redirected toward social reform measures such as old age pensions. Because of the Anglo-German naval race, the First Sea Lord, Sir John Fisher, pleaded not only for a concentration on bigger ships—with the qualitative leap represented by HMS Dreadnought—but also, in the November 1905 Cawdor program, for a continuous building rate of four ships a year. "Our own ship-building programme now depends mainly upon Germany. We have no intention of losing our naval position, and if no change takes place we shall, in a few years, be spending 10 million a year more on our Navy than we are at present. And so the competition between Germany and us will go on until one of us is bankrupt. I do not think we shall break first...."[18]

Because of this domestic competition for scarce financial resources between armaments and social reform, the question of arms limitation had to be considered seriously. By pursuing a disarmament initiative, the factional conflict within the British government could be externalized. Thus, Grey felt himself to be under pressure, but he thought it an excellent idea to shift the onus of responsibility to a future Hague conference. On 9 May 1906, the House of Commons passed a resolution to bring the question of armaments before the conference, followed two weeks later by the House of Lords. A domestic compromise was reached to limit the long-term building rate to three capital ships a year, and possibly to build only two, depending on the results achieved at The Hague. The "two-power standard" of superiority over the next two largest fleets had become obsolete since the entente with France and the virtual annihilation of the Russian navy. For these reasons, Grey officially reserved the right to bring up the armaments question at the conference, although it had not been included in the Russian agenda of April 1906. Privately he argued: "Of course there can be no such thing as disarmament; what is wanted is to make clear that it is Germany and not us which [sets] the pace."[19]

The German perception of this British debate was very different. For navy circles in Germany, the agitation for higher civilian expenditure showed that the Royal Navy could not build as much as it wanted as a result of domestic pressure. In the Reichsmarineamt, officers argued that Great Britain could not sustain the arms race; the German challenge had exposed British weakness and German efforts should be accelerated. They did not reflect on the opportunity to lessen the burden on both British and German taxpayers. All the same, there were real possibilities for a limitation of armaments at this point. "They remained theoretical not because the British Foreign Office advanced them only half-heartedly, but also for the reason that they interpreted the motives of German politics more clearly than did an important part of British public opinion at that time, which aimed at a peaceful balance of interests."[20]

Nevertheless, the German leaders after their diplomatic isolation at the 1906 Algeciras conference refrained from openly rejecting the British initiative. Emperor Wilhelm II declared: "Therefore our old program from the last Hague conference must be upheld. Only if 'questions of disarmament' are completely excluded, shall I go to the conference, otherwise not." Opposition to Wilhelm's view came from Friedrich von Holstein, one of the dominating influences on the formulation of German foreign policy over the previous two decades. He resigned over the issue of his dissenting judgment on this question. For him, it was "ridiculous nonsense" to try to separate Great Britain and France by building a fleet. The German navy, according to Holstein, was now strong enough. "Our finances are in a very unsatisfactory status and every expenditure on the fleet would make them worse." The navy was only a "children's toy" for the Emperor.

The American leaders were also unhappy about developments in naval armaments. The introduction of the *Dreadnought* type battleship by the British navy could intensify the arms race in battleships. The extra costs were not welcome, in addition to the fact that the planned Central American canal at Panama might not be navigable for larger battleships. Hence whereas in 1899 the idea of a limit of fifteen thousand tons for capital ships had not found any resonance, when Alfred Mahan proposed it now, it convinced his President. Roosevelt was completely uninterested in (not to say adamantly opposed to) restrictions on the number of ships constructed and to disarmament, on the grounds that armaments were essential to national sovereignty. But qualitative limits were a different matter. Great Britain and the United States, which had avoided confrontation in the first Venezuela crisis of 1895–97 and had cooperated in resolving the second Venezuela crisis in 1902–03, now tried to raise the armaments question in mutual solidarity. Because there was no advantage in a direct diplomatic confrontation between Great Britain and Germany, Grey tried to pass the initiative to the US President who, likewise, wanted to place the armaments question on the agenda at the next Hague conference. The United States could act as a kind of neutral in this case of Anglo-German contention. In the meantime, Emperor Wilhelm tried to incite his British counterpart King Edward VII against any discussion of armaments—and indeed Edward is said to have spoken of "humbug" in this regard—but Wilhelm II insisted on maintaining absolute freedom to determine the number of ships built.

The idea of naval armaments limitation was dropped for various reasons; one being that Roosevelt himself became doubtful about the whole matter. In 1906, tensions between Japan and the United States increased and America now felt the necessity of building larger ships for transoceanic warfare. In Britain, the idea gained predominance that economies could be made by concentrating on enhancing the quality of battleships rather than competing purely quantitatively. Both quantitative and qualitative arms limitations, as well as budgetary limitations were all now seriously discussed, but failed because all sides saw disadvantages in them.

France was also involved in the armaments question in 1906. The leaders in Paris, however, refrained from promoting the issue as Grey suggested they should. In December 1906, Foreign Minister Stephen Pichon finally refused to broach the armaments question formally, on the grounds that it was not included in the official Russian program of April 1906. Respect for the Entente partner Great Britain played an important role in this course, but it was *not* the result of French unwillingness to discuss arms limitation. On the contrary, an intense public debate ranged Baron d'Estournelles de Constant and Léon Bourgeois—who again became the principal French delegates at the Second Hague Conference—against the Minister of the Navy, Thomson. While the navy ministry vehemently pleaded against any limitations on armaments, the politicians argued publicly for an alternative navy based on submarines. This proposal revived notions associated with the "jeune école" of French naval thinking two decades earlier, and was based on ideas about alternative forms of naval warfare for a weaker power. However, such ideas were defeated in the public debate, as simultaneously were their counterparts in Germany, where like-minded naval officers such as Karl Galster or Lothar Persius were ostracized by the dominant Tirpitz faction. Another, even more interesting, French debate had purely internal dimensions. A military and a naval committee discussed the possibility of arms limitation, regardless of the political will to implement it. In a completely new assessment for the military elite of a great power, following extensive debates, Admiral Arago and General Amourel endorsed limitation in principle. The French navy could contemplate a ceiling on the tonnage of its larger ships (thus leaving open the questions of number and size, quality vs. quantity), if the army was ready to accept a fixed peacetime strength. Furthermore, Amourel judged it would be possible, beginning from 1907, to embark on a reduction by one twentieth in the number of army personnel and to continue reductions on a five-year cycle. A potential explanation for France's receptivity to disarmament could be seen in the country's slower economic expansion, which generated lesser revenue growth than in Germany. In any case, this pro-disarmament view of the army and naval committees was disregarded in the official French political position adopted at The Hague.

The question of arms limitation had failed in 1899 and was again being postponed for another conference, but it now won the attention of a part of public opinion. In the first months of 1907, the British journalist William Stead tried to promote an international "peace crusade." He worked in two ways. By traveling to all the major countries of Europe and to the United States, he strove to mobilize the public. It was Grey who somewhat disingenuously encouraged Stead by saying that only the pressure of organized public opinion could induce governments to discuss the armaments question at The Hague. Stead's other tactic was to meet with monarchs, presidents, and foreign ministers, thus trying to recruit them for his cause of arms limitation. In both respects he finally failed, but a new kind of public diplomacy formed a counterweight to official debates and constituted one of the first examples of a new style of international diplomacy from below in a peace-directed question.[21]

In the opening months of 1907, international relations were divided into two camps over the question of arms control: states and diplomats on the one hand vs. public pressure and social movements on the other. The Austro-Hungarian, Russian, and German governments tried to induce the British government to abandon the question as well as the whole approach of cultivating public opinion. It should be remembered that the arms question was not included in the Russian program for the peace conference—especially in the light of Russia's defeat in the Russo-Japanese war. Foreign Minister Aleksandr Isvolski did not conceal his contempt for the idea. Hence, a complicated and exhausting diplomatic struggle took place. The three Eastern powers, with Germany at the forefront, categorically refused to discuss the armament question at all. In the increasingly polarized situation, neither Russia's partner France nor Britain (with whom Russia was in the process of negotiating an entente) had any incentive to antagonize St. Petersburg. A "first-class burial"—as the internal language of the three conservative Imperial powers put it—of the arms limitation question was therefore the only possible outcome.

Grey once again tried to introduce other approaches to arms discussion that did not mention the word "disarmament." The idea of limiting armaments budgets was one of them, with far-reaching impacts on the future in the 1920s and 1930s. Another was exchanging information about building programs, which even later, in the 1970s and 1980s, became a key component of "confidence building measures." In 1907, both ideas remained stillborn. A burial of the arms control question by referring it to a committee of the great powers would at least have restored the basic structure of the contemporary international system in place of the "ochlocracy of the small states" at The Hague, which Germany had so despised in 1899. An ostentatious German refusal (by means of a public declaration in the Reichstag on 30 April 1907) to take part in any form of discussion in armaments cleared the scene and the responsibilities. Thus, only a *voeu* to study further the question, similar to that of 1899, could be renewed. The question of what would happen if, in the final official session of the second Hague meeting, diplomats asked the floor to comment on or even discuss the whole question received ample consideration. Russian president Nelidow chaired the second Hague conference's concluding session on 17 August 1907. The British first delegate, Sir Edward Fry (a Quaker) introduced the arms limitation resolution with a metaphor-laden speech. Nelidov gave notice that the US, Spanish, Argentinian, and Chilean delegations had written letters indicating their support. Things could have ended there. It was the French first delegate, Léon Bourgeois, who felt bound somewhat to depart from the pre-arranged proceedings by stressing that he had been the person who had already in 1899 found the formula for the *voeu*.

IV. The System of Arms Races and the Failure of a Third Meeting at The Hague

The arms race continued after 1907. The Anglo-German naval competition led to various bilateral negotiations, which centered on the ratio of battleships between each side and on the exchange of information. The military build-up continued after the return of tension to the continent in the aftermath of the First Moroccan Crisis, and reached its peak in the years after 1911.

At The Hague, the Scottish-American businessman Andrew Carnegie paid for the building of the Peace Palace, which from 1913 housed the Permanent Court of Arbitration. Sir Edward Fry's final speech, in which he had quoted Virgil's fourth eclogue about the coming golden age, found its material embodiment in four stained-glass windows that Great Britain had dedicated to the building.[22]

The second Hague conference had also concluded with the wish that there should be a third conference to reconsider the developments of the previous years. Indeed many governments instituted preparatory commissions for a third conference scheduled for 1915 or 1916. Armaments were not prominent in the various agendas. Instead, pacifists hoped to further a new general organization of the international system that was already underway. The German professor of international law, Walther Schücking, in this sense discerned a World Federation of States as already existing in 1913. In his opinion, this development would probably lead to a permanent organization of the Hague conferences as a kind of world parliament. "The system of people's armies armed against each other will be changed to a system of a common army of the world federation of states. This will ensure the maintenance of a peace of justice in the civilized world."[23] In a situation of intensifying international tension, this idea could refer only to a utopia that could hardly have been less relevant to the course of events after the Balkan wars.

It was only in the French scheme for a League of Nations after 1918 that the new organization was to be provided with armed forces of its own. Because the Anglo-American powers opposed such an idea, only a mutual pact of assistance was concluded, which failed before ratification. International peacekeeping forces had not been completely out of consideration in the period before 1914. Common blockades and landings by peacekeeping detachments had taken place in the Cretan crisis of 1896–97. A common European army was deployed to China during the so-called Boxer Rebellion in 1900. A local concert of the European powers which successfully intervened under common military command was a general habit in many extra-European capitals from Constantinople to Beijing. Yet these factors had more to do with imperialistic power politics than with the maintenance of peace. It would take another two generations before the United Nations created the institution of common international troops with peacekeeping purposes. The limits and usefulness of such operations may be debated even today.

V. Conclusion

There were three phases in multilateral debates about armaments control before 1914. Around the turn of the century, the relevant conceptual categories were developed and discussed for the first time. In the great-power system, none of the constituent members of international society had a concrete interest in this question. Of course, armament costs were high and in theory could be diverted to other civilian purposes. But neither optimism about a developing new peaceful system nor pessimism about a dangerous road to the abyss led to institutionalizing devices against the arms race.

Five years later, real armaments races were under way, real wars had been fought, and the international system tended to increasing polarization. At this point—in 1906–07—there were some real ideas for arms control. But they were not introduced into international politics, as leaders worked precisely to avoid exacerbating the situation by posing such a divisive question. It seemed that Britain and the

United States confronted the Eastern Powers, led by the German empire, but the confrontation was more apparent than real.

In the third phase, armaments talks were bilateral and thus had a practical focus on naval armaments, particularly battleships. They remained a sideshow, alongside other peripheral questions, but encouraged a limited relaxation of tensions.[24] The preparations for a third Hague conference did little to end the armaments race. But the idea that in the future there might be genuine international armed forces was developed for the first time in international politics. It took a world war to bring this notion to the attention of the Paris Peace Conference in 1919—unfortunately, under the developing League of Nations system, without any practical results at the time.

Before 1914, although armaments were considered as a preparation for war, the idea prevailed that they might be only necessary and inevitable tools in international power politics. None of the major powers was interested in a limitation of its sovereignty. For that reason, the Hague conferences had, at least in this regard, no chance of success. But they served as a catalyst and a forum for an international public opinion that grew stronger with the years and allowed hope for the future.

Notes

1. *The Hague Peace Conferences of 1899 and 1907*, ed. James Brown Scott (Baltimore, 1909), Vol. II, 1–2.
2. These and the following dates in this style are related to the old Russian (Julian) and to the Gregorian calendar.
3. Rolf Hobson, *Imperialism at Sea: Naval Strategic Thought, the Ideology of Sea Power and Tirpitz Plan, 1875–1914* (Boston, 2002), 43.
4. Ultima Cumaei venit iam carminis aetas
   magnus ab integro saeclorum nascitur ordo
   iam redit et virgo, redeunt Saturnia regna.
   In: *Rapports faits aux conférences de La Haye de 1899 et 1907*, introduction by James Brown Scott (Oxford, 1920), 892–894 (893).
5. For similar hopes among pacifists, see the contribution of Hartmut Lehmann in this volume.
6. James Brown Scott, ed., *Texts of the Peace Conferences at Hague, 1899 and 1907: With English Translation and Appendix of Related Documents* (Boston, 1908), 233–234.
7. *Rapports*, 892.
8. Scott, *Texts of the Peace Conferences*, 301–02.
9. Ibid.
10. *Proceedings of the Hague Peace Conferences: The Conference of 1899*, ed. James Brown Scott (New York, 1920), 308–309.

11. Arthur Eyffinger, *The 1899 Hague Peace Conference: 'The Parliament of Man, The Federation of the World'* (The Hague, 1999), 248.
12. Jost Dülffer, *Regeln gegen den Krieg? Die Haager Friedenskonferenzen 1899 und 1907 in der internationalen Politik* (Berlin, 1981), 78 f. Here as elsewhere in this chapter I rely heavily on this book.
13. Eyffinger, *The 1899 Hague Peace Conference*, 222.
14. Frederic W. Holls, *The Peace Conference at The Hague, and its Bearings on International Law and Policy* (New York, 1914), 119.
15. Scott, *Texts of the Peace Conferences*, 343.
16. Scott, *Texts of the Peace Conferences*, 264–66.
17. William I. Hull, *The Two Hague Conferences and their Contributions to International Law* (Boston, 1908), 69.
18. Grey to Ferguson, 19 September 1906, NA State Dept., R. G. 59, Case 40, Vol. 5–14.
19. Dülffer, *Regeln gegen den Krieg*, 290; Grey, referring to a report of the "Vossische Zeitung," 18 May 1906, that remarked positively on the resolution of the House of Commons.
20. Translated from Dülffer, *Regeln gegen den Krieg?* 291.
21. International movements for the independence of Greece in the 1820s, over the question of Bulgarian "atrocities" in the 1870s and 1880s, or the "pro-Boer" movement had specific cases of national self-determination or repression to deal with.
22. Eyffinger, *The 1899 Hague Peace Conference*, 253.
23. Jost Dülffer, "Efforts to Reform the International System and Peace Movements Before 1914," *Peace & Change* 14, 1 (1989), 25–45.
24. Concerning European detente before 1914, see the contribution of Friedrich Kiessling in this volume.

Chapter 6

WAS A PEACEFUL OUTCOME THINKABLE?
The Naval Race before 1914

Michael Epkenhans

In his *Memoirs*, published at the same time in Germany and Britain in October 1919, Grand Admiral Alfred von Tirpitz, the so-called father of the German battle fleet, entitled the last paragraph of his chapter dealing with Anglo-German relations before 1914 "Relief." Thus he wanted to emphasize in this book, as well as in many publications to follow, that Germany's naval build-up was not responsible for the outbreak of World War I in July 1914.[1] In Tirpitz's opinion, this change in Anglo-German relations was merely the corollary of a new policy toward Great Britain, embodied by the new German ambassador to the Court of St. James, Baron Marschall von Bieberstein:

> His appearance in London ... put a stop for a time to the German method of kow-towing to the English and being impressed by their ways. Marschall knew that the Briton becomes more respectful, the more resolutely his competitor maintains his own standpoint. He declared that Germany could not carry out her economic policy without possessing a power at sea which could protect us against the necessity of yielding to England at every turn.

Strangely enough, his main adversary on the opposite coast of the North Sea, Winston S. Churchill, First Lord of the Admiralty between 1911 and 1915, held similar views on this issue. In his book *The World Crisis*, first published in 1923, he left no doubt that Anglo-German relations had seriously deteriorated due to Germany's naval aspirations, but he also stressed that in 1914, "naval rivalry had at the moment ceased to be a cause of friction." He also explained why: "We were proceeding inflexibly for the third year in succession with our series of programmes according to scale and declaration. Germany had made no further increases since the beginning of 1912. It was certain that we could not be overtaken as far as capital ships were concerned."[2]

These views differ completely from the feeling of many contemporaries before and after the war. They felt that the Anglo-German naval race would eventually lead to war. In 1909, for example, the German cartoon magazine "Der wahre Jakob" ("The Real McCoy")—a Social Democratic magazine, of course—published a cartoon showing both the German Emperor and the English King in a race ending in hell.[3] In the eyes of contemporaries the outbreak of war in 1914 and the fact that Great Britain had joined France and Russia right at the beginning seemed to vindicate this Social Democratic cartoonist. So, who was right? The cartoonist, or Churchill and Tirpitz, who emphasized their mutual perseverance in naval matters, though for completely different reasons? Whereas Germany wanted to challenge the world's leading naval power, Great Britain wanted to defend its status against its rival. In order to answer this question, it seems necessary to discuss three interrelated issues.

1. Why did both countries have or want a powerful navy?

2. How did the naval race develop?

3. What steps were taken to stop this race and to alleviate political tensions?

This chapter will address these issues in this order, before returning to the problem of whether the naval race made the outbreak of war in 1914 more probable.

I. Why did both countries have or want a powerful navy?

Since the seventeenth-century, British politicians had been unanimous in their views on the importance of sea power, which, according to Alfred Thayer Mahan, had laid the foundations for the British Empire. In 1901, to give only one example, before the naval race actually started, Lord Selborne, the First Lord of the Admiralty and a leading Unionist, argued, "our stakes are out of all proportions to those of any another Power. To us defeat in a maritime war would mean a disaster of almost unparalleled magnitude in history. It might mean the destruction of our mercantile marine, the stoppage of our manufactures, scarcity of food, invasion, disruption of Empire. No other country runs the same risks in a war with us."[4]

At the height of Anglo-German tension in late 1911, one of his successors, the newly appointed First Lord of the Admiralty, Winston Spencer Churchill, a Liberal,

Illustration 6.1: Der Wahre Jakob, 22 June 1909

again described both the origins and the importance of Britain's naval supremacy in his first speech to the House of Commons: "The maintenance of naval supremacy is our whole foundation. Upon it stands not the Empire only, not merely the commercial property of our people, not merely a fine place in the world's affairs; upon our naval supremacy stands our lives and the freedom we have guarded for nearly a thousand years."[5] Accordingly, the British government expected the Royal Navy to perform three main tasks: first, to dominate the narrow seas and approaches to the British Isles and so prevent invasion; second, to secure communications with the colonies; and third, to preserve the security of the global trading system.[6]

In order to fulfil these tasks, the Royal Navy had been maintained during the eighteenth and nineteenth centuries as the most powerful navy in the world in every respect, and so it remained. As the Naval Defence Act of 1889 had stipulated, in 1900 it continued to be as strong as the combined navies of the second- and third-largest sea powers.[7] Moreover, the Royal Navy controlled what Sir John Fisher described as the five keys to the world, namely Dover, Gibraltar, Singapore, the Cape, and Alexandria.[7] These and all other outposts of the Empire were linked by modern cables enabling the Admiralty to respond immediately to imminent dangers arising anywhere in the world. Moreover, due to the devastating consequences of the loss of naval supremacy, the Admiralty had always carefully watched the development of rivals. Last but not least, in order to defend its supremacy, the Royal Navy, which could rely on an efficient shipbuilding industry, had also always tried to put into service the best vessels available.

Whereas Britain was the world's leading sea power in the nineteenth century, Germany had become the most powerful nation on the continent by defeating France in 1871. However, being aware of the inherent dangers of this position, Bismarck had steered a careful course between the European Great Powers, thus hoping to preserve peace, which he regarded as essential for the existence of the German Empire.[8]

Bismarck's successors, however, did not share his deep-rooted conviction that a moderate course in foreign affairs was a prerequisite for the status of the Empire among the European Powers. Rather, the early years of Wilhelm II's reign marked the end of a long era of land power thinking and relative decline in the navy. After many years of heavy infighting within both the navy and the government, as well as between the government and the Reichstag, in 1897–98 Germany finally embarked on a completely new course. The Austrian ambassador in Berlin described this change in German foreign policy in a long memorandum to his political masters in Vienna:

> The leading German statesmen, and above all Kaiser Wilhelm, have looked into the distant future and are striving to make Germany's already swiftly growing position as a world power into a dominating one, reckoning hereby upon becoming the linear successor to England in this respect. People in Berlin are however well aware that Germany would not be in a position today or for a long time to assume this succession, and for this reason a speedy collapse of English world power is not desired since it is fully recognised that Germany's far-reaching plans are at present only castles in the air. Notwithstanding this, Germany is already preparing with speed and vigour for her self-appointed future mission. In this connection I may permit myself to refer to the constant concern for the growth of German naval forces. ... England is now regarded as the most dangerous enemy which, at least as long as Germany is not sufficiently armed at sea, must be treated with consideration in all ways ... but because of the universally dominant Anglophobia, it is not easy [to convince public opinion of this.].[9]

On the whole, the Austrian ambassador was right, though one should not forget the impact of the Boer War on public opinion in Germany.

What were the reasons for this change? First, the young Kaiser was a naval enthusiast, and he could hardly resist imitating the example of his British relatives. Second, like their Kaiser, many contemporaries were proud of their political, economic, and military achievements since the unification of the German states in 1871, and they felt that Imperial Germany was a vigorous young nation which had to embark on "world policy" and to secure a "place in the sun" in order to preserve its achievements and, above all, its status in the Concert of the Great Powers, by building a powerful navy. Third, sea power, or as Tirpitz more often put it, maritime presence (*Seegeltung*), was allegedly a prerequisite for the protection of the German colonies as well as of economic wealth, industrial progress, and commerce. Without a strong navy, Tirpitz insisted (and many people believed him), Germany would be unable to preserve its steadily rising "sea interests" and, consequently, would inevitably decline to the status of a pre-industrial, "poor farming country."

Finally, sea power also had important domestic political implications. The government hoped that the acquisition of sea power and the envisaged great success of world policy through the plan, carefully designed by Tirpitz, would safeguard the overall expansion of German industry, foreign trade, colonies, and the navy, and, most importantly, offer a permanent solution to the "social problem" which threatened the existing political and social order.

In order to achieve these ambitious aims, and to succeed Spain, Holland, and now Britain as the leading world and sea power, Germany began to build the High Seas Fleet in 1897–98. The main architect of this fleet was Admiral von Tirpitz, who was appointed Secretary of the Navy in 1897. In many respects, the concept he developed in the mid 1890s was congruent with Mahan's ideas, though because of Tirpitz's own experience in High Command, it is unlikely that he simply adopted Mahan's thinking.[10] Like Mahan, Tirpitz was convinced that only a battle fleet could defeat the enemy's fleet, gain command of the sea, and attain naval supremacy.[11] Accordingly, this fleet was intended to comprise 41 battleships, 20 large cruisers, 40 small cruisers, 144 torpedo boats, and 72 submarines in twenty years' time.[12]

Of course, this remarkable force would still be inferior to the Royal Navy, but Tirpitz was convinced that Britain could not outbuild Germany because of financial restraints and a lack of personnel, and that, therefore, the margin of inferiority between the Imperial Navy and its future enemy would not exceed one-third. With a fleet of high quality ships unfolding "its greatest military potential between Helgoland and the Thames," superior tactics, and better-trained crews, Tirpitz regarded victory over the Royal Navy as possible. This optimistic view, however, was based on two important assumptions. First, he assumed that the Royal Navy would only be able to bring roughly half of its strength into action, due to its overseas commitments.[13] Second, in order to keep the costs of his ambitious shipbuilding program within certain limits, he hoped that the design of capital ships would not change dramatically. Any change in either respect would have dramatic repercussions on this whole program. Strategically, the Royal Navy might thus undermine his chances of successfully challenging Britain's naval supremacy. Politically, any cost increase would raise again the old question of whether Germany did in fact need a fleet and, moreover, might even disturb the fragile balance of domestic politics. At the turn of the century, Tirpitz was, of course, optimistic that he could avoid falling into any of the traps that might lie in the path to his ultimate aim. Step by step, building three capital ships every year, he skillfully began to realize his ambitions.

II: The Anglo-German Naval Race, 1908–1912

In 1898, Germany began to build up a powerful navy by passing the first naval law.[14] The second bill, amending this law by doubling the size of the fleet, followed only two years later. According to this law, the fleet was to consist of fifty-two ships of the line and armoured cruisers. Since many of the vessels under commission were more or less outdated, this was by no means an immediate menace to Britain's naval supremacy. However, the building rate of three ships a year ensured that the fleet would very soon consist of modern vessels. Moreover, by adding six armoured cruisers in 1906, accelerating the building tempo from three to four ships a year in 1908, and reducing the date of automatic replacement from twenty-five to twenty years, Tirpitz further accelerated the build-up of this formidable force. Most important of all, however, was Tirpitz's decision to follow Britain's lead in constructing a completely new type of battleship, the *Dreadnought*, launched at Portsmouth in 1906. This decision meant that Germany and Britain, unless the latter accelerated its building rate (which, as Tirpitz knew, the Liberal cabinet did not want for domestic reasons), would soon possess almost equal numbers of modern vessels. How would Britain react to this menace?

Much earlier than is often assumed both the public and, of course, the naval authorities had closely watched the development of the German Navy. As early as September 1901, the Director of Naval Intelligence, Admiral Sir Reginald Custance, had argued with respect to the future strength of the German Navy, "as the German Navy will be at that date a much greater danger to this country than the fleet of Russia," it would be necessary "to maintain a force in the North Sea sufficient to mask the German Fleet."[15] For the time being, however, the Admiralty watched the build-up of the German Fleet with relative calm, despite the rising Germanophobia amongst the public as well as among leading politicians. However, under the leadership of a new First Sea Lord, Admiral Sir John Fisher, the Admiralty did begin to redistribute its fleet and to rethink its construction policy.

According to Nicholas Lambert and Jon Sumida,[16] in this process the German Fleet still played only a minor role.[17]

The more Anglo-German relations deteriorated due to misunderstandings or direct clashes over differing interests in world affairs, the more important the naval question became. Strangely enough, when Russian warships fired at British trawlers (which they had mistaken for Japanese torpedo boats) on the Dogger Bank, a public outcry against Germany soon followed. For the first time, even leading politicians such as the First Lord of the Admiralty, Lee, openly warned of a preemptive strike.[18] This warning, in turn, caused Tirpitz and the German Admiralty staff to prepare for a naval war against Great Britain in the early months of 1905.[19] Though tensions soon abated, the naval question now loomed large in Anglo-German relations. Wisely, Tirpitz, who since 1903 had played with the idea of adding two more double squadrons to the existing fleet, restricted the 1906 *Novelle* (amending law) to a demand for six armoured cruisers for service on foreign stations, and, of course, for the appropriation of funds to launch new battleships of the *Dreadnought* type.

III. The Naval Race—A "Vicious Circle"? Anglo-German Negotiations, 1908–14

In midsummer 1908, after the passing of another naval bill which had accelerated the building rate from three to four capital ships a year, thus quickly closing the margin in modern vessels of the *Dreadnought* type, the situation seemed so tense that the chief of staff of the High Seas Fleet actually feared that the Kaiser's vessels would be attacked by the Royal Navy when passing the Straits of Dover during the fleet's annual summer cruise.[20] Though these apprehensions were not shared by the majority of the navy's leadership, there could be no doubt that Anglo-German relations were now at a crossroads. Germany could either continue to challenge Britain with the High Seas Fleet, even if this meant running deadly risks, or it could start to negotiate some kind of agreement in order to improve Anglo-German relations in general. For the time being, the German government inclined toward the latter option. Nevertheless, in August, the Kaiser refused outright the discussion of a naval agreement during the visit of King Edward VII. As a result, Anglo-German relations quickly deteriorated. Hostile newspaper articles, as well as direct warnings from politicians and those in charge of the navy in Britain, were a clear sign both of Britain's preparedness and its willingness to take up the gauntlet represented by Germany's naval build-up. Against this background the *Wahre Jakob* published the aforementioned cartoon, hoping thus to warn against the risks statesmen and admirals were running by entering a race they could not ultimately control.

It would be wrong, however, to assume that statesmen and admirals on both sides of the North Sea failed to appreciate the risks that they were running.[21] In midsummer 1908, chancellor Bülow, one of the leading architects of German world policy, began to realize that Germany could not afford to maintain both the strongest army and the second strongest navy in Europe, and that a further rise in tension could prove detrimental to the nation's freedom of action in international politics. In late 1908, Bülow therefore cautiously approached Tirpitz, then probably still the strongest personality within the German political and military hierarchy. The chancellor asked Tirpitz whether he could either clearly say that Germany was about to get through the so-called "danger zone," which meant the space of time during which Germany could only helplessly watch a preemptive strike by the Royal Navy—a "Copenhagen-ing" of the fleet as it was called in allusion to Nelson's attack on the Danish Fleet during the Napoleonic Wars—or whether Tirpitz was willing to consider some kind of naval agreement in exchange for a political agreement in which Britain promised its neutrality in case of a war on the continent.[22] Moreover, in order to defuse the impending crisis, Bülow even suggested shifting the emphasis away from battleships and toward mines, submarines, and coastal defences. Obviously briefed by the chief of the Admiralty staff, as Tirpitz later bitterly remarked, the chancellor thus tried to save money while also removing the main obstacle to better relations with Britain. Though Tirpitz, who in 1912 described Bülow's behaviour as outright "desertion,"[23] could not reply affirmatively to the first question, he refused to endorse Bülow's idea of a naval agreement. Nor did he accept Bülow's assumption that the naval question, and not commercial rivalry (as Tirpitz had always maintained), lay at the root of the conflict. In contrast to Bülow, the secretary of state of the Imperial Navy Office argued that only constant pressure, exerted through a formidable force of battleships, could force Britain to make concessions to Germany.

Bülow temporarily dropped the matter, but he returned to it shortly before his dismissal by the Kaiser in July 1909. "The only black cloud," he argued during an interdepartmental conference held on 3 June between high-ranking members of the government and the military (among them the chief of the Great General Staff, General Moltke), "lies over the North Sea, but this one might cause a thunderstorm."[24]

Tirpitz remained obdurate for the time being. He did, however, change his mind when he was approached by the new chancellor, Bethmann Hollweg, after Bülow's dismissal. Bethmann Hollweg also regarded a détente as necessary and, with the Kaiser's approval, eventually took up negotiations with the British ambassador in Berlin, Sir Edward Goschen. Yet these negotiations dragged on for almost two years without any result. The positions of the British cabinet and of the German government proved irreconcilable for a number of reasons. While the British cabinet wanted to conclude a naval agreement before discussing political concessions, the German government wanted to sign a far-reaching political agreement before entering into discussions about an agreement restricting its naval build-up.

Whereas the political leadership had eventually realized that Germany was isolated on the continent and was taking incalculable risks both politically and financially, as well as—at least for the time being—from a military point of view, without even knowing whether Tirpitz's concept would ever pay off, the secretary of state of the Imperial Navy Office had also begun to realize that he faced either disaster or triumph. In his opinion, which never wavered, he could only stay firm. Any agreement, unless it contained really substantial British concessions—as he would soon call them—was likely to prove disadvantageous for the navy in one way or another.

First, the law, with its rigid stipulations about the size and the building rate of the navy's vessels, was the foundation stone of Tirpitz's naval policy. In his opinion, any change in the navy law would open the floodgates for the increasing number of both politicians and high-ranking naval officers who were critical of the political, military, and strategic assumptions of his building program and encourage them to enforce a turnabout in a policy that had obviously proved futile. Second, against the background of scarce financial resources, as well as a deteriorating land military balance on the continent, there was a real danger that the navy might again lose its priority in defence spending to the army. Third, Tirpitz was afraid that by admitting that a smaller navy or a slower building rate would be sufficient to achieve its aims, the Imperial government would immediately face fierce protests from both the left and the right, which might eventually prove disastrous. While the left would argue that huge sums had simply been wasted, the right would accuse the government of giving up its aim of acquiring colonies for Germany. Fourth, he was afraid that everything he had achieved in previous years would in fact be lost. "If we ourselves undermine the navy law which is already in great danger due to the whole situation, we do not know where the journey is going to take us to," he told one of his close confidants in September 1909.[25]

Nevertheless, in summer 1909, he was willing to negotiate an agreement on one condition: Britain should declare that it would accept the limitation of its own fleet at a ratio of three : four capital ships. How did this change come about? By spring 1909, Tirpitz had realized that Germany, as many observers had warned, could not keep up with Britain if the latter decided to increase the tempo and outbuild Germany, as it had eventually done. In 1906–7 and in 1907–8 the Liberal cabinet had laid down three capital ships. In 1908–9, the number was reduced to only two, mostly for financial reasons, but also in order to demonstrate that Britain was willing to slacken the impending naval race. When all such attempts to convince Germany of the need to reduce naval expenditure had failed, and when, moreover, rumours reached the Admiralty that Germany might even accelerate its building rate by secretly collecting material for building warships and preparing to launch new ones prematurely, the cabinet after fierce internal conflicts finally decided to lay down eight capital ships in 1909–10. Even if one leaves aside the evidence that the Admiralty, in order to get its vessels, had calculated Germany's building capacity very generously, and had thus misled both the public and Parliament, there was unanimous agreement in Britain that its naval supremacy had to be defended against Germany.

For Tirpitz this unexpected great increase was, in fact, a severe blow. From a different perspective, however, this blow provided an incentive to try to bind Britain by an agreement that would fix the strengths of the two fleets at a ratio that favored Germany. The new chancellor, however, thwarted this attempt by letting Tirpitz know that he expected proposals that would not impede negotiations before they had actually begun. Nevertheless, the prospects for these negotiations were bleak, for although Bethmann Hollweg had nothing substantial to offer to the British, he had much to demand from them in order to satisfy the domestic critics—"ultras" as he called them in a report to the Kaiser—of any agreement. It is hardly astonishing that these negotiations never made any progress. While the chancellor regarded a political agreement as a prerequisite for a naval agreement (which, under the given circumstances, meant only a slackening in the construction tempo, not a change in the naval law), the Liberal government wanted to conclude a naval agreement first and give some vague political promises subsequently. Even though it was finally decided to negotiate on both the naval and the political agreement simultaneously, these talks never achieved a breakthrough.

From the German point of view, a leading Berlin foreign ministry official was right when he summarized the dilemma that the politicians and Tirpitz alike faced at that time: "No one here likes to renounce all ideas of great power."[26] In this respect, Britain was in a much better position. As Charles Hardinge, undersecretary of state in the foreign office, proudly commented on a report by Edward Goschen, Britain's ambassador in Berlin, in November 1909: "The position of Great Britain on the Continent is happily very different to that of Germany. At the present moment England's only possible foe is Germany, while Germany might under certain circumstances have to reckon with England, France or Russia, or a combination of two or more of these Powers."[27] Compared to Britain's isolation only a few years before, this was in fact both a strategic and a diplomatic advantage they were unwilling to risk. Moreover, Bethmann's proposals were not very attractive either from a military or a financial point of view:

> We are therefore still face to face with a situation in 1918 when Germany will have 38 Dreadnoughts and England will presumably have to have 60 capital ships, or approximately 50 more than we now have. This will entail further expenditure during the next few years of over 100 million sterling, or roughly speaking 10 millions per annum for the next ten years. With the best and most friendly intentions in the world, one may ask whether it is really worthwhile to talk of a naval agreement, except as an empty platitude, so long as it is regarded in Germany as an essential part of German policy that there must be 38 Dreadnoughts by 1918.[28]

Whereas negotiations on the "big issue" made no progress, those on a minor though by no means unimportant question, the exchange of information about naval building, in fact did. The 1909 "navy scare" had highlighted the dangers of rumors and false reports and their repercussions on both the public and decision makers. Though these negotiations also dragged on, some kind of understanding was eventually reached, even though, in the aftermath of the debacle of the Haldane mission (discussed below), no agreement was signed.[29]

In spite of these meagre results and the naval race, Anglo-German relations slowly seemed to improve in 1910–11. Both sides had shown their willingness to move from confrontation to negotiation, thus paving the way to political stabilization. In absolute terms, the more vessels Tirpitz launched and commissioned, the less was the danger of a British preemptive strike, and yet relatively the greater the British advantage in modern capital vessels, the more the Royal Navy's superiority was assured. However, generally speaking, the lessening in tension was due to the fact that Tirpitz had proved vulnerable both to the constant pressure from the new chancellor (who was deeply convinced of the need to improve Germany's situation in international politics), and, more importantly, to the financial strain caused by the qualitative leap into *Dreadnought* construction.

This Anglo-German détente—as one might call it—rested on two assumptions: first, that Tirpitz would not introduce another *Novelle* to enlarge the navy when the tempo fell from four to two vessels a year in 1912, and second, that Germany would not "cause mischief" again—as Grey once put it—by embarking on a more offensive policy. Both assumptions soon proved wrong.

It was precisely the lack of success in foreign affairs that prompted Bethmann Hollweg in midsummer 1911 to exploit French difficulties in Morocco to bolster the prestige of the Imperial government, as well as to demonstrate that Germany was a world power whose interests must not be neglected by its rivals.[30] The impact of the crisis caused by the so-called "Panther leap" at Agadir in July was, of course, disastrous. Chancellor of the Exchequer David Lloyd George's Mansion House speech was a clear warning of Britain's attitude in the event of a German attack on France. Whatever aims Bethmann Hollweg may have hoped to achieve, they now proved castles in the air. Moreover, the whole affair backfired upon the Imperial government, for Britain's reaction and the lack of visible gains unleashed a wave of unprecedented nationalism on the part of the German public. These circumstances in turn finally proved an almost golden opportunity for Tirpitz to introduce another *Novelle*.[31] Hesitant at first, he eventually seized the opportunity and demanded three additional battleships and the replacement of three armoured cruisers by modern battle cruisers. Moreover, he intended to increase the number of active battle squadrons from two to three.

Since Bethmann Hollweg was convinced that these demands would have a disastrous impact upon Anglo-German relations, he tried to prevent the introduction of the *Novelle* as best he could. What followed was an inter-departmental struggle that dragged on until April 1912. The result was a compromise: Tirpitz dropped his demand for the early replacement of the battle cruisers, but he could add three new battleships to the fleet and, most important from his point of view, he was able to increase the latter's battle readiness.

Why did the chancellor have to give in, and what did this new *Novelle* mean for Anglo-German relations? The underlying problem was very similar to the pattern set in previous years. Though the chancellor could, with at least partial success, invoke the financial strain that would be caused by a new big *Novelle*, and moreover could convince the Kaiser that, due to the deteriorating situation on land, more money should be allotted to the army than to the navy in the future, he, once again, could offer no substantial gains if the *Novelle* was dropped completely. Though the secret visit to Berlin by Britain's secretary of state for war, Richard Burdon Haldane, in early 1912 was in many ways a remarkable success, it did not further an understanding on the two great interrelated questions: a naval agreement and in exchange for it a far-reaching political agreement.[32]

It is true that for a few days after the Haldane mission even Tirpitz wavered, for even his closest confidants advised him to drop the *Novelle* if Britain delivered what Haldane seemed to have promised in the political sphere, namely more places in the sun such as the islands of Zanzibar, Timor, and several others. Then, Admiral Capelle argued, the *Novelle* would be completely "illogical. ... Then we will hitch up 3 horses at the front of the carriage and 4 at the back, and then the carriage will stop and eventually move backwards."[33] However, not only did Tirpitz eventually refuse to drop the *Novelle*, but also the negotiations between the chancellor and the London government made no headway. Germany's and Britain's naval and political demands proved as incompatible as in the years before. Against the background of anti-English feeling in Germany, the chancellor simply had no choice but to ask for an agreement that would guarantee Britain's neutrality in a war between Germany and France. This position was unacceptable to the Liberal government, however, and difficult for it even to understand. "What we offer them is quite sufficient to show friendliness and that should be quite enough for them if they have no designs upon other people," Goschen wrote to the permanent undersecretary of state in the Foreign Office, Arthur Nicolson, in late March 1912.[34] In theory, the British ambassador was right. In practice, however, he completely misjudged the domestic aspects of Bethmann's foreign policy, not to speak of the latter's difficult position within the "polycratic chaos," as Haldane had described the structure of the German political system after his return. Eventually both sides dropped the matter.

The doves in Germany, it seems, had again lost to the hawks. Subsequently the Royal Navy once again increased its building rate in 1912, in spite of the financial strain this entailed, and withdrew its modern vessels from the Mediterranean in order to strengthen its position in the North Sea theatre, thereby making Britain more dependent on naval cooperation with France and impeding the country's freedom of action in the event of a continental war. Nevertheless, the two years following the Haldane mission were in fact a period of a kind of détente. Part of the reason, paradoxically, was that neither Grey nor Bethmann Hollweg thought it wise to touch on the naval question again. Both of them were convinced that negotiations would do more harm than good. Moreover, they had realized that a higher level of mutual confidence was necessary to deal with such difficult matters as the reduction of naval expenditure or even a far-reaching political agreement. This understanding, however, rested on a number of unspoken assumptions.

First, Germany was expected to introduce no new *Novelle* and to instigate no public agitation for another increase of the navy, which was likely to touch on a sore point. Second, the governments on the opposing shores of the North Sea concentrated on successful negotiations over less contentious questions such as the Baghdad Railway and the Portuguese colonies as a test for better relations in general. Third, both governments agreed to collaborate in minor, and perhaps even major, diplomatic crises instead of seeking open confrontation. Bethmann Hollweg and Grey more or less agreed upon these points. Both of them especially tried not to put the naval question on the agenda again. Consequently in late 1912, when Tirpitz once again wanted to introduce a new *Novelle* (this time following an order from the Kaiser), Bethmann Hollweg thwarted him by referring to the greater needs of the army. Ironically, though on the one hand he thereby helped avoid a new naval race, on the other he helped to accelerate the arms race on land. Moreover, neither Grey nor the chancellor took up Churchill's repeated proposals for a "naval holiday" in 1913–14, in spite of Tirpitz's public acceptance of this idea, though on the basis of a ratio of "5:8 squadrons."[35] This response to Churchill already indicated that negotiations would prove difficult and were likely to cause resentment instead of inspiring mutual confidence. To avoid any kind of misunderstanding, Grey also objected to Churchill's idea of going to Germany himself in June 1914 in order to take up negotiations with Tirpitz directly. The chancellor, in turn, almost instantly intervened whenever there were any further rumours about a new *Novelle*.[36] Apart from the fact that negotiations about minor issues as well as collaboration during international conflicts—such as the Balkan Wars—proved successful, the smooth working of Anglo-German relations in this period was mainly due to two developments.

For the time being the Royal Navy had preserved its supremacy—on the basis of a new ratio, "+ 60 percent"—by taking a number of important measures: laying down powerful new battleships; redistributing its ships; adopting a complete change in operational planning which, in turn, would keep the High Seas Fleet ineffectively bottled in the North Sea.

Tirpitz in turn was on the defensive in every respect, und thus indirectly and against his own intentions supporting the chancellor's policy towards Great Britain. Most important of all, he had lost the confidence of the Kaiser, as he bitterly remarked after his annual report (*Immediatvortrag*) in 1913.[37] Equally important, in 1914, he realized that he was running out of money. "The situation is collapsing over the navy,"[38] he wrote in a memorandum in May. A little later he complained that, "We cannot build the vessels any more that we have planned."[39] The costs of new battleships—hulls and machinery alone—had risen from 30 to 32.7 million marks, those of battle cruisers from 29 to almost 35 million marks, and there was no end in sight. Subsequently, Tirpitz could hardly disguise his envy of Churchill in 1914. While the First Lord of the Admiralty, though with great difficulties, again had pushed through the House of Commons his naval estimates, which now amounted to roughly 1 billion marks, Tirpitz's budget was cracking at the seams. According to his own estimates, at least 150 to 200 million marks were necessary within the next six to eight years in order to build the vessels planned under the existing naval law. Finally, he had begun to realize that his strategic concept, developed in the 1890s in completely different circumstances, would probably prove futile. Obviously, the Royal Navy would not offer battle in the "wet triangle" of sea between the German and Danish coasts and Helgoland, but it could be expected to establish a distant blockade, which the High Seas Fleet would be unable to break. Its commanders openly admitted this fact without perceiving any alternative. Tirpitz proved that he completely misjudged the situation when he nevertheless still argued that "only permanent strength can help us. We must let them come and not look for them. I am sure, they will come."[40]

Germany and Britain had now reached some kind of modus vivendi, which resembled a tacit agreement about each other's respective naval strengths. Yet against the background of the fierce conflict that seemed imminent only a few years before, this might seem to present a good prospect for the future of Anglo-German relations.

IV. Did the Naval Race make War Inevitable?

There can be no doubt that the naval race was not responsible for the outbreak of war in 1914. Britain had successfully defended its naval supremacy against Germany. Whether Tirpitz would have renewed the uphill struggle—and there are some indications that he was at least playing with this idea—and whether he would again have been successful are matters for speculation. From the admiral's point of view, Bethmann Hollweg's policy was wrong. In a secret speech, Tirpitz told his officers in October 1913 that the policy of the chancellor would reduce Germany to a second-rate power depending upon Britain's goodwill. Instead, he preferred to fight for a "supreme aim and perish honourably instead of renouncing the future ingloriously."[41]

There is, however, no doubt that the naval question decisively helped to frame the grouping of the powers before 1914. Though former Chancellor Bülow was deeply convinced that his successor had completely mishandled the situation in July 1914, he did, at least, privately point out to Tirpitz in 1924 that "there is the question whether France and particularly Russia would have let it come to war had public opinion in England not been so greatly enraged precisely at the construction of our great ships."[42]

Bülow's judgement was right, for, as Paul Kennedy has correctly observed, the real reason why the Tories and Liberal-Imperialists advocated a continental commitment was naval. In 1911, Grey explained to the representatives of the Dominions:

If a European conflict, not of our own making, arose, in which it was quite clear that the struggle was one for supremacy in Europe, in fact, that you got back to a situation something like that in the old Napoleonic days, then ... our concern in seeing that there did not arise a supremacy in Europe which entailed a combination that would deprive us of the command of the sea would be such that we might have to take part in that European war. That is why the naval position underlies our European policy.[43]

Table 6.1 Naval Expenditure of the European Powers, 1900–13 (£ million, current prices)

	Britain	France	Russia	Austria-Hungary	Germany	Italy
1900	29.5	14.9	9.4	1.9	—	—
1901	31.0	13.7	9.8	1.9	10.2	5.0
1902	31.2	11.9	10.6	2.1	10.6	4.9
1903	35.5	12.1	12.1	2.1	11.0	4.7
1904	36.8	11.7	11.9	2.3	10.7	4.7
1905	33.3	12.6	12.3	2.7	12.0	4.9
1906	31.4	12.2	12.3	2.9	12.7	4.8
1907	31.1	12.6	9.3	2.6	14.9	5.8
1908	32.2	13.2	9.9	3.1	17.0	5.9
1909	35.8	13.9	9.8	4.2	20.6	6.6
1910	40.4	14.5	11.9	4.2	21.3	6.3
1911	42.9	20.7	12.8	5.0	22.1	8.2
1912	44.4	17.1	18.6	7.1	22.7	11.2
1913	48.8	—	25.9	8.7	23.5	14.4

Source: David Stevenson, *Armaments and the Coming of War, Europe 1904–1914* (Oxford 2000) p. 7.

Table 6.2 Cumulative *Dreadnought* Battleship and Battle Cruiser Starts: Britain, Germany, and the United States, 1905–14

Fiscal year (April–March)	Britain	Germany	USA	Germany * USA	Germany * USA * 10*	Germany + 60 percent
1905–06	3 [15]	0	0	0	0	0
1906–07	8 [10l]	0	2	2	2.2	0
1907–08	9 [11]	5	4	9	9.9	8.0
1908–09	12 [14]	10	6	16	17.2	16.0
1909–10	15 [17]	12	8	20	20.2	19.2
1910–11	25 [27]	17	8	25	27.5	27.2
1911–12	27 [29]	21	10	31	34.1	33.6
1912–13	34 [36l]	23	12	35	38.5	36.8
1913–14	40 [42]	26	14	40	44.0	41.6

Source: Jon T. Sumida: *In Defence of Naval Supremacy: Finance, Technology, and British Naval Policy 1889–1914* (London, 1989).

Table 6.3 Cumulative *Dreadnought* Battleship and Battle Cruiser Starts: Britain, Germany, and the United States, 1905–14

Calendar year	Britain	Germany	USA	Germany + USA	Germany + USA t 10«	Germany + 60 percent
1905	1 [3]	0	0	0	0	0
1906	5 [7]	0	2	2	2.2	0
1907	9 [11]	4	4	8	8.8	6.4
1908	10 [12]	9	4	13	14.3	14.4
1909	16 [18]	11	6	17	18.7	17.6
1910	22 [24]	16	8	24	26.4	25.6
1911	27 [29]	20	10	30	33.0	32.0
1912	34 [36]	23	12	35	38.5	36.8
1913	40 [42]	26	13	39	42.9	41.6

*Bracketed figures include the 2 semi-Dreadnoughts of the *Lord Nelson* class.

Source: Jon T. Sumida, *In Defence of Naval Supremacy: Finance, Technology, and British Naval Policy 1889–1914* (London, 1989).

Notes

1. Alfred v. Tirpitz, *My Memoirs* (London, 1919), vol. I, 232–235.
2. Winston S. Churchill, *The World Crisis* (London, 1938 [first published 1923]), vol.I, 143–44.
3. Cf. the attached cartoon.
4. Selbourne memo, 16 November 1901, cited in Paul M. Kennedy, *The Rise of the Anglo-German Antagonism 1860–1914* (London, 1980), 416.
5. Churchill in the House of Commons, 10 November 1911, cited in Nicholas Lambert, *Sir John Fisher's Naval Revolution* (Columbia, South Carolina, 1999), 15.
6. Cf. Lambert, *Sir John Fisher's Naval Revolution*, 15.
7. Churchill in the House of Commons, 10 November 1911, ibid.
7. Cf. Paul M. Kennedy, *The Rise and Fall of British Naval Mastery* (London, 1976 [reprinted 1992]), 206.
8. The best book on German foreign policy in this era is Klaus Hildebrand, *Das vergangene Reich: Deutsche Außenpolitik von Bismarck bis Hitler* (Stuttgart, 1995), 13–146.
9. Szögyeny to Goluchowski, 5 February 1900, cited in Kennedy, *Anglo-German Antagonism*, 241.
10. Cf. Tirpitz, *Memoirs*, 55.
11. Ivo N. Lambi, *The Navy and German Power Politics, 1862–1914* (London, 1984), 62–90.
12. According to the last amendment in 1912 to the navy law 1898, cf. Alfred von Tirpitz, *Politische Dokumente*, vol. I, *Der Aufbau der deutschen Weltmacht* (Stuttgart, Berlin, 1924), appendix.
13. Cf. Berghahn, *Tirpitz-Plan*, 184ff.; Paul M. Kennedy, "Maritime Strategieprobleme der deutsch-englischen Flottenrivalität," in *Marine und Marinepolitik im kaiserlichen Deutschland 1871–1914*, 2nd ed., Herbert Schottelius and Wilhelm Deist, eds. (Düsseldorf 1981), 181–83.

14. On the buildup of the German navy, cf. also Volker R. Berghahn, *Der Tirpitz-Plan: Eine innenpolitische Krisenstrategie unter Wilhelm II* (Düsseldorf, 1971) and Michael Epkenhans, *Die wilhelminische Flottenrüstung 1908–1914: Weltmachtstreben, technischer Fortschritt, soziale Integration* (Munich, 1991).
15. Kerr to Selborne, 24.September 1901, enclosing Custance memo of the same date, cited in Kennedy, *Anglo-German Antagonism*, 251.
16. Jon T. Sumida, *In Defence of Naval Supremacy: Finance, Technology, and British Naval Policy 1889–1914* (London, 1989), 3–70.
17. Cf. Lambert, *Naval Revolution*, 77–164. In my opinion, however, both Lambert and Sumida seem to underestimate the impact of the development of the High Seas Fleet upon British policy makers. In spite of their fear of Russia, Germany, at least after 1905, seemed a greater danger to British interests than the tsarist empire.
18. Cf. Kennedy, *Anglo-German Antagonism*, 275.
19. For details cf. Lambi, *The Navy*.
20. Cf. the entries of 13 to 15 July 1908 in the Hopman diary, in Epkenhans, *Hopman*, 148–149. However, the quotation also attributes the following phrase to Prinz Heinrich: "Im Kriegsfalle, der aber völlig unwahrscheinlich sei ...." (13 July 1908).
21. For details of Anglo-German negotiations between 1908–09 and 1912 cf. Epkenhans, *Flottenrüstung*, 31–142.
22. Epkenhans, *Flottenrüstung*, 31–142.
23. Undated memo (November 1912 ?), BA-MA Tirpitz papers N 253-9.
24. Quoted in Epkenhans, *Flottenrüstung*, 50.
25. Tirpitz to Capelle, 19 September 1909, BA-MA, Tirpitz papers, N 253-8.
26. Stemrich to Kiderlen-Wächter, 6 October 1909, cited in Epkenhans, *Flottenrüstung*, 62.
27. Hardinge memo, 10 November 1909, in *British Documents on the Origins of the War 1898–1914*, G.P. Gooch and Harold Temperley, eds., vol. 6: *Anglo-German Tensions, 1907–1912* (London, 1930), no. 204.
28. Hardinge memo, 24 October 1909, ibid., no. 200.
29. For details cf. Epkenhans, *Flottenrüstung*, 72–82.
30. Ibid., 93–113.
31. Ibid., 113–42.
32. Ibid., 113–37.
33. Hopman diary, 10 February 1912, in Epkenhans, *Hopman*, 198f.
34. Goschen to Nicolson, 29 March 1912, in *British Documents on the Origins of the War*, vol. 6, no. 561.
35. Cf. Epkenhans, *Flottenrüstung*, 19; footnote 36, 325–336; John Maurer, "Churchill's Naval Holiday: Arms Control and the Anglo German Naval Race, 1912–1914," *Journal of Strategic Studies* 15 (1992), 102–127.
36. Epkenhans, *Flottenrüstung*, 313–65.
37. Hopman diary, 28 September 1913, in Epkenhans, *Hopman*, 336.
38. Tirpitz memo, May 1914 (?), BA-MA Tirpitz papers N 253-29.
39. Note by Tirpitz on a memo by Capelle, 17 May 1914, ibid.
40. Hopman diary, 24–30 November 1913, in Epkenhans, *Hopman*, 343f.
41. Speech by Tirpitz, October 1913, BA-MA Tirpitz papers N 253/423.
42. Bülow to Tirpitz, 26 November 1924, cited in Kennedy, *Anglo-German Antagonism*, 423.
43. Grey to the Dominion representatives, 11 July 1911, cited in Kennedy, *Anglo-German Antagonism*, 428–29.

Chapter 7

WAS A PEACEFUL OUTCOME THINKABLE?
The European Land Armaments Race before 1914

David Stevenson

The previous chapter focused on naval rivalry; here the spotlight turns to competition between armies. This chapter will consider not the more conventional question of whether the arms races caused the war that broke out in 1914, but rather the more speculative and counterfactual problem of whether the land arms race made such a war inevitable. By so framing the issue, it addresses the general hypothesis considered in this volume that World War I was "improbable," and the possibility that its outbreak was not a direct and logical consequence of mounting international tension.[1] The ominous military trends in pre-1914 Europe represent a major difficulty for such a thesis, and in recent years have been the most intensively researched aspect of the period.[2] In summary it will be argued here that by 1914 European land armaments competition had indeed created a dangerous situation, in which another diplomatic crisis—if it occurred—was likely to trigger armed conflict. Such a crisis was not a certainty, however, and although the play of counterfactuals is finely balanced, it is plausible to envisage an alternative scenario in which the arms race did not culminate in hostilities. This approach goes some way toward meeting the improbability thesis, although with reservations. What follows will examine the reasons for believing that a war was likely as well as those for maintaining that it was not inevitable and that the question remains open: but it will commence with an analysis of the arms race itself.

I. The Arms Race in Overview

We begin with the statistical data:

Table 7.1 Real Defence Burden (Defence Expenditure/Net National Product), 1900–13 (percent)

	Britain	France	Russia	Austria	Germany	Italy
1900	6.9	4.4	4.0	2.7	—	3.1
1901	7.1	4.6	3.9	2.7	4.1	3.2
1902	5.8	4.5	3.7	2.7	3.9	3.3
1903	4.2	4.1	4.1	2.8	3.6	2.9
1904	3.9	4.0	9.2	2.8	3.6	3.0
1905	3.5	3.9	13.8	2.5	3.6	2.9
1906	3.1	3.9	8.7	2.3	3.8	2.7
1907	2.9	4.2	5.4	2.2	4.2	2.7
1908	3.1	4.1	4.7	2.4	3.8	2.8
1909	3.3	3.8	4.3	3.0	4.0	2.9
1910	3.4	4.1	4.0	2.6	4.2	3.0
1911	3.4	4.1	4.3	2.4	3.9	3.3
1912	3.3	4.0	4.5	2.6	3.8	4.0
1913	3.4	4.3	5.1	3.5	4.9	5.1

Source: D. Stevenson, *Armaments and the Coming of War: Europe, 1904–1914* (Oxford, 1996), 7. The "Austrian" series is for the Austrian half of the Habsburg Monarchy, as Net National Product figures are not available for the Hungarian half.

Table 7.2 Naval Expenditure of the European Powers, 1900–13 (£ million, current prices)

	Britain	France	Russia	Austria-Hungary	Germany	Italy
1900	29.5	14.9	9.4	1.9	—	—
1901	31.0	13.7	9.8	1.9	10.2	5.0
1902	31.2	11.9	10.6	2.1	10.6	4.9
1903	35.5	12.1	12.1	2.1	11.0	4.7
1904	36.8	11.7	11.7	2.3	10.7	4.7
1905	33.3	12.6	12.3	2.7	12.0	4.9
1906	31.4	12.2	12.3	2.9	12.7	4.8
1907	31.1	12.6	9.3	2.6	14.9	5.8
1908	32.2	13.2	9.9	3.1	17.0	5.9
1909	35.8	13.9	9.8	4.2	20.6	6.6
1910	40.4	14.5	11.9	4.2	21.3	6.3
1911	42.9	20.7	12.8	5.0	22.1	8.2
1912	44.4	17.1	18.6	7.1	22.7	11.2
1913	48.8	—	25.9	8.7	23.5	14.4

Source: Stevenson, *Armaments*, 7. The figures include the cost to Britain of the South African War and to Italy of the Libyan War, but not those to Russia of the war with Japan.

Table 7.3 Army Expenditure of the European Powers, 1900–1913 (£ million, current prices)

	Britain	France	Russia	Austria-Hungary	Germany	Italy
1900	91.5	26.8	35.1	15.2	—	—
1901	92.3	29.0	35.4	16.4	33.2	9.8
1902	69.4	29.2	36.3	16.9	38.0	10.8
1903	36.7	28.1	37.1	17.2	37.6	11.3
1904	29.2	28.0	39.4	17.6	36.6	9.7
1905	28.9	28.5	40.0	17.4	39.7	10.1
1906	27.8	34.2	41.5	17.4	41.5	10.1
1907	27.1	32.7	42.9	18.5	46.0	10.3
1908	26.8	33.3	54.4	21.1	47.0	10.9
1909	27.2	34.7	57.0	27.4	49.0	12.0
1910	27.4	36.4	56.6	24.2	47.3	13.5
1911	27.6	40.5	58.1	22.4	46.9	14.7
1912	28.1	43.4	67.6	25.4	52.1	18.7
1913	28.3	—	75.8	34.4	78.3	25.3

Source: ibid, 8.

Table 7.4 Peacetime Effectives of the European Powers, 1904–13 (Officers and Enlisted Men—Thousands)

	Britain	France	Russia	Austria-Hungary	Germany	Italy
1904	209	575	1,900	362	607	221
1905	214	595	1,900	362	610	221
1906	197	590	1,000	362	614	250
1907	179	602	1,000	367	617	250
1908	183	611	1,000	366	619	c.247
1909	182	567	1,209	369	610	c.247
1910	182	574	1,303	371	610	239
1911	183	594	1,345	353	613	254
1912	193	611	1,332	391	646	256
1913	192	c.700	1,300	—	782	256

Source: D. G. Herrmann, *The Arming of Europe and the Making of the First World War* (Princeton, 1996), 234.

The figures confirm that something significant was happening. In constant prices, total defence spending by the six European powers rose by 6.4 percent in the five years from 1903 to 1908 but by 39.4 percent between 1908 and 1913, by far the fastest rate since 1870.[3] Army expenditure preponderated in the defence budgets of all five Continental powers, and accounted for the major part of those budgets' pre-war increases (except in Russia, where the army and navy contributed about equally to the expansion). Most of the upsurge in army spending was concentrated in the final pre-war years and it contrasted with relative stagnation during the first decade of the twentieth century, leaving aside the cost of the

South African and the Russo-Japanese Wars. It is therefore unsurprising to see the main increase in army peacetime strengths (at least in France, Germany, and Austria-Hungary) also coming in the later part of the period. The suddenness, accelerating pace, and simultaneity that characterized the growth of the Continental armies strongly suggest a competitive process, driven by a deteriorating external environment that every country viewed as menacing. In short, there *was* an arms race. A qualitative comparative analysis of European defence policies confirms this impression. Three sub-periods in their evolution may be distinguished: c. 1904–08, 1908–12, and 1912–14.

The first period was one of unstable equilibrium in land armaments. It witnessed little underlying growth in Continental army budgets despite one major technological change: the reequipping of the field artillery with quick-firing guns modelled on the revolutionary French 75mm cannon. Characteristic of this period was the strength of the domestic forces inhibiting army expansion. In Russia economic depression and revolutionary unrest delayed reequipment after the defeat by Japan, and forced the military to concentrate on internal repression. In France a post-Dreyfus Affair reaction was still in train against the officer corps, one manifestation being a law of 1905 that reduced the active military service term from three years to two. In the Habsburg Monarchy the central authorities in Vienna clashed with the Hungarian government in Budapest, which resisted a new army bill unless accompanied by concessions over the use of Magyar as the language of command. Finally, in Germany the war ministry acquiesced in the navy's increasing share of the defence budget, in part because it feared that expansion would oblige the army to absorb more working-class (rather than rural) conscripts and more middle-class (rather than aristocratic) officers, thus reducing its dependability as a bulwark of authority at home. Yet this apparent overall equilibrium rested in part on the abnormal circumstances created by Russia's discomfiture, which made it easier for Germany and Austria-Hungary to cap their total defence spending and to focus respectively on arms races against Britain and Italy, the first of which was wholly naval and the second substantially so. It is true that after the First Moroccan Crisis of 1905–06, France and Germany accelerated reequipping against each other, but in both countries this upturn proved to be a temporary blip.

The second period, between 1908 and 1912, was one of transition. During these years, in both Eastern and in Western Europe, equilibrium broke down and armaments policies were reorientated. In the east the first shock to the system was the Bosnian Crisis of 1908–09. Following their humiliation in the crisis, Serbia and Montenegro intensified their military preparations with the assistance of French loans and weapons deliveries, whereas the leaders of Austria-Hungary agreed on a new expenditure program in the "Schönaich Pact" of 1911, the basis of the army law (*Wehrgesetz*) of 1912.[4] That law was not passed, however, until the rising tension that preceded the First Balkan War, by which time Italy was bogged down in conquering Libya and therefore obliged to curtail its military programmes and to mend its fences with Vienna. Meanwhile a second shock was administered to the Eastern European balance by Russia's economic and political recovery, and especially by its major military reorganization of 1910, which among other things significantly enhanced Russian preparedness through the adoption of a territorial mobilization system. Germany and Austria-Hungary quickly revised upward their assessments of the tsarist strategic threat, and arguably the 1910 reorganization was the most significant single turning point in the origins of the land arms race. As for Western Europe, this sub-period saw the climax of the Anglo-German naval rivalry, Admiral Alfred von Tirpitz's decision to follow Britain's lead in constructing *Dreadnought*-style capital ships soon prompting a panic fear in Whitehall that Germany was secretly accelerating its building program. By retaliating with a decision to lay down eight new dreadnoughts in 1909–10 the British gained a lead that Germany could not match, and against this backdrop the Second Moroccan (or Agadir) Crisis of 1911 prompted the *Rüstungswende* or "armaments turning point": a crucial reappraisal in Berlin in the winter of 1911–12. Its outcome was a decision to scale down construction starts from four to two new capital ships a year and to switch priorities to land armaments with Germany's 1912 army law, which stepped up reequipping and expansion from the very cautious pace set in the army's five-year program (*Quinquennat*) that had been adopted only one year before.

In the third phase, between 1912 and 1914, the land arms race was at its height. The stage had now been set for a major round of competition between the two great Continental military blocs: the Austro-German and the Franco-Russian alliances. It may therefore be characterized as a "central" arms race, in contrast to the "peripheral" Anglo-German and Austro-Italian ones that had previously been the most dynamic features of the European scene. Britain and Germany slowed their naval construction tempos and attempted a political détente: the Rome-Vienna rivalry similarly lost impetus. Conversely, not only were Austria-Hungary and Germany increasingly alarmed about Russia, but also in both France and Germany the Agadir Crisis had touched off agitation for greater military preparedness. The event that brought these trends together and linked developments in Eastern and Western Europe was the First Balkan War, which together with its aftershocks caused a year of diplomatic confrontation from autumn 1912 to autumn 1913. The war precipitated Germany's decision to pass yet another army law in 1913 (the largest in the Reich's peacetime history), which in turn precipitated France's 1913 law restoring a three-year term of military service (the *Loi des trois ans*), as well as hardening Belgium's resolve to implement a major new measure (the *Loi sur la milice*). The Balkan upheaval also prompted another Austro-Hungarian army law, passed in March 1914. Finally, it led to further expansion in Russia, which reacted to the 1913 German law and to the Liman von Sanders crisis over the Turkish Straits in the winter of 1913–14 by adopting two measures. The first was a Franco-Russian strategic railway construction agreement concluded in January 1914, and the second was Russia's "Great Program" (*bol'shaya programma*) of army enlargement, approved by the Duma in July. In short, the years from 1912 to 1914 offer an exceptionally clear example of what the theoretical literature on arms races refers to as the "action-reaction model": German initiatives encouraging French, Belgian, and Russian responses. Yet the next step in the escalation process was not a further round of German armaments expansion but war. We now need to scrutinize more closely the connections between the land arms race and the onset of hostilities.

II. The Arms Race Made War Probable

This connection can be analyzed under two headings. The first is the general contribution of the land arms race to international insecurity. The second is its more specific impact on decision makers' perceptions of the military balance in July 1914.

The land arms race was an integral and essential component of a broader complex of developments that ratcheted up European tension in the decade before the war. In the celebrated (but contestable) judgement of the British Foreign Secretary Sir Edward Grey, "The enormous growth of armaments in Europe, the sense of insecurity and fear caused by them—it was these that made war inevitable. This, it seems to me, is the truest reading of history, and the lesson that the present should be learning from the past in the interests of future peace, the warning to be handed on to those who come after us."[5] Actually it is difficult to separate armaments from the other factors, which included the growth of a militarist and extreme nationalist mood on the right wing of public opinion (voiced through pressure groups, political parties, and the press); the intensifying diplomatic isolation and "encirclement" of Austria-Hungary in the Balkans and of Germany in Europe as a whole; a succession of crises and local conflicts in the Balkans and the Mediterranean; and the adoption by the military in France, Germany, and Russia of more offensive war plans. Army laws required more money and manpower than did naval increases and therefore needed selling to legislatures that had previously resisted them, the associated publicity serving to strengthen public perceptions of a heightened risk of conflict. This was not simply a top-down process. The German Army League (*Deutscher Wehrverein*), founded after the Agadir Crisis, contended that the navy had failed as a power-political instrument to support Germany's diplomatic demands and that the army should be expanded instead: the League was never under official control and its campaigning skills were formidable. Similarly, a disquieting development in spring 1914 was the "press war" between leading German, Russian, and Austro-Hungarian newspapers, which began with a warning in the *Kölnische Zeitung* that Russia might start a war when it had completed its arms increases. Although the German government did not initiate this article, it let the controversy run until the St. Petersburg foreign ministry placed a retaliatory commentary in the *Birshevaia Viedomosti* that infuriated Wilhelm II by insisting that

Russia would not be intimidated. A further common feature of the army bills was their value for crisis management. They aimed to make armies more crisis-ready by bringing them up to higher levels of peacetime strength and facilitating rapid mobilization, thus reducing the danger from a surprise attack but also enabling immediate action if tension exploded into hostilities. (A similar development could be seen at sea with the German 1912 amending naval law or *Novelle*, which raised the fully-manned and active battle fleet from two to three squadrons, to which the First Lord of the Admiralty Winston Churchill replied by redeploying British warships from the Mediterranean to home waters. Both steps were prompted by the naval alert that took place during the Agadir episode.)[6] But as military readiness grew, governments supposed that they were better positioned for brinkmanship. Moreover, army increases were intended not merely to protect the home territory, but also to accompany more aggressive war plans. The connection was perhaps most obvious in France, between the Three-Year Law and the General Staff's new Plan XVII, but Russia likewise adopted the more offensive Plan 19 altered in 1912, and in 1913 Germany suspended work on the more cautious eastern alternative to its ambitious Schlieffen-Moltke plan for striking out to the west.[7]

This interplay between crisis management, public opinion, and strategic developments was exemplified in the origins of the 1913 German and French army laws. In the first instance, Germany's measure was prompted by the winter emergency caused by the First Balkan War, during which Russia partially mobilized in Poland and unexpectedly kept under arms its senior conscript cohort, exposing the Prussian eastern provinces to invasion. The German army therefore needed reinforcement to ensure the integrity of the national territory at times of tension (and Austria-Hungary's 1914 law had similar motives). Yet more fundamentally, the law responded to the power shift caused by the Balkan states' defeat of Turkey, which meant that in a general war Austria-Hungary would now be heavily committed on its south-eastern border, obliging Germany to take on France and Russia virtually single handed. To win the Reichstag over, the government briefed the deputies in secret sessions and exaggerated the country's danger, thereby fanning the flames of hysteria. But meanwhile the news of the German bill enabled the French government to introduce its three-year military service law and to undercut opposition to the longer conscription term, which it portrayed to the National Assembly as essential to protect the borders by strengthening the *couverture* (covering force) and deterring a surprise attack, but whose underlying purpose was to move the army to a higher state of readiness and to give it the extra trained men needed to implement Plan XVII's aspiration to invade Germany at once if war began. In addition the Three-Year Law demonstrated the role of alliance politics, as President Raymond Poincaré viewed it as an earnest to the Russians of France's commitment to them, and the latter treated it in the same way. Later the French treated the 1914 strategic railway agreement as a similar touchstone of commitment on the Russian side. In many ways, therefore, "armaments fever" (as statesmen referred to it at the time)[8] contributed to the psychological preparation of both the public and their leaders for hostilities. It also encouraged a perception that military preparation was becoming an intolerable burden, and that war might actually be more cost effective. Most war ministries had estimated the cost of the first three months of operations, and for the Austrian leaders by 1913, for example, the likely expense of a Balkan war seemed scarcely higher than that of endless precautionary alerts.[9] The French minister in Munich reported that the capital levy used to finance Germany's 1913 law had caused great pessimism, and cited the Bavarian press: "Where we are going the Gods alone know. It is really astonishing that more and more people do not prefer a resolution at the price of catastrophe to a catastrophe without resolution, to which the people are continually exposed."[10]

The second point is that in addition to these more general considerations the development of the arms race appeared to create for Germany a "window of opportunity"—a transient strategic advantage—in 1914. The basic reason was that Germany's 1913 law was a front-end loaded measure that, in addition to accelerating the implementation of the 1911 and 1912 laws, introduced new provisions, many scheduled to be carried out in the first year, and which by 1914 were progressing well toward completion.[11] Austria-Hungary was less favorably placed, as its 1912 law was being implemented more gradually and its 1914 law had only just reached the statute book; but Austria-Hungary also mattered less, as it would not have risked military action unless assured of German backing. Hence Berlin's perception of the military balance was crucial, and the Prussian Great General Staff (*Grosser Generalstab*—GGS) was very well informed about the country's potential enemies. As of summer 1914 the *Loi sur la milice* had made little difference to Belgian capabilities; the strategic railway agreement would improve Russian transport capacity in at earliest three to four years; and the Great Program was still in gestation.[12] The Three-Year Law was being put into effect, but in the short term it disrupted and weakened the French army. To head off unrest among the serving conscripts the French government had accepted the "Escudier amendment," which meant that the standing army would be enlarged not by retaining the existing men for an extra year but instead by calling up two new cohorts of raw young recruits in autumn 1913, with the result that the proportion of experienced and fully trained soldiers was temporarily diminished.[13] Moreover, whereas the German 1913 law approved expenditure on both manpower and weaponry, the French dealt with manpower first and passed a large equipment credit only on 15 July 1914. Indeed on 13 and 14 July respectively, a speech by the French Senator Charles Humbert and a remarkably unguarded statement by the head of French military intelligence to the German attaché in Paris both testified to their army's severe under-equipment in several respects.[14] Among these the GGS Chief Helmuth von Moltke the Younger singled out the shortcomings of the Lebel rifle and the French army's lack of modern heavy artillery, whereas the Germans possessed heavy field weapons and were taking delivery of Krupp 42cm and Skoda 30.5cm fortress-smashing mortars.[15] The longer-term benefits for the French of a larger standing army that combined two trained-age cohorts with one newly-enlisted would be felt only from 1915–16; those for the Russians of the railway agreement and the *bol'shaya programma* would not be felt until 1917–18 even if they kept to their ambitious schedule, which was unlikely.

If the Germans let slip the opportunity and waited, however, their prospects were bleak. Within another three or four years it would be questionable whether their plan to send most of the army westward and leave only a defensive screen for Berlin in the east could any longer be safely implemented. Moltke was well aware of this danger, and ensured that Wilhelm II and civilians such as Chancellor Theobald von Bethmann Hollweg and Foreign Minister Gottlieb von Jagow were likewise alerted. Certainly, the Berlin leaders in early 1914 agreed that France and Russia did not want war now and there was no immediate threat to the Reich's security, Moltke's deputy Alfred von Waldersee concluding that the current military position was favorable.[16] But their fear was for the medium term. During the July Crisis itself, in a private letter to the ambassador in London, Prince Karl Max Lichnowsky, Jagow referred to the military balance as justification for backing Austria-Hungary, as in retrospect did Bethmann.[17] In short, the European blocs were approaching a point of "power transition": a shift in the balance of advantage from the Austro-German to the Franco-Russian group.[18]

This analysis can be reinforced by Niall Ferguson's influential thesis that "the decisive factor in 1914 which pushed the German Reich over the brink into war was the conviction of both military and civilian leaders that Germany could not win the arms race against its continental neighbours. ... This conviction was justified in terms not only of the size and capability of Germany's military forces, but more particularly in terms of the financial effort Germany was making toward its own defence."[19] According to Ferguson it would have been *technically* feasible for Germany to finance a continuing arms race, but it had reached the limits of the *politically* possible with the 1913 army law and the accompanying capital levy (*Wehrbeitrag*), the latter passing the Reichstag only with support from the Social Democrats whereas the Catholic Centre Party abstained and the Conservatives voted against it. In December 1913 the Bavarian prime minister called publicly on financial grounds for a moratorium on further armaments increases. In the German federal system the Reich authorities faced resistance from the Conservatives to higher direct taxes and from the Social Democrats (after 1912, the largest Reichstag party) to higher indirect ones: many revenue sources were reserved to the state governments, to whom the centre had to turn for supplementary contributions. The Empire's short-term indebtedness was increasing and its credit worthiness, as evidenced in the international market for its paper, was deteriorating. Conversely, the unitary French, Russian, and British states faced fewer obstacles in generating support for tax increases, whereas the cumbersome Austro-Hungarian

Dual Monarchy was in an even worse financial predicament than its ally. If to such internal politico-financial constraints was added the external evidence that France and Russia would gain strategic superiority by 1917–18, the arguments for fighting now might indeed have seemed overwhelming.

The stress here must be on the central powers, as it was they who took the lead in escalating the July 1914 crisis.[20] None the less, it took two sides to make a war and it may seem puzzling that the French and Russians rose to the challenge, even though for them 1914 was far from an optimum moment. During the Liman von Sanders affair the Russian General Staff still felt unready to fight, and it wanted another at least two to three years to implement existing and projected military reforms.[21] What mattered more, however, was that the situation was no longer as in 1909, when at the climax of the Bosnian Crisis the Russian military had urged upon their government that a European war must be avoided at almost any cost, and had admitted as much to the Austrian and German representatives in St. Petersburg.[22] In the July Crisis, although the war and navy ministers (Vladimir Sukhomlinov and I. K. Grigorovich) were unenthusiastic about hostilities, they joined with the consensus in the Russian Council of Ministers that it was better to take a stand than let Austria-Hungary overrun Serbia.[23] Probably one reason for their acquiescence was that the French General Staff (*Etat-major de l'armée*—EMA) had become more confident since 1911 that the scales were tipping in favor of France and Russia and that they could now contemplate fighting and winning. The French government, including the pivotal figure of Poincaré, had been made aware of this appreciation, and it seems likely that it was forwarded to the Russians, whom the French met for annual staff talks and regularly communicated with via the attaché system.[24] On the other hand, the May–June 1914 French parliamentary elections had produced a swing to the left in the Chamber of Deputies and the formation of a new government headed by René Viviani, who agreed provisionally to maintain the Three-Year Law, but had voted against it. Hence a showdown may have been impending between Poincaré and the new premier in the autumn, when the law (which arguably had provided more manpower than the army needed) stood to be amended.[25] However, the main development to underline on the Franco-Russian side is less the burst of new measures in 1913–14 (the Three-Year Law, the railway agreement, and the Great Programme) than the progress already made in strengthening the armed forces, which meant that by 1914 war if not optimal was at least conceivable and might be preferable to backing down. On both sides in the July Crisis, only by taking account of armaments developments is it possible to appreciate the underlying forces for war.

III. The Arms Race did not make War Inevitable

The land arms race played an essential role in determining the timing and the circumstances of the conflict's outbreak. Yet this does not mean that it made hostilities inevitable, either in 1914 or later. Certainly, once the Sarajevo outrage had been perpetrated, and especially once Germany had given its "blank cheque" on 5 to 6 July assuring military support to Austria-Hungary, the chances for a peaceful resolution were slim: the Austrians were scarcely likely now to draw back from invading Serbia, and Russia was equally unlikely to stand by while they carried the operation through. The best prospect for diplomacy lay in a firm warning from London, but new evidence confirms that Germany at first supposed it could avoid British intervention and Sir Edward Grey's cautious response to the crisis encouraged that illusion,[26] while the Germans encouraged him in that caution by deliberately deceiving him.[27] Hence Grey's admonition to Berlin on 29 July came too late, for by this time Russia's pre-mobilization military measures were well under way and to all intents and purposes European peace was dead, Bethmann's and Wilhelm's last-minute jitters being of little significance. Sarajevo was *not*, however, simply a "streetcar" in the sense applied by President Lyndon Johnson's National Security Adviser, McGeorge Bundy, to the Pleiku incident (the Viet Cong rocket attack that precipitated the American ground-troop commitment in Vietnam): i.e. if this one had not been the precipitant, sooner or later another would have come along.[28] On the contrary, Wilhelm II accepted that a suitable rallying cry—such as Russian aggression—was crucial for his people to support mobilization,[29] and Moltke agreed that a war must start in circumstances that made it seem defensive and with Austria-Hungary standing at Germany's side. Skillful stage management might help create such circumstances—and to an extent in 1914 it did—but they could not be manufactured from nothing and without Gavrilo Princip's bullets there can be no certainty that war would have broken out that summer. On the eve of the July Crisis the diplomatic options still remained open, as until then no power had decided to launch hostilities.

    This conclusion is supported by what we know about the motives for the arms build-up. Among those motives were deterrence, securing the borders, managing crises, and enabling more offensive strategies; but none of them (not even the last) necessarily entailed a political commitment to initiate a conflict. Thus the Russians appear to have carried out their 1910 reorganization without foreseeing how it would galvanize their potential enemies. War Minister Vladimir Sukhomlinov, the reform's key architect, wanted better to prepare the army for use in Asia, as much as in Europe, by speeding its mobilization but also by withdrawing its strategic concentration line to a zone lying much further behind the western border. Initially the reorganization went together with a defensive operational war plan.[30] Even after 1912, when the Russians adopted a much bolder scheme to invade East Prussia and Austrian Galicia at the outset of hostilities, this new design was still a contingency plan, offering no more evidence than France's Plan XVII of an *intention* to launch aggression.[31] On the Central Powers' side the position is admittedly more ambiguous. It indeed seems that by autumn 1913 most of Austria-Hungary's leaders (except for the Archduke Franz Ferdinand and the

Hungarian premier, István Tisza) had concluded that only war remained as a solution to the Serbian problem, and that Germany's leaders feared that unless they stood by Vienna in the next Balkan crisis they might lose it as an ally.[32] On the Dual Monarchy's south-eastern frontier another "window of opportunity" had opened, in that the Balkan Wars had almost doubled Serbia's and Montenegro's surface area but much of the new territory was ethnically Albanian or Bulgarian and therefore tied down occupation forces without providing new conscripts to compensate; moreover, both the South Slav countries needed to reequip but they lacked the requisite finance.[33] For a larger war against Russia, on the other hand, Austria-Hungary's circumstances were much less favorable than a few years earlier, and even the Vienna hawks hesitated to start a Balkan blitzkrieg unless assured of German backing. Franz Conrad von Hötzendorff, the Chief of the General Staff, appreciated his army's weaknesses and that it was lagging behind in the arms race: although still willing to advocate war in 1914, he regarded it as a "break-the-bank game" (*Vabanquespiel*), far riskier than in 1912 or 1909.[34]

Hence Germany, once again, was crucial; and it has been argued that both the 1912 and 1913 German laws were introduced with the acceptance and even in the expectation that they might lead to a general war.[35] This is the nub of the issue and remains the subject of debate.[36] This author's view is that although from 1912 the German military and civilian leaders increasingly contemplated a preventive strike against France and Russia as a possible option, they were not committed to it at any time before the Sarajevo assassinations. Even the "blank check" represented a decision to provoke a localized Balkan war but only to accept the risk of a general European conflict rather than actively to provoke one as the preferred outcome to the crisis, and the German decision to ignite a Continental conflagration did not come until 31 July 1914.

Recent research has exposed two problems with the argument that the military balance and domestic fiscal considerations were impelling Germany into a preventive war. First, although Jack Snyder pointed out two decades ago the paradox that the military establishments of the period favored offensive strategies when the technology of the period advantaged the defensive, it now seems that European General Staffs were far less optimistic than once was thought.[37] The evidence suggests that Moltke and the GGS lacked confidence in their ability even to defeat France swiftly, let alone to triumph against the entire Triple Entente.[38] In itself this is not conclusive, as they appear neither to have communicated these misgivings to their political chiefs nor to have been inhibited by them from urging a preventive strike, although possibly only to maximize Germany's initial advantage in a life-and-death struggle that they believed was coming anyway. But second—and possibly allied to this point—despite Berlin's financial constraints, the GGS in spring and summer 1914 was still considering with great seriousness the possibility of further rounds of armaments competition, and two projects in particular. The first was for yet another manpower law to call up and train the approximately forty thousand fit young men in each annual age cohort who still escaped military service, thus enlarging both the army's peacetime and mobilized strength. Waldersee demanded such a step (if possible from the coming October) in a forceful memorandum on 18 May, and Moltke pressed the case on Wilhelm and Bethmann.[39] The Emperor was sympathetic and supported raising taxes to pay for it, and the *Deutscher Wehrverein* lobbied for an increase. The chief resistance came from War Minister Erich von Falkenhayn, who informed Moltke on 8 July that he agreed with the principle of training all able-bodied men but that in order to avoid diluting the army's quality the increase should be phased in after October 1916 and spread over ten years.[40] However, the military authorities were united over the second project, which was a massive program of strategic railway building to be completed in stages down to 1917–20. Moltke presented it as the corollary of the 1913 law and as a riposte to the Franco-Russian railway agreement. It would entail three new Rhine bridges, eight more double-tracked lines to the western concentration zone and one more to East Prussia, and the widening of bottlenecks in the interior, thus hastening both the initial strategic concentration against France and the subsequent eastward redeployment. The investment needed was estimated at 500 million marks, whereas the one-off costs of the 1913 law had been 895 million and its additional recurrent costs 184 million.[41] Although Moltke and Falkenhayn both recommended this proposal, the finance ministry pleaded that it could spare nothing until 1916, obliging Bethmann to resort to top-secret discussions with the state governments. Prussia said it could bear some of the cost, but Bavaria jibbed at contributing anything significant. On 16 June the GGS decided to send out envoys to brief the state war ministers orally, in order to avoid written communication.[42] In fact the evidence is nicely ambiguous, suggesting that the German military continued to pursue long-term rearmament schemes regardless of the difficulties, but also that the latter were formidable. Given that the obstacles were primarily political rather than that Germany had genuinely reached the limits to its financial capacity, however, the outcome of a hypothetical debate over the railway plan in winter 1914–15 remains open.[43] The key point is that alternatives to preventive war stayed on the table.

This inference assists us in constructing a counterfactual scenario, and at this point it is valuable to consider analogies with other arms races. The pre-1914 land race was one of the most dramatic examples of such a competition in modern history, and ranks among the best cases available for testing the links between armaments rivalry and the outbreak of major wars. The Soviet-American Cold War race included several similar periods of recurrent diplomatic confrontation, heightened popular anxiety, intensified weapons deployment, and reorientation of strategic planning (notably in the years c. 1947–53, 1957–62, and 1979–83). Yet especially by its later stages all concerned could see that going to war must be a suicidal enterprise, whose destructiveness would be wholly disproportionate to any conceivable gains. On the other hand, the European arms race of c. 1936–39 differed fundamentally from that of 1912–14 in that the Nazi German leadership was committed to a major war from the beginning, albeit against the Soviet Union rather than the West. Even an analysis confined to pre-1914 cases, however, brings out the perhaps elementary point that arms races do not invariably end in wars. On the contrary, they may terminate when one competitor is crippled by insolvency or revolution, or turns to face a more pressing threat elsewhere.[44] Britain's late nineteenth-century naval race against France and Russia was ended by entente with France and by defeat and revolution in Russia in 1904–5; the Austro-Italian race was suspended after Italy invaded Libya and Austria-Hungary again faced danger from Russia and Serbia; and the Anglo-German naval race lost much of its impetus after 1912 when Germany ran into budgetary crisis and felt more threatened on land. It may be objected that naval contests were inherently safer affairs, being conducted over more peripheral conflicts of interest between antagonists who were separated by water, and proceeding at a slower tempo because of the lengthy lead times before spending decisions were translated into capital ships. If we seek a firmer basis for generalization by restricting ourselves to land races, perhaps the closest comparators with 1912–14 are the Franco-Prussian race in the 1860s and especially the German-Austro-Franco-Russian competition in the 1880s. Analysis of the three cases is suggestive. One of the most disturbing features of the pre-1914 land arms race was its speed. Within a few years the relative stability of the early twentieth century collapsed, and an intense competition superseded it.[45] The arms race of the 1860s was similarly dramatic and arguably culminated in a potential "power transition" comparable to that of 1912–14, as the Prussian advantage created by Albrecht von Roon's 1864 reform was threatened when the French Second Empire at last began to organize its superior resources.[46] Still more intriguing is the comparison with the 1880s, a period also characterized by interlocking diplomatic crises in Eastern and Western Europe and by a succession of army bills, albeit entailing much smaller increases in spending and in recruitment.[47] Yet that rivalry appears to have stabilized in the 1890s with all the combatants at a higher level of preparedness but polarized in approximate parity between the Austro-German alliance and a newly forged Franco-Russian bloc. This historical excursion not only illuminates the most dangerous characteristics of the pre-1914 land race but also underlines that arms race can have many outcomes.

What were the prospects for the pre-1914 land race ending peacefully? There was some evidence in early 1914 that the two "peripheral" races were regaining momentum: Britain approved monies for four new capital ships while Italy was recovering from its Libyan imbroglio and its army received a new equipment credit. But neither the Germans nor the Austrians responded by diverting resources from the central competition against Russia and France. If Europe had remained peaceful until the autumn, France might have revised the Three-Year Law, though it is unlikely that the change would have been great. Russia faced an internal strike wave, but the authorities were containing it. Austria-Hungary's nationalist discontents still had little impact on its defence policy. There was scant evidence that any participant in the land arms race was about to drop out. Although expenditure levels were high by previous peacetime standards, as percentages of national income they were lower than in the later 1930s or during much of the Cold War. Nor does a new "diplomatic revolution" severing Britain from Russia (although speculated about at the time) seem to have been likely in the next few years. Hence the most pertinent question is whether the arms race might have settled down without a political upheaval, as did that of the 1880s. Multilateral diplomacy would have been unlikely to have a role: the proposals at the 1899 and 1907 Hague Peace Conferences (discussed in Jost Dülffer's chapter in this volume) for agreed limitations on military budgets and on weapons innovation had achieved next to nothing, in part because all the powers objected on principle to such initiatives as intrusions on their sovereignty. Bilateral diplomacy had likewise failed between Britain and Germany, even though a two-power naval rivalry in which capital ships provided an easily detectable and measurable unit of strength was much more susceptible to negotiation than was an inter-bloc contest on land. Yet in fact after 1912 Britain and Germany were approaching an eight to five ratio in capital ships that was acceptable to both sides; if one way of interpreting wars is as tests of disputed power relationships between states, the naval race had fulfilled such a function without resort to bloodshed.[48] On land, however, no such stabilization around a mutually acceptable numerical ratio was in prospect. On the contrary, Germany acted as it did in the July Crisis precisely because it foresaw otherwise an impending shift to its irrevocable disadvantage. The French and Russians had almost immediately trumped its 1913 law, and if it did nothing its remaining margin of military superiority would dissipate. German anxiety would have remained acute even if there had been no Balkan crisis or European war in summer 1914, and that anxiety would have made containing any future crisis extremely difficult. Yet because the Germans would have hesitated to precipitate hostilities without a pretext adequate to carry the Austrians and their own public opinion with them, if the Balkans had remained quiet it remains conceivable that the arms race might have continued without a war. In such a scenario it seems implausible, however, that the Germans would have placidly resigned themselves to strategic inferiority and to forfeiting their great-power status. The most likely outcome would probably have been a further "armaments turning point" in Berlin like that of 1911–12, further downgrading the navy and releasing the relatively affordable sums needed for Moltke's railway program and another recruitment expansion. New political coalitions had formed to counter an external threat before, and they might have done so again. And that outcome, if France and Russia had acquiesced in it (and refrained from preventive war themselves), might have restored equilibrium by the end of the decade, as both sides secured their borders with much stronger garrisons and both endowed their armies with modernized artillery and transport and built fortification infrastructures that could support both attacking and defensive operations. In other words, stable mutual deterrence, as appears to have been established between the European powers in the 1890s and would be so again between Moscow and Washington in the 1960s, was a possible alternative world.

Holger Afflerbach has rightly emphasized the will for peace among the European governments, which showed itself in their determination to subordinate military sabre rattling to diplomatic exigencies through the run of crises that preceded 1914. None of these crises was beyond the control of the governments of the day; and of those governments it was arguably the German one that controlled its military most tightly and perceived most clearly the danger that such crises might run away from statesmen and propel them inadvertently into hostilities.[49] Yet the Germans' earlier caution makes the risks they ran in 1914 appear all the more striking, and underlines how fundamentally the land arms race had altered international politics. Ironically—and tragically—there was no need for Germany to respond as drastically as it did to security dilemmas that were less acute than it feared and were in substantial measure of its own making. That a peaceful alternative scenario is plausible strengthens the contention that the arms race need not have culminated in bloodshed. But this conclusion leads us back to the question of the quality and integrity of leadership, and to the ruinously irresponsible gamble for which the German authorities opted. And it was precisely with this question that the debate over war origins began.

Notes

1. Holger Afflerbach, *Der Dreibund: Europäische Grossmacht- und Allianzpolitik vor dem Ersten Weltkrieg* (Vienna, Cologne, and Weimar, 2002); and his *Das Deutsche Reich, Bismarcks Allianzpolitik und die europäische Friedenssicherung vor 1914* (Friedrichsruh, 1998), 3, 25–6. See also his contribution to this volume. The view has points in common with that of A. J. P. Taylor in his *The Struggle for Mastery in Europe, 1848–1918* (Oxford, 1954), and *War by Timetable: How the First World War Began* (London, 1969), although Afflerbach expounds it more systematically.
2. Matthew S. Seligmann, "'A Barometer of National Confidence': a British Assessment of the Role of Insecurity in the Formulation of German Military Policy before the First World War," *The English Historical Review* 117, 471 (2002), 333–36 for a recent overview. On the land race itself, David G. Herrman, *The Arming of Europe and the Making of the First World War* (Princeton, 1996); David Stevenson, *Armaments and the Coming of War: Europe, 1904–1914* (Oxford 1996); Dieter Storz, *Kriegsbild und Rüstung vor 1914: Europäische Landstreitkräfte vor dem Ersten Weltkrieg* (Herford, 1992).
3. Calculated from table 4 in Stevenson, *Armaments*, 4; for figures since 1870 see John M. Hobson, "The Military-Extraction Gap and the Wary Titan: The Fiscal Sociology of British Defence Policy, 1870–1913," *Journal of European Economic History* 22, 3 (1993), 461–506.
4. Franz von Schönaich was the Austro-Hungarian common war minister from 1906 to 1911.

5. Edward Grey, *Twenty-Five Years, 1892–1916*, 2 vols. (London, 1925), vol. I, 90. It will be seen that Grey was no supporter of the Afflerbach thesis. However his belief in the war's inevitability was arrived at retrospectively.
6. Stevenson, *Armaments*, 197, 209–10, 214.
7. On war plans see Jack Snyder, *The Ideology of the Offensive: Military Decision Making and the Disasters of 1914* (Ithaca, NY, 1984). Terence Zuber, *Inventing the Schlieffen Plan: German War Planning, 1871–1914* (Oxford, 2002) suggests that the Germans had a defensive-offensive western war plan, but overstates its case.
8. The phrase was used by Count Leopold Berchtold (the Austro-Hungarian foreign minister) and by Bethmann Hollweg: Stevenson, *Armaments*, 283, 364.
9. Stevenson, *Armaments*, 270.
10. Allizé to Viviani, 14 July 1914, *Documents diplomatiques français, 1871–1914*, 41 vols. (Paris, 1929–59), 3rd series, vol. 10, doc. 510; cf., Herrmann, *Arming*, 226, 228: "The arms race and the rhetoric that accompanied it quickly created a new attitude toward the use of armed force in Europe. … The changed atmosphere brought about by the armaments race and its accompanying rhetoric added a crucial difference. In this sense, the arms race did precipitate the First World War. It had many of the destabilizing effects that theorists predict for such competitions."
11. Stevenson, *Armaments*, 295, 298. Herrmann, *Arming*, 200–1. However, in 1915 Germany's relative position would arguably have been even stronger.
12. Stevenson, *Armaments*, 301, 322–26; David Stevenson, "War by Timetable? The Railway Race before 1914," *Past & Present* 162 (1999), 179–80.
13. Stevenson, *Armaments*, 311; see Gerd Krumeich, *Armaments and Politics in France on the Eve of the First World War: The Introduction of Three-Year Conscription, 1913–1914*, Stephen Conn, trans. (Leamington Spa, 1984), chap. 5.
14. Stevenson, *Armaments*, 313, 359.
15. For GGS analyses of French military developments see memoranda in Bayerische Hauptstaarsarchiv Munich—Militärarchiv, KAM MKr 992 (12 August 1913 and 18 February 1914); also October 1913 in KAM Gstb 166. For appreciations of Russia, memorandum of 4 July 1914 on "Die wachsende Macht Russlands," in Politisches Archiv des Auswärtigen Amtes (PAAA) R. 996, and of 15 December 1913 on Russian railways, PAAA R. 11011.
16. Stevenson, *Armaments*, 360, 364; Waldersee to Moltke, 18 May 1914, BA-MA W-10/50279, doc. 94.
17. Stevenson, *Armaments*, 358, 363–4; Jagow to Lichnowsky, 18 July, 1914, Immanuel Geiss, ed, *July 1914: The Outbreak of the First World War. Selected Documents* (New York, 1967), doc. 30. Cf. the retrospective statements made by German officials to the Berlin newspaper editor Theodor Wolff, summarized in John C. G. Röhl, "Germany," in Keith M. Wilson, ed., *Decisions for War, 1914* (London, 1995), 32–7.
18. On "power transition" theory, see Jack S. Levy, "Declining Power and the Preventive Motivation for War," *World Politics* 40, 1 (1987), 82–107.
19. Niall Ferguson, "Public Finance and National Security: The Domestic Origins of the First World War Revisited," *Past & Present*, 142 (1994), 143; cf, Niall Ferguson, *The Pity of War* (London, 1998), chap. 5, esp. 140: "the domestically determined financial constraint on Germany's military capability was a—perhaps *the*—crucial factor in the calculations of the German General Staff in 1914." The idea appeared in less elaborate form in Dieter Groh, "'Je eher, desto besser!': Innenpolitische Faktoren für die Präventivkriegsbereitschaft des deutschen Reiches, 1913/14," *Politische Vierteljahresschrift* 13, 4 (1972), 501–21.
20. See the contribution in this volume by Samuel Williamson, which underlines the importance and independence of Austria-Hungary's role.

21. M. Pokrowski, ed., *Drei Konferenzen (zur Vorgeschichte des Weltkrieges)* (1920), 32ff. S. Dobrorolsky, "La Mobilisation de l'armée russe en 1914," *Revue d'histoire de la guerre mondiale*, I (1923).
22. Stevenson, *Armaments*, 127–29.
23. Dominic B. C. Lieven, *Russia and the Origins of the First World War* (Basingstoke, 1983), 141–44.
24. Stevenson, *Armaments*, 220, 307. See especially Conseil supérieur de la défense nationale, Section d'études, "Note de presentation," 9 January 1912, Service historique de l'armée de terre, Vincennes (SHA) 2.N.1; EMA 3rd Bureau, "Plan XVII: Bases du Plan," (n.d. but April 1913?), SHA I.N.11.
25. Krumeich, *Armaments and Politics*, 215.
26. I owe this to a conversation with Michael Epkenhans, who has edited the diaries of Albert Hopman.
27. Michael Ekstein, "Sir Edward Grey and Imperial Germany in 1914," *Journal of Contemporary History* 6, 3 (1971), 121–31.
28. Cited in George C. Herring, *America's Longest War: The United States and Vietnam, 1950–1975* (New York, 1979), 130.
29. Stevenson, *Armaments*, 249.
30. Stevenson, *Armaments*, 157–8.
31. No such intention is suggested in the latest study, using new Russian archival sources: Bruce E. Menning, "Pieces of the Puzzle: the Role of Iu. N. Danilov and M. V. Alekseev in Russian War Planning before 1914," *The International History Review*, 25, 4 (2003), 775–98. For a recent restatement of the limits to the French "nationalist reawakening" (*réveil national*) before 1914, see Bertrand Joly, "La France et la revanche (1871–1914)," *Revue d'histoire moderne et contemporaine*, 46, 2 (1999), 325–47.
32. For these points, Stevenson, *Armaments*, 275–8; Samuel R. Williamson, Jr., *Austria-Hungary and the Origins of the First World War* (Basingstoke, 1991), 154–6; Richard J. Crampton, *The Hollow Détente: Anglo-German Relations in the Balkans, 1911–1914* (London, 1979), 117.
33. For further information, Katrin Boeckh, *Von den Balkankriegen zum Ersten Weltkrieg: Kleinstaatenpolitik und ethnische Selbstbestimmung auf dem Balkan* (Munich, 1996). I am indebted to Holger Afflerbach for this reference.
34. Franz Conrad von Hötzendorff, *Aus Meiner Dienstzeit, 1906–1918*, 5 vols. (Vienna, 1921–25), vol. 4, 53–7, 72.
35. For the 1912 law, Herrman, *Arming*, 161–2, 226; for the 1913 law, see chap. 9 "Der vertagte Krieg" of Fritz Fischer, *Krieg der Illusionen: Deutsche Politik von 1911 bis 1914* (repr. Düsseldorf, 1987).
36. For the latest contribution, Mark Hewitson, *Germany and the Causes of the First World War* (Oxford and New York, 2004).
37. Jack Snyder, "Civil-Military Relations and the Cult of the Offensive, 1914 and 1984," *International Security* 9, 1 (1984), 108–46.
38. For details, Stig Förster, "Der deutsche Generalstab und die Illusion des kurzen Krieges, 1871–1914. Metakritik eines Mythos," *Militärgeschichtliche Mitteilungen*, 54 (1994), 61–95; Hew Strachan, *The First World War. Volume I: To Arms* (Oxford, 2001), 1005–14.
39. Waldersee to Moltke, 18 May 1914; Moltke notes (n.d.) on audience with Wilhelm; Moltke to Bethmann, 18 July 1914: Bundesarchiv-Militärarchiv, Freiburg-im-Breisgau (BA-MA), W-10/50279, docs. 94, 95, 97. Moltke was still urging this case nearly two weeks after Germany gave its "blank check" to Vienna.
40. Falkenhayn to Moltke, 8 July 1914, ibid., doc. 96; Stevenson, *Armaments*, 361.
41. Stevenson, *Armaments*, 294, 362; Stevenson, "War by Timetable?" 186–9.
42. Ritter von Wenninger to Bavarian War Minister, 16 June 1914, KAM MKr 41 (This is a covering note—the report itself is missing from the file.): "Strategic Railways: Presentation of

15.6.14. No. 2360: In today's discussion Quartermaster-General Count Waldersee asked for written reports to the War Ministries to be refrained from. The War Ministers of the Federal States would be informed orally by special emissaries from the Great General Staff. First Lieutenant Krause of the Railway Department will present himself in Munich on the 25th." For another interpretation of this source, see the contribution of John Röhl in this volume, p. 79, 90.

43. Intriguingly, Conrad was also pushing in Vienna for a long-term scheme to create a trained reserve (*Reservearmee*) of 450,000 men, capable of fighting alongside active troops, which would begin to be deployable from 1919–20. Alexander Krobatin, the war minister, warned that funds would be unlikely to be available before 1916–17 and gave higher priority to a plan for building strategic railways up to the frontier in Bosnia-Herzegovina. Both projects were marking time as of June 1914. Stevenson, *Armaments*, 282–5, 357.

44. Cf. the classic analysis in Samuel P. Huntington, "Arms Races: Prerequisites and Results," reprinted in R. J. Art and K. N. Waltz, eds., *The Use of Force: International Politics and Foreign Policy* (Lanham, MD, 1983), 439–77. For a recent review of the theoretical literature that includes pre-1914 case studies, Charles L. Glaser, "When are Arms Races Dangerous? Rational versus Suboptimal Arming," *International Security* 28, 4 (2004), 44–84.

45. Mark Hewitson has similarly stressed the suddenness of the growth of insecurity: the German military were accustomed to measuring themselves against the French, and assumed that provided they comfortably outmatched their western neighbor their country was in no great danger. Abruptly, with Russia's recovery and the growing Balkan challenge to Austria-Hungary, this assurance was gone. Mark Hewitson, "Germany and France before the First World War: A Reassessment of Wilhelmine Foreign Policy," *The English Historical Review*, 115 (2000), 576.

46. On the pre-1870 race, see Michael Howard, *The Franco-Prussian War: The German Invasion of France, 1870–1871* (London, 1961), chaps. 1–2. Similar points, *mutatis mutandis*, can be made about the arms race of the 1930s. See Joseph Maiolo, "Armaments Competition," chap. 16 in Robert Boyce and Joseph Maiolo, eds., *The Origins of World War II: The Debate Continues* (Basingstoke and New York, 2003) for a new discussion.

47. Germany passed army laws in 1887 and 1893, Russia in 1888, and Austria-Hungary and France in 1889. Italy's army spending reached its nineteenth-century peak in 1889–90. Stevenson, *Armaments*, 45–59.

48. This is the argument in Geoffrey Blainey, *The Causes of War* (London, 1973).

49. See David Stevenson, "The Militarization of European Diplomacy before 1914," *International Security* 22, 1 (1997), 125–161, and the major study by Jost Düllfer, Martin Kröger, and Rolf-Harald Wippich, *Vermiedene Kriege: Deeskalation von Konflikten der Grossmächte zwischen Krimkrieg und Erstem Weltkrieg (1856–1914)* (Munich, 1997).

Chapter 8

THE GERMAN AND AUSTRO-HUNGARIAN GENERAL STAFFS AND THEIR REFLECTIONS ON AN "IMPOSSIBLE" WAR

Günther Kronenbitter

In May 1914, Helmuth von Moltke, the chief of the German General Staff, was enjoying the waters at the Bohemian spa of Karlsbad. Since 1905, when he had taken over from Alfred von Schlieffen, the political and strategic situation of Germany had been changed for the worse. As a result of the Russo-Japanese War and the 1905–6 Russian Revolution the leverage of military superiority on the European continent had made it possible for the German General Staff to present war as an effective political tool to the civilian leadership. Without the imminent threat of a two-front war against France and Russia, Moltke had been able to base Germany's deployment plans on the concepts of his predecessor and rely on a "France-first" strategy. By 1914, the formation of the Triple Entente, the Russian rearmament program, diplomatic setbacks, the growing isolation of Germany, and worries about the internal stability and deteriorating international situation of Austria-Hungary, its closest ally, had weakened the German Reich politically and militarily. Not prone to unsound outbursts of optimism at the best of times, in 1914 Moltke feared the worst was yet to come. Before leaving for Bohemia, he had asked for the introduction of actual universal conscription as the only way to counter the military build-up of the Entente in general and Russia in particular.

Otherwise, in a few years Germany would have to bow to the overwhelming superiority of its foes in any international crisis to come.[1]

Moltke did not expect the outbreak of a general war in Europe in the short run. But he was deeply convinced that sooner or later the Entente powers would be well prepared for a war. As a military leader, he could not think of a situation in which an alliance strong enough to win a war would not choose to use its military power to subjugate or to destroy its foes. As soon as it seemed possible to win a European war, the stronger alliance would be likely to wage it or at least threaten to wage it. The General Staff's dire warnings concerning Russia's armament program and its consequences were based on the assumption that international politics were shaped by power blocs struggling for mastery.[2] In 1914, the Entente powers' military build-up was still incomplete; an offensive war against Germany was improbable. A memorandum written in May 1914 by Georg Graf von Waldersee, Moltke's *Generalquartiermeister I* and his right hand man in political matters, followed this line of thought. Waldersee wanted to make the case for a renewed effort to increase the fighting power of the German army, and therefore he gave a rather pessimistic picture of Germany's relative decline in the near future. His prognosis, that the Entente would be ready for war against Germany and its allies in a few years, came with a more favorable view of the situation in 1914 attached to it. This opened what political scientists used to call a window of opportunity: "From these considerations it can be deduced that Germany will not have to endure an attack in the immediate future in the normal course of events; on the other hand, she not only has no reason to avoid a conflict whatever the situation, rather, the prospects for coming out of a great European war quickly and victoriously are today still very favourable for Germany and also for the Triple Alliance. Soon this will no longer be the case."[3]

This analysis was shared by Alberto Pollio, Moltke's opposite number in Italy, who compared the situation of Germany and its allies in 1914 to Prussia's encirclement on the eve of the Seven Years War, suggesting a preemptive strike as the best way to deal with the strategic threat.[4] Franz Conrad von Hötzendorf, the chief of the Austro-Hungarian General Staff since 1906, did not have to be converted to this assessment. Relentlessly, Conrad had been advocating preemptive wars as the only viable solution to Austria-Hungary's security dilemma, to the point of provoking his dismissal in 1911.[5] The Balkan War of 1912 and the international crisis triggered by Austria-Hungary's response to Serbian expansionism had brought Conrad back to office. To his great disappointment, Austria-Hungary's "militant diplomacy" (as Sam Williamson has described it) in 1912–13 had not provoked a war against Serbia or Montenegro.[6] According to Conrad, this was partly due to the lack of resolve within the political elite in general and in the foreign office in particular. But he also had to blame the heir apparent to the throne, Archduke Francis Ferdinand, and Germany's rather lukewarm support. This experience shaped his expectations when he paid a visit to Moltke on 12 May. Conrad and Moltke knew each other quite well, having cooperated closely since 1908–09. At their meeting in Karlsbad, they came to the conclusion that there was still a window of opportunity open to the Triple Alliance but that the strategic position would deteriorate rapidly. Unfortunately, the political leaders in Berlin, Vienna, and Budapest would not muster the resolve to provoke a war in time.[7]

In the July crisis, monarchs and politicians in Germany and Austria-Hungary proved Conrad and Moltke wrong. The military did not need to prod civilian decision makers to provoke a "Third Balkan War" and to risk a Great European War in the July Crisis. Rulers and statesman, diplomats and opinion leaders were already accustomed to defining security almost exclusively in terms of military power. Only at the very end of July did Moltke play an important role in the escalation of the crisis. To be sure, Moltke had tried hard to make the political leaders in Berlin aware of the advantages of preventive war. As Annika Mombauer argues convincingly, he was not just a reluctant military leader, shying away from politics, and no one ever doubted that Conrad did his very best to propagate his credo of preventive war.[8] But for years, Conrad—and to a lesser degree Moltke—had tried to influence foreign policy without tangible results. The July Crisis and the decision to go to war seemed to them somewhat belated—it would have been much more timely some years earlier. A close look at Moltke's memorandum written on 28 July, reveals his ambiguous feelings when he contemplated the dangerous road ahead of him, leading on from the *coup de main* against Liège to the devastating effects of modern warfare on human civilization.[9] And even Conrad, distracted by a love affair, seemed muted in the July Crisis, at least by comparison with his usual warmongering in the years before. The Great War was a hazardous gamble, Conrad conceded.[10] It could destroy the social and political order of Europe or even human civilization. But neither Conrad nor Moltke wanted to lose their credibility by opposing the decision to go to war.

Why were the chiefs of the General Staffs in Berlin and Vienna willing to risk such a war? The most popular explanatory tool for historians dealing with this question used to be the "short war illusion."[11] According to Lancelot Farrar and those who followed his line of interpretation, war—even a great power war—seemed to be a viable option because up to 1914, military experts were still expecting the next war to be short. Offensive war plans should pave the way for swift, decisive campaigns. The German war plan looks like the epitome of such an approach. With hindsight, it is obvious that general staffs in Europe had failed to learn the lessons of the American Civil War, the second part of the French-German War, the Boer War, and the Russo-Japanese War. Industrialized warfare, people's war, the effect of modern infantry fire, machine guns, and quick-firing artillery were not taken into account by military planners as thoroughly as they should have been. Future war, the argument goes, was still expected to be based on the model of the Wars of German Unification. The "ideology of the offensive" provided the military elite in Europe with a coherent thought pattern.[12] It could be applied to tactical, operational, strategic, and political aspects of warfare and war planning. The German General Staff, which had to live up to its reputation and find a way to deal with a two-front war, opted for an offensive operation against France along the lines of Schlieffen's plan of 1905. Based on rigid timetables and implemented without the number of troops envisaged by Schlieffen, this plan proved to be a recipe for disaster in 1914. Gerhard Ritter's harsh criticism of Schlieffen and his disciples, who had accused Moltke of tinkering with Schlieffen's infallible plan, became received wisdom in the 1960s and 70s.[13] That the German General Staff honestly believed in a quick, decisive strike against the French army and the subsequent redeployment of troops to the Eastern Front, was part of the generally accepted historical account. If Europe's general staffs had confidence in their plans—or in those of their allies—it was not difficult to see why they were hoping for victory.

In recent years, several aspects of this traditional view have been subjected to criticism. Terence Zuber's thesis on the Schlieffen Plan—or to put it more precisely: on its non-existence—provoked a debate which need not be dealt with here. Zuber's wide-ranging conclusions concerning the allegedly defensive posture of Germany in 1914 have drawn a lot of fire. Aside from those rather far-fetched assertions, Zuber pointed out that there was more flexibility in Germany's war preparations than many historians used to imagine.[14] The changes made in Germany's war plans between 1905 and 1914 were to a high degree reactions to political and strategic considerations. Annika Mombauer is certainly right to propose the term "Moltke Plan" or "Moltke-Schlieffen Plan" as more appropriate for the war plans of 1914.[15] Both modifications of the traditional account of German war planning should make historians aware of the fact that we still do not know enough about the way the General Staff worked and how decisions on war preparations were actually made. Informal hierarchies and networks should be subjected to closer scrutiny. Stig Förster has recently pointed out that the German General Staff was characterized by different approaches to warfare and war planning, one in the tradition of the Elder Moltke and rather sceptical about operational recipes for all-out victory, the other embodied by Schlieffen. The complex interaction between different cliques and different concepts of war in the time of the Younger Moltke calls for a detailed analysis. According to Förster there is evidence for Moltke being closer to his uncle's school of thought.[16]

This would fit in with another aspect of Förster's revisionist interpretation: the chief of the German General Staff did not really share the "short war illusion." The Elder Moltke doubted that there was a viable military solution to Germany's strategic problems in case of a two-front war. Preventive war against France or Russia at a favorable situation seemed to be an option to Moltke and his deputy and successor, Waldersee the Elder. Nevertheless, Moltke came to acknowledge the consequences of modern warfare in the age of mass armies and improved firepower: France was able to emulate Germany's military innovations and a rapid annihilation of the French army could become almost impossible to achieve. The General Staff had to face a difficult task. As Major General Friedrich Köpke put it in 1895, "We cannot expect rapid and decisive victories. Army and nation will have to get used to that thought early on in order to avoid alarming pessimism right at the beginning of the war that could become a great danger for the outcome. Positional warfare in general, the struggle surrounding long fronts of field fortifications, the siege of large fortresses, must be carried out victoriously."[17]

Schlieffen, desperate to avoid a war of attrition, worked on an operational solution to the strategic dilemma. When he finally devised his plan of a campaign against France in the *Große Denkschrift*, Russia could be neglected—but only for a short time. In the longer run, it became clear to Moltke the Younger that Schlieffen had failed to square the circle. This called for an adjustment of German war plans. The offensive against France might fail to bring about the annihilation of the French army as quickly as scheduled by the General Staff, and it would be wise to prepare for a war that would take longer. Moltke's decision to respect Dutch neutrality in order to keep open a "windpipe" for German overseas trade—as well as plans to store huge amounts of grain—indicate a growing expectation of a prolonged conflict. Yet although Moltke was unsure that Germany would be able to wage a victorious and short war, he did not fight desperately for the human and financial resources needed in a long one.[18] And whatever was on Moltke's mind in the last days of July 1914, as soon as the outbreak of war became an irreversible fact, the mood in the General Staff was cheerful.[19]

In the Austro-Hungarian General Staff, too, a high degree of optimism was in the air at the end of July, but feelings were somewhat less euphoric.[20] Given the Habsburg Monarchy's military record in the nineteenth century, Russia's military potential, and the belated decision to redeploy the 2nd Army from the Balkan theater of war to the northeast, it is no surprise to find some officers having second thoughts. Ever since the 1870s, planning for war case "R," war against Russia, had been the Austro-Hungarian General Staff's most difficult task. Only with the promise of German assistance and a moderate expansion of the railway system in Galicia, could the General Staff hope to defeat the Russians in the early stages of the war. Other war scenarios caused little concern—a victory against the Italians or the Serbs was considered to be a foregone conclusion. Under the leadership of Conrad, the General Staff started to produce new war plans for a broad range of possible cases. As long as Russia did not get involved, any war could be won by the *k.u.k.* (Imperial and Royal) Army. Moreover, the agreement between Conrad and Moltke in 1909 on coalition warfare in the east provided the Austro-Hungarian General Staff with a solid basis for planning a war against the Tsar's army. Now, even a two-front war against Russia and Italy or Serbia seemed to be manageable, and the question as to how to switch deployment plans during mobilization caused the biggest headache for Conrad and his officers. In such an eventuality, close cooperation between the foreign office and the general staff would be crucial to the deployment. It would be difficult to get the timing right but this did not appear to be an unsolvable problem.[21]

When Conrad took over from Beck in 1906, he aimed at a root-and-branch reform of the army. His achievements were quite impressive, and he earned the respect of many officers. The usual infighting between different cliques within the general staff did not stop in 1906, but younger officers in particular admired Conrad's courage and energy. He became a role model and instilled self-confidence in the officer corps. In many ways, the German-Prussian system of war preparations set a benchmark for the *k.u.k.* Army. In comparison with its mighty ally, Austria-Hungary was still lagging behind in 1914, but there were remarkable improvements in most fields of war preparations, ranging from new armament programs and a higher number of recruits to more "realistic" training for troops and more rigorous standards for the selection of senior officers. Whereas the cohesion of the multiethnic army seemed to be endangered by modern nationalism in the longer run, the Habsburg Empire's ground forces were in much better shape in 1914 than in 1906. Conrad was an ardent believer in the "ideology of the offensive," promoting preventive war, offensive operations, and the superiority of the offensive on the battlefield. The lessons of the Napoleonic Wars and the wars of 1859, 1866, and 1870–71 were still considered to provide young officers with valuable operational and tactical principles. There was an abundance of evidence to the contrary from the Boer War and the Russo-Japanese War, but the general staff in Vienna refused to learn the lesson about the effects of modern weaponry on warfare. What Conrad and his staff did not try to contemplate were the repercussions of tactical innovations for operational and strategic war preparations. Manchuria confirmed them—just as their colleagues in France and Germany—in their preferences. To them, the Japanese victories bore witness to the superiority of the offensive and to the overwhelming importance of morale. It was possible to win a war.[22]

But how long would it take to force the enemy to surrender? This was not discussed explicitly, but the most basic strategic model—fighting a two-front war as a sequence of two one-front wars—was based on the expectation that some kind of a decisive victory could be achieved in a couple of weeks. "Decisive" is a ubiquitous term in documents related to war planning but the precise meaning of the term is somewhat hard to define. Obviously, it implied the severe disruption of the enemy's military forces. However, even a war on one front, not to mention a two-front war, could not simply be decided by successful campaigns. As long as the enemy refused to give up, the war could not be ended. The second part of the Franco-Prussian War was a case in point, and military planners in Berlin and Vienna were aware of the problem. And in contrast to France in 1871, Germany's and Austria-Hungary's enemies in a future war could rely on allies to come to their support. Military innovations and alliances would make it even harder to predict the duration of a war.[23]

Otto Berndt, a *k. u. k.* general staff officer who published a textbook on military statistics in 1897, expected any future war to last for several months but probably not for more than a year.[24] We do not know whether Conrad would have agreed with this rough estimate. As in Germany, business people, politicians, and the military in Austria-Hungary started to prepare for the economic and administrative effects of war. Looking at these plans and regulations discussed in the last three years of peace, it is quite clear that they were not prepared to deal with the consequences of a protracted war.[25] This comes as no surprise because a long war was perceived to be a disaster for the economically vulnerable and politically unstable Dual Monarchy, something that Austria-Hungary could not survive. But neither would Russia, the Habsburg Monarchy's most dangerous potential foe. Like the German military leadership, the General Staff in Vienna came to hope that the turmoil of war would ignite a revolution in Russia. Only extreme reactionaries like Francis Ferdinand, who wanted to preserve the remnants of Europe's traditional political order, came to the conclusion that a war against Russia had to be avoided at all costs. Most general staff officers could console themselves with the thought that the Tsar's regime was at least as fragile as the Habsburg Monarchy. A long war might seal Russia's fate well before the collapse of Austria-Hungary.[26]

The mobilization and deployment plans of the general staffs in Berlin and Vienna were based on the assumption that it was possible to prepare for victorious opening rounds in a fight for existence. Some high-ranking officers were just eager to fight and prove that they could live up to the principles of Europe's martial traditions. Those military leaders with a higher degree of sensitivity felt a shiver when they were writing and talking about the calamity that an all-out war would bring about. Moltke the Younger and Blasius Schemua, who replaced Conrad as Chief of the General Staff in 1911–12, are perfect examples. They were both in touch with esoteric and anthroposophist circles, which were as fashionable around the turn of the century as they now seem obscure to us. We should resist the temptation to make too much of this specific background when we are looking for the ideological sources of belligerence in the military elite. Moltke and Schemua were a little bit more prone to gloomy predictions but when it came to drawing a conclusion and giving advice, they offered exactly the same solution to the political and strategic problems as their less high-minded colleagues: unless you are willing to surrender, sooner or later you will have to fight for the survival of the traditional political order in Europe; given the deteriorating strategic situation, it would be better to fight. In their reflections on future war, Conrad, Schemua, Moltke, and many other high-ranking officers argued for war along the lines of Social Darwinism. War was inherent in man's nature and all the destructive energies mobilized in fighting were nature's tool to foster progress.[27]

It might seem strange to find Austro-Hungarian officers waxing lyrical about "the survival of the fittest," but there was hope that the new "sick man of Europe" would be able to muster up the courage to counter the forces of destruction. After the assassination of Francis Ferdinand, Austria-Hungary's military attaché in Greece, Gabriel Tánczos, cast in the same Social Darwinist mould as Conrad or Schemua, called for war as the only way to defend Austria-Hungary's very existence. According to him, the fight against Serbia might be the beginning of a longer period of war in Europe, but Austria-Hungary had to accept this risk. Fighting for survival might even rejuvenate the Habsburg Monarchy. Then he explained why he did not even bother to reflect on a possible failure: he believed in success, Tánczos wrote, and even a partial failure would be less harmful than inaction. To be sure, in a war against Russia, Austria-Hungary might face destruction and not only a partial failure. But even at the end of the July Crisis, when the plans for case "R" had to be implemented, the same kind of logic prevailed: doing nothing would make it impossible to save the Habsburg Monarchy from destruction; war was a high-risk gamble but at least it offered a chance to win.[28]

Some military experts and publicists, who were cast in the same Social Darwinist and belligerent mould, called for a massive build-up of the armed forces and a more thorough militarization of society in order to make Germany—and to a lesser extent Austria-Hungary—ready for modern warfare.[29] The chiefs of the general staffs in Berlin and Vienna pressed their armament programs on the ministries of war and on civilian decision makers up to the end of July 1914. The dire warnings in their memoranda on the balance of power in Europe were a classical dual-purpose argument and justified calls for preventive war *and* for a systematic military build-up. There is no need to discard one of the alternatives presented to the civilian leaders as a tool of deception. From Conrad's and Moltke's point of view, both options, to wage war or to invest in the military forces on a massive scale, would have improved Germany's and Austria-Hungary's strategic situation. It was hard to calculate the consequences of a military build-up for the balance of power, not just because of the not so distant possibility that the Entente might out-spend Germany and the Habsburg Monarchy. Much closer to Conrad's and Moltke's mind was the fact that shifts in the pattern of alliances might undo the effects of a spending spree overnight.

Fearful of losing important alliance partners, Moltke and Conrad entered on a new wave of negotiations with their opposite numbers in Rome and Bucharest—in vain, as we now know. The governments of Rumania or Italy did not let their decisions be swayed by this kind of military diplomacy. Staff conversations were no substitute for a reliable political commitment. Nevertheless, by 1914 both Conrad and Moltke had grown accustomed to thinking of future war in terms of alliances and the repercussions of Balkan politics. At their meeting in Karlsbad, they discussed the changing international situation and concluded unanimously that war was inevitable in the long run, but its outbreak improbable for the next couple of months, and that it would be possible to win a war if it were started immediately. Neither Moltke nor Conrad questioned the feasibility of their ally's war plans.

When Conrad wanted to learn from Moltke how long it would take to defeat the French field army and to start the redeployment of German troops, Moltke's reply was evasive to say the least. This is less astounding than the fact that Conrad did not even try to obtain a more precise answer. Moltke, on his part, never dared to doubt that the k.u.k. Army would be capable of fighting the Russians successfully. Politics had become more important than purely military considerations—as the politicians went to war because they followed a restricted, militarized concept of security, the general staffs in Berlin and Vienna had become too politicized to assess the military situation properly. War *had* to be possible.

Notes

1. Robert T. Foley, *German Strategy and the Path to Verdun: Erich von Falkenhayn and the Development of Attrition, 1870–1916* (Cambridge, 2005), 69, 77; Annika Mombauer, *Helmuth von Moltke and the Origins of the First World War* (Cambridge, 2001).
2. Mombauer, *Moltke*, 172–79. For the perception of international politics as dominated by the ability to wage war successfully or to pretend to do so, see J. J. Ruedorffer (Kurt Riezler), *Grundzüge der Weltpolitik*, 4th ed., (Stuttgart, 1920), 220–22.
3. Cited in Mombauer, *Moltke*, 178.
4. Waldersee to Kageneck, 31 May 1914, cited in Günther Kronenbitter, "Die Macht der Illusionen: Julikrise und Kriegsausbruch 1914 aus der Sicht des deutschen Militärattachés in Wien," *Militärgeschichtliche Mitteilungen* 57, 2 (1998), 525.
5. Lawrence Sondhaus, *Franz Conrad von Hötzendorf: Architect of the Apocalypse* (Boston, 2000); August Urbanski von Ostrymiecz, *Conrad von Hötzendorf: Soldat und Mensch* (Graz, 1938).
6. Samuel R. Williamson, Jr., *Austria-Hungary and the Origins of the First World War*, 3rd ed. (London, 1993), 121–63.
7. Franz Conrad von Hötzendorf, *Aus meiner Dienstzeit*, 5 vols. (Vienna, 1921-25), vol. 3, 669–73.
8. Annika Mombauer, "A Reluctant Military Leader? Helmuth von Moltke and the July Crisis of 1914," *War in History* 6, 4 (1999): 417–46.
9. Mombauer, *Moltke*, 201f.
10. Conrad, *Dienstzeit*, vol. 4, 72.
11. L. L. Farrar, *The Short War Illusion: German Policy, Strategy and Domestic Affairs, August–December 1914* (Santa Barbara, 1973).
12. Jack Snyder, *The Ideology of the Offensive: Military Decision Making and the Disasters of 1914* (London, 1984).
13. Gerhard Ritter, *The Schlieffen Plan: Critique of a Myth* (London, 1958).
14. Terence Zuber, *Inventing the Schlieffen Plan: German War Planning, 1871–1914* (Oxford, 2002). For Zuber and his critics see *Der Schlieffenplan: Analyse und Dokumente*, Hans Ehlert, Michael Epkenhans, and Gerhard P. Groß, eds., (Munich, 2006).
15. See Annika Mombauer, "Der Moltke-Plan—Modifikation des Schlieffenplans bei gleichen Zielen?" in *Schlieffenplan*, Ehlert, Epkenhans, and Groß eds.
16. Stig Förster, "Germany," in *War Planing: The Lessons of 1914*, ed. Richard Hamilton and Holger Herwig, (Cambridge, forthcoming). See Foley, *German Strategy*, 14–81.

17. Cited in Stig Förster, "Dreams and Nightmares: German Military Leadership and the Images of Future Warfare, 1871–1914," in *Anticipating Total War: The German and American Experiences, 1871–1914*, Manfred F. Boemeke et al, eds. (Cambridge, 1999), 355f.
18. Foley, *German Strategy*, 79–81.
19. Holger Afflerbach, *Falkenhayn: Politisches Denken und Handeln im Kaiserreich* (Munich, 1994), 161–71; Mombauer, *Moltke*, 227.
20. Günther Kronenbitter, *"Krieg im Frieden": Die Führung der k. u. k. Armee und die Großmachtpolitik Österreich-Ungarns, 1906–1914* (München, 2003), 484–86.
21. Graydon A. Tunstall, Jr., *Planning for War Against Russia and Serbia: Austro-Hungarian and German Military Strategies, 1871–1914* (New York, 1993); Diether Degreif, *Operative Planungen des k. u. k. Generalstabes für einen Krieg in der Zeit vor 1914 (1880–1914)* (Wiesbaden, 1985).
22. Kronenbitter, *"Krieg im Frieden,"* 79–120.
23. Foley, *German Strategy*, 16–25.
24. Otto Berndt, *Die Zahl im Kriege: Statistische Daten aus der neueren Kriegsgeschichte in graphischer Darstellung* (Wien, 1897), 132–34.
25. Kronenbitter, *"Krieg im Frieden,"* 279–332.
26. Ibid., 276.
27. Ibid., 126–42.
28. Tánczos to Conrad, 3 July 1914, cited in Günther Kronenbitter, "Nur los lassen: Österreich-Ungarn und der Wille zum Krieg," in Johannes Burkhardt et al., eds., *Lange und kurze Wege in den Ersten Weltkrieg: Vier Augsburger Beiträge zur Kriegsursachenforschung* (Munich, 1996), 182.
29. Colmar Freiherr von der Goltz, *The Nation in Arms* (London, 1906); Friedrich von Bernhardi, *Germany and the Next War* (London, 1912).

Part III

Hopes and Fears of War and Peace
Subjective Expectations and Unspoken Assumptions in European Societies before 1914

Chapter 9

THE TOPOS OF IMPROBABLE WAR IN EUROPE BEFORE 1914

Holger Afflerbach

I. The Golden Age of Security

"I will never forget 1 August 1914. The memory of this day will always recall a profound feeling of quietness, of lost tension, of 'all is well.'" Surprisingly, this was how Sebastian Haffner described the day World War I broke out in his book, *Memories of a German*. His family spent their holidays in the countryside of Pomerania, well removed from world affairs. In fact, newspapers did not arrive there until the next day. And so, on this August evening, there was a feeling of safety in comparison to the preceding days. Haffner wrote:

> I will not forget the quiet and confident sound of their voices, the clear voice of my father and the sonorous bass of the landowner, and how reassuring the aromatic smoke of their slowly consumed cigars was as it rose in small columns into the air. And the more they talked, the clearer, the better and more consoling things became. Yes, in the end it had become obviously clear that war was impossible. And for that reason, we would not be afraid, but would remain here until the end of our holidays, as always.[1]

At the moment Haffner's father and his host were drawing to these conclusions, the German government was issuing ultimata to France and Russia, and the outbreak of war was only hours away. But the deceptive feeling of security, the idea that war could not come, that it was highly improbable, most likely impossible, was widespread in Europe that summer. Stefan Zweig, on a beach holiday in July, wrote in his *Memoirs of a European*,

> If I try to find a handy formula for the times before 1914, in which I was raised up, I hope to be most precise if I say, 'it was the golden age of security. ... Nobody believed in wars, in revolutions, or overthrows. Everything radical, everything violent seemed already impossible in an age of reason.[2]

Zweig described a Europe that held a somnambulistic belief in progress: "Nobody believed in barbarous atavisms like wars between the peoples of Europe, as nobody believed in witches or ghosts; our fathers were very deeply influenced by faith in the unfailing strength of tolerance and conciliation."[3]

It might be questioned whether either impression was typical of 1914 Europe. Both writers were of very liberal political inclinations and wrote down their memories in the 1930's, many years after the events and in the shadow of new and dangerous political developments. It is therefore reasonable to debate the reliability of these sources. But in their tenor they agree with numerous other documented recollections of that period. Europe was on holiday in summer 1914, and the diaries and sources of high-ranking politicians, diplomats, and military officials did not express undue concern before the Austrian government delivered the ultimatum to Serbia. The Bavarian general Wenninger was on holiday in Bornholm and wrote in his diary that he saw no reason to be worried about international politics.[4] Fritz Endres, a historian who was "fanatically interested in politics," wrote several postcards on 30 July 1914 from his holiday residence in Oberammergau. He mentioned the "usual holiday business," made scholarly remarks and harmless requests for books, and showed no sign of being worried about war.[5] Dominik Richert was stationed in the summer of 1914 as a German soldier in an army barracks in Württemberg. He had no premonition about the coming conflict, and neither did his comrades. They were woken by their master sergeant on the night of 30 July, at 10:00 PM, greatly surprised to hear about an imminent war: "War? Where? Against whom? Naturally, we soon came to an understanding that we would probably have to fight the French again."[6] The French President and Prime Minister were, in the meantime, on their way back from a state visit to Russia. The junior minister Abel Ferry wrote on 29 July 1914: "When they landed at Dunkirk, neither Viviani, nor Poincaré wanted to believe in war" and they thought he had overreacted in calling army units from Morocco back to France.[7] The French socialist leader Jean Jaurès—who was assassinated soon afterwards—was also optimistic on 30 July 1914: "It will be like Agadir. There will be ups and downs, but things will rearrange themselves."[8] Very well-informed German contemporaries also thought a war was improbable. When Arthur Zimmermann, Undersecretary of State in the German Foreign Office, heard for the first time from Hoyos about Vienna's plans, he said that any Austrian action against Serbia would lead to escalation and European war.[9] But the feeling of security soon got the upper hand: he repeatedly said in these July weeks that the situation was "still quite earnest," but he did not believe "in great European conflicts" or the "great continental war." He thought Austria Hungary would "slap the Serbs on the fingers" and in that way become a strong member of the Triple Alliance again.[10]

The German military leadership was on holiday as well. Chief of Staff Helmuth von Moltke, the German government's leading advocate of a preventive war, was in Carlsbad for health treatments. An interruption of his stay was considered to be unnecessary.[11] His colleague, Erich von Falkenhayn, Prussian minister of war, was on the island of Juist with his family. He did not expect war either. He was busy with peacetime army plans for 1916, and so was his ministry.[12] General von Lyncker, chief of the Imperial military cabinet, had travelled with Wilhelm II to Norway. On 21 July 1914, shortly before the Austrians handed over the ultimatum to Serbia, he believed that the voyage would continue as in the years before, and that a premature return was possible, but not probable.[13]

Some historians speculate that these were merely tactics of deception by the German government and argue that Berlin wished to allay any international suspicion of war plans by sending the Kaiser and the military chiefs on holiday.[14] But just as high-ranking German military officers did not expect war at the beginning of July 1914, nearly no one abroad believed the Sarajevo affair would escalate into a continental war. The British Prime Minister, Herbert Henry Asquith, spent the month working on the Ulster question, examining religious statistics of the border counties in Ireland in order to draw a line acceptable to both parties. "A war seemed unthinkable to me in that moment."[15] When the Italian senator Alberto Pansa, former Italian ambassador in Berlin, was informed of the Austrian ultimatum, he still refused to believe in the possibility of war, calling it in his diary "una tale follia" (such a crazy thing).[16]

That nobody seemed to believe in the possibility of a great war between the great powers was claimed by David Lloyd George in his memoirs.[17] Ernst von Salomon, in his autobiography *The Questionnaire*, later mocked those in 1914 who had believed "it was impossible that a war could break out in the twentieth century."[18] This, for example, had been the conviction of Joyce Cary, the novelist, who, just down from Trinity College, Oxford in October 1912, had taken part in the First Balkan War: "I wanted the experience of war. I thought there would be no more wars."[19] It would be possible to add here hundreds of similar quotations to prove that this common belief, this "topos" of the improbability of war, was as firmly held as the belief of the *Titanic*'s passengers in the infallibility of modern technology. Both beliefs proved to be ill founded. In reality, there was much in Europe that pointed to war: the relentless armaments race, imperialist designs to dominate other countries, colonial rivalries, exacerbated nationalism, and intensifying diplomatic crises.[20] Does it not seem much more probable that contemporaries would have talked of the inevitability of a coming Great War; and that people would think its outbreak was only a question of time, a natural and inevitable outcome of the era of European imperialism? Such opinions were indeed expressed in 1913 and 1914 by Albert Ballin and Colonel House, who said that the European army and naval arms race must lead "to conflict."[21] Marxists were warning of an inevitable conflagration as well, as, for other reasons, were military leaders.[22]

Such opinions turned out to be more accurate predictions of the future, but this chapter will explore how far they were representative or genuine. One thing is certain: they have strongly influenced the historiography and the interpretation of World War I as an inevitable outcome of the pre-1914 domestic and international order. Nobody made this case better than did James Joll, Eric Hobsbawm and especially Wolfgang J. Mommsen, in whose essay "The "Topos of Inevitable War,"[23] we can read:

> "But above all, the view gained ground that the inevitable imperialist expansion of the major states into the still undeveloped areas of the globe, regarded as indispensable for the survival of the homeland in future eras, could not be carried out without severe warlike encounters between the rival major powers. Under the influence of these developments a tendency emerged, fostered by imperialist enthusiasm, towards the use of violence and war. Violence was increasingly regarded as an essential element in international relations and indeed positively welcomed. On the other hand, as a sort of reflex of these ideas, a basically fatalistic attitude developed which began to see a world war as sooner or later inevitable. ... This weakened, from a formal point of view, resistance to aggressive tendencies. The widespread assumption that war must come sooner or later, whatever particular policies might be pursued, had, in the final analysis, the effect of a 'self-fulfilling prophecy.'"[24]

Especially after the Agadir crisis of 1911 there was, according to Mommsen, a very real "cult of inevitability."[25] The symptomatic German title of the book in which his essay appeared, was, "Ready for War."[26]

But how do we reconcile this "cult of inevitability," which made war possible by creating a fatalistic atmosphere, with the somnambulant belief in the stability of European civilization, in the improbability of a great war? In recent years, historical research has raised doubts about the thesis of a "topos of inevitable war" and a general war mood in Europe before 1914, and has suggested the need for revision, giving more attention to factors of political détente.[27]

It is absolutely necessary to recognize that leaders then, as they do now, considered scale when contemplating conflicts. Distinctions were made between the "small" wars of the period and a hypothetical "Great War," a generalized conflict between the European great powers. Here we will concentrate just on the latter, the coming Great War. There is unanimous consensus that nearly everyone at the time expected that such a Great War, should it occur, would be a catastrophe, an

"Armageddon."[28] Not only convinced pacifists, but also the bellicose high-ranking military leaders expected that a great continental conflict would devastate Europe for decades.

Yet this chapter will try to demonstrate that such a great war was considered to be highly improbable at the time—precisely because of the devastating effects that it would wreak on the whole of European civilization. It will examine a variety of perspectives on the prospect of a future Great War: those of the foreign ministries, of the military leaders, and of the press and elements of public opinion. It will also consider some reasons for enthusiasm for war in the summer of 1914, after which it will draw some conclusions.

II. The European Cabinets and the "Improbable War"

An effective way to study whether or not European cabinets were expecting the Great War is to analyze their alliances—which have frequently been considered to be one of the leading causes of the catastrophe of 1914—and especially to examine their contingency plans for a possible war. For example, let us look at the Triple Alliance, one of the two main diplomatic blocs in Europe, whose last renewal had been in December 1912. The renewal negotiations took place after the Agadir crisis and the Libyan war and during the First Balkan war—a time at which the pre-1914 international tension undoubtedly reached a peak. In preparation for the negotiations between the Triple Alliance partners, top secret analyses of the alliance were made, for internal use only, in Berlin, Rome, and Vienna; and each touched on the possibility of a Great War.

In Italy, the renewal of the treaty was strongly advocated by all involved. King Vittorio Emanuele III, Prime Minister Giovanni Giolitti, Foreign Minister Antonino di San Giuliano, and the ambassadors to Germany and Austria Hungary agreed for a number of reasons to continue the alliance. All the protagonists were concerned only with the fields of internal, foreign, and colonial policy, and their focus can be described as a "policy of stability." It is striking that in the whole debate, the casus foederis (i.e. a European War) was not discussed in detail, as it was considered to be highly unlikely. The ambassador in Berlin, Alberto Pansa, concluded in a secret dossier that the casus foederis was "most improbable in the foreseeable future." The recent Moroccan crisis had shown "how much the common aversion to European War had progressed."[29] According to the celebrated Italian historian of this period, Luigi Albertini, Giolitti, like Pansa, could absolutely not believe in a danger to the European peace at the end of 1912.[30]

Italy's antagonistic Triple Alliance partner, Austria-Hungary, viewed many political problems very differently, but not the question of the likelihood of a Great War. European peace was not seen as being in danger. An official from the Vienna Foreign Ministry, Julius Szilassy von Szilas, prepared a memorandum in which he wrote that the only goal of the Triple Alliance was the "conservation of world peace." From a historical point of view, this comment could be seen as the greatest possible compliment for the Triple Alliance. But Szilassy meant it negatively as a sign of the fruitlessness of an alliance limited to a "negative goal," the preservation of a peace that was not endangered. Szilassy wrote: "Today the [Habsburg] monarchy is bound to Italy only by its interest in keeping world peace and the peace between themselves!" He held this peacekeeping function of the Triple Alliance in low esteem because he did not consider the peace to be in danger, and therefore saw the alliance as somewhat superfluous. Furthermore, if Italy were to drop out of the Triple Alliance and join the French-Russian-English group, the consequences would be tolerable as no tendencies of the time pointed in the direction of a Great War. Szilassy wrote: "Today neither France nor Russia want war, the former because it has become pacifistic; the latter because it has other problems."[31] His judgment that a Great War was improbable was widely shared among the Austro-Hungarian diplomatic corps.[32]

The Austrian and Italian judgments agreed on the decisive points. Both considered the alliance an ineffective tool to further either partner's individual goals. But the ability of the Triple Alliance to preserve the European equilibrium and peace was estimated to be high. That the alliance was very useful as an instrument of European peace keeping was a belief held not only in Vienna and Rome, but also in Berlin. Alfred von Kiderlen-Wächter, Secretary of State in the German Foreign Office and leading the renewal negotiations for Germany, also considered a European war to be improbable given the actual situation.[33] These observations offer a significant challenge to the notion that the "Topos of inevitability of war" accurately characterizes the mood of Europe between the Agadir crisis and Sarajevo.[34]

In order to show how improbable German government and diplomatic circles considered a war to be, we can look to two books from the period in which these thoughts are reflected. *German World Policy and No War* (*Deutsche Weltpolitik und kein Krieg*), was the title of a booklet published under a pseudonym in 1913 by the German diplomat Richard von Kühlmann,[35] in which he denied any national necessity for war. We can look particularly to the famous little book by Kurt Riezler, the secretary of Bethmann Hollweg, entitled *Basic Characteristics of World Politics in our Times* (*Grundzüge der Weltpolitik in der Gegenwart*).[36] This book, written in the autumn of 1913, dealt with the competition between nations, nationalistic fervor, and the necessity for a world policy, as well as with the inevitability of colonial rivalries, the European arms race, and the lack of effective supranational tendencies that might have balanced out these other factors. Nevertheless, Riezler repeatedly drew the conclusion that a great war between the European alliance systems was surely improbable, and that the fear of devastating consequences made it practically impossible.[37] The existing system of alliances, he believed, made hostilities between any two nations impossible without leading to a broad escalation, and for this reason alone effectively conserved the peace. All the necessary and desirable changes in power politics, he felt, were possible and realizable by slow, tenacious pressure. Riezler wrote: "Wars between great powers will no longer be started in order to gain advantages, but only in the case of emergency. There is only a small possibility that such an emergency will befall a great power, because no enemy will be interested in provoking this case of emergency. It is typical, in modern conflicts between great powers, that neither side has an interest in a solution that involves the prospect of war."[38] This opinion appears to have been, as Mommsen claims, "naïve"[39] and indeed was proven false by the outbreak of World War I only a few months after the book was published. But it is a very good example of both the topos of improbable war in Europe before 1914 and the dangerous implications of this topos, namely, that powers might attempt to obtain their political goals by threatening—as a bluff—the war that everybody feared.[40]

At this point, let us leave this overview of the political leadership of these three powers. It would be possible, as can be shown by existing research, to demonstrate that the policies of the Great Powers were dominated by the belief that a Great War was improbable despite the armaments race and political tension. This was recently shown to be true in the case of France by Klaus Wilsberg.[41] The political expectations of the nation as a whole were summed up in a French school book dating from 1912: "War is not probable, but possible. For that reason France is armed and always ready to defend itself."[42]

All this illustrates that even at a moment of extreme polarization in European diplomacy after the second Moroccan crisis, after the Libyan War, and during the Balkan War, the leading foreign office politicians considered a Great War to be improbable, and did not anticipate the conflict to come.

III. The Militaries and their Fear of an Enduring Peace

We have discussed the perspectives of diplomats and foreign politicians, but what about those of the military leaders? Did not Moltke, the German Chief of Staff, and his Austro-Hungarian counterpart Conrad von Hötzendorff plan for, if not dream of war before 1914? Did not their Italian counterpart Alberto Pollio support a preventive war, citing the example of Frederick the Great and the Seven Years War? And did not some Russian and French generals have very similar designs?[43]

Here we turn to a different method of exposition. So far, the civilians we have cited, such as Stefan Zweig, and the diplomats and politicians, such as Giolitti, Szilassy, or Kiderlen-Wächter, were men whose interests—and even official obligations—were to preserve the peace. However, the military officers that we will now deal with, particularly the high-ranking German officers, actually desired war. Of this there can be no doubt. They despaired at the thought of missing the chance to demonstrate their abilities, and feared that as a result, the social reputation of the military would fade in a protracted period of peace.

Such concerns were related, in Imperial Germany, to the phenomenon of *Epigonentum*, or an "epigone complex," a conflict of generations analyzed by Thomas Rohkrämer in his study of the German veterans' associations. The "Wilhelmine Germans," born between 1859 and 1866,[44] were too young to have participated in the wars of unification and wished to escape the long shadow of the founding generation by performing heroic deeds of their own.[45]

Many Wilhelmine military officers desired war because of their high self-esteem and confidence in their chances for a victory. It is easy to show that all German Chiefs of Staff, from Waldersee, and Schlieffen, to Moltke the Younger, claimed that war was "inevitable" and frequently insisted that the sooner the war came, the better it would be for Germany.[46] Many military leaders were enthusiastic when war broke out. Many predicted a quick victory and others morbidly believed that "Even if we perish, it will have been wonderful."[47] But we are not questioning whether the military community desired war, but whether they believed that it was likely. And again we are referring not to the possibility of small colonial conflicts, perhaps in Africa, but to a great war in Europe.

In fact, in 1914 many soldiers indeed felt that the tide of time was working steadily against the outbreak of war. Yet in books and articles, they tried to convince themselves and others that war, a Great War, despite all the signs that it was improbable, would serve to maintain the military culture's importance to society. The most famous example is probably Friedrich von Bernhardi's *Germany and the Next War (Deutschland und der nächste Krieg)*,[48] which attempted to construct a philosophical argument, using Social Darwinism, that war was necessary, elemental, and desirable. This book was considered by contemporaries, and is referred to by historians, as a sign of the readiness for war in Germany. This is understandable, but the book can also be interpreted in another way: high-ranking officers, afraid that no major wars might occur in the future, chose, not to lose hope, but to try to spread more widely their desire for armed conflict. What everyone else would consider a catastrophe, they argued was philosophically and politically necessary and for that reason it was to be hoped that it was more probable than anyone thought it to be.

Naturally, it is difficult to measure soldiers' love of war for war's sake, and to prove that the military was therefore desperate precisely because of the enduring peace. In writings after 1918, many of these explosive opinions were omitted, when reflected upon, or were replaced in retrospect by more legitimate reflections. However, we can get an idea of the views of a political die hard by examining a letter by the later Prussian War Minister and Chief of Staff Erich von Falkenhayn. It was written in March 1912, after the second Moroccan crisis and during the Libyan War. Falkenhayn, who passionately wanted war, wrote on March 22:

> I do not share the opinion of the inevitability of war any longer. His Majesty is firmly decided to maintain peace under any circumstances, and there is no one in his

entourage who can change this dangerous decision. England is... absorbed by internal problems, so that it cannot hope to measure up with us in the foreseeable future. The crazy mood in Paris is the only hope that it can start. And perhaps the French are correct in their desire to take advantage of their partially illusory, partially very real superiority, gained from their advances in aviation. But if they are really so convinced of their success, that they will start without England is doubtful. Lastly, they have absolutely no cause. The emperor pleases them wherever and as much he can, because he instinctively feels that they are the chief threat to his humanitarian ideal. Our passive policy will give them no opportunity either. So, according to logic, war is unthinkable. But often it comes differently, as Berlin people say, differently than you think. Hopefully, this will be the case. I say, hopefully, because I think that we will win in the long run."[49]

Falkenhayn believed that "according to human calculation ... war was unthinkable." Again we observe here, and from a totally different perspective, the topos of improbable war. This Great War was even more improbable, because, as Falkenhayn wrote in another letter dated 30 September 1912, all the European powers would only suffer whereas "the USA and Japan would easily gain the upper hand in the event of a great European war." His only hope was that the desired war would break out, against all logic. And he concluded: "For me it will be all right. I am most tired and extremely bored by this lazy peacetime life."[50] Also Captain Albert Hopman, a close collaborator of Admiral von Tirpitz, did not believe in war either, and wrote on 9 December 1912: "I do not believe in the inevitability of war; I believe that it will not happen. ... The City (of London) does everything to avoid war, in which it would only suffer for years to come. And so do the bankers of all the other countries."[51]

Another example will also show how deeply rooted was the common belief in the improbability of a Great War in the minds of the German military leaders. On 1 August 1914, the German leadership received news from London that Great Britain wanted to remain neutral should the Germans abstain from military actions to the west.[52] Naturally, all the members of the hastily-gathered German leadership wanted to take advantage of this offer, which meant war against Russia alone, and with Austro-Hungarian help, and this seemed to guarantee a victory. Only Moltke opposed accepting the offer because, on the one hand, he feared it would complicate his existing war and mobilization plans, and on the other, he was afraid war might be averted altogether at the very last moment: "I always feared this; we would have won the two-front war....The only thing lacking now is that Russia slips away, too."[53] This illustrates perfectly how, at this critical moment, Moltke still believed that the war, which he personally expected to devastate European cultural life for decades, might after all be avoided. Here, a bizarre parallel can be drawn with Sebastian Haffner's father, who at the same moment, sitting in Pomerania, came to the conclusion that war was improbable, not to say impossible, and would therefore not take place.[54]

IV. The Improbable War in Newspapers, Political Parties, and Public Opinion

It would be interesting to analyze a broad spectrum of opinion from societies across Europe. However, the representativeness of such a survey is bound to be questionable. The problem is that historians can show the opinions of single persons if they are lucky enough to have good sources, but must limit themselves if they deal with whole societies to incomplete and impressionistic overviews. Wolfgang J. Mommsen draws on some comments by James Joll,[55] to demonstrate the limits of an analysis of public opinion: "It is, of course, extraordinarily difficult to filter out as independent elements from the multiplicity of historical factors enthusiasm for war on the one hand and fatalistic expectation of war on the other. This is precisely because they extend into the realm of the 'unspoken assumptions,' but more particularly because models of argument of this sort have usually been reflexes of the most diverse political and social interests."[56] Similarly, the common belief in the improbability of war was tightly interconnected with and dependent on the ever-changing political events of the time, which caused nearly daily changes in opinions, analyses, and expectations for the future.

Nevertheless, the question is important, because, as James Joll concluded: "To understand the people of 1914, we must understand the values of 1914: and by these values their deeds must be judged."[57] This chapter will now try to demonstrate, mainly with arguments of plausibility, that the European population as a whole also shared a common belief in the improbability of a Great War. Recent regional studies claim that the local populations feared war.[58] But the question of exactly what people anticipated from a prospective Great War cannot be answered simply: the education, interests, and expectations of the population were too diverse. People in the countryside saw things differently from the educated urban population; women differently from men; married people differently from single ones; and young people differently from the elderly. Military specialists were also sharply divided in their expectations of the duration and the outcome of a Great War.[59] Nevertheless, in spite of all these differences, historians agree that the European populations feared the prospect of a great war,[60] and that the advocates of such a war were a minority.[61] In addition, all historians who address the "topos of inevitable war" speak of war fatalism, not of war enthusiasm, which was cultivated only by eccentrics such as Italian futurists, German military diehards, and political extremists.[62] Admittedly we should keep in mind that radical pacifists, such as Bertha von Suttner, were also a small minority.[63] The majority of educated people saw the current political circumstances as imperfect but acceptable and improving, and thought in terms of national sovereignty, of a political and military "balance of power" (or "equilibrium")[64] and also of military deterrence.

But as always, we are concerned not with the question of whether Europeans desired or wanted to avoid the Great War, but whether they considered it to be possible. Josef Redlich, an Austrian hardliner, provided us with an answer on 17 October 1912, when, with some regret, he wrote in his diary that, "The general public does not believe in the possibility of war between the great powers."[65]

To further address this question, it is useful to examine the analysis of Bernhard Rosenberger, who tried to provide in his book *Zeitungen als Kriegstreiber* an example of how German newspapers helped to spread the "topos of inevitable war."[66] He analyzed five publications that were representative of the various German sociocultural milieus.[67] He tried to prove that these newspapers, particularly when they warned about the prospect of a Great War (as did the Social Democratic paper *Vorwärts*), increased the possibility of war by fostering fatalistic expectations. But in reality, his own material proves the contrary, and supports the topos of the improbability of a Great War. We can see this when he tells us that in the newspapers he analyzed while studying the second Moroccan crisis, there were only nineteen mentions of the possibility of war. Moreover, of these nineteen mentions only two referred to war as probable, eleven considered the situation as uncertain, and six considered war improbable.[68]

The same picture is seen during the July crisis. In agreement with all other scholarly works about the European press at that time,[69] Rosenberger also says in the initial period after Sarajevo, the newspapers he analyzed did not deal intensively with the prospects of a world war. Only after the Austrian ultimatum and the Serbian rejection of it did the tenor of the newspapers change. Rosenberger writes, "We can conclude that the press was reluctant to provide a direct or indirect prognosis of whether a war was imminent or not until the last week of July. In fact, two thirds (65 percent) of all quotations about the probability of war during the July Crisis of 1914 are from the period between 26 July and 2 August."[70] And his own evidence shows that when newspapers spoke in July 1914 about war, they were frequently anticipating a limited Austro-Serbian conflict and not a great war.[71] Jean-Jacques Becker conducted a similar analysis of French newspapers, and his results were also similar.[72] Here we can put the thesis of the topos of inevitable war to the test. If a great war was widely considered to be inevitable, after Sarajevo everyone, or at least a vast majority of Europeans, would have expected an outbreak of war to come soon. But despite this, they still went on holiday; the news about Sarajevo disappeared from the headlines, and was replaced in German, Austrian, and Italian newspapers by discussion of Albanian affairs. In France, public opinion as a whole was almost exclusively consumed with the Caillaux trial,[73] and in Great Britain, the Ulster question dominated the headlines. These indisputable facts do not suggest (as Mommsen, Hobsbawm, and others have claimed) an atmosphere of fatalism about a coming war, or that a Great War was seen as inevitable, or that the political elites were condemned to impotence in the face of the boiling over of nationalism, making alternatives impossible. On the contrary, it is obvious that in the first half of July 1914 no one expected that this crisis would escalate into a Great War. Contemporaries did, of course, consider an Austrian-Serbian conflict to be possible, which is important for understanding German and Austrian policy. In fact it was precisely because they believed in the improbability of a Great War that all parties involved assumed that it would be avoided; they could risk a local war against Serbia to stabilize both Austria-Hungary and, as a result, their own Triple Alliance system.

Signs of enthusiasm for war in the summer of 1914 also fit into this interpretation.[74] The extent of such enthusiasm has been questioned by recent research, but it cannot be denied entirely;[75] it certainly existed among at least parts of the bourgeois, urban population.[76] But it was not the end result of an enthusiasm for war that had accumulated over the years, fed by nationalist fervor or a fatalistic acceptance of an inevitable Great War. On the contrary, the Great War was considered to be improbable and for that reason also unnecessary. The greatest crime was seen to be the waging of such a war. It seemed natural that the other side should be blamed for doing so, and there was a strong desire to punish any enemy that could cause such a catastrophe, once the war had broken out. Theodor Heuss described the general mood as "willing earnestness" rather than "enthusiasm."[77] And the German historian Karl Alexander von Müller wrote, "I remember that I myself was a testimony to the feelings of the whole German population at the outbreak of this World War, which was deeply and honestly dominated by the necessity to fight, against their will, a defensive war, a forced war against enormously superior enemies."[78] In Great Britain, "even the Labour members, despite their sworn devotion to neutrality, were unfavorably impressed by this sample of German methods. [i.e. by the German aggression against neutral Belgium.] A Scotch Radical member, who hates war, said 'Germany leaves us no alternative but to fight. We are standing for public law; she is trampling upon it.'"[79]

As may be seen, it can be demonstrated that some contemporaries had the impression that Europe was sliding, against its will, into war. First made public by David Lloyd George on 20 December 1920,[80] this impression has not been confirmed as accurate by modern historians, who consider it to be overly generous, and are less inclined to show lenience to the statesmen in charge at the time, especially on the German and Austrian side. It should also be considered that it simply recalls the familiar Fischer controversy.[81] Today, however, the question of where the guilt lies should play a smaller role in historiography, as the debate over who was responsible has become a much less explosive controversy.[82] But another issue, because it deals with the broad evaluation of European cultural development and civilization over the last two hundred years, is still relevant; and that is whether the individual failures by particular politicians, diplomats, and military officers can be related to the European cultures that they represented. Were these cultures so infected by a desire for war and by fatalism about it that individual responsibility can be seen as less important than the overwhelming tide of time? Or was the catastrophe the result of very grave professional mistakes, which in turn created an uncontrollable dynamic? And were these professional mistakes provoked by optimism, an unjustified optimism, a common belief shared in both Berlin and Vienna, that a Great War was "impossible"?

V. The Socialists, their Warnings of an "Inevitable War," and their Surprise in 1914

The only factions in pre-1914 Europe that did *not* seem to share this common belief in the improbability of a Great War, and who constantly warned of a coming conflict, were the socialists and Marxists. Friedrich Engels apparently foresaw World War I when he wrote:

> Eight to ten million soldiers will fight each other and will ravage Europe like no swarm of locusts we have ever seen. The devastations of the Thirty Years War will be compressed into three or four years and cover the continent; hunger, disease, and the common de-civilization of armies and people, will be brought about by acute misery. The hopeless breakdown of our artificial machinery of trade, industry, and credit will end in bankruptcy and the overthrowing of old states and their traditional state's wisdom, so that crowns will roll by the dozens into the streets, and there will be no one to pick them up. It is an absolute impossibility to predict where it will end and who will be the victor in this fight. Only one result is guaranteed: general exhaustion and the creation of the conditions necessary for the final victory of the working class.[83]

Very similar words were spoken by August Bebel, who, though mocked by conservatives, said in November 1911 to the German parliament:

> So there will be armament and re-armament on all sides until one day, one side or the other will say, 'Rather an end in terror than terror without end'.... They might also say, 'Listen, if we wait any longer, we'll be the weaker side instead of the stronger.' Then the catastrophe will come. Then the great general march will be embarked upon in Europe, in which 16–18 million men, the blossoming male youth of the different nations, equipped with the best murder weapons, will turn against one another as enemies in the field. ... The twilight of the gods of the bourgeois world is within sight.[84]

As mentioned above, similar warnings could be found continuously in the main Social Democratic newspaper, *Vorwärts*.

But here the question is whether the Social Democrats really thought that a Great War was inevitable, or whether their warnings were just a very effective and striking argument against the costly arms race, deployed in the political struggle against the government and the bourgeois majority in the Reichstag whom they held responsible; a tool used against the commanding power of the Kaiser and the class privileges of the army, the nobility and the Imperial guard.[85] The Social

Democrats certainly considered the army to be an excellent target for their political propaganda because they believed "that most workers, due to the harsh military service, will automatically become Social Democrats."[86] And James Joll correctly pointed out that the Social Democrats could never convincingly solve their dilemma of whether they should "welcome war, as the catalyst for revolution, or try to avoid it."[87] Georges Haupt showed that Lenin wavered similarly concerning war and revolution.[88] As did the Marxists, for in the summer of 1914, socialists in all countries were as greatly surprised by the war as everyone else. "At the end of July, *after* Austria had already declared war on Serbia, the leaders of international socialism met, deeply troubled but still convinced that a general war was impossible, that a peaceful solution to the crisis would be found. 'I personally do not believe that there will be a general war,' said Victor Adler, who was the chief of Habsburg Social Democracy, on 29 July."[89] This evidence does not speak very well for the view that the socialists had believed war was "inevitable." The French historians Jules Isaac and (later) Jean-Jacques Becker asked of French socialists of the time: "How do you explain, if the war was expected, predicted since 1905, that when it came in the summer of 1914, it surprised the world like an avalanche?"[90]

VI. Expectations of Improbable and Inevitable War in July 1914— an Impossible Interaction?

Finally, we raise a question that may seem to be, on first inspection, slightly paradoxical. Is it possible that *both* common beliefs, the "topos of improbable war" *and* that of "inevitable war," existed side by side? Logically, this seems to be difficult. Nevertheless, it could be true. The same individuals could have had sharply contrasting, perhaps even contradictory, expectations of the future depending on their mood and the current political circumstances at any one time. And it is unlikely that everyone always had, at every moment, only one set of opinions and expectations. Maybe, for a better understanding of the events, we need a model that can incorporate these constantly oscillating, ambiguous expectations; a model that shows how the belief in a probable war alternated with the belief that a war was improbable, depending on the situation.[91] Robert Wohl wrote: "Among Europeans ... optimism about the future could be 'allied insanely' with the expectation of Armageddon."[92] As I have tried to demonstrate, the "horizon of expectation," to use an expression by Reinhard Koselleck, in 1914 was, by far, dominated by the common belief in an *improbable* Great War. However, this belief in the endurance of European peace did not dominate in a static, rigid, monolithic way over other expectations, but rather in a dynamic and mobile way.

Perhaps we can present an example of how these two expectations could coexist by examining the July crisis of 1914. The mistake that was made by German and Austrian leaders—by Berchtold, Bethmann Hollweg, and their subordinates—was based on their assumptions both of how widespread the fear of a Great War in Europe was, *and* how improbable it seemed. They thought, as a result, that they could carry out the maneuver against Serbia without further consequences. The July crisis was a huge bluff on the part of the Central Powers—a bluff that ended in catastrophe, of course—which would allow them to realize a local war that they considered necessary for the political stabilization of the Habsburg monarchy. But there was an afterthought: if, against all expectations, the other powers could not be intimidated, and would break the European consensus that a Great War must be avoided, it would simply prove that they had evil designs for the future anyway, and thus a Great War was imminent and it was better to fight now rather than later. It should be noted that this outcome was not seriously considered and was thought to be unlikely precisely *because* decision makers believed, as can be seen in the atmosphere at the beginning of the July crisis, in the topos of an improbable Great War. However, if a Great War did result, it would be perfect proof that it had, indeed, been inevitable. An example of this relationship between the ideas of improbable and inevitable war can be seen in a 29 July 1914 report by the Austrian ambassador to Rome, Kajetan von Mérey. He wrote: "I will consider it very lucky if it comes to war against Serbia. If the result is a European conflagration, this will be proof for me that it was in the air, that it would have come sooner or later on some pretext or other, and there is no doubt that for the Triple Alliance today is a better moment than later."[93] It should be noted that Mérey did not believe that the Great War was probable; but that *should* it come, he would consider it to have been inevitable. He experienced a complete nervous breakdown at the outbreak of the "improbable" Great War and had to be relieved of his office.[94] It is legitimate to speculate whether this personal crisis was the direct result of the event he did not expect to occur.[95]

VII. Conclusion

In analyzing European politics before 1914, we must consider *both* views: the topos of inevitable *and* of improbable war. Which assumption was more dangerous? On the one hand, the illusory belief in security, the topos of an improbable Great War, the optimistic faith in progress, rationality, humanity, and reason; *or* on the other hand, the fatalistic belief in an inevitable Great War, which seduced politicians into taking great risks? This is difficult to determine. In order to adequately explain the catastrophe, one must carefully utilize both ideas, much as a gymnast needs not just one, but both sides of his parallel bars to perform his routine. It was this very *combination* of expectations that provided the volatile mixture that led to world war.

As a last consideration, if one ultimately prefers the topos of an *improbable* Great War, one must be skeptical about one of Mommsen's central conclusions: his basic belief that nationalist public opinion, especially in Germany and Austria-Hungary, forced their weak and feeble governments toward war, and that this war mood was widespread in pre-war societies.[96] The decisions for war were made by the governments, not by the people.

The "seminal catastrophe" of the twentieth century changed everything in European politics. The people of Europe saw that their political system was unable to protect them from a cataclysm they had considered to be improbable; and therefore, it was natural to see that system as bankrupt. Disillusioned, and despairing at the failure of reason, too many Europeans were ready to open their minds to deeply irrational ideas. Their "fatal, calamitous reaction against the rationalistic humanism of the nineteenth century"[97] made possible the even greater catastrophes that followed.

Notes

Most English readers might be less familiar with the term "topos." I use it here in the sense of a "commonly held belief" held by the Europeans before 1914. The term relates to one of Wolfgang J. Mommsen's most influential essays: "The Topos of Inevitable War in Germany before 1914" (note 27 see below). Mommsen had agreed to participate in this conference and subsequent volume, but was unable to do so because of his sudden death in August 2004. I use his term "topos" here to make it clear to whom I refer, and also out of respect for and as a dedication to my long time teacher.

1. Sebastian Haffner, *Geschichte eines Deutschen: Die Erinnerungen 1914–1933* (Stuttgart-München 2000), 15f.
2. Stefan Zweig, *Die Welt von Gestern: Erinnerungen eines Europäers*, (1st edition, Stockholm 1944; special edition, Grankfurt 1992), 14–15.
3. Ibid., 16f.
4. Holger Afflerbach, *Falkenhayn: Politisches Denken und Handeln im Kaiserreich* (München, 1994), 152, with other examples.
5. Georg Alexander von Müller, *Aus Gärten der Vergangenheit: Erinnerungen 1882–1914* (Stuttgart, 1952), 545.
6. Dominik Richert, *Beste Gelegenheit zum Sterben: Meine Erlebnisse im Kriege 1914–1918*, Angelika Tramitz and Bernd Ulrich, eds. (München, 1989), 15.
7. Jean Jacques Becker, *1914 : Comment les Français sont entrés dans la guerre* (Paris, 1977), 138. ('A leur débarquement à Dunkerque, ni Viviani, ni Poincaré ne voulaient croire à la guerre.')
8. James Joll, *Die Ursprünge des Ersten Weltkriegs* (München, 1988), 304. (…mais les choses ne peuvent ne pas s'arranger.)
9. Graf Alexander Hoyos, "Meine Mission nach Berlin," printed in Fritz Fellner, "Die Mission Hoyos," in Fellner, *Vom Dreibund zum Völkerbund: Studien zur Geschichte der internationalen Beziehungen 1882–1919* (München 1994), 112–141, 137.
10. See Albert Hopman, *Das ereignisreiche Leben eines Wilhelminers: Tagebücher, Briefe, Aufzeichnungen 1901 bis 1920*, Michael Epkenhans, ed. (München, 2004), 386 (7 July 1914), 388 (13 July 1914), 389 (16 July 1914).

11. Afflerbach, *Falkenhayn*, 150.
12. Ibid., 134f. (planning for 1916), 151 (holiday on Juist).
13. Lyncker to his wife, 21 July 1914, in Holger Afflerbach, ed., *Kaiser Wilhelm II: als Oberster Kriegsherr. Quellen aus der militärischen Umgebung des Kaisers 1914–1918* (München, 2005), Nr. L 1.
14. Afflerbach, *Falkenhayn*, 149–51. See also Anscar Jansen, *Der Weg in den Ersten Weltkrieg: Das deutsche Militär in der Julikrise 1914* (Marburg, 2005), 512 f. This latest analysis of the role of German military during the July crisis of 1914 concludes that the deception theory is not credible because the German armies were caught by surprise by the outbreak of war.
15. Henry Herbert Asquith, *Memories and Reflections, 1852–1927* (Boston, 1928), vol. 2, 4–12; William Hayden Edwards, "Die Kriegsschuld der Nerven"(manuscript), 31. Manuscript in BPH Rep. 53, Nr. 28 (old Sign. HA Rep. 53a Nr. 16).
16. Holger Afflerbach, *Der Dreibund: Europäische Großmacht- und Bündnispolitik vor 1914* (Wien, 2002), 842.
17. David Lloyd George, *War Memoirs*, vol. I, 1914–1915 (Boston, 1933), 49, wrote: "Not even the most astute and intuitive statesman foresaw in the early summer of 1914 that the autumn would find the nations of the world interlocked in the most terrible conflict that had ever been witnessed in the history of mankind; and if you come to the ordinary men and women who were engaged in their daily avocations in all countries, there was not one of them who suspected the imminence of such a catastrophe.... The nations slithered over the brink into the boiling cauldron of war without any sign of apprehension or dismay."
18. Ernst von Salomon, *Der Fragebogen* (Reinbek, 1951), 11.
19. Joyce Cary, *Memoir of the Bobotes* (London, 2000), 7.
20. On these questions see Paul Schroeder's chapter in this volume.
21. Hopman, *Wilhelminer*, 270; Colonel House to Wilson, May 1914, in *The World War I Document Archive*, Brigham Young University, <http://www.lib.byu.edu/~rdh/wwi/index.html>; Afflerbach, *Dreibund*, 765–67. Concerning the European armaments race, see the analysis by David Stevenson, *Armaments and the Coming of War: Europe, 1904–1914* (Oxford, 1996), and his chapter in this volume. See also David G. Herrmann, *The Arming of Europe and the First World War* (Princeton, 1996).
22. Annika Mombauer, *Helmut von Moltke and the Origins of the First World War* (Cambridge, 2001).
23. Joll, *Ursprünge*, passim; Eric Hobsbawm, *The Age of Empire 1875–1914* (London, 1987), esp. Chapter 13 "From Peace to War," 302–27. He not only deals with the "topos of inevitable war," but almost creates his own topos when he writes on p. 312: "in the summer of 1914 … peace had been written off by all the powers.... None of the great powers would have given peace the coup de grâce even in 1914, unless they had been convinced that its wounds were already fatal."; Wolfgang J. Mommsen, "The Topos of Inevitable War in Germany in the Decade before 1914," in Volker R. Berghahn, Martin Kitchen, eds., *Germany in the Age of Total War: Essays in Honor of Francis L. Carsten*, (London, 1981), 23–46. German translation, Mommsen, "Der Topos vom unvermeidlichen Krieg: Außenpolitik und öffentliche Meinung im Deutschen Reich im letzten Jahrzehnt vor 1914," in Jost Dülffer and Karl Holl, eds., *Bereit zum Krieg: Kriegsmentalität im wilhelminischen Deutschland 1890–1914* (Göttingen, 1986), 194–224. Also in Wolfgang J. Mommsen, *Der autoritäre Nationalstaat. Verfassung, Gesellschaft und Kultur des deutschen Kaiserreiches* (Frankfurt am Main, 1990), 380–406. Very similar or identical opinions in Wolfgang J. Mommsen, *Großmachtstellung und Weltpolitik 1870–1914. Die Außenpolitik des Deutschen Reiches* (Frankfurt am Main/Berlin, 1993), and in Wolfgang J. Mommsen "Deutschland," in Gerhard Hirschfeld/ Gerd Krumeich/Irina Renz, *Enzyklopädie Erster Weltkrieg* (Paderborn/München/Wien/Zürich, 2003), 15–30; Wolfgang J. Mommsen, *Der erste Weltkrieg: Anfang vom Ende des bürgerlichen Zeitalters* (Frankfurt am Main, 2004).
24. Mommsen, *Topos*, 24. (Mommsen, *Nationalstaat*, 381f.)
25. Ibid., 30.

26. Dülffer, Holl, *Bereit zum Krieg*.
27. Holger Afflerbach, "Der Dreibund als Instrument der europäischen Friedenssicherung vor 1914," in Helmut Rumpler, Jan Niederkorn, eds., *Der "Zweibund" 1879: Das deutsch—österreichisch-ungarische Bündnis und die europäische Diplomatie (Zentraleuropa-Studien, Band 2, Tagungsband des 3. Deutsch-Österreichischen Historikergesprächs in Wien, 27–29 Oktober 1994)* (Wien, 1996), 87–118; Afflerbach, *Dreibund*; Friedrich Kießling, *Gegen den "grossen Krieg"? Entspannung in den internationalen Beziehungen 1911–1914* (München, 2002); Friedrich Kießling, "Wege aus der Stringenzfalle: Die Vorgeschichte des Ersten Weltkriegs als 'Ära der Entspannung,'" in *Geschichte in Wissenschaft und Unterricht* 55 (2004), 284–304; Klaus Wilsberg, *"Terrible ami—aimable ennemi": Kooperation und Konflikt in den deutsch-französischen Beziehungen 1911–1914* (Bonn, 1998), especially 81–94. Critical of such views, Volker Ullrich, "Ein Weltkrieg wider Willen? Der Streit der Historiker über den Kriegsausbruch 1914 geht in eine neue Runde," in *Die Zeit* Nr. 2, 2 (January 2003).
28. Geoffrey Barraclough, *From Agadir to Armageddon: Anatomy of a Crisis* (New York, 1982).
29. Pansa to San Giuliano, 24 September 1911, in Archivio Storico del Ministero degli Affari Esteri (ASMAE), Cassette Verdi, Cassetta 4: "Per parlare francamente, il governo Imperiale sa benissimo che solo fino ad un certo punto e con qualche riserva esso potrebbe fare assegnamento sulla attiva cooperazione dell'Italia quando il casus foederis si presentasse. Ma se, poco probabile che ciò avvenga entro un termine calcolabile ad occhio nudo,—ed i recenti casi del Marocco hanno provato quali progressi abbia fatti la ripugnanza ad una guerra europea,—non c'è dubbio che ove questa disgraziatamente scopiasse tra la Francia e la Germania, sarebbe pur sempre un'immensa guarentigia per quest'ultima l'avere nell'Italia un'alleata, sia pure un po' tiepida e restia." Cited in Afflerbach, *Dreibund*, 715.
30. Luigi Albertini, *The Origins of the War of 1914*, 3 vols., Isabella M. Massey, trans., (London New York Toronto, 1952, 1953, 1957), vol. I, 431–32.
31. Afflerbach, *Dreibund*, 717.
32. See Manfred Tobisch, *Das Deutschlandbild der Diplomatie Österreich-Ungarns von 1908–1914* (Frankfurt am Main/ Berlin/ Bern u.a., 1994), 277–86 (summary), esp. p. 281.
33. On Kiderlen's opinions about a European war, see Ralf Forsbach, *Alfred von Kiderlen-Wächter (1852–1912): Ein Diplomatenleben im Kaiserreich*, 2 vols. (Göttingen, 1997) (Schriftenreihe der Historischen Kommission bei der Bayerischen Akademie der Wissenschaften, 59), esp. vol. 2, 512, 540, 682–699 (*Die unterschätzte Kriegsgefahr*), 773 (see there note 44). Flotow, 23 April 1912, in *Österreich-Ungarns Außenpolitik von der Bosnischen Krise 1908 bis zum Kriegsausbruch 1914. Diplomatische Aktenstücke des österreichisch-ungarischen Ministeriums des Äußern. Ausgewählt von Ludwig Bittner, Alfred F. Pribram, Heinrich Srbik und Hans Uebersberger. Bearbeitet von Ludwig Bittner und Hans Uebersberger, Band 1–9, Wien/Leipzig 1930 (Veröffentlichungen der Kommission für Neuere Geschichte Österreichs, Band 19–27)*, vol. 4, Nr. 3469.
34. Afflerbach, *Dreibund*, 719.
35. Joll, *Ursprünge*, 244.
36. J. J. Ruedorffer (i.e. Kurt Riezler), *Grundzüge der Weltpolitik in der Gegenwart* (Stuttgart and Berlin, 1914; unchanged new edition 1916).
37. Riezler, *Grundzüge*, 224, 229, "Die Bündnissysteme verdunkeln also jede Kalkulation und sind schon deshalb eminent friedenserhaltend."
38. Ibid., 221, "Kriege zwischen Großmächten werden nicht mehr um der durch sie zu erringenden Vorteile willen begonnen, sondern nur mehr aus Not. Der Fall der Not tritt für eine Großmacht nur mit sehr geringer Wahrscheinlichkeit ein, da kein Gegner da ist, der ein Interesse daran hat, diesen Fall der Not herbeizuführen. Es ist für die modernen Konflikte zwischen Großmächten durchaus typisch, daß keiner der beiden streitenden Teile ein Interesse an einer kriegerischen Lösung hat."
39. Mommsen, *Topos*, 29 (German version, 387).

40. Afflerbach, *Falkenhayn*, 77, with a letter from Falkenhayn to Arlabosse, 27 October 1911, in which he interpreted the second Moroccan crisis as a "bluff." And Kiderlen-Waechter wrote during the Balkan wars: "Das kennen Sie doch! Bluff, alles Bluff! Ich erlebe das nun zum dritten Male: Algeciras, Marokko und jetzt. Nur, jetzt versucht immer einer den andern im Bluffen zu übertrumpfen! Krieg gäbe es nur, wenn einer so mordsdämlich wäre, sich so zu verbluffen, daß er nicht mehr zurück kann und schießen muß. Für einen solchen Ochsen halte ich aber keinen der jetzt in Frage kommenden Staatsmänner!" Newspaper article from 11 January 11, 1913, cited by Forsbach, *Kiderlen-Wächter*, vol. 2, 773.
41. Wilsberg, *Terrible ami*, passim.
42. Joll, *Ursprünge*, 294.
43. Afflerbach, *Dreibund*, 769–85.
44. Martin Doerry, *Übergangsmenschen. Die Mentalität der Wilhelminer und die Krise des Kaiserreichs*, 2 volumes (Weinheim and München, 1986).
45. Thomas Rohkrämer, *Der Militarismus der "kleinen Leute." Die Kriegervereine im Deutschen Kaiserreich, 1871–1914* (München, 1990); Johannes Burkhardt, "Kriegsgrund Geschichte? 1870, 1813, 1756—historische Argumente und Orientierungen bei Ausbruch des Ersten Weltkrieges," in Johannes Burkhardt u.a.: *Lange und kurze Wege in den Ersten Weltkrieg* (München, 1996) (Schriften der Philosophischen Fakultäten der Universität Augsburg, Band 49), 9–86.
46. Afflerbach, *Dreibund*, 829f.
47. Afflerbach, *Falkenhayn*, 147.
48. Friedrich von Bernhardi, *Deutschland und der nächste Krieg* (Stuttgart, 1912). English translation, *Germany and the Next War* (New York, 1914).
49. "Ich teile übrigens die Ansicht von der Unausbleiblichkeit des Krieges nicht mehr. S.M. ist fest entschlossen, den Frieden unter allen Umständen zu erhalten und in seiner ganzen Umgebung befindet sich kein Mensch, der ihn von diesem gefährlichen Entschluß abzubringen vermochte. England ist ... so durch die inneren Verhältnisse in Anspruch genommen, dass es in absehbarer Zeit kaum versuchen kann, sich mit uns zu messen. An der verrückten Stimmung in Paris liegt die einzige Hoffnung begründet, dass es doch noch losgehen wird. Und sicherlich haben die Franzosen Recht, wenn sie die zum Teil vermeintliche, zum Teil sehr reelle Überlegenheit, die ihnen die Fortschritte im Fliegerwesen geben, ausnutzen wollen. Aber ob sie so von ihrem Erfolg überzeigt sind, dass sie ohne England anfangen werden, ist doch eine große Frage. Es fehlt ihnen am Ende jeder Grund. Der Kaiser kajoliert sie in dem instinktiven Gefühl, dass seiner Humanitätsidee von dort die größte Gefahr droht, wo er nur kann nach Leibeskräften. Unsere passive Politik aber wird ihnen keine Blöße bieten, wo sie einsetzen könnten. Nach menschlichem Ermessen ist also an einen Krieg nicht zu denken. Aber es kommt ja häufig, wie der Berliner sagt, erstens anders und zweitens als man denkt. Hoffen wir, dass er in diesem Fall Recht behält. Ich sage, hoffen wir, weil ich annehme, dass wir in the long run doch oben bleiben würden." Cited in Afflerbach, *Falkenhayn*, 99f.
50. Ibid., 100f.
51. Hopman, *Wilhelminer*, 43, 269. That Hopman's impression was accurate is shown also by Boris Barth, *Die deutsche Hochfinanz und die Imperialismen. Banken und Außenpolitik vor 1914* (Stuttgart, 1995).
52. This was of course due to a misunderstanding.
53. Afflerbach, *Falkenhayn*, 164; Afflerbach, *Wilhelm II*, 133.
54. Winston Churchill, another proponent of war, had a similar moment of crisis at the end of July 1914. Allegedly he reflected on suicide after the moderate Serbian reply to the Austrian ultimatum, and said, "If war can be avoided, I lived for nothing." I have not been able to verify this anecdote in any of the established Churchill biographies. It derives from the already mentioned manuscript, William Hayden Edwards, *Die Kriegsschuld der Nerven*, p. 30. Normally

Hayden worked quite meticuously. In the file of the BPH, the following remark is found, "Die Veröffentlichung nicht nachzuweisen; unbekannt, wie Manuskript mit kritischer Tendenz 1931 in das Hausarchiv gelangt ist." Support for the story comes from the letter that Churchill wrote to his wife on 28 July 1914, "Everything tends towards catastrophe and collapse. I am interested, geared up and happy. It is not horrible to be built like that? The preparations have a hideous fascination for me. I pray to God to forgive me for such fearful moods of levity." In Randolph S. Churchill, *Winston S. Churchill, Volume II: Companion, Part 3: 1911–1914* (London, 1969), 1989.
55. Joll, *Ursprünge*, 306.
56. Mommsen, *Topos*, 24f.; James Joll, *1914 – the Unspoken Assumptions* (London, 1968), 24.
57. Joll, *Ursprünge*, 316.
58. Volker Ullrich, *Kriegsalltag* (Köln, 1982); Benjamin Ziemann, *Front und Heimat. Ländliche Kriegserfahrung im südlichen Bayern 1914–1923* (Essen, 1997).
59. Analyzing the expectations of war before 1914, the following historians stress the expectation of a short war: Gerhard Ritter, *Staatskunst und Kriegshandwerk: Das Problem des "Militarismus" in Deutschland*, 4 vols. (München, 1954–1968), 2, passim; L. L. Farrar, *The Short War Illusion: German Policy, Strategy, and Domestic Affairs August–December 1914* (Oxford, 1973); Detlev Bald, "Zum Kriegsbild der militärischen Führung im Kaiserreich," in Jost Dülffer, Karl Holl, eds., *Bereit zum Krieg: Kriegsmentalitäten im wilhelminischen Deutschland, 1890–1914* (Göttingen, 1986), 146–159. For doubts about this thesis of a short war illusion, see Lothar Burchardt, *Friedenswirtschaft und Kriegsvorsorge: Deutschlands wirtschaftliche Rüstungsbestrebungen vor 1914* (Boppard, 1968); Dieter Storz, *Kriegsbild und Rüstung vor 1914: Europäische Landstreitkräfte vor dem Ersten Weltkrieg* (Herford, 1992); Afflerbach, *Dreibund*, 823f. Hew Strachan balances these theories, with a tendency toward an expectation of a somewhat longer war in *The First World War: Volume I: To Arms* (Oxford, 2001), Chapter 11, "The Short-War Illusion," 1005–14.
60. Joll, *Ursprünge*, 282; Becker, *1914*, 286–91.
61. Bernhard Rosenberger, *Zeitungen als Kriegstreiber? Die Rolle der Presse im Vorfeld des Ersten Weltkrieges* (Köln Weimar Wien, 1998) (Medien in Geschichte und Gegenwart, Band 11), shows on 266–68 that during the July crisis, all newspaper articles, with only very limited exceptions of around 2 percent, were against war.
62. Mommsen, *Topos*; Rosenberger, *Zeitungen*; Joll, *Ursprünge*.
63. The limits of a policy of armaments control are shown by Jost Dülffer in his contribution in this volume. See also his book, *Regeln gegen den Krieg? Die Haager Friedenskonferenzen von 1899 und 1907 in der internationalen Politik* (Berlin/Frankfurt am Main/Wien, 1981). Regarding the peace movement in Germany, Roger Chickering, *Imperial Germany and a World without War: The Peace Movement and German Society, 1892–1914* (Princeton, 1975).
64. See Paul W. Schroeder, *The Transformation of European Politics 1763–1848* (Oxford, 1994); Afflerbach, *Dreibund*, 824.
65. Fritz Fellner, ed., *Schicksalsjahre Österreichs 1908–1919: Das politische Tagebuch Josef Redlichs, 1. Vol.: 1908–1914*, 2 vols., (Graz-Köln, 1953–1954) (Veröffentlichungen der Kommission für neuere Geschichte Österreichs, Band 39 und 40), vol. 1, diary entry from 17 October 1912.
66. Rosenberger, *Zeitungen*.
67. Rainer Lepsius, *Parteiensystem und Sozialstruktur: Zum Problem der Demokratisierung der deutschen Gesellschaft* (first 1966), in Gerhard A. Ritter ed., *Deutsche Parteien vor 1918* (Köln, 1973), 56–80.
68. Rosenberger, *Zeitungen*, 203.
69. E. M. Carroll, *Germany and the Great Powers 1866–1914: A Study in Public Opinion and Foreign Policy* (New York, 1940); Klaus Wernecke, *Der Wille zur Weltgeltung: Aussenpolitik und Öffentlichkeit im Kaiserreich am Vorabend des Ersten Weltkrieges* (Düsseldorf, 1970); A. Jux, *Der Kriegsschrecken des Frühjahrs 1914 in der europäischen Presse* (Berlin, 1929); Risto Ropponen, *Die russische Gefahr: Das Verhalten der öffentlichen Meinung Deutschlands und Österreich-Ungarns gegenüber der Aussenpolitik Russlands in der Zeit*

zwischen dem Frieden von Portsmouth und dem Ausbruch des Ersten Weltkriegs (Helsinki, 1976); J. F. Scott, *Five Weeks: The Surge of Public Opinion on the Eve of the Great War* (New York, 1973).
70. Rosenberger, *Zeitungen*, 272.
71. Ibid., 263.
72. Becker, *1914*, 139f.
73. Ibid., 131–36.
74. On war enthusiasm in summer 1914, see Roger Chickering's contribution in this volume.
75. Wolfgang J. Mommsen, *Der große Krieg und die Historiker: Neue Wege der Geschichtsschreibung über den Ersten Weltkrieg* (Essen, 2002), 12f.
76. Strachan, *War*, Chapter 2, "Willingly to War," 103–62; Jeffrey Verhey, *The Spirit of 1914: Militarism, Myth, and Mobilization in Germany* (Cambridge, 2000).
77. Theodor Heuss, *Erinnerungen 1905–1933* (Tübingen, 1963), 199.
78. Karl Alexander von Müller, *Mars und Venus: Erinnerungen 1914–1919* (Stuttgart, 1954), 17f.
79. *New York Times*, 5 August 1914.
80. Cited in Kurt Zentner, *Kaiserliche Zeiten: Wilhelm II. und seine Ära in Bildern und Dokumenten* (München, 1964), 192.
81. The best example is Ullrich, "Weltkrieg." Fritz Fischer, *Wir sind nicht hineingeschliddert: Das Staatsgeheimnis um die Riezler-Tagebücher. Eine Streitschrift* (Reinbek, 1983).
82. Mommsen, *Krieg*, 10 f. Also Hobsbawm, *Age*, 310, finds the war guilt question somehow banal: "If we are interested in why a century of European peace gave way to an epoch of world wars, the question whose fault it was is as trivial as the question whether William the Conqueror had a good legal case for invading England is for the study of why warriors from Scandinavia found themselves conquering numerous areas of Europe in the tenth and eleventh centuries."
83. Joll, *Ursprünge*, 276.
84. Mommsen, *Topos*, 31. (German translation: Mommsen, *Nationalstaat*, 390). Original in *Verhandlungen des Reichstages*, vol. 268, 7730 C.
85. Jürgen Lampe et al., eds., *Diesem System keinen Mann und keinen Groschen. Militärpolitik der revolutionären deutschen Arbeiterbewegung 1830–1917* (Berlin, 1990). An example of a highly-tactical use of anti-war propaganda was Bebel's advice of September 1911, "not to shoot too early" (das Pulver nicht zu früh [zu] verschießen) and to use the Moroccan crisis "as good publicity in the upcoming elections" (werbewirksam in der bevorstehenden Reichstagswahl) (325). A highly-tactical motive seemed also to lie behind Rosa Luxemburg's writing that suggested it was the duty of Social Democracy "not to calm down public opinion, but to agitate it and to warn against the dangers of today's world politics. We should not count on the peace interests of some capitalists, but only on the resistance of the enlightened working class as a peace factor." (nicht die öffentliche Meinung zu beruhigen, sondern umgekehrt, sie aufzurütteln und vor den in jedem solchen Abenteuer der heutigen Weltpolitik schlummernden Gefahren zu warnen. Nicht auf die Friedensinteressen irgendeiner Kapitalistenclique, sondern lediglich auf den Widerstand der aufgeklärten Volksmassen als Friedensfaktor geziemt es uns, zu rechnen" (326f.).
86. Lampe, *System*, 317.
87. Joll, *Ursprünge*, 276. A good example is the final resolution of the International Socialist Congress in Stuttgart, 18–24 August 1907, in, Lampe, *System*, 302f.
88. Georges Haupt, "War and Revolution in Lenin", in Georges Haupt: *Aspects of International Socialism 1871–1914* (Cambridge, 1986), 132–53.
89. Habsbawm, *Age of Empire*, 304.
90. Becker, *1914*, 125. ("Comment expliquer que la guerre, tant de fois prévue, prédite depuis 1905, quand elle éclata dans l'été 1914, parut tomber sur le monde comme une avalanche?") Also "Lenin may not have anticipated … the sudden outbreak of war in Europe…," see Haupt, *War*, 145.
91. Robert Wohl, *The Generation of 1914* (Cambridge, MA 1979), 211, had a similar thought, although his whole argumentation goes in a different direction. He wrote: "War among the major

European powers seemed both inevitable (because of Germany's determination to dominate the continent and challenge England's control of the world's seas and markets) and impossible (because of the complex economic interrelationships that bound the great powers to each other and made the prosperity of one dependent on the prosperity of all). This was the paradox that defined European international relations between 1900 and 1914."

92. Wohl, *Generation,* 212.
93. Afflerbach, *Dreibund,* 831. "Ich werde es also für ein wahres Glück halten, wenn es zum Kriege mit Serbien kommt. Entwickelt sich daraus die europäische Konflagration, so wird mir dies beweisen, dass dieselbe in der Luft lag, früher oder später bei irgend einem Anlasse doch gekommen wäre, und da unterliegt es wohl keinem Zweifel, dass für den Dreibund der heutige Moment ein günstigerer ist als ein späterer."
94. Ibid., 811.
95. On Wilhelm II's nervous breakdown at the outbreak of war, see Afflerbach, *Kaiser,* 14f.
96. Mommsen, *Topos,* 380.
97. Thomas Mann, *What is German?* in *The Atlantic Monthly,* May 1944, 82.

Chapter 10

Unfought Wars
The Effect of Détente before World War I

Friedrich Kießling

Victor Klemperer, the German scholar of Romance studies, is famous mostly due to his diaries from the Third Reich. But Klemperer, born in 1881, kept a diary even before 1933. On 30 July 1914, two days before Germany declared war on Russia, thus launching World War I, the 32-year-old wrote: "I still believe that finally peace will be kept in what is real Europe. Everyone will mobilize and then stop, and after that they will get on with each other, though growling."[1] Even in his memoirs, which were written some decades later, Klemperer reports that his "convictions of the impossibility of a European war" had "not been seriously shaken for several days" even after Austria had declared war on Serbia on 28 July.[2] German novelist Thomas Mann wrote in a famous letter to his brother Heinrich in the first week of the war, "Still I feel as if I am dreaming—but now it seems as if one has to feel ashamed for not having thought that it might happen and for not having seen that the disaster was to come."[3] Moreover, we also know the surprise of the European peace movement—the minor German movement included—at the outbreak of war in 1914.

It would be easy to cite more examples—and certainly not only in the German case. There is a mass of evidence that many contemporaries all across Europe were surprised by the outbreak of war in August 1914. Yet, most historians have found this reaction difficult to understand. In retrospect, developments in the years before 1914 seemed only too obviously to have been leading to war. One international crisis followed another, as the European powers built up armaments on land and sea as fast as their finances permitted. Militarism, nationalism, and a growing "war mentality" set the tone for public opinion. There seemed no cause for contemporaries to have been taken unawares.

Nevertheless, in many cases, this apparent insouciance was not at all due to naiveté, ignorance of the real situation, or the general holiday atmosphere of July 1914. Quite the opposite, many people were absolutely aware of how dangerous the international situation had become. The fact that they still did not believe war would come makes the matter even more perplexing. Such sentiments should keep us from regarding astonishment at the events of 1914 as being merely a historical curiosity.

Several reasons for this optimism (which seems so strange in retrospect) may be stated. Among them were the expectations of the likely dimensions of a general war. Today we know that the horrors of modern warfare between the European Great Powers were widely discussed before 1914. For example, the British Secretary of State for Foreign Affairs, Sir Edward Grey, wrote in his memoirs that foreboding about what an unprecedented disaster such a conflict would represent had been increasingly depressing for him. In 1914 itself he suggested that this thought "had, in the difficult years from 1905 till now, made the Great Powers recoil from pressing anything to the point of war."[4] In addition, the fact that the last war between the Great Powers in Europe had taken place some forty years before—and that even the Franco-Prussian War of 1870–71 had not been a general conflict—certainly played a role. Meanwhile, the idea of a war between the Great Powers seemed fantastic. As Eric Hobsbawm put it: In the years before 1914, "there had been a lot of writing on the war but nobody had really been ready to believe it."[5] Finally and most relevant for this chapter, the optimism of many people rested on certain developments in the international politics of the pre-war period, which contemporaries considered manifestations of a détente.

In the following essay, it is this tendency toward détente that I would like to examine in more detail. What were its dimensions? What motives lay behind it? How was it perceived and what were the implications for our interpretation of the outbreak of war in 1914? In the following pages, I will first outline the characteristics of international détente before 1914. Then, I will investigate the significance of this détente in the history of international relations and more particularly in the origins of World War I. Because détente was an international political phenomenon, the perspectives of all the leading European powers should be included.[6] Nevertheless, in various respects the German example is of particular interest, and will therefore be considered especially closely.

I. Great Power Détente before 1914: Definition and Extent

First, we must establish the terminology: before 1914, détente was possible between Austria-Hungary and Great Britain, Austria-Hungary and Russia, or France and

Germany.[7] The term was not normally applied to developments within the two diplomatic camps (the Triple Entente on the one hand, and the Dual—alternatively the Triple Alliance—on the other). A number of terms denote the phenomenon, among them "rapprochement," "improvement," "better understanding," or in German "Annäherung" and "Entspannung." Nevertheless, the expression most often used internationally—and the most precise term for diplomats and politicians—was détente. The term was used with reference to improvements in relations between powers belonging to different camps (or between the two camps as a whole) below the level of agreements of greater political significance. A further crucial aspect of détente was that diplomats and politicians saw it as a process. Thus, détente was more than just crisis management. Indeed, it could be seen—although not invariably—as the starting point for an entente.[8]

Within this context it is very important to realize that détente before 1914 was not a matter of simply a few isolated cases in a limited timeframe, represented primarily by the well-known relaxation of tension between Britain and Germany. On the contrary, phenomena of détente were discernible across the gamut of relationships *between* the European Great Powers in different diplomatic camps. Between 1911 and 1914, for example, Austro-Hungarian political leaders made several attempts to improve relations with Great Britain and similar attempts can be observed in relations between Austria-Hungary and Russia.[9] In the autumn of 1912, diplomats sounded out the possibilities for convergence and cooperation between the tsarist empire and the Hapsburg monarchy in the Balkans.[10] On the multilateral plane, the years 1912–13 in particular witnessed various efforts at détente. Especially important was the famous London Ambassadors' conference from December 1912 to August 1913 during the two Balkan Wars, which succeeded in getting representatives of the six Great Powers of the two European blocs to meet together around one table.[11] Moreover, further multilateral conferences of ambassadors took place in St. Petersburg and in Constantinople.

As regards the German Reich, the most prominent initiatives for détente were certainly those directed toward Great Britain. In February 1912, the British Secretary of State for War, Lord Haldane, visited Berlin for political and naval talks. In 1913 and in 1914, two colonial agreements regarding the Portuguese colonies and the Baghdad Railway were initialed. At the London Conference of ambassadors, Anglo-German cooperation played a major role.[12] For German foreign policy, however, détente also had more than one facet. The German-Russian summits at Potsdam in November 1910 and at Baltic Port in July 1912 must also be counted as détente initiatives, as should contacts with the French government. In the spring and summer of 1913, Berlin and Paris made two arrangements for the quiet, bilateral settlement of minor incidents between them. In February 1914 they initialed an agreement over railroad building in Turkey.[13] Thus, détente played a role in practically every aspect of the country's relations with the Triple Entente powers during the last years before the outbreak of war.

II. Perceptions

Even more than listing examples of détente, it is crucially important to consider contemporary perceptions of the phenomenon. Thus, when analyzing diplomatic crises, the arms race, or bellicose nationalism before World War I, one should not forget the fact that contemporaries were also quite aware of the dangers of such developments. As regarded politico-military alignments, the situation had completely changed after the end of the nineteenth century. On the eve of World War I, two political-military blocs, laden with weapons, confronted one another. On the one hand was the French-Russian-British Triple Entente; opposing it was the Triple Alliance, despite doubts about Italy.[14] The perils arising from this situation were evident to contemporaries long before the summer of 1914. In fact, the alliance system did not improve the member states' security. Just the opposite was true: because cabinets looked for solidarity from the other members of their blocs, the number of possible conflicts that each state might be involved in actually expanded. Increasingly governments became entangled in their partners' struggles. This aspect of the pre-1914 "security dilemma" turned out to be abundantly evident after 1911.[15] Repeatedly, international crises, however restricted at first, seemed to threaten a general European war.

In these circumstances, it is not surprising that apparent or real efforts at détente were regular occurrences. They were noted not only in the press, where reports of them appeared frequently, but also by politicians and diplomats, who all over Europe were suspiciously eyeing one another and were constantly ready to check their counterparts' statements for evidence of "détente offers" to themselves or others. Thus the visit of a Russian Grand Duke to Vienna at the beginning of 1912 prompted a debate in the British Foreign Office on the possibility and the implications of an Austro-Russian détente.[16] Count Thurn, the Austro-Hungarian ambassador in St. Petersburg, interpreted a number of brief remarks uttered by several of his Russian partners in conversation as a "long-term initiative for making the bilateral relationship closer" which was "unmistakable,"[17] and he interpreted certain polite phrases by the Tsar as an "announcement of great political significance" which indicated a wish for détente.[18] However, symptoms of détente were more than only noted; sometimes governments tried to profit for their own purposes from the excitement that rumors of détente always caused. During the Balkan wars, in Austro-Russian relations this was true for the spectacular delivery of a handwritten letter from Emperor Franz Joseph to Nicholas II by a special envoy at the beginning of 1913.[19] From the perspective of the substantive political issues, things had already improved by this point. The letter's purpose was merely to display Austro-Russian détente to the world (and to public opinion in the two countries).

Perceptions of détente varied in the German context too and from time to time all governments tried to profit from rumors of détente. Thus, in the triangular relationship between Germany, France, and Russia, gestures of good will were engineered repeatedly in order to demonstrate or to counteract signs of détente. Before Wilhelm II met the Tsar at Baltic Port in July 1912, the French Ambassador hastened to see Nicholas II. Some weeks later, the French Prime Minister came to Russia, and the German Ambassador provided himself with an audience with the Russian monarch just after the Premier's visit. On both occasions, the press reacted as intended.[20] One and a half years later, the German government was confronted with supposed signs of an Austro-French détente. German diplomats reacted nervously when at the end of 1913 and the beginning of 1914 talks took place between Austrian and French banks. Berlin quickly interpreted these economic talks as having political significance and warned Vienna against rapprochement with Paris. The argument was that such action would play the game of the Dual Alliance's diplomatic opponents.[21] But vice versa, the government in Berlin was repeatedly subjected to criticisms from Vienna, alleging that Germany's policy of détente toward the Triple Entente was a betrayal of common interests. Especially revealing in this regard was a confidential memorandum by Count Szápáry (Sektionschef at the Austrian Ministry of Foreign Affairs and later ambassador to Russia) dating from autumn 1912, in which he saw the "foundations" of the Dual Alliance as being endangered by Germany's policy toward Russia.[22] In May 1914, he again criticized the "new German policy of conflict-free arrangement" (neu-deutsche Politik der streitlosen Auseinandersetzung), which he said affected Austrian interests.[23] Now German policy toward Great Britain too was the focus of criticism.

Thus, Austrian official observers interpreted German overtures toward Russia or Great Britain not as isolated instances but rather as a major aspect of German foreign policy, i.e. of a policy of détente. Other observers saw matters in a similar way. For many people, détente was an important aspect of international relations. The French President acknowledged the "harmonious interaction of the powers" and the "trustful atmosphere thereby created" during the Balkan crisis.[24] In January 1914, Szápáry spoke of a "general tendency towards détente,"[25] the British Under-Secretary of State for Foreign Affairs, Sir Arthur Nicolson, commented several times on the great international calm and the powers' wish for peace.[26] On Germany's side, similar judgments—confidential and public—may be cited. In May 1914, the State Secretary for Foreign Affairs, Gottlieb von Jagow, spoke in the Reichstag of progress concerning "general détente."[27] Since the Balkan Wars, his diplomats had repeatedly reported on the wish for peace in Europe.[28] In April 1914, the publisher and historian Emil Daniels likewise spoke of an "era of détente."[29] To express the outcome in a different way: Before 1914, détente had become a readily available interpretative template that determined readings of international relations.

III. Motivations and Expectations

By now it should be clear that, given the prevalence of this view, it did not matter whether such interpretations corresponded with the reality. But what were the motives for the real attempts to ease international tension? Here again we can find a wide range of answers. There were economic motives,[30] as well as the personal ambitions of particular diplomats,[31] and there were genuine desires to strengthen peace. Doubtless too, a number of European politicians tried to extricate themselves from the "security dilemma." The imperative was to keep the system of alignments sufficiently flexible by keeping open a channel to the other side in case of crises, despite the continuing polarization between the respective blocs. The British Secretary of State repeatedly spoke publicly in favor of such a strategy, arguing that "separate diplomatic groups need not necessarily be in opposing diplomatic camps." This was, for example, what he stated in a speech in the House of Commons in July 1912.[32] In such cases, today's political science speaks of a détente on the basis of the existing structure of relations.[33] But détente could also be motivated by tactical considerations. On the one hand, new leverage might be achieved against one's own ally; on the other hand, détente might weaken the opposite camp. This variety of motivations can be easily demonstrated by examining the German case, with one peculiarity: for Berlin, tactical considerations became especially important.

The starting point of the German policy of détente before 1914 was the second Moroccan crisis in 1911. When the German Reichskanzler Bethmann Hollweg and the British Secretary of State for Foreign Affairs started afterwards to consult each other beforehand on their speeches to their parliaments,[34] this was simply a way for both men to get their countries' mutual relations back on to an even keel. In German-French relations, the situation was similar. Here too, both sides were mainly interested in reducing the danger of war. When in September 1912 the follow-up talks between both countries on the Morocco agreement were concluded, one German diplomat was already satisfied by the fact that the talks had not caused any further frictions.[35] Besides avoiding war and a general wish for reestablishing "normal"[36] relations, another motivation must be emphasized in the German case. Tactical calculations concerning the alliances particularly centered on relations with Great Britain and Russia. The goal was to improve the alliance situation of the Reich. Thus, after the German-Russian summit conference at Baltic Port the German State Secretary for Foreign Affairs, Alfred von Kiderlen-Wächter, complained that the common communiqué (about which he had not been consulted) had been too reassuring for other governments. Evidently, Kiderlen-Wächter would have preferred to cause mistrust in the opposing camp through an ostentatious German-Russian agreement.[37] German policy toward Great Britain aimed even more at improving Berlin's alliance situation and not simply at reducing tension. After the Haldane mission had failed, the advocates of seeking détente with London—of course there were also opponents—still wanted to base relations with Great Britain on a new more stable and stronger foundation, now through agreements concerning colonial matters.

Was such an objective aggressive? Probably not, or at least not necessarily. This policy of détente did not mean preparing for a war in the sense of purposefully forcing Great Britain into neutrality if war broke out.[38] Yet, there was of course a hope of calling into question the existing alliances and ententes, and this was also something that the leaders of the German Reich wanted. However, this was not the only motivation, and ambitions for success in the field of colonial policy also played a role. Moreover, such views of alliance politics were not purely a German phenomenon: in some instances, they were also evident elsewhere, as in French policy toward Austria-Hungary or on the part of the British Ambassador in Vienna, Sir Fairfax Cartwright.[39]

Before turning to interpretation, a final aspect should be added to this analysis of the various dimensions of détente. Détente was not only widely recognized by contemporaries but also during the last years before 1914 it increasingly became a part of political expectations. Thus, during 1913 the experience of détente began to have an important influence on how the governments of the European powers perceived one another. In August 1913 Germany's Wilhelm II concluded that the Balkan crisis had revealed that "Europe's true interests" could be defended "by the two leading powers of the groups" and that "the wish for peace of all the Great Powers is much more important than had been expected and that alternative poses could be called a bluff."[40] The German Ambassador in Paris, von Schön, considered France to be peaceful after the middle of 1913 and explained this by citing, among other things, French policy in recent years which had shown a willingness to negotiate.[41] Regarding Russia, there was scope for similar perceptions: "Russia's entire behavior during the Balkan Wars showed how much war is feared here," a German diplomat reported from St. Petersburg in September 1913.[42]

More examples from other governments could be added. "Today's tendency for peace in Europe," the Austrian Ambassador to Russia wrote in January 1914, "also exists in the Russian empire";[43] "fortunately all Powers are anxious for peace," Sir Arthur Nicolson—one of the leading "Germanophobes" in the British Foreign Office—noted four months later.[44] This does not mean that in the Sarajevo crisis of July 1914 the European leaders considered an intervention by the opposing camp improbable. But opinion was quite ambivalent. Before 1914, besides a "topos of inevitable war"[45] there was also a "topos of repeatedly avoided war."[46]

IV. Détente and the Outbreak of World War I

Was détente successful before 1914? Did it have a chance of preventing World War I? In answer to these questions about the significance of pre-war détente, it must first be said that the major problems of European policy were not solved by the kind of détente described here. However, in many cases this was not the goal. We may recall Grey's statement that a situation should be created in which the diplomatic camps were not "opposing" each other, even while being "separate." Similarly, Germany's leaders tried to reestablish "normal" relations with France. If judged by such criteria, détente really seemed to achieve something in the years after 1911. From the viewpoint of contemporaries, in important respects the danger of war was decreasing. The diplomatic blocs still existed, but overall the situation seemed to have calmed down. At least in the field of German-British and German-French relations the immediate danger of war had largely disappeared by the spring of 1914. "Even if the two groups of powers themselves continue to exist and this system remains a factor in dealing with European problems," the Austrian Minister of Foreign Affairs, Count Berchtold, commented on the situation in April 1914, "in this field a 'certain easing of tension' can be felt."[47]

With the advantage of hindsight, any judgment must be much more skeptical. Though the danger of war between Germany and France or Germany and Great Britain was indeed diminishing after 1911, as regarded German-Russian and Austrian-Russian relations all efforts at détente had failed. Even more important were the structural problems that détente had to contend with. The Anglo-French and the Anglo-Russian settlements of 1904 or 1907 provided the major historical precedent, which was the beacon for détente initiatives during the final pre-war years. But in those instances, an entente had followed détente. Moreover, in the changed international scene precisely this development was a problem for every indication of détente, no matter how small. Every time an improvement in relations between two governments in opposing blocs was observed, all the other powers asked themselves if détente would again be followed by an entente and therefore whether the existing alignments were endangered.[48] As it was conventionally implemented, the policy of détente was bound to fail under the weight of such suspicions, but a new practice of détente—which Grey's wording envisaged—did not (or could not) yet assert itself.

An additional problem was that, except in isolated instances, governments planned and carried out détente initiatives without public knowledge or input, or even excluded public opinion by means of the "old diplomacy." In the conditions of foreign policy at the beginning of the twentieth century, when public opinion was playing an ever-increasing role, precisely this factor endangered the success of détente. Even so, diplomats and politicians were unable—or unwilling—to change their traditional political style.[49] Thus in Germany, ironically the leaders of the Reich would not permit the publication of their 1913 colonial agreements with Great Britain (originally concluded to improve relations), as they feared a public outcry and further damage to Anglo-German détente.[50]

But my main interest is not in answering the hypothetical question of whether détente could have prevented the war (if it had been implemented differently or if it had been allowed more time to work), and Crampton's term "hollow détente," which he used to characterize the German-British relationship before World War I, is also inapplicable to this analysis as set out thus far.[51] To concentrate on assessing the success of pre-1914 détente does not permit a full examination of its significance.

Instead, for the interpretation of détente in pre-war Europe it must be borne in mind that the international system before 1914 was still not a system of solid diplomatic camps based on clear ideological distinctions or—regarding the Triple Entente—on long-lasting alliances. It was still a system in transformation that can be best described as an "unstable system of blocs." The crucial point is that contemporaries did not consider "important alliances to be so strong as historians have considered them in retrospect."[52] Viewed in this light, détente proves to have been an integral factor in pre-war international systems. In other words: to describe and to explain the history of international relations on the eve of World War I we need détente.

On the one hand, there was great insecurity in international politics during the last years of peace. To an extent that seems paranoid to the modern viewer, the actors followed other governments' every move, or every rumored move. In particular, this can be shown with the perception of real or apparent symptoms of détente. Several examples have already been mentioned. The Germans became nervous because an Austrian and a Russian group of banks were talking to one another. The British Ambassador in Vienna ascribed far-reaching implications to the length of the visit of a Russian Grand Duke, just as his colleagues in the Foreign Office and elsewhere feared the specter of a renewed German-Austrian-Russian alliance of the three emperors.[53] In addition, the European press used even the smallest incident as an opportunity to speculate about a "renversement des alliances." Indeed, reports of détente kept alive the thought of alternatives to the existing alignments. Repeatedly, the German position was the focus of such hopes and fears. The latent anxiety at the Foreign Office about again losing the connection with St. Petersburg, which was so vital for the British Empire, centered on the state of German-Russian relations. In both Paris and Vienna, the improvement of relations between Berlin and London was viewed with increasing distrust, and eventually the annoyance felt was clearly articulated.

At this point, it becomes clear that détente and its perceptions before 1914 must be considered not only as a symptom of the state of relations between the powers, but also as a factor contributing in its own right to the deterioration of the international situation. Détente not only highlighted the instability and nervousness in Europe, but actually contributed to them. Thus, governments felt obliged to react to their own partners' uneasiness. The German government did so by communicating a compilation to the Vienna diplomats, which summed up all the cases when it had supported the Hapsburg monarchy in Balkan policy.[54] During their constant arguments with the German Ambassador in London, Fürst von Lichnowsky, over the appropriate policy toward Great Britain, Jagow and Bethmann-Hollweg repeatedly referred to the necessity to consider the interests of Austria-Hungary in order to counterbalance Anglo-German détente.[55] Moreover, when the Austrian Sektionschef Forgách was visiting Berlin in September 1913, Jagow tried to convince him that German-British détente was also useful for Vienna. Jagow did not succeed, and Austrian protests continued to pour in.[56] On the Triple Entente side, it must be borne in mind that between Britain and France and Britain and Russia, no formal alliances existed. From a political point of view, there were only the colonial agreements of 1904 and 1907 respectively. Thus, as each political problem appeared, the inter-connections between colonial and European policy had to be reaffirmed. Furthermore, a German-British colonial agreement might have been more difficult to achieve than the ententes of 1904 and 1907 had been. Under these circumstances, each Anglo-German understanding, no matter how unimportant, potentially threatened the existence of the Triple Entente and accordingly Paris and St. Petersburg constantly voiced their uneasiness about British-German talks or cooperation in colonial or Balkan matters. In this way, détente was inseparable from the sources of international tension and—being confronted with their partners' complaints—more and more governments were forced to demonstrate bloc solidarity somewhere else. Détente was an integral factor in international relations before 1914 and it was widely recognized by contemporaries. It is now time to consider its influence on the July Crisis.

It is likely that in the spring of 1914, the British government was the only government that really envisaged repeating the methods of crisis management of previous years in the case of a new confrontation. Although in this sense British policy in the July Crisis reflected the influence of the détente process,[57] in Germany and Austria-Hungary[58] matters were rather different.

There has been prolonged debate over why the German leaders pursued so dangerous a course in the summer of 1914, when compared to the other crises of the pre-war period.[59] I think the history of détente may contribute to answering this question. For if in the spring of 1914, the Berlin decision makers reviewed developments over previous years, they would have seen a double image. On the one hand, there had been serious international crises, the arms race had begun another round, and aggressive nationalism was gaining popularity all over Europe. Yet on the other, general war had repeatedly been avoided; from Berlin's viewpoint, governments had proven their willingness to work at détente and keeping the peace. The Balkan Wars in particular, when Europe had escaped a general conflagration against all expectations, seemed to be prime evidence of this. The continent had become used to danger—and to passing it by. As early as after the second Moroccan crisis, Alfred Fried, the Austrian pacifist and chairman of the German peace movement, wrote that the "tally of unfought wars" had been increased by a "new, highly important case."[60] Later, at the beginning of 1914, the previously mentioned conservative publisher and historian, Emil Daniels, remarked that the Balkan Wars had shown that "at the moment the ruling powers of the great states were all working towards European peace."[61] Among decision makers after the Balkan crisis, not only those British politicians and diplomats who until then had been skeptical now considered the German leaders peaceful, but also in Berlin in the second half of 1913, the conclusion was drawn that besides Great Britain,

France and Russia too did not want war. But, of course, there were also contraindications, particularly during the weeks and months before Sarajevo. Rumors of British-Russian naval talks had reached the German capital. Despite all efforts, the diplomatic-military situation of the Reich was menaced by further deterioration, the détente achieved with Great Britain in particular was endangered,[62] and Russia also seemed to have become more threatening.[63] Altogether, in 1914 both aspects—tension and détente—suggested to the Reich leaders a policy of aggressive deterrence verging on full-fledged war, which then influenced their calculations during the July Crisis. The perceived impending deterioration of Germany's international position made for a new and even more powerful attempt to break through the "encirclement" of the Reich. At the same time, the experiences of the recent "era of détente" seemed still valid and Berlin hoped to profit from it perhaps for the last time. Thus, in July 1914 within a calculation based on the perception of tension and of relaxation of tension, détente and the supposed willingness of the Triple Entente powers to keep the European peace facilitated the German (and Austrian) decision to run a high-risk policy on the brink of general war. Though threatened, in Berlin's viewpoint, détente in summer 1914 provided the opportunity to take strong diplomatic action without general conflagration as its necessary outcome.

To be sure, such an approach was the complete antithesis of an active policy of détente. From Berlin's point of view, in the summer of 1914 détente was the other side's business. Additionally, Austrian allegations of a sell out of Hapsburg interests as the price of the détente process were still ringing in German ears. This is another link between the pre-war détente policy and the July Crisis. Maybe the most notorious consequence of this is the comment by Wilhelm II on Tschirschky's report from 30 June, in which the ambassador said he was warning the Austrians against overhasty steps. "That's very stupid!" the emperor wrote. "How to react is Austrians' business only. If it fails, in the end it will be said that Germany had not wanted action!! Tschirschky should stop that nonsense! The Serbians must be sorted out, and I mean soon."[64]

Thus, investigating a phenomenon like détente may contradict the historian's instinct to concentrate first on the more obvious factors of escalation in causing World War I. But studying the role of détente can open the way for new interpretative approaches. These new approaches do not impair the validity of previous views. No one would seriously deny the significance of militarism, a war mentality, or internal and international polarization. But, I think attempts to explain the war solely through these older views must be abandoned. Instead, the new complexity of our image of the outbreak of war in 1914 can enrich our understanding of that event. Taking both the signs of tension and those of détente into account carries conviction primarily in three respects. First, it allows a more precise description of the mechanisms of the international system before 1914, which remained an "unstable bloc-system" characterized by a high degree of nervousness even within the two diplomatic camps. Second, it enables us to integrate the different scenarios employed during the July Crisis by the Austrian and particularly by the German leaders, the often-described mixture of optimism and pessimism.[65] And last but not least, it enables us in part to demonstrate what made the crisis so dangerous exactly in that fateful summer of 1914.[66] Thus, the seemingly irrational, volatile, or rather cavalier attitude of the German leaders can best be understood as expressing a juxtaposition of aggressive militarism, fear of being threatened, and hope for gaining profit from international détente for one last time.[67]

Such an interpretation would have another advantage—and with this, we return to the beginning—it would enable us to take up again the experiences of the contemporaries. In 1914, people also foresaw how dangerous the international situation had become. However, that war was near was something that many refused to believe until the end.

Conclusion

"So there will be armament and rearmament on all sides until one day one or other side will say: rather an end in terror than terror without end ... then the catastrophe comes. The twilight of the gods of the bourgeois world is in prospect." It was August Bebel, the leader of the German Social Democratic Party who spoke these rather gloomy words in the German Parliament in autumn 1911.[68] In the following year Friedrich von Bernhardi published his famous book *Germany and The Next War*, which culminated in statements such as: "There is no way in which we can avoid going to war for the sake of our position as a world power and ... we should not be concerned with postponing it for as long as possible, but rather should concentrate on bringing it about under the most favorable conditions possible."[69]

Clearly, not everyone was surprised by the war in 1914.[70] Besides hopes for lasting peace there had also been a widespread expectation of (and sometimes a wish for) a great war. As the quotations at the beginning of my essay indicate, it would be easy to find numerous examples of either viewpoint. But European society as a whole has only been mentioned in passing in this essay, and I have not tried to assess or to review the warlike and peaceful tendencies. Of course, this might also be a very worthwhile task—and one that will have to be done anyway. Nevertheless, acknowledging the coexistence of influences for peace on the one hand with a more warlike spirit on the other is crucial if we want to understand the situation in Europe before 1914. Furthermore, we must study not only the simultaneous occurrence of these tendencies, but also their interdependence and relative impact. Finally, it is possible to add some further general thoughts about the way in which we interpret the outbreak of war in 1914.

In recent historiography, our understanding of the history of World War I has also become more differentiated on other points of interpretation. The enthusiasm in Europe at the beginning of hostilities now seems more qualified, some of the bilateral relationships seem less antagonistic,[71] and even the image of Wilhelm II has become somewhat more positive;[72] more recent investigations of the image of war before 1914 have already been mentioned.[73] Altogether, these examples show that investigating phenomena such as détente before 1914 may prevent us from blundering into two possible traps that research has not always escaped. The first one I call the trap of monumentality, the second, the trap of linear causality.

World War I was *the* disaster in European history at the beginning of the twentieth century. Not everything, but overwhelmingly many things had changed by 1918. Yet the fact that World War I was such a monumental historical rupture should not mislead us into thinking that it must have had monumental causes. Because many historians have succumbed to this tendency, they have neglected to understand the period before 1914 on its own terms and have projected multiple developments that arose only during the war back into its prehistory. Usually, however, history is not so simple.

Thus, it would also be a mistake to restrict oneself to the factors apparently making for escalation when seeking the causes of the war. For example, the case of détente shows that steps intended to deescalate the situation could actually increase the risk of hostilities. As a result, in the international scenery of the early twentieth century détente was often counterproductive, and the influence of détente also contributed to the faulty calculations of the July Crisis. Hence, it is inadequate to pursue solely the seemingly compelling straight lines of investigation. Especially in analyzing the dichotomies of the pre-war situation, there are additional alternative interpretations that offer a much more satisfying complexity.

Notes

The essay is based on: Friedrich Kießling, *Gegen den "großen Krieg"? Entspannung in den internationalen Beziehungen 1911–1914* (Munich, 2002), and Friedrich Kießling, "Wege aus der Stringenzfalle. Die Vorgeschichte des Ersten Weltkriegs als 'Ära der Entspannung,'" *Geschichte in Wissenschaft und Unterricht* 55 (2004), 284–304. Thank you to Holger Afflerbach, Chad Fulwider, Herbert Sirois, and David Stevenson for comments and suggestions.

1. Victor Klemperer, *Curriculum vitae: Erinnerungen 1881–1918*, Walter Nowojski, ed., (Berlin, 1996), vol. 2, 177.
2. Ibid., 171.
3. Thomas Mann and Heinrich Mann, *Briefwechsel 1900–1949*, Hans Wysling, ed., enlarged edition (Frankfurt am Main, 1984), 131.
4. Sir Edward Grey, *Twenty-Five Years, 1892–1916*, vol. I (London, 1925), 302. On the image of war, mostly as perceived in Germany, see Jost Dülffer, "Die zivile Reichsleitung und der Krieg:

Erwartungen und Bilder 1890–1914," in *Gestaltungskraft des Politischen: Festschrift für Eberhard Kolb*, Wolfram Pyta and Ludwig Richter eds., (Berlin, 1998), 11–28. Stig Förster, "Der deutsche Generalstab und die Illusion des kurzen Krieges, 1871–1914: Metakritik eines Mythos," in *Lange und kurze Wege in den Ersten Weltkrieg: Vier Augsburger Beiträge zur Kriegsursachenforschung*, Johannes Burkhardt et al., eds. (Munich, 1996), 115–58.

5. Eric J. Hobsbawm, *The Age of Empire 1875–1914* (London, 1987), 303–04.
6. I.e. Austria-Hungary, Germany, Great Britain, France, and Russia. In the last years before 1914 Italy—still not wholly accepted as a great power by the others—had strong ties to both diplomatic camps and was of minor importance in the debate among contemporaries about détente that I will analyze here. For the role of Italy in international relations before 1914, see Holger Afflerbach, *Der Dreibund: Europäische Großmacht- und Allianzpolitik vor dem Ersten Weltkrieg* (Vienna, 2002).
7. In studies on the outbreak of World War I which mention détente in more detail, all in all the interpretation has dominated that though there were some symptoms of improvement, détente could not alter the general increase of tension. For example: A. J. P. Taylor, *The Struggle for Mastery in Europe, 1848–1918* (Oxford and New York, 1954), 518–20; Luigi Albertini, *The Origins of the War of 1914*, 3 vols. (London,1952–57), vol. I, 540; Dwight E. Lee, *Europe's Crucial Years: The Diplomatic Background of Wold War I, 1902–1914* (Hanover, NH, 1974), 336, 354; Klaus Hildebrand, *Das vergangene Reich* (Stuttgart, 1995), 292. Emphasizing peaceful tendencies before 1914: Jean-Jacques Becker, *La première guerre mondiale* (Paris, 1985), 140; and (very far reaching) Niall Ferguson, *The Pity of War* (London, 1998). Recently Klaus Hildebrand has particularly stressed the role of détente in international relations before 1914, Hildebrand, "*Staatskunst und Kriegshandwerk": Akteure und System der europäischen Staatenwelt vor 1914*, Friedrichsruher Beiträge, vol. 24 (Friedrichsruh, 2005).
8. On terminology see also, Gordon A. Craig and Alexander L. George, *Force and Statecraft. Diplomatic Problems of Our Time* (Oxford, 1983), 238–45.
9. Toward Great Britain mostly in the summer of 1912, e.g. dispatch to London 8 August 1912. *Österreich-Ungarns Außenpolitik von der Bosnischen Krise 1908 bis zum Kriegsausbruch 1914: Diplomatische Aktenstücke des österreichisch-ungarischen Ministeriums des Äußern*, selected by Ludwig Bittner et al., Ludwig Bittner and Hans Uebersberger, eds. 9 vols. (Vienna and Leipzig, 1930), vol. 4, no. 3674. (ÖUA vol., no.).
10. See e.g. ÖUA 4, 4063 and 4076.
11. Still valuable is Ernst Christian Helmreich, *The Diplomacy of the Balkan Wars 1912–1913* (Cambridge, MA, 1938).
12. On the German-British détente before 1914: Richard J. Crampton, *The Hollow Détente: Anglo-German relations in the Balkans, 1911–1914* (London, 1979). Michael Fröhlich, *Von Konfrontation zur Koexistenz: Die deutsch-englischen Kolonialbeziehungen in Afrika zwischen 1884 und 1914* (Bochum, 1990). Gregor Schöllgen, *Imperialismus und Gleichgewicht: Deutschland, England und die orientalische Frage 1871–1914* (Munich, 2000).
13. On Franco-German relations, emphasizing the détente aspect: Klaus Wilsberg, "*Terrible ami— aimable ennemi": Kooperation und Konflikt in den deutsch-französischen Beziehungen 1911–1914* (Bonn, 1998).
14. See also: Francis Roy Bridge, "Transformation of the European States System, 1856–1914," in *"The Transformation of European Politics, 1763–1848": Episode or Model in Modern History?* Peter Krüger and Paul W. Schroeder, eds., (Münster int. al., 2002), 255–72. Klaus Hildebrand, "Europäisches Zentrum, überseeische Peripherie und Neue Welt: Über den Wandel des Staatensystems zwischen Berliner Kongreß (1878) und dem Pariser Frieden (1919–20)," in *Historische Zeitschrift* 248 (1989), 53–94.
15. Klaus Hildebrand, "Julikrise 1914: Das europäische Sicherheitsdilemma. Betrachtungen über den Ausbruch des Ersten Weltkrieges," in *Geschichte in Wissenschaft und Unterricht* 36 (1985), 469–502.

16. Kießling, *Gegen den "großen Krieg,"* 81–83.
17. ÖUA 3, 3257.
18. Telegram from St. Petersburg, 14 January 1912, ÖUA 3, 3223.
19. E.g. ÖUA 4, 5789.
20. National Archives London, FO 371/1469, report from Paris, 8 July 1912 or Auswärtiges Amt, Politisches Archiv, R 2061, telegram from St. Petersburg, 8 August 1912.
21. *Die große Politik der europäischen Kabinette 1871–1914. Sammlung der Diplomatischen Akten des Auswärtigen Amtes.* Im Auftrag des Auswärtigen Amtes ed. by Johannes Lepsius int. al. 40 vol. (Berlin, 1922–27), vol. 37/II, no. 15138, report from Vienna, 2 February 1914. (GP vol., no.)
22. ÖUA 7, 9219.
23. Report from St. Petersburg, ÖUA 8, 9656.
24. Auswärtiges Amt, Politisches Archiv, R 7070, telegram, Paris, 21 February 1914.
25. ÖUA 7, 9219.
26. See Zara S. Steiner, *Britain and the Origins of the First World War* (Basingstoke and London, 1995), 215–217. (First edition 1977)
27. *Schulthess' Europäischer Geschichtskalender* 55 (1914), 281.
28. E.g. Auswärtiges Amt, Politisches Archiv, R 6908, report from Paris, March 1914. Ibid., R 10981, report from St. Petersburg, 6 September 1913.
29. Emil Daniels, "Rußland—Die Republik Nordepirus—Die innere Lage der Westmächte," in *Preußische Jahrbücher* 156 (April–June 1914), 167–84.
30. E.g. for the Austrian policy toward France, see ÖUA 3, 2954.
31. Concerning the German Reich, including the Counsellor at the embassy in Paris, Oscar Freiherr von der Lancken-Wakenitz, or Richard von Kühlmann, Counsellor at the embassy in London, should be mentioned. See Gerhard Keiper, *Biographische Studien zu den Verständigungsversuchen zwischen Deutschland und Frankreich am Vorabend des Ersten Weltkrieges* (Frankfurt am Main et al., 1997). Gregor Schöllgen, "Richard von Kühlmann und das deutsch-englische Verhältnis 1912–1914: Zur Bedeutung der Peripherie in der europäischen Vorkriegspolitik," in *Historische Zeitschrift* 230 (1980), 293–337.
32. Sir Edward Grey, *Speeches on Foreign Affairs 1904–1914* (London, 1931), 207.
33. Wilsberg, *"Terrible ami—aimable ennemi,"* 356. For a similar definition of détente regarding the Cold War, see Richard L. Stevenson, *The Rise and Fall of Detente: Relaxations of Tensions in US-Soviet relations, 1953–1984* (London, 1985), 10.
34. G. P. Gooch and Harold Temperley, eds., *British Documents on the Origins of the War 1898–1914*, 11 vols. (London, 1926–38), vol. 7, no. 657, 659, 663, 665, 666.
35. Auswärtiges Amt, Politisches Archiv, R 6970, report from Paris, 30 September 1912.
36. This term probably best describes in particular the German policy toward France before 1914.
37. Alfred von Kiderlen-Wächter, *Kiderlen-Wächter der Staatsmann und Mensch: Briefwechsel aus dem Nachlaß*, 2 vols., Ernst Jäckh, ed. (Berlin and Leipzig, 1924), vol. 2, 152.
38. To this most of all Imanuel Geiss, *Der lange Weg in die Katastrophe: Die Vorgeschichte des Ersten Weltkriegs 1815–1914* (Munich and Zürich, 1990), 260–61.
39. National Archives, FO 800/356, Nicolson Mss., Cartwright to Nicolson, 11 April 1912 and ibid. 800/357, 20 June and 19 July. Jean Bérenger, "Die Österreichpolitik Frankreichs von 1848 bis 1918," in *Die Habsburgermonarchie 1848–1918*, vol. VI, *Die Habsburgermonarchie im System der internationalen Beziehungen*, Adam Wandruszka and Peter Urbanitsch, eds. (Vienna, 1993), 491–538, see 532–38.
40. GP 36/I, 13781, telegram by Wilhelm II, 16 August 1913.
41. E.g. GP 39, 15657, report from Paris, 15 November 1913.
42. Auswärtiges Amt, Politisches Archiv, R 10981, report, 6 September 1913.

43. ÖUA 7, 9219.
44. Goschen to Grey, 4 May 1914, National Archives, FO 371/1990, minute Nicolson.
45. Wolfgang J. Mommsen, "The Topos of Inevitable War in Germany in the Decade before 1914," in *Germany in the Age of Total War: Essays in Honour of Francis Carsten*, Volker R. Berghahn and Martin Kitchen, eds. (London, 1981), 23–45.
46. Kießling, *Gegen den "großen Krieg,"* 306. For the broader context of "avoided wars" since 1856, see, Jost Dülffer et al.: *Vermiedene Kriege: Deeskalation von Konflikten der Großmächte zwischen Krimkrieg und Erstem Weltkrieg 1856–1914* (Munich, 1997); Stephan R. Rock, *Why Peace Breaks Out: Great Power Rapprochement in Historical Perspective* (Chapel Hill and London, 1989).
47. Graf Berchtold, addressing the Austrian delegation, 29 April 1914, *Stenographische Sitzungsprotokolle der Delegation des Reichsrates*, 46.–49. Session 1911–14. Vienna 1912–14, 49. Session, p. 3.
48. See Craig and George, *Force and Statecraft*, 240–42.
49. On this see (as an attempt at offering indications for describing a "diplomatic culture"), Friedrich Kießling, "Self-perceptions, the Official Attitude towards Pacifism, and Great Power Détente: Reflections on Diplomatic Culture before World War I," in *Decentering America: New Directions in Culture and International History*, Jessica Gienow-Hecht, ed. (New York and Oxford, forthcoming).
50. Richard Langhorne, *The Collapse of the Concert of Europe: International Politics 1890–1914* (New York, 1981), 105.
51. Crampton, *The Hollow Detente*.
52. Thomas Nipperdey, *Deutsche Geschichte 1866–1918*, vol. 2, *Machtstaat vor der Demokratie* (Munich, 1992), 697.
53. National Archives, Nicolson Mss., FO 800/353, Nicolson to Hardinge, 22 February 1912 and ibid. FO 371/1490, Buchanan to Grey, 21 February 1912.
54. Auswärtiges Amt, Politisches Archiv, R 14344, record, 15 September 1913.
55. On this controversy, GP 34/I, 12708, 12740 or 12763.
56. Auswärtiges Amt, Politisches Archiv, R 9016, records by von Jagow, 26 September 1913.
57. Additionally, now and then it has been pointed out that at the Foreign Office the crisis was probably underestimated in the beginning, due to the experience from the past years. See Michael Ekstein, "Some Notes on Sir Edward Grey's Policy in July 1914," *Historical Journal* 15 (1972), 321–24.
58. Indications in Friedrich Kießling, "Österreich-Ungarn und die deutsch-englischen Détentebemühungen 1912–1914," in *Historisches Jahrbuch* 116 (1996), 102–25. Günther Kronenbitter, "'Nur los lassen': Österreich-Ungarn und der Wille zum Krieg," in *Lange und kurze Wege in den Ersten Weltkrieg: Vier Augsburger Beiträge zur Kriegsursachenforschung*, Johannes Burkhardt et. al., eds. (Munich, 1996), 159–87. John Leslie, "Österreich-Ungarn vor dem Kriegsausbruch: Der Ballhausplatz in Wien aus der Sicht eines österreichisch-ungarischen Diplomaten," in *Deutschland und Europa in der Neuzeit: Festschrift für Karl Otmar von Aretin zum 65. Geburtstag*, Ralph Melville et al., eds., (Stuttgart, 1988), 661–84.
59. Standing for this and summing up, Stig Förster, "Im Reich der Absurden: Die Ursachen des Ersten Weltkrieges," in *Wie Kriege entstehen: Zum historischen Hintergrund von Staatenkonflikten*, Bernd Wegner ed.(Paderborn et al., 2000), 211–52. Richard F. Hamilton, ed., *The Origins of World War I* (Cambridge, 2003). Hildebrand, *"Staatskunst und Kriegshandwerk."*
60. Alfred Fried, "Das Marokkoabkommen," in *Die Friedens-Warte* 13 (1911), 313–15.
61. Emil Daniels, "Enver der Seraskier—Eine französische Stimme über den Zukunftskrieg," in *Preußische Jahrbücher* 155 (January–March 1914), 382–98.
62. Volker Ullrich, "Das deutsche Kalkül in der Julikrise 1914 und die Frage der englischen Neutralität," in *Geschichte in Wissenschaft und Unterricht* 34 (1983), 79–97.
63. On this, if a bit overstated, Thomas Lindemann, *Die Macht der Perzeptionen und Perzeptionen von Mächten* (Berlin, 2000).

64. *Julikrise und Kriegsausbruch 1914*, vol. I, Imanuel Geiss ed. (Bonn, 1976), 58–59. ("das ist sehr dumm! geht ihn gar nichts an, da es lediglich Österreichs Sache ist, was es hierauf zu thun gedenkt. Nachher heißt es dann, wenns schief geht, Deutschland hat nicht gewollt!! Tschirschky soll den Unsinn gefälligst lassen! Mit den Serben muß aufgeräumt werden, und zwar bald.")
65. See, Klaus Hildebrand, *Deutsche Außenpolitk 1871–1918* (Munich, 1994), 44. Johannes Burkhardt, "Kriegsgrund Geschichte? 1870, 1813, 1756—historische Argumente und Orientierungen bei Ausbruch des Ersten Weltkriegs," in *Lange und kurze Wege in den Ersten Weltkrieg*, Bukhardt et al., eds., 9–86, 36.
66. Holger Afflerbach urges such "situative" explanations. Holger Afflerbach, *Der Dreibund.*
67. In so far, my thoughts go along with the results of a number of colleagues, who recently worked out a differentiated image of the pre-war period. Besides the already mentioned work by Wilsberg, most of Joachim Radkau's work on the attitude of the German elite toward the war before 1914 should be mentioned. Joachim Radkau, *Das Zeitalter der Nervosität: Deutschland zwischen Bismarck und Hitler* (Darmstadt, 1998), see 407–46.
68. *Stenographische Protokolle der Verhandlungen des Reichstages*, vol. 268, 7730 C.
69. Friedrich von Bernhardi, *Deutschland und der nächste Krieg* (Stuttgart and Berlin, 1913), 125.
70. Both above-mentioned quotes were cited also in Mommsen, *The Topos of Inevitable War in Germany.*
71. Even between Germany and France. Besides Wilsberg, see Mark Hewitson, *National Identity and Political Thought in Germany: Wilhelmine Depictions of the French Third Republic 1890–1914* (Oxford, 2000).
72. Lothar Reinermann, *Der Kaiser in England: Wilhelm II. und sein Bild in der britischen Öffentlichkeit* (Paderborn et al., 2001).
73. Hobsbawm, *The Age of Empire.* (see footnote 5).

Chapter 11

"WAR ENTHUSIASM?"
PUBLIC OPINION AND THE OUTBREAK OF WAR IN 1914

Roger Chickering

"In August 1914 a powerful surge of war enthusiasm gripped the Germans." As he committed these words to paper in 1991, Thomas Nipperdey embraced practically every one of the myths that have surrounded the beginning of World War I in Germany. "National unity was a primal experience in a moment of threat and crisis," he wrote. "The war itself had something liberating about it; it offered escape from the stifling atmosphere of tensions, of middle-class respectability [*Bürgerlichkeit*], of class conflict. Hardly anyone could escape this mood, this 'experience' of August 1914."[1] The pressure of illness is perhaps the most charitable explanation for the great historian's credulity, for a large body of literature was available even then to demonstrate the untenability of these judgments. Since Nipperdey's death, this literature has continued to grow, to the point now that—in the German case at least—the public reaction to the outbreak of World War I has been so thoroughly and competently researched that it seems difficult to add much in a short essay. One point is worth emphasizing in the context of this volume, however. The dramatic scenes of the summer of 1914 ought to be understood in the light of their own political and cultural dynamics. They should not be taken as evidence that an inveterate German war enthusiasm made war probable or inevitable.

The remarks that follow first offer a brief review of the literature. They begin with some reflections on the historiography of "war enthusiasm" in 1914. They address in particular some of the enduring problems that have survived even into the recent critical literature. The essay then turns to an empirical case—which has itself been the subject of a fine recent study[2]—to offer some thoughts that might elucidate these problems.

The most striking feature in the historical literature on the popular attitudes toward the coming of the war is its imbalance. By a wide margin, the greatest portion of the studies have been devoted to public reactions in Germany—to the popular demonstrations that began with the announcement of the Austrian ultimatum to Serbia on 24 July, reached a peak with the declaration of mobilization a week later, then modulated into the rush of volunteers to the colors. The major anomaly in this literature is the monumental work of Jean-Jacques Becker, who carefully reconstructed public opinion in six French departments during the summer crisis of 1914.[3] Elsewhere, outside Germany, there is nothing comparable. Perhaps because an awareness of the situation's gravity developed only late in Britain, as armed intervention became likely during the first days of August, the state of research on public sentiment in this country has remained, as one scholar recently observed, "largely an unstudied problem."[4] The duration of popular awareness of the crisis has evidently not, however, dictated the disproportions in the historiography, for aside from several brief analyses, there is also a dearth of work on the dramatic, conflict-ridden events in Russia, and even less on popular attitudes in the Habsburg monarchy, where the crisis originated.[5] The war-guilt debate has doubtlessly contributed to the imbalance: the crowd scenes in Berlin and other German cities could be cited in evidence of long-building popular support for an aggressive war in Germany, while Becker's volume seemed conclusively to document the weakness of bellicose sentiment in France.

For Germany the work of Jeffrey Verhey is the place to start.[6] In addition to a thorough account of the public demonstrations in Berlin and other cities in late July and early August, Verhey presents a compelling analysis of why the German case has attracted such a large share of the interest. What he calls "the myth of the 'spirit of 1914'" began to take shape in Germany virtually the moment the war broke out. The crowd scenes became icons of a transcendent moment in German history, the triumph of national unity and resolve, the suspension of domestic strife, and the spontaneous birth of collective enthusiasm for a war of national defense. Images that were recorded in diaries, newspaper accounts, and photographs quickly gave way to oratory and learned exegesis from the country's leading scholars and intellectuals.[7] The myth of collective enthusiasm then guided German propaganda throughout the war, and its purchase on collective memory survived defeat in 1918. During the Weimar era the myth lived on. Popular enthusiasm in the summer of 1914 served at once as a fleeting moment of national fulfillment and as the *terminus a quo* in another myth—this one a narrative of wartime betrayal and subversion, whose culmination was the *Dolchstoss* in 1918. Verhey has suggested that the myth died in 1945, but a case can be made—with Nipperdey as a witness—

Illustration 11.1: Max Beckmann: *Der Kriegsausbruch*, 1914, Radierung, 19,8 × 24,8 cm. © SESAM, Paris, 1998.

that it lived on. It did so commonly either in the guise fashioned for it by Friedrich Meinecke, who wrote of the country's last, tragic moment of innocence in the summer of 1914, or on the more extravagant terms of some cultural historians, who have folded German war enthusiasm in that summer into a broader, European narrative of transcendence, conceived now as the collective abandonment of civilized constraints and reasoned argument, the triumph of primitivism, and the flight into modernity (or from it).[8]

These bold assertions have usually taken the writings and graphic art of the German expressionists as a litmus test of popular attitudes, but they are not supported by the findings of scores of historians, who have investigated popular reactions to the war more systematically in a variety of German venues.[9] These scholars have shown that enthusiasm for war was by no means universally shared, and was confined primarily to young males in the big cities. Studies of sentiments within other segments of urban populations, as well as in smaller towns and rural communities—among workers, women, and peasants—have disclosed a much more complex mix of attitudes. Reluctance, anxiety, panic, or opposition were more common than enthusiasm for military action—at least until the German declaration of mobilization on 1 August transformed war from a prospect into a fact.[10] Even then, however, the numbers of volunteers for the army have proved to be far fewer than the "myth" implied.[11] At the very least, these historical studies have thrown a shadow over comprehensive generalizations of any kind about popular attitudes before the war (even among German expressionists).[12] Consensus reigns, on the other hand, that once war was declared, there was practically no popular resistance to it in Germany—or anywhere else in Europe west of the Polish lands.

Still, despite all the attention that has been devoted to it, an air of hesitancy and inconclusiveness hovers over the question of popular responses in Germany and elsewhere to the outbreak of war. The conclusions of even the most substantial recent work leave doubts. The principal problem is that historians have remained committed to an agenda that was set by the German commentators who first framed the "myth of 1914." These observers were interested above all in questions of *"Gesinnung"*—a word that is difficult to translate from the German but implies convictions and character traits deep enough to motivate. Guided by this interest, early commentators interpreted the urban crowd scenes as revelations of fundamental attitudes in the German people, as evidence of a genuine *"nationale Gesinnung,"* which had long lain latent among the population, and had been activated in the supreme moment of crisis.

Although they were much more careful about generalizing from their evidence, later historians engaged in a similar exercise. They, too, sought to analyze crowd behavior in order to draw conclusions about basic popular attitudes and motivations. As it did in 1914, this goal challenged them to draw psychological conclusions—generalizations about individual motivations—from sources that make this a risky undertaking at best. Becker's study of French opinion was the most impressive attempt to meet the challenge, but it laid bare the methodological difficulties. His conclusions rested in significant part on an analysis of notes compiled by French school teachers, whom the ministry of public education instructed in September 1914 to record their perceptions of attitudes that they had witnessed as the crisis developed in July and August. The problems in Becker's strategy were several. One was the potential political bias of his sources, particularly as these teachers looked back from the fall of 1914 on the events of the summer. Becker's approach begged the question whether the French school teachers' perceptions represented in principle any more an unbiased guide to popular attitudes than the writings of Rudolf Eucken, Johann Plenge, Ulrich von Wilamowitz-Moellendorff, and the countless other German professors who were likewise quick to record their observations of these fateful moments.[13] This question became acute in view of the impressionistic conclusions that the French school teachers were instructed by their superiors to draw. Becker counted the recurrence of attributes recorded in the reports, such as "consternation," "stupefaction," "anxiety," "sadness," "agitation," "seriousness," "resolve," "confidence," "patriotism," "vigor," and "enthusiasm." He then arrayed these attributes along his own impressionistic spectrum of sentiments about the war, from "negative" through "composed" to "favorable." The composite of these individual attributes, he argued, signified French collective opinion about the outbreak of the war. However, the significance of these attitudes themselves—individual or collective—remained unclear. Did they indicate mental dispositions or fleeting reactions? Where they, for that matter, mutually exclusive? Could one not be "anxiously patriotic" or "vigorously consternated" about the war?

The controversy in German scholarship has focused on only one of the attributes that Becker considered. The word *"Kriegsbegeisterung"* also surfaced in 1914 in the discourse on the "spirit of 1914." Translating it into English as "war enthusiasm" has proved less troublesome than the effort to document its motivating force in the crowds, or to fix its historical meaning. One sign of trouble came in 1991, when the organizers of a German symposium on *Kriegsbegeisterung* confessed after the event that the participants had tried but failed to answer the basic question "what is war enthusiasm?"[14] Verhey's frustration with the same question was evident in the quotation marks that he affixed to the word "enthusiasm," while he coupled it with attributes of his own, such as "apprehensive," "naïve," or "engendered by relief." While he wrote of "a certain enthusiasm in the population," he insisted that "it was an 'enthusiasm' which required no sacrifices. It was an enthusiasm for enthusiasm's sake."[15] Thomas Raithel's analysis of collective attitudes in six German cities wrestled with the same problem and overcame it only by means of semantic relocation. "Whether it is justified to see the demonstrations of 25–26 July as an expression of 'war enthusiasm,'" he wrote, "depends on how one defines this term." In the sense of "passionate fervor" (leidenschaftlicher Eifer) or "diffuse joyful excitement" (diffuse freudige Erregung), he found signs of its presence (more in Germany than France), but questions as to its significance persisted.[16] Christian Geinitz's study aimed at a more in-depth analysis of attitudes in Freiburg during the opening phases of the war. As the book's title, *Kriegsfurcht und Kampfbereitschaft*, suggested, his object was to explain the apparent contradictions in collective attitudes, the simultaneity of enthusiasm and anxiety about war. His goal, he wrote, was to describe the "psychic structures in which the war was processed."[17] This formulation revealed the extent to which issues of individual psychology were at stake; and at times the author seemed to be reaching for Freud. The spy scare of the war's first weeks, an often noted aspect of collective behavior in these excited times, he diagnosed as the "exaggerated, irrational, abnormal processing of reality through hallucinations and outbursts of paranoia."[18]

To fault recent scholarship on these grounds is neither generous nor fair. These excellent studies have drawn a compelling picture of the ambiguity and confusion that reigned on the streets of Germany in the summer of 1914. They represent crucial contributions to an established professional discourse on the outbreak of war. If they have not answered central questions about the motivations of participants, the fault lies less with them than with a discourse that has generated unanswerable questions. Conclusions about the emotions of individuals, let alone long-standing collective beliefs about the desirability of war, rest insecurely on an analysis of the crowd scenes in the cities in 1914, whether in Germany or anywhere else.

The same discourse has also obscured other questions that can now be answered with a little more confidence, thanks in large part to this same scholarship, particularly to the work of Christian Geinitz, which is also set in Freiburg.

When Freiburg's newspapers announced the Austrian ultimatum to Serbia on 24 July, they riveted public attention on developments in southeast Europe. News of the break in diplomatic relations between the two countries came the next evening, 25 July (a Saturday), and let loose the first demonstrations. The axis of the commotion was the city's main street, the Kaiserstrasse. At its north end, this street was anchored in the Karlsplatz, where the central barracks were close to the monument of the German victory of 1870 (the Siegesdenkmal), and at its south end in the building that housed the liberal *Freiburger Zeitung*. While the one site was the town's patriotic center of gravity, the other was a principal source of the news bulletins that fed the growing crowds. The demonstration on the evening of 25 July began at the newspaper office, where crowds gathered at six o'clock, as the Austrian ultimatum was due to expire. When the news of the diplomatic rupture arrived several hours later, the demonstration turned into a parade that undulated to patriotic song up and down the street, its ranks swelled by several thousand curious and excited men, women, and children. As a cloudburst drove many demonstrators inside, the taverns, restaurants, and wine bars on adjacent streets in the city center, particularly the student dives at the "Briem" and "Rappen," also became central sites in the spectacle—as sources of information, rumor, musical accompaniment, and nourishment for the participants. The rain and cool weather failed to discourage the carnival, which increasingly resembled an extravagant student frolic, a swollen outgrowth of the revelries that had accompanied the approach of the summer break in this university town. Many, perhaps a majority, of the celebrants came in fact from the university, whose corporations arrived bedecked in their colors, as well as from the upper forms of the city's male secondary schools. When the rain stopped, the crowds returned to the streets. At two o'clock in the morning their declamations and patriotic singing at the Siegesdenkmal could still be heard almost a kilometer away in the district of Herdern, where the listeners included curious inmates of the penitentiary.[19]

These scenes established the pattern for demonstrations during the rest of July. In the daylight hours, crowds gathered in search of the latest bulletins at kiosks and the offices of the city's newspapers, most of which lay not far from the Kaiserstrasse, while sales boys hawked special editions. As singing students roamed the streets, the celebrations resumed at night, particularly on Monday, 27 July, when news arrived of the Austrian declaration of war on Serbia.

Social Democrats were conspicuously absent from the demonstrations. The Socialist paper, the *Volkswacht*, criticized the Austrian ultimatum; and on Sunday, 26 July, windows in the paper's offices posted the national party's proclamation against war. To this provocation the students replied with a loud rally outside this building on the following evening.[20] The sides were not evenly matched, for the police, who had smiled on the patriotic multitudes as they jammed the Kaiserstrasse without a permit, forbade the Socialists to march. The Socialist response in Freiburg came on Tuesday, 28 July (as it did in Berlin and many other German cities).[21] The party rented the Saalbau, a large hall across the river to the south, where they staged an indoor rally in favor of a peaceful resolution of the diplomatic crisis. Here an Alsatian Socialist from the Reichstag, Joseph Emmel, addressed an audience that, according to some reports, amounted to several thousand participants.[22] They were joined by university students in sufficient numbers to ensure a commotion inside the hall, while additional student protesters gathered outside. Angry verbal exchanges, the expulsion of one of the protesters, and a brick through a window punctuated the meeting, which culminated in the Socialists' singing of the "Arbeitermarseillaise" (to the melody of the French national anthem) and a resolution to support "most energetically" the efforts of the national party on behalf of peace.[23]

If this scene did not belie images of patriotic unity in Freiburg at this stage in the proceedings, the sequel did.[24] As the Socialists dispersed in small groups after the meeting, the protesters paraded as a group back up the Kaiserstrasse via the Siegesdenkmal to the offices of the *Volkswacht*, which lay several blocks away. Here, in the most violent episode of the whole carnival, the mood turned ugly as rocks and beer bottles rained onto the building. One of the occupants, the sister of Reinhard Zumtobel, an editor of the paper, thereupon turned a hose on the demonstrators from the window of the printery. Although the crowd then broke up, the Socialists posted a squad of workers around the building for protection; they also had further reason to complain about the behavior of the police, who were nowhere to be seen. News several days later that the state prosecutor was bringing charges against some of the student demonstrators afforded little comfort, for the same official also initiated action against Zumtobel himself for an article that appeared in his paper on 30 July. Here Rosa Luxemburg declared, with a nod to the Russian experience in 1905, that the only guarantee of peace was the organization of "emphatic mass action against war."[25]

These events reflected the extent of the public volatility during the last week of July. In view of their own history, however, it was unlikely in the extreme that Freiburg's Social Democrats would follow the call for a mass strike against war. The same issue of the *Volkswacht* that carried Luxemburg's article published an unambiguous declaration of the local party's views in line with those appearing elsewhere in the Social Democratic press; namely, that the party "stands man for man behind the Fatherland" and that, in the event of "real danger, it will be surpassed by no one in its willingness to sacrifice."[26]

The volatility of local sentiments was elsewhere in evidence, too. Tourists and other visitors fled the city.[27] "The crush was indescribable," wrote one diarist of the scene at the train station on 31 July, "vast numbers of tourists were leaving."[28] Banks were faced with a storm of nervous depositors and ceased to make loans.[29] After over a thousand customers emptied their accounts on 30 July, the Municipal Savings Bank was compelled to restrict withdrawals.[30] Some shop owners refused to accept paper money. Food stores throughout the city faced panic buying. All of them raised their prices; many shut their doors. Whether they were members or not, anxious customers throughout town descended on the twelve outlets of the Consumer Cooperative, which ordinarily kept stocks sufficient for a month but were now compelled to ration foodstuffs.[31] "Buyers are behaving irrationally," complained the semi-official local bulletin, the *Tagblatt*, speaking for the city council, "and sellers are committing an injustice when they exploit the anxiety of the little people to fill their own pockets. We assure you, there is no cause for worry."[32]

No one was interested in this advice. Instead, tensions rose in town as the crisis played out to more news from the east. By 31 July, rumors of mobilization, war, and German efforts at mediation had engulfed the city in "an oppressive anxiety," as the city's chronicler reported, "[an] attentiveness [*Horchen*] to any sign of relaxation" of the crisis.[33] Resolution, if not relaxation, began that morning when the bulletins announced the general mobilization of the Russian armies. In the afternoon the crowds grew at the usual spots, awaiting the German response. At six o'clock in the evening, a police officer in an automobile, who was accompanied by a trumpeter, toured the city's main public squares to read out the formal German declaration of a state of war (*Kriegszustand*). The parades through the old city to the Siegesdenkmal thereupon resumed. While the demonstrations continued well into the night, they took place this time, observers noted, in a more serious mood, even among the young men, for the latest announcement had immediate practical consequences for everyone.[34]

What conclusions, if any, can one draw from these events during the final week of July, which, as the literature has now made amply clear, resembled scenes reported in other cities around the country? Certainly, like the editors of the non-Socialist newspapers, the demonstrators who flocked to the Kaiserstrasse and Siegesdenkmal were excited. To judge at least from their actions against the Socialists, who undertook the main action in opposition to war, many of these demonstrators were also doubtless *kriegsbegeistert*, in the aggressive sense that they happily greeted, in Raithel's words, "the prospect of German participation in war."[35] Other than signs that the participants' enthusiasm was well watered with alcohol, however, the demonstrations themselves offered no conclusive evidence about the roots of this sentiment. Although a number of historical studies have suggested plausible reasons why German university students, who made up a large part of the revelers, had embraced aggressive nationalism before the war, the demonstrators left no recorded clues as to whether they were indulging in some heroic male fantasy or regarded war as an opportunity to flee boredom, modernity, civilized values, or their fathers.[36]

Several other features of these festivities are worth noting. The first is the obvious fact that the demonstrations in this city were molded to local conditions, as they were in other towns—such as Cologne, where the excitement conjured up images of the local carnival season, or Königsberg, where it was accompanied by band music.[37] Freiburg was in this respect like other university towns, insofar as an institution of higher education provided a large font of enthusiastic participants—probably between two and three thousand young men. The topography of the demonstrations was well suited to the carnival atmosphere as well. The Kaiserstrasse was like a small replica of Unter den Linden in Berlin. It was an area concentrated enough for crowds to dominate it; its two poles also set the crowds in motion, from sources of information to sites of emotional outlet, while the spaces in between energized them with food and drink.

Another, related dimension of the spectacle has to do with what one might call, with Christian Geinitz and Thomas Raithel, the "structures of communication" that underlay the demonstrations.[38] During the last week of July, from the announcement of the ultimatum to the declaration of German mobilization, information was a precious commodity. On it—and about this truth there was no dissent—hinged the fate of everyone in town. As elsewhere, events in Freiburg were governed by the scarcity of information and the uncertainties to which it gave rise. Because they offered the earliest points of access to information, the offices of the local newspapers invited large gatherings of curious people; and none of these offices lay far from the Siegesdenkmal, where this community of uncertainty could collect for catharsis. The taverns were also critical props on this stage. They could not compete with the newspapers for information, but they did compete with one another to communicate the latest news bulletins to their customers; and they could offer liquid means of coping with the uncertainty.[39] What the bulletins failed to communicate became the object of collective speculation, rumor, and the kind of panic that began even in July to find vent not only in parades to the Siegesdenkmal, but also in spy scares, and exaggerated fears about the illicit consumers of precious information.[40] This dimension of the crowd scenes was common, in other words, both to patriotic demonstrators and panicky consumers; and it poses the question of whether a range of sentiments that seemed contradictory—war enthusiasm, anxiety, and panic—could not be parts of a single, volatile complex of reactions.

A final, central facet of these demonstrations is better analyzed with an eye to its ethnography than its psychology. It has less to do with the motives of the demonstrators than with the meaning and practical effects of the rituals of street politics in which they engaged.[41] In this respect, the pivotal moments during the last week of July were the confrontations between the students and the Socialists at the Saalbau and then at the offices of the *Volkswacht*. More than any other episodes in the final crisis, these gave lie to the myth that the demonstrations represented the forging of a patriotic community. In fact, they were rituals of intimidation and exclusion. They set the domestic bounds of patriotic community, established the rules of political language that operated within it, and emphasized the claims of the patriotic demonstrators to establish these rules. In Freiburg the demonstrations registered the climax of long-held local antagonisms, which had pitched the guardians of the national symbols, whose fortress was the university, against the sector of the local political landscape that had long functioned as a national counter-symbol. It was not an equal contest. In Freiburg and other German cities, the patriotic demonstrators could count on the support of the police, who either forbade the Socialists to demonstrate in the open or kept them out of "sanctified" spaces, like the Kaiserstrasse or Unter den Linden (or the Place de la Concorde in Paris).[42] Had the police not done so, the scenes that subsequently gave rise to the "myth of 1914" would likely have been marred, in Freiburg as in Berlin, to a much greater extent by street violence.

The dynamic of street politics thus placed the Socialists in Freiburg and elsewhere in a difficult position. Only if they were to abandon their opposition to war would they be able to escape from political marginalization. Inclusion in the *Volksgemeinschaft* required them to speak a new political language. While they had, as Sven Oliver Müller has argued, long employed their own language of patriotism to articulate their political demands and expectations, the new accents of war amounted to a different syntax, which prescribed the inversion of the Socialists' traditional political priorities and the subordination of domestic social conflict to the basic, implacable hostility of the nation's foreign enemies.[43] The traditional custodians of this aggressive language of patriotism, the "semantic hegemons," immediately used their power—and the Socialists' apparent acceptance of it—to construct the "myth of 1914."

As Wolfgang Kruse has shown, the leaders of the German Social Democratic Party tried to resist this interpretation of what they were doing, but they were dealing with forces beyond their control. Their decision to accept the new semantic logic, to embrace a war of national defense in these terms, was in part a product of the nationalist demonstrations at the end of July. Kruse writes of the Socialists' "fear of being overwhelmed in the growing national enthusiasm for war, which now completely dominated the non-Socialist public in Germany."[44] To this extent, and whatever the deeper emotional roots of their behavior, the patriotic demonstrators who claimed the streets in Freiburg and other German cities achieved practical political results. They encouraged a major shift in official Socialist thinking about the relationship between domestic conflict and international strife and about the viability of the domestic institutions of capitalism. If some Socialist leaders persisted in the belief that they could achieve their long-held domestic goals under the new linguistic auspices of patriotic unity, they were indulging, as subsequent events made clear, in their own "myth of 1914."

In Freiburg and other German cities, the dramatic scenes in July and August 1914 reflected similar dynamics. Far from being socially comprehensive, they were exclusionary rituals directed in the main at Socialist workers. They reflected further the play of uncertainties bred in the shortage of reliable information. Beyond these observations, conclusions about the motivation of those who populated the crowds are difficult to draw. It would in all events overtax the evidence from the street to conclude that their enthusiasm reflected long-standing, deep-seated, or universal attitudes about the probability or desirability of war.

Notes

1. Thomas Nipperdey, *Deutsche Geschichte 1866–1918: Machtstaat vor der Demokratie* (Munich, 1992), 778–79.
2. Christian Geinitz, *Kriegsfurcht und Kampfbereitschaft: Das Augusterlebnis in Freiburg: Eine Studie zum Kriegsbeginn 1914* (Essen, 1998).
3. Jean-Jacques Becker, *1914: Comment les Français sont entrés dans la guerre: Contribution à l'étude de l'opinion publique, printemps-été 1914* (Paris, 1977); cf. Becker, "'That's the Death Knell of Our Boys…'" Patrick Fridenson, ed., *The French Home Front, 1914–1918* (Providence and Oxford, 1992), 17–36. See also Richard Cobb, "France and the Coming of War," R. J. W. Evans and Hartmut Pogge von Strandmann, eds., *The Coming of the First World War* (Oxford, 1988), 125–44; P. J. Flood, *France, 1914–1918: Public Opinion and the War Effort* (London, 1990), 5–16.
4. Sven Oliver Müller, *Die Nation als Waffe: Nationalismus in Deutschland und Großbritannien im Ersten Weltkrieg* (Göttingen, 2002), 70; cf. J. F. V. Keiger, "Britain's 'Union sacrée' in 1914," in Jean-Jacques Becker and Stéphan Audoin-Rouzeau, *Les Sociétés européennes et la guerre de 1914–1918* (Nanterre, 1990), 39–52; D. C. Watt, "The British Reactions to the Assassination at Sarajevo," *European Studies Review* 1 (1970), 233–47. Most of Niall Ferguson's discussion of the general phenomenon dwells on the British case: *The Pity of War: Explaining World War I* (New York, 1999), 174–211.
5. Joshua Sanborn, "The Mobilization of 1914 and the Question of the Russian Nation: A Reexamination," *Slavic Review* 59 (2000), 267–89; Dittmar Dahlmann, "Russia at the Outbreak of the First World War," in Becker and Audoin-Rouzeau, *Sociétés*, 53–63; Bernard Michel, "L'Autriche et l'entrée dans la guerre en 1914," *Guerres mondiales et conflits contemporaines* 45 (1995), 5–11; R. J. W. Evans, "The Habsburg Monarchy and the Coming of War," in Evans and Pogge von Strandmann, *Coming*, 42–55; Edmond von Glaise Horstenau, *Die Katastrophe* (Zurich, 1929), 29–36.
6. Jeffrey Verhey, *The Spirit of 1914: Militarism, Myth, and Mobilization in Germany* (Cambridge, 2000). This work represents a revision of Verhey's dissertation, which has served as a foundation for much of the work done during the last decade: Verhey, "The 'Spirit of 1914': The Myth of Enthusiasm and the Rhetoric of Unity in World War I Germany" (PhD Diss., University of California, Berkeley, 1991).
7. See Kurt Flasch, *Die geistige Mobilmachung: Die deutschen Intellektuellen und der Erste Weltkrieg* (Berlin, 2000).
8. Friedrich Meinecke, *Die deutsche Katastrophe: Betrachtungen und Erinnerungen* (Wiesbaden, 1947), 43–45; Modris Eksteins, *Rites of Spring: The Great War and the Birth of the Modern Age* (Boston, 1989), 55–94; cf. Peter Graf Kielmannsegg, *Deutschland und der Erste Weltkrieg* (Frankfurt, 1968) 146–

47; Gunther Mai, *Das Ende des Kaiserreichs: Politik und Kriegführung im Ersten Weltkrieg* (Munich, 1987), 14–18; Michael Jeismann, *Das Vaterland der Feinde: Studien zum Feindbegriff und Selbstverständnis in Deutschland und Frankreich 1792–1918* (Stuttgart, 1992), 316.

9. For a survey of the earlier work see Gerd Krumeich, "L'entrée en guerre en Allemagne," in Bekker and Audoin-Rouzeau, *Sociétés européennes*, 65–74; Wolfgang Kruse, "Die Kriegsbegeisterung im Deutschen Reich zu Beginn des Ersten Weltkrieges: Entstehungszusammenhänge, Grenzen und ideologische Strukturen," in Marcel van der Linden and Gottfried Mergner, eds., *Kriegsbegeisterung und mentale Kriegsvorbereitung: Interdisziplinäre Studien* (Berlin, 1991), 73–87.
10. Wolfgang Kruse, *Krieg und nationale Integration: Eine Neuinterpretation des sozialdemokratischen Burgfriedensschlusses 1914/15* (Essen, 1993), 30–42, 54–61; Benjamin Ziemann, *Front und Heimat: Ländliche Kriegserfahrungen im südlichen Bayern 1914–1923* (Essen, 1997), 39–54.
11. Verhey, *Spirit*, 97–8.
12. Seth Taylor, *Left–Wing Nietzscheans: The Politics of German Expressionism, 1910–1920* (New York, 1990).
13. See Reinhard Rürup, "Der 'Geist von 1914' in Deutschland: Kriegsbegeisterung und Ideologisierung des Krieges im Ersten Weltkrieg," Bernd Hüppauf, ed., *Ansichten vom Krieg: Vergleichende Studien zum Ersten Weltkrieg in Literatur und Gesellschaft* (Königstein i. T., 1984), 1–30.
14. Marcel van der Linden and Gottfried Mergner, "Kriegsbegeisterung und mentale Kriegsvorbereitung," in van der Linden and Mergner, *Kriegsbegeisterung*, 22.
15. Verhey, *Spirit*, 97–114.
16. Thomas Raithel, *Das Wunder der inneren Einheit: Studien zur deutschen und französischen Öffentlichkeit bei Beginn des Ersten Weltkrieges* (Bonn, 1996), 235–36.
17. Geinitz, *Kriegsfurcht*, 128.
18. Ibid., 173.
19. Generallandesarchiv Karlsruhe, 234/10931, Georg Sältzer, Tagebuch, 13 October 1914; Stadtarchiv Freiburg im Breisgau (hereafter cited StadtAF), B1(H), Nr. 317, Kriegs-Chronik, 25 July 1914; Oskar Haffner, *Kriegschronik der Stadt Freiburg im Breisgau 1914–1919* (Freiburg, 1924), 2; *Freiburger Bote* (hereafter cited FB), 27 July 1914; *Freiburger Volkswacht* (hereafter cited VW), 27 July 1914; Geinitz, *Kriegsfurcht*, 57–69.
20. VW, 25 July 14; *Breisgauer Zeitung* (hereafter cited BZ), 27 July 1914.
21. Raithel, *Wunder*, 244–48.
22. Kruse, *Krieg*, 32; cf. Geinitz, *Kriegsfurcht*, 81.
23. VW, 29 July 1914.
24. On the episode VW, 29 July 1917; Reinhold Zumtobel, *Vom Gemeindebub zum Ehrenbürger: Kurvenreicher Lebensweg eines Hebelverehrers* (Schopfheim, 1953), 97–99; Wilhelm Engler, *Freiburg, Baden und das Reich: Lebenserinnerungen eines südwestdeutschen Sozialdemokraten, 1873–1938* (Stuttgart, 1991), 23–24; Geinitz, *Kriegsfurcht*, 80–88; Kruse, *Krieg*, 32, who, on the basis of a report in the Socialist *Volksfreund* in Karlsruhe, cites a figure of seven thousand Socialist demonstrators. This figure strikes me as too high.
25. "Der Friede, der Dreibund und wir," VW, 30 July 1914.
26. "Verschiedene Vaterlandsliebe," VW, 30 July 1914.
27. *Freiburger Zeitung* (hereafter cited FZ), 1 August 1914.
28. Charlotte Herder, *Mein Kriegstagebuch 1914–1918* (Freiburg, n.d.), 5.
29. StadtAF, B1(H), Nr. 317, Kriegs-Chronik, 27 July 1914.
30. Städtische Sparkasse, Freiburg, *Rechenschafts-Bericht für das Jahr 1914* (Freiburg, 1915), 4; Josef Wysocki, *150 Jahre Sparkasse Freiburg* (Freiburg, 1976), 181.
31. VW, 31 July 1914.
32. *Freiburger Tagblatt*, 30 July 1914.
33. StadtAF, B1(H), Nr. 317, Kriegs-Chronik, 31 July 1914; FB, 1 August 1914.
34. FZ, 1 August 1914; FB, 1 August 1914.

35. Raithel, *Wunder*, 235–36.
36. Norbert Kampe, *Studenten und "Judenfrage" im Deutschen Kaiserreich: Die Entstehung einer akademischen Trägerschicht des Antisemitismus* (Göttingen, 1988); Konrad H. Jarausch, *Students, Society, and Politics in Imperial Germany: The Rise of Academic Illiberalism* (Princeton, 1982); Sonja Levsen, "Männlichkeit als Studienziel: Männlichkeitkonstruktionen englischer und deutscher Studenten vor dem Ersten Weltkrieg," *Zeitschrift für Geschichtswissenschaft* 51 (2003), 109–30.
37. Müller, *Nation als Waffe*, 62.
38. Ibid., 96; Raithel, *Wunder*, 222–33; cf. Kruse, "Kriegsbegeisterung," 75.
39. TB, 27 July 1914.
40. BZ, 30 July 1914.
41. See Thomas Lindenberger, *Strassenpolitik: Zur Sozialgeschichte der öffentlichen Ordnung in Berlin 1900 bis 1914* (Bonn, 1995).
42. Raithel, *Wunder*, 239–40; Kruse, *Krieg*, 41.
43. Müller, *Nation als Waffe*, 62–63.
44. Kruse, *Krieg*, 63.

Chapter 12

EDUCATION FOR WAR, PEACE, AND PATRIOTISM IN RUSSIA ON THE EVE OF WORLD WAR I

Joshua A. Sanborn

On 13 October 1893, a Russian naval squadron arrived in Toulon for a two-week visit. Officially, they were simply returning the favor paid two years earlier when the French navy spent ten celebratory days docked at Kronstadt, the Russian naval base not far from the capital St. Petersburg. Unofficially, the visit was to seal the secret military convention that the two countries were about to sign. Never before had such a secret compact seen such an enormous public celebration. From the moment they landed, George Kennan would later note, the Russian sailors were subjected to "an uproarious and continuous round of formalities, receptions, ceremonies, luncheons, dinners, visits, invitations, toasts, and speeches ... all to the accompaniment of mass popular demonstrations reaching, on many occasions, an intensity that can only be described as delirium."[1]

Kennan was not the only one to think so. One Russian correspondent covering the event for the newspaper *Novoe vremia*, stunned to be welcomed by thousands of Frenchmen shouting "Vive la Russie! Vive le Tsar!" was prompted to write that "[i]t was not rapture, the word is too commonplace; it was better than rapture. More picturesque, deeper, happier, more various."[2] Telegraph lines were kept humming with the details of every event: the menus, the drinks of choice, and the pompous speeches. Even the salacious comments were proudly reported, as one correspondent wrote that "he had been informed at a ball that there was scarcely a woman in Paris who would not have been ready to forget her duties to satisfy the desire of any of the Russian sailors."³ Diplomatic silence aside, these promises of dalliance were also promises of alliance: "From the time of the Toulon visit down to 1914, the Franco-Russian Alliance may be said to have existed as a reality in the eyes of the public, even though the documentary basis for it remained concealed."⁴

The Franco-Russian Alliance was an important strategic event, but the enthusiasm surrounding the mutual military visits indicates that it was also an important part of open discussions across Europe about the role that the public at large would play in future armed conflicts. This question was as central in Russia as it was in France, despite the fact that public activism in Russia was hindered by the actions of a traditionally repressive state and by relatively low levels of practical and political literacy in the population at large. These conditions were looked at with horror by modernizers in the Russian political system, who believed as the nineteenth century came to a close that the world had changed, that warfare had changed, and that Russia needed to change as well. Above all, in an age of mass warfare, they felt it was necessary to create a society in which the young men who would fight Russia's wars would be taught not only passive loyalty but also active support. This would entail both a social and cultural reorientation of the country in a process of militarization that would be long and arduous.

Not surprisingly, much of this discussion centered on the process of inculcating patriotism in the Russian population. Patriotism in its simplest manifestation is the love of one's country, and in this broad respect patriotism had been a part of Russian political life from the beginning.⁵ But at the start of the twentieth century, Russian patriotism was transformed by the expectation that lower-class citizens would have to adopt the conscious and active brand of patriotism that had previously been practiced only by the nobility. The expansion of patriotism in a military key was a political project, and this chapter aims to recover some of the tension surrounding the process, the reasons for its success, and the obstacles it faced both from autocratic conservatives and Russia's nascent pacifist movement. I conclude that the desire to increase Russia's military power led to policies that encouraged the development of mass politics (in part through the creation of grass-roots paramilitary youth organizations) and mass communication (through military propaganda campaigns). This concerted engagement with all sectors of Russian society led to a vast increase in the amount of political energy in the country, and with it an increase of both the potential for war and the potential for peace. In the end, the development of a militarized society and of patriotic politics made Russia's involvement in World War I much more likely than it otherwise might have been. As we shall see, few Russian politicians thought that war in 1914 was desirable or that protecting Serbia from Habsburg wrath was in itself worth the enormous risk that military conflict with the Germanic powers posed. But in the midst of the July Crisis, soldiers and political leaders went to war because they were conditioned by the rhetoric of martial patriotism to believe that real men went to war when they were called, even if it might mean their own death, and that responsible politicians had to protect the Great Power status of the Russian Empire, even if it might mean political and social ruin.

I. Education for War in Russia before 1914

For both technological and political reasons, the last generation of young men to come of age in tsarist Russia was the first to be systematically subjected to martial propaganda. The shaping of the souls of teenage boys, once left to the family and parish church, was now seen by military leaders as the key to social survival in the apocalyptic times that many felt were soon to come. The adoption of universal military conscription in 1874 had been the painful and controversial admission by the autocracy that old regime institutions were outdated and that wars between mobilized armies of citizen soldiers would ultimately decide the Great Power rivalries. With the masses now brought into war politically as well as physically, the stage was set for a massive effort to teach Russia's youth to love swords as well as plowshares.

Because they realized that future wars would be total wars, military ideologues understood that improving the performance of the army depended on the success of pre-war social reforms. As scholars in the General Staff Academy never tired of repeating, Europe was experiencing a period of "spectacular change." New technologies and new military strategies meant that "the role of the state and people now equaled the role of the army."[6] Not surprisingly, military men were most interested in the soldiers they would be drafting in the near future and targeted most of their activities at teenage and even preteen boys. Military outreach programs therefore focused on improving and militarizing Russia's educational system. Here they faced a double-edged sword. Knowing that good primary education would make their soldiers easier to train and more likely to take the initiative on the battlefield, staff officers supported an expansion of Russia's rudimentary education system and created their own literacy training programs in military units to teach some of the illiterate young men who came their way. Increasing the number of schools in the Russian empire required increasing the number of teachers, however, and one of the few enticements the state created to attract candidates to poorly paid jobs in distant villages was a draft exemption for schoolteachers. Thus, young teachers whose martial fervor was in question were teaching future soldiers in village schools. This fact was not lost on military reformers as the twentieth century began, who always (and not without cause) doubted the loyalty of Russia's intelligentsia. As General E. I. Martynov lamented in 1904, many of Russia's leading cultural figures held that a love of country was "obsolete," that war was a "remnant of barbarism," and that the army was the "main drag on progress." Martynov consequently urged that military officers become more deeply involved in shaping potential recruits, or the disease of pacifism might spread to the lower ranks.[7]

Though the attitudes of village teachers and the Russian intelligentsia worried the army, militarizers still held many advantages in the struggle for the souls of young men. The most prominent of these was consensus on the part of state officials in the educational and military bureaucracies alike on the necessity and inevitability of war. School textbooks, public celebrations, and the emerging Russian patriotic narrative all placed the feats of Russian arms at the center of attention. The string of enormous public celebrations staged by the imperial court in the first years of the twentieth century also centered on martial glory, as Nicholas II made ceremonial circuit rides around the country to remind all of Russia of the three hundredth anniversary of the expulsion of Polish troops and the establishment of the Romanov dynasty (1913), the two hundredth anniversary of Peter the Great's important victory at Poltava (1709), and of course the centenary of the trouncing of Napoleon (1912). As Richard Wortman noted regarding these celebrations, the "Russian monarchy entered the modern era of mass publicity to an extent that has hardly been remarked on in the historical and biographical literature. Nicholas II broke with traditional forms of representation and made the image of the emperor available in the market place, participating in the 'commodity culture' that arose with the growth of commerce and industry."[8] In this respect, at least, Russia was very similar to other continental powers. In France and Germany too, rapidly expanding public culture acquired a strong military flavor in the years following the introduction of male conscription.[9] Russian educational officials also shared an interest with other pedagogues in introducing military history as a core component of the curriculum. From the much embellished and sanitized accounts of Muscovite clashes with Mongol hordes to the grand tales of the defeat of Napoleon, stories of duty, honor, and glory on the battlefield were part of every young Russian's education. These lessons in martial masculinity were very important, and Russia's young men learned them well. By the time the Great War broke out, the mechanisms of mass education and mass politics had increased the war potential of Russian society by solidifying the link between manhood, statehood, and military performance.[10]

But how much had they increased Russia's military power, and was it enough? As planners across Europe were aware, there was no good way short of war to test how successful their projects of militarization had been. In contrast to many other belligerents, however, Russia took this exam of war in 1904–05 in its contest with Japan. The outcome shook state officials throughout the Russian bureaucratic apparatus. On the one hand, the creaky mobilization system produced unsatisfactory results. Many reservists failed to show up for the war, and even those older reservists who did appear proved ornery and insubordinate. Military officials felt that, young or old, enlisted men were insufficiently fired with zeal for either the martial or the patriotic cause. The stunning defeats on land and at sea only seemed to confirm that Russian society was not producing modern soldiers. On the other hand, there was enough public mobilization and mass political sentiment to fuel a revolution. In the wake of defeat, armed political conflict broke out throughout the empire. Only a combination of unprecedented carrots (the formation of a parliament and the guarantees of religious and certain political freedoms in particular) and enormous sticks (the wave of state repression under the cover of martial law resulted in more than one thousand executions) kept the Romanovs on the throne. Conservatives throughout the empire, particularly in the Ministry of Internal Affairs, became convinced that mass mobilization had to be prevented at all costs.

The stage was therefore set for a bureaucratic struggle between the two most important "power" ministries on the question of militarizing society, a struggle that became apparent when military reformers intent on restructuring the links between army and society put forward major reform plans between 1908 and 1914. Though space does not permit an examination of these plans in depth, we can take a brief look at two ways in which military officials attempted to influence the Russian educational system. The mixed results show both the resistance army planners faced and the limited success they achieved.[11]

The first political initiative was the General Staff's effort to eliminate the existing draft exemption for schoolteachers. The exemption that had been in place since 1874 was a peculiar one. Teachers received not a blanket exemption but the right to be enrolled directly in the reserves without having to serve on active duty. The justification for this policy was that, being educated, they would not need the training that regular conscripts received. The real reason was that officials at the Ministry of Popular Enlightenment and at the Holy Synod (church school teachers were exempted as well) had forced these concessions during the horse trading that occurred in the 1870s prior to the law's passage. After embarrassing incidents of draft dodging, desertion, and military incompetence on the part of these untrained reservists during the Russo-Japanese War, the army now insisted that teachers be required to serve in the armed forces like all other citizens, not only out of reasons of fairness and military efficiency, but also as part of a larger program of "militarizing the schools." Teachers, the war ministry asserted, should serve in the army so that they could "inculcate the proper attitude toward military service into the teenage generation."[12]

For their part, the education ministries lobbied Prime Minister Petr Stolypin hard to block the change. Stolpyin was persuaded by the educators, and he told the army frankly that he believed that these thousands of men were more necessary in village schools than in the armed forces. Still, he also admitted that the military's desire to militarize the schools was important and their concerns in this respect "weighty." He tried to parry the army's claim that revoking the exemption would lead to more militarization by pointing out that by taking away the primary incentive for men to become teachers, the measure would in fact lead to a further feminization of a teaching profession that was already dominated by women. Thus, lifting the exemption would be counterproductive, since women were "hopeless from the point of view of instilling military spirit or military discipline."[13] The army was unmoved, and it won a five-year phase out of the teacher exemption in 1912, too late to make any difference in World War I.

If the army's ultimate victory regarding the militarization of schoolteachers was more in principle than in practice, the same was not true for students. From 1874 on, the military had been indirectly influencing primary education both in the halls of power and on the ground, a fact confirmed by teachers in Moscow province in the 1890s, who noted that army needs shaped the content of their courses.[14] After the Russo-Japanese War, military men looked for ways to have direct contact with their future conscripts. Starting in 1909, for instance, lower and middle school students in the Caucasus and Central Asia spent part of their summer learning gymnastics and military affairs under the supervision of army officials. Most of the students were recent Slavic immigrants to Russia's Asian colonies, but some students in native schools received instruction as well.[15] By 1911, the movement to militarize youngsters was building steadily. An interministerial commission was established to work out a plan for introducing all teenagers to physical education and military affairs.[16] In Odessa, in the same year, the First Congress on Physical Development and Sport proclaimed that the great significance of physical education and sport was becoming clearer to Russian "society" with each passing year and that immediate and serious measures needed to be taken to popularize and organize the physical "upbringing" *(vospitanie)* of adolescents.[17]

It is a sign of the success that the militarizers were enjoying that the public response to these plans was enthusiastic and that even conservative ministries like the Holy Synod and the Ministry of Popular Enlightenment were forced to admit that physical education was needed in all schools.[18] In all the discussions, the armed forces played a crucial role, from participating in commission debates to authoring manuals for village teachers to use when teaching physical education to their charges.[19]

The most striking change, however, came not from initiatives to expand the militarizing capacity of previously existing schools but from the movement to create new paramilitary institutions outside of the schools to increase physical fitness and teach military affairs. Two groups arose at roughly the same time in 1909 to take up the task of physically developing the younger generation. One of these institutions was a direct borrowing from Britain; Russian officers created Boy Scout troops on Baden Powell's model almost immediately after Baden Powell himself formed the first troops in England in 1908.[20]

Domestic initiative was also important in the rise of measures to militarize the teenage generation, as a host of "play companies" *(poteshnye roty)* sprung up around the country. The name rang with the echoes of Russia's martial past, as the founders of the movement borrowed the name from the mock units that Peter the Great created as a young boy in the late seventeenth century to experience military life.[21] These new companies were a specific response to the growing perception that Russian adolescents were physically inferior to their western counterparts and that they lacked the patriotic fervor and sense of duty that the teenagers of Russia's threatening enemies possessed.

Play companies originated in Ekaterinoslav province during the 1908–09 school year, and within two years they had spread like wildfire across the empire. By 1912, about one hundred thousand boys had signed up.[22] Young men who enrolled experienced the joys of physical training, discipline, and marching with groups of their peers. The army leadership and the government remained largely reactive while enthusiastic citizens (the majority of whom were either retired military men or officers working on their own time) formed these new groups. The increased attention toward adolescents was welcome to military officials, but conservatives were plagued by anxieties that the new "spontaneous" mass organizations would spin out of control and lead to disorder. As the St. Petersburg governor warned, "the mob is always impressionable, it easily changes mood and still more easily falls under the charm of leaders. The same people who raised red flags in our time of troubles enthusiastically are now prepared to participate in expressions of loyal feeling. … Introducing, therefore, organization into a mob of children, of young people, is acceptable only with exceeding caution. Unfortunately, this caution is not apparent."[23]

One man's patriotic initiative was another man's recklessness.

The tsar's response to the conflict between energetic officers and anxious conservatives was to allow play companies to be formed, but only under strict, occasionally suffocating, observation. As the numbers of these units multiplied, so too did government concern. Finally, in July 1911, the tsar and the War Ministry came out with a statute regulating the companies, requiring all units to inculcate the same values, follow the same regulations, and be subject to the watchful eye of the army. The right to form these troops was also strictly limited to high-ranking officers on active duty or the reserves, sporting societies approved by the state, fire brigades, special military training societies, and "trustworthy people."[24] Despite these limiting statutes, youth paramilitary organizations continued to grow in size and importance. With each trained boy and proud parent, the potential not only for military success but also for public support for military action grew.

II. Education for Peace

This expansion of military training and martial propaganda disturbed more people than just the fearful conservatives who envisioned these armed young men carrying red flags. It also proved repugnant to Russia's infant pacifist movement, a movement that had been brought into being in large part by the militarization drive itself. Prior to 1874, it was impossible to speak of a Russian pacifist movement. There were certain isolated groups like the Mennonites and Dukhobors (a homegrown religious movement that rejected the hierarchical and ornate trappings of the Orthodox church for a communal religious experience) who rejected military service in principle, but they had little impact on the political scene and were in any case assuaged by draft exemptions granted by the state on the condition that they colonize and cultivate the rich agricultural lands the empire was seizing from the Ottoman domains in the late eighteenth and early nineteenth centuries. Pacifist dissent from other sources was totally insignificant.

Universal conscription and mass politics changed all of that. As state officials attempted to make military service the uniform obligation of all citizens of the empire, they ran foul of the pacifist religious sects and jarred the consciences of Russia's emerging liberals as well. Modern pacifism became more political and more evangelical, and as it did so, education and persuasion became its favorite tools. At the same time, as we have seen, state and military officials turned to education and persuasion as means to produce autonomous and "conscious" citizen soldiers who would be proficient in war, understand the reasons for it, and perhaps even grow to love it as they had. The questions of war and peace were thus not only entering the public sphere, but the sphere of publicity as well.

This emergence into the public sphere gave greater visibility and energy to the traditional Christian pacifists, but it also caused problems for them. As peace became part of a broader political discourse that was rapidly secularizing, Christian resisters lost their monopoly on war objection. As Sandi Cooper has most exhaustively demonstrated, the expansion of mass politics across Europe during the course of the nineteenth century created a powerful strand of peace movements that both desired peace and accepted the primacy of the state in political affairs.[25] In Russia, this phenomenon was both visible and precocious. Liberal bureaucrats within the Russian government took the lead in seeking international political solutions to the moral problems of war, not just at the Hague Conferences described by Jost Dülffer in this volume, but earlier in the century as well.[26] Non-state actors were just as vigorous and important. The most famous of these was Jan Bloch, the Polish magnate who wrote *The Future of War*, a sober tract that argued that technological and social change had rendered wars so deadly, so inconclusive, and so expensive that only irrational or suicidal policymakers would begin them.[27] But others were active too. Pavel Miliukov, the noted historian and liberal politician, served on the Carnegie Commission sent to document the horrors of the Balkan Wars of 1912–13. The Carnegie Commission's stated aim was "to inform public opinion and to make plain just what is or may be involved in an international war carried on under modern conditions. If the minds of men can be turned even for a short time away from passion, from race antagonism and from national aggrandizement to a contemplation of the individual and national losses due to war and to the shocking horrors which modern warfare entails, a step and by no means a short one, will have been taken toward the substitution of justice for force in the settlement of international differences."[28]

III. Patriotism or Peace?

The knowledge that modern war was horrible and an abiding faith in reason were the hallmarks of the patriotic pacifists, who held firm to the notion that they should prefer their own country and countrymen even as they rejected war. But this faith in reason rather than God divided those who sought peace in Russia at the fin-de-siècle. For the patriotic pacifists, it was precisely the love of country that should spur the love of peace (through the "contemplation of the individual and national losses due to war"). But the Christian pacifists saw patriotism as a cause of war, not a handmaiden of peace. This difference of opinion was far more than doctrinal squabbling, for the terms on which the propaganda battle for young Russian souls would be fought were at stake. There were more than a few men in the Russian military who thought that war was a positive force and disputed the claims of the patriotic pacifists that it was both horrible and unnecessary, but this was not the theme of the militarizing program, which instead focused directly on building up patriotic sentiments. In essence, then, the question of the desirability or moral status of war was passed over in favor of the seemingly benign education in patriotism that military officials urged upon schools and newly formed paramilitary formations.

It fell to Leo Tolstoy, Russia's most prominent Christian pacifist, to state the pacifist case against patriotism. Even prior to his spiritual crisis and turn to radical Christianity in 1880, Tolstoy had been a critical but conflicted observer of the war fever that preceded the Russo-Turkish War of 1877–78.[29] The picture Tolstoy painted in *Anna Karenina* (1877) on this theme was mixed. On the one hand, Tolstoy mocked the Panslavic upsurge as "one of those fashionable fads which, supplanting one another, always serve as a subject of concern for society … much here was frivolous and ridiculous." On the other, he also "saw and recognized the unquestionable, ever growing enthusiasm which united all classes of society, with which one could not but sympathize."[30]

By the 1890s, however, all traces of ambiguity regarding patriotism and war had disappeared. In two articles, "Christianity and Patriotism" (1894) and "Patriotism, or Peace?" (1895), Tolstoy directly confronted the threat that the rise of patriotic feelings in Russia in the 1890s posed to the cause of peace.[31] Reading the reports of the Toulon visit disturbed him, and he admitted his astonishment that it "came to pass that not only those who ate, drank and spoke, but every one who was present, and even those who merely heard or read in the papers of these proceedings—all these millions of French and Russians—imagined suddenly that in some especial fashion they were enamored of each other; that is, that all the French love all the Russians, and all the Russians all the French."[32] Most painfully for Tolstoy, all of this patriotic and martial fervor was dressed in Christian clothing. "Since the time of the Concordat scarcely so many prayers can have been offered as during this short period. All the French suddenly became extraordinarily religious, and carefully deposited in the rooms of the Russian mariners the very images which a short time previously they had as carefully removed from their schools as harmful tools of superstition."[33]

All of this "hurrah-patriotism" was, in Tolstoy's opinion silly and thoughtless, something to be expected of the effeminate elites of France and Russia, whom he had been lampooning even before his sudden turn to the Gospels.[34] In his fictional and nonfictional works alike, Tolstoy used the good sense and simple morals of commoners to puncture the absurdity of this elite. The conviction that the masses were undeceived and unimpressed by the games of their rulers normally made Tolstoy an optimist. Indeed, in "Christianity and Patriotism," he included a lengthy account of a French agitator who visited him in 1890 to talk up the Franco-Russian rapprochement.[35] Neither Tolstoy nor Prokofii, the local peasant to whom the envoy turned after failing to convince the sage novelist, was much impressed by the Frenchman's exhortations to help him recover Alsace and Lorraine. Prokofii even became angry momentarily before asking the agitator to instead get members of all three countries to work in the fields together. Homespun wisdom won the day, at least in Tolstoy's mind.

But Tolstoy also knew that the waves of modernity were washing over Russian villages with increasing strength and that new Russians were emerging. On the face of it, increased literacy, education and social communication seemed to be good for the pacifist cause, because both war and patriotism were irrational and degrading, and as a result "the fraud of patriotism ought daily to become more difficult and at length impossible to practice." "But," he continued, "the truth is that these very means of general external education, facilitated locomotion and intercourse, and especially the spread of literature, being captured and constantly more and more controlled by government, confer on the latter such possibilities of exciting a feeling of mutual animosity between nations, that in degree as the uselessness and harmfulness of patriotism have become manifest, so also has increased the power of the government and ruling class to excite patriotism among the people."[36] If Prokofii's generation had been cool to Panslavism as young men in the 1870s and dismissive of French élan in the 1890s, their sons might be a different story.

It was clear to Tolstoy that the "inevitable consequence of patriotism" was war, both because it was based in selfishness and hatred and because it was dedicated to preserving territorial states that had been formed through unrelenting violence. Every practicing Christian who believed instead in selflessness, love, and nonviolence would have to realize that patriotism was evil and corrosive. But even Tolstoy had to admit that the issue at present was not nearly so clear to either young Russian peasants or to others of all levels of education across Europe.[37] As Tolstoy himself observed, Russian reporters in Toulon ardently declared that the patriotic upsurge they were experiencing was making their souls "throb with that love which sees in men brothers, which hates blood, and violence, and the snatching of children from a beloved mother.... Is not this the sensible presence of the God of love and of fraternity, the presence of the loftiest ideal descending in His supremest moments upon man?"[38]

These statements, like the martial prayers mentioned earlier, touched Tolstoy to the quick. The capacity of patriots to appropriate the Christian sentiments of love and fraternity as their own and the willingness of so many people to listen to them worried him, even as he insisted that at some time the "cobweb of lies" must be swept away. Patriotism would be exposed as a fraud, soldiers and statesmen would be revealed as brigands, and the good men of Europe and the "Christian world" would disarm, thereby "showing the Oriental nations an example, not of savage patriotism and ferocity, but that one of brotherly life which has been taught to us by Christ."[39] Tolstoy himself dedicated his life to promoting this message around the world, virtually abandoning his career as a novelist to pursue the goal. He had no small degree of success. He was the best known pacifist in the world as the twentieth century began and was one of the most widely read authors in Russia, thanks not so much to his massive novels as to the short little Christian pacifist fables he published cheaply and sold widely in the last years of his life.[40] Many a young Russian's first success in reading came from a Tolstoy pamphlet, and a large number of religious followers emerged, calling themselves "Tolstoyans" and promoting his views.[41]

Tolstoy died in 1910, still believing that peace would soon reign on earth. It was just as well, as the war that would break out four years later showed to anyone who cared to see that, Tolstoy's efforts notwithstanding, the militarizers had won the propaganda battle. Their success was not only over Tolstoy and other pacifists, but was also over the rather more powerful conservatives at the apex of the tsarist political system. The battle within the elite was sharp during the reform process as the specter of revolution loomed over Petersburg politicians. In those final years and months before the Great War, conservatives did more than protest the revoking of their favorite draft exemptions. Many protested against the slide to war itself, seeing the danger that continental war posed to the political order and urging the tsar to disentangle himself from the looming conflict. As Petr Durnovo argued in a memorandum to the tsar in February 1914, if Russia continued to be aligned with France and England, it would bear the brunt of the war for no good reason, since "the vital interests of Russia and Germany do not conflict." Instead, the two powers shared an interest in preserving "the conservative principle in the world of which the above-named two great powers are the only reliable bulwarks," and in dampening down the nationalist demands of smaller peoples in Eastern Europe. If present trends continued and war with Germany occurred, Durnovo claimed, the military prospects were not great. Any possibility for Russian victory would come in a long war that would prove costly in terms of lives and treasure. Battlefield success would bring only economic dislocation and social upheaval. Defeat would certainly bring revolution. The only patriotic course that made sense for the country was to stay out of the titanic battle that was sure to come between Germany and England.[42]

Durnovo was just one member of a substantive and powerful conservative group at court that Baron Taube, a fellow member, described as a "choir of 'pacifists.'"[43] As Taube's scare quotes suggest, it is going too far to call Durnovo a pacifist, even a "patriotic pacifist." Still, the strength of antiwar sentiment among conservatives in 1914 demonstrates that there were constraining factors at all levels of the Russian political scene as the fateful summer of 1914 approached. Russian elites well knew the danger of war. Commoners too had living memories of a painful and bloody war less than ten years in the past and a rich bank of oppositional ideas and movements from which they could draw if they wished to resist the rush to war. Tolstoy's message was part of the public fund of knowledge, and the visible socialist movement had actively been opposing the arms race and imperial scramble that had produced the parlous situation at hand. Even Nicholas II was of two minds on the question. His hesitation during the July Crisis was evident in the cautious advice he sent to Serbia, his personal appeal to the Kaiser for peace, and his attempt to take a middle road of partial mobilization against Austria (but not Germany). Indeed, his ministers were so worried about further tergiversation that Sergei Sazonov, the foreign minister, urged the General Staff to "smash the telephone" after sending out the full mobilization orders.[44]

Russia's participation in the war was therefore not inevitable as the July Crisis came to a head. Even the spread of patriotic sentiment that had occurred over the previous two decades by no means predetermined the catastrophic decision to fight. Indeed, if patriotism had simply been what its proponents claimed it was—an essentially rational and preservative (if not conservative) force based in self-worth and love of the fatherland—war would probably not have occurred. But Russian patriotism also included a love of Russia's empire and its Great Power status and an inclination to see that status tied fundamentally to military prowess. These latter factors proved decisive in the crucial cabinet meeting on July 24 (n.s.)[45] that presented the tsar with a request to take a hard line in the crisis. Sazonov explicitly argued that Russian concessions in the past had emboldened the Central Powers and that if Russia abandoned the Balkans "she would be considered a decadent state and would henceforth have to take second place among the powers." Other ministers, including the moderate A. V. Krivoshein, also argued that Russia had to take a "firmer and more energetic attitude towards the unreasonable claims of the Central European powers." Even the finance minister, while noting that economic disaster was a real possibility, supported the firm line because "the honour, dignity and authority of Russia were at stake."[46]

Nicholas II concurred with his cabinet and went to war. Though many at the time (and many more later) doubted that Russia was patriotic enough to sustain the war effort that was required, Russia in the Great War was in fact patriotic. This does not mean, of course, that every Russian supported either the war or the government, but it does mean that Russian public life was deeply colored by patriotism. Those deemed unpatriotic were marginalized, and patriotic ideals did indeed inspire many Russians of all stations during the war years.[47] Patriotism was also transformed over the same years, becoming more "modern" and egalitarian, and less conservative and monarchical. Indeed, over the course of the war, the political implications of patriotism changed dramatically. In 1914, patriotism mostly meant support for the tsar and his government. By 1915, anguished ministers were privately telling the tsar that they thought his policies were leading the country to ruin. By 1916, the idea that the government itself had become unpatriotic was being publicly stated even by moderates like Vasilii Maklakov, who declared to the Duma in November 1916 that serving both Russia and the regime was "just as impossible as serving both Mammon and God."[48] In the midst of this political crisis, the nexus between patriotism and soldiering only grew stronger. Even those who despised the tsar loved his soldiers. Indeed, martial content was probably the only constant of patriotic culture during this time of tremendous political and ideological change.

Conclusion

Objectively speaking, Russia's entry into the war was the most improbable of all. Russia had the least to gain from continental conflict and the most to lose. With the exception of the Straits Question, the ambitions of Russian policy makers in geostrategic terms were either foolish or slight. Most of those put forward early in the war (annexation of East Prussia, the establishment of Russian hegemony in the Balkans, and the "unification of Poland" under Russian oversight) were on the foolish side. Annexing East Prussia would only serve as a stimulant to a future Russo-German war, the new Balkan states had already demonstrated quite clearly in 1912–13 that they were capable of ignoring Russia when pursuing their own strategies, and the last thing the Russian Empire needed was to expand its Polish problem. As for the Straits, war with the Central Powers was a rather roundabout way of securing free passage to the Mediterranean. To make just the most obvious point, successful resolution of the problem depended most heavily on two countries: Great Britain and the Ottoman Empire, who were not even engaged in the war when Russia entered it. Achieving any of these goals would also depend on military success, a very unsure prospect. The armed forces had not yet fully recovered from their embarrassment a decade before and were still in the midst of a substantial reorganization. For its part, the Russian public had very bitter memories of a recent, bloody war, was increasingly antagonistic toward its government, and saw little good coming from a titanic clash with German and Austria-Hungary. Most importantly, all of these reasons not to go to war were visible at the time and were clearly articulated prior to the declaration of hostilities.

Still, I have argued here that Russia's entry into the war in the conditions that existed during the July Crisis was very probable, not only at the state level but down to the level of the soldier as well. This was not, I will stress again, the result of ignorance. It was the outcome produced by the change in subjective conditions, in "political culture," that had occurred over the previous generation. What is striking about Russia's mobilization is that though almost no one thought that the war was a good idea, virtually everyone responded to the emergency by participating in the war effort. This was as true for the tsar as it was for his lowliest soldier, as true for conservative ministers as it was for the members of the liberal and socialist opposition.[49] As we have seen, the Council of Ministers was united in its support for the war. The Duma would show its enthusiasm through patriotic oratory and then by closing itself down. And, in sharp contrast to the Russo-Japanese War, more than 95 percent of Russian reservists of all stripes would respond to the wartime call-up.

The change in political culture that facilitated the march to war was the insertion of martial patriotism into the center of the emerging mass culture and mass political system of the Russian Empire. We have seen that this was a conscious project targeted mainly at young men. Schools were militarized, paramilitary groups were formed, and the grand narrative of Russian history taught in textbooks and in public celebrations alike focused on the exploits of the Russian military. Part of the intent of the program was to make newly literate peasants aware of the importance of a powerful and respected state to their identity as Russians, but part was also to make adolescent boys aware of the importance of military service to their identity as men. The overwhelming Russian response to the German declaration of war was based on these subjective concerns, not on the fantastic and indeed barely known "objective" war aims.

It turns out, then, that Tolstoy was right to be alarmed as a pacifist by the rise in patriotism that he was witnessing. He understood that "patriotic pacifists" were not really worthy of the name. The July Crisis proved how quickly patriotic pacifists could become patriots in a crisis. More importantly, he saw that patriotism and war were indelibly linked. And the two proved close friends during the succeeding convulsive years. Without patriotism, it is hard to see how the cobbled Russian political system, that mish-mash of old regime structures and mass political institutions, imperialists and nationalists, elites and commoners, could have sustained even a brief war. Without war, it is hard to see what else Russian patriots could agree upon. Whatever else we may say about Russian patriotism, it is difficult to deny that it was strong enough to lead Russians to war and strong enough to keep them there for three and a half years. Tolstoy was wrong about the ability of simple Russians to resist patriotism's seductive charm.

In the end, however, patriotism proved both pernicious and self-defeating. As the war years would show, full as they were in German and Jewish pogroms, atrocities against civilians and self-righteous puffery, it was pernicious in the humanitarian terms that Tolstoy described. But patriotism was also self-defeating. It brought words of unity without the substance of true political consensus. It sponsored human destruction while providing surprisingly few resources for community building. Patriotism had helped bring war, but war ravaged Russian society, the Russian economy, and especially the Russian political system. At the end of the day, all that was left was war itself, as the world war was succeeded by a civil war that, almost unbelievably, proved more devastating to the country than the titanic confrontation that had ruined the continent.

Notes

1. George F. Kennan, *The Fateful Alliance: France, Russia, and the Coming of the First World War* (New York, 1984), 221.
2. Cited in Leo Tolstoy, "Christianity and Patriotism," in *Writings on Civil Disobedience and Nonviolence* (Philadelphia, 1987), 55–56. The publishers of this volume translated the article title (Khristianstvo i patriotism) as "On Patriotism." I am using the more literal translation here.
3. Cited in Ibid., 63.
4. Kennan, *Fateful Alliance*, 223.
5. Similar (though not identical) questions arise when considering the question of the rise of nationalism in Russia in the years surrounding World War I, and this has been the focus of much recent work (including my own). I examine patriotism here because it has a broader application. In more general terms, I agree with Rogers Brubaker that patriotism and nationalism have distinctive qualities, but also that they are flexible and dynamic ideologies that overlap more than those who stress rigid definitional characteristics usually admit. See here Rogers Brubaker, "In the Name of the Nation: Reflections on Nationalism and Patriotism," *Citizenship Studies* 8, 2 (2004), 115–27.
6. Peter Von Wahlde, "Military Thought in Imperial Russia" (PhD diss., Indiana University, 1966), 212.
7. E. I. Martynov, "V chem sila Iaponii i slabost' Rossii?" in "... *Khorosho zabytoe staroe": sbornik statei*, O. A. Bobrakov, ed., (Moscow, 1991 [1904]), 8–9.
8. Richard Wortman, *Scenarios of Power: Myth and Ceremony in Russian Monarchy*, 2 vols., Studies of the Harriman Institute (Princeton, N.J., 1995), 481.
9. Jakob Vogel, "Military, Folklore, Eigensinn: Folkloric Militarism in Germany and France, 1871–1914," *Central European History* 33, 4 (2000), 487–504.
10. I have explored this question in detail in chapter 4 ("The Nationalization of Masculinity") of Joshua A. Sanborn, *Drafting the Russian Nation: Military Conscription, Total War, and Mass Politics, 1905–1925* (DeKalb, 2003).
11. For more on this reform process, see ibid., 25–29, 133–34, 42–45. Much of this section is adapted from the corresponding parts of that work.
12. War ministry request excerpted in Petr Stolypin, Letter to the War Ministry (27 March 1910), Russian State Military History Archive (RGVIA) f. 2000, op. 3, d. 71, ll. 254–55.
13. Ibid.

14. Ben Eklof, *Russian Peasant Schools: Officialdom, Village Culture, and Popular Pedagogy, 1861–1914* (Berkeley, 1986), 125.
15. "Otchet o pervykh kratkosrochnykh kursakh gimnastiki dlia uchashchikhsia v nizshikh i srednykh uchebnykh zavedeniiakh Kavkazskogo uchebnago okruga sostoiavshikhsia letom 1909 goda," RGVIA f. 2000, op. 2, d. 794, ll. 415–457ob; Excerpts from the 1910 report to the tsar on the condition of Semirechenskaia oblast, RGVIA f. 2000, op. 2, d. 800, ll. 44–45.
16. See "Zhurnal zasedaniia mezhduvedomstvennoi komissii, uchrezhdennoi dlia detal'noi razrabotki voprosov o fizicheskom razvitii molodezhi i obuchenii ee voennomu stroiu," (1911) RGVIA f. 2000, op. 2, d. 795, ll. 347–48.
17. "K s"ezdu po fizicheskomu razvitiiu o sportu," (1911) RGVIA f. 2000, op. 2, d. 795, ll. 120.
18. See the declarations of the Holy Synod and the MNP to this effect, 29 December 1911 and 19 June 1912, RGVIA f. 2000, op. 2, d. 795, l. 2ob, 7ob.
19. See for instance, Major-General Dubenskii, *Uchebnik dlia vedeniia stroevykh i gimnasticheskikh zaniatii v narodnykh shkolakh i drugikh uchebnykh zavedeniiakh* (St. Petersburg, 1911).
20. The first Boy Scout troop was formed in Tsarskoe Selo by army officers in 1909. James Riordan, *Sport in Soviet Society: Development of Sport and Physical Education in Russia and the Ussr* (Cambridge, 1977), 35.
21. Vasilii Kliuchevskii, *Peter the Great*, Liliana Archibald, trans (New York, 1961), 10–12.
22. David R. Jones, "Forerunners of the Komsomol: Scouting in Imperial Russia," in *Reforming the Tsar's Army: Military Innovation in Imperial Russia from Peter the Great to the Revolution*, David Schimmelpenninck van der Oye and Bruce W. Menning, eds., Woodrow Wilson Center Series (Cambridge, 2004), 67.
23. Report from governor of St. Petersburg to the chairman of the Council of Ministers (1910) RGVIA f. 2000, op. 2, d. 794, l. 5ob; see similar expressions of hope and fear regarding *poteshnye roty* in "Osobyi zhurnal soveta ministrov," (1911) RGVIA f. 2000, op. 2, d. 794, ll. 58–61.
24. "Polozhenie o vneshkol'noi podgotovke Russkoi molodezhi k voennoi sluzhbe, 18 July 1911," in *Ustavy o voinskoi povinnosti*, S. M. Gorianov and P. P. Lebedev eds., (St. Petersburg, 1913), appendix, 3–7.
25. Sandi E. Cooper, *Patriotic Pacifism: Waging War on War in Europe, 1815–1914* (New York, 1991).
26. Geoffrey Best, *Humanity in Warfare* (New York, 1980), 156.
27. Jan Gotlib Bloch, *The Future of War in Its Technical, Economic, and Political Relations: Is War Now Impossible?* (New York, 1899).
28. International Commission to Inquire into the Causes and Conduct of the Balkan Wars, and George Frost Kennan, *The Other Balkan Wars: A 1913 Carnegie Endowment Inquiry in Retrospect* (Washington, DC, 1993). From unpaginated preface by Nicholas Murray Butler [1914].
29. Tolstoy's inner conflict over morality was long evident in many respects. His "conversion" in 1880 was simply the dramatic moment in which he attempted to resolve the conflict once and for all. See Rene Fueoloep-Miller, "Tolstoy the Apostolic Crusader," *Russian Review* 19, 2 (1960), 108.
30. Leo Tolstoy, *Anna Karenina*, Richard Pevear and Larissa Volokhonsky, trans. (New York, 2000), 771.
31. Tolstoy, "Christianity and Patriotism"; Leo Tolstoy, "Patriotism, or Peace?" in *Writings on Civil Disobedience and Nonviolence* (Philadelphia, 1987).
32. Tolstoy, "Christianity and Patriotism," 52.
33. Ibid., 59.
34. Tolstoy, who was growing increasingly misogynist at this time, did not hesitate to assert that during the Franco-Russian festivities (which Tolstoy did not witness personally), "the women on all these occasions played the leading part." Ibid., 63.
35. Ibid., 80–85.

36. Ibid., 105.
37. Tolstoy, "Patriotism, or Peace?," 137.
38. Tolstoy, "Christianity and Patriotism," 55.
39. Tolstoy, "Patriotism, or Peace?," 144–47.
40. Tolstoy's publishing house, Posrednik, which mainly (but not exclusively) sold Tolstoy's didactic works, published more than twelve million copies in its first four years of existence. These were available not only in urban shops but from peddlers at country fairs as well. Jeffrey Brooks, *When Russia Learned to Read: Literacy and Popular Literature, 1861–1917* (Princeton, NJ, 1985), 105, 338.
41. For a collection of Tolstoyan memoirs and an introductory history of them, see William Benbow Edgerton, *Memoirs of Peasant Tolstoyans in Soviet Russia*, Indiana-Michigan Series in Russian and East European Studies (Bloomington, 1993).
42. P. N. Durnovo, "Memorandum to Tsar Nicholas II, February 1914," in *Documents of Russian History, 1914–1917*, Frank Golder ed. (New York and London, 1927), 12, 19. For more on the significance of this memorandum, see David M. McDonald, "The Durnovo Memorandum in Context: Official Conservatism and the Crisis of Autocracy," *Jahrbücher für Geschichte Osteuropas* 44, 4 (1996).
43. Baron Taube, cited in McDonald, "The Durnovo Memorandum in Context: Official Conservatism and the Crisis of Autocracy," 496.
44. W. Bruce Lincoln, *Passage through Armageddon: The Russians in War & Revolution, 1914–1918* (New York, 1986), 38.
45. n.s. (new style) relates to a date according to the Gregorian calendar.
46. D. C. B. Lieven, *Russia and the Origins of the First World War* (New York, 1983), 142–43.
47. See Jahn for an exploration of patriotism in visual culture during the war; on another aspect of this new patriotic inspiration, see Melissa K. Stockdale, "'My Death for the Motherland is Happiness': Women, Patriotism, and Soldiering in Russia's Great War, 1914–1917," *American Historical Review* 109, 1 (2004).
48. V. A. Maklakov, "Speech on the Duma Floor, November 3, 1916," in *Gosudarstvennaia Duma, 1906–1917: Stenograficheskie Otchety*, 4 vols., V. D. Karpovich, ed., (Moscow, 1995). vol 4, 63–67.
49. The Bolsheviks were remarkable (and as a result deeply isolated) by their immediate and persistent refusal to hop on the bandwagon of war.

Part IV

Culture, Gender, Religiosity, and the Coming of War

Chapter 13

HONOR, GENDER, AND POWER
The Politics of Satisfaction in Pre-War Europe

Ute Frevert

⁕

The power of political structures has a specific internal dynamic. On the basis of this power, the members may pretend to a special "prestige," and their pretensions may influence the external conduct of the power structures. Experience teaches that claims to prestige have always played into the origin of wars. Their part is difficult to gauge; it cannot be determined in general, but it is very obvious. The realm of "honor," which is comparable to the "status order" within a social structure, pertains also to the interrelations of political structures... The sentiment of prestige is able to strengthen the ardent belief in the actual existence of one's own might, and this is important for positive self-assurance in the case of conflict. Therefore, all those having vested interests in the political structure tend systematically to cultivate this prestige sentiment.[1]

In these dry words, Max Weber assessed the role of honor in national and international politics. Large political units, he claimed, develop pretensions of honor and prestige that tend to become an irrational element of international relations. The "honor of power" (*Ehre der Macht*) typically bears an expansive character and is highly flammable. At the same time, it is self-affirmative and thus acts as a strong amplifier. As a contemporary example, Weber (who wrote this before 1914) cited the German-French antagonism during the early years of the twentieth century.

A few years later, Weber found himself immersed in a fresh case of honor politics. This time, however, he cast off the role of a distant analytic observer but rather played an active role in propagating and cultivating the "prestige sentiment."

Although he constantly urged his fellow citizens to think rationally rather than let themselves be overwhelmed by emotions, he did not shy away from using strong language in his own wartime writings and speeches. In October 1916, he spoke at a rally organized by left liberals in Munich. The war, he claimed, was a war of honor, at least for Germany. Germany did not fight for territorial changes or economic profit; instead, it fought "for honor" (um die Ehre). It would have been a cause of shame (*Schande*) if the nation had not taken up arms to defend its claim to power against countries like Britain and Russia that were about to conquer the world. As a country with a large population and a vibrant economy, Germany had no choice but to be a *Machtstaat* and cast its vote in deciding on the world's future.[2]

Max Weber was not the only contemporary to think and talk about World War I in terms of honor and shame. The conflict between European states that erupted in July 1914, and resulted in multiple declarations of war a month later was largely framed in a language of honor. This language was spoken by all participants, who—despite severe differences of interest—communicated in a common vocabulary, grammar, and syntax. Unlike future antagonists, they were socialized in the same sphere of norms and values; their "unspoken assumptions" and their "ideological furniture" showed similar patterns.[3] They shared a cultural understanding of what honor meant and how it was displayed. And they were extremely sensitive to allegations of dishonorable and shameful behavior.

My thesis is that the language of honor as it was traditionally spoken in times of strife was very badly suited to solving the massive conflicts in 1914. Rather than offering a way out, it forced the participants into a deadlock that resulted in war. Once the war had started, the language of honor served, along Weber's lines, to instil an "ardent [*pathetisch*] belief in the real existence of national power" among those who fought, financed, and endured the war. The pathos, so my argument goes, largely stemmed from gendered images of honor that appealed directly to people's emotions and senses and was one of the central underlying cultural preconditions for the outbreak of World War I.

I. From Personal Honor to National Honor: Duels and Wars

With regard to the events of July and early August 1914, many historians have stressed the impact of militant nationalism: "Love of one's country and hatred for its enemies proved the most potent rationalization for aggression the long nineteenth century produced."[4] Indeed, passionate emotions, both positive and negative, were pronounced in the oral and written declamations, declarations, and proclamations that accompanied the diplomatic tug of war during those crucial weeks of summer. Speeches, poems, and newspaper articles all spoke of love and hatred. The enemy was dealt with in highly despicable words, metaphors, and images, whereas one's own country was applauded and cherished beyond all measure.

This emotional divide was not restricted to the outbreak of war, but intensified during its course; posters and postcards, often commissioned by the government, lent it a visual expression that grasped people's imagination and pervaded public communication.

True, this nationalistic fervor could draw on an eminent tradition. For France and Germany, it has been traced back, through the 1870–71 war, to the late eighteenth century. In order to construct national consciousness and identity, both nations needed an enemy: no "patrie sans ennemi," no "Vaterland ohne Feind." The language of patriotism and nationalism that gained currency during and after the French Revolution dwelt on a deeply antagonistic imagery. With minor alterations, it basically stayed the same between 1792 and 1918, except for the introduction of ethnic-anthropological notions during World War I.[5] For other countries, similar national antagonisms and stereotyped enmities can be established.[6] Thus, Europeans in 1914 were well equipped with an arsenal of politically framed emotions that could be easily evoked and expressed in times of crisis.

What has escaped most historians, though, is the dominance of "honor" in the language that was used to whip up national feelings.[7] As a matter of fact, wars could be legitimated much more effectively as acts of defense rather than aggression. The defensive logic, in turn, was deeply ingrained in the idea and practice of honor. Honor (which we can, for the sake of brevity, define as "a right to respect"),[8] was attacked, insulted, and offended—and thus had to be defended, saved, and rescued. Reading the documents that were produced during the crucial stages of decision making in July and August 1914, one cannot help noticing how often contemporaries alluded to honor in order to justify what they were thinking and doing. Rather than love for one's fatherland and hatred of the respective enemy, it was honor, dishonor, and shame that served as powerful explanatory concepts and frames of reference.

Evidence can be provided for all sides. The manifesto that the Austrian Emperor Franz Josef issued to his "peoples" on 28 July 1914 justified the war against Serbia as being "in the defence of the honor of my Monarchy."[9] When the Russian ambassador at Vienna announced his country's military mobilization on 29 July 1914, he added that Russia had been slighted in its honor as a major power, urging the nation to take the necessary steps.[10] This allegation was refuted by Kaiser Wilhelm II, who, in a telegram to the tsar, assured him that "nobody is threatening the honor or power of Russia."[11] For his part, the kaiser explained on 5 August that he was "forced to draw the sword in order to ward off an unjustified attack and fight for ... our national honor."[12] One day later, he issued a proclamation to the German people in which he argued that Germany's enemies did not want the nation to "stand, in resolute fidelity, by our ally which is battling for its reputation as a great power, and with whose humiliation our power and honor, too, would be lost."[13] On the very same day, the British prime minister Asquith told the Commons: "We are fighting ... in the first place to fulfil a solemn international obligation which, if it had been entered into between private persons in the ordinary concerns of life, would have been regarded as an obligation not only of law but of honour, which no self-respecting man could possibly have repudiated." He knew himself to be in keeping with public opinion and the Unionist shadow cabinet that had earlier on declared it "fatal to the honour and security of the United Kingdom to hesitate in supporting France and Russia at the present juncture."[14]

The arguments were indistinguishable and interchangeable. First, all politicians claimed that by declaring war they were acting in defense. They were responding to an attack that was launched from outside, by an enemy who in turn was held to be pursuing aggressive aims. Second, this attack was not just endangering the existence and security of one's own country or its vital interests; above all, it affected its honor. It came as an insult and was intended as such. It thus demanded a sharp rebuff. Quite obviously, this could not happen in the form of diplomatic deliberations; rather it called for war. War, for all participants, seemed to be the only adequate answer when national honor was at stake.

We might dismiss this as purely rhetorical, as a formal reminiscence of far older practices that had actually lost their meaning in the modern world of national power dynamics. And we might find support from critical contemporaries who seriously doubted the validity of references to honor when it came to preparing for war. When on 3 August the House of Commons was discussing Sir Edward Grey's speech concerning the position of His Majesty's Government with regard to the European crisis, members of the Labour Party explicitly questioned his argument that, not only obligations or interests, but also honor compelled Britain to go to war. Keir Hardie reminded the House that "the plea that our honour was involved in entering into war was always the excuse." Mentioning both the Crimean and the Boer War that had allegedly been fought "because of our honour," Ramsay MacDonald queried whether Grey's argument could be taken at face value. Defying "Ministerial and Opposition cheers," he sarcastically remarked that statesmen usually and traditionally appealed "to their nation's honour" in order to cloak a crime.[15]

At the same time, however, MacDonald did not generally dismiss honor as a valid motive and reason. "If," he said, "the nation's honour is in danger, we would be with him" (meaning the Foreign Secretary). He only questioned that honor *was* in danger in the present situation, just as he was not persuaded by Grey's argument that "the country is in danger." Even for Labour MPs (as much as for German social democrats or French socialists), thus, honor was a value that was recognized as such and that could necessitate immediate action.

Still, there were some reservations about whether the concept of honor was still timely and appropriate. For poets like Rupert Brooke, it was coated with a patina of old and faded traditions that he was only too happy to see rejuvenated:

> Honour has come back, as a king, to earth
> And paid his subjects with a royal wage;

And nobleness walks in our ways again;
And we have come into our heritage.[16]

As if he did not trust this reappearance, Foreign Secretary Grey often referred to "our respect and good name and reputation before the world."[17] Max Weber, too, used "honor" synonymously with "prestige" and "reputation." In his theoretical writings he thus modernized a concept that to him seemed somewhat old-fashioned in a world allegedly governed by the rational assessment of prosaic interest. In his wartime political speeches, however, he talked about honor as a given fact, just as the British Liberal David Lloyd George called honor a "reality."[18]

Honor, as Weber saw it, was part and parcel of a pre-modern world that was stratified in estates or status groups (*Stände*) rather than classes defined by the market situation. In contrast to the latter, the status situation (*ständische Lage*) was not determined by economic conditions, but by honor. Both principles "normally" excluded each other in that status honor "stands in sharp opposition to the pretensions of sheer property." It was based on a "specific conduct of life" that favored "distance and exclusiveness" and rested on a "distinctive traditional ethic reinforced by education." This ethic, as Weber observed with regard to medieval aristocracy, "made personal relations central to the conduct of life and impressed every individual with the obligations of a status honor that was jointly held and thus a unifying bond for the status group as a whole." The medieval tradition, according to Weber, had proved powerful in influencing the European upper classes ever since. Both in Great Britain and on the Continent the current "ideal of manliness" and "conduct of life" clearly demonstrated that "feudal knighthood" with its strong sense of "personal honor" and chivalry still served as a crucial "center of orientation."[19]

While Weber acknowledged, somewhat perplexed, the persistence of honor in the modern market-oriented world, his colleague Georg Simmel pointed to the functions that honor performed in society. Honor, to him, mediated between the individual and the group in which he or she belonged. It translated "social duty" into "individual weal" by infusing the individual "with the conviction that the maintenance of his honour constitutes his most intrinsic, most profound and most personal self-interest." Although honor resided in the group and guaranteed its cohesion, it was felt and practised by each group member individually.[20] This analysis helps us to understand the inner dynamics of honor-based social or status groups. Within nineteenth century European societies, there were quite a number of these groups adhering to strict codes of honor. The officer corps counted among them as well as academic circles, administrative elites and the nobility. Classes, however, which formed in the market and were economy driven, proved less prone to sharing and exhibiting these codes.

This said, it is not difficult to locate the men charged with political decision making in 1914 in social milieus that socialized their members in the language and practice of honor. The military—who became more and more influential as the crisis evolved—thought of honor as their "inviolable possession."[21] The diplomatic corps, whose ranks were mostly filled with aristocrats, was equally bathed in honor, and so were the politicians who eventually decided on war and peace or advised the heads of state (mostly monarchs) on the decision. Not surprisingly, the interaction within and between these groups in July and August 1914 was intensely marked by the language of honor. It was not only the word itself that, as quoted above, was used time and again in official, semi-official, and secret communication. Other concepts and practices that were part of the lexicon of honor were even more frequently employed and alluded to. "Humiliation," "insult," "shame," "challenge," "satisfaction," "offense"—there was barely a telegram or a conversation that did not include these notions. Every member of the upper (middle) classes in Europe could easily identify them as what they were: components of the early modern language of honor that had focused on the practice of duelling. Even in countries like Great Britain where the duel had fallen out of fashion since mid-century, the language was still spoken and understood.[22]

On the other hand, though, the subject of honor and shame as it was addressed in this communication was no longer the male individual (and member of a respective status group); instead, it was the nation. Politicians, diplomats, officers, and public opinion did not speak in their own name; rather, they spoke on behalf of the "nation," the "fatherland," the state, the country. It was "us" rather than "I," "our" honor rather than "mine" that was at stake. A code of conduct, a concept of behavior that had been utterly individualistic (though rooted in and backed by social groups) was thus collectivized. The nation, i.e. the citizens of a given state, had become the target of insults and offenses and was called upon to defend itself. It could do so by issuing a "challenge" and engaging in a fight that was meant to restore its honor. On national terms, the challenge amounted to a declaration of war, and through war, the humiliating insult could be washed away. War thus resembled the duel, except that it was fought not between two men, but between millions.

There were other differences, too. While the duel was a highly formalized and controlled practice, war was not. There were no neutral observers who made sure that the rules were obeyed. Even the rules themselves were not clearly defined, despite attempts since the 1860s to codify internationally valid norms of conduct in warfare. Most important of all, there was no predetermined end of war. Whereas a duel's end was agreed on before it even started, wars did not know that kind of previous negotiation. The results of the fighting also differed. A duel, especially in modern times, did not necessarily entail physical damage. It was not meant to kill. Certainly, there were situations in which participants were eager to harm one another, and in such cases, the conditions under which duels were fought (and which both opponents had to accept) were particularly severe. But even then, a fatal outcome was never guaranteed. It was possible, but not certain. Only one in four duels that were brought to the attention of the public persecutor in Germany during the nineteenth century had ended with death.²³ The basic idea of the duel was not punishment, or revenge; even if strong emotions were involved, they had to be controlled and brought under a strict regimen of outside checks and balances.

In contrast, wars were fought until one party gave up and either asked for an armistice or surrendered its military forces in a formal capitulation.²⁴ There were clearly winners and losers, as much as there was victory and defeat. This logic, again, was completely absent in a duel which could neither be lost nor won. A duel was something to be endured. Its participants had to confront and stand up to the situation without flickering and showing a trace of fear or nervousness. Through the defiance of death, they mutually acknowledged their honor. They showed their respect for each other and upheld that they were both men of honor who did not shy away from physical danger in order to fend off insults and offenses. If injuries or even death occurred and stopped the duel, this was not interpreted as victory or defeat. And it by no means delivered a verdict on the actions that had provoked the duel.

Wars as they were fought since the late eighteenth and early nineteenth century followed an altogether different logic. According to military theoretician Carl von Clausewitz, modern war as it was initiated by Napoleon came ever closer "to its true nature, its absolute perfection." Its driving force was the will to "annihilation," its goal being the "defeat of the opponent" which had to be energetically and ruthlessly pursued. While the eighteenth century had transformed war into a mere political "game" of limited risks, the wars of revolution had unleashed "absolute violence." Rather than allowing for a "moderate advantage" in order to negotiate a favorable peace, the new idea of war was to "annihilate" the opponent. Even if this did not mean "absolute destruction," it entailed enough violence to thrash the enemy so that their armies could not go on fighting.²⁵

Here again, it becomes evident that this kind of warfare had nothing to do with how and for what ends duels were fought. Clausewitz's initial statement that "war is nothing but an extended duel" thus proved more and more unrealistic.²⁶ Modern weaponry, its industrialized supply and amassment during the final decades of the nineteenth century, made it even more theoretical. If there had been anything like the "military code of honour of civilised nations" that the *Times* alluded to one year after the outbreak of the Great War, it was eradicated by the accumulated means and strategies of destruction since August 1914. Germany was not alone in "employing her rich technical resources in a manner regardless of the traditions of war," as the British paper reproachfully and nostalgically claimed.²⁷ Even before 1914, each war had brought about changes and innovations both in tactics and weapons; the "traditions" that the *Times* journalists referred to, including the "military code of honour," quite obviously were those that were established in pre-Napoleonic times and had been eroded ever since. Although the Geneva Convention of 1864, the Brussels Declaration of 1874, and the Conventions on

Land Warfare signed at The Hague in 1899 and 1907 had newly set up "laws and customs" that should be observed in warfare, they were never unanimously and unequivocally agreed on, let alone abided by.[28]

Still, it is interesting and revealing that contemporaries of the Great War could and did refer to a "code of honor" allegedly inherent in warfare. It tells us something about the mindset of those who lived through these dramatic events, and it testifies once more—and even more directly—to the prevalence and omnipresence of chivalrous concepts of behavior among members of the upper and middle classes. Although they should have known—and did know—better, they obviously chose to envisage war as an "extended duel." German students who had volunteered for front-line service expected the latter to resemble a *Mensur*: "It takes rigid self-discipline," a 24-year-old medical student wrote home, "to stand your ground in a duel without batting an eyelid."[29] And Ernst Jünger, a highly decorated young officer in the German army and author of the widely acclaimed *Storm of Steel* (1920), more than once described combat experiences on the Western Front as "duels."[30]

It would be a subject of its own to analyze the clash between traditional codes of honor and the industrialized mode of warfare that gained momentum during World War I. Shared norms of honorable conduct that still prevailed at the beginning of military action appear to have soon broken down.[31] This clash and the ensuing disillusionment (which was formidably captured in Jean Renoir's 1937 movie, *La Grande Illusion*) contributed greatly to the negative image of war that emerged after 1918.[32] What came as a surprise to men who had grown up in cultures of honor, though, could have been obvious to everyone reading Clausewitz (and other military theoreticians and practitioners after him). Clausewitz's writing in the 1820s had linked the brutalization of war to what he perceived as its "nationalization." When citizens were addressed as soldiers and wars became "peoples' wars," war changed its "nature." National "enthusiasm" linking citizens and governments unleashed "energies" that knew no bounds. Traditional "boundaries" of warfare were trespassed due to the democratic participation of the whole population. Since the citizens themselves identified with the war, considered it of national interest, and imbued it with strong emotions, the means of warfare became unlimited, both technically and morally. As to the future of military conflicts, Clausewitz was extremely pessimistic. Once those boundaries had been torn down, it would be very hard to erect them anew. Whenever "great interests" were involved, mutual enmity would probably be acted out in the same unrestrained way that he and his contemporaries had witnessed since 1793.[33]

What had actually happened during and after the French Revolution can be described as two closely intertwined developments: the nationalization of politics, and the nationalization of war. First, enthroning the nation as sovereign meant transforming politics from a business of the government (i.e. the king's cabinet) into the concern of (male) citizens who, through their elected representatives, took decisions on war and peace. Some contemporary observers quickly concluded that under these conditions wars would become less and less frequent since they contradicted the citizens' proper interest. Their "commercial spirit" (rather than morality) would eventually foster peaceful relations between states and nations.[34] These predictions, however, proved wrong. As mentioned above, nationalist ideas turned out to be powerful means of evoking feelings of belonging and antagonism. Propaganda evoking "national honor" had a strong feedback. Public opinion as it was expressed in daily papers, party rallies, and demonstrations depicted a high degree of sensibility and vulnerability when it dealt with alleged attacks against this honor. Even in Germany, whose citizens remained largely excluded from political decision making throughout the nineteenth century, similar developments took place. In 1890, Helmuth von Moltke (the elder), an eminent military figure and a conservative member of the Reichstag, emphatically warned his fellow parliamentarians against new wars that, as he claimed, would be instigated not by governments and princes, but by peoples. "Nationalist and racial endeavours" could, at any moment, provoke the outbreak of war, even against the will of those in charge of declaring war.[35]

Moltke was not only a critical observer of the nationalization of politics and the strong wave of nationalism that gripped European societies since the final decades of the nineteenth century.[36] He had also been a witness to the nationalization of war as he experienced it in 1870–71. Originally, this development too was rooted in the French Revolution that had merged the roles of citizens and soldiers. By declaring every citizen a soldier, the French had been able to draft mass armies and imbue them with a spirit of national commitment that had utterly surprised their opponents. During the course of the nineteenth century, most European countries (except for Great Britain) adopted the practice of general conscription. This meant that wars were no longer fought by mainly professional soldiers but by civilians who for the time being put on a military uniform and obeyed their superiors' orders. This new type of recruitment bore great potential, both in terms of numbers and motivation. Citizen soldiers were supposed to know what they were fighting for: it was their own national interest that allegedly kept them going. This held especially true for those who did not wait to be drafted but entered the army as volunteers.

What Moltke, as Prussian chief of staff, experienced in 1870/71, though, was a further stage of development. After most of the French regular army had been taken prisoner by the Germans, the new French government declared *"la guerre à outrance"* and started arming civilians in great numbers. For Moltke, this "armed crowd" lacked all legitimacy. He called them *"franctireurs," "francvoleurs,"* and "terrorist gangs" and fought them "by severe reprisals." Even if he acknowledged their "patriotism" and "bravery," he detested the "anarchy" and destruction they brought about and that was to be answered by "merciless severity." The war, he wrote to his brother in October and November 1870, "is ever growing more bitter and hateful." "The war is assuming a horrible aspect. It is bad enough when armies have to tear each other to pieces; but to set nations against each other is not an advance, but a lapse into barbarism."[37]

In a way, Moltke drew too strict a line between what he called a war of armies and a war of nations. Gambetta's policy only meant a gradual radicalization of what had come into being eight decades earlier. Whenever a government called on its citizens to join the armed forces, it helped to nationalize war. Moltke's predecessors, venerable Prussian officers like Blücher, Scharnhorst, or Gneisenau, had already talked about a "national army" and "national war," and the law that institutionalised conscription in 1814 had elevated the army to be the "main training school for war for the entire nation."[38] The emotional excitement that Moltke found so upsetting in 1870 had a much longer tradition as well. Military reformers in Prussia advertised universal conscription as a "national desire … welcome to all who love their country and hate the oppressor." And self-appointed propagandists like Ernst Moritz Arndt or Ludwig Jahn did not hesitate to evoke strong emotions both positive and negative in their attempts to incite their fellow citizens for a German *Volkskrieg* against the French.[39]

In order to achieve this goal, they constantly referred to notions of German honor that had been violated and desecrated by Napoleon. By invading and occupying German lands, the French had branded the country. Now it was up to German men to take up arms and reclaim the fatherland's lost honor. At the same time, they were called upon to protect their "parents, women and children" who could not help themselves but depended on their sons', husbands', and fathers' manly shield. This shield, Arndt remonstrated, had failed when the French enemy had raided Germany and "disgraced your wives and daughters." To eventually drive the enemy out of the country and restore German honor was thus an urgent duty that should be performed out of "fiery hatred against the French" and "intimate love for the Germans." Only when motivated by those emotions and fought for "fatherland and justice and freedom" did war bear any legitimacy.[40]

2. Honor and Gender

These arguments exhibit notions of honor and shame that are outspokenly gendered. Both the fatherland and the family were described in feminine terms. The fatherland had been invaded and overrun; it had been occupied by foreigners who had enslaved its men and raped its women. Therefore it needed a new generation of men to stand up, fight off the slander, and restore national as well as female honor to their former glory and integrity.

One hundred years later, the language of international relations sounded very much the same. While heads of state, diplomats, and national governments were deliberating war in July 1914, they used a highly gendered vocabulary. In Berlin,

Austria's answer to the Sarajevo murder was closely watched and judged in categories of strengths and weaknesses. The Foreign Office saw Austria's "prestige" waning because of its continuous lack of action and its "timid and undecided" behavior. This was considered a serious weakness which ultimately divested Austria of its status as a great power and downgraded the nation to "the Sick Man of Europe." The only way out was to react strongly to the Serbian challenge and thus achieve "political rehabilitation."[41] On the other hand, Serbia, which was held to be a "small" but "provocative" country, had to be "humbled" and "chastised" by all means. Only a "deep humiliation" could reduce them to their proper status and in turn lift Austria's "prestige."[42]

The language of honor as it was spoken among diplomats was thus strongly associated with gender images. To act as Austria had done prior to the July crisis obviously rendered it effeminate. It was in danger of losing its masculine character and being abated to a weak and helpless state that would eventually be torn apart and swallowed by greedy neighbors. Honor was identified with strength, courage, and decisiveness, whereas weakness, anxiousness, and a lack of initiative were inviting dishonor and shame.

Quite obviously, these characteristics were part of a gender lexicon that had been compiled and communicated since the late eighteenth century. Women, as a general rule, were thought of as weak creatures who due to their physical nature were neither in control of their bodies nor of their emotions. This made them into helpless victims of male seduction and aggression. Men, in contrast, were perceived as taller, more robust, and muscular beings whose relative physical strength translated into feelings of power and courage. They consequently developed higher ambitions to impose their will and their force on others which made them into good hunters and warriors. The male character, in short, proved itself both in "creating and destroying" structures and people.[43]

The categorical gender differences that the nineteenth century was so proud to set up encompassed honor and dishonor, too. As much as honor differed among social status groups, it also differed between men and women. While female honor was basically rooted in sexual integrity, male honor was held to reside in a man's readiness to stand up fearlessly and courageously to challenges of any kind. Nature, so common opinion went, had based "the whole moral existence of the woman on decency and chastity while the man's rested on courage and strength." This was why "a woman lost her honor and reputation if her decency [*Schamhaftigkeit*] and chastity were harmed, while a man lost his through unmanly cowardice."[44]

To act like a coward and to be named one were thus the deepest insults and humiliations that a man could endure. He had, by all means, to do everything he could to prevent this from happening. Strength and the determination to speak and act strongly were considered major prerequisites of manhood, and it was absolutely necessary not to shy away from danger. Especially when it came to protecting weaker beings, manhood had to stand the test. As fathers, husbands, sons, and brothers, men were in a position to take care of women who could not defend themselves against attacks. If they failed to fend off these attacks and safeguard women's honor, their own honor was lost or at least seriously questioned.

This mode of thinking and feeling was not restricted to German, French, Austrian, Italian, or Russian upper (and) middle classes, among whom the duel—as a perfect method to demonstrate manly courage and save male honor—enjoyed a high reputation well into the twentieth century. It also applied to English gentlemen, who despite renouncing the duel resorted to other means of self-assertion. Public schools that educated the country's social and political elite were well known for their unwavering emphasis on so-called masculine virtues. Students were socialized in an atmosphere of "rough-and-tumble" and were taught early on that they should by no means show fear: "If you're afraid, you'll get bullied." Such was the advice that Tom Brown, the archetypical nineteenth-century school boy, passed on to an incoming student.[45] The gospel of "muscular Christianity" as it was preached in the wake of Thomas Arnold's reforms favored toughness, endurance, courage, and steadfastness. When Harry Count Kessler entered Saint George's School at Ascot in 1880, he first had to undergo a ritual that proved his courage: a boxing fight with an older student who wanted to test both his fairness and his bravery. The education that he received from both his teachers and his fellow students emphasized "chivalry, steadfastness, and honesty." Team sports played a huge role and offered, among other things, a field where the gentlemanly virtues had to be acted out. Fair play was highly valued, as well as a behavior that strictly followed the rules. Above all, a gentleman was compelled never to lose his composure, never to break down or loosen his tenacious will. He had to stand up to all kinds of danger and threats. Under any circumstances, he was asked, according to Kessler, "to keep his nerve, to be 'plucky,' to lead and not duck." He should be absolutely polite and considerate toward weaker people, and he should always be in full command of his senses and emotions.[46]

Despite some institutional and practical differences, the rules of manly behavior appear to have been remarkably similar in Britain and on the European continent. The basic components of masculine honor were valued and shared on both sides of the Channel. And, it seems, they were not restricted to those men who as members of the upper (and) middle classes were educated in institutions that preached them day in and day out. Especially when it came to differences between male and female honor, the meaning was understood by broad sections of the population. That men should not be cowards and back down, and that they should not take advantage of women's weakness was general opinion and easily transcended the class line.

This common understanding of a gender-specific honor made it easier in 1914 to rally support for the decision to go to war. The language of honor that was spoken among the powerful elites also appealed to the public. When the German chancellor addressed a huge crowd gathering in front of his palace around midnight on 30 July, he promised to fight for Germany's existence and "our national honor" to the last drop of blood; the crowd answered with "enthusiastic cheers." Even the (rare) critical voices that denounced the "vague notion of honor" ex negativo testified to its power to send "hundreds of thousands" (a gross underestimate) to death.[47] Especially when explicitly linked to gendered modes of behavior, honor proved an irresistible means of alignment. When Max Weber in 1916 explained the inevitable logic of Germany's decision to go to war, he evoked her duty to protect the independent existence of smaller countries that could exist only in the shadow of great powers counterbalancing one another. It was a question of honor, then, to make sure that this counterbalance was not destroyed by other powers' quest for dominance.[48]

In the same vein, British politicians placed national honor in the decision to stand up for Belgian independence. When David Lloyd George, Chancellor of the Exchequer (and future Prime Minister), addressed a large audience at Queen's Hall, London, on 19 September, 1914, he chose to talk about "Honour and Dishonour." "National honour," he claimed, was not just a pretension, but "a reality, and any nation that disregards it is doomed." For Britain, it was "an honourable obligation" to defend Belgium's liberty and integrity: "We could not have avoided it without national dishonour." When German troops invaded the country and thus broke the treaty that had granted Belgium's neutrality, Britain was "in honour bound to stand by it." If they had not come to Belgium's rescue, "our shame would have rung down the everlasting ages." It was not just a matter of keeping treaties, Lloyd George insisted, but also a moral duty to protect a small, weak country that was "peaceable, industrious, thrifty, hard-working" and gave "offence to no one." When it was "treated brutally" by its strong German neighbor, Britain had to throw in the glove, draw its sword, and hurry to the battlefield. It was an act of chivalry, then, and the British Chancellor did not forget to mention the slaughtered "women and children" who had to be avenged.[49]

Gendered images of strong and courageous men protecting weak women were omnipresent when it came to legitimizing the war on all sides. As Lloyd George put it, standing up for the weak and militantly defending their existence was "the only answer that becomes a man." Conversely, the "insult against British courage" that came with German descriptions of Britain as an "unheroic," "timorous, craven" nation had to be hurled "on the battlefields of France and of Germany."[50] Casting doubt on a nation's courage, then, was tantamount to attacking its honour.

For Russia, it was "little" Serbia that had to be protected as a matter of honor, and Germany likewise referred to its word of honor that bound it to Austria-Hungary in case of danger. For France, it was a *point d'honneur* to reclaim Alsace-Lorraine that had been annexed by Germany in 1871. This had dealt a heavy blow to French national honor, which was finally to be restored. The failure to protect one's own territorial integrity had severely "shamed" the French nation, and the "lost provinces" had been mourned ever since. Again, gendered images were used to color Alsace-

Lorraine's sufferings under German rule. The provinces were represented as young girls in traditional costumes desperately waiting to be rescued and returned to the motherland. Occupation and annexation were thus seen as a violation of their honor and a threat to the honor of mother France. This spurred strong emotions and the urge to liberate the land from the German masculine presence.[51]

Even blunter sexual allusions were used to describe what happened to Belgium and Northern France in August 1914. After German troops had crossed the Belgian border and crushed the resistance with, as officials declared, "unrelenting severity," the French and British public were flooded with images of German soldiers brutally trampling women and infants underfoot. Again and again, the country was depicted as a defiled woman. Obsessively, men who shaped public discourse as investigators of war crimes, as journalists and illustrators, told horrible tales about the mutilated bodies of girls and women. In a myriad of widely distributed pamphlets, posters, postcards, and newspaper articles, "two pictures went in tandem— that of the rolling, gentle Belgium or France invaded and the innocent, virtuous Belgian or Frenchwoman violated."[52] Men (except for the German perpetrators) were notably absent in these pictures. In the rare cases where they showed up, they had either been killed themselves or appeared as impotent victims helplessly watching what happened to their wives and daughters. Quite obviously, they had failed in their assigned role as heroic protectors of female honor and were now called upon to make up for their misbehavior by rendering their support to the war machine.[53]

Even in Germany whose administration tried to dismiss these images as crude propagandistic fabrications and whose intellectuals rallied behind the government "with our name and with our honour,"[54] the sexual connotations of warfare were readily invoked. Max Weber, who was a fervent critic of annexations, spoke of Belgium's *"Vergewaltigung"* (rape) and *"Kastration."*[55] In an altogether different perspective, Professor Philipp Witkop, in his 1915 address to teachers, not only approvingly quoted the song "Jungfer Lüttich," but also recommended it to be used in German classes as an excellent example to connect current and traditional war lyrics. In barely concealed sexual terms the song described the fall of Lüttich (Liège) as the violent conquest of a woman who was courted by Germany, but chose another lover (France) before eventually (and lustfully) falling for the German invaner who took her by force.[56]

This must have reminded teachers and students of Friedrich Schiller's famous *Reiterlied*, which had used similar images but placed them in the early modern milieu of Wallenstein's mercenaries. In fact, the language (and, evidently, practice) of rape, invasion, and conquest has had a long tradition in European warfare, and as much as the conquerors were painted as strong and reckless men, their victims (both male and female) were held to be weak and helpless creatures. If it were not for the intervention of a chivalrous knight, neither virtuous ladies nor humble peasants were in a position to fend off an attack. The nineteenth century had substantially modified this pattern when it declared all men responsible for defending their fatherland and family. Now, every man had to act as a knight protecting those who as women, children, and elderly people could not fight for themselves.

Along these lines, governments in 1914 issued propaganda posters portraying soldiers as knights in shining armor on horseback. By invoking the medieval tradition of bravery, chivalry, and nobility, they depicted their troops as the physical embodiment of honor while reducing the enemy to the figure of the barbarian rapist.[57] At the same time, official manifestos called upon men to defend "home and hearth," meaning the physical integrity and honor of their families and the land that they inhabited. Apparently, this ideology was well received. Both volunteers and conscripts often explained their soldierly role as fighting and dying "for the sake of the women and children."[58]

On the reverse side, those men who tried to stay out of the war were treated with disdain and contempt. In Britain, women handed out white feathers to those who in the absence of general conscription did not enlist voluntarily.[59] This meant that young men not wearing a uniform were considered as cowardly shying away from their foremost duty: protecting the honor of the fatherland and the honor of its women. By shaming them in public, women reminded men of their true honor which lay in fighting for those who were worth fighting for and who could not fight for themselves. If a woman's honor largely depended on her male guardian's determination and courage, a perceived lack of courage logically meant an insult and was interpreted as dishonorable behavior. When men complained about "horrible women" who sent them to war instead of screaming and begging them to stay at home, they did not seem to understand what was at stake. It was not so much the desire to be "in fashion" and the fear "to stand there without a hero" that compelled women to act as they—or at least some of them—did. Rather, it was the intimate connection between male and female honor that made women utterly dependent on men's courage and strength. If men could not be motivated to defend their wives', daughters', or sisters' honor, that honor was definitely in danger.[60]

3. Honor, Shame, and No Compromise: A Conclusion

The argument that has been presented so far has gone as follows: First, honor was shown as being a major concern of those men who, in July and August 1914, decided on war and peace. Honor and shame ranked highly on their list of motives that legitimized their declarations of war. This was not just meant as a camouflage of "real" interests or as a marketing trick. The war was not only "sold" as a war of honor to those who had to fight it, to work and pay for it. Rather, honor was already present in the deliberations and negotiations that diplomats and government officials engaged in during the crucial weeks after Sarajevo.[61] The vocabulary borrowed from the lexicon of honor (which reached back to the Middle Ages and the cult of knightly chivalry) could be traced along all lines of communication that spread through Europe and connected its centers of political decision making.

Second, the language of weakness and strength, of humiliation and satisfaction, of challenge and offense bore heavily gendered undertones. To stand in for the weak (and female) and to defend their honor was an essential and defining part of male honor. In turn, the impaired honor of a weaker being—be it an individual or a state—seriously harmed and questioned the honor of those who were called upon to protect it. Male honor, thus, was linked to a code of courage, bravery, and chivalry. It was inherent both in the fair play ethics of an English gentleman and in the duelling culture of continental Europe. And it transcended class lines, being understood by all social groups and genders.

This said, it still remains to be seen how far the deeply gendered language of honor not only permeated political communication before and during World War I, but also played a part in actual decision making. The argument here is that the language spoken and the metaphors used made it extremely difficult to find a compromise in the diplomatic exchanges preceding the declarations of war. Honor, as it stands, is a matter of all or nothing. Unlike a more sophisticated morality, which shows many shades of grey, is ambiguous and is open to different outcomes, an honor-based ethics only offers two ways out of a conflict: Either the offender steps back and apologizes, or he has to be challenged and called out. Given the gendered nature of honor, stepping back is extremely difficult and generally associated with weakness and lack of courage. It means "losing face," i.e. being shamefaced, which, in societal terms, is tantamount to social death.[62] Somebody who has lost face has also lost credit, confidence, and respect among his peers. His position in the world is severely shattered and not easily, if at all, repaired. The more generalized honor is, the more ubiquitous are the social results of a failure to act in accordance with it.

If we speak of honor in the context not of a social group but of a whole nation or state, the pressures that it exerts become all the more obvious. That nations and states were imbued with honor was a common perception in pre-war Europe, and so was the idea that states bore a genuinely masculine character. Heinrich von Treitschke stated very clearly that "any insult offered, even if only outwardly, to the honour of a State, casts doubt upon the nature of the State." Therefore, "if the flag is insulted, the State must claim reparation; should this not be forthcoming, war must follow, however small the occasion may seem; for the state has never any choice but to maintain the respect in which it is held among its fellows."[63] Even if British politicians and academics after 1914 tried to read a particularly German essence into Treitschke, his concepts were widely shared by contemporary theoreticians and practitioners of the nation-state all over Europe.[64]

Although Treitschke lectured in the 1880s and early 1890s, his ideas about insults, reparation, and satisfaction seem like a perfect illustration of what actually happened in 1914. The occasion was trivial even if it cost the lives of two people. The assassination of the Austrian crown prince and his wife was a single terrorist act committed by a group of young pro-Serbian nationalists. It was duly condemned as such by all governments. That it was blown up into a major national offence and into an attack on the vital interests of the Austrian-Hungarian Empire had a lot to do with domestic issues, with the inner frailty of the multi-ethnic state and the attempt to strengthen internal cohesion through forceful foreign politics. This was a factor that played a huge role in all countries that got involved in the ensuing diplomatic hassles (and that Treitschke had overlooked).[65] To rally citizens behind the flag that had allegedly been insulted was a clever move of those who otherwise feared that the citizens would turn against each other or against their own government.

But it was more than that. The audience of the language of honor was not only composed of national citizens, but also and primarily, I would argue, of foreign states. The diplomatic exchanges that took place in July and early August 1914 mainly took place between diplomats, heads of state, and government officials. Even if some information leaked out or was intentionally passed on to journalists, it was above all the "state system" in Treitschke's terms that was addressed. To ensure its "respect," every nerve had to be "strained," or, in Weber's terms, the "actual existence of one's own might" had to be ascertained. The "sentiment of honor" served this goal very well: It not only provided positive self-assurance, but also signalled to others that one would not flinch.

Talking honor meant just this: One would not voluntarily abandon one's position but on the contrary would fight for it until the last drop of blood. There was no "honor play" involved of the kind that recent anthropologists have gone far to analyze.[66] It was not a matter of outdoing one another by answering an insult with an even harsher one. Honor was not about competition or about attempting to appear more honorable than the offender. It did not translate itself into a zero-sum situation. Rather, it was taken to be an asset that could either be lost or saved but not gradually diminished or enhanced. It was "either or" rather than "less or more."[67]

If we keep honor's specific grammar in mind, it becomes clearer what terms like "humiliation," "insult," "challenge," "weakness," and "satisfaction" actually meant during the July crisis. Those who spoke or wrote these words were profoundly aware of their codified meanings, and so were those who heard or read them. The message was unequivocal: I am not a weakling, I will defend my place as a great power, I will not let others doubt my standing, and I command respect. If offended, I will demand satisfaction and, if it is not given voluntarily, I will compel the offender to face my arms.

The nature of the offense, as it became obvious in July 1914, was not open to negotiation. As soon as it was defined as such, it had to be accepted as such, and the necessary steps had to follow suit. The language of honor did not allow for compromise because this was considered as giving in, as abandoning the principles that safeguarded one's existence as a great power.[68] This would have been interpreted as a sign of weakness, and would have shamefaced the insulted party even further. In his memoirs, Bethmann Hollweg tellingly called it "self-emasculation" if Germany had yielded to Russian pressure in 1914 and not stood by its ally.[69] What was needed, instead, was a posture of "fermeté persévérante et un impassible sang-froid,"[70] of "absolute and decided firmness," of "cool and sincere courage." "Stand firmly and steadfastly" was the motto that was followed by all participants.[71]

This manly posture made attempts to peacefully solve the crisis extremely difficult. This does not mean, however, that it rendered war inevitable. Former disputes that had been wrapped up as conflicts of honor had not resulted in war while others, like the 1870 crisis between France and Prussia, had done.[72] Even the language of honor, though rather resolute and formal, knew means and ways of mediation. Not every insult among "men of honour" resulted in a duel. There were seconds involved whose task it was to look, if possible, for an "honorable" yet peaceful solution. It then depended on the goodwill of the seconds, on their communication, and on their power to convince the potential duellists that they should settle the dispute without taking up arms. In the July Crisis, the seconds' task was poorly performed. Instead of calming the insulted, Germany encouraged Austria to take strong action in order to compensate for previous weaknesses. Russia, acting as Serbia's second, initially did a much better job of restraining Serbia, but eventually entered the scene as a combatant in its own right. France, as Russia's ally, supported this move rather than seeking to avert it. And Britain, which had put in the most effort to soothe the waters and summon the opponents to a joint conference, ended up starring, too, in the theatre of war whose curtains opened in early August 1914.

Postscript

The history of honor as an element of national and international politics does not end here. Honor was at stake when Germany signed the armistice in 1918, when the German navy sank its ships in Scapa Flow in 1919, when the Weimar national assembly voted on the Versailles treaty, when the national right campaigned against the "peace of shame" and denounced (and murdered) those who had signed it. Honor and shame continually accompanied the internal and external struggle of the Weimar Republic. And it showed in 1936 when Hitler staged the *"Parteitag der Ehre"* in order to celebrate Germany's final liberation from the "chains" of the Versailles peace settlements. It came to the fore again in June 1940 when the Germans had the French sign the armistice in the same railway carriage that hosted the 1918 event. The question of how far this pathetic story of honor and shame was peculiar to those nations that had lost World War I, needs further research.

Notes

1. Max Weber, *Economy and Society: An Outline of Interpretive Sociology*, Guenther Roth and Claus Wittich, eds., (Berkeley, 1978), vol. 2, 910–12.
2. Max Weber, *Zur Politik im Weltkrieg: Schriften und Reden 1914–1918* (Tübingen, 1988), 40, 77.
3. As to the role of "unspoken assumptions" and the influence of general ideas (above all, Darwin's and Nietzsche's) on the "ideological furniture" of the decision-making elite in July 1914, see James Joll, *1914: The Unspoken Assumptions* (London, 1968).
4. Peter Gay, *The Cultivation of Hatred* (New York, 1993), 518.
5. Michael Jeismann, *Das Vaterland der Feinde: Studien zum nationalen Feindbegriff und Selbstverständnis in Deutschland und Frankreich 1792–1918* (Stuttgart, 1992).
6. Birgit Aschmann and Michael Salewski, eds., *Das Bild "des Anderen": Politische Wahrnehmung im 19. und 20. Jahrhundert* (Stuttgart, 2000); cf. for Britain Sven Oliver Müller, "Who is the Enemy? The Nationalist Dilemma of Inclusion and Exclusion in Britain During the First World War," *European Review of History* 9, 1 (2002), 63–83.
7. An exception is Joll, *Unspoken Assumptions*. But even he mentions "honor" only in passing, and especially Avner Offer, "Going to War in 1914: a Matter of Honour?" *Politics and Society* 23 (1995), 213–41.
8. Frank Henderson Stewart, *Honor* (Chicago, 1994), 21, passim.
9. *The Times*, 30 July 1914, 7.
10. Imanuel Geiss, ed., *July 1914: The Outbreak of the First World War: Selected Documents* (New York, 1967), 280. The tsar's manifesto published 2 August 1914, not only referred to Russia's duty to protect Serbia against "unjust" Austrian attacks, but also mentioned that "we must also safeguard the honour, dignity, and integrity of Russia and her position among the Great Powers" (*The Times*, 4 August 1914, 3).
11. Geiss, *July 1914*, 324.
12. Ernst Johann, ed., *Innenansicht eines Krieges: Deutsche Dokumente 1914–1918* (Munich, 1973), 24.
13. Gay, *Cultivation*, 515.
14. Michael Brock, "Britain Enters The War," in *The Coming of the First World War*, Robert J. W. Evans and Hartmut Pogge von Strandmann, eds., (Oxford, 1990), 145–78, quotes 177, 156. In the same vein, Britain's Ambassador at Berlin, Sir Edward Goschen, told the German Chancellor Bethmann Hollweg on 4 August "that it was, so to speak, a matter of 'life and death' for the honour of Great Britain that she should keep her solemn engagement to do her utmost to defend Belgium's neutrality if attacked." Bethmann had, for his part, stressed that the British policy "was like striking a man from behind while he was fighting for his life against two assailants"—which was among the most dishonorable acts that one could think of. Quotes in *Why We are at War: Great Britain's Case*, by Members of the Oxford Faculty of Modern History (Oxford, 1914), 200.
15. *The Times*, 4 August 1914, 6f. Grey's speech was reprinted in Viscount Grey of Fallodon, *Twenty-Five Years 1892–1916*, vol. 3 (London, 1935), 296–319. MacDonald's and Hardie's reservations were shared by David Lloyd George, who, in a speech on 19 September 1914, declared himself "fully alive to the fact that whenever a nation has been engaged in any war she has always invoked the sacred name of honour. Many a crime has been committed in its name; there are some crimes being committed now. But, all the same, national honour is a reality, and any nation that disregards it is doomed." In *Honour and Dishonour: A Speech*, David Lloyd George (London, 1914), 2.
16. Rupert Brooke, *1914 and other poems* (London, 1918), 13.
17. Grey, *Twenty-Five Years*, 316.
18. Lloyd George, *Honour*, 2.

19. Weber, *Economy and Society*, vol. 2, 932–37, 1068 f. Where the translation speaks of "styles of life," I have changed it to "conduct of life," which comes closer to the German *"Lebensführung."*
20. Georg Simmel, *Soziologie: Untersuchungen über die Formen der Vergesellschaftung* (Frankfurt, 1992), 485ff. Stewart, *Honor*, 54ff. concisely speaks of "honor groups."
21. Ute Frevert, *Men of Honour: A Social and Cultural History of the Duel* (Cambridge, 1995), 47.
22. D. T. Andrew, "The Code of Honour and its Critics: The Opposition to Duelling in England, 1700–1850," *Social History* 5 (1981), 409–34; Ute Frevert, "Honour and Middle-Class Culture: The History of the Duel in England and Germany," in *Bourgeois Society in Nineteenth-century Europe*, Jürgen Kocka and Allan Mitchell, eds.(Oxford, 1993), 207–40. As to the French "culture of honor" before 1914, see Edward Berenson, *The Trial of Madame Caillaux* (Berkeley, 1992), ch. 5, as well as Robert A. Nye, *Masculinity and Male Codes of Honor in Modern France* (New York, 1993)
23. Frevert, *Men of Honour*, 234. If we take into account that official record taking only set in when duellists were severely injured or killed, we can assume that the overall proportion of fatal duels was far below 25 percent.
24. Bernd Wegner, ed., *Wie Kriege enden: Wege zum Frieden von der Antike bis zur Gegenwart* (Paderborn, 2002).
25. Carl von Clausewitz, "Vom Kriege," in *Kriegstheorie und Kriegsgeschichte*, Reinhard Stumpf, ed., (Frankfurt, 1993), 15–423 (important quotes 54f., 253—definition of "annihilation"). *Absolute Destruction* is the title of Isabel Hull's recent book on German military culture (Ithaca, 2005) in which she claims that Imperial Germany developed both the theory and practice of military extremism. Notwithstanding her generally convincing argument, I would hold against it that (1) those extremes were actually thought and acted out during the Napoleonic Wars, (2) that they were not peculiar to Germany, but shared by most European countries, (3) and that the concept of Vernichtung and Vernichtungskrieg was not per se synonymous with physical eradication of the enemy.
26. Clausewitz, "Vom Kriege," 15.
27. *The Times*, 2 August 1915, quoted in Aribert Reimann, *Der große Krieg der Sprachen: Untersuchungen zur historischen Semantik in Deutschland und England zur Zeit des Ersten Weltkriegs* (Essen, 2000), 264.
28. The Hague Ordinances, for example, introduced the extremely elastic concept of "necessities of war" that offered signatory states the opportunity to get around the precepts of humane warfare under certain circumstances. See Leon Friedman, ed., *The Law of War: A Documentary History*, vol. 1 (New York, 1973), esp. 229; Geoffrey Best, *Humanity in Warfare* (New York, 1980); Jost Dülffer, *Regeln gegen den Krieg? Die Haager Friedenskonferenzen von 1899 und 1907 in der internationalen Politik* (Berlin, 1981).
29. Philipp Witkop, ed., *Kriegsbriefe gefallener Studenten* (Munich, 1928), 11. A *Mensur* was a students duel that was fought with swords rather than pistols (Frevert, *Men of Honour*, 102–15).
30. Ernst Jünger, *In Stahlgewittern* (1920) (Stuttgart, 1986), esp. 73, 241, 267.
31. This is not only supported by accounts of the Western Front but also by naval warfare. Initially, German submarines attacking Allied merchant ships surfaced and let the crew and passengers leave in life boats before they blew up the ship. This changed during the period of unrestricted submarine warfare (Robert K. Massie, *Castles of Steel: Britain, Germany, and the Winning of the Great War at Sea* (New York, 2003), 514ff.
32. This is deplored and heavily criticized by James Bowman whose recent book, *Honor: A History* (New York, 2006) launches an ardent attack on the "anti-honor culture" that has prevailed ever after.
33. Clausewitz, "Vom Kriege," 193, 240f., 337–40.
34. Immanuel Kant, "Zum ewigen Frieden. Ein philosophischer Entwurf," in *Ewiger Friede? Dokumente einer deutschen Diskussion um 1800*, Anita and Walter Dietze, eds., (Munich, 1989), esp. 89f.,102.
35. Moltke's speech in parliament, 14 May 1890, quoted in *Kriegstheorie und Kriegsgeschichte*, 504–07.

36. See Eugen Weber, *The Nationalist Revival in France, 1905–1914* (Berkeley, 1968); Jost Dülffer and Karl Holl, eds., *Bereit zum Krieg: Kriegsmentalität im wilhelminischen Deutschland 1890–1914* (Göttingen, 1986); Paul Kennedy and Anthony Nicholls, eds., *Nationalist and Racialist Movements in Britain and Germany before 1914* (London, 1981).
37. *Letters of Field-Marshal Count Helmuth von Moltke to His Mother and His Brothers*, translated by Clara Bell and Henry W. Fischer (New York, 1892), 197–209.
38. Ute Frevert, *A Nation in Barracks: Modern Germany, Military Conscription and Civil Society* (Oxford, 2004), 15, 19, 40.
39. Ibid., 15, 25. Cf. Karen Hagemann, "Of 'Manly Valor' and 'German Honor': Nation, War and Masculinity in the Age of the Prussian Uprising against Napoleon," *Central European History* 31 (1998), 187–220.
40. Ernst Moritz Arndt, *Kurzer Katechismus für teutsche Soldaten, nebst einem Anhang von Liedern* (n.l., 1812), 9, 15, 22, 24; Arndt, *Zwei Worte über die Entstehung und Bestimmung der Teutschen Legion* (n.l., 1813), 22f.
41. Geiss, *July 1914*, 122f. (Jagow); 128f. (Schoen paraphrasing Zimmermann).
42. Ibid., 82, 129.
43. *Universal-Lexikon oder vollständiges encyclopädisches Wörterbuch*, H. A. Pierer, ed., (Altenburg, 1835), vol. 13,161f. See Ute Frevert, *"Mann und Weib, und Weib und Mann." Geschlechter-Differenzen in der Moderne* (Munich, 1995), 25–50.
44. Ibid., 215f. (quotes from 1808 and 1838). See, as a reflection on these beliefs, the arguments about male and female honor that were made in the famous Caillaux trial in Paris, July 1914, Berenson, *Trial*, 23f.
45. Thomas Hughes, *Tom Brown's Schooldays* (London, 1906), 197; J. A. Mangan, *Athleticism in the Victorian and Edwardian Public School* (Cambridge, 1981).
46. Harry Graf Kessler, *Gesichter und Zeiten: Erinnerungen* (Frankfurt, 1988), 102, 104, 113. Cf. Mark Girouard, *The Return to Camelot: Chivalry and the English Gentleman* (New Haven, 1981).
47. See the editorial "The obsessed" (Die Besessenen) in the left-liberal journal *Die Aktion*, 1 August 1914, quoted in Johann, *Innenansicht*, 15f. For Bethmann Hollweg's speech and the reaction, see ibid., 15.
48. Weber, *Zur Politik im Weltkrieg*, 77.
49. Lloyd George, *Honour*, 1, 5, 7. Even relatively unemotional publications used strong language to label the German violation of "weak"countries' neutrality as "cowardly" (*Why We are at War*, 88).
50. Lloyd George, *Honour*, 7, 10. That Germans did question Britain's heroism and the courage of its male citizens is evident in a multitude of brochures, articles, and pamphlets published the beginning of the war. For Britain, the standard argument went, the war was just "business" in order to make money, let others do the fighting, and reap the benefits. See, pars pro toto, Adolf von Trotha, *Volkstum und Staatsführung: Briefe und Aufzeichnungen aus den Jahren 1915–1920* (Berlin, 1928), 18, 48.
51. Ouriel Reshef, *Guerre, mythes et caricature: Au berceau d'une mentalité francaise* (Paris, 1984), ch. 1; Michael Burns, "Families and Fatherlands: The Lost Provinces and the Case of Captain Dreyfus," in Robert Tombs, ed., *Nationhood and Nationalism in France* (London 1991), 50–62. Berenson, *Trial*, 114–17, even argues that French men felt personally emasculated and dishonoured by the 1870 defeat.
52. Ruth Harris, "The 'Child of the Barbarian': Rape, Race and Nationalism in France during the First World War", *Past & Present* 141 (1993): 170–206, quote 179. Cf. also Nicoletta F. Gullace, "Sexual Violence and Family Honour: British Propaganda and International Law during the First World War," *American Historical Review* 102 (1997), 714–47.
53. *The Times*, 29 August 1914, 9 ("The March of the Huns"); *Punch*, 26 August 1914: "The Triumph of 'Culture'"; *Punch*, 9 September 1914: "God (and the Women) Our Shield." As for

French propaganda graphics, see "Les Atrocités Allemandes" (1914–15), in *Die letzten Tage der Menschheit: Bilder des Ersten Weltkrieges*, Rainer Rother, ed., (Berlin, 1994), 468–71. Cf. John Horne and Alan Kramer, *German Atrocities, 1914: A History of Denial* (New Haven, 2001), ch. 5.

54. "An die Kulturwelt. Ein Aufruf," quoted in Bernhard vom Brocke, "Wissenschaft und Militarismus," in *Wilamowitz nach 50 Jahren*, William M. Calder III et al., eds., (Darmstadt, 1985), 649–719, 718. See Horne and Kramer, *Atrocities*, chs. 4, 6.

55. Weber, *Politik im Weltkrieg*, 18, 21, 22, 70.

56. "Und das war der Herr von Emmich, / Dieser sprach: 'Die Festung nehm ich. / Jungfer, mach den Laden auf. / Heißgeliebte Jungfer Lüttich, / Laß mich ein zu dir, ich bitt dich, / Hochzeitsgäste warten drauf.' / Doch die Jungfer Lüttich süße / Wollte nicht Herrn Emmichs Grüße, / Wollt ein ander Ehgemahl; / Einen andern, einen Franzen, / Wollt nur mit dem Schranzen tanzen, / Der sich durch das Pförtlein stahl. / Aber sprach der Herr von Emmich: / 'Deine Hochzeitstüre stemm ich', / Gab das Zeichen zu dem Tanz. / Und mit Fetzen und mit Scherben / Tat er um die Jungfrau werben, / Schoß ihr ab den Hochzeitskranz. / Blümlein warf er an die Mauer, / Rosen blühten rot, mit Schauer / Zuckten Hochzeitsfackeln auf. / Ja, das war ein herzhaft Schießen / Und ein großes Blutvergießen / Bei der Hochzeit und der Tauf. / Herr von Emmich mag nicht spaßen, / Tat sie um die Taille fassen; / Fräulein Lüttich schrie vor Lust. / Und sie hat sich ihm ergeben / In dem Jahr, in dem wir leben, / An dem siebenten August." The song was written by P. Ansgar Pöllmann and sung after the popular melody of "Prinz Eugen." Philipp Witkop, "Der deutsche Unterricht," in *Der Weltkrieg im Unterricht* (Gotha, 1915), 53–67, quote 60f.

57. Maurice Rickards, *Posters of the First World War* (New York, 1968); Joseph Derracott, *The First World War in Posters: From the Imperial War Museum* (London, 1974).

58. From a letter of Will Orchard, 5 May, 1917, quoted in Reimann, *Krieg der Sprachen*, 290.

59. Nicoletta F. Gullace, "White Feathers and Wounded Men: Female Patriotism and the Memory of the Great War," *Journal of British Studies* 16 (1997), 178–206.

60. Andreas Latzko, *Men in War* (New York, 1918), 40–42.

61. Here, my argument contradicts Hartmut Pogge von Strandmann's that "ideas and principles which seemed to some to be worth fighting for were introduced mainly after hostilities had begun in order to justify the entry into the war" ("Germany and the Coming of War," in Evans and Pogge von Strandmann, *Coming*, 92).

62. See, on the relation between face and honor, Erving Goffman, "On face-work," in Goffman, *Interaction Ritual: Essays on Face-to-Face Behaviour* (Harmondsworth, 1972), 5–45, esp. 9f.

63. Heinrich von Treitschke, *Politics* (New York, 1916), Vol. 2, 595; as to the masculinity of states and power, see ibid., vol. 1, 252–55; more references in Ute Frevert, "Das Geschlecht des Politischen," in *Männerbund und Bundesstaat*, Lynn Blattmann and Irène Meier, eds., (Zürich, 1998), 36–52.

64. James Joll, *The Origins of the First World War* (London, 1992), 217 f.; *Why We are at War*, ch. 6 ("The new German theory of the State").

65. Ibid., ch. 5; Hew Strachan, *The First World War* (Oxford, 2001), Vol. I, ch. 1.

66. See, above all, Pierre Bourdieu, "The sentiment of honour in Kabyle Society," in *Honour and Shame: The Values of Mediterranean Society*, John G. Peristiany, ed., (London, 1966), 191–241; John G. Peristiany and Julian Pitt-Rivers, eds., *Honor and Grace in Anthropology* (Cambridge, 1992).

67. This is a different logic from that one suggested by Avner Offer, who confronts the passion-led "short term consideration of honor" with the "prudential, longer term preference for survival" ("Going to War," 223, passim.)

68. Cf. Max Weber who, in his "Parliament and Government in Germany" (1917–18), argued that when positions were "fixed as if it were a point of *honour*," they destroyed "the possibility of any substantive understanding" in international relations: Weber, *Political Writings*, Peter Lassman and Ronald Speirs, eds,(Cambridge, 1994), 203.

69. Theobald von Bethmann Hollweg, *Betrachtungen zum Weltkriege*, (Berlin, 1919), vol. I, 142f.
70. Gerd Krumeich, *Aufrüstung und Innenpolitik in Frankreich vor dem Ersten Weltkrieg* (Wiesbaden, 1980), 264 (quoting here Poincaré).
71. Quotes from *The Daily Mail*, 27 July 1914, *The Daily Chronicle*, 31 July 1914, and *The Daily Mail*, 3 August 1914, in Reimann, *Krieg der Sprachen*, 30 f.
72. See, for the many cases of averted wars, Jost Dülffer et al., *Vermiedene Kriege: Deeskalation von Konflikten der Großmächte zwischen Krimkrieg und Erstem Weltkrieg* (Munich, 1997). As to the 1870 crisis which, from the very beginning, was played out as classical case of *point d'honneur*, see Birgit Aschmann, "Ehre – Das verletzte Gefühl als Grund für den Krieg: Der Kriegsausbruch 1870," in *Gefühl und Kalkül: Der Einfluß von Emotionen auf die Politik des 19. und 20. Jahrhunderts*, Aschmann, ed., (Munich, 2005), 151–74.

Chapter 14

INTERNATIONAL SOLIDARITY IN EUROPEAN AND NORTH AMERICAN PROTESTANTISM BEFORE 1914 AND AFTER

Hartmut Lehmann

As the Great War began in August 1914, European governments proclaimed declarations of war, mobilized troops, and rushed them to the battlefields, while the churches of all states involved in this conflict of yet-unknown proportions performed enthusiastically what they considered to be their duty. They arranged special services for the departing troops, assured those at home that God was on their side, and assigned some members of the clergy to serve as army chaplains.[1] No one had expected a conflict of this magnitude, and everyone was shocked that peace could not be preserved; but Protestant clergy and the members of Protestant churches in particular, with few exceptions, accepted the war as if it had been sent by God, and they asked God for peace but above all for victory as each side believed that its own cause was just.

Of the countries at war, both Germany and Great Britain had the longest and strongest Protestant tradition. The established churches of both countries had broken away from Rome in the sixteenth century (though Germany retained some of its Catholic ties), and in both countries a close relationship between state power and state interests on the one hand and the role of the church on the other hand had developed during the Reformation. As a result, Lutheran and Reformed churches in German territories and the Anglican Church in England were conceived of and constructed as state churches or state institutions. Solidarity with Protestants in other countries counted less than loyalty to the prince or monarch of one's own country, and this tradition remained unbroken until 1914.

However, new religious movements created new forms of contact between English and German Protestants as early as the seventeenth and the eighteenth centuries. Pious German Protestants eagerly read edifying literature written by English Puritan authors.[2] German Pietists understood their own cause as being similar to the religious efforts of Puritans, while English Methodists, in turn, were inspired by the success of German Pietism. Beyond the limits set by the state churches, therefore, a new kind of solidarity between pious Protestants of both countries began to grow many decades before the French Revolution. This solidarity crystallized around the belief that they were all working toward the establishment of God's Kingdom on Earth. This second tradition also lasted until 1914. Moreover, and as we will see, it continued to grow considerably in the course of the nineteenth century.

As early as the seventeenth century, some Protestants in England were involved in a third tradition, though less strongly than were Protestants in Germany. This was what became the tradition of "peace churches": a tradition shaped most notably by Quakers and Mennonites, and also to a certain degree by Baptists. These groups shared a strong belief in peace and peacekeeping. Some nonconformist Protestants in Germany were inspired by the same kinds of ideas, but secular and church authorities suppressed them by force. Most persons sympathetic to these ideas therefore migrated to the British colonies in North America, where they were able to find places of refuge. In the late seventeenth century, William Penn even toured Germany and successfully invited nonconformist German Protestants to settle in his new colony of Pennsylvania.

During the eighteenth and nineteenth centuries, congregations in England, Scotland, and North America became partners in this third tradition of Protestant peace churches, but congregations in Germany did not. Certainly, the Herrnhuter (or Moravians as they were known in the English-speaking world), a branch of German Pietism, also believed in pacifism as a Christian virtue. Within a few decades, the Herrnhuter had succeeded in becoming an international free church with a special dedication to missionary work. But their energies were almost completely exhausted when their leader, Count Zinzendorf, died in 1760. Although the Herrnhuter remained active until 1914, they never won the kind of influence in matters of peace that the Quakers acquired during the nineteenth century in both the United States and Great Britain as well as internationally. Not surprisingly, therefore, in 1914, when the German Herrnhuter were called to arms, they did not object. The Herrnhuter had failed to develop a policy of objection to any kind of war on the ground of reasons of conscience before 1914, and they were not strong enough as a movement to mobilize the members of Herrnhuter communities all over the world for the cause of peace as war erupted.

Many of the more conservative Protestants in Europe were alarmed by the events of the French Revolution. Between the 1790s and the 1820s London became the most important international center for establishing publishing-houses for the printing and distribution of large numbers of Bibles. These Bibles were considered the best possible remedy against revolutionary activities. Furthermore, almost all of the missionary activities of the following decades were first started in London. Very soon, however, other centers were created in Amsterdam, Basel, Boston, Edinburgh, and Philadelphia. By the 1830s, what can be called the "Pious International" had assumed significant influence and contours that distinguished its followers' activities from the rest of Protestantism. Those who participated believed that the Bible contained all the knowledge they needed for their faith, they were active in missionary work, and they considered themselves born-again Christians. The "Pious International" was led by members of the free churches of England, Scotland, and the United States, by members of the Réveil in Switzerland, and by members of religious revival movements associated with the Great Awakening, or *Erweckungsbewegung* in Germany and Scandinavia. It took on a concrete manifestation when in 1846, the so-called Evangelical Alliance was founded in London. Of 920 delegates who were present at this meeting, 786 came from Great Britain, 87 from North America, 13 from the German-speaking countries of Central Europe, and 34 from other European countries. In 1855, moreover, as a subsidiary of the Evangelical Alliance, the Young Men's Christian Association (YMCA) was founded in Paris. All members of the Evangelical Alliance were, it seems, convinced that the Protestant nations had a special mission. For them, it was the historical role of Protestantism to overcome medieval superstition on the one hand and to support the progress of civilization on the other. This role, they believed, was not yet fulfilled but had to be continued in their own time. Luther and Calvin were their heroes. Building God's Kingdom at home and abroad, through social reform and missionary activities in Africa, Asia, and Australia, had, in their view, blended with anti-Catholicism into a common cause. Whereas the British, French, Belgian, and French Swiss branches of the Evangelical Alliance were constituted as early as 1846 and 1847, however, the German branch came alive only after the Revolution of 1848. Nonetheless, in the 1850s, the German branch held regular meetings in various German cities. When it met in Berlin in 1853, the Prussian king Frederick William IV provided a reception, thus indicating that he supported the cause of international solidarity among pious Protestants.

In the same years as the Evangelical Alliance flourished, new and additional ties were created between the Protestants of Europe and North America. For example, a sizeable number of young Americans came to German universities to study Protestant theology; American Protestants, but also Protestants from other countries toured Geneva and Wittenberg, which was called by some the "Mecca of Protestants."[3] As Luther's four hundredth birthday was celebrated in 1883, the festivities staged in England and in many cities in the United States were almost as impressive as those in Germany.[4] Books written by leading German theologians were translated into English. Philip Schaff, who had migrated from Berlin to Mercersburg in Pennsylvania in 1846 and later taught at Union Theological Seminary in New York, becoming perhaps the most prominent among American theologians, served as a kind of ambassador between the scholars of both nations. Protestant solidarity between English, American, and German missionaries and their effective cooperation on the ground can also be observed in many mission fields in that period. No one could have imagined in the mid nineteenth century that Germany and England would ever be at war and that the United States would join the British side against Germany.

In retrospect, however, we can observe that relations between the Protestants of these countries began to change in the 1870s and the 1880s. After the Franco-German war of 1870–71 and German unification under the leadership of Prussia, many German Protestants believed that they had received a special blessing from God and that they were now first among the Protestant nations of the world. By contrast, as early as the 1870s, American evangelists, as they came to England, also began to preach in Germany. They did so because it seemed to them that, under the strong influence of liberalism and socialism, Germany was a country drifting away from true Christian faith and true Christian practice. At the same time on the other side of the Atlantic, the communities of Germans who had emigrated to the United States and had set up their own churches became ever more resistant to assimilating into American society. Many of the communities of German-Americans considered themselves as Germans abroad (*Auslandsdeutschen*). The way of life they cherished was either non-religious, as in the case of those who attempted to create a socialist movement in the United States, or devoutly orthodox, as in the case of the Lutherans who united to form the Missouri synod. Most pastors sent from Germany to serve the congregations of Germans in America after 1870–71 were convinced that it was their task to preserve pure Lutheranism against what they called American sects, and pure German customs against the American way of life. Nineteenth century German immigrants, with very few exceptions, never joined the traditional American peace churches or the American peace society, founded in 1828.

Other changes in the relationships between German, English, and American Protestants were even more significant. From 1867 onward, delegates of the Anglican churches in all countries of the world met regularly every ten years. The World Alliance of the Reformed Churches holding the Presbyterian Faith was created in 1875, the Ecumenical Methodist Conferences were begun in 1881, the International Congregational Council was established in 1891, and the Baptist World Alliance in 1905. In all of these ventures, Protestants from the United States, England, and Scotland were the primary participants, while Protestants from Germany were not active, or only to a marginal degree. Indeed, it was not until 1947 that the Lutherische Weltbund (Lutheran World Federation) was founded. (The

Mennonite World Conference was created in 1925.) The Quakers, to be sure, needed no such new bodies. They had maintained their own international system of cooperation since the eighteenth century, and Quaker ties between England and the United States had always been especially close. In general, however, while communication and contacts between the members of the various denominations in England, Scotland, and the United States were strengthened in the last decades of the nineteenth century, no such new bridges between German, British, and American Protestants were built before 1914.

Admittedly, there were a number of exceptions to this generalization, even though the various initiatives were unsuccessful if one takes the prevention of war in 1914 as a measure of success. The first of these initiatives was the founding of the World's Student Christian Federation in 1895. The guiding spirit in this venture was John R. Mott, an American born in 1865 who had been active in the YMCA since the early 1880s, and who had served first as student as President of the Cornell University Christian Association and then as National Secretary of the Intercollegiate YMCA of the United States after 1888.[5] Mott admired Luther,[6] and in his eyes, any international body of Protestant Christians without German participation was unthinkable. As his plans to create a World's Student Christian Federation became more concrete, he therefore traveled to Germany where he met with German students who were active in the Gnadauer Gemeinschaftsverband, a new religious revival movement especially strong among Protestants of Northern Germany. Mott convinced the German students he spoke to of two things: that they should form a new organization of their own (which they did, as they created the Deutsch-Christlichen Studentenverein, the DCSV[7]), and that they should take part in an international body of Christian students. From Germany, Mott traveled to Sweden where the World's Student Christian Federation (WSCF) was founded. Karl Fries from Sweden became the first president of this organization, and Mott the secretary general. From the German DCSV, Dr. Johannes Siemsen was present.

In the following years, the WSCF met regularly: in 1898 at Eisenach, in 1900 at Versailles, in 1902 at Soroe in Denmark, in 1905 at the Herrnhuter community in Zeist in the Netherlands, in 1907 in Tokyo, in 1909 at Oxford, in 1911 in Constantinople and in 1913 at Lake Mohonk in upstate New York. The 1915 meeting that had been called in Prague had to be cancelled. In the course of these years, Mott returned to Germany just once when he attended the Eisenach meeting in 1898, on which occasion he visited Wartburg castle. During his 1898 visit, Mott realized how difficult it was to implement there the aims of the WSCF "to unite students' Christian movements or organizations throughout the world," by deepening "the spiritual life of Christian students and fitting them to win others," thus developing "a world-wide student fellowship in Christ."[8] Thus, after the meeting in Eisenach, Mott spoke to groups of members of the DCSV at the universities of Göttingen, Breslau, Leipzig, Halle, and Berlin. "It is not surprising," he wrote once he was back in the United States, "that the weeks spent in Germany constituted one of the most difficult and exhausting experiences I ever had." According to Mott, "the multitude of student secular societies which have a first and very strong hold on students render it almost impossible for the Christian movement to get a foothold. The fact that the influence of many of these organizations is positively against Christianity makes them a still greater hindrance. The indifference of students to things spiritual, coupled with their great reserve in speaking about religious matters, constitutes another very real barrier." In sum, in Mott's words: "We know of no land which presents such an array of problems and obstacles."[9] It has to be added that this negative experience did not alter Mott's Christian optimism. In 1900 he published a book in which he proclaimed "The Evangelization of the World in This Generation." When the WSCF met, however, German students were hardly ever present, and Christian students from Germany played no significant part in Mott's plans, which soon centered on large-scale missions to China and the Muslim world.

As the British branch of the WSCF met in Liverpool in 1912, a member of the German delegation, Karl Axenfeld, director of the Berlin mission, mentioned the possibility of war between Great Britain and Germany. As a response, "cables were exchanged between the German and the British delegations during the conference, expressing their determination to pray and work for peace between their nations."[10] None the less, when Mott spoke at the meeting of the WSCF at Lake Mohonk in 1913, he chose as a motto for his speech, "Our best days lie in front of us."[11] He argued, "The Austrian Empire, the Balkan states, and the Turkish Empire are the 'danger zone' of Europe." However, for Mott "these regions constituted not only a zone of danger but also a large promise for the Federation" and he concluded, "how strikingly true both views [i.e. both zones of danger and promise] were and still are." Certainly, political tensions could not be overlooked. In Mott's view, however, "happily these countries have also been the scenes of some of the most striking advances in the onward movement of Christ among the students of the nations."[12] To Mott, therefore, as for the vast majority of the Christian students, "the outbreak of war [in August 1914] was a thunderclap out of a clear blue sky,"[13] and one of the experts on the history of the ecumenical movement, Ruth Rouse, has remarked that in her view, "most [of the] Federation leaders were as blind as the students." There had been any number of severe international crises prior to 1914; within the WSCF, however, "only in 1913 did the British Movement begin to air the subject of peace in its magazine."[14]

As war erupted in August 1914, Mott did not hesitate to act. In September 1914, he traveled from New York to Rotterdam and on to Berlin where he met the new head of the German branch of the WSCF (the DCSV), Georg Michaelis. From Michaelis, who would succeed Bethmann Hollweg as Chancellor of the Reich for a brief period in 1917, Mott heard "a full, almost fanatical defense of the German attitude toward England and Russia." Mott also met Adolf von Harnack, the most famous of German theologians, who "gave him an almost as impassionate defense of the German course of action as had Michaelis, but attributed the stance of the English Christians to ignorance."[15]

Mott's own feelings in August 1914 can perhaps best be described through the words of a letter that he received from his friend Joseph H. Oldham, who had prior to 1914 spent his energies, like Mott, in supporting international missionary work. In a passage that Mott marked especially, Oldham wrote, "It is impossible yet to take in the meaning of this terrible blow to all that we have been working for during the past few years. Our deepest need, I feel sure, is to continue to have faith in God, and to believe that not even human sin and madness can ultimately defeat His purpose of love for the world." Oldham continued that he was "sure that the first feeling in all our hearts must be one of penitence and contrition. We need not trouble about the distribution of responsibility. We need to get behind that to the fundamental fact that Christian Europe had departed so far from God and rejected so completely the rule of Christ that a catastrophe of this kind is possible." According to Oldham, in this situation Christians "need to bow in deep humility before God": they "must strive," as he wrote, "to maintain the international fellowship and love."[16] It was in this spirit that Mott attempted to continue his mission after 1918.

As Mott reported to the general meeting of the WSCF that met near Thun in Switzerland in 1920, all members of the World's Student Christian Federation had served their countries during the war. "The German movement," for example, had, as Mott explained, "at the time of Christmas, 1914, sent a specially prepared booklet, Deutsche Weihnacht, to 40,000 mobilized German students in the trenches."[17] What Mott did not mention was that the Christian students in Germany had, as in other countries, volunteered in large numbers to serve as soldiers, that they had been especially keen advocates of the war effort as they believed that their cause was just and that God was on their side, and also, that many Christian students had lost their lives in combat.

Mott had also been the presiding officer in the First World Missionary Conference that was held in Edinburgh, 14–23 June 1910. By 1910, for Mott, as he called a new publication, "The Decisive Hour of Christian Missions" had started. The ambitious aim of the Edinburgh event was to carry the gospel to all peoples of the non-Christian world. Yet most of the participants and speakers who discussed at Edinburgh how foreign missionary work could best be organized and how foreign missions could best be promoted came from the English-speaking part of the world. The German presence there was minimal. It is true that among the recipients of honorary doctorates from the University of Edinburgh presented because of the occasion were three Germans: Carl Meinhof from Hamburg, Julius Richter from Berlin, and Johannes Warneck, the renowned German authority on the history and tasks of Christian missions. Indeed, Warneck did not fail to write a letter to the participants of the conference in which he commended the aims of their gathering.[18] In his papers, Mott also mentions a telegram sent by the German Colonial Office to the participants at the Edinburgh conference. "The German Colonial Office is following the proceedings of the World Missionary Conference with lively interest, and desires that it be crowned with blessing and success"; furthermore, the German Colonial Office "recognizes with satisfaction and gratitude that the endeavors for the spread of the gospel are followed by the blessings of civilization and culture in all countries."[19] Yet this sentence indicates clearly that the persons in the German Colonial Office responsible for this telegram believed that missionary work had to serve secular ends. Although Mott did not comment on this, one can be sure that he did not fail to see the differences between his views and the official German position. Moreover, no German belonged to the Continuation Committee that was elected at the end of the Edinburgh conference and to which the task was entrusted to put in practice what the delegates had decided and agreed upon.[20] After war had broken out, Entente forces occupied the German colonies. German missionaries, some of whom had taken up arms against Entente troops, were interned. Most of them were not able to return to Germany until after the war was over in 1919. Resentments were strong. For many years to come among German missionaries, nothing was left from the spirit of Edinburgh.

Another major initiative to preserve international peace had been launched before 1900 by an American Quaker, Albert Smiley, a graduate of Haverford College, former principal of the Friends' School in Providence, Rhode Island, and a friend of Andrew Carnegie. Smiley had bought a large tract of land on Lake Mohonk in upstate New York on which he built a hotel that could be used as a conference center. In 1883, in true Quaker spirit and following the Quaker tradition, Smiley initiated a series of "Friends of the Indian" conferences: that is, of course, the American Indian. Twelve years later, in 1895, in an attempt to do something toward the preservation of world peace, Smiley started "The Lake Mohonk Conferences on International Arbitration." In the following years, these conferences gave strong impulses toward the success of the Hague conference movement.[21] Much to the satisfaction of Smiley and his friends, the Lake Mohonk Conferences on International Arbitration became the most important meeting-place of American peace activists. Yet as far as this author has been able to discover, no German delegate was ever there.

As the Second Peace Conference took place at The Hague in 1907, delegates from many English churches prepared a peace memorandum that they sent to the governments as well as to the President of the Hague Conference. This formed part of a larger initiative in which J. Allen Baker, a Quaker MP, played the leading role. After having made a fortune in manufacturing, Baker had entered politics. The preservation of peace was his main interest, and he believed that peace could best be secured through direct contact with the leading statesmen. Therefore, he met the kaiser in Berlin, who helped him to arrange two meetings between German and English clergymen. In the spring of 1908, under the leadership of the Berlin court-preacher Ernst von Dryander, a group consisting of 95 German Protestants, 15 Catholics, and 19 representatives from Free Churches visited Great Britain. In the following year (1909) a similar number of representatives of the various bodies of Christian churches in Great Britain traveled to Germany.[22] In addition, in 1909, in both countries, a new organization called the "Church Council for Promoting Friendly Relations between Great Britain and Germany" was founded. In Germany, Friedrich Siegmund-Schultze, a student of Harnack in Berlin and a friend of Martin Rade, the well-known publisher of the weekly *Christliche Welt*, was instrumental in the creation of the "Kirchliches Komitee zur Pflege freundschaftlicher Beziehungen zwischen Großbritannien und Deutschland" (Church Committee for the Cultivation of Friendly Relations between Great Britain and Germany).[23] According to a pamphlet published by the American Council of the World Alliance for Promoting International Friendship through the Churches in 1919, between 1909 and 1914 in Great Britain some twelve thousand persons joined this body, of which the Archbishop of Canterbury was the President, and some four thousand persons in Germany.[24] However, the practical consequences of this remarkable initiative in the pre-war years have yet to be researched.

In the years before 1914, no one advocated the aims of the international peace movement more than Dryander's godson Friedrich Siegmund-Schultze. Strongly influenced by some of the religious socialists from Switzerland, especially by Hermann Kutter; Siegmund-Schultze also admired John Mott. In 1905, Siegmund-Schulze had taken part for the first time in the yearly meetings of the DCSV where he heard the preaching of an American evangelist, Reuben Archer Torrey (1856–1928), who impressed him a great deal. In 1909, he helped Dryander in hosting the British church delegation in Germany. In 1912–13, Siegmund-Schultze served as the secretary of the DCSV responsible for foreign students. In those years, he also came to know some of the more conservative German theologians who were active in the DCSV, such as Karl Heim from the University of Tübingen, and he met the new leader of the DCSV, Georg Michaelis. Clearly, however, what mattered more to Siegmund-Schultze than dogmatic questions was the cause of peace. He believed that war was the result of hatred between the nations and peoples. Therefore, in his view everything had to be done to overcome such hatred.[25]

As plans were made by the British and the German Church Council to send delegates to the next Lake Mohonk conference on International Arbitration in 1913, Andrew Carnegie became actively involved. Carnegie paid a visit to Berlin on the occasion of the kaiser's Silver Jubilee. In a meeting with the kaiser, Carnegie promised a gift of hundred thousand dollars for the cause of peace. The kaiser was astonished and requested advice from court-preacher Dryander, who pointed to Siegmund-Schultze as a capable young man to whom this matter could be entrusted. The next day Siegmund-Schultze met Carnegie, who promised him an annual subvention of twenty thousand dollars for the purpose of promoting the cause of peace in Germany. Because of this donation, Siegmund-Schultze was able to begin the publication of *Die Eiche*, a journal exclusively devoted to the cause of international peace.

Back in the United States, Carnegie developed further plans. After having established the Carnegie Endowment for International Peace in 1910, he now conceived "a proposal for a society that would campaign for peace through an appeal to religious convictions." In pursuing this plan, in February 1914 Carnegie assembled at his house in New York "representatives of the Protestant, Catholic, and Jewish faiths, many of whom were leaders in the peace movement." He promised to support financially two preliminary conferences to discuss the unification of Christian forces for the purpose of organizing the churches against the use of war as a means for settling international disputes.[26]

A month earlier, in January 1914, the body of Swiss Reformed Churches, the Schweizerische Kirchenkonferenz, taking up a suggestion first made by the Reformed Church of the Swiss canton of Waadtland, had invited Christian leaders interested in peace to a conference in Bern. In spring 1914, the Carnegie and the Swiss initiatives were synchronized. Again, J. Allen Baker played a crucial role. It was his idea that this conference should be held in Germany and the organization should be entrusted to Siegmund-Schultze. As a result, an invitation was issued to an international peace conference of Christian representatives in the city of Constance, a place sacred to many Protestants for the memory of Johann Hus. The date set for this conference was 1 August 1914.

A total of 148 delegates had originally planned to come to Constance: 50 from the United States, 29 from Britain, 22 from Germany, 14 from France, 7 from Belgium, 7 from Switzerland, 4 from Austria-Hungary, 4 from the Netherlands, 4 from Norway, 3 from Denmark, and 2 each from Italy and Sweden. Friedrich Siegmund-Schultze was a member of the German delegation that consisted mainly of representatives of the Prussian Union Church. There were two members of Reformed Churches in the German delegation, and one from the Methodist Church of Germany, but none from the Herrnhuter, the Seventh Day-Adventists, the Baptists, the Mennonites, or the Quakers.[27]

Of the 148 who had intended to come to Constance, less than half did in fact arrive. On Sunday, 2 August 1914, they assembled in the Hotel Insel to consider the relationship of Christianity to international peace, but everything was completely overshadowed by the news of mobilization for war. Therefore, the delegates sat in an upstairs room of the hotel and worried mainly how they would be able to get back home. But they also prayed for peace in English, French, German, and Swedish. Moreover, before the delegates departed hurriedly on Monday, 3 August, they made far-reaching decisions. They passed four motions: the first declared the obligation of the churches to use their influence in furthering friendship amongst nations; the second asked for united action by the churches in preserving peace; the third demanded that a permanent organization for carrying these objects into effect be set up; and the fourth appointed an international and inter-denominational

Committee to carry on this work and arrange future conferences. The participants at the Constance meeting also unanimously agreed to send the following telegram to the Crowned Heads and Prime Ministers of Europe and to the President of the United States: "This conference of members of Christian Churches representing twelve countries and thirty confessions assembled at Constance to promote friendly relations between nations, solemnly appeals to Christian rulers to avert a war between millions of men, amongst whom friendship and common interests have been steadily growing, and thereby to save from disaster Christian civilization, and assert the power of the Christian spirit in human affairs."[28]

As the Constance meeting was adjourned on 3 August, most delegates took the train to Cologne from where they headed for the Netherlands and on to Great Britain.[29] Some of the delegates who had been in Constance were able to reassemble in London as early as 5 August 1914, where they discussed the statutes for the World Alliance for Promoting International Friendship through the Churches. The stated purpose of this new body was "to organize the religious forces of the world so that the weight of all churches and Christians can be brought to bear upon the relations of governments and peoples to the end that the spirit of peace and goodwill may prevail, and that there may be substituted arbitration for war in the settlement of international disputes; friendship in place of suspicion and hate; co-operation instead of ruinous competition; and a spirit of service and sacrifice rather than that of greed and gain in all transactions between the nations." At the London meeting, these statutes were officially approved, although—needless to say—no German delegate was present at this occasion.[30]

The World Alliance for Promoting International Friendship through the Churches received from Andrew Carnegie an endowment of 2 million dollars. It became best known as "The Church Peace Union." In the years after World War I, it exercised a dominating influence on the American Federal Council of Churches. The German branch of the Church Peace Union, led by Friedrich Siegmund-Schultze, pursued matters of peace with more vigor than the mother organization. It became known as the Internationaler Versöhnungsbund (Fellowship of Reconciliation). According to an official report by the American Council in 1919, during World War I the German members had worked at times "under personal danger of imprisonment."[31] After the war Adolf Deissmann (a professor of theology in Berlin, and formerly at Heidelberg University) and Friedrich Albert Spiecker (a leading manager from the firm Siemens & Halske) reactivated the German branch.[32] Friedrich Siegmund-Schultze continued to serve as its secretary. There can be no doubt, however, that after 1918, despite Siegmund-Schultze's unceasing efforts, German participation in the activities of the Church Peace Union always remained marginal. The effects were, at best, indirect. For example, Adolf Deissmann was one of Dietrich Bonhoeffer's academic teachers.

In conclusion, two questions have to be addressed. First, were European and North American Protestants aware of the danger of an impending "big war"?

Second, could World War I have been prevented had the leaders of Protestant Churches of all countries been united in opposition against war prior to 1914? The answer to the first question is "no"; to the leaders of the international Protestant community, the war of 1914 came almost as a total surprise. Certainly, there had been some indications that international tensions were rising, and the leaders of Protestant Churches knew this as well as everybody else. But they never expected the outbreak of a "big" international conflict, and they never expected a war in which English-speaking Protestants would be confronted by their German brothers and sisters in a bitter struggle for survival.

The answer to the second question is equally clear. The sad truth is that the leaders of Protestantism in Europe and North America were not strong enough to influence the political course of their countries and they were also not united in promoting international peace. For the older generation of church leaders, close cooperation between the churches and the state was a sacred duty. This is how they interpreted what Luther and Calvin had taught. Even as the foreign policy of their states became more and more aggressive in the era of imperialism, with few exceptions this position was not modified. The members of the younger generation, too, at the end of the nineteenth century and in the decade before 1914 still thought in terms of national categories. In short: it was self-evident that nationalism had become the guiding principle of international politics. This was as true for those Protestants who continued to employ religious categories and perceive their own nation as a people chosen by God,[33] as it was for those who distanced themselves from religion altogether and borrowed from the ideas of social Darwinism.[34]

By contrast, international peace churches had gained little influence in Germany before 1914, while new religious groups like the Seventh-Day Adventists or the Pentecostal movement were more interested in conversion and in winning new members than in the preservation of international peace. By 1914, moreover, one of the most remarkable German religious nonconformists and pacifists, Christoph Friedrich Blumhardt, was too old and too ill to be able to organize any kind of resistance against the war, despite his bitter opposition to the conflict.

Pacifists in America however, were no better prepared when the war came. Since the Civil War, peace groups like the Mennonites had had no experience of military service and conscription. As Ray Abrams put it in 1933, "in the halcyon days just prior to 1914 a glorious optimism pervaded the peace movement," with the result that "most of the pacifists seem to have been either ignorant of or to have ignored the realities of the situation." According to Abrams, "the religious groups and peace societies, in common with the majority of the American people, were astounded that such a catastrophe could come about so suddenly."[35] Even the large sums of money Andrew Carnegie had invested in peace projects had accomplished nothing. In 1917, Carnegie too supported the American decision to enter the war on the side of the Entente: "He shared the conviction of many Americans that the Germans were chiefly responsible and had to be defeated before real peace was possible."[36]

After the first weeks of war, a most bitter controversy erupted between British and German theologians. Leading German theologians like Adolf von Harnack and Adolf Deissmann, who were much admired in Britain, signed the "Declaration of the 93,"[37] in which German war guilt was flatly denied and all the blame was put on British arrogance and aggression. British theologians were antagonized. When they wrote to Harnack personally and asked him to explain his position, Harnack reiterated what he had signed up to in the Declaration and opposed further German-British communication until the British side showed more insight.[38] Why was there so much bitterness from German theologians toward their British colleagues? One answer is that the poison of nationalism (or perhaps the "religion of nationalism," as C. J. H. Hayes has put it as early as 1926), had corrupted Christian belief in keeping peace and Christian solidarity across national borders.[39]

In the early days of August 1914, many German theologians, just like many German politicians, hoped that their friends and partners on the other side of the Channel would safeguard the preservation of peace even in a situation when the German and the Austro-Hungarian side decided to settle open accounts—or what they believed to be open accounts—with Serbia, Russia and France. When the British government decided to enter the war on the side of France and Russia, they were deeply disappointed. Most certainly, after war broke out, both sides were convinced that their cause was just. They even called the conflict a "Holy War" in which God was on their side.[40]

After 1918, it would take a long time before the wounds inflicted verbally and in writing especially during the first weeks of the conflict would begin to heal. The German delegates who came to the ecumenical conference at Stockholm in 1925, organized by Nathan Söderbloom, attempted to use the occasion for propaganda against the Versailles Treaty. Only a few German delegates attended the international missionary conference in Jerusalem in 1928. However, by 1937, when the next large meeting of Protestants devoted to matters of peace and missionary work gathered at Oxford, the German churches were engaged in a new conflict. Those opposing Hitler now needed every kind of help that they could get from British Protestants, and despite the divisions of the past, this help was generously extended.

Notes

1. Wolfgang J. Mommsen, "Die christlichen Kirchen im Ersten Weltkrieg," in Mommsen, *Der Erste Weltkrieg: Anfang vom Ende des bürgerlichen Zeitalters* (Frankfurt am Main, 2004), 168–180.
2. Udo Sträter, *Sonthom, Bayly, Dyke und Hall* (Tübingen, 1987), 4–57.

3. Hartmut Lehmann, "A Pilgrimage to Wittenberg, the so-called Protestant Mecca," Anmerkungen zum amerikanischen Deutschland-Tourismus im 19. Jahrhundert, in Nobert Finzsch and Hermann Wellenreuter, eds., *Liberalitas: Festschrift für Erich Angermann zum 65. Geburtstag* (Stuttgart, 1992), 223–37.
4. Hartmut Lehmann, *Martin Luther in the American Imagination* (München, 1988), 176–93.
5. C. Howard Hopkins, *John R. Mott, 1865–1955*, vol. I (Grand Rapids, 1979).
6. Lehmann, *Luther in the American Imagination*, 250–53.
7. Karl Kupisch, *Studenten entdecken die Bibel:. Die Geschichte der Deutschen Christlichen Studenten-Vereinigung (DCSV)* (Hamburg, 1964), 39.
8. See Ruth Rouse, *The World's Student Christian Federation* (London, 1948), 68; and John Raleigh Mott, *Addresses and Papers of John R. Mott*, (New York, 1947), vol. 2, 14, 18.
9. Ibid., 335.
10. Ruth Rouse, *WSCF*, 176. In 1912 Axenfeld published two important pieces: "Der Kampf des Christentums um Afrika wider Heidentum und Islam," in Karl Axenfeld and Julius Richter, eds., *Vom Kampf des Christentums um Asien und Afrika* (Berlin, 1912), 20–35; Karl Axenfeld, *Die Aussaat des Gotteswortes in Heiden- und Mohammedanerherzen*, 2nd ed. (Berlin, 1912). According to these titles, Axenfeld's missionary aims were quite similar to those of Mott in the years prior to 1914.
11. Ibid., 579.
12. Ibid., 144.
13. On the argument of surprise, see the contribution of Holger Afflerbach, "The Topos of Improbable War in Europe before 1914," in this volume.
14. Ruth Rouse, *WSCF*, 176–77.
15. Hopkins, *John R. Mott*, vol. I, 439–41.
16. Letter from 5 August 1914, quoted by C. Howard Hopkins, *John R. Mott*, vol.I, 433; also by Keith Clements, *Faith on the Frontier: A Life of Joseph H. Oldham* (Edinburgh, Geneva, 1999), 123.
17. Mott, *Addresses and Papers*, vol. 2, 201.
18. Mott, *Addresses and Papers*, vol. 5, 15–16.
19. Ibid.,13.
20. Joseph H. Oldham served as secretary of the Continuation Committee. About the Edinburgh Conference and Oldham's activities 1910–14 see Keith Clements, *Faith on the Frontier*, 73–119.
21. See the contribution of Jost Dülffer in this volume.
22. John S. Conway, "The Struggle for Peace," *The Ecumenical Review* 35 (1983), 25–26; Roger Chickering, *Imperial Germany and a World without War: The Peace Movement and German Society 1892–1914* (Princeton, 1975), 210–17.
23. Friedrich Siegmund-Schultze, *Friedenskirche, Kaffeeklappe und die ökumenische Vision: Texte 1910–1969*, Wolfgang Grünberg, ed.(Munich, 1990), 48–50.
24. The World Alliance for International Friendship through the Churches, *The American Council: History, Work, Plans and Program* (New York, [1919]), 2–3.
25. Stefan Grotefeld, *Friedrich Siegmund-Schultze: Ein deutscher Ökumeniker und christlicher Pazifist* (Gütersloh, 1995).
26. Carnegie Endowment for International Peace, *Perspectives on Peace 1910–1960* (New York, 1960), 12–13. See also Ruth Rouse and Stephan Charles Neill, *Geschichte der ökumenischen Bewegung 1517–1948*, (Göttingen, 1958), Vol.6, part 2, 136–43.
27. I am most grateful to Dr. Juergen Kloeckler from the Stadtarchiv Konstanz for providing me with this information, which is based on reports in the daily newspapers in Konstanz in August 1914. However, exact numbers are hard to find. The Official Report of the World Alliance of Churches for Promoting International Friendships is now part of the Swarthmore College Peace Collection. According to this report entitled, "'The Churches and International Friendship' Report of Conference held at Constance, 1914," published by World Alliance of Churches

for Promoting International Friendship (London and New York, n.d.), 153 delegates had planned to come to Constance, and 80 had in fact managed to get there by 1 August 1914. See "The Churches and International Friendship," 10–11.
28. For a complete account, see the Report of Conference held at Constance, 1914, that includes the text of the four motions and the telegram, 19–46.
29. Without the help of the Grand Duchess of Baden, the kaiser's aunt, who lived near Constance on the island of Mainau, Friedrich Siegmund-Schultze would not have been able to arrange that a special train would take the delegates from Constance to Cologne and to the Dutch border.
30. See *Official Report*, 46–48. Another report, also deposited in the Swarthmore College Peace Collection, was written by Dr. Benjamin Battin from Swarthmore College (privately printed in November 1915). Battin paid special attention to the events prior to the Constance meeting as well as to the actions of the various national chapters of the World Alliance of Churches for Promoting International Friendship until the fall of 1915.
31. World Alliance, *The American Council*, 7.
32. Jochen-Christoph Kaiser, *Friedrich Albert Spiecker (1854–1937)*. "Eine Karriere zwischen Großindustrie und freiem Protestantismus," in *Christliche Unternehmer*, Francesca Schinzinger ed. (Boppard am Rhein, 1994).
33. Hartmut Lehmann, "The Chosen People Theme in Late Nineteenth- and Early Twentieth-Century German Nationalism," in William R. Hutchison and Hartmut Lehmann, eds., *Many Are Chosen: Divine Election and Western Nationalism* (Harrisburg, PA, 1994), 85–107.
34. Cf. Peter van der Veer and Hartmut Lehmann, eds., *Nation and Religion: Perspectives on Europe and Asia* (Princeton, 1999); Michael Geyer and Hartmut Lehmann, eds., *Religion und Nation: Nation und Religion* (Göttingen, 2004).
35. Ray H. Abrams, *Preachers Present Arms* (New York, 1933), 15.
36. Carnegie Endowment, *Perspectives on Peace*, 13.
37. Wolfgang von Ungern-Sternberg, *Der Aufruf "An die Kulturwelt": Das Manifest der 93 und die Anfänge der Kulturpropaganda im Ersten Weltkrieg* (Stuttgart, 1996).
38. Adolf von Harnack als Zeitgenosse, ed. Kurt Nowak, part 2: *Der Wissenschaftsorganisator und Gelehrtenpolitiker* (Berlin, New York, 1996), 1435–44.
39. See Abrams, *Preachers*, 245–46.
40. See Irene Willis, *England's Holy War* (New York, 1928); Gerd Krumeich, "'Gott mit uns?' Der Erste Weltkrieg als Religionskrieg," in Gerd Krumeich and Hartmut Lehmann, eds., *"Gott mit uns": Nation, Religion und Gewalt im 19. und frühen 20. Jahrhunder* (Göttingen, 2000), 273–83.

Chapter 15

AN IMPROBABLE WAR?
INTERNATIONAL RELATIONS, ARTS, AND CULTURE BEFORE 1914

Jessica C. E. Gienow-Hecht

"Whenever I hear Wagner," Woody Allen is rumored to have said, "I want to march into Poland."[1] It is open to speculation whether Allen meant to emphasize the political content of Wagner's compositions. But in any case, he failed to mention that the composer's largest contingent of fans used to reside in the United States. Here, Wagner remained en vogue long after he had fallen out of grace with most of his European admirers.

In this essay, I wish to argue that in the long run World War I mattered very little to the development of cultural relations between Europe and the United States. As I will show, before the war European nations competed with one another for cultural preponderance in the United States. French, British, and German officials offered much leeway to non-governmental cultural exports. As we shall see, not only the content of these ventures determined their outcome but the degree of state control: the less the state got conspicuously involved in cultural exports, the more effective they turned out to be. As a result, British literature and love, French art and craftsmanship, as well as German music and musicology dominated the cultural canon of the turn of the century. They all constituted a lingua franca that supposedly transcended borders, furthered mutual understanding, and avoided military conflicts. And while these cultural relations did not help avoid the war, they survived the trench warfare almost intact. I will outline three programs of European cultural expansion before turning to the significance of German music in the United States.

On a larger level, my argument defies the notion of a probable war. For all the nationalist tendencies in European and American culture around the turn of the century, no musician anticipated, wished for, or expected a military conflict, or believed war to be a likely and probable scenario in 1913–14. German-born conductors, soloists, and orchestra musicians in the United States freely and enthusiastically traveled on the concert circuit, accepting regular engagements and guest appearances on both sides of the Atlantic Ocean. Conductors like Emil Oberhoffer (of the Minneapolis Symphony Orchestra) or Karl Muck (Boston Symphony Orchestra) spent summers in Wiesbaden, Bayreuth and elsewhere all the way up to 30 July 1914. Whatever politicians may negotiate or say, whatever military leaders may plan, whatever our newspapers report, many believed, art leads a life on its own. While cultural nationalism had been a theme in the nineteenth century and while the two decades prior to World War I witnessed intensive debates around the creation of an "American music," there were no signs for cultural pessimism or any hint of the coming catastrophe.

The scholarship on European-American diplomatic and economic relations before World War I has concluded that this period was one of dramatically changing political flirtations: European nations such as Great Britain increasingly wooed US leaders in order to win their political support.[2] This courtship affected both the diplomatic and the cultural arena. France and Germany in particular came to see the fin-de-siècle as an international competition for the export of national culture.[3] In this conflict, the United States emerged as one of the foremost targets of the European competition for cultural preponderance. Indeed, in the eyes of European cultural missionaries, America was a cultural wasteland ready to be civilized. But it was also a suitable battlefield of foreign cultures.

In 1870, France's reputation staggered to an all-time low. The Germans, in contrast, enjoyed a high popularity among most Americans. France was seen as a corrupt and weak country, ruled by opportunist republicans. From a social and economic point of view, France seemed to lack the spirit of innovation while its population stagnated.[4]

French officials were not happy with this point of view. To counter these charges and win the minds of US audiences, US-based French propagandists zealously tried to lure the upper crust of American society into their cultural domain. Though influenced by state policy, their strategies delegated the government to the backbench. The *Alliance Française*, an association founded in 1883 to promote French language and culture abroad, had no equal in Europe. Early on, the Alliance targeted the United States as its most fertile ground for proselytization. Between 1880 and 1900, the Alliance established so called "committees" in San Francisco, Boston, Los Angeles, Texas, Chicago, Denver, Brooklyn, and New York, while also inspiring seminars in San Francisco, Kansas City, and Dallas. The Alliance counted more than twenty five thousand adherents in the United States in 1904.[5] In this way, the Alliance became an influential tool in the export of French culture because it functioned like a non-governmental organization while simultaneously following state objectives.

The fine arts represented another venue for informal French cultural diplomacy. From the 1850s, salesmen and representatives of French impressionism exerted a strong influence on American culture, notably art and architecture, that lasted well into the twentieth century (and much longer than in France proper).[6] Again, the French government played a minor role without totally yielding control. Its foremost instrument of influence was the École des Beaux-Arts, its Academy, and the annual or biannual salon. While the participation of both critics and the middle classes increased the publicity of the salons in the nineteenth century, it was the state, that is the Ministry of Fine Arts, that selected the range of exhibitioners, encouraged particular themes, and it was the state who awarded individual art works. The winners of the awards given out by the state provided the works that were most likely to be selected for export to the United States.[7]

Furthermore, the central administration of the arts in France developed a fullfledged yet informal advertising program for national artwork abroad catering to the lack of art in the United States. Despite the discouraging US tariff on foreign art, professional Paris dealers like Cadart, Gambart, Durand-Ruel, and Goupil, Vibert & Cie. established renowned galleries along the US east coast dedicated to the sale of French paintings.[8]

This strategy proved enormously successful. According to a study produced by the German Generalkonsulat (which took a great interest in the matter) in New York in 1906, 57.2 percent of all paintings imported to the United States originated in France; while Germany supplied 5.1 percent. The following year, French art merchants exported four million marks worth of art works into the United States. By comparison, the German figure stagnated: it hovered somewhere around four hundred thousand marks.[9]

Scholars and art experts agree that the export of visual art never constitutes a purely cultural phenomenon. Instead, it has a double effect: the education of sensibility and the global colonization of taste and mind through the medium of the image or the painting. French art merchants, perhaps even more than French painters, were keenly aware of their influence in the United States.[10] As one journal wrote: "To this still young country which sends us republican ideas, gold and novels [an allusion to Poe's popularity, translated by Baudelaire] France will send paintings."

French efforts were not limited to language and art. The French government also made a concerted effort to attract American students, offering them a first-rate and inexpensive education. US painters like Frank W. Benson, William Glackens, and countless others dutifully spent part of their formative years in France. Broken French tinged with an American accent became a commonplace sound in the streets of Paris. Indeed, many young French artists grumbled that American students were trying to become more French than they themselves.[11]

This overall strategy worked wonders. At the end of the nineteenth century, France's prolific informal efforts to boost its culture in America had proven successful and by 1900, the country's reputation in the United States was thriving. French naturalist novels, French symbolist poetry, and, above all, French impressionist painting now commanded the attention of US artists as well as the public at large.[12] Equipped with the message that France was the cultural capital of the world, for the next four decades French propagandists would attempt to foster goodwill among American leaders. As Robert Young has argued, they consciously manipulated America's sense of cultural inferiority in the face of European history and tradition.[13]

Meanwhile, British leaders faced their own challenges in their rather thorny relationship with the United States. Quite a few US observers portrayed Great Britain as an undemocratic regime run by the landed aristocracy. England's ambivalent stand during the Civil War, economic competition, disagreements over American tariffs and fishery interests in the Bering Sea, the British presence in Canada, as well as conflicting goals in the Far East and the Caribbean put a strain on the "special relationship."

Curiously, these crises served to foster the will for an intensifying cultural rapprochement. British culture had enjoyed a special place in the imagination of American elites since the early days of the republic.[14] In the nineteenth century Anglo-American Victorianism turned into a transatlantic "middle-class," English-speaking culture. It included a set of values such as Protestantism and an orientation toward the future. It thrived on a clearly defined behavioral code that encompassed self-righteousness and competition. And it embraced common taste, fashion, and customs. For all the political disagreements, England was America's foremost cultural point of reference. When Americans acquired furniture, selected clothes and styles, worried about appropriate behavior and language, or searched for proper literature for their offspring to read, they continuously looked to Great Britain.[15] Henry James has immortalized US elites' craving for a bicultural consciousness in classic stories such as *The Bostonians*. To this day, Frances Burnett's *Little Lord Fauntleroy* still brings tears to the eyes of readers (and television viewers).[16] An avalanche of lesser Victorian novels abounded with heroes dangling between London and Chicago, creating transatlantic liaisons and mutual appreciation.

Victorianism promoted the popular interest and use of technological inventions such as mass printing. The "Victorian internet"—the telegraph—enabled immediate communication between England and the United States. And the steamer made it possible for Anglo-American Victorians to travel back and forth across the Atlantic to an unprecedented extent.[17] Since the early nineteenth century, British actors had engaged in theatrical tours up and down the eastern coast and into the

Midwest. US writers like Mark Twain were often hailed across the Atlantic before they became acceptable in the United States.[18]

Anglo-American cultural rapprochment had an impact on the educational sector as well. Throughout the nineteenth century, American elites had enrolled their offspring at German universities. But in search for an ivy-covered education for their children, at the end of the century upper-class Americans sent students increasingly to British elite schools rather than to Göttingen or Leipzig. The estate of Oxford philosopher Cecil Rhodes founded a scholarship that enabled, from 1902–03 on, more than one hundred US students to study at Oxford in order to solidify, as Rhodes called it, "[t]he extension of British rule throughout the world."[19]

On another informal level, marriage and kinship deepened the racial ties between both countries, as did the British aristocracy's increasing need of cash. Marriage brokers on both sides of the Atlantic matched up British blue blood and American money in matrimony.[20] For example, Mary Endicott married Joseph Chamberlain, Mary Leiter wed Lord Curzon, Consuelo Vanderbilt said "yes" to the Duke of Marlborough, and Jennie Jerome exchanged vows with Lord Randolph Churchill. We know now that more than one hundred such weddings were celebrated during the years before World War I. Every single one of them produced enduring political ties between British and American elites.[21]

German politicians and intellectuals monitored these activities and they increasingly feared that they would lose out in the European cultural courtship for American affection.[22] The language barrier blocked German poetry and literature from the broader American public. American students increasingly stayed away from German institutes of higher education. Save for a few exceptions, German painters had never made a significant inroad in the United States that could compete with the influx of French paintings. And German counts did not constitute a particularly good catch among the wealthy heiresses of the United States.[23]

Around the turn of the century the German imperial government became increasingly interested in cultural contacts to the United States. The Reich's early cultural export efforts centred on a—rather unsuccessful—academic exchange program. The Prussian cultural ministry and the German kaiser created this program in the early 1900s. But the exchange did more to alienate American elites than to attract them to German culture. Many US students could not attend German lectures because they did not speak or understand the language. Worse, much to the contempt of their US colleagues, German professors abroad did not always adjust their behavior to local democratic etiquette. Instead they brushed their egos and insisted on their scholastic and social superiority.[24]

The German Reich's cultural program also contained an art exchange program that proved equally worthless. It did not help that Reich officials were divided in their interpretation of such exchanges. Some believed that the function of art was to soothe international frictions, while others, notably the Foreign Office, had little interest in an art exchange.[25] On the more practical level, German artists could simply not compete with the French monopoly. Apart from nineteenth century painters such as Adolph Menzel, Arnold Böcklin, and Franz von Lenbach, German painters had not made significant inroads in the United States. The Imperial (i.e. Reich) government deemed contemporary artists like Max Beckmann or Lovis Corinth inappropriate for an international exhibition. Landscapes inspiring spectators with the spirit of *Heimat*, such as the ones by Ludwig Dill and Gustav Schönleber, seemed more appropriate politically to policymakers in the German capital.[26]

Two things matter about all these initiatives in the context of German cultural diplomacy: first, in their motivation, content, and strategy they did not differ much from French and British activities. As we have seen above, the British, too, developed an academic exchange program, the remnants of which are still with us today in the form of the highly prestigious Rhodes scholarship program. And when exporting their art, the Germans simply followed the French model. What was different, though, and this is the second point, was that for all their reluctance to get involved, German government officials kept a close eye on these initiatives. It was precisely this level of control that may have made these enterprises fail in the end. Collectively, the activities of private individuals and NGOs amounted to a political force that worried Reich officials who feared they might do more harm than good to Germany's prestige abroad.[27]

Curiously state officials remained much more diffident vis-à-vis a third sector that in the past had cemented Germany's reputation as a *Kulturnation* (nation of culture), and that was the case of "serious" music. Their reluctance coupled with the enormous prestige of the German symphony in the United States explains why this particular export received such a formidable press throughout the nineteenth century and beyond.

Since the early nineteenth century, music has occupied a special place in German history. While until about 1800 music was typically associated with either the church or entertainment, after the turn of the century, music turned increasingly into an end of itself. Celia Applegate has shown how in the early nineteenth century, music became instrumental to the shaping of German national identity. Music loomed large as the centerpiece of German *Kultur*, larger than art, painting and sculptures ever would.[28] During Napoleon's occupation, when French civilization and language seemed to threaten German cultural independence, the compositions of Beethoven's symphonies consoled millions of Germans, convincing them of their cultural superiority in the face of political and military defeat. And throughout the nineteenth century, musicians, music critics, and musicologists argued that German music was vital to the development of a German national consciousness, long before there was a German national state.[29]

Yet for all the musical enthusiasm on the part of the German kaiser and his subjects the Reich government remained lukewarm to proposals for musical exports.[30] Private societies, concert agencies, individual sponsors, and artists appealed in vain to the government to support their cultural aspirations. Venturing tours across the world, including all of Europe, Asia, and the Americas, these NGOs sought to spread German music and they hoped to solicit the moral and administrative support of local embassies, consulates, and the foreign offices.[31] For example, the Deutsche Bank of Berlin expressed a desire to send several military bands to the World Exhibition in Chicago in 1893. The bank even authorized Wolf's concert agency in Berlin to obtain the necessary permission from the emperor, but nothing came of it.[32] The primarary reason for the failure of most proposals was their presumed lack of quality or a lack of qualification on the part of the organizers. Officials were so worried that state-sponsored performances would distort the essence and reputation of German music abroad that they preferred to stay altogether out of such missions.[33]

Nonetheless, between 1850 and 1918, classical music composed in German-speaking countries, German conductors, German musicians, musicology, and music pedagogy virtually monopolized the American music scene. Appreciating music was synonymous with being German. To be German meant to be musical, to sing, to play an instrument, and to master the secret of conveying emotion through sound.[34]

While during the first half of the nineteenth century, Italian opera and occasionally French composers had fascinated US audiences, after mid century, American audiences increasingly worshipped composers from the northern half of the European continent, including Wolfgang Mozart, Johann Strauss, Richard Wagner, and others. Before World War I, New York (1842), St. Louis (1879), Boston (1881), Chicago (1891), Cincinnati (1895), Pittsburgh (1895), Philadelphia (1900), Minneapolis (1903), and San Francisco (1911) established permanent philharmonics, most of these under the tutelage of German conductors like Theodore Thomas in Chicago or Leopold Damrosch in New York.[35]

These German conductors were often driven by an almost missionary zeal to educate US audiences in classical music, a zeal that echoed the German Reich's increasing propensity to spread *Kultur* across the globe. "For that alone is it, that attracts me to come there," wrote the Mainz musician Felix Volbach when applying for the position of conductor at the Cincinnati Symphony Orchestra, in 1894, "namely to bring our rich treasures of our great masters there to the world of the future and help that they conquer the world." Evidently, an army of German musicians saw themselves appointed to trumpet down the walls of Jericho, or rather, the United States, a country that many believed lacked cultural taste and refinement.[36]

This infatuation with the world of German music created an array of spin-off effects fostering a sympathetic perception, not just of German artistry but of Germany in general. Newspapers and journals were swamped with sketches, biographies, and photographs of distinguished-looking pianists, violinists, and singers from Germany who, presumably, led a purified life dedicated to "the higher arts." German male performers like Rudolph Ganz or Emil Sauer were idolized to the same extent as were Bono, U2, or the Backstreet Boys, one hundred years later.[37] The image of the German musician as an attractive man able to express his feelings became a symbol for Germany's cosmopolitan culture. "The waltz king, personally, is evidently a good fellow," wrote one journalist during Johann Strauss' visit to America. "He talks only German, but he smiles in all languages."[38]

In retreating to a preference for German classical music, American audiences acted the way Imperial cultural administrators and immigrant musicians hoped they would. The art of "the three Bs" or Wagner evoked the respect for German greatness, *Heimat,* and emotionalism that Reich officials wanted to convey.[39] In this context it matters little whether or not the organizers and representatives of music, such as Theodore Thomas or Leopold Damrosch, acted under the explicit order of the kaiser. While their efforts may not have represented a diplomatic act, they clearly had precisely the diplomatic effect desired by the Imperial government. Germany's informal "sound diplomacy" became its most powerful tool of cultural influence and its legacy lasted long beyond the German Kaiserreich.[40]

The summer of 1914 was sweltering hot in Bayreuth. Of course, the heat could not keep away the armada of Wagner fans. From the United States, conductor Karl Muck had arrived to lead his operatic showpiece, *Parsifal.* Those who knew him must have noticed that his performance on 28 July was one of the most unusual ones ever displayed. Muck was a handsome, dashing man in the prime of his life. He was also known as the former Kapellmeister of the Royal Opera in Berlin and a personal favorite of the kaiser. His style originated in the nineteenth century: Muck continuously displayed a reserved manner, both in his personal behavior as well as his conducting. But on that day, 28 July, Muck conducted the orchestra with a rarely displayed air of emotion. Suddenly, cries of "War" sounded from the audience. A tormentous excitement began. People began running into all directions. Women fainted as men threw away their instruments, champagne glasses, and evening gowns to report for army duty at once. Muck managed to finish *Parsifal* that day with only a few musicians remaining, then fled from Bayreuth. His performance was the last rendition that year at Bayreuth. The Festspiele had to be prematurely terminated: half of the orchestra players and all of the stage hands were soldiers or eligible for military duty.[41]

Men like Muck did not expect war in the summer of 1914. To him and thousands of other artists, peace, international audiences, and transportation across the open sea was the key to their success. The war ended all of this. The fact that these musicians went to Europe indicates their ignorance—otherwise, they would not have chosen to spend their seasonal break in what would soon turn into a gigantic battlefield.

In August and September 1914, hundreds of German and American soloists, orchestra players, and conductors who had permanent engagements in the United States but spent their vacations abroad suddenly found themselves stranded in Europe or had just managed to sneak out. When war broke out, twenty-four of the orchestra players of the Boston Symphony Orchestra were still in Europe for their summer breaks and engagements, including seven first violins, two second violins, four violas, four cellos, one bass, two oboes, two clarinets, one fagot, three bass winds, and a harp. The manager of the Symphony personally rushed to Europe in order to reassemble the players and, above all, the orchestra's star conductor who, it turned out, was eager to march off to Belgium but then agreed to return.[42] Entire orchestras found themselves depleted of personnel on account of the war. When the 1914–15 season began, the Philadelphia Orchestra announced that of the twenty members of the orchestra who had traveled to Europe during the summer, only four men had been able to return to the United States.[43] Many of those who stayed in Europe joined the war effort on either one side or the other—and most of them did not have a choice. What began as a summer vacation dedicated to the art of music unexpectedly turned into a four-year inferno with little music other than the sound of gunfire, gas grenades, and exploding mines.

For most international musicians, the consequences were often devastating, both economically and personally. Pianist Ferrucio Busoni, a favorite with American audiences, was forced to cancel a fifty thousand dollar tour. Polish pianist Leopold Godowski, for six years a resident of Chicago, fled from his Brussels home without a cent. Famous pianist Joseph Weiss was now playing at a third class café.[44] Violinist Jacques Thibaud spent nineteen months in the trenches along the Marne, the Aisne, at Ypres, Arras, Verdun, and in the Champagne, where he became temporarily half blind and "as deaf as Beethoven" due to the explosion of the new French mortars.[45] Meanwhile, world-class soprano Johanna Gadski hurried to assure reporters that the war would not affect music, and music would not affect the war because "Musical harmonies have no effect on bursting shells."[46]

In conclusion, on the eve of the Great War non-governmental groups and individual artists busily traveled on the transatlantic culture circuit. Officials and political observers offered diplomatic advice, attempted to control the arts and academic exchange sector, then left the bulk of cultural exchange to non-governmental initiatives. In more than one way, German policy followed British and French models and no one put this more concisely than the German Reichskanzler, Theobald von Bethmann Hollweg, in 1913. He observed that if the Germans wanted to outdo British and French cultural propaganda, not the government but the nation as a whole would have to assume a stronger role. "What France and England accomplish in this area, is not due to the accomplishment of their governments but to the national whole, the unity and closeness of their cultures, the unerring desire for prestige of the nation itself. We have not come quite as far yet. We are not yet as certain and as conscious of our culture, our inner self, and our national ideal."[47]

To what an extent did cultural exports reflect or soothe the tensions of the times? Most artists and administrators would agree that the arts should transcend national borders and constitute a lingua franca designed to build bridges. Words and pictures and melodies are beyond mathematical calculations. Their impact cannot be measured the way we measure the effect of trade treaties, military alliances, and declarations of war.

But what we can say is this: While cultural relations mattered very little to the direct outbreak of World War I—least of all they were able to anticipate or prevent it—the war, in turn, affected these relations very little. French art, particularly impressionism and then expressionism, had a profound impact on the emergence of bohemian culture in America after World War I. And while many of the Anglo-American Victorian artifacts went out of vogue after the war, the cultural consensus remained firmly in place. Quite a few of the transatlantic academic fellowships and marriages led to lasting Anglo-American ties, the most famous of which produced Sir Winston Churchill, tireless advocate of the "special relationship" in World War II. As to the case of German music, America today is the home of some of the most influential highbrow musical institutions in the world—Carnegie Hall, the Metropolitan Opera, the Juilliard School of Music, the Curtis Institute—as well as a number of internationally acclaimed orchestras, such as the Boston Symphony Orchestra, all of whom continue to celebrate the nineteenth-century German masters.

Cultural relations lead a life on their own and the nineteenth century has a story to tell of how state involvment is only of peripheral significance for the results of cultural exchange. Perhaps cultural relations occasionally overlap with but they certainly do not merely reflect political realities. Perhaps we need to consider the quality of every international involvement and every international conflict on several levels, among those the non-military and non-political ones. Perhaps Johanna Gadski's hope that music and shells existed in different universes bore a grain of truth. And perhaps Woody Allen was right as well: hearing *The Flying Dutchman* makes audiences want to go places. Which is okay as long as they behave.

Notes

1. I am indebted to Richard Pells for this hint.
2. Alfred Vagts, *Deutschland und die Vereinigten Staaten in der Weltpolitik*, 2 vols. (New York, 1935); Ragnhild Fiebig-von Hase, *Lateinamerika als Konfliktherd der deutsch-amerikanischen Beziehungen 1890–1903 vom Beginn der Panamerikapolitik bis zur Venezuelakrise von 1902/03*, 2 vols. (Göttingen, 1986); Fiebig-von Hase, "Die deutsch-amerikanischen Wirtschaftsbeziehungen, 1890–1914, im Zeichen von Protektionismus und internationaler Integration." *Amerikastudien* 33 (1988), 329–57; Fiebig-von Hase, "Amerikanische Friedensbemühungen in Europa, 1905–1914," in *Liberalitas: Festschrift für Erich Angermann*, Norbert Finzsch and Hermann Wellenreuther eds.(Stuttgart, 1992), 285–318; Fiebig-von Hase, "The United States and Germany in the World Arena, 1900–1917," in *Confrontation and Cooperation: Germany and the United States in the Era of World War I*,

1900–1924, Hans-Jürgen Schröder ed.,(Providence, 1993), 33–68; Nancey Mitchell, "The Height of the German Challenge: The Venezuela Blockade, 1902–1903," *Diplomatic History* 20 (1996), 185–209; Torsten Oppelland, "Der lange Weg in den Krieg (1900–1918)," in *Deutschland und die USA im 20. Jahrhundert: Geschichte der politischen Beziehungen*, Klaus Larres and Torsten Oppelland eds., (Darmstadt, 1997), 1–30; Otto Pflanze, "Germany—Bismarck—America," in *Deutschland und der Westen*, vol. I *Transatlantische Beziehungen*, Jürgen Elvert and Michael Salewski, eds., (Stuttgart,1993), 67–84; Reinhard R. Doerries, "Empire and Republic: German-American Relations Before 1917" in *America and the Germans: An Assessment of a Three-Hundred Year History*, Frank Trommler and Joseph McVeigh, eds., (Philadelphia, 1985), vol. 2, 3–17; Doerries, *Imperial Challenge: Ambassador Count Berstorff and German-American Relations, 1908–1917*, Christa D. Shannon, trans., (Chapel Hill, NC, 1989); Raimund Lammersdorf, *Anfänge einer Weltmacht: Theodore Roosevelt und die transatlantischen Beziehungen der USA, 1901–1909* (Berlin, 1994).
3. Nancy Troy, *Modernism and the Decorative Arts in France: Art Nouveau to Le Corbusier* (New Haven, CT, London, 1991).
4. Of course, one needs to be careful with notions such as "the American perception" or "the French view." American perceptions of European countries and cultures depended to no small degree on the ethnic, geographical, educational, social, and political background of the observer. In the context of this work, I am specifically referring to Anglo-American elites, unless noted otherwise.
5. Peter Grupp, "Voraussetzungen und Praxis deutscher amtlicher Kulturpropaganda in den neutralen Staaten während des Ersten Weltkrieges," in *Der Erste Weltkrieg: Wirkung, Wahrnehmung und Analyse*, Wolfgang Michalka, ed., (Munich, 1994), 802.
6. Marc Fumaroli, *L'Etat culturel: une religion moderne* (Paris, 1991); Guy Debord, *La société du spectacle* (Paris, 1992). I am indebted to Patrice Higgonet for this observation.
7. Lois M. Fink, *American Art at the 19th Century Paris Salons* (New York, 1990), 61, 113–15, 130–31, 160; Pierre Miquel, *Art et argent 1800–1900: l'école de la nature*, vol. 6 (Maurs-La-Jolie, 1986, 1987), 9–84, 303–410.
8. Lois M. Fink, "French Art in the United States, 1850–1870: Three Dealers and Collectors," *Gazette des Beaux Arts* (September 1978), 87.
9. Reiner Pommerin, *Der Kaiser und Amerika: Die USA in der Politik der Reichsleitung, 1890–1917* (Cologne, Vienna, 1986), 292–93; Ekkehard Mai, "Präsentation und Repräsentativität: Interne Probleme deutscher Kunstausstellungen im Ausland (1900–1930)," *Zeitschrift für Kulturaustausch* 31.1 (1981), 107–23; 112–13; Fink, *American Art at the 19th Century Paris Salons*, 277–78; Paul Lefort, "Les Écoles Étrangeres de la Peinture—Etats Unis," *Gazette des Beaux-Arts* 43 (1879): 483–87; Fink, "French Art in the United States, 1850–1870," 87–100.
10. Miquel, *Art et argent*, 355–60. See also Annie Cohen-Solal, *Un jour, ils auront des peintres: L'avènement des peintres américains, Paris 1867–New York 1948* (Paris, 2000).
11. Barbara H. Weinberg, Doreen Bolger, and David Park Curry, eds, *American Impressionism and Realism: The Painting of Modern Life, 1885–1995* (New York, 1994); Jean-Paul Carlhian, "L'Ecole des Beaux-Arts and Its Influence on American Architects and American Architecture, 1886–1936," *Two Hundred Years of Franco-American Relations: Papers of the Bicentennial Colloquium of the Society for French Historical Studies in Newport, Rhode Island, September 7–10, 1978*, Nancy L. Roelker and Charles K. Warner, eds. (n.p., n.d.,[1978?]), 185–206; Fink, *American Art at the 19th Century Paris Salons*, 64–65, 93–94, 114, 130–32, 271.
12. Frank Trommler, "Inventing the Enemy: German-American Cultural Relations, 1900–1917," in Schröder, *Confrontation and Cooperation*, 103; Jacques Portes, "L'européanisation des Etats-Unis vue par les Français (1870–1914)," *Revue française d'études américaines* 12 (1982), 51–64.
13. Robert J. Young, *Marketing Marianne: French Propaganda in America, 1900–1940* (New Brunswick, NJ, 2004).
14. Christopher Hitchens, *Blood, Class, and Nostalgia: Anglo-American Ironies* (New York, 1990), 8. See also Kevin Phillips, *The Cousins' Wars: Religion, Politics, and the Triumph of Anglo-America* (New York, 1999).

15. Daniel Walker Howe, "Victorian Culture in America," in Geoffrey Blodgett et al., eds., *Victorian America* (Philadelphia, 1976), 3–28. Victorianism was "middle class" only in a limited sense. England's landed aristocracy was politically at least as influential as the East-Elbian junker elite in Germany, and retained the absolute veto power in the House of Lords until shortly before World War I. I am indebted to Wolfram Kaiser for this observation.
16. Henry James, *The Europeans: A Sketch* (Boston, 1979); James, *The Bostonians* (London, 1886); Frances H. Burnett, *Little Lord Fauntleroy* (London, 1886).
17. Tom Standage, *The Victorian Internet: The Remarkable Story of the Telegraph and the Nineteenth Century's On-Line Pioneers* (New York, 1998); David P. Nickles, *Under Wire: How the Telegraph Changed Diplomacy* (Cambridge, MA, 2003).
18. Hitchens, *Blood, Class and Nostalgia*, 5.
19. Hitchens, *Blood, Class and Nostalgia*, 298–99; Thomas A. Kohut, *Wilhelm II and the Germans: A Study in Leadership* (New York, Oxford, 1991), 152; Frank Aydelotte, *The American Rhodes Scholarships: A Review of the First Forty Years* (Princeton, NJ, 1946).
20. Hitchens, *Blood, Class, and Nostalgia*, 120–22.
21. Hitchens, *Blood, Class, and Nostalgia*, 134, 162, 174, 358; Stolberg-Wernigerode, *Germany and the United States*, 194–95; Bernhard vom Brocke, "Der deutsch-amerikanische Professorenaustausch: Preußische Wissenschaftspolitik, internationale Wissenschaftsbeziehungen und die Anfänge einer deutschen auswärtigen Kulturpolitik vor dem Ersten Weltkrieg," *Zeitschrift für Kulturaustausch* 31 (1981), 131.
22. "Acta betreffend: die von auswaertigen Behörden gg. über die dortigseitigen wissenschaftlichen und Kunst Anstalten erhaltenen Nachrichten," I HA, Rep. 76 Ve, Sekt. I, Abt. X, No. I, Bd. I, Bl. 190–97, Geheimes Staatsarchiv, Preußischer Kulturbesitz, Berlin Dahlem (GStPK); W. Loehr (?), Kaiserlich Deutsches Konsulat, St. Louis, Missouri, 11 February 1907, R 901/37069, Bl. 81–83, BA
23. "Marriage in Germany," n.p., n.d., Adelaide Kalkman, musical scrapbooks, VI, Missouri Historical Society, St. Louis (MHS). Of course, the same could be said for women in France where women's activism was even less developed than in Germany or Great Britain.
24. Pommerin, *Der Kaiser und Amerika*, 279–80.
25. Mai, "Präsentation und Repräsentativität," 110–16; Pommerin, *Der Kaiser und Amerika*, 292.
26. Mai, "Präsentation und Repräsentativität," 107–23.
27. Military attaché, German embassy, Washington, DC, to Auswärtiges Amt, 30 November 1914, cited in Pommerin, *Der Kaiser und Amerika*, 281.
28. Pamela Potter, *Most German of the Arts: Musicology and Society from the Weimar Republic to the End of Hitler's Reich* (New Haven, 1998), ix–xvii.
29. Celia Applegate, "What Is German Music? Reflections on the Role of Art in the Creation of the Nation," *German Studies Review*, special issue on "German Identity" (Winter 1992), 29; Sanna Pederson, "A. B. Marx, Berlin Concert Life, and German National Identity," 19th-Century Music XVIII (Fall 1994), 87–107; David B. Dennis, *Beethoven in German Politics, 1870–1989* (New Haven, 1996), 32–85.
30. Timotheus Fabri, Berlin, to Herr Staatsminister (10–20 February 1904); von Studt to Lucanus (9 March 1904), both in R 901/37069, Bl. 75–82, Bundesarchiv Berlin Lichterfelde (BA).
31. Berliner Liedertafel and Reichskanzler, 27 September 1907, R 901/37854, AA, BA.
32. "In the Realm of Tone," n.p., n.d. (approx. September 1892), CSO scrapbooks, MF Columbia Exposition, Rosenthal Archives, Chicago Symphony Orchestra (CSO).
33. Bezirkspräsident J. W. Kilinger, Straßburg, 16 April 1902, R 901/37853, AA, BA.
34. See, for example, Abram Chasins, *Leopold Stokowski: A Profile* (New York, 1979), xv.
35. Philip Hart, *Orpheus in the New World: The Symphony Orchestra as an American Cultural Institution* (New York, 1973); Lawrence Levine, *Highbrow/Lowbrow: The Emergence of Cultural Hierarchy in America*

(Cambridge, MA, 1988),104–42, 219. During World War I, Baltimore, Cleveland, and Detroit followed suit (Baltimore hired Gustav Strube in 1917).
36. Felix Volbach, Mainz, to "Madam" (Taft?), 14 July 1894, Wulsin Family Papers, Series I, Box 24, Folder 1, Cincinnati Historical Society.
37. Boston Symphony Orchestra (BSO) scrapbooks, MF Pres, reels 1–18; Jessica C. E. Gienow-Hecht, "Trumpeting Down the Walls of Jericho: The Politics of Art, Music and Emotion in German-American Relations, 1870–1920," *Journal of Social History* 36, 3 (Spring 2003), 585–613
38. Harold Schonberg, *The Lives of Great Composers*, 3rd ed. (New York, 1997), 317.
39. John Higham, "The Reorientation of American Culture in the 1890s," in *The Origins of Modern Consciousness*, John Weiss, ed., (Detroit, 1965), 46.
40. Jessica C. E. Gienow-Hecht, *Sound Diplomacy: Music and Emotions in German-American Relations Since 1850* (Chicago, forthcoming).
41. Mary Lawton, *Schumann-Heink: The Last of the Titans* (New York, 1928), 264–65.
42. Gayle Turk, "The Case of Dr. Karl Muck: Anti-German Hysteria and Enemy Alien Internment During World War I" (undergraduate thesis, Harvard University, 1994), 23, 24; Charles Elllis, Munich, to Higginson, 9 August 1914, HHC, MF BSO/3, Barker Library, Harvard University (BL); Higginson to Otto Braunfels, Frankfurt am Main, ibid.; Charles Ellis, Rotterdam, to Higginson, HHC, XII-15; 26-8-191+, BL.
43. "President's Report," 8 December 1914, Treasurer's Report, Board of Trustees, Minutes, box 1, vol. 1, CSO; "The Orchestra and the War," WWI Activities, Philadelphia Orchestra Archives (POA).
44. "Musicians of World Fame Ruined by War," *Minneapolis Journal*, 30 September 1914, MNSO scrapbooks, vol. 29, 12 Home season, 1914–15, Performing Arts Archives, University of Minnesota (UMN).
45. "Thibaud Found that Trench Life Had Not Interfered With Talent," *Pioneer Press*, 19 November 1916, Minneapolis Symphony scrapbooks, vol. 47, St. Paul concerts, 1916–18, UMN.
46. "Daughter of Opera Singer for Germany," *Morning Tribune*, Duluth, MN, 18 November 1915, MNSO scrapbooks 38, 13th home season, newspaper clips, UMN.
47. "Aus einem Briefe des Reichskanzlers an Prof. Lamprecht vom 21. Juni 1913," Friedrich Schmidt-Ott collection, I. HA, Rep. 92, A LXXVII, Bl. 2, GStA PK.

Part V

THE PERSPECTIVE FROM AFAR: THE OUTBREAK OF WAR IN EUROPE IN THE EYES OF OTHER CONTINENTS

Chapter 16

WAR AS THE SAVIOR?
HOPES FOR WAR AND PEACE IN
OTTOMAN POLITICS BEFORE 1914

Mustafa Aksakal

> The West, very soon, will be subject to a terrific and big war. Then, while weak nations will be destroyed ... it will only be strong nations which will survive this struggle.... To live is to fight.[1]
>
> Major Ali Fuad, 1908–09

I. Introduction

On 13 July 1914, about two weeks after the assassination of Franz Ferdinand in Sarajevo, the Ottoman grand vizier and foreign minister, Said Halim Pasha, dispatched a confidential note, written in his own hand, to the Ottoman war minister, Enver Pasha, conveying the strong possibility of the outbreak of war between Austria-Hungary and Serbia. Said Halim rang the alarm bells based on information he had received from an "authoritative" and "high-ranking" source in the German Foreign Ministry itself. The German official had disclosed remarkable news: "I can tell you confidentially that next week war will break out between Austria and Serbia. ... We hope that the war is no longer avoidable, because it [a war] is perhaps the final chance for Austria to deal with Serbia. But one does not have full confidence that Vienna will demonstrate the energy necessary for this decision."[2] While this note may reveal something about the attitudes of some in Berlin during the July Crisis, it also demonstrates that the Ottoman government remained by no means benighted regarding the outbreak of a major European war in late July 1914.

Based on Ottoman internal correspondence, the documents of the German-Ottoman alliance negotiations, and Ottoman newspapers, journals, and books appearing on the eve of World War I, perhaps few events seemed more probable, in the Ottoman case, than yet another war in the near future. By no means do I intend to suggest, however, that the Ottoman military and political elite were fatalistic in their decision-making or irrational, or, by definition, thinking in terms that were any less strategic than the decision making elites in any of the other belligerent powers. And I should hasten to add that *a* war seemed very probable in the Ottoman context, and not necessarily the *world* war that in fact ensued.

What considerations, then, determined Ottoman policy in 1914? The partition of the Ottoman Empire by 1914 had been discussed for so long, so publicly, and so unabashedly, that it is not difficult to understand that the Ottoman leadership saw as its duty nothing less than the task of saving the empire from dismemberment and destruction. In fact, the dismemberment of the Ottoman Empire in many ways had begun already. Thus, the Ottoman political agenda on the eve of the Great War centered on the establishment of a sovereign, economically and politically independent state that enjoyed full membership in the international states system and equal status under international law. In some sense, the Ottoman Empire had been a member of the Concert of Europe since 1856, when the Ottoman government had been a signatory to the Treaty of Paris ending the Crimean War. In practice, however, Great Power status and membership in this club had not prevented the Ottoman Empire from suffering a long series of territorial and diplomatic losses throughout the late nineteenth and early twentieth centuries, a series of defeats that left the country utterly demoralized and in financial ruin.

These losses included Cyprus (British administration under Ottoman sovereignty, 1878); Kars, Batum, and Ardahan (to Russia, 1878); Montenegro, Romania, Serbia (all gaining independence, 1878); Bosnia-Herzegovina (Austro-Hungarian occupation, 1878; Austro-Hungarian annexation, 1908); Tunisia (French protectorate, 1881); Egypt (British occupation, 1882); Crete (Great Powers impose autonomy, 1898); Kuwait (British protectorate, 1899); Bulgaria (independence, 1908); Tripolitania (Italian annexation, 1912), Dodecanese islands (Italian occupation, 1912); Western Thrace (to Bulgaria and Greece, 1912); Aegean islands including Chios and Mitylene (to Greece, 1912); Albania (independence, 1912); and Macedonia (partitioned among Bulgaria, Greece, and Serbia, 1912–1913). It should also be noted, however, that the great powers intervened on behalf of the Ottoman Empire at the Berlin Congress of 1878, when the powers stepped in to curb Russian expansion by reversing the creation of a Greater Bulgaria.

In 1914, the July Crisis appeared to offer an escape route from what many Ottomans perceived to be a dead end. With the support and guidance of the German Empire, Ottoman leaders hoped to carry through the kind of radical transformation of the Ottoman state and its people that a modern, sustainable state required. Wartime, some of these leaders believed, presented a suitable, even ideal, environ-

Hopes for War and Peace in Ottoman Politics • 289

ARMAGEDDON: A DIVERSION.

Turkey. "Good! if only all those other Christian nations get at one another's throats, I may have a dog's chance yet."

Illustration 16.1: Punch, 4 December 1912

ment for the realization of such drastic changes. The Young Turks intended to transform the Ottoman Empire into a politically and economically independent, modern country by removing foreign control and cultivating a citizenry that would be loyal to the state. These individuals imagined that conditions of war could offer an appropriate pretext for the expulsion of foreign businesses and the nullification of fiscal and legal exemptions for foreign nationals, the so-called "capitulations"; and these capitulations indeed were proclaimed annulled on 9 September 1914. Wartime, moreover, presented the state with additional practical tools for the mobilization of the citizenry behind the Istanbul government.[3]

This chapter examines the Ottoman political and military culture that provided the context for the Ottoman decision for war in 1914. But since this volume is meant not only to illuminate the past but to offer also some insight into the state of contemporary affairs, the deep significance of the Great War in the history of Middle Eastern societies in the twentieth century and now in the twenty-first century should be stressed. The Great War in the Middle East and the end of the Ottoman Empire saw the destruction of a political and cultural system that had successfully held together a religiously, ethnically, and linguistically diverse population. Admittedly, this Ottoman system had come under increasing strains already by the time the Great War broke out, but the complete abolition of the Ottoman system meant the creation of radically new structures of social organization that have arguably served the region less well.

II. Historiography

The most pressing questions regarding the entry of the Ottoman Empire into the war have received a good deal of attention from historians. Most such historical interpretations have depicted the Ottoman leaders as having been utterly foolish, and/or corrupt, in their decision for war in 1914. Instead of treating the European war as an opportunity to concentrate on domestic reforms and to re-strengthen Ottoman society, the Ottoman leaders pushed the empire into a war it did not want. In this depiction of Ottoman decision making, the Ottoman war minister and acting commander in chief, Enver Pasha, has played a crucial role. I will say a little bit more about this traditional historical interpretation in general terms, but I would then like to present some new evidence on the Ottoman decision for war and offer some suggestions for rethinking our understanding of the Ottoman entry into the war.

Turkish historiography has judged rather harshly the Ottoman leadership whose actions led to the empire's entry into World War I.[4] Enver Pasha, in particular, has frequently been presented as "selling out" the country to Germany and forcing the Ottomans into war for his own lofty personal ambitions.[5] The history of the late Ottoman period written after the war was, in a way, itself a casualty of the Great War, as the tragic outcome of the war experience defined the historiography of the Ottomans at war. In looking back, historians of the new Turkish Republic were eager to break with the Ottoman past and to build a new state; for them, it was self-evident to condemn the Ottoman decision as a terrible mistake.

However, in this case, as is so often the case in the writing of history, hindsight was decidedly not 20/20. Rather, hindsight had a clear political bent, as the new Turkish elite sought to distance itself from the responsibility for bringing upheaval to the entire region by waging war on the Allied powers and, of course, from the accusation and responsibility for murdering the Armenian population of Anatolia. In the words of the father of modern Turkish diplomatic history, the Ottoman statesmen who decided for war in 1914 were "below average" and "simple-minded" individuals.[6] He argued that the Ottoman leaders could and should have steered a course of neutrality in 1914 but instead they entered the war "without any compelling reason." In this explanation of the Ottoman entry into the war, the Ottoman war minister, Enver Pasha, received the brunt of the criticism. Enver and the Ottoman leaders were judged guilty of pushing the empire into war in pursuit of "ideals like Turanism and pan-Islamism," the unification, in other words, of all Turks and/or Muslims of Eurasia and Africa under a single state.[7]

This view has largely persisted down to our own day and shaped scholarship outside of Turkey as well. A recent work published by Harvard University Press, for example, posited: "Greed rather than necessity drove the Ottoman Empire into the First World War. Its war aim was to realize the imperialist vision of the powerful minister of war Enver Pasha: a tangled web of grievances and *revanchist* hopes geared toward reassertion of Ottoman imperial glory and unification of the Turkic peoples within an expanded empire."[8] In sum, Enver Pasha has emerged in the historiography as a military dictator who concluded the secret alliance treaty with Germany on 2 August 1914 and subsequently strong armed the Ottoman Empire into war.

From the perspective of the German archives, Ulrich Trumpener made this argument as well in an influential book and several articles. The effect of Trumpener's work was to downplay the role Germany played in the Ottoman decision to enter the war. In part, this interpretation absolved Berlin from any responsibility for Ottoman intervention, and was also a defense against the charge that Berlin had forced the Ottomans into the war: not Berlin but Enver Pasha, Trumpener's work strongly suggested, was the reason behind the Ottoman entry into the war.

III. The Ottoman Decision for War

My own view is that in portraying Enver Pasha as a reckless, pro-German war hawk, and by placing primary responsibility on his shoulders, both German and Turkish historians have found a convenient method of explaining away the German-Ottoman relationship of 1914 and the Ottoman entry into the war. But from closer study of the German-Ottoman negotiations following the Sarajevo assassination and from Ottoman contemporary publications, a different picture emerges. Here, the evidence suggests that the policy so closely and so exclusively linked with Enver was shared by his colleagues and by that part of the Ottoman public that expressed political views through newspapers, journals, and books, and through the staging of political demonstrations.

Said Halim Pasha, who frequently is depicted as having been "duped" and "tricked" by Enver and the Germans, was actually instrumental in arranging and negotiating the German-Ottoman alliance of 2 August 1914. Nor did the Ottomans plunge into the war enthusiastically, moreover. Once the Ottoman leaders secured the alliance with Germany that August, the Ottomans did not enter the war until 29 October, almost three months later. In the alliance treaty itself, the Ottomans had promised to enter the war more or less immediately. While the German officials in the Ottoman capital mounted their pressure to get the Ottomans to enter the war immediately, the latter, led by Enver and Said Halim, argued that they were not yet sufficiently prepared to fight in the war with any success; Enver made this argument repeatedly and asked for more time from Berlin.[9]

In so doing the Ottoman leaders delayed Ottoman entry into the war in the hope that the war would end while the alliance with Germany continued. In fact, the evidence strongly suggests that it was this alliance with Germany, initially intended to last until 1918 but then extended until 1920 and 1926, which represented the great Ottoman objective. In exchange for committing itself to support Germany in the Great War, the Ottomans hoped to receive future German diplomatic and economic support and desperately needed security in a hostile international system. By June 1914, each of the Great Powers, including Italy, had negotiated its sphere of control in the partition of the Ottoman Empire, and color-coded partition maps had been drawn up and circulated among the European capitals.[10] Thus the most important determinants of Ottoman policy in 1914 were the Ottomans' deep concern for the long-term security of their borders, on the one hand, and for sustained economic development, on the other. In this great irony, the Ottoman road to peace and stability led only through war.

The ultimately tragic outcome and long duration of the Great War led historians to depict the Ottoman decision for belligerency as a high-stakes gamble or a suicidal plunge into the abyss. Yet such a view overlooks the fact that despite the militarism and armaments race in Europe many contemporaries believed that a general war, if it broke out at all, might well last no more than "a matter of months" and would have to be concluded by a negotiated peace rather than decisive military victory.[11] If the Ottoman leaders could have plausibly expected a shorter confrontation, therefore, we might allow for the possibility that they were not seeking territorial expansion, as has been charged, but rather that their main goal was a long-term alliance with a Great Power, that is, with Germany.

During the summer of 1914, Germany provided the Ottomans with two powerful warships (the famous *SMS Goeben* and the *SMS Breslau*), a military mission, and a naval mission; amounting in total to over one thousand German officers, military specialists, and personnel. In addition, the Ottomans received considerable amounts of military equipment and over five million Ottoman pounds. In exchange, the

Ottoman government promised Germany's representatives to intervene in the war as soon as Ottoman troops were ready: either in a campaign against Russia, or in a campaign against the British in Egypt, or alongside Bulgaria in the Balkans against Greece or Serbia. By October 1914, however, Ottoman forces had still not entered the war, and the German government had not only stopped any further supply of military aid but also had threatened to pull out of the alliance.[12]

When the Ottomans finally entered the war through the medium of a naval raid led by the *Goeben* and the *Breslau* on 29 October against the Russian city of Odessa, they insisted on revising and expanding the German-Ottoman alliance treaty. As part of that revision, the alliance was extended from a duration of four to twelve years. The Ottomans also insisted on a written guarantee from their German allies pledging to support the Ottoman Empire financially "for the entire duration of the war." And indeed, the German ambassador, Hans von Wangenheim, issued such a written guarantee to Said Halim Pasha shortly after the Black Sea naval raid. A revised treaty of alliance, moreover, was signed on 11 January 1915.[13]

Despite Said Halim's opposition to the timing of intervention, therefore, it did not take long before the grand vizier rejoined his colleagues in their decision. Top Ottoman military commanders such as Kazım Karabekir, Hafız Hakkı, and Ali İhsan, who favored a later campaign in Spring 1915, had also called for delaying intervention.[14] In the general decision to win Germany's long-term support, however, the Ottoman leaders were thus united in their decision making in 1914. This point is also illustrated in a *New York Times* interview, appearing on 22 February 1915, in which Said Halim declared that in their decision for war the Ottoman leaders had been "tired of the hypocrisy actuating the powers of the Triple Entente when dealing with Turkey." The grand vizier added that the Ottoman Empire "knew that to enter into relations with Great Britain, France, and Russia would have been a harmful factor in respect to the country's interest." Finally, the grand vizier stated, the Ottoman "people want a chance to work out their destiny."[15] In entering the Great War the Ottomans, perhaps influenced by common expectations that the war would not (in fact could not) last very long, were pursuing a deliberate policy. They believed that in the aftermath of the war Ottoman state and society would benefit from a peacetime alliance with Germany that would offer the Ottomans long-term territorial integrity, diplomatic support, and economic development.

IV. Ottoman Political and Military Culture on the Eve of the Great War

My second argument is based on Ottoman publications appearing during and following the Balkan Wars. An examination of the political literature during this time supports the argument that Enver Pasha was not unique in his views of the international system and the Ottoman place in it. In Ottoman newspapers, journals, books, and parliamentary remarks, authors frequently expressed the view that an alliance with Germany and participation in a general war was a desirable, even preferred course of action. Ottoman publications, moreover, reflected a deep conviction that the country's survival could eventually only be secured on the battlefield.

In such publications, writers employed arguments depicting the Ottoman Empire as engaged in a final struggle of life and death, and one finds a strong linkage between the questions of modernity, liberation, and war. The discussions surrounding the creation of a "new society" and a "new life" (*yeni hayat*), were intertwined with the idea of waging war and gaining independence from the imperialist powers: Austria-Hungary, Great Britain, France, Italy, and Russia. Much of Ottoman political discourse preceding World War I aimed at broad segments of the population and intended to mobilize Ottoman society against the state's external (and some allegedly internal) enemies. Intellectuals and politicians alike viewed as their role the mobilization and education of the people, a process to which contemporaries, in rhetoric common to nationalists everywhere, referred as the "awakening" (*intibah*).[16] To overcome the difficulty of spreading their message to countrymen who were often illiterate, popular authors like the sharp-minded critic of the dominant Committee of Union and Progress (CUP), Şehbenderzade Ahmed Hilmi, added bylines to their book titles such as "May every patriot read and relate this booklet to the Turks."[17] Ahmed Hilmi, whose book appeared between March 1913 and March 1914, urged his readers to rise up and rally behind the Ottoman state (*Osmanlı Devleti*). A new age, he insisted, had opened, and the new age demanded that the people unite under one flag. Addressing the reader as "Turk" (*Türk*), he explained that the national groups in the Balkans had ended Ottoman rule there because the peoples of the Balkans had "awoken after centuries of slumber" and were regaining their national consciousness.[18] Now, Ahmed Hilmi claimed, those nations had "become people of this age while we have remained the people of a past age," an age he labeled "the age of knowledge and struggle" (*bilgi ve çabalama zamanı*). According to the author, such struggle was inevitable and required the selfless effort and sacrifice of each and every Turk. "The struggle [in the Balkans] is over, but struggle will start again. Living means struggling. Absence of struggle can only be found in cemeteries. Only the dead are without struggle."[19]

By 1914, the defining characteristics of the age were part of Ottoman common knowledge. Darwinian ideas had been elaborated upon and transferred, if pseudo-scientifically, to the realms of government and international relations. The importance of this theme, however, that Ottoman society must organize itself and prepare its every aspect for war, cannot be overemphasized; it was the predominant theme of Ottoman political discourse on the eve of World War I.[20] While today's student of the Ottoman political literature may ask what exactly authors had in mind when they referred to "the nation," some authors, like Ahmed Hilmi, left no doubt. The intended audience was the Turkish-speaking Muslim population of Anatolia:

The Crimea, Rumania, Algeria, Tunisia, Egypt, Serbia, Bulgaria, the Caucasus all went one by one. … Finally Tripolitania [in Libya] and three-fourths of the Balkans also were lost. These areas were all rich and valuable places; we gained them at the cost of our blood. But those territories, however rich they may be, were not the heart and soul of our homeland [*yurdumuzun yüreği*] … Anatolia is the heart and soul of our homeland. O Turk! If we continue in our old ways, if we face the enemy again in slumber, unprotected, then this time the enemy's sword will come to our [homeland's] heart and soul and kill each one of us.[21]

Mobilization and unification of the people, in other words, topped the agenda. In the foreword to the translation of a French work, the writer Recai made an argument similar to Ahmed Hilmi's. Under the title, *How Germany Revived and How it is Preparing for War*, Recai criticized writers and intellectuals for not writing sufficiently about topics that could contribute to the formation of an "Ottoman nation." Novels and plays must never be purely literary or artistic, but needed to fulfill a social purpose, illustrating didactically the importance and ways of being a true patriot.[22] Those intellectuals who put their services in the nation's interest should join together and form a National Literature Association, he proposed.[23]

Recai, in fact, elevated the task of writing and thinking in the nation's interest to be a matter of life and death. Prussian history provided a most instructive lesson in this regard, he argued. Following Prussia's defeat at the hands of Napoleon Bonaparte, Prussian writers and poets had given shape to a German spirit capable of uniting the German people and of defeating France in 1870–71. The Ottoman nation, too, he continued, had to be educated about the meanings of state and nation, as well as about foreign countries and their people.[24] In the writings of the day, a consensus existed that an army could only be as powerful as the level of education and the vitality of the society it represented. Writing just before the outbreak of the Second Balkan War, Major Hafız Hakkı, who served as Enver's assistant in the general staff in 1914, argued that "the army may try as hard as it wishes to improve a society's military strength. The army's officers may be the most skilled in the world, but if the society's material and moral standards are low, the army will certainly enter the battlefield in a deficient and disorderly manner and quickly meet with defeat."[25]

Hafız Hakkı decried the crops of impoverished and uneducated recruits who entered the army's ranks for regular military service year after year and returned later as reserves during periods of mobilization. The army's problems, he believed, reflected those of Ottoman society itself: the need for education, economic development, and the improved situation of women.[26] Hafız Hakkı argued that the Ottoman people needed a shared, supreme ideal that defined Ottoman life and towards whose purpose all Ottomans could strive together,[27] a purpose that was frequently simply referred to as the "national ideal" (*mefkûre-i milliye*).[28] Hafız Hakkı sketched out a vision of a "people in arms," as the German general Colmar von der Goltz had done before him, and whose book by that title had been translated into Ottoman.[29] Like Recai, Hafız Hakkı, too, invoked the Prussian example of recovery and victory. Such recovery was available to the Ottoman Empire as well, but only provided that Ottoman society, as a totality, prepared itself for war unconditionally during times of peace.[30]

Cami [Baykut], a former delegate to the Ottoman Chamber of Deputies who had co-founded in 1912 the National Constitution Party, the first party to be openly Turkish nationalist, argued along similar lines. In a work entitled, *The Ottoman Future: Its Enemies and Its Friends*, published in 1913, Cami argued that the Ottoman Empire was an Asian country, and that the Balkans, now lost, had been colonies separate from the true homeland (*vatan*). Like Hafız Hakkı, Cami, a former officer, also was well acquainted with the ideas of Goltz. Cami praised the German general's suggestion that the empire's center of gravity should formally be shifted southward by moving the capital to Konya, or perhaps even farther south.[31] When it came to Great Power politics, Ottoman political writers gravitated toward Germany. Together they found a great deal of irony in the Ottoman dilemma, namely that only Europe stood in the way of the "Turk's Europeanization" (*Türkün Avrupalılaşmasına*). Through constant interference in Ottoman internal affairs, politically and financially, the Great Powers of Europe had tied the hands of the Ottoman government and prevented it from implementing lasting reforms, despite Ottoman attempts dating back to, at least, the beginning of the nineteenth century. The Triple Entente, and Britain in particular, Cami argued, was waging an all-out attack on the Ottomans.[32] Cami described this dynamic sarcastically:

"Yes, in order to be friends with Britain we must recognize that the Red Sea is a British sea. And we must also cede [to the British the region stretching from] Egypt to Syria, [and from] Iraq to India, and permit the British sphere of influence in Iran to extend westward, that is, extend to the port of Alexandretta. And we must be satisfied with an Anatolian princedom based in Konya. [Once we do all that] we can begin to speak of a friendly British policy towards us."[33] Nothing but harm, therefore, could be expected from Britain and its partners in the Triple Entente.

As for Germany, the author expressed a widely held perspective:

> Germany is not simply pursuing its economic interests by maintaining the status quo in the Near East, but Germany also intends to take advantage of the Ottoman state's [strategic] position in its [own] hostile relationship with Slavdom. In fact, the Slavic world is growing more rapidly than its neighbors and poses a threat in Europe to the Germans, Hungarians, and Romanians; and it poses the same threat, or perhaps even a greater calamity, to the Ottomans. A strong Ottoman state must form an alliance with Germany and take a defensive position against the Russian and Balkan Slavs; this is the foundation for a correct policy.[34]

Further evidence of public opinion's orientation toward Germany was offered on the occasion of the German battle cruiser *SMS Goeben*'s visit to Istanbul in May 1914. It was rumored that the powerful ship might be sold to the Ottoman navy, and that in the event of war between the Triple Alliance and the Triple Entente the

Goeben would assume certain duties of the Ottoman navy, even if a sale would not take place and the ship would remain in German possession.[35] Hence, about six weeks prior to the assassination of the Habsburg heir apparent Franz Ferdinand in Sarajevo, Ottoman participation in a general war alongside Germany was presented in a major Istanbul daily as a reasonable and acceptable course of action.

Among Ottoman political writers, the Balkan Wars were increasingly regarded as proof that coexistence of Christians and Muslims in the Ottoman Empire was no longer possible, as Muslim writers perceived many Christians to be sympathetic to the Balkan powers, especially the Greek Orthodox population (*Rum*, or *Rumlar*). In fact, relations between Greek and Turkish Ottomans had turned so violent in certain areas that Greek Ottomans were compelled to leave the Ottoman Empire forever, particularly those Greek Ottomans living in Izmir and Thrace.[36]

V. The Journal *Büyük Duygu* (The Great Longing)

The emotional and intellectual environment that emerged during the Balkan Wars can be illustrated by the journal *Büyük Duygu*. Its first issue appeared in Istanbul in March 1913, and was followed by twenty-five further issues before publication came to an end in January 1914. Subtitled "The Turk's Journal," *Büyük Duygu* employed nationalist rhetoric throughout its articles on politics, history, and literature. The journal's first issue declared as its purpose the fostering of awareness of Turkish history and of national consciousness. These needed development, it was argued, because the Turks would soon be taking their place on the battlefield, where they would fight for their national survival. Women, in particular, were accorded a major role in the formation of the new society.[37]

What did the journal's title, "the great longing" refer to? Was it "revenge" (*intikam duygusu*), as the title of several lead articles seemed to suggest?[38] Or did it refer to a perceived need to "return" to a primordial Turkish identity (*türklük duygusu*)? Whichever facet one might want to emphasize, there can be no doubt that the journal sought to grip its readers with gory descriptions of the recent past and to instill a deep sense of violation in an attempt to build a collective identity. The unity of the nation, the editors proclaimed, was the only reliable foundation for its survival. Continuous "battle" (*kavga*), moreover, constituted the essence of any meaningful existence. "Peace and tranquility" could only be found in death.[39] The journal continued in social Darwinian terms: "Only the nation armed with national feelings (*milliyet duygularıyla*) can participate in the struggle and gain as a result of it the right to remain alive. But let us not spend much time on the word 'right,' for there is no one left who does not believe that 'right' (*hak*) is anything other than 'might' (*kuvvet*). 'The most obvious truth is that those who do not crush will be crushed.' The inevitable place of those who do not heed this proverb is the cemetery and history. Thus in order to live we must not strive for 'right' but for power."[40]

Throughout the issues of *Büyük Duygu*, the authors' message was unequivocal. Everything rested on self-reliance and the ability to assert oneself: "Right can only be derived from power, civilization only from power, happiness only from power. Power is everything."[41] The views of Ottoman intellectuals in this respect coincided with the views of their statesmen. In a letter of 8 May 1913 Enver Pasha wrote: "My heart is bleeding.... If I could tell you all the atrocities which the enemy has committed right here at the gates of Istanbul, you would understand the sufferings of the poor Muslims farther away. But our hatred is intensifying: revenge, revenge, revenge, there is nothing else."[42]

Typical of the authors in this genre, *Büyük Duygu*'s editors were mobilizers and activists, and far from being resigned to Ottoman demise. To illustrate their arguments, such writers turned to history for examples of peoples that had reemerged successfully from defeat.[43] Successful recovery demanded an active, not a passive policy. "Crushed and defeated nations must rise up without delay and act swiftly ... crying Revenge, Revenge!" As a nation that had reasserted itself, Germany, in particular, served as the example to be followed. Thus the writers of *Büyük Duygu* called their readers to action: "Oh Turkish nation! ... Has the blood of Oğuz, Genghis, and Fatih [Mehmed the Conqueror] dried up in your veins? Will you forget the blows that have been dealt against your Turkish soul (*Türklüğüne*]), will you forget the wounds that have been inflicted upon your heart?!"[44] Evidently, some parts of the Turkish elite in Istanbul believed not only that the Ottoman Empire faced a historic military confrontation in the near future, but that the Ottomans should seek out that confrontation rather than passively await its appearance.

While the size and make-up of *Büyük Duygu*'s readership remains unknown, it is significant that the journal supported public lectures and meetings in an effort to involve broad segments of the populations. One such meeting was held in an Istanbul suburb in early April 1913, organized by the local women's branch of the Society for National Defense (*Müdafaa-i Milliye Cemiyeti*), another prominent and very popular organization that promoted the values of the publications under discussion. At the meeting, the Branch Chairwoman, N. Sebiha, delivered an address that was subsequently published in *Büyük Duygu*. The topic of Sebiha's address, that the people were "still asleep" and must be awakened to the dangers facing the empire, was also the defining theme running through the contemporary political literature and the public discourse in the capital. She called on her listeners and readers to demonstrate to the Europeans that Turks were strong enough to "face the Europeans head-on, both militarily and economically."[45]

VI. Conclusion

Although it remains impossible to gauge the importance and appeal of each of the works examined here, this sample of contemporary publications reflects a deep conviction in the necessity of fighting a "war of independence" and demonstrates that this conviction had become a widely-discussed, if not an accepted, reality.[46] In holding that sentiment, the views of the Ottoman elite did not differ from the outlook held by War Minister Enver Pasha. Because of its recent historical experience and the continued expansion of European power worldwide, and because of the weak place it occupied on the margins of the European states system, the Ottoman Empire and its leaders viewed their involvement in war in the near future with great probability. There is little to suggest, however, that the Ottoman leaders anticipated the *world war* that broke out in August 1914.

Tragically, the outbreak of World War I became the opportunity through which Ottoman hopes for restoring a militarily powerful and politically independent empire could be achieved; the Ottoman Empire had entered a crucial point in its history between salvation and destruction. Nations and states were thought to exist in a Darwinian struggle that no one could escape, and by 1914 a broad consensus had formed around these issues, at least in the Ottoman capital.

Like the drive to modernize its armies beginning in the late eighteenth century, nascent Turkish nationalism on the eve of World War I stemmed from the external imperative to gear up the country for military conflict. In promoting this mobilization movement, the Ottoman elite created an environment in which war was increasingly seen as an inevitable and potentially unifying and liberating experience. In 1914 Ottoman public life was charged with feelings of despair, and of violation at the hands of the Great Power system. These strong emotions also imbued Ottoman diplomacy. The empire's statesmen sought revenge against an international system that they thought had betrayed them, while at the same time imagining that war would set the stage for national renewal and reinvigoration. The assassination of the Austro-Hungarian heir apparent on 28 June 1914 in Sarajevo unleashed a new international dynamic that afforded the Ottomans an historic opportunity for self-assertion. While the empire's demise after the war has been understood as a sign of the Ottoman leaders' failure, the tenets by which they operated did not die with them. Militarism, nationalism, and modernism continued to define the political landscape of the Turkish nation-state that emerged after World War I.

Notes

I would like to acknowledge with gratitude the Institute of Turkish Studies, Washington, DC, and the Kluge Center for Scholars at the Library of Congress, which generously supported research for this paper.

1. Major Ali Fuad, "Felsefe-i Harb [Philosophy of War]," *Asker* 3 (1324/1908–09), 109–10, quoted in Handan Nezir Akmeşe, *The Birth of Modern Turkey: The Ottoman Military and the March to World War I* (New York, 2005), 72.

2. Genelkurmay Askeri Tarih ve Stratejik Etüt Başkanlığı Arşivi (ATASE), BDH, Klasör 243, Yeni Dosya 1009, Fihrist 1 and 1-1. Said Halim received Berlin's letter via the Ottoman consul at Bremen.
3. M. Şükrü Hanioğlu, *Preparation for a Revolution: The Young Turks, 1902–1908* (New York, 2001), 302–05; Zafer Toprak, *Milli İktisat-Milli Burjuvazi: Türkiye'de Ekonomi ve Toplum (1908–1950)*. Türkiye Araştırmaları, no. 14 (Ankara: Tarih Vakfı Yurt Yayınları, 1995), 4–6, 51–54, 66–74; Fikret Adanır, "Der jungtürkische Modernismus und die nationale Frage im Osmanischen Reich," *Zeitschrift für Türkeistudien* 2 (1989), 79-91.
4. Şevket Süreyya Aydemir, *Makedonya'dan Ortaasya'ya Enver Paşa* (Istanbul, 1971), vol. 2, 505–06.
5. See, for example, the front page headline in a prominent Turkish daily, "Savaşın bedeli 5 milyon altın [The War's Price: Five Million in Gold]," *Cumhuriyet*, 11 August 1996, reporting a "smoking gun" found in the archives of the German Foreign Ministry proving that Cemal-Enver-Talat, the ministers of the navy, war, and the interior, respectively, accepted five million Ottoman pounds from Germany in exchange for entering the war.
6. Yusuf Hikmet Bayur, *Paylaşmalar*, vol. 2/3, *Türk İnkılâbı Tarihi* (Ankara, 1991; 1951), 2, 5.
7. Bayur, *1914–1918 Genel Savaşı*, vol. 3/1, *Türk İnkılâbı Tarihi* (Ankara, 1991; 1953), 268 for the quote, and see ibid., 267–74, where he addresses the question "Was the Ottoman government correct in entering the war?"
8. Efraim Karsh and Inari Karsh, *Empires of the Sand: The Struggle for Mastery in the Middle East, 1789–1923* (Cambridge, 1999), 138; Baykara, "Birinci Dünya Savaşı'na Girişin Psikolojik Sebepleri," in *Bildiriler*, 363–65; Aydemir, *Makedonya'dan Ortaasya'ya*, vol. 2, 11–21, 505–06; Jacob M. Landau, *Pan-Turkism: From Irredentism to Cooperation*, 2d ed. (Bloomington, 1995), 51–56, and, for a more balanced presentation, Landau, *The Politics of Pan-Islam: Ideology and Organization* (New York, 1994), 94–103; cf. discussion above of Bayur.
9. For one such instance, see Politisches Archiv des Auswärtigen Amts (PA/AA), R 22402, Zimmermann to Jagow, 20 August 1914, no. 32.
10. Harry N. Howard, *The Partition of Turkey: A Diplomatic History, 1913–1923* (Norman, 1931), 50–60.
11. David G. Herrmann, *The Arming of Europe and the Making of the First World War*, Princeton Studies in International History and Politics (Princeton, 1996), 1.
12. PA/AA, R 22402, Jagow to Wangenheim, 10 September 1914, no. 121.
13. PA/AA, R 22403, Zimmermann to Bethmann Hollweg, 17 November 1914, Report no. 12, conveying Wangenheim's request, and Zimmermann's and Jagow's support for it.
14. Kemal H. Karpat, "The Entry of the Ottoman Empire into World War I," *Belleten* 58 (December 2004), 720–22.
15. "Turkey Distrusted Allies, Says Halim," *New York Times*, 22 February 1914.
16. Tüccarzade İbrahim Hilmi, *Türkiye Uyan* [Turkey Awake], Kütübhane-i İntibah, no. 13 (Dersaadet, 1329 [March 1913-March 1914], 1-2 and passim; Mehmed Emin, *Ey Türk Uyan* [Turk, Awake!]; see also the addresses to the Ottoman Chamber of Deputies by the sultan and by the grand Vezir, e.g. Mehmed Reşad V, "Muhterem Âyân ve Mebusan [Honored Senators and Deputies]," *Meclis-i Mebusan Zabit Ceridesi* (MMZC) [Proceedings of the Ottoman Chamber of Deputies], address delivered 1 Mayıs 1330 [14 May 1914], and the government program of the Said Halim Pasha cabinet, *MMZC*, address delivered by Talat Bey, 6 Temmuz 1330 [19 July 1914]; "İğne Darbeleri," *Tanin*, 21 April 1914. For an expanded discussion of these publications see my "Not 'by those old books of international law, but only by war': Ottoman Intellectuals on the Eve of the Great War," *Diplomacy and Statecraft* 15 (September 2004), 507–44.
17. Özdemir [Şehbenderzade Filibeli Ahmed Hilmi], *Türk Ruhu Nasıl Yapılıyor? Her Vatanperverden, Bu Eserciği Türklere Okumasını ve Anlatmasını Niyaz Ederiz* [How the Turkish Spirit is Formed: We Ask of Each Patriot to Read and Relate this Booklet to the Turks], İkaz-ı Millet Kütübhanesi, no. 1 (Darülhilâfe, 1329 [March 1913–March 1914]); see also Jones Moll [attrib.], *Anadolu'da Türkiye*, Habil Adem, trans., [Naci İsmail Pelister], 15–21, 78–79.

18. Ibid., 16.
19. Ibid., 4.
20. Besides the works discussed here in detail, see also A., *Balkan Harbi'nde Neden Münhezim Olduk* [Why We Were Defeated in the Balkan War], Kütübhane-i İntibah, Tüccarzade İbrahim Hilmi, no. 9 (Istanbul, 1329 [March 1913–March 1914]), 4, as well as İbrahim Hilmi's afterword in ibid., 92.
21. Özdemir [Şehbenderzade Filibeli Ahmed Hilmi], *Türk Ruhu Nasıl Yapılıyor?*, 6–7.
22. Recai, foreword to *Almanya Nasıl Dirildi? Harbe Nasıl Hazırlanıyor?* [How Germany Revived and How it is Preparing for War], translation of *La préparation de la lutte économique par l'Allemagne*, by Antoine de Tarlé (Dersaadet, 1329 [March 1913–March 1914]), 7.
23. Ibid., 10.
24. Ibid., 8. Recai writes the following about the Prussian victory over the French: "Bu kıyamı hazırlayan işte bütün Prusya mütefekkirleri, ve onların içinde de en ziyade edibleri, şairleridir." [Those who prepared the rise of Prussia were Prussian intellectuals, and amongst these most importantly their writers and poets.]
25. Hafız Hakkı, *Bozgun* [Morale and Defeat], Tüccarzade İbrahim Hilmi Series (Dersaadet, 1330 [March 1914–March 1915]), 37.
26. Ibid., 39–42, 66–67.
27. Ibid., 51–53.
28. "Şevketmeab [Your Majesty]," *MMZC*, 10 Mayıs 330 [23 May 1914].
29. Hafız Hakkı, *Bozgun* [Morale and Defeat], 80–81. Goltz's book, *Das Volk in Waffen: ein Buch über Heerwesen und Kriegsführung unserer Zeit*, 3rd Edition (Berlin, 1884) appeared in Ottoman as *Millet-i Müselleha* (Kostantiniye, 1301 [March 1885–March 1886]).
30. Ibid., 105–06.
31. Cami [Abdurrahman Cami Baykut], *Osmanlılığın Âtisi: Düşmanları ve Dostları* [The Ottoman Future: Its Enemies and Its Friends] (Istanbul, 1331 [5 Kanunisani 1328/18 Jan 1913]), 6–8, 12.
32. Ibid., 21–29.
33. Ibid., 30.
34. Ibid., 34; "Asabiyet Alâmetleri [Signs of Nervousness]," *Tanin*, 30 April 1914.
35. "Bu Günlerde Tekrar Limanımıza Gelecek Olan *Goeben* Drednotu [The Dreadnought *Goeben*, Which is to Call on our Port Once Again]," *Tanin*, 7 May 1914; "Amiral Suşon [Admiral Souchon]," *Tanin*, 17 May 1914; the rumor of the *Goeben*'s sale to the Ottoman Empire had also been discussed in diplomatic circles, see *Die Internationalen Beziehungen im Zeitalter des Imperialismus* (Berlin, 1931–43), Series I, vol. I, no. 72, Gulkevich to Sazonov, 24 January 1914, 62–63, and ibid., Series I, vol. I, no. 140, Sazonov to Sverbeyev, 30 January 1914, 123, and ibid., Series I, vol. I, no. 175, Sverbeyev to Sazonov, 4 February 1914, 164.
36. Mehmed Şerif, *Edirne Vilayetinden Rumlar Niçin Gitmek İstiyorlar? İzmir Mebusu Emanuelidi Efendi'ye* [Why Do Greek Ottomans Want to Leave Edirne Province? A Letter to Emanuelidi Efendi, Member of the Chamber of Deputies from Izmir] (Edirne, 1330 [March 1914–March 1915].
37. The journal's founders were listed as Dündar Alp, Ş Uluğ, and M. Fazıl, see the first issue of *Büyük Duygu: Onbeş Günde Bir Çıkar, Türkün Risalesidir* [The Great Longing: The Turk's Bimonthly Journal], Cemiyet Kütüphanesi, Sayı 1, 2 Mart 1329 [15 March 1913], 1.
38. "İntikam Duygusu [Feelings of Revenge]," *Büyük Duygu*, Sayı 2, 16 Mart 1329 [29 March 1913], 17–18, and "Acımak Yok ... İntikam![No Mercy ... Revenge!]," *Büyük Duygu*, Sayı 8, 6 Haziran 1329 [19 June 1913], 113–14.
39. "İntikam Duygusu [Feelings of Revenge]," *Büyük Duygu*, Sayı 2, 16 Mart 1329 [29 March 1913], 17–18.
40. Ibid., 17.

41. Ibid.
42. M. Şükrü Hanioğlu, ed., *Kendi Mektuplarında Enver Paşa* (Istanbul, 1989), 242.
43. See Naci İsmail, Belak [pseud.], *Mağlub Milletler Nasıl İntikam Alırlar* [How Do Defeated Nations Take Revenge?], Habil Adem, trans. [Naci İsmail Pelister] (Dersaadet, 1332 h. [November 1913–November 1914]).
44. "İntikam Duygusu," *Büyük Duygu*, 18.
45. "Türk Hanımlarının Toplantısı," *Büyük Duygu*, no. 2, 16 Mart 1329 [29 March 1913], 31–32; on the *Müdafaa-i Milliye Cemiyeti*, which was formed during the height of the Balkan Wars by some of the most influential intellectuals and politicians of the time, and its women's groups, see Nazım H. Polat, *Müdafaa-i Milliye Cemiyeti*, Kaynak Eserler, no. 52 (Ankara, 1991), 16–33, 71–81.
46. See also Nezir Akmeşe, *Birth of Modern Turkey*, 172, where the author reaches a similar conclusion: "By 1914, it seems clear, at least some of the Empire's political and military leaders were already convinced that a further war was inevitable and even desirable," and ibid, 64–86, for a discussion of the military press.

Chapter 17

THE VIEW FROM JAPAN
War and Peace in Europe around 1914

Frederick R. Dickinson

Far from the principal locus of activity on the Western front, Japan seems an unlikely arena to weigh cultures of war and peace in August 1914. But Japanese observers closely followed events in Europe and participated passionately in speculation over the causes and probable consequences of the war. Although Western historians have subsequently crafted a more comfortable Western-centric vision of the conflict, Western belligerents, in turn, eagerly sought Japanese participation in hostilities. Few World War I buffs will recall how fervently British, French, and American policy-makers appealed for direct Japanese aid.[1] At their most ambitious, these requests envisioned up to five hundred thousand Japanese troops in the Balkans.[2]

Tokyo would ultimately decline all requests for Japanese troops to fight in Europe. But Japanese participation in the war was not negligible. Responding to his ally Britain's request to hunt down German armed merchant cruisers in Chinese waters, Foreign Minister Kato Takaaki by 8 August persuaded the Japanese cabinet and elder statesmen to issue an ultimatum to Berlin.[3] The Japanese cabinet subsequently declared war on Germany on 23 August.

Although Japanese operations against the kaiser paled by comparison with those of their European allies, Japan would eject the German navy from the Marshall, Mariana, and Caroline Islands (German Micronesia) in the South Pacific in August 1914, defeat German ground forces at Qingdao, Shandong province (China) by November 1914 and ultimately play a critical role ferrying British Commonwealth troops from the Pacific to the Indian Ocean, hunting German U-boats in the Mediterranean, and sending badly-needed arms aid to Russia.

Japanese participation clearly had much less effect upon the outcome of the war than Allied leaders had hoped. But the reverse—the impact of the conflict on Japan—was, as recent research has shown, profound.[4] Most importantly, the new wave of internationalism that swept the post-war world had a momentous effect upon Japanese politics, diplomacy, and national culture.

From the perspective of Tokyo, in other words, the twelve thousand kilometers that separated the Japanese archipelago from the Western front belied the actual proximity of the "European War" in Japanese national affairs. An examination of material contributions in World War I reveals critical Japanese support with a fervent Allied desire for more. Likewise, a study of the Japanese national discussion immediately before and after the outbreak of hostilities provides an intriguing new perspective on the cultures of war and peace in Europe and Japan in 1914.

I. Japanese Adaptation of a European Pattern

A member of the Japanese Upper House, Viscount Tani Kanjo, best captured the mood of Japan in August 1914 in what is commonly referred to as the Tani Memorial. Tani urged the authorities to "encourage and protect the people at home, and then wait for the time of the confusion of Europe which must come eventually sooner or later, and although we have no immediate concern with it ourselves we must feel it, for such an event will agitate the nations of the Orient as well, and hence, although our country is not mixed up in the matter, so far as Europe is concerned, we may become the chief nation of the Orient."[5] Submitted in resignation after an internal dispute over Japan's "unequal treaties" with the powers, the memorandum is extraordinary for its calm and calculating attitude toward the "confusion" that Tani considered probable in Europe. Most remarkably, Tani penned the brief in 1887.

Although submitted less than ten years after the advent of modern Japan (the Meiji Restoration of 1868) and almost three decades before the assassination of Archduke Franz Ferdinand, Tani's memorial anticipated three critical elements in the general Japanese response to war in 1914: a sense of predictability, an exaggerated portrayal of the principal belligerents, and anticipation of an exceptional opportunity. Each of these trends mirrored developments in the capitals of Europe. But Japan's special geographic and political circumstances guaranteed important divergences. These departures would have a momentous effect upon the cultures of war and peace in post-World War I Japan.

II. Shock of War

Despite the impressive speed with which the Japanese cabinet declared war on Germany in August 1914, most Japanese policy makers and pundits echoed their European counterparts in their initial shock at the suddenness and scale of the conflagration in Europe. The president of the largest party in the Japanese parliament (the Seiyukai [Association of Political Friends]), Hara Takashi, described the conflict as "an unexpectedly large disturbance."[6] And the semi-official journal of the Japanese Foreign Ministry, the *Diplomatic Review* (Gaiko jiho), expressed alarm at the "great world disturbance like never before in history" that "has come circling like an unstoppable ring of fire."[7]

As in Europe, war appeared to come suddenly to the Japanese because of assumptions held before August 1914. Commentators in Tokyo were as familiar as their European counterparts with the animated European discussions regarding the probability of war and with the many efforts aimed at guaranteeing peace. "There are few sudden events as unpredictable as this European War," declared Japanese Christian and president of Aoyama Gakuin University, Takagi Mizutaro, in November 1914. But in light of Norman Angell's hope that war would disappear with the realization of its economic costs and the peace efforts of such men as Alfred Nobel and Andrew Carnegie (founder of the Carnegie Foundation for Peace), "the enormous surprise of the world" was understandable.[8] Referring to the writings of the pacifist Ivan Bloch, peace conferences in Holland and Russia, and the work of the Carnegie Foundation, the conservative bi-weekly *Japan and the Japanese* (Nihon oyobi Nihonjin) noted wryly that, "soon after the construction of these temples to peace, we see Europe plunge into war."[9]

As in Europe, incredulity in Tokyo was accentuated by the unprecedented scale of the conflict. Seiyukai president Hara described it as possibly "the largest war since Napoleon I."[10] Waseda University historian Kemuyama Sentaro noted that although European history had been a history of wars, none of these conflicts had reached beyond the continent. The present clash was the first "world war," possible only after a certain level of political development.[11]

Closer to home, the popular mouthpiece of political reform in Japan, the *Osaka Daily News* (Osaka Mainichi shinbun), described the Great War as the largest military engagement, up to that point, in modern Japanese history. It found a violence that "far outstrips that of the Russo-Japanese War."[12] Accentuating the novelty of the situation in Japan, the daily *Peoples' News* (Minpo) noted at the end of August that "these days, even the most remote countryside is animated by the talk of war. ... Even dogs get excited when a newspaper extra is delivered."[13] In downtown Tokyo, major department stores marked the occasion with displays of military accoutrements and images of aerial bombings and sieges.[14]

III. Explaining the Outbreak of War

If Japanese politicians, pundits (and pets) marveled at the suddenness and scale of events in August 1914, like their counterparts in Europe, they were not caught entirely unawares. Modern Japan was forged in the last three decades of the nineteenth century from political, military, and economic models painstakingly studied and transported from Europe to the Japanese archipelago. And most Japanese statesmen were painfully aware of the axiom enunciated by the founder of the modern Japanese army, Yamagata Aritomo, in 1895, that "the affairs of the world are decided in Europe."[15] Japanese political and opinion leaders, therefore, faithfully kept abreast of developments in the heart of the Western world. As Viscount Tani's memorial indicates, they were well aware of the persistence of European rivalries.

As recently as January 1914, the semi-official publication of the Japanese Foreign Ministry warned of "great change" (*dai hendo*) to visit European politics in the near future. Citing the French poem "La Marche de l'Est," the editors of *Diplomatic Review* mistakenly identified the likely source of disturbance as an international struggle over Africa.[16] But commentary following the outbreak of general hostilities referenced more relevant recent discussion in Europe. The September issue of *Diplomatic Review* noted a 1913 publication by a French general predicting an imminent Austro-Russian War accompanied by a Franco-German conflict. The former German Chancellor von Bülow had, moreover, promised to "surpass the other continental powers and take on Britain."[17] Anyone who had heard the pronouncements of retired German cavalry officer Friedrich von Bernhardi before 1914, declared liberal journalist Kayahara Kazan in Japan's most popular monthly journal, *Central Review* (Chuo koron), "would have no need for surprise [by the war]."[18]

If the persistence of European rivalries gave the great "European war" a certain tinge of predictability, so too did the massive military build up before the war. Retired Major General Yamaguchi Keizo characterized the conflict as something that he had "absolutely no doubt" would occur. Since the Franco-Prussian War, he explained, peace in Europe had been maintained by a balance of power between Russia and France on the one hand and Germany, Austria, and Italy on the other. But as Britain joined the Entente and Italy began to drift from the Central Powers, the balance disintegrated into an arms race. When the competition became too onerous, the powers decided to act.[19] Another Japanese general, writing anonymously in the pages of the popular bi-monthly, *Sun* (Taiyo), argued that "Europe seemed preoccupied with preparations for an inevitable war and decided that this was the perfect time for a fight."[20]

The sense of predictability expressed by Japanese commentators following the outbreak of war in Europe related closely to a larger discussion of reasons for the conflagration. If observers located a high probability of conflict in the breakdown of a balance of power and in a pre-war arms buildup, it was to those factors that many naturally attributed the principal causes of war. Echoing the comments of General Yamaguchi, the editors of *Japan and the Japanese* highlighted the annual expansion of armaments before the war and described peace as "simply an interval for [war] preparation."[21] The 1 August *Osaka Daily News* offered a feature on the Entente and the Central Powers to underscore the centrality of alliances. Peace had been maintained as long as there had remained a balance of power between these two camps.[22]

IV. Cultural Explanations for the European War

Japanese explanations for the outbreak of war in Europe were, of course, varied. But just as European pundits accentuated the sinister distinctiveness of their new battlefield enemies, Japanese observers fashioned their own images of difference. Given their cultural distinctiveness from the Western powers, Japan's version of wartime branding covered an impressive range. For many observers in Tokyo, the war was the direct result not of the peculiarities of one or two nations but of an entire European culture.

In describing the importance of a balance of power, for example, the most popular monthly, *Central Review*, characterized it as a "peculiarly European phenomenon."[23] It was neither apparent in current relations between the United States and Canada nor characteristic of diplomacy in ancient China, where, despite a history of wars between states, the norm remained a unity of the realm under one monarch. "Given that the maintenance of a balance of power in Europe is the guarantor of the powers' existence," the editors declared, "destruction of this balance is the public enemy of Europe."[24]

Likewise, according to some Japanese observers, European culture was distinguished by its materialism and lack of spirituality. A member of the *Sun* editorial staff, Asada Emura, credited the "dazzling luster of European civilization" for maintaining peace for forty years. And he had no doubt of the superiority of standards of living in Europe. But the Europeans, he insisted, remained "ardent believers in Machiavellism."[25] The president of the private Methodist university, Aoyama Gakuin, asked rhetorically how it was possible that all of the main belligerents in the European conflict were Christian. Modern European civilization, Takagi Mizutaro offered, had diverged enormously from Christianity, "The present war does not mark the bankruptcy of Christian civilization. It marks the bankruptcy of anti-Christian civilization, that is, materialist, individualist civilization. It is the bankruptcy of modern civilization that developed over the last three hundred years and reached its apex in the nineteenth century."

Although there were many positive elements to this civilization, there was also one great deficiency: "the absolute disregard for spiritual aspects." The result was the ruinous war.[26]

V. Racial Explanations for the European War

European belligerents accentuated the differences between themselves and their enemies by making frequent references to race, whether it be to the German "Hun" or to "Slavic" hordes. Likewise, Japanese observers often prioritized race. In a 1 August article for the daily *Tokyo Asahi News* (Tokyo Asahi shinbun) titled, "The Slav Spirit," an anonymous Japanese military officer noted that "Slavs are a kind of mysterious race, seemingly capable and incapable—impossible to tell whether they are asleep or awake." But because they could be "astonishingly clever with one blow of the wind," they had to be watched. Russia had been obstructed in its long desire to expand south into the Balkans and now spied a chance for "the development of the Slav race against Austria."[27] The daily *Osaka Asahi News* (Osaka Asahi shinbun) predicted that "the conflict between the Slav and Teutonic peoples will increasingly threaten the peace of the Balkan peninsula and Europe."[28] With the outbreak of full-scale war, the editors of *Japan and the Japanese* confirmed that it was "a battle between the Germanic and Slav peoples."[29] Likewise, retired Tokyo University law professor Tomizu Hirondo located the long-term cause of the war in "the competition between the Germanic and Slavic races in the eastern Balkans."[30]

But while many in Japan subscribed to the Germanic-Slav distinction propagated in some quarters in Europe, Japanese visions of race, like Japanese perceptions of European culture, often accentuated the fault lines not within Europe but outside it. Given Japan's status as the only Asian power among a host of Western imperial powers and in light of increasing opposition in the United States and Australia to Japanese immigration, some Japanese continued to brood about their country as a racial outlier in world politics. Thus, the September *Japan and the Japanese* hinted that developments in Europe were not simply a war between two European "races," but also a harbinger of more directly threatening battles to come: "The great trend of the twentieth century is racial war. The cause of this Great European War absolutely lies here. Even though we are in the Far East, they (the Europeans) will certainly not look cheerfully upon the sudden rise of the yellow peoples."[31]

Even more outspoken about the implications of a European race war was one of Japan's most influential policy makers, Field Marshal Yamagata. As the most powerful of the four Japanese "elder statesman" (*genro*), Yamagata remained a formidable political force in 1914. In the 8 August genro-cabinet deliberation on Japanese participation in the war, Yamagata made a powerful case for "firm" relations with China in anticipation of an eventual East-West conflict. "Although the current European war has many causes," he allowed, "we must identify racial competition as the principal motive." Echoing earlier assessments, Yamagata described a war between the Germanic peoples and the Slavs. It was, admittedly, a struggle between two Caucasian "races." But given British discrimination against Indians in Britain, South Africa, and Canada, and in light of American persecution of Japanese on American soil, "we cannot say that [those races] will not come together."

Yamagata foresaw in the not-so-distant future "a contest between the yellow and white races."[32]

VI. Admiring Kaiser Wilhelm

If the outbreak of war in Europe spurred an animated discussion in Japan over the causes of the conflict, it also focused ample attention on the primary protagonist, Germany. From the beginning, a consensus in Tokyo identified Germany as the principal instigator of hostilities. As the *Diplomatic Review* declared on 15 August, "We have no hesitation in locating Germany at the center of present events. Germany must bear responsibility for being the 'power behind the veil,' pushing Austria toward an uncompromising attitude."[33] And Japanese observers condemned Germany and Kaiser Wilhelm II for all manner of sins: a lack of caution, impatience, political ineptness, prevarication, arrogance, and political backwardness. "No matter what the outcome of this great European disturbance," declared German language specialist Muko Gunji in September, "it will surely carry a great lesson for world history," namely, "the extent to which absolute monarchy is an anachronism in the twentieth century." Wilhelm II had resorted to "rash behavior" (*keikyo modo*) because he considered himself a servant of God, above the will of the people.[34] A political cartoon in the same September issue of *Japan and the Japanese* portrayed Germany as a devil behind a mask of civilization.[35]

But despite a certain antipathy in Japan for Germany's pivotal role in disturbing world peace, there remained abundant appreciation for its impressive accomplishments. The sheer audacity of Germany's initiatives left many observers breathless. Reacting to German persistence in the face of great losses at the Battle of Liège, the *Osaka Daily News* marveled at "the power of a losing Kaiser!"[36] Given the enormous stakes involved, the German monarch's gamble, argued Papal law authority and Lower House MP Tomizu Hirondo, "is not something an average person could accomplish."[37] By November, rapid advances by the German army had Tomizu hailing German power as "magnificent" (*subarashii*).[38]

This power was all the more conspicuous in light of Germany's very recent development. As political historian Kemuyama Sentaro noted, although the Germans, like their French and British counterparts, counted among the "civilized" peoples of Europe, as a modern nation-state, Germany was relatively young. German development had, moreover, reached a level of "ferocity" (*domo*) since unification, despite being surrounded and pressured by great powers.[39] Japanese observers hailed Germany most often for its military and technological accomplishments. But many also applauded German prowess in the realm of culture and in the cultivation of the spirit.[40]

If Japanese pundits were struck by German power, culture, and rapid development, they were particularly fascinated by the principal embodiment of those

Illustration 17.1: Nihon oyobi Nihonjin (Japan and the Japanese), 15 September 1914, 154

accomplishments, Kaiser Wilhelm. The Japanese media highlighted Allied leaders from French president Poincaré to Belgian king Albert. But they paid special attention to the head of their erstwhile foe, Wilhelm. Like the German empire itself, Wilhelm II captivated Japanese analysts for his sheer will. "Even if he is an enemy," declared Upper House MP Nakashoji Ren in a special issue of the *Central Review* dedicated to the German monarch, "one must praise someone with the qualities of an outstanding leader." In particular, Nakashoji urged his countrymen to "devote ourselves single-mindedly to the object of avoiding defeat," following the "perfect model" of Wilhelm.[41] According to liberal journalist-cum-politician Tagawa Daikichiro, the talents of this "most extraordinary hero" (fuseshutsu no eishu) were many. He was highly perceptive, exceedingly cultured, good at painting and oratory, a fan of learning, an aficionado of military affairs, and deeply religious.[42]

Although most observers recognized the difficulty of the Kaiser's current position against the Entente, they considered him symbolic of the formidable successes already recorded by Imperial Germany. As noted by *Japan and the Japanese*, the German empire "was constructed, maintained and expanded by the two Wilhelms." And although Wilhelm I was the most exalted founding father of Imperial Germany, his grandson "must be seen as just as important a figure."[43]

For Japan, Wilhelm II's leadership role was more than just an academic matter. At the heart of Japanese fascination with Germany and its supreme leader lay the close historical affinity between Imperial Germany and Japan. Like Germany, Japan was a late-developer. The founders of Imperial Japan had, in fact, looked to an earlier generation of German leadership for inspiration in constructing some of Japan's most important political and military institutions. Two of modern Japan's founding fathers, Ito Hirobumi and Yamagata Aritomo, had met Otto von Bismarck on fact-finding tours of Europe and had subsequently incorporated German principles into the Japanese constitution and modern army, respectively.

It is no surprise, therefore, that some Japanese analysts found Kaiser Wilhelm very familiar. The editors of *Japan and the Japanese* described the legacies of Wilhelm I and II as being very similar to the pivotal role played by the first and third shoguns, Tokugawa Ieyasu and Tokugawa Iemitsu, in establishing the foundations of Tokugawa Japan (1600–1868).[44] Journalist and Europhile Gorai Motokawa viewed Wilhelm II as an "Asian-style emperor," sharing many of the principles found in the reign of Japan's own monarch: the emperor as a living god and as the father of his people, and the important place of both spirituality and militarism in the national polity. Echoing forecasts of an eventual East-West split, Gorai found such a division already a reality in the battle between Germany, as the embodiment of "Asian-style" rulership in Europe, and the liberal polities represented by the Entente.[45]

VII. War as Opportunity

Despite such sympathy in Japan for the kaiser, the Japanese cabinet, as we have seen, wasted no time in issuing an ultimatum to Germany at the beginning of August 1914. The man most responsible for Japan's decision for war, Foreign Minister Kato Takaaki, hoped to join the battle against Germany, in part, to solidify Japan's alliance with Great Britain. Kato had served as Japan's minister, then ambassador to the Court of St. James and had played a pivotal role in crafting the Anglo-Japanese alliance in 1902.[46] But Japanese ties to Britain were only one of a host of issues raised by Japanese commentators as they debated Japan's response to the war.

As in European capitals, the Japanese debate accelerated with the realization of the gravity of the situation in Europe. And, as with their European counterparts, Japanese observers expressed great enthusiasm for an opportunity in the first months of conflict. According to elder statesman Inoue Kaoru, "The present great disturbance is the divine aid of the new Taisho era for the development of the destiny of Japan."[47]

In its most limited sense, the war offered an opportunity for revenge. As the first-page editorial of the 15 September issue of *Japan and the Japanese* noted, "the current [German] emperor's pressure [on Japan] nineteen years ago to return Liaodong is still fresh in our memory."[48] Indeed, a "tri-partite intervention" of Russia, France, and Germany had forced Japan to retract its demand for China to cede the Liaodong peninsula (southern Manchuria) following the Sino-Japanese War. This was a golden opportunity to repay the favor.

But it was not simply that Berlin had conspired with the powers against Japan in 1895. As the popular monthly *Central Review* reminded its readers, Germany had, immediately thereafter, laid claim to territory in Shandong province, thus beginning the scramble for spheres of influence in China that had not only threatened to tear China apart, but had also sparked the Russo-Japanese War. Germany's subsequent economic development and militarization of the Kiaochow concession in Shandong meant that "just as Germany is the root of evil [*kongen*] in Europe, Kiaochow is truly the bane of the Far East."[49]

The opportunity to eject Germany from Kiaochow was only a small part of a larger desire to expand Japanese influence in Asia. Japan had astounded the world by militarily defeating China and Russia in 1895 and 1905, respectively. With those victories, Japan catapulted from the status of victim of great power imperialism to an imperial power in its own right. Japan had acquired a formal colony in Formosa in 1895 and established a foothold in China for the first time with the transfer of Russian interests in South Manchuria in 1905.

Despite these impressive gains, the post-Russo-Japanese War years brought significant setbacks to Japanese regional influence. Tokyo was unable to steer China toward a constitutional monarchy in its own image following the 1911 Chinese Revolution. And the Taft administration's "dollar diplomacy" aggressively challenged Japan's newly acquired interests in South Manchuria. The first reaction of the *Diplomatic Review* to the outbreak of war in Europe was, therefore, to cheer the opportunity for Japan to take charge on the continent, "As long as China remains under the guarantee of several powers, we must forever be prepared for disturbances. To cut this root of evil, we must build an irrevocable foundation of unity with this old country. Today is the perfect opportunity to push this through."[50]

Nationalist politician Nakano Seigo echoed this sentiment when he noted that Japan could mobilize troops against Kiaochow with "no danger of attack from the enemy." The effect upon Japanese commerce and trade would, moreover, be limited. "A disturbance in Europe means a perfect opportunity to expand our capabilities in Asia."[51] Liberal journalist-cum-politician Ishikawa Hanzan could not help but "welcome" news of "the great European War, contemplate its effect upon the East, and wish for the Japanese people to seize this opportunity for great action."[52]

A critical component of the aspiration for expanded Japanese influence in China was the hope for increased commercial opportunity. Although the immediate impact of the war in Japan was, as in the capitals of Europe, negative, more than a few observers spied ample potential rewards. As legal scholar Watanab Manzo noted, given the disruption of European trade and shipping, this was the time to "energetically establish and expand our commercial supremacy [shoken] in China."[53] Among the early opportunities making the news was the dramatic headway made by Japanese breweries. The war radically reduced British and American beer exports and forced the suspension of operations in Japan's two greatest competitors in Asia, Union Breweries of Shanghai and Qingdao Breweries of Qingdao. By the end of September, the daily *Central News* (Chuo shinbun) reported a practical Japanese monopoly on beer sales in China, the Russian Far East, the Philippines, Thailand, and Borneo.[54]

If a flurry of Japanese analysts spied opportunity for increased market share in China, many also anticipated a boon for Japanese shipping. Given the dramatic reduction of European bottoms east of the Suez Canal, educator Wada Kikuo urged Japanese shipping to "great activity." National interests, he argued, should "increasingly reclaim the sea lanes from the European powers, and seize control of the seas."[55]

The most fundamental foreign policy aspiration of Japanese observers in August 1914 was for Japan to seize the opportunity, once again, to increase its international status. Such had, indeed, been the ultimate consequence of both the Sino- and Russo-Japanese Wars. Japan's 1895 victory over China had inspired Western onlookers to describe the nation as the "pioneer of progress in the Orient."[56] The 1905 victory over Russia famously drove President Theodore Roosevelt to exclaim that "this is the greatest phenomenon the world has ever seen."[57] And it prompted the powers to raise their legations in Japan to full-fledged embassies.

But despite Japan's victory over both the principal East Asian hegemon and a major European empire, not even Japanese commentators in August 1914 ventured to place the country in the ranks of the world's great powers. Writing from Paris on the eve of the war, Kyoto University professor Kanbe Masao noted that "the farther abroad one peers from at Japan, the lower one feels (its international status)." To Kanbe, Japan stood clearly below Europe in both a material and spiritual sense. But what vexed him most was the fact that, while in some ways Western powers viewed Japan as an equal, there remained a clear atmosphere of prejudice.[58] As if to confirm this bias, word spread in Tokyo on the eve of the Great War of a caustic report about Japan written by the correspondent of the London *Times* in Tokyo. "Although the Japanese emerged on the world stage ten years ago as a people with unbelievable courage," read the *Times*, "as the effect of the war dissipated, so too have those singing Japan's praises. Japan is now completely forgotten."[59]

If Japan's international status left much to be desired, even more so did the place of Asia in the world. Chronicling the history of Western colonization of Asia and Africa from the sixteenth century, the *Diplomatic Review* lamented several months before Sarajevo that an "Asia for the Asians" would not materialize for another "several hundred years."[60] On the eve of war, the *Central Review* urged its readers to "understand the fate of the Asian peoples, think of the opportunity of a major turning point in world history and strive from now on to energetically cultivate our power."[61]

In this context, many in Japan understandably viewed the outbreak of war in Europe as the historic turning point that might finally grant Japan and Asia the international status they deserved. "The day our troops disembark in Shandong," proclaimed Uma Kakunari in early September, "will be a time of great honor for our people."[62] Commenting on Japan's recent declaration of war, an anonymous writer in the *Central Review* rejoiced that "We are truly on the road to victory. This is a sense of honor that our people have not felt since the founding of our empire."[63] Referring explicitly to the most recent humiliation of Japan, journalist Shibukawa Genji insisted that, "the Taisho era, which the London *Times* criticized as an age of Japan on the decline is, from today, again on an upward slope of hope."[64] As for Asia, Japanese governor-general of Korea and soon-to-be prime minister General Terauchi Masatake wrote excitedly to Vice-Chief of the Army General Staff Akashi Motojiro at the end of August that, "although we will not insist upon excluding Europeans and Americans, it is proper to inform the Westerners that, up to a point, Asia should be under the control of Asians."[65]

VIII. Conclusion

As in the principal European belligerents, Japanese reactions to the outbreak of war in Europe were varied. National discussion in Japan, in fact, mirrored familiar patterns of debate long discussed by historians of Europe. If, on the one hand, Japanese policy makers and pundits marveled at the suddenness and scale of the conflict, they also greeted it with a certain presentiment. And they shared with European prognosticators both trepidation and hope for the opportunities generated by general conflict.

Japan's geographic and cultural remoteness from the heart of battle and relatively light level of participation guaranteed a distinct twist in Japanese perception. Rather than simply censure their wartime enemies, many in Japan highlighted the inadequacies of European culture overall. Although Tokyo had been quick to declare allegiance to the Allied cause, Japanese observers were, moreover, as likely to echo German concerns over the expansion of "Slav" power as they were to condemn German "militarism." German criticism of the lack of spirituality in Western Europe found expression in a larger Japanese condemnation of the materialism of modern European civilization. And numerous commentators in Tokyo marveled at both German power and the accomplishments of its "heroic" monarch. This robust interest in Germany offers more indirect evidence that one of Foreign Minister Kato Takaaki's principal motives in moving so swiftly for a declaration of war against Berlin may have been to head off a counter initiative to act in concert with the Kaiser.[66]

Tokyo was not, on the eve of the Great War, poised for another continental initiative on the scale of the Sino- or Russo-Japanese Wars. But most Japanese policy makers and opinion leaders in August 1914 were eager to seize the opportunity to further Japan's most critical long-term foreign policy goal: boosting the continental presence that would, in the words of Viscount Tani, make Japan the "chief nation of the Orient." Historians continue to revile Foreign Minister Kato Takaaki for his ambitious attempt to negotiate a comprehensive list of Japanese "rights" in China in the first half of 1915 (the notorious "Twenty-One Demands").[67] But these must be understood in the context of this "culture of opportunity" in Tokyo in the late summer and fall of 1914.

Tokyo's "culture of opportunity" mirrors a similar phenomenon in capitals throughout Europe in 1914. But while European expectations of benefits quickly dissolved in the appalling carnage of the Western front, Japanese hopes received no such chastening. Rather, Japan became the only power that saw all initial expectations of opportunity not only fulfilled but surpassed. Japanese forces handily dispatched Germany from Kiaochow, China, and German Micronesia by November 1914—at a cost of less than two thousand dead. Seven months later, Beijing signed a treaty granting sweeping new rights to Japan throughout China (in response to the "Twenty-One Demands"). As anticipated by many, the war provided a major boost to Japanese trade, shipping and, in turn, to the economy. By 1916, Tokyo enjoyed a balance of payments surplus and could fully participate in the vital game of international finance for the first time. Japanese financiers eagerly floated loans to Russia, France, Britain, and China. At the Paris Peace Conference, Japanese delegates sat at an international conference, for the first time, as equals of those from the four greatest world powers.

Japan's rise to the status of global power in 1919 was predicated upon a strong identification with the new internationalist trend of the world. Despite significant wartime Japanese fascination with Germany, post-war Japan was dominated by men such as Doshikai party elder, Shimada Saburo, who had in 1914 viewed Kaiser Wilhelm II as "the epitome of old authoritarian monarchy, an anachronism in the twentieth century."[68] For Shimada and those fighting for an end to the monopoly privileges of Japan's established elite, the battle against Germany was, fundamentally, a fight to ensure more representative rule at home. To engage Germany at Kiaochow had been to "destroy the land and sea defenses, which commemorate the dangerous [militarist] thought of Germany."[69]

Although Shimada and his allies in the political party movement prevailed in 1920s Japan, compliance with the new internationalist world order did not go uncontested. For every reproach of German "militarism" during World War I, there had been those like Lieutenant General Izu Tsuneo who hoped the conflict would "breathe life into patriotism and military preparedness."[70] General Izu and his friends among the military-bureaucratic establishment continued in inter-war Japan to challenge every new step toward democracy and internationalism.

The dramatic 1920s turn toward retraction of empire, arms reductions, economic expansion, universal male suffrage, and political party rule indicated that Izu and his allies waged a losing battle throughout the decade. But given the real benefits of Japanese involvement in the Great War, the "culture of opportunity" of August 1914 remained. "The Japanese like war," remarked the Chief of the War Ministry's Military Affairs Bureau Koiso Kuniaki in August 1931. "If the guns start firing, they'll all jump in for a good fight."[71] One month later, members of the Japanese army in Manchuria deliberately set an explosion along the South Manchuria Railway that demonstrated the devastating consequences of Japan's "culture of opportunity." Hailed in Tokyo as the beginning of new possibilities,[72] the Manchurian Incident, in fact, ushered in fourteen years of war that would ultimately invite the destruction of Imperial Japan.

Notes

1. Following his August 1914 request for Japanese help against German warships in Asia, British Foreign Secretary Sir Edward Grey made several appeals in November 1914 for Japanese troops to be sent to France, Belgium, and Germany, "in the same way as our Army is doing, and to fight alongside our soldiers on the continent of Europe." See Grey telegram to Japanese Ambassador Inoue Katsunosuke, 2 November. 1914; Grey telegram to British Embassy, Tokyo, 7 November 1914, both in File 5-2-2-51, "Oshu senso no sai teikoku no shuppeiron kankei

ikken" (Documents Relating to Discussions on a Japanese Expedition during the European War), Japanese Ministry of Foreign Affairs. In July 1918, the US navy described the participation of Japanese battle cruisers in the protection of US troop transports en route to Europe as "a matter of vital necessity." Letter from Secretary of the Navy Edwin Denby to Secretary of State Charles E. Hughes, 23 September 1921. Stanley K. Hornbeck papers, Box 255, "Japan: War Costs and Contributions" file, the Hoover Institution on War, Revolution and Peace.

2. Payson Jackson Treat, "Japan, America and the Great War," *A League of Nations*, vol. 1, no. 8 (December 1918), 8. Stanley K. Hornbeck Papers, Box 238, "Japan: War, 'Japan in the War,' by P. J. Treat" file.

3. For details on Anglo-Japanese negotiations in August 1914 on Japanese participation in the war, see Peter Lowe, *Great Britain and Japan 1911–15* (London, 1969), 181.

4. See, for example, Frederick R. Dickinson, *War and National Reinvention: Japan in the Great War, 1914–1919* (Cambridge, 1999).

5. Quoted in Tyler Dennett, *Americans in Eastern Asia* (New York, 1941), 527.

6. Hara Keiichiro, ed., *Hara Takashi nikki* [Diary of Hara Takashi], 6 vols. (Tokyo, 1981), vol. 4, 25–26 (diary entry for 4 August 1914).

7. Editors, "Zen-O doran to teikoku seifu no taido" [Our Government's Attitude toward the All-European Disturbance], *Gaiko jiho* (15 August 1914), 1–2.

8. Takagi Mizutaro, "Oshu senran to kirisutokyo" [Christianity and the European War], *Nihon oyobi Nihonjin* (15 November 1914), 30. For another reference to Norman Angell, see Nakano Seigo, "Taisenran to kokumin no kakugo" [The Great War and the Peoples' Preparedness], *Nihon oyobi Nihonjin* (15 September. 1914), 23.

9. Editors, "Ichi seneki wa ichi seneki yori daikibo" [This War is One on a Scale Greater than War], *Nihon oyobi Nihonjin*, no. 637 (1 September 1914), 12–13.

10. Hara, ed., *Hara Takashi nikki*, vol. 4, 26.

11. Waseda remains one of Japan's most prestigious private universities. Kemuyama Sentaro, "Doran kanchu no ni kanso" [Two Impressions of the Disturbance], *Gaiko jiho* (1 September 1914), 27.

12. "Rieju de uketa Dokugun no daigisei" [The Great Sacrifice Paid by the German Army at Liège], *Osaka Mainichi shinbun*, 9 August 1914; found in Taisho nyusu jiten hensan iinkai, ed., *Taisho nyusu jiten* [Dictionary of Taisho news], 8 vols. (Tokyo, 1986), vol.I, 391.

13. "Tatakaibanashi ni yoru ga fukeru" [The Night Goes on with the Talk of War], *Minpo*, 25 August 1914; found in Watanabe Katsumasa, ed., *Shinbun shuroku Taishoshi* [Newspaper compilation of Taisho history], 15 vols. (Tokyo, 1978), vol. 2, 317.

14. Among the accoutrements were knapsacks, swords, guns, bugles, medals, epaulets, and crests. "Sen gokko no omocha ryu" [The Toys of War Games], *Yomiuri shinbun*, 25 September 1914; printed in ibid., 350.

15. Yamagata was reacting to the intervention of Russia, France, and Germany following the Sino-Japanese War (1894–95), forcing Japan's retrocession of the Liadong Peninsula (southern Manchuria) to China. Quoted in Oka Yoshitake, *Yamagata Aritomo: Meiji Nihon no shocho* [Yamagata Aritomo: Symbol of Meiji Japan] (Tokyo, 1958), 62–63.

16. "Hentenshi iku oshu seikyoku" [A Changing Europe], *Gaiko jiho* (1 January 1914), 6–7.

17. "O-A tairan shimatsuki" [Note on the Circumstances of the Great Disturbance of Europe and Asia], *Gaiko jiho* (1 September 1914), 109–10.

18. Kayahara Kazan, "Bunmeishiteki kokusaishiteki ni kansatsu shitaru Oshu senso" [The European War as Viewed from the Perspective of the History of Civilization and International Relations], *Chuo koron* (Fall 1914), 72. Bernhardi's 1912 publication, *Germany and the Next War*, had stressed the importance of war in maintaining Germany's advantage in the struggle for world power.

19. Yamaguchi Keizo, "Gaiko to senryaku to no chowa o kakeru Doku gun" [The German Army, which Lacks Balance between Diplomacy and Strategy], *Chuo koron* (Fall 1914), 111.

20. Anonymous Major-General, "Chinmoku no senryaku" (The Hidden Strategy), *Taiyo* (1 September 1914), 147.
21. "Ichi seneki wa ichi seneki yori dai kibo" (This War is One on a Scale Greater than War), 13.
22. "Sankoku domei to sankoku kyosho yurai" [Origins of the Central Alliance and Entente], *Osaka Asahi shinbun*, 1 August 1914; printed in *Shinbun shuroku Taishoshi*, vol. 2, 279.
23. Editors, "Oshu no doran o ronzu" [On the Great European Disturbance], *Chuo koron* (Fall 1914), 5.
24. Ibid., 2.
25. Asada Emura, "Oshu rekkyo no kosenjutsu" [The European Powers' Passion for War], *Taiyo* (1 September 1914), 18–20.
26. Takagi, "Oshu senran to kirisutokyo" [Christianity and the European War], 33.
27. "Surabu damashii" [The Slav Spirit], *Tokyo Asahi shinbun*, 1 August 1914; printed in Meiji Taisho Showa shinbun kenkyukai, ed., *Shinbun shusei Taishohen nenshi* [Taisho History Compilation of Newspapers], (Tokyo, 1980), 1914, vol. 2, 235.
28. "Sankoku domei to sankoku kyosho yurai" [Origins of the Central Alliance and Entente], 280.
29. Editors, "Zen oshu no taisenran" [The Great All-European War], *Nihon oyobi Nihonjin* (15 August 1914), 4.
30. Tomizu Hirondo, "Oshu rekkyo no daikaisen ni taishite" [Looking at the Outbreak of a Great War among the European Powers], *Chuo koron* (Fall 1914), 100.
31. Editors, "Oshu senkyoku hi ni shinten" [The Daily Unfolding European War], *Nihon oyobi Nihonjin* (1 September 1914), 5.
32. Ito Takashi, ed., *Taisho shoki Yamagata Aritomo danwa hikki* [Record of Yamagata Aritomo's Conversations in Early Taisho], (Tokyo, 1981), 60.
33. Editors, "Zen-O doran to teikoku seifu no taido" [Our Government's Attitude toward the All-European Disturbance], 4.
34. Muko Gunji, "Oshu senran no atauru kyokun" [The Lesson of the European War], *Nihon oyobi Nihonjin* (15 September 1914), 32–36.
35. "Jiji manga" [Cartoons of Current Events], ibid., 154.
36. "Rieju de uketa Dokugun no daigisei" [The Great Sacrifice Paid by the German Army at Liège], 391.
37. Tomizu Hirondo, "Oshu rekkyo no daikaisen ni taishite" [Looking at the Outbreak of a Great War among the European Powers], 105.
38. Tomizu Hirondo, "Sengo ni okeru gunbi mondai" [The Problem of Arms after the War], *Chuo koron* (November 1914), 96.
39. Kemuyama, "Doran kanchu no ni kanso" [Two Impressions of the Disturbance], 31.
40. See, for example, Tanaka Masahira, "Ekken o tamawatta toki no kioku" [Memories of My Audience with the Kaiser], *Chuo koron* (Fall 1914), 89–91 and Anonymous, "Kaiza" (Kaiser), ibid., 73–77, respectively.
41. Nakashoji Ren, "Doitsu otei wa eiketsu nari" [The German Emperor is an Outstanding Leader], *ibid.*, pp. 88–9.
42. Tagawa Daikichiro, "Nan to moshitemo fuseshutsu no eio" [A Truly Extraordinary Hero], *Chuo koron* (Fall 1914), 78.
43. Editors, "Iren issei, iren nisei no ido" [The Difference between Wilhelm I and Wilhelm II], *Nihon oyobi Nihonjin* (15 September. 1914), 7.
44. Ibid., 10.
45. Gorai Motokawa, "Toyo kunshufu no Doitsu kotei" [The Asian-style German Emperor], *Chuo koron* (Fall 1914), 82–84.
46. For more on Kato's initiatives and motives at the outbreak of the Great War, see Frederick R. Dickinson, "Japan," in Richard Hamilton and Holger Herwig, eds., *The Origins of World War I* (Cambridge, 2003), 300–36.

47. Speaking in August 1914. Inoue Kaoru ko denki hensankai, ed., *Segai Inoue ko den* [Biography of the Late Lord Inoue], 5 vols. (Tokyo, 1968) vol. 5, 367.
48. Editors, "Nihon tai Doku O no seneki" [Japan's War against Germany and Austria], *Nihon oyobi Nihonjin* (15 September 1914), 1.
49. Editors, "Oko Koshuwan" [The Crying Kiaochow], *Chuo koron* (Fall 1914), 1.
50. Editors, "Zen-O doran to teikoku seifu no taido" [Our Government's Attitude toward the All-European Disturbance], 9.
51. Nakano Seigo, "Taisenran to kokumin no kakugo" [The Great War and the Peoples' Preparedness], 24.
52. Ishikawa Hanzan, "Kekkyoku shina mondai" [In the End, it is the China Problem], *Chuo koron* (Fall 1914), 71.
53. Watanabe Manzo, "Oshu senran to zaikai no eikyo" [Effect of the European War on the Business Community], *Nihon oyobi Nihonjin* (15 August 1914), 30.
54. "Honpo biiru no hanro kakucho wa ima nari" [Expansion of the Japanese Beer Market is Now], *Chuo shinbun*, 28 September 1914, in *Shinbun shuroku Taishoshi*, vol. 2, 355.
55. Wada Kikuo, "Oshu no senkyoku to waga zosengyo" [Our Ship-building Industry and the European War], *Nihon oyobi Nihonjin* (1 September 1914), 32.
56. John L. Stoddard, *John L. Stoddard's Lectures*, 10 vols. (Chicago, 1897), vol. 3, 116.
57. Roosevelt was referring specifically to Japan's sinking of the Russian Baltic Fleet at the Battle of Tsushima Straits on 27 May 1905. Quoted in Shumpei Okamoto, *The Japanese Oligarchy and the Russo-Japanese War* (New York, 1970), 119.
58. Kanbe Masao, "Nihon oyobi Nihonjin no taigaiteki taido" [The Attitude of Japan and the Japanese toward the World], *Taiyo* (1 September 1914), 114–17. Kanbe's comments were originally dated 21 July.
59. As quoted in "Taimusu shin Nihonron" [The London *Times*' Theory of a New Japan], *Tokyo nichinichi shinbun*, 29 July 1914, in *Shinbun shusei Taishohen nenshi*, 1914, vol. 2, 221.
60. Editors, "Ajia wa mezamezaru ya" [Won't Asia Awaken?], *Gaiko jiho* (1 January 1914), 19.
61. Editors, "Ajia minzoku no kakugo o unagasu" [Urging the Preparation of Asian Peoples], *Chuo koron* (August 1914), 13.
62. Uma Kakunari, "Kaizeru no kaoiro" [The Kaiser's Facial Hue], *Nihon oyobi Nihonjin* (1 September 1914), 115.
63. Kuro Zukin (pen name), "Kono toki" [At this Time], *Chuo koron* (Fall 1914), 32. The article was originally written on 15 August.
64. Shibukawa Genji, "Nihon no noborizaka" [Japan's Upward Slope], *Chuo koron* (Fall 1914), 40. Article dated August 16.
65. Akashi Motojiro monjo 32–11, Terauchi to Akashi, 22 August 1914; in Nihon seiji gaikoshi kenkyukai, "Akashi Motojiro monjo oyobi kadai" [Papers of Akashi Motojiro and Bibliography], *Kaio daigaku hogaku kenkyu*, (September 1985) vol. 58, no. 9, 96.
66. For a full statement of this argument, see Dickinson, "Japan."
67. For more on these, see Dickinson, *War and National Reinvention*, ch. 2.
68. Shimada Saburo, "Jikyoku gaiken" [Survey of the Situation], *Chuo koron* (November 1914), 63.
69. Ibid., 70.
70. Izu Tsuneo, "Oshu taisenkan" [Perspective on the Great European War], *Nihon oyobi Nihonjin* (15 October 1914), 80.
71. Quoted in Saburo Ienaga, *The Pacific War, 1931–1945* (New York, 1978), 63.
72. For more on this, see Louise Young, *Japan's Total Empire: Manchuria and the Culture of Wartime Imperialism* (Berkeley, 1997).

Chapter 18

WAR, PEACE, AND COMMERCE
The American Reaction to the Outbreak of World War I in Europe 1914

Fraser J. Harbutt

Europeans naturally look back to August 1914 as an irredeemable moment, tragic in all its consequences and implications. The decline of Europe as a primary force in the world, notwithstanding its turbulent second wind in the inter-war period, is reasonably dated from this point. For Americans too there was necessarily at the time, if only by virtue of their multifarious associations with the old continent, a tragic dimension. But for the United States, in the long run of history, 1914 may be said to mark a new beginning, opening up for the first time as a realizable prospect, the ascension of the Republic to a position of hegemonic, global power.

There was not, however, in the classic political sense, any discernible American will to power in August 1914 or any widespread expectation of it. Most Europeans were shocked and surprised by the sudden onset of war, although a few had long anticipated it and the excitement with which some greeted it suggests a sense of relieved tension. Americans, with very few exceptions, had not expected war and, viewing developments from afar, they were stunned by the sudden abdication of reason and diplomatic sophistication so clearly on display. The historian John Milton Cooper remarks: "The outbreak of the World War in August 1914 provoked comparison with a natural catastrophe or a supernatural occurrence."[1] Even as the war intensified and it began to seem that the Great Powers were engaged in a kind of suicidal death struggle, few Americans saw this as a political opportunity for the United States. That would come later with full belligerency in 1917 and

Woodrow Wilson's vigorous post-hostilities diplomacy. In 1914 the opportunity Americans saw, dimly at first and then beckoning brightly was, as any close student of American history up to that moment might have predicted, almost exclusively economic in character.

In the end both economic and political impulses would propel the United States into the struggle. And in retrospect we can easily enough identify certain structural factors that, even before the war began, made it likely that America would line up with the Allies. Here, after all, were its primary economic partners, long used to communicating directly and profitably across the open Atlantic. Here too was both the geopolitical rapprochement with Britain, carefully consolidated since the Venezuela incident of 1895, and a persisting emotional tie to the French ally of the Revolutionary War.

This lack of political inappetence may seem, from our vantage point today, rather surprising. After all, many Americans had from the founding of the Republic, and indeed long before that, taken a Promethean view of their destiny. Foreign observers from Simon Bolivar to Alexis de Tocqueville in the early nineteenth century, had predicted America's eventual emergence as a dominating world power.[2] The British writer W. T. Stead's famous book, *The Americanisation of the World*, published in the United States in 1902, registered an accelerating European awareness of this process.[3] The facts seemed to confirm the impression. As early as the 1870s the United States, already embarked on its remarkable, rapid industrialization, was by far the world's leading producer of steel. And the expansionary impulses associated with the 1898 war with Spain and its imperial outcome, as well as the robust subsequent leadership of Theodore Roosevelt, all seemed to many Europeans to point toward a fuller, more assertive engagement with the world.

Yet much of this was deceptive. The power, at least latently, was there. The will to power was another matter entirely. The 1898 adventure had in fact divided Americans, revealing deep reservations about empire, about the use of the military, and about following European modes of international politics. There was, largely as a result of the burgeoning industrialism and the surge of immigration that characterized the pre-war years, a growing and distracting concern about the coherence and unity of American society and consequently, counterpointing the new but still limited interest in world affairs, a growing preoccupation with domestic problems. This was particularly true of the new Democratic administration of Woodrow Wilson that took power at the beginning of 1913. The brief era of Republican assertiveness in foreign affairs that had begun with McKinley in 1898 and had shone brightly with Theodore Roosevelt and even to some extent with William Howard Taft, was now passing into what one historian has aptly called "a twilight."[4] The Wilsonians were bent on curbing the interests, on domestic reform, and on moral regeneration. Roosevelt's chronic lament from August 1914 onward was that fate had capriciously cast him aside in this moment of supreme challenge and left Woodrow Wilson, the supposedly thin-blooded academic from Princeton

University, to lead the country. But the fact is that the Rooseveltian moment was by 1914 very much a thing of the past.

What then, to come now to specifics, do we see in the American response to the outbreak of war in 1914? The first reactions of the Wilson administration are well known: a firm, express commitment to neutrality together with a strong assertion of neutral rights; a determination not to get politically involved; and a concern for political and economic stability at home. In the nation generally three impulses were clearly visible. First, there was a widespread attempt to stamp some definitional imprint upon the shocking event. Then there was, inevitably, a preoccupation with the likely economic repercussions. And third, much less noticeable at this stage and confined to a tiny politico-academic elite, there was an early flurry of interest in the possibilities of some regenerative American initiative to mediate the dispute or lay some basis for a better post-war world. And while the overlapping character of these impulses, and the fast-moving nature of the crisis itself, counsel against any overly schematic explanation of their significance we may identify two dominating practical concerns. One was the threat of a divided society. A vast number of Americans, without demonstrating any desire to participate in the struggle, quickly identified with one of the two great warring alliances in Europe. The larger of these, reflecting the ethnic/ancestral background of most Americans (especially in the more Anglicized South) sided with the British and French allies. But the sizable German-American community, notably in its mid-Western stronghold, naturally inclined to the Central Powers, as did many Irish, deeply antagonistic to Great Britain, and Jewish-Americans who were strongly hostile to Imperial Russia. It was therefore more from a down-to-earth determination to ensure American domestic solidarity than from any abstract aspirations to Solomonic equilibrium that President Wilson (distracted in these early days by his wife's illness and death on 6 August) declared the nation's neutrality and urged additionally that "We must be impartial in thought as well as in action."[5]

The more immediate initial concern was with the economic outlook. The prevailing emotion in the commercial community upon the outbreak of war was alarm, and inevitably in some sensitive sectors a degree of panic. Contemporary observers put it that history gave no example of such a general interruption of trade and all other international intercourse. Already in the last days of July, fear of war had suddenly driven commodity prices up sharply. It was of course understood immediately that unprecedented disruptions were likely. There was a human side to this. It was estimated that about one hundred thousand American tourists were suddenly stranded in Europe—unable to cash their checks or have their drafts honored, unable in many cases to arrange convenient passages home, or even to communicate with their families. Two extraordinarily vivid letters to Wilson Ambassador Walter H. Page described the chaos in London as thousands of Americans sought assistance in turbulent scenes that were repeated at United States embassies in Paris, Berlin, and Vienna. The impact on financial markets at home was dramatic, involving very large withdrawals of gold and capital as Europeans called in their holdings. The New York Stock Exchange was forced to close to arrest an accelerating decline. On the other hand, wheat and corn prices soared in anticipation of an increased European demand for foodstuffs. Innumerable businesses, however, especially importers, were suddenly deeply compromised, their assets often frozen or otherwise at risk, their contacts severed and their future dubious in the extreme.[6]

As Americans struggled to adjust to these disruptions they were also, after a few days of what one contemporary called "bewilderment," trying to define the causes and character of their new dispensation. A certain amount of respect was paid, at least by government spokesmen, to Wilson's injunction to be "impartial." In the press it was honored mainly in the breach. Historians have tried somewhat inconclusively to capture the precise character of the media response. Most newspapers expressed some contempt for Europe in a general way. But the majority appear to have gathered rather quickly around a pro-Allied explanation. Thus, the *New York Globe*, as representative as any, blamed Germany. It found (as many historians have since) a moral and political culpability in the kaiser's having licensed if not encouraged Austrian pressure upon Serbia, even though he knew, or should have known, that Russia, and therefore France, would intervene. It was for these reasons that *The Literary Digest*'s review of the American press found on 15 August that "American opinion is almost solidly arrayed against Germany as the aggressor." This judgment seems in retrospect to have been something of an exaggeration. For the press in the mid West was in fact deeply skeptical of British and French motives and there was considerable sympathy there for the German dilemma in the face of the supposed Russian or Slavic menace. Nevertheless, the weight of American sentiment was almost from the start strongly pro-Allied.[7]

The dramatic German advance through Belgium and northern France substantially reinforced that tendency. This is hardly surprising. Whatever its justifications Germany was, after all, the obvious aggressor in Western Europe. Along with the invasion of Belgium came the Imperial chancellor's provocative characterization of the treaty (to which Germany was itself party) that guaranteed that country's neutrality, as "a scrap of paper." To a people schooled during the Progressive era to a belief in the morality and efficacy of international law this was shocking, and it led directly to the epidemic charges of German "militarism" one finds throughout the United States in the first days of the war. In a press review article on 22 August entitled "Blaming Germany for the War" the *Literary Digest* drew attention to the imbalance. It found a tendency among both newspapers and weekly magazines to distinguish between the honorable German people and their immoral government, which they were inclined to hold responsible for the war. The prevalent American imagery of German conduct thus moved through August from an initial perception of gross illegality, then to charges of unrestrained militarism, and finally to accusations of "barbarism."

What weight then should be given to the well-documented British efforts to manipulate news reports and propagate exaggerated atrocity stories in the early days of the war? Historians have argued about this. John Bach McMaster, professor of history at the University of Pennsylvania, wrote in 1919 of the German advance in Belgium, "Everywhere their path had been marked by murder, raping, brutality, and crime. The details of what was done need not be retold. The whole world knows it."[8] This appears to be the authentic voice of the wartime generation. But modern historians have been skeptical about the impact in 1914 of these allegations. Ernest May concludes that "Long before biased news or propaganda could possibly have any effect, the public had demonstrated its profound sympathy for Belgium, and the Allied cause had come to seem righteous in the eyes of a large number of Americans." Another scholar, John Milton Cooper, credits Arthur Link (long the dean of Wilson era historians) with having "demolished" the idea that London's sophisticated atrocity propaganda was a primary influence with American opinion.[9] The decisive opinion-forming element, on this view, was not only the German violation of a treaty but also the destruction of such iconic monuments as the famous Library at Louvain and Rheims Cathedral as well as a considerable degree of well-attested aggressive behavior at civilian expense. It was, in short, the overt reality of German action, not British propaganda, that was most influential with Americans.[10]

Nevertheless, British influence was a significant factor. For one thing London was, so far as European events were concerned, America's "newspaper capital." Few newspapers before the war had maintained correspondents on the continent. The common practice was to establish a well-stocked London bureau from which almost all European news, often augmented by material taken straight from British publications, flowed directly to the United States. As soon as hostilities broke out journalistic travel to the continental fronts was almost entirely confined to officially approved British correspondents. A strict censorship was also imposed by the London authorities. And to ensure the absence of a competing narrative the Royal Navy, on the day after Britain entered the war, dredged up and cut the German cables to North America. The plain intention, so far as information about the war was concerned, was to lock the American audience into a kind of British echo chamber. Some newspapers were able to draw on assigned or roving correspondents of various nationalities to give some semblance of the Central Powers' perspective. But in its crucial early stages the war was seen by Americans very much as the British wished them to see it. And it was within this controlled journalistic environment that the first and lasting images of German behavior were indelibly established.[11]

The German government and its American supporters fought back as best they could. So far as Belgium was concerned a steady stream of explanatory and exculpatory material issued from Berlin. Only fragments reached the American people but at least they were made aware that some sort of defense case was being presented. The Wilson administration was aware of the news imbalance and

Secretary of State William Jennings Bryan, exceptional among Cabinet members in his concern for equal treatment, took a personal hand in the negotiations that kept two German radio stations in operation for American listeners. The heart of the Germans' effort was both to try and put a better light on their Belgian activities and more generally to fix blame for the war itself on Britain and France, who had—it was alleged—opened up a road for the barbaric Slavic invasion of Europe. German publicists, relying a great deal on racial justifications, referred incessantly to their necessary mission of defending their superior civilization (and Europe's) from the Tartar and Mongolian hordes pouring in from the east. At the same time, even as they raised the specter of Russian "barbarism" they endeavored in their approach to the United States to exploit chronic Anglo-American grievances, reminding Americans of Britain's "imperial egotism" and commercial selfishness. As the British, eager from the start to restrict German and Austrian commerce, had as early as 6 August presented their first list of contraband items to an outraged State Department, this was a promising line of argument. For the British had already upset the Wilson administration by refusing to abide by the terms of the 1909 Declaration of London, which they had themselves largely shaped, and which took a very expansive view of neutral rights and a correspondingly narrow interpretation of contraband. Now they came up against the wish of American exporters, supported by their government, to trade worldwide with only minimal constraints. Bitter charges of "unfair treatment" at British hands came from German-American newspapers and institutions and German-American individuals of high standing. By late August, as British economic controls in the Atlantic began to trench severely on American freedom of action, these charges began to have an impact upon moderate opinion.[12]

A curious feature of these early struggles to define the alarming new realities and establish responsibility for the war was a bitter debate between distinguished British and German intellectuals that was fully ventilated in the United States and drew a variety of philosophers, professors, and writers into the argument. Here too the British were quicker off the mark. Among the first protagonists was the writer H. G. Wells who published in the *New York Times* on 5 August an elaborate justification of the crucial British declaration of war as a necessary response to "that tramping, drilling foolery in the heart of Europe that has arrested civilization and darkened the hopes of mankind for forty years—German imperialism and German militarism. Never was a war so righteous as is the war against Germany now."[13] A stream of similar articles from such patriotic British luminaries as Rudyard Kipling, John Galsworthy, Arnold Bennett, and many others, poured out from the British government's propaganda office near Victoria Station to waiting American journalists who were frustrated by the wartime censorship and desperate for something to satisfy the expectancies aroused at home by the war. These passionate, transparently sincere, and well-written essays were widely disseminated in the United States.[14]

Gradually the answering charges of distinguished German philosophers, historians, and writers found their way across the Atlantic. They echoed the German press in stressing the Slavic threat and took their stand on the superiority of German culture. Their wrath fell especially upon Britain for encouraging, as the poet and playwright Gerhard Hauptmann put it, "the assault of Mongolian Cossacks upon European civilization." The writer Ludwig Fulda addressed Americans directly, stressing that what the British maliciously called German "militarism" was simply "the iron commandment of self-preservation" in the face of "the Mongolian people, the most dangerous enemy of the white race and its culture." "America," he asked rhetorically, "does your racial feeling, at other times so sensitive, remain silent in view of this unexampled shame?" In September, somewhat more temperately, several dozen German professors published a statement addressed "To the Civilized World." They identified themselves as "heralds of truth" condemning the lies and calumnies spread by the Allies. "Have faith in us" they concluded, "Believe that we shall carry on this war to the end as a civilized nation, to whom the legacy of a Goethe, a Beethoven, and a Kant is just as sacred as its own hearths and homes."[15]

What is particularly striking here is the stridency, especially among the Germans, but also among several of the British, of these culture-oriented effusions, as well as the extraordinary patriotic solidarity of men hitherto accustomed to consider themselves sophisticated international figures. This sudden cleaving to the national cause, so dramatic in the vigorous public displays of patriotic emotion in the streets of Berlin, Paris, London, and Vienna, so familiar to us also in the case of the hitherto supposedly international socialists, is no less remarkable here. One senses, in the almost hysterical patriotism on view, a high degree of anxiety as well as excitement, and, on the part of the German intellectuals at least, a premonition of disaster and a felt need to fix blame well in advance of a dreaded denouement. Above all one has a poignant sense of a general awareness among all these luminaries of a collapsing civilization. "Christianity has been thrown to the dogs," one American church leader declared, "and the nations have gone mad."[16]

These Anglo-German arguments were widely read in the United States and stimulated a similar debate among American intellectuals. Reflecting general trends already established in the political and newspaper arenas, most American academics and intellectuals appear to have favored the Allies. Here a prominent, authoritative figure was Charles W. Elliot, emeritus president of Harvard. In a series of articles in the *New York Times* early in the war, Elliot, while paying elaborate tribute to Germany's cultural achievements, castigated its military "barbarism" and insisted that Britain and France were "fighting for freedom and civilization."[17] His lead was followed by David Starr Jordan, the former president of Stanford University, who claimed that "The Germany of today is an anachronism. Her scientific ideals are of the 20th century. Her political ideals hark back to the 16th." These were representative intellectual views, reflecting a general cultural critique that firmly resisted the invitation of the German professors to meditate on Goethe and Beethoven. It came to focus rather on the "might is right" and "blood and iron" formulations of Bismarck's day, then on the kaiser's greed, vanity, and irresponsibility, often coming to rest finally on a trinity of suspects—General Friedrich v. Bernhardi, the evil inspiration of German militarism, Heinrich v. Treitschke, the hyper-nationalistic historian, and of course Friedrich Nietzsche, still in the early stages of his career as one of the twentieth century's favorite intellectual scapegoats.[18]

From the other side, somewhat belatedly and defensively, came an array of commentators, some of non-German ancestry, favoring the Central Powers. The eminent Columbia philosopher and political scientist John W. Burgess passionately defended the kaiser and his policies. His colleague, the historian William Sloane, called for a "stricter neutrality" and presented a detailed explanation of the roots of German militarism, which he saw as the necessary defensive posture of an exposed, vulnerable nation surrounded by hostile powers. A number of German professors working in American universities also published heartfelt defenses of the Fatherland, variously condemning Russian savagery and British deceit. The leading Jewish-American banker, Jacob Schiff, also declared himself pro-German and entered into a polite controversy with Elliot in the columns of the *New York Times*.[19]

By mid September, however, the first, visceral mostly pro-Allied reactions were spent. America was beginning to adjust to the new situation and we may identify a new, more sober stage in its definitional response. The German protests of misrepresentation were now beginning to come through. Reports came in from a group of American journalists who had been stranded in Belgium and thereafter accompanied the German troops, declaring that they had witnessed no atrocities. Some embarrassed British official acknowledgments that their reports of early German excesses had been exaggerated were circulated, as were reminders that the Schlieffen Plan, which had openly anticipated the violation of Belgian neutrality, had been no secret and had in fact been common knowledge in Europe for several years. Another moderating influence at this time was the leading German religious institution, The Evangelical Lutheran Church of North America, which issued a statement noting that all the contending nations had long been actuated by rivalry, fear, and jealousy and shared responsibility for the disaster.[20]

It is a question whether these more measured and balanced assessments appearing in September were due to deep thought or to a growing awareness that there was a good deal of political manipulation in the news, or to the quite sudden realization, especially among those in the mercantile community, that "the European war" (as it was very properly called in America during its early stages) might after all have a positive dimension for the United States. What is clear is that by early September many businessmen were beginning to catch the sweet scent of economic recovery and beckoning opportunity. Yes, there had been brief, temporary disruptions, and some of these were expected to continue. But wheat and coal were now in immediate demand in Europe. A boom in cotton seemed likely. The early outflow of capital to Europe was already being tempered by an inflow from non-European sources seeking security in a country, as one observer put it, "4000 miles from the crossed bayonets of Europe." Some importers would certainly suffer. But exporters, farmers, industrialists, and American shipping would surely prosper. The first regular commercial shipment on 18 August through the newly opened Panama Canal was enthusiastically celebrated and seemed to many an augury of America's brilliant globally-oriented future.[21]

Many of these very upbeat scenarios looked to what one leading economist called "the beginning of a new commercial and industrial era in the United States."[22] The growing expectation, expressed in much political and press comment, was that as the apparently suicidal Europeans moved out of South America, Africa, and Asia, the United States would move in. Certainly an augmented merchant marine would be needed. But the ultimate result was easily predicted. The Columbia economist E. R. A. Seligman pointed out the connection between war and economic progress. British command of the seas dated from the Napoleonic wars; Germany's industrial and commercial rise followed the war of 1870. The present war, he felt sure, would launch the United States into a position of primacy. By October there was some solid evidence to sustain the bright new mood. The *Wall Street Journal* reported "Indications are multiplying that a turning of the financial tide is in sight." The 1 October settlements showed record food shipments overseas, a rise in cotton exports, and an easing in the money markets. Wheat, flour, and corn were now selling at two and a half times their 1913 prices. Meat was in demand. Thousands of horses were already being shipped, whether for food or other purposes, to the belligerent powers. The *New York Sun* reported, "All talk of stagnation in our export trade has ceased and alarm over the settlement of our debts to Europe is disappearing as millions of credits are transferred to New York to pay for the huge purchases that England, France, and Russia are making or planning to make here."[23]

The significant words here are "England, France, and Russia." It was perhaps inevitable that trade with them rather than the Central Powers would predominate from the start. The Allies and their possessions had accounted for 77 percent of United States trade during 1913, Germany and its allies for only 13 percent. Moreover, ships of British registry typically carried over 60 percent of American transatlantic freight compared with Germany's 17 percent share. Furthermore, the initial British contraband list, though it provoked complaints, was comparatively modest in early August, only becoming more restrictive as British trade with the United States became more commercially binding for both parties.[24]

The Wilson administration, despite early reservations and later spasms of anger over British policy, was more than pleased with the turn of events. For all the pious commitments to "impartiality" the president himself, both in private statements (except for occasional exasperated criticisms of the Royal Navy's excesses) and in his policies (again with occasional, mostly inconsequential, exceptions) was firmly pro-Allied and inclined to follow in this, as he thought, about 90 percent of American opinion. Thus he stood strongly against the German-American and pacifist campaign for an arms embargo that could have crippled an increasingly lucrative trade with the Allies. He did not complain when the Royal Navy mined the North Sea and, quickly reversing the initial ban on loans, he systematically eased the ability of the British to raise the necessary financial credits in the United States in order to sustain the flow of material. All these measures helped the Allies and also seemed to many commentators to serve American interests. The *Investor's Chronicle*, representatively ebullient, thought the United States was about to enter "the greatest era of prosperity in its history. . . . We will capture the major portion of the trade opportunities abandoned by the belligerents and repay ourselves for our losses many times over." The Europeans, it predicted, would dissipate their capital. American capital on the other hand, "will go through the war unscathed. As a result we shall become the dominating financial power of the globe. The financial center of the globe will move from London to New York." From London came the reinforcing affirmation of Norman Angell, more successful in this prophecy than in his pre-war insistence that globalized commerce had made war impossible, declaring that "New York will henceforth be the center of credit."[25]

All this did of course come true in the end. But not without a price. The price would turn out to be nothing less than American involvement in the war itself. This had been predicted by some of the calmer heads in August 1914. The *Saint Louis Globe-Democrat*, for instance, had pointed out that "the risk we run of being dragged into Europe's wars is no idle dream. No mere declaration of neutrality safeguards us. If the war is prolonged the desperation of the combatants . . . might easily lead us into complications with one or more of the warring powers." Similarly The *Baltimore News* warned that complications were inevitable "for our relations with each country, if advantageous to her, are as distasteful to her enemies."[26]

But these were lonely voices in the summer of 1914. For what is most striking in all the swelling optimism of September and October, as the exciting range of new economic opportunities seemed to open up, is the almost complete absence, with only a few exceptions, of any awareness of the possible political implications for the United States of the growing stream of trade that was already flowing strongly toward the Allies and away from the Central Powers. As we have seen, there was an initial American expectation that full neutral rights, notably the right to trade with all belligerents except in the restricted contraband enshrined in the Declaration of London, would be accepted by all parties. Only in March 1915, with the transformation of an ad hoc policy of graduated restrictions into a full British blockade of Germany, did this give way to a reluctant acceptance of the fact that Britain would not permit this expansionary conception and had the power to prevent almost all American trade with Germany and its allies. But by that time the American economy was firmly attached to the Allied cause.

The blockade policy, especially in its fully developed form in early 1915, was, of course, risky for the British. The United States government might be tempted to move beyond its habitual protests to some embargo or, more plausibly, targeted restrictions on the flow of supply to the Allies. Historian Ernest May notes of Foreign Secretary Sir Edward Grey's diplomacy that "During the autumn of 1914 ... the policy of preserving American friendship at almost any cost was not Grey's alone but that of virtually the entire government." But by 1915 the experience of what was now clearly going to be a drawn-out war of attrition argued the need for the much tighter blockade powerfully urged on London by its ever more desperate French and Russian allies. The British Cabinet now judged that the United States was sufficiently yoked to the Allied economically to accept the new situation.[27] To make their increasingly restrictive policies palatable to the Wilson administration the British relied on two elements. The first was a sharply self-interested but energetically maintained conception of international law. Grey worked hard and, for the most part, successfully to drive the sometimes acrimonious Anglo-American exchanges into a mutually congenial, courtly arena of negotiation, contract, equity, and familiar common law precepts that was intended not only to achieve British goals but also to make a telling contrast with the supposed German practice of naked power politics.

This carefully constructed legal arena was essentially a facilitating instrument. The principal incentive the British put before the Wilson administration was a willingness, on the part of its allies as well as itself, to buy almost all America had to offer even if it meant going deeply in debt to American bankers and bondholders. For this, to be sure, the British would pay the profound price of submission at last to the rising economic and financial transatlantic hegemon. But by a skillful policy of calculated blockade maintenance, by carefully measuring at each stage how far the restive Americans could be made to comply, on the one hand, and by keeping up an extraordinary, more than compensatory volume of sustained demand for American goods and credit on the other, the British and their allies were able to achieve their short-term objective.

In truth, though, a kind of nemesis seems already in 1914 to have been stalking all the powers—pushing the United States into a honeyed politico-economic trap that would result in a largely unforeseen belligerency, and driving Britain toward a respected but severely diminished place in the world. In the short term, certainly, the heaviest price would be paid by Germany. The first serious crisis in her relations with the United States came in early 1915. It was at this point that the British contraband rules were beginning to bite hard and to antagonize American exporters who, compromisingly engaged already with the Anglo-French war effort, nevertheless wanted to inflate their profits by trade with the Central Powers. A serious upset came in late October 1914 when the Royal Navy suddenly seized three American tankers bound for Denmark. As these seizures multiplied, Anglo-American tensions rose. But the Germans then botched the opportunity by announcing a blockade of the British Isles. The British took advantage of this perhaps clumsy (and at this stage in the early build-up of the U-boat fleet, not very meaningful) move to declare and justify in March 1915 their full blockade, effectively shutting off almost all prospect of substantial American commerce with Germany. This nevertheless created a storm of protest from almost all the American political establishment and press. It seemed for a few weeks that there might indeed be a serious Anglo-American rupture.[28]

Once again, however, a German error came to the rescue. For it was in the midst of this unresolved dispute, on 7 May, that the British-owned *Lusitania* was sunk by a U-boat with the loss of 128 American lives. This sensational event transformed the situation. Two more years of argument and occasional tensions lay ahead in Anglo-American relations. But these paled in comparison with the bitter emotions set in train by the destruction of the *Lusitania*. From May 1915 the British abridgment of American commercial rights, its impact already veiled by international law and softened by the rising prosperity associated with the ever-growing traffic from the United States to the Allies, came to seem to most Americans much less censurable than the very apparent German willingness to violate human rights and to carry out seemingly murderous policies on the high seas, a willingness that reinforced and perhaps crystallized for millions the already preexisting images of German barbarism.[29]

May 1915 then, as a practical matter, seems to mark the end of the comparatively fluid early stage in American relations with the warring European powers, a kind of diplomatic analog to the early mobile phase in the war itself. But it is not quite the end of our brief review here. For in addition to the various attempts to define the war, and to seize the economic opportunities it offered, there was a third impulse in the American response to the outbreak of the war that deserves at least a passing mention. This was the notion that the United States might have a leading part to play in mediating an end to the struggle, and laying some groundwork for an improved post-war international order.

President Wilson was, as is well known, eager to assume a peace-making responsibility. He had upon the outbreak of war offered all the belligerents his "good offices."[30] Finding virtually no response he drew back, reemerging tentatively in 1915 with the first wartime House mission and then much more vigorously as the conflict intensified in 1916. The point to note here is that this constructive tendency was visible from the earliest stages of the war and was exhibited not only by the president but by many other Americans. This is significant because it qualifies to some extent the various notions prominent in the historiography of American diplomacy in this period that the United States was either basically self-interested in pursuing its own interests and in exploiting the opportunities presented by the crisis, or alternatively was the sleepwalking victim of calculated manipulation by Sir Edward Grey and his colleagues in London. It reminds us that there was, in other words, along with the exaggerated legalism and moral complacency and the commercial opportunism, a distinctive high-minded strain in the early American response, one that emphasized peace and a progressive internationalism.

Indeed the different elements of what we have come to view as the Wilsonian dispensation were appearing here long before the president himself took up the cause publicly. As early as August 1914, John Milton Cooper reminds us, Wilson was already privately advocating "an association of nations, all bound together for the integrity of each, so that anyone breaking this bond will bring upon herself war: that is to say, punishment, automatically."[31] Secretary Bryan was eager from the outset to launch mediation efforts. Meanwhile, Charles W. Elliot fulminated robustly in the latter months of 1914 against the arms traffic, against secret diplomacy, and against the violations of international law now so openly on display in Europe. He called for a federation of the European states, backed by an "overwhelming" international force that would be subject to the orders of an international tribunal. David Starr Jordan urged "the rule of law," as did the distinguished international jurist John Bassett Moore who was already in 1914 busying himself preparing and publishing a series of annotated reports of the pre-war international arbitration tribunals so that governments and judges would have a record of decided cases which, in the anticipated post-war nirvana of law and institutionalized reason, could be used as precedents. Meanwhile the eminent sociologist Franklin Giddings called for a new Europe founded on "the rise of democracy," while Columbia's Nicholas Murray Butler looked to a "United States of Europe."[32] Thus, even as President Wilson was stepping forward tentatively as a would-be peacemaker, many respected Americans—officials, editorialists, pundits, as well as professors—were trying not only to define the issues of the war but to offer characteristically American solutions for the post-war world.

At this point, of course, the principal focus of attention was not upon the minds of visionaries and pedagogues but on the Western Front and on the Atlantic. By the spring of 1915 the war was settling into its own destructively enduring rhythm. As one commentator surveying the stagnation on the Western Front aptly put it, "the time is past when the issue can be decided by the tiger's leap." It would now, he said, "be decided by stupendous attrition rather than by brilliant strokes of arms."[33] In other words it would in the end be a struggle of material at least as much as of human resources. In that struggle the United States, its political options critically narrowed by the way in which it had defined the war and responded to it in its first months, would nevertheless come to be the decisive instrument.

Historians trying to reconstruct American reactions in the first months of the war face a familiar professional dilemma: how to strike a balance between the dramatic and richly causative events that capture attention very easily on the one hand, and on the other the less visible but enduring structural impulses we noted briefly earlier as constituting a congeries of foundational prompts to association with the Allies rather than the Central Powers. Some of these were economic, such as the comparative primacy in volume of a long-standing Anglo-American commerce that still seemed, in these early stages, to be conveniently protected by British sea power. Some were political, notably the Anglo-American diplomatic rapprochement of the 1890s and the accompanying intimacy of the two elites. Some were cultural. Bismarck's celebrated aphorism about the dominating significance in international politics of the fact that Britain and the United States shared a common language can be properly cited under this head. It should perhaps be reinforced with a corollary of peculiarly 1914 vintage, namely that the specialized language of the Anglo-American conception of international law proved, in these early months, to be an almost perfect facilitating and legitimizing medium for the consolidation of an already logical collaboration.

Notes

1. John Milton Cooper, *The Vanity of Power: American Isolationism and the First World War, 1914–1917* (Westport, CT, 1969), 19.
2. Theodore Draper, "Idea of the Cold War and its Prophets," *Encounter* (February, 1979), 34–45.
3. W. T. Stead, *The Americanisation of the World* (London, 1902).
4. Walter Millis, *Road to War: America, 1914–1917* (Boston and New York, 1935), 6; For political divisions see Robert Beisner, *Twelve Against Empire: The Anti-Imperialists, 1898–1900* (New York, 1968).
5. Wilson press conference, 3 August 1914, *Woodrow Wilson Papers*, (Princeton, 1966), vol. 30, 332.
6. *New York World*, 31 July 1914; Page to Wilson, 2, 9 August 1914 in *Wilson Papers*, vol. 30, 329–31, 366–71. For general reactions see the *New York Times* through August 1914. For economic issues see *Wall Street Journal*, *Investor's Chronicle*, and the *Journal of Commerce* in August 1914. For reviews of press reactions see *Literary Digest*, 8, 15, 22, 29 August 1914.
7. *Literary Digest*, 15 August 1914.
8. John Bach McMaster, *The United States in the World War* (New York, 1919), 27
9. Ernest May, *The World War and American Isolation, 1914–1917* (Cambridge, MA, 1966), 36; John Milton Cooper, *The Vanity of Power: American Isolationism and the First World War, 1914–1917* (Westport, CT, 1969), 48, n. 39.
10. See John Horne, Alan Kramer, *German Atrocities, 1914: A History of Denial* (New Haven, 2001) for a recent treatment.
11. Millis, *Road to War*, 42–44.
12. For radio stations see May, *The World War*, 38 and see chapters 1 and 2 for general context.
13. *New York Times*, 5 August 1914
14. Millis, *Road to War*, 63; *The New York Times, Current History, The European War*, vol. I, *August–December, 1914* (New York, 1917) for Galsworthy (102), Kipling (106–107), and Bennett (60). See also letter "British Authors Defend England's War," signed by fifty three leading intellectuals, ibid., 82–86.
15. Ibid., 181, 185–87. See also Hauptmann's defense of German conduct in Belgium in *New York Times*, 5 and 22 August 1914, and his "Reply to R. Rolland" in ibid., 26 September 1914.

16. *New York Times, Current History*, vol. I, contains the views of many British, German, and other academics and intellectuals in the first months of the war. For the churchman (Reverend F. Lynch) see *Literary Digest*, 12 September 1914.
17. For Elliott's influential 1914 articles see *New York Times*, 4 September ("Causes of the War"); 6 September ("Perils of Militarism"); 22 September ("Imperialism and Democratic Ideals"); 2 October ("America and the Issues of the European War"); and 11 December ("Hopeful Road to Lasting Peace in Europe").
18. *New York Times, Current History*, Vol., I, 502–03.
19. *New York Times*, 17 October 1914 (Burgess); 3 December 1914 (Sloane); 20 December 1914 (Schiff).
20. For these developments see *Literary Digest*, 19 September 1914.
21. Ibid., 15 and 22 August 1914.
22. *Journal of Commerce*, 23 August 1914.
23. *Literary Digest*, 29 August 1914 (citing Seligman); 17 October 1914 (citing *Wall Street Journal*); and 31 October 1914 (citing *New York Sun*).
24. Millis, *Road to War*, 84; News Report, 1 August 1914, *Wilson Papers*, Vol. 30, 326. For a critique of Wilson's supposed partiality to the Allies see John W. Coogan, *The End of Neutrality: The United States, Britain and Maritime Rights, 1899–1915* (Ithaca, 1981), 209–10, 247.
25. May, *World War*, 36, 45; *Literary Digest*, 29 August, 24 October 1914. For Treasury Secretary William McAdoo's supportive views see John A. Thompson, *Woodrow Wilson: Profiles in Power* (London, 2002), 127–28.
26. *Literary Digest*, 22 August 1914.
27. May, *World War*, 19, and see, more generally, chapter 1.
28. *Literary Digest*, 24 October 1914.
29. For the impact of the *Lusitania*'s destruction see Thompson, *Woodrow Wilson*, 110–16.
30. Press Release, 4 August 1914, *Wilson Papers*, Vol. 30, 342.
31. Cooper, *Vanity of Power*, 37.
32. *New York Times*, 11, 18, 25 October; 1 November; 11, 30 December 1914. Cooper, *Vanity of Power*, 38.
33. *New York Press*, cited in *Literary Digest*, 12 December 1914.

Contributors

Holger Afflerbach currently teaches Modern European History at the University of Leeds. From 2002–2006 he was DAAD Professor of History at Emory University. Afflerbach specializes in late nineteenth and twentieth Century German history; international relations; military history, particularly World War I and World War II; and Austrian and Italian history. He has spent several years at Italian and Austrian universities as well as spring 2001 as Visiting Fellow at the University of Sussex in Great Britain. Among his publications are the political biography of the Prussian War Minister and Chief of General Staff Erich von Falkenhayn (Munich 1994, second edition 1996); his study of the Triple Alliance, entitled *Der Dreibund. Europäische Grossmacht- und Allianzpolitik vor dem Ersten Weltkrieg* (Vienna 2002); and a popular book on the history of the Atlantic published under the title *Das entfesselte Meer* (Munich, 2002). He edited an edition of the diaries and letters of two World War I generals under the title *Kaiser Wilhelm II: als Oberster Kriegsherr während des Ersten Weltkrieges – Quellen aus der militärischen Umgebung des Kaisers* (Munich, 2005).

Mustafa Aksakal is Assistant Professor of History at American University in Washington, DC. Previously he taught at Monmouth University. Aksakal received his PhD from Princeton University. He specializes in Near Eastern History, Ottoman and Turkish History, Diplomatic History, and World War I. His dissertation, which won the Bayard and Cleveland E. Dodge Best Dissertation Award and is currently being revised for publication, focuses on the Ottoman decision to enter World War I. Aksakal enjoys teaching courses on the social and political history of the Middle East, especially on the period after 1800. In particular, he is interested in the ways Middle Easterners have responded to the rise of Western global influence in the Modern Age.

Jimmy Carter, the thirty-ninth president of the United States and winner of the 2002 Nobel Peace Prize, is founder and chairman of the board of trustees of The Carter Center, as well as University Distinguished Professor at Emory University.

Roger Chickering is professor of history in the BMW Center for German and European Studies at Georgetown University. His publications include *Imperial Germany and a World without War: The Peace Movement and German Society, 1892–1914*; *We Men Who Feel Most German: A Cultural Study of the Pan-German League, 1886–1914*; and *Imperial Germany and the Great War, 1914–1918*. He has joined Stig Förster in convening a series of conferences on the history of total war. With Thomas A. Brady, Jr., of the University of California at Berkeley, he is also co-editor of the monograph series, "Studies in Central European Histories," which is published by Brill. Dr. Chickering is vice-president of the Conference Group for Central European History and vice-president of the Friends of the German Historical Institute, Washington. His latest book *The Great War and Urban Life in Germany. Freiburg, 1914–1918*, Cambridge 2007 has been met with great acclaim.

Frederick R. Dickinson is Associate Professor of Japanese History at the University of Pennsylvania. Born in Tokyo and raised in Kanazawa and Kyoto, Japan, he teaches courses on modern Japan, East Asian diplomacy, and politics and nationalism in Asia. He received an MA (1987) and PhD (1993) in history from Yale University and holds an MA in International Politics from Kyoto University (1986). He is the author of *War and National Reinvention: Japan in the Great War, 1914–1919* (Harvard University Press, 1999). Currently, he is working on a study of the politics and culture of Japanese imperialism, 1919–31. He has won a number of prizes and fellowships and served as a National Fellow at the Hoover Institution at Stanford University in the 2000–01 academic year.

Jost Dülffer, Professor of Modern European History at the University of Cologne, specializes in International History and conflict and peace research in the nineteenth and twentieth centuries. He has published numerous books, including: *Vermiedene Kriege: Deeskalation von Konflikten im europäischen Mächtesystem 1856–1915* (with others, 1997); *Die Haager Friedenskonferenzen im internationalen System 1899 und 1907* (1981); and *Im Zeichen der Gewalt* (2003).

Michael Epkenhans, Director of the Otto-von-Bismarck-Foundation, Friedrichsruh; Honorary Lecturer in modern German History at Hamburg University. He received his PhD from Münster University in 1989. His books include *Die wilhelminische Flottenrüstung, 1908–1914: Weltmachtstreben, technischer Fortschritt, soziale Integration* (Munich 1991), and *Vizeadmiral Albert Hopman: Ein typischer'Wilhelminer': Tagebücher, Briefe und Aufzeichnungen 1901–1920* (Munich, 2004). He has published frequently on German naval history in the nineteenth and twentieth centuries. He is currently working on a biography of Grand Admiral Alfred von Tirpitz and an edition of the private letters of the Bismarck family.

Ute Frevert, Professor of History at Yale University, received her PhD from Bielefeld University in 1982. Her books include *Krankheit als politisches Problem 1770–1880: Soziale Unterschichten in Preußen zwischen Medizinischer Polizei und staatlicher Sozialversicherung* (1984); *Women in German History: From Bourgeois Emancipation to Sexual Liberation* (1986); *Men of Honour: A Social and Cultural History of the Duel* (1995); *Mann und Weib, und Weib und Mann: Geschlechter-Differenzen in der Moderne* (1995); (with Alida Assmann) *Geschichtsvergessenheit – Geschichtsversessenheit: Vom Umgang mit deutschen Vergangenheiten nach 1945* (1999); *Die kasernierte Nation: Militärdienst und Zivilgesellschaft in Deutschland* (2001); and *Eurovisionen: Ansichten guter Europäer im 19. und 20. Jahrhundert* (2003). Her seminars at Yale include courses in modern German and European history.

Jessica Gienow-Hecht is Heisenberg Fellow at ZENAF at the University of Frankfurt and a Fellow at the Charles Warren Center for Studies in American History at Harvard University. She has published articles in the *Journal of Social History and Diplomatic History*, among others. Her study, *Transmission Impossible: American Journalism as Cultural Diplomacy in Postwar Germany, 1945–1955*, won several awards in diplomatic history. She is currently completing a study on transatlantic emotions since 1850.

Fraser J. Harbutt, Professor of History at Emory University, (BA, LL., University of Otago, New Zealand, 1960; LLM., University of Auckland, New Zealand, 1967; PhD, University of California, Berkeley, 1976), specializes in international history and United States diplomatic and political history with a main scholarly concentration is U.S.-Soviet relations. His publications include *The Cold War Era* (2001) and *The Iron Curtain: Churchill, America and the Origins of the Cold War* (1986), which received the Stuart L. Bernath Memorial Book Prize for 1986 from the Society for Historians of American Foreign Relations. He expects to publish *Yalta's Shadow: the Decline and Fall of Traditional Diplomacy, 1939–1945* in 2003. Dr. Harbutt is currently interested in definitions of the American diplomatic tradition, and in the general problems of transition between successive international orders.

Friedrich Kießling, Wissenschaftlicher Assistent at Friedrich-Alexander-University Erlangen-Nuremberg, was educated in Munich and Erlangen, where he received his PhD in 2001. He specializes in the history of international relations and modern German intellectual history. Among his publications are his study of great power détente before World War I, *Gegen den großen Krieg? Entspannung in den internationalen Beziehungen 1911–1914* (Munich, 2002) and an edition of primary sources of Nazi-Germany foreign policy, (*Quellen zur deutschen Außenpolitik 1933–1939, Darmstadt 2000: Ausgewählte Quellen zur deutschen Geschichte der Neuzeit Bd. XXXIV*).

Günther Kronenbitter is Professor of History at the University of Augsburg where he received his PhD in 1992. He was Visiting Professor at the University of

British Columbia in 1997, at the University of Salzburg in 1999, the University of Vienna in 2002, and the University of Berne in 2003–04. He specializes in nineteenth century intellectual history; international relations; military history; German and Austrian history. His publications include: *Wort und Macht: Friedrich Gentz als politischer Schriftsteller* (Dunker and Humblot, 1994); ed. *Friedrich Gentz: Gesammelte Schriften*, 12 vols. (Olms, 1997–2004); *"Krieg im Frieden": Die Führung der k. u. k. Armee und die Großmachtpolitik Österreich-Ungarns 1906–1914* (Oldenbourg, 2003).

Hartmut Lehmann studied History, English, and Political Science at the universities of Tübingen, Bristol (England), Vienna, and Cologne. He received his PhD from the University of Vienna in 1959. From 1959–68 he was assistant professor at the university of Cologne; 1967 Habilitation. From 1969–93 Lehmann was Professor of Medieval and Modern History at the University of Kiel (chair). He was visiting fellow at the University of Chicago, at the Institute for Advanced Study in Princeton and at the Humanities Research Center of the Australian National University in Canberra. Lehmann was visiting professor at UCLA, Harvard, Emory University, Hebrew University in Jerusalem and numerous other places. From 1987–93 he was director of German Historical Institute, Washington, DC. From 1993 to 2004 he was the Director at the Max-Planck-Institute of History, Göttingen, and a member of the Academy of Science in Göttingen. His main publications are: *Pietismus und weltliche Ordnung in Württemberg vom 17. bis zum 20. Jahrhundert* (1969); *Das Zeitalter des Absolutismus* (1980); *Martin Luther in the American Imagination* (1988); *Alte und Neue Welt in wechselseitiger Sicht* (1995), *Religion und Religiosität in der Neuzeit* (1996); *Max Weber's ‚Protestantische Ethik* (1996); *Protestantische Weltsichten* (1998); and *Protestantisches Christentum im Prozeß der Säkularisierung* (2001).

John C.G. Röhl is Research Professor of German History at the University of Sussex. After military service in the Royal Air Force, he took up his studies at Corpus Christi College, Cambridge, receiving a First Class in both Parts of the Historical Tripos. The supervisor of his doctoral dissertation at Cambridge was Professor Sir Harry Hinsley; his examiners were James Joll and Geoffrey Barraclough. In 1964 he was appointed to a lectureship in European History at the then new University of Sussex. He was promoted to a Chair in 1979. In 1986 he was elected to a Fellowship at the Historisches Kolleg in Munich. For the academic year 1989–90 he was a Fellow of the Woodrow Wilson International Center for Scholars in Washington, DC. In 1994 he spent a term at the Institute for Advanced Study at Princeton, in late 1996 he was attached to the Moses Mendelssohn Zentrum für Europäisch-Jüdische Studien at Potsdam, and in 1997–98 he was a Fellow at the National Humanities Center in North Carolina. In 1999 he retired from his teaching post at the University of Sussex, but still maintains close links with the University. His book *The Kaiser and His Court* won the Wolfson History Prize for

1994 and has now been translated into Chinese. In 1999 he was awarded a grant of £95,000 by the Arts and Humanities Research Board in support of his three-volume biography of Kaiser Wilhelm II, which he is writing in both German and English. The two volumes which have appeared so far, *Wilhelm II: Die Jugend des Kaisers 1859–1888* (Munich, 1993, English translation, Cambridge, 1998), and *Wilhelm II. Der Aufbau der Persönlichen Monarchie 1888–1900* (Munich, 2001, English translation, Cambridge, 2004) have received international recognition. The biography was awarded the £25,000 Gissings Prize in 2002.

Joshua A. Sanborn is Associate Professor of History at Lafayette College in Pennsylvania. A member of the Lafayette faculty since 1999, Sanborn holds a PhD in Russian history from the University of Chicago, a master's degree in history from the University of Chicago, and a bachelor's degree with a major in history from Stanford University. Sanborn has received fellowships from Lafayette, Princeton University, the University of Chicago, the Social Science Research Council, the Council for Advanced Studies in Peace and International Cooperation, and the Mellon Foundation. He has published *Drafting the Russian Nation: Military Conscription, Total War, an Mass Politics, 1905–1925*, (Northern Illinois UP, 2003), and written numerous articles and reviews for academic journals, including *Slavic Review, Kritika: Explorations in Eurasian History, Revolutionary Russia, Russian History/Histoire Russe, Canadian Ethnic Studies/Etudes Ethniques au Canada*, and *Journal of Modern History*, as well as for edited volumes in his field, including essays last year in *Military and Society in Russia and History in Dispute, Volume 8: World War I*, the First Series. He has given presentations at a number of conferences, including the Conference in Honor of the 100th Anniversary of the Nobel Peace Prize, the Great War Society Convention, the American Association for the Advancement of Slavic Studies Convention, the American Historical Association Convention, the Western Social Science Association Conference, the Russian and Soviet Studies Workshop, the Nations and Nationalism Workshop, the Shelby Cullom Davis Center for Historical Studies, and an international colloquium on "Russia in the First World War" held in St. Petersburg, Russia.

Paul W. Schroeder, Professor Emeritus of History at the University of Illinois at Urbana-Champaign, specializes in late sixteenth- to twentieth-century European international politics, Central Europe, and the theory of history. His current research focuses on European international politics, 1648–1945, emphasizing systemic evolution and development. Selected publications include *Austria, Great Britain and the Crimean War: The Destruction of the European Concert* (Cornell University Press, 1972); "AHR Forum: Did the Vienna Settlement Rest on a Balance of Power?," in *American Historical Review*, (June 1992), and *The Transformation of European Politics, 1765–1848* (Clarendon Press, 1994). Professor Schroeder received his doctorate from the University of Texas at Austin in 1958.

Matthias Schulz, DAAD Visiting Associate Professor of History at Vanderbilt University, specializes in nineteenth and twentieth Century German and European history; the history of European integration and of international relations; and the social and economic history of Europe. His monographs include: *Regionalismus und die Gestaltung Europas: Die europäische Integration im Spannungsfeld zwischen Integration und Desintegration* (Hamburg, 1993); *Deutschland, der Völkerbund und die Frage der europäischen Wirtschaftsordnung 1925–1933* (Hamburg, 1997). His essays and articles include: "The Merton-Plan for a European Central Bank System: German Commercial Elites and the Beginning of European Integration 1947–1957," in Eric Bussière and Michel Dumoulin eds., *Milieux économiques et integration européenne en Europe occidentale au XXe siècle* (Arras 1998), "Die politische Freundschaft Jean Monnet – Kurt Birrenbach, die Einheit des Westens und die 'Präambel' zum Elysée-Vertrag von 1963," in: Andreas Wilkens, eds., *Interessen verbinden: Jean Monnet und die europäische Integration der Bundesrepublik Deutschland*. (Bonn, 1999).

David Stevenson, Professor of International History at the London School of Economics and Political Science, specializes in the history of international relations in Europe since c.1900, with special reference to World War I. Two of his recent books are: *Armaments and the Coming of War: Europe, 1904–1914* (Oxford, 1996) and *The Outbreak of the First World War: 1914 in Perspective* (New York, 1997). His latest publication was *Cataclysm: The First World War as Political Tragedy* (New York, 2004).

Samuel R. Williamson, Robert M. Ayres, Jr. Distinguished University Professor and Vice-Chancellor Emeritus at Sewanee University, is a specialist in European diplomatic and military history in the nineteenth and twentieth centuries, as well as intelligence and foreign policy. He graduated with honors from Tulane University and received further education at the University of Edinburgh as a Fulbright Scholar and Harvard University where he earned his PhD in 1966. Before coming to Sewanee, he held significant teaching and administrative posts at the US Military Academy, Harvard University, and the University of North Carolina at Chapel Hill. He has received numerous awards for his historical work, including the George Louis Beer Prize of the American Historical Association for the best book in international history, *The Politics of Grand Strategy: Britain and France Prepare for War, 1904–1914* (Cambridge, MA: Harvard University Press, 1969). His work, *Austria-Hungary and the Origins of the First World War* (London and New York: Macmillan) appeared in 1991 and a formerly classified study, *The Origins of U.S. Nuclear Strategy, 1945–1953* (with Steve Rearden) (New York: St. Martins) appeared in 1993. His new study on civil-military relations in the July 1914 crisis appeared in early 2003.

Selected Bibliography

Abrams, Ray H. *Preachers Present Arms.* New York, 1933.
Afflerbach, Holger. *Der Dreibund: Europäische Grossmacht- und Allianzpolitik vor dem Ersten Weltkrieg.* Vienna, Cologne, and Weimar, 2002.
Afflerbach, Holger. *Falkenhayn. Politisches Denken und Handeln im Kaiserreich.* Munich, 1994.
Afflerbach, Holger. *Das Deutsche Reich, Bismarcks Allianzpolitik und die europäische Friedenssicherung vor 1914.* Friedrichsruh, 1998.
Afflerbach, Holger, ed. *Kaiser Wilhelm II als Oberster Kriegsherr im Ersten Weltkrieg. Quellen aus der militärischen Umgebung des Kaisers 1914–1918.* Munich, 2005.
Akmeşe, Handan Nezir. *The Birth of Modern Turkey: The Ottoman Military and the March to World War I.* New York, 2005.
Aksakal, Mustafa. "Not 'by those old books of international law, but only by war': Ottoman Intellectuals on the Eve of the Great War," *Diplomacy and Statecraft* 15 (September 2004), 507–44.
Albertini, Luigi. *The Origins of the War of 1914,* 3 vols. London, 1952–57.
Albrecht-Carrié, René. *The Concert of Europe 1815–1914.* London, Melbourne, 1968.
Andrew, Christopher. *Théophile Delcassé and the Making of the Entente Cordiale: A Reappraisal of French Foreign Policy, 1898–1905.* New York, 1968.
Andrew, D. T. "The Code of Honour and its Critics. The Opposition to Duelling in England, 1700–1850." *Social History* 5 (1981), 409–34.
Angelow, Jürgen. *Kalkül und Prestige: Der Zweibund am Vorabend des Ersten Weltkrieges.* Cologne, 2000.
Applegate, Celia. "What Is German Music? Reflections on the Role of Art in the Creation of the Nation," *German Studies Review,* special issue on "German Identity" (Winter 1992).
Arndt, Ernst Moritz. *Kurzer Katechismus für teutsche Soldaten, nebst einem Anhang von Liedern.* n.l., 1812.
Arndt, Ernst Moritz. *Zwei Worte über die Entstehung und Bestimmung der Teutschen Legion.* n.l., 1813.
Aschmann, Birgit and Michael Salewski, eds. *Das Bild "des Anderen": Politische Wahrnehmung im 19. und 20. Jahrhundert.* Stuttgart, 2000.
Asquith, Henry Herbert. *Memories and Reflections, 1852–1927.* Vol. 2, Boston, 1928.
Axenfeld, Karl. "Der Kampf des Christentums um Afrika wider Heidentum und Islam," in *Vom Kampf des Christentums um Asien und Afrika.* Karl Axenfeld and Julius Richter, eds., Berlin, 1912.
Axenfeld, Karl. *Die Aussaat des Gotteswortes in Heiden- und Mohammedanerherzen,* 2nd ed. Berlin, 1912.
Aydelotte, Frank. *The American Rhodes Scholarships: A Review of the First Forty Years.* Princeton, NJ, 1946.
Aydemir, Şevket Süreyya. *Makedonya'dan Ortaasya'ya Enver Paşa.* Istanbul, 1971.
Balfour, Sebastian. "The Impact of War within Spain: Continuity or Crisis?" in *The Crisis of 1898.* Angel Smith and Emma Davila-Cox, eds., New York, 1999.
Balfour, Sebastian. *The End of the Spanish Empire, 1898–1923.* Oxford, 1997.
Barraclough, Geoffre. *From Agadir to Armageddon: Anatomy of a Crisis.* New York, 1982.

Barth, Boris. *Die deutsche Hochfinanz und die Imperialismen: Banken und Außenpolitik vor 1914.* Stuttgart, 1995.
Baumgart, Winfried. *Europäisches Konzert und nationale Bewegung: Internationale Beziehungen 1830–1878.* Paderborn, 1999.
Baumgart, Winfried. *The Crimean War 1853–1856.* London, Sidney, Auckland, 1999.
Bayur, Yusuf Hikmet. *Paylaşmalar,* vol. 2/3, *Türk İnkılâbı Tarihi.* Ankara, 1991; 1951.
Bayur. Yusuf Hikmet. *1914–1918 Genel Savaşı,* vol. 3/1, *Türk İnkılâbı Tarihi.* Ankara, 1991; 1953.
Becker, Jean-Jacques. *1914: Comment les Français sont entrés dans la guerre: Contribution à l'étude de l'opinion publique, printemps-été 1914.* Paris, 1977.
Becker, Jean-Jacques. *La première guerre mondiale.* Paris, 1985.
Becker, Jean-Jacques and Audoin-Rouzeau, Stéphane, eds. *Les Sociétés européennes et la guerre de 1914–1918.* Nanterre, 1990.
Behnen, Michael. *Rüstung, Bündnis, Sicherheit: Dreibund und informeller Imperialismus, 1900–1908.* Tübingen, 1985.
Beisner, Robert. *Twelve Against Empire: The Anti-Imperialists, 1898–1900.* New York, 1968.
Beller, Steve. *Francis Joseph.* New York, 1996.
Benson, Arthur C. and Viscount Esher, eds. *The Letters of Queen Victoria, a selection from Her Majesty's correspondence between the years 1837 and 1861, published by authority of His Majesty the king.* London, 1907.
Bérenger, Jean. "Die Österreichpolitik Frankreichs von 1848 bis 1918," in *Die Habsburgermonarchie 1848–1918,* vol. VI, *Die Habsburgermonarchie im System der internationalen Beziehungen.* Adam Wandruszka and Peter Urbanitsch, eds., Vienna, 1993.
Berghahn, Volker R. *Der Tirpitz-Plan: Eine innenpolitische Krisenstrategie unter Wilhelm II.* Düsseldorf, 1971.
Berghahn, Volker R. and Kitchen Martin, eds. *Germany In The Age Of Total War: Essays In Honor Of Francis L. Carsten.* London, 1981.
Berghahn, Volker R. and Wilhelm Deist, eds. "Kaiserliche Marine und Kriegsausbruch 1914. Neue Dokumente zur Juli-Krise," *Militärgeschichtliche Mitteilungen* I, I (1970).
Berenson, Edward. *The Trial of Madame Caillaux.* Berkeley, 1992.
Berndt, Otto. *Die Zahl im Kriege: Statistische Daten aus der neueren Kriegsgeschichte in graphischer Darstellung.* Vienna, 1897.
Bernhardi, Friedrich von. *Deutschland und der nächste Krieg.* Stuttgart, 1912, Berlin, 1913. English version, *Germany and the Next War.* London, 1912, New York, 1914.
Best, Geoffrey. *Humanity in Warfare.* New York, 1980.
Bihl, Wolfdieter. "Zu den österreichisch-ungarischen Kriegszielen 1914," *Jahrbücher für die Geschichte Osteuropas* XVI, 4 (1968), 505–30.
Bittner, Ludwig and Hans Uebersberger, eds. *Österreich-Ungarns Außenpolitik von der Bosnischen Krise 1908 bis zum Kriegsausbruch 1914: Diplomatische Aktenstücke des österreichisch-ungarischen Ministeriums des Äußern,* 9 vols. Vienna and Leipzig, 1930.
Blainey, Geoffrey. *The Causes of War.* London, 1973.
Bled, Jean-Paul. *Franz Joseph,* translated by Teresa Bridgeman. Oxford, 1992.
Bloch, Jan Gotlib. *The Future of War in Its Technical, Economic, and Political Relations: Is War Now Impossible?* New York, 1899.
Blodgett, Geoffrey et al., eds. *Victorian America.* Philadelphia, 1976.
Boeckh, Katrin. *Von den Balkankriegen zum Ersten Weltkrieg: Kleinstaatenpolitik und ethnische Selbstbestimmung auf dem Balkan.* Munich, 1996.
Boemeke, Manfred F. "Woodrow Wilson's Image of Germany, the War-Guilt Question, and the Treaty of Versailles," in Manfred F. Boemeke, Gerald D. Feldman, and Elisabeth Glaser, eds., *The Treaty of Versailles: A Reassessment after 75 Years.* New York, 1998.
Bowman, James. *Honor: A History.* New York, 2006.
Boyce, Robert and Joseph Maiolo, eds. *The Origins of World War II: The Debate Continues.* Basingstoke and New York, 2003.

Boyer, John W. *Culture and Political Crisis in Vienna: Christian Socialism in Power, 1897–1918*. Chicago, 1995.
Bridge, F. R. "Isvolsky, Aehrenthal and the End of the Austro-Russian Entente, 1906–8," *Mitteilungen des Österreichischen Staatsarchivs* 29 (1976), 315–62.
Bridge, F. R. *The Habsburg Monarchy among the Great Powers, 1815–1918*. New York, 1990.
Bridge, F. R. "'Tarde venientibus ossa': Austro-Hungarian Colonial Aspirations in Asia Minor 1913–14," *Middle Eastern Studies* 6, 3 (October 1970), 319–30.
Bridge, F. R. "Transformation of the European States System, 1856–1914," in *"The Transformation of European Politics, 1763–1848": Episode or Model in Modern History?* Peter Krüger and Paul W. Schroeder, eds., Münster, 2002.
Bridge, F. R. *Great Britain and Austria-Hungary, 1906–1914: A Diplomatic History*. London, 1972.
Brock, Michael. "Britain Enters The War," in *The Coming of the First World War*, Robert J.W. Evans and Hartmut Pogge von Strandmann, eds., Oxford, 1990.
Brocke, Bernhard v. "Der deutsch-amerikanische Professorenaustausch: Preussische Wissenschaftspolitik, internationale Wissenschaftsbeziehungen und die Anfänge einer deutschen auswärtigen Kulturpolitik vor dem Ersten Weltkrieg," *Zeitschrift für Kulturaustausch* 31 (1981).
Brooke, Rupert. *1914 and Other Poems*. London, 1918.
Brooks, Jeffrey. *When Russia Learned to Read: Literacy and Popular Literature, 1861–1917*. Princeton, NJ, 1985.
Brubaker, Rogers. "In the Name of the Nation: Reflections on Nationalism and Patriotism," *Citizenship Studies* 8, 2 (2004), 115–27.
Burchardt, Lothar. *Friedenswirtschaft und Kriegsvorsorge: Deutschlands wirtschaftliche Rüstungsbestrebungen vor 1914*. Boppard, 1968.
Burckhardt, Johannes, et al., eds. *Lange und kurze Wege in den Ersten Weltkrieg*. München, 1996.
Burkhardt, Johannes. "Kriegsgrund Geschichte? 1870, 1813, 1756—historische Argumente und Orientierungen bei Ausbruch des Ersten Weltkriegs," in *Lange und kurze Wege in den Ersten Weltkrieg*, ed. Burkhardt et al., München, 1996.
Burnett, Frances H. *Little Lord Fauntleroy*. London, 1886.
Cami-Baykut [Abdurrahman Cami Baykut]. *Osmanlılığın Âtisi: Düşmanları ve Dostları* [The Ottoman Future: Its Enemies and Its Friends]. Istanbul, 1331 [5 Kanunisani 1328/18 Jan 1913].
Carroll, E. M. *Germany and the Great Powers 1866–1914. A Study in Public Opinion and Foreign Policy*. New York, 1940.
Cary, Joyce Cary. *Memoir of the Bobotes*. London, 2000.
Chasins, Abram. *Leopold Stokowski: A Profile*. New York, 1979.
Chickering, Roger. *Imperial Germany and a World without War: The Peace Movement and German Society 1892–1914*. Princeton, NJ 1975.
Churchill, Randolph S. *Winston S. Churchill, Volume II: Companion, Part 3: 1911–1914*. London, 1969.
Churchill, Winston S. *World Crisis*, vol. I. London, 1938 (1923).
Clark, Ian. *The Hierarchy of States: Reform and Resistance in the International Order*. Cambridge, 1989.
Clausewitz, Carl von. "Vom Kriege," in *Kriegstheorie und Kriegsgeschichte*, Reinhard Stumpf, ed., Frankfurt, 1993.
Clements, Keith. *Faith on the Frontier: A Life of Joseph H. Oldham*. Edinburgh and Geneva, 1999.
Cohen-Solal, Annie. *Un jour, ils auront des peintres: L'avènement des peintres américains, Paris 1867–New York 1948*. Paris, 2000.
Conway, John S. "The Struggle for Peace," *The Ecumenical Review* 35 (1983), 25–26
Coogan, John W. *The End of Neutrality: The United States, Britain and Maritime Rights, 1899 1915*. Ithaca, 1981.
Cooper, John Milton. *The Vanity of Power: American Isolationism and the First World War, 1914–1917*. Westport, CT, 1969.
Cooper, Sandi E. *Patriotic Pacifism: Waging War on War in Europe, 1815–1914*. New York, 1991.

Cornwall, Mark, ed. *The Last Years of Austria-Hungary: A Multi-National Experiment in Early Twentieth Century Europe*, 2nd ed. Exeter, 2002.

Craig, Gordon A. and Alexander L. George. *Force and Statecraft: Diplomatic Problems of Our Time*. Oxford, 1983.

Crampton, Richard J. *The Hollow Détente: Anglo-German Relations in the Balkans, 1911–1914*. London, 1979.

Daikichiro, Tagawa. "Nan to moshitemo fuseshutsu no eio" [A Truly Extraordinary Hero], *Chuo koron* (Fall 1914).

Dakin, Douglas. "British Sources on the Greek Struggle in Macedonia," *Balkan Studies* 2, 1 (1961).

Daniels, Emil. "Enver der Seraskier - Eine französische Stimme über den Zukunftskrieg," *Preußische Jahrbücher* 155 (January–March 1914).

Daniels, Emil. "Rußland - Die Republik Nordepirus - Die innere Lage der Westmächte," *Preußische Jahrbücher* 156 (April–June 1914).

De Tarlé, Antoine. *La préparation de la lutte économique par l'Allemagne*. Turkish translation *Nasıl Dirildi? Harbe Nasıl Hazırlanıyor?* [How Germany Revived and How it is Preparing for War], Dersaadet, 1329 [March 1913–March 1914].

Debord, Guy. *La société du spectacle*. Paris, 1992.

Degreif, Diether. *Operative Planungen des k. u. k. Generalstabes für einen Krieg in der Zeit vor 1914 (1880–1914)*. Wiesbaden, 1985.

Dennett, Tyler. *Americans in Eastern Asia*. New York, 1941.

Dennis, David B. *Beethoven in German Politics, 1870–1989*. New Haven, 1996.

Derracott, Joseph. *The First World War in Posters: From the Imperial War Museum*. London, 1974.

Dickinson, Frederick R. "Japan," in Richard Hamilton and Holger Herwig, eds., *The Origins of World War I*. Cambridge, 2003.

Dickinson, Frederick R. *War and National Reinvention: Japan in the Great War, 1914–1919*. Cambridge, 1999.

Diószegi, István. *Hungarians in the Ballhausplatz: Studies on the Austro-Hungarian Common Foreign Policy*, translated by Kornél Balás and Mary Boros. Budapest, 1983.

Dobrorolsky, S. "La Mobilisation de l'armée russe en 1914," *Revue d'histoire de la guerre mondiale*, 1 (1923).

Doering-Manteuffel, Anselm. *Vom Wiener Kongreß zur Pariser Konferenz: England, die deutsche Frage und das Mächtesystem 1815–1856*. Göttingen, 1991.

Doerries, Reinhard R. *Imperial Challenge: Ambassador Count Berstorff and German-American Relations, 1908–1917*, translated by Christa D. Shannon. Chapel Hill, NC, 1989.

Doerry, Martin. *Übergangsmenschen: Die Mentalität der Wilhelminer und die Krise des Kaiserreichs*, 2 vols. Weinheim and Munich, 1986.

Dubenskii, Major-General. *Uchebnik dlia vedeniia stroevykh i gimnasticheskikh zaniatii v narodnykh shkolakh i drugikh uchebnykh zavedeniiakh*. St. Petersburg, 1911.

Dülffer, Jost. "Die zivile Reichsleitung und der Krieg: Erwartungen und Bilder 1890–1914," in *Gestaltungskraft des Politischen: Festschrift für Eberhard Kolb*, Wolfram Pyta and Ludwig Richtern, eds., Berlin, 1998.

Dülffer, Jost. "Efforts to Reform the International System and Peace Movements Before 1914," *Peace & Change* 14, 1 (1989).

Dülffer, Jost. *Regeln gegen den Krieg? Die Haager Friedenskonferenzen von 1899 und 1907 in der internationalen Politik*. Berlin, 1981.

Dülffer, Jost and Karl Holl, eds. *Bereit zum Krieg: Kriegsmentalität im wilhelminischen Deutschland 1890–1914*. Göttingen, 1986.

Dülffer, Jost, Martin Kröger, and Rolf-Harald Wippich, eds. *Vermiedene Kriege. Deeskalation von Konflikten der Großmächte zwischen Krimkrieg und Erstem Weltkrieg 1856–1914*. Munich, 1997.

Dupuis, Louis. *Le principe d'équilibre et le Concert européen*. Paris, 1909.

Durnovo, P. N. "Memorandum to Tsar Nicholas II, February 1914," in Frank Golder, ed., *Documents of Russian History, 1914–1917,* New York and London, 1927.
Edgerton, William Benbow. *Memoirs of Peasant Tolstoyans in Soviet Russia.* Indiana-Michigan Series in Russian and East European Studies. Bloomington, 1993.
Ehlert, Hans, Michael Epkenhans, and Gerhard P. Groß, eds. *Der Schlieffenplan: Analyse und Dokumente.* Munich, 2006.
Eklof, Ben. *Russian Peasant Schools: Officialdom, Village Culture, and Popular Pedagogy, 1861–1914.* Berkeley, 1986.
Ekstein, Michael. "Sir Edward Grey and Imperial Germany in 1914," *Journal of Contemporary History,* 6, 3 (1971), 121–31.
Ekstein, Michael. "Some Notes on Sir Edward Grey's Policy in July 1914," *Historical Journal* 15 (1972).
Eksteins, Modris. *Rites of Spring: The Great War and the Birth of the Modern Age.* Boston, 1989.
Elias, Norbert. *Über den Prozeß der Zivilisation: Soziogenetische und psychogenetische Untersuchungen.* Frankfurt am Main, 1976.
Elrod, Richard B. "The Concert of Europe: A Fresh Look at an International System," *World Politics* 28 (1976), 159–74.
Elvert, Jürgen and Michael Salewski. *Deutschland und der Westen,* vol. I: *Transatlantische Beziehungen.* Stuttgart, 1993.
Emura, Asada Emura. "Oshu rekkyo no kosenjutsu" [The European Powers' Passion for War], *Taiyo* (1 September 1914).
Engler, Wilhelm. *Freiburg, Baden und das Reich: Lebenserinnerungen eines südwestdeutschen Sozialdemokraten, 1873–1938.* Stuttgart, 1991.
Epkenhans, Michael. *Die wilhelminische Flottenrüstung 1908–1914. Weltmachtstreben, technischer Fortschritt, soziale Integration.* Munich, 1991.
Epkenhans, Michael, ed. *Albert Hopman: Das ereignisreiche Leben eines "Wilhelminers." Tagebücher, Briefe, Aufzeichnungen 1901 bis 1920.* Munich, 2004.
Erdmann, Karl Dietrich, ed. *Kurt Riezler, Tagebücher, Aufsätze, Dokumente.* Göttingen, 1972.
Evans, R. J. W. and Hartmut Pogge von Strandmann, eds. *The Coming of the First World War.* Oxford, 1988.
Eyffinger, Arthur. *The 1899 Hague Peace Conference: "The Parliament of Man, The Federation of the World."* The Hague, 1999.
Farrar, L. L. *The Short War Illusion: German Policy, Strategy and Domestic Affairs, August–December 1914.* Santa Barbara, 1973.
Fellner, Fritz, ed. *Schicksalsjahre Österreichs 1908–1919: Das politische Tagebuch Josef Redlichs, 1. Vol.: 1908–1914,* 2 vols. Graz-Köln, 1953–1954.
Fellner, Fritz. "Die 'Mission Hoyos,'" in *Vom Dreibund zum Völkerbund: Studien zur Geschichte der internationalen Beziehungen, 1882–1919.* Heidrun Maschl and Brigitte Mazohl-Wallnig, eds., Vienna, 1994 [1984].
Fellner, Fritz. *Vom Dreibund zum Völkerbund: Studien zur Geschichte der internationalen Beziehungen 1882–1919.* Munich, 1994.
Ferguson, Niall. "Public Finance and National Security: the Domestic Origins of the First World War Revisited," *Past & Present,* 142 (1994).
Ferguson, Niall. *The Pity of War: Explaining World War I.* London, 1998, New York, 1999.
Fiebig-von Hase, Ragnhild. "Die deutsch-amerikanischen Wirtschaftsbeziehungen, 1890–1914, im Zeichen von Protektionismus und internationaler Integration," *Amerikastudien* 33 (1988).
Fiebig-von Hase, Ragnhild. "Amerikanische Friedensbemühungen in Europa, 1905–1914," in Norbert Finzsch und Hermann Wellenreuther, eds., *Liberalitas.* Stuttgart, 1992.
Fiebig-von Hase, Ragnhild. *Lateinamerika als Konfliktherd der deutsch-amerikanischen Beziehungen 1890–1903 vom Beginn der Panamerikapolitik bis zur Venezuelakrise von 1902/03,* 2 vols. Göttingen, 1986.
Fink, Lois M. *American Art at the 19th Century Paris Salons.* New York, 1990.

Fink, Lois M. "French Art in the United States, 1850–1870: Three Dealers and Collectors," *Gazette des Beaux Arts* (September 1978), 87.
Finzsch, Norbert and Hermann Wellenreuther, eds. *Liberalitas: Festschrift für Erich Angermann*. Stuttgart, 1992.
Fischer, Fritz. *Krieg der Illusionen: Die deutsche Politik von 1911 bis 1914*. Düsseldorf, 1987, (1969).
Fischer, Fritz. *Wir sind nicht hineingeschliddert: Das Staatsgeheimnis um die Riezler-Tagebücher: Eine Streitschrift*. Reinbek, 1983.
Flasch, Kurt. *Die geistige Mobilmachung: Die deutschen Intellektuellen und der Erste Weltkrieg*. Berlin, 2000.
Flood, P. J. *France, 1914–1918: Public Opinion and the War Effort*. London, 1990.
Foley, Robert T. *German Strategy and the Path to Verdun: Erich von Falkenhayn and the Development of Attrition, 1870–1916*. Cambridge, 2005.
Forsbach, Ralf. *Alfred von Kiderlen-Wächter (1852–1912): Ein Diplomatenleben im Kaiserreich*. 2 vols. Göttingen, 1997.
Förster, Stig et al., eds. *Europe and Africa: The Berlin Congo Conference 1884–1885 and the Onset of Partition*. Oxford, 1989.
Förster, Stig. "Der deutsche Generalstab und die Illusion des kurzen Krieges, 1871–1914: Metakritik eines Mythos" *Militärgeschichtliche Mitteilungen*, 54 (1994), 61–95.
Förster, Stig. "Der deutsche Generalstab und die Illusion des kurzen Krieges, 1871–1914: Metakritik eines Mythos," in *Lange und kurze Wege in den Ersten Weltkrieg: Vier Augsburger Beiträge zur Kriegsursachenforschung*, Johannes Burkhardt et. al., eds., Munich, 1996.
Förster, Stig. "Dreams and Nightmares: German Military Leadership and the Images of Future Warfare, 1871–1914," in *Anticipating Total War: The German and American Experiences, 1871–1914*. Manfred F. Boemeke et al., eds., Cambridge, 1999.
Förster, Stig. "Germany," in *War Planning: The Lessons of 1914*, Richard Hamilton and Holger H. Herwig, eds., Cambridge, forthcoming.
Förster, Stig. "Im Reich der Absurden: Die Ursachen des Ersten Weltkrieges," in *Wie Kriege entstehen. Zum historischen Hintergrund von Staatenkonflikten*, Bernd Wegner, ed., Paderborn et al., 2000.
Franke, Lydia. *Die Randbemerkungen Wilhelms II in den Akten der auswärtigen Politik als historische und psychologische Quelle*. Berlin, 1933.
Frevert, Ute. *A Nation in Barracks: Modern Germany, Military Conscription and Civil Society*. Oxford, 2004.
Frevert, Ute. "Das Geschlecht des Politischen," in *Männerbund und Bundesstaat*, Lynn Blattmann and Irène Meier, eds., Zürich, 1998.
Frevert, Ute. *"Mann und Weib, und Weib und Mann": Geschlechter-Differenzen in der Moderne*. Munich, 1995.
Frevert, Ute. *Men of Honour: A Social and Cultural History of the Duel*. Cambridge, 1995.
Frevert, Ute. "Honour and Middle-Class Culture: the History of the Duel in England and Germany," in *Bourgeois Society in Nineteenth-century Europe*, Jürgen Kocka and Allan Mitchell, eds., Oxford, 1993.
Fridenson, Patrick, ed. *The French Home Front, 1914–1918*. Providence and Oxford, 1992.
Fried, Alfred. "Das Marokkoabkommen," *Die Friedens-Warte* 13 (1911).
Friedman, Leon, ed. *The Law of War: A Documentary History*, vol. 1. New York, 1973.
Fröhlich, Michael. *Von Konfrontation zur Koexistenz: Die deutsch-englischen Kolonialbeziehungen in Afrika zwischen 1884 und 1914*. Bochum, 1990.
Fueoloep-Miller, Rene. "Tolstoy the Apostolic Crusader," *Russian Review* 19, 2 (1960).
Fuller, William C. *Civil-Military Conflict in Russia, 1881–1914*. Princeton, NJ, 1985.
Fumaroli, Marc. *L'Etat culturel: une religion moderne*. Paris, 1991.
Gaebler, Ulrich. *Geschichte des Pietismus*, vol. 3: *Das neunzehnte und zwanzigste Jahrhundert*. Göttingen, 2000.
Gay, Peter. *The Cultivation of Hatred*. New York, 1993.
Geinitz, Christian. *Kriegsfurcht und Kampfbereitschaft: Das Augusterlebnis in Freiburg: Eine Studie zum Kriegsbeginn 1914*. Essen, 1998.
Geiss, Imanuel. *Der lange Weg in die Katastrophe. Die Vorgeschichte des Ersten Weltkriegs 1815–1914*. Munich and Zürich, 1990.

Geiss, Imanuel, ed. *Julikrise und Kriegsausbruch 1914*. 2 vols. Hanover, 1963–6, Bonn 1976.
Geiss, Immanuel Geiss, ed. *July 1914: The Outbreak of the First World War. Selected Documents*. New York, 1967.
Genji, Shibukawa. "Nihon no noborizaka" [Japan's Upward Slope], *Chuo koron* [Fall 1914].
Geyer, Michael and Hartmut Lehmann, eds. *Religion und Nation: Nation und Religion*. Göttingen, 2004.
Girouard, Mark. *The Return to Camelot: Chivalry and the English Gentleman*. New Haven, 1981.
Glaise Horstenau, Edmund von. *Die Katastrophe*. Zurich, 1929.
Glaser, Charles L. "When are Arms Races Dangerous? Rational versus Suboptimal Arming," *International Security* 28, 4 (2004), 44–84.
Godsey, Jr., William D. *Aristocratic Redoubt: The Austro-Hungarian Foreign Office on the Eve of the First World War*. West Lafayette, IN, 1999.
Goffmann, Erving. "On face-work," in Goffmann, Erving. *Interaction Ritual: Essays on Face-to-Face Behaviour*. Harmondsworth, 1972.
Göhler, Gerhard. "Einleitung: Politische Ideengeschichte – institutionentheoretisch gelesen," in Göhler, Gerhard; Lenk, Kurt; Münkler, Herfried; Walther, Manfred Walther, eds. *Politische Institutionen im gesellschaftlichen Umbruch: Ideengeschichtliche Beiträge zur Theorie politischer Institutionen*. Opladen, 1990.
Goltz, Colmar Freiherr von der. *The Nation in Arms*. London, 1906.
Goltz, Colmar von der. *Das Volk in Waffen: ein Buch über Heerwesen und Kriegsführung unserer Zeit*. 3rd Edition. Berlin, 1884. Translated as *Millet-i Müselleha*. Kostantiniye: Matbaa-i Ebüzziya, 1301 [March 1885–March 1886].
Gong, Gerrit W. *The Standard of 'Civilization' in International Society*. Oxford, 1984.
Gooch, G. P. and Harold Temperley. *British Documents on the Origins of the War 1898–1914*, vol. 6: Anglo-German Tensions, 1907–1912. London, 1930.
Görlitz, Walter, ed. *Regierte der Kaiser? Kriegstagebücher, Aufzeichnungen und Briefe des Chefs des Marine-Kabinetts Admiral Georg Alexander von Müller 1914–1918*. Göttingen, 1959.
Grewe, Wilhelm. *Epochen der Völkerrechtsgeschichte*. Baden-Baden, 1988.
Grey, Sir Edward. *Twenty-Five Years, 1892–1916*. 2 vols. London, 1925.
Groh, Dieter. "'Je eher, desto besser!': Innenpolitische Faktoren für die Präventivkriegsbereitschaft des deutschen Reiches, 1913/14," *Politische Vierteljahresschrift* 13, 4 (1972), 501–21.
Grotefeld, Stefan. *Friedrich Siegmund-Schultze: Ein deutscher Ökumeniker und christlicher Pazifist*. Gütersloh, 1995.
Gunji, Muko Gunji. "Oshu senran no atauru kyokun" [The Lesson of the European War], *Nihon oyobi Nihonjin* [15 September 1914].
Gutsche, Willibald. *Wilhelm II: Der letzte Kaiser des Deutschen Reiches*. Berlin, 1991.
Haffner, Oskar. *Kriegschronik der Stadt Freiburg im Breisgau 1914–1919*. Freiburg, 1924. Zumtobel, Reinhold. *Vom Gemeindebub zum Ehrenbürger: Kurvenreicher Lebensweg eines Hebelverehrers*. Schopfheim, 1953.
Haffner, Sebastian Haffner. *Geschichte eines Deutschen. Die Erinnerungen 1914–1933*. Stuttgart and Munich, 2000.
Hagemann, Karen. Of 'Manly Valor' and 'German Honor': Nation, War and Masculinity in the Age of the Prussian Uprising against Napoleon," *Central European History* 31 (1998), 187–220.
Hakki, Hafız. *Bozgun* [Morale and Defeat]. Tüccarzade İbrahim Hilmi Series. Dersaadet: Matbaa-i Hayriye, 1330 [March 1914–March 1915].
Hamilton, Richard F., ed. *The Origins of World War I*. Cambridge, 2003.
Hanioğlu, M. Şükrü, ed. *Kendi Mektuplarında Enver Paşa*. Istanbul, 1989.
Hantsch, Hugo. *Leopold Graf Berchtold*. 2 vols. Graz, 1963.
Hanzan, Ishikawa. "Kekkyoku shina mondai" [In the End, it is the China Problem], *Chuo koron* (Fall 1914).
Harnack als Zeitgenosse, Adolf von, ed. *Kurt Nowak, part 2: Der Wissenschaftsorganisator und Gelehrtenpolitiker*. Berlin, New York, 1996.
Harris, Ruth. "The 'Child of the Barbarian': Rape, Race and Nationalism in France during the First World War," *Past & Present* 141 (1993), 170–206.

Hart, Philip. *Orpheus in the New World: The Symphony Orchestra as an American Cultural Institution.* New York, 1973.
Haupt, Georges. *Aspects of International Socialism 1871–1914.* Cambridge, 1986.
Helmreich, Ernst Christian. *The Diplomacy of the Balkan Wars 1912–1913.* Cambridge, MA, 1938.
Herder, Charlotte Herder. *Mein Kriegstagebuch 1914–1918.* Freiburg, n.d.
Herring, George C. *America's Longest War: the United States and Vietnam, 1950–1975.* New York, 1979.
Herrmann, David G. *The Arming of Europe and the Making of the First World War.* Princeton Studies in International History and Politics. Princeton, NJ, 1996.
Herwig, Holger. *The First World War: Germany and Austria-Hungary, 1914–1918.* London, 1997.
Heuss, Theodor. *Erinnerungen 1905–1933.* Tübingen, 1963.
Hewitson, Mark. *Germany and the Causes of the First World War.* Oxford and New York, 2004.
Hewitson, Mark. *National Identity and Political Thought in Germany: Wilhelmine Depictions of the French Third Republic 1890–1914.* Oxford, 2000.
Hewitson, Mark. "Germany and France before the First World War: A Reassessment of Wilhelmine Foreign Policy," *The English Historical Review*, 115 (2000), 576.
Hildebrand, Klaus. "Europäisches Zentrum, überseeische Peripherie und Neue Welt. Über den Wandel des Staatensystems zwischen Berliner Kongreß (1878) und dem Pariser Frieden (1919/20)," *Historische Zeitschrift* 248 (1989).
Hildebrand, Klaus. "Julikrise 1914: Das europäische Sicherheitsdilemma. Betrachtungen über den Ausbruch des Ersten Weltkrieges," *Geschichte in Wissenschaft und Unterricht* 36 (1985).
Hildebrand, Klaus. *"Staatskunst und Kriegshandwerk": Akteure und System der europäischen Staatenwelt vor 1914.* Friedrichsruher Beiträge, vol. 24. (Friedrichsruh, 2005).
Hildebrand, Klaus. *Das vergangene Reich: Deutsche Außenpolitik von Bismarck bis Hitler.* Stuttgart, 1995.
Hildebrand, Klaus. *Deutsche Außenpolitik 1871–1918.* Munich, 1994.
Hilmi, Tüccarzade İbrahim. *Türkiye Uyan* [Turkey Awake]. Kütübhane-i İntibah, no. 13 Dersaadet: Kütübhane-i İslam ve Askerî, 1329 [March 1913–March 1914].
Hirondo, Tomizu. "Oshu rekkyo no daikaisen ni taishite" [Looking at the Outbreak of a Great War among the European Powers], *Chuo koron* (Fall 1914).
Hirondo, Tomizu. "Sengo ni okeru gunbi mondai" [The Problem of Arms after the War], *Chuo koron* (November 1914).
Hirsch, Gerhard, Gerd Krumeich, and Irina Renz, eds. *Enzyklopädie Erster Weltkrieg.* Paderborn, Munich, Vienna, and Zürich, 2003.
Hitchens, Christopher. *Blood, Class, and Nostalgia: Anglo-American Ironies.* New York, 1990.
Höbelt, Lothar. "'Well-tempered Discontent': Austrian Domestic Politics," in *The Last Years of Austria-Hungary: A Multi-National Experiment in Early Twentieth Century Europe*, 2nd ed., Mark Cornwall, ed., Exeter, 2002.
Höbelt, Lothar. "Parteien und Fraktionen im Cisleithanischen Reichsrat," in *Die Habsburgermonarchie, 1848–1918*, vol. VII: *Verfassung und Parlamentarismus*, 2 vols., pt.I: *Verfassungsrecht, Verfassungs-Wirklichkeit, Zentrale Repräsentativkörperschaften*, Helmut Rumpler and Peter Urbanitsch, eds., Vienna, 2000.
Hobsbawm, Eric J. *The Age of Empire 1875–1914.* London, 1987.
Hobson, John M. "The Military-Extraction Gap and the Wary Titan: The Fiscal Sociology of British Defence Policy, 1870–1913," *Journal of European Economic History* 22, 3 (1993), 461–506.
Hobson, Rolf. *Imperialism at Sea: Naval Strategic Thought, the Ideology of Sea Power and Tirpitz Plan, 1875–1914.* Boston, 2002.
Hoffmann, Stanley. *Organisations internationales et pouvoirs politiques des Etats.* Paris, 1954.
Holbraad, Carsten. *The Concert of Europe: A Study in German and British International Theory, 1815–1914.* London, 1970.
Holls, Frederic W. *The Peace Conference at The Hague, and its Bearings on International Law and Policy.* New York, 1914.
Hopkins, C. Howard. *John R. Mott, 1865–1955*, vol I. Grand Rapids, 1979.

Hopman, Albert. *Das ereignisreiche Leben eines Wilhelminers: Tagebücher, Briefe, Aufzeichnungen 1901 bis 1920.* Michael Epkenhans, ed., Munich, 2004.

Horne, John and Alan Kramer. *German Atrocities, 1914: A History of Denial.* New Haven, 2001.

Hötzendorf, Franz Conrad von. *Private Aufzeichnungen: Erste Veröffentlichungen aus den Papieren des k. u.k. Generalstab-Chefs,* edited by Kurt Peball. Vienna, 1977.

Hötzendorf, Franz Conrad von. *Aus Meiner Dienstzeit, 1906–1918.* 5 vols. Vienna, 1921–25.

Howard, Harry N. *The Partition of Turkey: A Diplomatic History, 1913–1923.* Norman, OK, 1931.

Howard, Michael. *The Franco-Prussian War: The German Invasion of France, 1870–1871.* London, 1961.

Hoyos, Graf Alexander. "Meine Mission nach Berlin," printed in Fritz Fellner, "Die Mission Hoyos," in *Deutschlands Sonderung von Europa 1862–1945.* Wilhelm Alff, ed., Frankfurt am Main, Bern, New York, 1984.

Hughes, Thomas. *Tom Brown's Schooldays.* London, 1906.

Hull, William I. *The Two Hague Conferences and their Contributions to International Law.* Boston, 1908.

Huntington, Samuel P. "Arms Races: Prerequisites and Results," reprinted in *The Use of Force: International Politics and Foreign Policy,* R. J. Art and K. N. Waltz, eds. Lanham, MD, 1983.

Hüppauf, Bernd, ed. *Ansichten vom Krieg: Vergleichende Studien zum Ersten Weltkrieg in Literatur und Gesellschaft.* Königstein im Taunus, 1984.

Ienaga, Saburo. *The Pacific War, 1931–1945.* New York, 1978.

Inoue Kaoru ko denki hensankai, ed. *Segai Inoue ko den* [Biography of the Late Lord Inoue]. 5 vols. Tokyo, 1968.

James, Henry. *Bostonians.* London, 1886.

James, Henry. *The Europeans: A Sketch.* Boston, 1979.

Jansen, Anscar. *Der Weg in den Ersten Weltkrieg: Das deutsche Militär in der Julikrise 1914.* Marburg, 2005.

Jarausch, Konrad H. *Students, Society, and Politics in Imperial Germany: The Rise of Academic Illiberalism.* Princeton, NJ 1982.

Jěrabék, Rudolf. *Potiorek: General im Schatten von Sarajevo.* Graz, 1991.

Jeismann, Michael. *Das Vaterland der Feinde: Studien zum Feindbegriff und Selbstverständnis in Deutschland und Frankreich 1792–1918.* Stuttgart, 1992.

Johann, Ernst, ed. *Innenansicht eines Krieges: Deutsche Dokumente 1914–1918.* Munich, 1973.

Joll, James. *1914: The Unspoken Assumptions.* London, 1968.

Joll, James. *The Origins of the First World War.* London, 1984.

Joll, James. *Die Ursprünge des Ersten Weltkriegs.* Munich, 1988.

Joly, Bertrand. "La France et la revanche (1871–1914)," *Revue d'histoire moderne et contemporaine* 46, 2 (1999), 325–47.

Jones, David R. "Forerunners of the Komsomol: Scouting in Imperial Russia," in *Reforming the Tsar's Army: Military Innovation in Imperial Russia from Peter the Great to the Revolution,* David Schimmelpenninck van der Oye and Bruce W. Menning, eds., Woodrow Wilson Center Series. Cambridge, 2004.

Jünger, Ernst. *In Stahlgewittern* (1920). Stuttgart, 1986.

Jux, A. *Der Kriegsschrecken des Frühjahrs 1914 in der europäischen Presse.* Berlin, 1929.

Kaiser, Jochen-Christoph. "Friedrich Albert Spiecker (1854–1937) : Eine Karriere zwischen Großindustrie und freiem Protestantismus," in *Christliche Unternehmer,* Francesca Schinzinger, ed., Boppard am Rhein, 1994.

Kakunari, Uma. "Kaizeru no kaoiro" [The Kaiser's Facial Hue], *Nihon oyobi Nihonjin* (1 September 1914).

Kampe, Norbert. *Studenten und "Judenfrage" im Deutschen Kaiserreich: Die Entstehung einer akademischen Trägerschicht des Antisemitismus.* Göttingen, 1988.

Kann, Robert A. *Dynasty, Politics and Culture: Selected Essays,* Stanley B. Winters, ed., Boulder, 1991.

Kann, Robert A. *Erzherzog Franz Ferdinand Studien.* Vienna, 1976.

Kant, Immanuel. "Zum ewigen Frieden: Ein philosophischer Entwurf." in *Ewiger Friede? Dokumente einer deutschen Diskussion um 1800,* Anita and Walter Dietze, eds., Munich, 1989.

Karpat, Kemal. "The Entry of the Ottoman Empire into World War I," *Belleten* 58 (December 2004).
Karsh, Efraim and Inari Karsh. *Empires of the Sand: The Struggle for Mastery in the Middle East, 1789–1923.* Cambridge, 1999.
Katsumasa, Watanabe, ed. *Shinbun shuroku Taishoshi* [Newspaper compilation of Taisho history]. 15 vols. Tokyo, 1978.
Kautsky, Karl, ed. *Die deutschen Dokumente zum Kriegsausbruch.* 4 vols. Berlin, 1919.
Kazan, Kayahara. "Bunmeishiteki kokusaishiteki ni kansatsu shitaru Oshu senso" [The European War as Viewed from the Perspective of the History of Civilization and International Relations]. *Chuo koron* (Fall 1914).
Keiichiro, Hara, ed. *Hara Takashi nikki* [Diary of Hara Takashi] 6 vols. Tokyo, 1981.
Keiper, Gerhard. *Biographische Studien zu den Verständigungsversuchen zwischen Deutschland und Frankreich am Vorabend des Ersten Weltkrieges.* Frankfurt am Main et al., 1997.
Kennan, George F. *The Fateful Alliance: France, Russia, and the Coming of the First World War.* New York, 1984.
Kennan, George Frost. *The Other Balkan Wars: A 1913 Carnegie Endowment Inquiry in Retrospect.* Washington, DC, 1993.
Kennedy, Paul M. *The Rise and Fall of British Naval Mastery.* London, 1976 (reprinted 1992).
Kennedy, Paul M. *The Rise of the Anglo-German Antagonism 1860–1914.* London, 1980.
Kennedy, Paul. *Aufstieg und Fall der großen Mächte: Ökonomischer Wandel und militärischer Konflikt von 1500 bis 2000.* Frankfurt, 1991.
Kennedy, Paul and Anthony Nicholls, eds. *Nationalist and Racialist Movements in Britain and Germany before 1914.* London, 1981.
Kessler, Harry Graf. *Gesichter und Zeiten: Erinnerungen.* Frankfurt, 1988.
Kiderlen-Wächter, Alfred von. *Kiderlen Wächter der Staatsmann und Mensch: Briefwechsel aus dem Nachlaß*, edited by Ernst Jäckh. 2 vols. Berlin and Leipzig, 1924.
Kielmannsegg, Graf Peter. *Deutschland und der Erste Weltkrieg.* Frankfurt, 1968.
Kießling, Friedrich. "Österreich-Ungarn und die deutsch-englischen Détentebemühungen 1912–1914," in *Historisches Jahrbuch* 116 (1996), 102–25.
Kießling, Friedrich. "Self-perceptions, the Official Attitude towards Pacifism, and Great Power Détente: Reflections on Diplomatic Culture before World War I," in *Decentering America*, Culture and International History II, Jessica Gienow-Hecht, ed., New York and Oxford, forthcoming.
Kießling, Friedrich. "Wege aus der Stringenzfalle: Die Vorgeschichte des Ersten Weltkriegs als 'Ära der Entspannung', "*Geschichte in Wissenschaft und Unterricht* 55 (2004), 284–304.
Kießling, Friedrich. *Gegen den "großen Krieg"? Entspannung in den internationalen Beziehungen 1911–1914.* Munich, 2002.
Kikuo, Wada. "Oshu no senkyoku to waga zosengyo" [Our Ship-building Industry and the European War], *Nihon oyobi Nihonjin* (1 September 1914).
Kinglake, Alexander W. *The Invasion of the Crimea.* 6 vols. Edinburgh, 1877.
Kissinger, Henry A. *Diplomacy.* New York, 1994.
Klemperer, Victor. *Curriculum vitae: Erinnerungen 1881–1918*, vol. 2, edited by Walter Nowojski. Berlin, 1996.
Kliuchevskii, Vasilii. *Peter the Great*, translated by Liliana Archibald. New York, 1961.
Klüber, Johann L. *Pragmatische Geschichte der nationalen und politischen Wiedergeburt Griechenlands, bis zu dem Regierungsantritt des Königs Otto.* Frankfurt am Main, 1835.
Klueber, Johann L. *Europäisches Völkerrecht.* Schotthausen, 1851 (1819).
Kohut, Thomas A. *Wilhelm II and the Germans: A Study in Leadership.* New York, Oxford, 1991.
Koskenniemi, Martti. *The Gentle Civilizer of Nations: The Rise and Fall of International Law.* Cambridge, 2002.
Kraehe, Enno, ed. *The Metternich Controversy.* New York, 1971.

Kratochwil, Friedrich. *Rules, Norms, and Decisions: On the Conditions of Practical and Legal Reasoning in International Relations and Domestic Affairs.* Cambridge, 1995 (1989).

Kronenbitter, Günther. "'Nur los lassen': Österreich-Ungarn und der Wille zum Krieg," in *Lange und kurze Wege in den Ersten Weltkrieg: Vier Augsburger Beiträge zur Kriegsursachenforschung,* Johannes Burckhardt et al., eds., Munich, 1996.

Kronenbitter, Günther. "Bundesgenossen? Zur militärpolitischen Kooperation zwischen Berlin und Wien 1912 bis 1914," in *Deutschland in den internationalen Beziehungen des 19. und 20. Jahrhunderts,* Walther L. Berneckker and Volker Dotterweich eds., Munich, 1996.

Kronenbitter, Günther. "Die Macht der Illusionen: Julikrise und Kriegsausbruch 1914 aus der Sicht des deutschen Militärattachés in Wien," *Militärgeschichtliche Mitteilungen* 57, 2 (1998).

Kronenbitter, Günther. *"Krieg im Frieden": Die Führung der k.u.k. Armee und die Grossmachtpolitik Österreich-Ungarns 1906–1914.* Munich, 2003.

Krueger, Peter and Paul W. Schroeder. *"The Transformation of European Politics, 1763–1848": Episode or Model in Modern History?* Münster, 2002.

Krumeich, Gerd. "Gott mit uns?" Der Erste Weltkrieg als Religionskrieg, in, *"Gott mit uns": Nation, Religion und Gewalt im 19. und frühen 20. Jahrhundert,* Gerd Krumeich and Hartmut Lehmann, eds., Göttingen, 2000.

Krumeich, Gerd. *Armaments and Politics in France on the Eve of the First World War: The Introduction of Three-Year Conscription, 1913–1914,* translated by Stephen Conn. Leamington Spa, 1984.

Kruse, Wolfgang. *Krieg und nationale Integration: Eine Neuinterpretation des sozialdemokratischen Burgfriedensschlusses 1914/15.* Essen, 1993.

Kupisch, Karl. *Studenten entdecken die Bibel: Die Geschichte der Deutschen Christlichen Studenten-Vereinigung (DCSV).* Hamburg, 1964.

Lambert, Nicholas. *Sir John Fisher's Naval Revolution.* Columbia, SC, 1999.

Lambi, Ivo N. *The Navy and German Power Politics, 1862–1914.* London, 1984.

Lammersdorf, Raimund. *Anfänge einer Weltmacht: Theodore Roosevelt und die transatlantischen Beziehungen der USA, 1901–1909.* Berlin, 1994.

Lampe, Jürgen et al., eds. *Diesem System keinen Mann und keinen Groschen: Militärpolitik der revolutionären deutschen Arbeiterbewegung 1830–1917.* Berlin, 1990

Landau, Jacob M. *Pan-Turkism: From Irredentism to Cooperation.* 2nd ed. Bloomington, 1995.

Landau, Jacob M. *The Politics of Pan-Islam: Ideology and Organization.* New York, 1994.

Langhorne, Richard. *The Collapse of the Concert of Europe: International Politics 1890–1914.* New York, 1981.

Larres, Klaus and Torsten Oppelland, eds. *Deutschland und die USA im 20. Jahrhundert: Geschichte der politischen Beziehungen.* Darmstadt, 1997.

Latham, Robert. "Nineteenth-century lessons," *RIS* 23 (1997), 419–43.

Lawrence, T. J. "The Primacy of the Great Powers," in Lawrence, T. J. *Essays on Some Disputed Questions in Modern International Law.* Cambridge, 1884.

Lawton, Mary. *Schumann-Heink: The Last of the Titans.* New York, 1928.

Lee, Dwight E. *Europe's Crucial Years: The Diplomatic Background of World War I, 1902–1914.* Hanover, NH, 1974.

Lefort, Paul. "Les Écoles Étrangères de la Peinture — Etats Unis," *Gazette des Beaux-Arts* 43 (1879), 483–5.

Lehmann, Hartmut. "The Chosen People Theme in Late Nineteenth- and Early Twentieth-Century German Nationalism," in *Many Are Chosen: Divine Election and Western Nationalism,* William R. Hutchison and Hartmut Lehmann, eds., Harrisburg, PA, 1994.

Lehmann, Hartmut. "A Pilgrimage to Wittenberg, the so-called Protestant Mecca": Anmerkungen zum amerikanischen Deutschland-Tourismus im 19. Jahrhundert, in *Liberalitas. Festschrift für Erich Angermann zum 65. Geburtstag,* Nobert Finzsch and Hermann Wellenreuter, eds., Stuttgart, 1992.

Lehmann, Hartmut. *Martin Luther in the American Imagination.* Munich, 1988.

Lepsius, Johannes, Albrecht Mendelsohn Bartholdy, Friedrich Thimme, eds. *Die Grosse Politik der Europäischen Kabinette 1871–1914*. 40 vols. Berlin, 1922–27.
Lepsius, Rainer. *Interessen, Ideen und Institutionen*. Opladen, 1990.
Leslie, John. "The Antecedents of Austria-Hungary's War Aims: Policies and Policy-Makers in Vienna and Budapest before and during 1914," in *Archiv und Forschung: Das Haus-, Hof- und Staatsarchiv in seiner Bedeutung für die Geschichte Österreichs und Europas*. Elisabeth Springer and Leopold Kammerhold, eds., Vienna, 1993.
Leslie, John. "Österreich-Ungarn vor dem Kriegsausbruch. Der Ballhausplatz in Wien aus der Sicht eines österreichisch-ungarischen Diplomaten," in *Deutschland und Europa in der Neuzeit. Festschrift für Karl Otmar von Aretin zum 65. Geburtstag*, Ralph Melville et al., eds., Stuttgart, 1988.
Levine, Lawrence. *Highbrow/Lowbrow: The Emergence of Cultural Hierarchy in America*. Cambridge, MA, 1988.
Levsen, Sonja. "Männlichkeit als Studienziel: Männlichkeitskonstruktionen englischer und deutscher Studenten vor dem Ersten Weltkrieg," *Zeitschrift für Geschichtswissenschaft* 51 (2003).
Levy, Jack S. "Declining Power and the Preventive Motivation for War," *World Politics* 40, 1 (1987), 82–107.
Levy, Jack S. *War in the Modern Great Power System, 1494–1975*. Lexington, 1983.
Lieven, Dominic B. C. *Russia and the Origins of the First World War*. Basingstoke and New York, 1983.
Linclon, W. Bruce. *Passage through Armageddon: The Russians in War & Revolution, 1914–1918*. New York, 1986.
Lindemann, Thomas. *Die Macht der Perzeptionen und Perzeptionen von Mächten*, Berlin 2000.
Linden, Marcel van der and Gottfried Mergner, eds. *Kriegsbegeisterung und mentale Kriegsvorbereitung: Interdisziplinäre Studien*. Berlin, 1991.
Lindenberger, Thomas. *Strassenpolitik: Zur Sozialgeschichte der öffentlichen Ordnung in Berlin 1900 bis 1914*. Bonn, 1995.
Lloyd-George, David. *War Memoirs*, vol. I, *1914–1915*. Boston, 1933.
Lorimer, James. *The Institutes of the Law of Nations: A Treatise of the Jural Relations of Separate Political Communities*. 2 vols. Edinburgh, London, 1883–84.
Lovett, Perry Glenn. *Justifying War: The Just War Tradition until 1919*. PhD diss., University of Oklahoma, 1982.
Lowe, Peter. *Great Britain and Japan 1911–15*. London, 1969.
Luard, Evan. *International Society*. New York, 1990.
Mai, Gunther. *Das Ende des Kaiserreichs: Politik und Kriegführung im Ersten Weltkrieg*. Munich, 1987.
Maklakov, V. A. "Speech on the Duma Floor, November 3, 1916," in *Gosudarstvennaia Duma, 1906–1917: Stenograficheskie Otchety*, 4 vols., V. D. Karpovich, ed., Moscow, 1995.
Mangan, J. A. *Athleticism in the Victorian and Edwardian Public School*. Cambridge, 1981.
Mann, Thomas and Heinrich Mann. *Briefwechsel 1900–1949*, edited by Hans Wysling. Enlarged edition. Frankfurt am Main, 1984.
Manzo, Watanabe. "Oshu senran to zaikai no eikyo" [Effect of the European War on the Business Community], *Nihon oyobi Nihonjin* (15 August 1914).
Marks, Sally. "'My Name is Ozymandias': The Kaiser in Exile," *Central European History* XVI, 2 (June 1983), 122–70.
Martel, Gordon. "Afterword: The Imperial Contract - an Ethology of Power," in *Great Powers and Little Wars: The Limits of Power*, A. H. Ion and E. J. Herrington, eds. Westport, CT, 1993.
Martynov, E. I. "V chem sila Iaponii i slabost' Rossii?," in "*... Khorosho zabytoe staroe": sbornik statei*, O. A. Bobrakov, ed., Moscow, 1991 (1904).
Masahira, Tanaka. "Ekken o tamawatta toki no kioku" [Memories of My Audience (with the Kaiser)], *Chuo koron* (Fall 1914).
Masao, Kanbe. "Nihon oyobi Nihonjin no taigaiteki taido" [The Attitude of Japan and the Japanese toward the World], *Taiyo* (1 September 1914).
May, Ernest. *The World War and American Isolation, 1914–1917*. Cambridge, MA, 1966.

McDonald, David M. "The Durnovo Memorandum in Context: Official Conservatism and the Crisis of Autocracy," *Jahrbücher für Geschichte Osteuropas* 44, 4 (1996).
McMaster, John Bach. *The United States in the World War.* New York, 1919.
Medlicott, W. Norton. *Bismarck, Gladstone and the Concert of Europe.* London, 1957.
Meiji Taisho Showa shinbun kenkyukai, ed. *Shinbun shusei Taishohen nenshi* [Taisho History Compilation of Newspapers]. Tokyo, 1980.
Meinecke, Friedrich. *Die deutsche Katastrophe: Betrachtungen und Erinnerungen.* Wiesbaden, 1947.
Menning, Bruce E. "Pieces of the Puzzle: the Role of Iu. N. Danilov and M. V. Alekseev in Russian War Planning before 1914," *The International History Review* 25, 4 (2003), 775–98.
Michalka, Wolfgang, ed. *Der Erste Weltkrieg: Wirkung, Wahrnehmung und Analyse.* Munich, 1994.
Michel, Bernard. "L'Autriche et l'entrée dans la guerre en 1914," *Guerres mondiales et conflits contemporaines* 45 (1995).
Millis, Walter. *Road to War: America, 1914–1917.* Boston and New York, 1935.
Miquel, Pierre. *Art et argent 1800–1900: l'école de la nature,* vol. VI. Maurs-La-Jolie, 1986, 1987.
Mitchell, Nancey. "The Height of the German Challenge: The Venezuela Blockade, 1902–1903," *Diplomatic History* 20 (1996), 185–209.
Mizutaro, Takagi. "Oshu senran to kirisutokyo" [Christianity and the European War], *Nihon oyobi Nihonjin* (15 November 1914).
Moll, Jones [attrib.]. *Anadolu'da Türkiye,* translated by Habil Adem [Naci İsmail Pelister].
Moltke, Helmuth von. *Erinnerungen, Briefe, Dokumente, 1877–1916.* Stuttgart, 1922.
Moltke, Helmuth von. *Letters of Field-Marshal count Helmuth von Moltke to His Mother and His Brother.* New York, 1892.
Mombauer, Annika. "A Reluctant Military Leader? Helmuth von Moltke and the July Crisis of 1914," *War in History* 6, 4 (1999), 417–46.
Mombauer, Annika. *Helmuth von Moltke and the Origins of the First World War.* Cambridge, England, 2001.
Mombauer, Annika. *The Origins of the First World War: Controversies and Consensus.* London, 2002.
Mombauer, Annika and Wilhelm Deist, eds. *The Kaiser: New Research on Wilhelm II's Role in Imperial Germany.* Cambridge, England, 2003.
Mommsen, Wolfgang J. *Der erste Weltkrieg: Anfang vom Ende des bürgerlichen Zeitalters.* Frankfurt am Main, 2004.
Mommsen, Wolfgang J. "Die christlichen Kirchen im Ersten Weltkrieg," in Mommsen, Wolfgang J. *Der Erste Weltkrieg. Anfang vom Ende des bürgerlichen Zeitalters.* Frankfurt am Main, 2004.
Mommsen, Wolfgang J. *Der autoritäre Nationalstaat: Verfassung, Gesellschaft und Kultur des deutschen Kaiserreiches.* Frankfurt am Main, 1990.
Mommsen, Wolfgang J. *Der große Krieg und die Historiker: Neue Wege der Geschichtsschreibung über den Ersten Weltkrieg.* Essen, 2002.
Mommsen, Wolfgang J. *Großmachtstellung und Weltpolitik 1870–1914: Die Außenpolitik des Deutschen Reiches.* Frankfurt am Main, Berlin, 1993.
Montgelas, Max and Walther Schücking, eds. *Outbreak of the World War: German Documents Collected by Karl Kautsky.* New York, 1924.
Motokawa, Gorai. "Toyo kunshufu no Doitsu kotei" [The Asian-style German Emperor], *Chuo koron* (Fall 1914).
Mott, John, R. *Addresses and Papers of John R. Mott,* vol. 2. New York, 1947.
Müller, Georg Alexander von. *Aus Gärten der Vergangenheit. Erinnerungen 1882–1914.* Stuttgart, 1952.
Müller, Karl Alexander von. *Mars und Venus: Erinnerungen 1914–1919.* Stuttgart, 1954.
Müller, Sven Oliver. *Die Nation als Waffe: Nationalismus in Deutschland und Großbritannien im Ersten Weltkrieg.* Göttingen, 2002.
Müller, Sven Oliver. "Who is the Enemy? The Nationalist Dilemma of Inclusion and Exclusion in Britain During the First World War," *European Review of History* 9, 1 (2002), 63–83.

Naci İsmail, Belak (pseud.). *Mağlub Milletler Nasıl İntikam Alırlar* [How Do Defeated Nations Take Revenge?], translated by Habil Adem [Naci İsmail Pelister]. Dersaadet: İkbal Kütübhanesi, 1332 h. [November 1913–November 1914].
Nardin, Terry. *Law, Morality, and the Relations of States*. Princeton, NJ, 1983.
Nickles, David P. *Under Wire: How the Telegraph Changed Diplomacy*. Cambridge, MA, 2003.
Nipperdey, Thomas. *Deutsche Geschichte 1866–1918: Machtstaat vor der Demokratie*. Munich, 1992.
Okamoto, Shumpei. *The Japanese Oligarchy and the Russo-Japanese War*. New York, 1970.
Okey, Robin. *The Habsburg Monarchy*. New York, 2001.
Oppenheim, L. *International Law*. London, 1905.
Osiander, Andreas. *The States System of Europe, 1640–1990: Peacemaking and the Conditions of International Stability*. Oxford, 1994.
Ostrymiecz, August Urbanski von. *Conrad von Hötzendorf: Soldat und Mensch*. Graz, 1938.
Özdemir [Şehbenderzade Filibeli Ahmed Hilmi]. *Türk Ruhu Nasıl Yapılıyor? Her Vatanperverden, Bu Eserciği Türklere Okumasını ve Anlatmasını Niyaz Ederiz* [How the Turkish Spirit is Formed: We Ask of Each Patriot to Read and Relate this Booklet to the Turks], İkaz-ı Millet Kütübhanesi, no. 1. Darül-hilâfe: Hikmet Matbaa-i İslamiyesi, 1329 [March 1913–March 1914].
Papers of Akashi Motojiro and Bibliography, "Akashi Motojiro monjo oyobi kadai," *Kaio daigaku hogaku kenkyu*, vol. 58, no. 9 (September 1985).
Pederson, Sanna. "A. B. Marx, Berlin Concert Life, and German National Identity," *Nineteenth Century Music* XVIII (Fall 1994).
Peristiany, John G. and Julian Pitt-Rivers, eds. *Honor and Grace in Anthropology*. Cambridge, 1992.
Phillips, Kevin. *The Cousins' Wars: Religion, Politics, and the Triumph of Anglo-America*. New York, 1999.
Pokrowski, M., ed. *Drei Konferenzen (zur Vorgeschichte des Weltkrieges)*. n.p., 1920.
Polat, Nazım H. Polat. *Müdafaa-i Milliye Cemiyeti*. Kaynak Eserler. No. 52. Ankara, 1991.
Pollard, Sidney. "Probleme der europäischen Integration im 19. und 20. Jahrhundert," in *Wirtschaftliche und politische Integration in Europa im 19. und 20. Jahrhundert*, Helmut Berding, ed.. Göttingen, 1984.
Pommerin, Reiner. *Der Kaiser und Amerika: Die USA in der Politik der Reichsleitung, 1890–1917*. Cologne, Vienna, 1986.
Portes, Jacques. "L'européanisation des Etats-Unis vue par les Français (1870–1914)," *Revue française d'études américaines* 12 (1982), 51–64.
Potter, Pamela. *Most German of the Arts: Musicology and Society from the Weimar Republic to the End of Hitler's Reich*. New Haven, 1998.
Pyta, Wolfram. "Konzert der Mächte und kollektives Sicherheitssystem: Neue Wege zwischenstaatlicher Friedenswahrung in Europa nach dem Wiener Kongreß," in *Jahrbuch des Historischen Kollegs*. Munich, 1996.
Radkau, Joachim. *Das Zeitalter der Nervosität: Deutschland zwischen Bismarck und Hitler*. Darmstadt, 1998.
Raithel, Thomas. *Das Wunder der inneren Einheit: Studien zur deutschen und französischen Öffentlichkeit bei Beginn des Ersten Weltkrieges*. Bonn, 1996.
Rauchensteiner, Manfried. *Der Tod des Doppeladlers: Österreich-Ungarn und der Erste Weltkrieg*. Graz, 1993.
Reimann, Aribert. *Der große Krieg der Sprachen: Untersuchungen zur historischen Semantik in Deutschland und England zur Zeit des Ersten Weltkriegs*. Essen, 2000.
Reinermann, Lothar. *Der Kaiser in England: Wilhelm II und sein Bild in der britischen Öffentlichkeit*. Paderborn et al., 2001.
Reshef, Ouriel. *Guerre, mythes et caricature: Au berceau d'une mentalité francaise*. Paris, 1984.
Richardson, James L. *Crisis Diplomacy: The Great Powers since the Mid-Nineteenth Century*. Cambridge, 1994.
Richert, Dominik Richert. *Beste Gelegenheit zum Sterben: Meine Erlebnisse im Kriege 1914–1918*, edited by Angelika Tramitz und Bernd Ulrich. Munich, 1989.
Rickards, Maurice. *Posters of the First World War*. New York, 1968.
Riordan, James. *Sport in Soviet Society: Development of Sport and Physical Education in Russia and the USSR*. Cambridge, 1977.

Ritter, Gerhard A., ed. *Deutsche Parteien vor 1918*. Köln, 1973.
Ritter, Gerhard. *Staatskunst und Kriegshandwerk: Das Problem des "Militarismus" in Deutschland*, vol. 1–4. Munich, 1954–68.
Ritter, Gerhard. *The Schlieffen Plan: Critique of a Myth*. London, 1958.
Rock, Stephan R. *Why Peace Breaks Out: Great Power Rapprochement in Historical Perspective.* Chapel Hill and London 1989.
Roelker, Nancy L. and Charles K. Warner, eds. *Two Hundred Years of Franco-American Relations: Papers of the Bicentennial Colloquium of the Society for French Historical Studies in Newport, Rhode Island, September 7–10, 1978.* n.p., n.d., (1978?).
Rohkrämer, Thomas. *Der Militarismus der "kleinen Leute": Die Kriegervereine im Deutschen Kaiserreich, 1871–1914.* Munich, 1990.
Röhl, John C. G. "Germany," in *Decisions for War, 1914*, Keith Wilson, ed. New York, 1995.
Röhl, John C.G. "Admiral von Müller and the Approach of War, 1911–1914," *The Historical Journal* 12,4 (1969), 651–673.
Ropponen, Risto. *Die russische Gefahr: das Verhalten der öffentlichen Meinung Deutschlands und Österreich-Ungarns gegenüber der Aussenpolitik Russlands in der Zeit zwischen dem Frieden von Portsmouth und dem Ausbruch des Ersten Weltkriegs.* Helsinki, 1976.
Rosenberger, Bernhard. *Zeitungen als Kriegstreiber? Die Rolle der Presse im Vorfeld des Ersten Weltkrieges.* Köln, 1998.
Rouse, Ruth and Stephan Charles Neill. *Geschichte der ökumenischen Bewegung 1517–1948*, vol. 6, part 2. Göttingen, 1958.
Rouse, Ruth. *The World's Student Christian Federation*. London, 1948.
Rother, Rainer, ed. "Les Atrocités Allemandes" (1914–15), in *Die letzten Tage der Menschheit: Bilder des Ersten Weltkrieges.* Berlin, 1994.
Ruedorffer, J. J. [i.e. Kurt Riezler] *Grundzüge der Weltpolitik in der Gegenwart.* Stuttgart and Berlin, 1914.
Rumpler, Helmut and Jan Niederkorn, eds. *Der "Zweibund" 1879: Das deutsch - österreichisch-ungarische Bündnis und die europäische Diplomatie: Zentraleuropa-Studien, Band 2, Tagungsband des 3: Deutsch-Österreichischen Historikergesprächs in Wien, 27–29 Oktober 1994.* Vienna, 1996.
Rumpler, Helmut. *Eine Chance für Mitteleuropa: bürgerliche Emanzipation und Staatsverfall in der Habsburgermonarchie.* Vienna, 1997.
Saburo, Shimada. "Jikyoku gaiken" [Survey of the Situation], *Chuo koron* (November 1914).
Saloman, Ernst von. *Der Fragebogen.* Reinbek, 1951.
Sanborn, Joshua A. *Drafting the Russian Nation: Military Conscription, Total War, and Mass Politics, 1905–1925.* DeKalb, 2003.
Sanborn, Joshua. "The Mobilization of 1914 and the Question of the Russian Nation: A Reexamination," *Slavic Review* 59 (2000).
Schöllgen, Gregor. "Richard von Kühlmann und das deutsch-englische Verhältnis 1912–1914. Zur Bedeutung der Peripherie in der europäischen Vorkriegspolitik," in *Historische Zeitschrift* 230 (1980).
Schöllgen, Gregor. *Imperialismus und Gleichgewicht: Deutschland, England und die orientalische Frage 1871–1914.* Munich, 2000.
Schonberg, Harold. *The Lives of Great Composers.* 3rd ed. New York, 1997.
Schottelius, Herbert and Wilhelm Deist, eds. *Marine und Marinepolitik im kaiserlichen Deutschland 1871–1914.* 2nd ed. Düsseldorf, 1981.
Schröder, Hans-Jürgen. *Confrontation and Cooperation: Germany and the United States in the Era of World War I, 1900–1924.* Providence, 1993.
Schroeder, Paul W. "Comment: The Luck of the House of Habsburg: Military Defeat and Political Survival," *Austrian History Yearbook* 32 (2001), 215–24.
Schroeder, Paul W. "Embedded Counterfactuals and World War I as an Unavoidable War," in *Systems, Stability and Statecraft: Essays on the International History of Modern Europe,* David Wetzel, Robert Jervis, and Jack S. Levy, eds. New York, 2004.

Schroeder, Paul W. *Austria, Great Britain and the Crimean War: The Destruction of the European Concert.* Ithaca, London, 1972.
Schroeder, Paul W. *The Transformation of European Politics, 1763–1848.* Oxford, 1994.
Schulte, Bernd-Felix. *Die Verfälschung der Riezler Tagebücher.* Frankfurt am Main, Bern, New York, 1985.
Schulte, Bernd-Felix. "Neue Dokumente zu Kriegsausbruch und Kriegsverlauf 1914," *Militärgeschichtliche Mitteilungen,* 25 (1979).
Schulthess' Europäischer Geschichtskalender 55 (1914).
Schulz, Matthias. "'Wächter der Zivilisation'? Institutionelle Merkmale und normative Grundlagen des Europäischen Konzerts im 19. Jahrhundert," in *Historische Mitteilungen* (HMRG), 17 (2004), 35–47.
Schulz, Matthias. "Normen und Netzwerke in der internationalen Geschichte," in *HMRG* 17 (2004), 1–13.
Schulz, Matthias. *Das Europäische Konzert der Großmächte als Sicherheitsrat: Normen und Praxis plurilateraler Konfliktlösung, 1815–1852,* post-doctoral dissertation [*Habilschrift*]. Rostock, 2001.
Scott, J. F. *Five Weeks: The Surge of Public Opinion on the Eve of the Great War.* New York, 1973.
Scott, James Brown, *Rapports faits aux conférences de La Haye de 1899 et 1907.* Oxford, 1920.
Scott, James Brown, ed. *Texts of the Peace Conferences at Hague, 1899 and 1907. With English Translation and Appendix of Related Documents.* Boston, 1908
Seigo, Nakano. "Taisenran to kokumin no kakugo" [The Great War and the Peoples' Preparedness], *Nihon oyobi Nihonjin* (15 September 1914).
Seligmann, Matthew S. "'A Barometer of National Confidence': A British Assessment of the Role of Insecurity in the Formulation of German Military Policy before the First World War," *The English Historical Review* 117, 471 (2002), 333–36.
Sentaro, Kemuyama. "Doran kanchu no ni kanso" [Two Impressions of the Disturbance], *Gaiko jiho* (1 September 1914).
Serif, Mehmed. *Edirne Vilayetinden Rumlar Niçin Gitmek İstiyorlar? İzmir Mebusu Emanuelidi Efendi'ye* [Why Do Greek Ottomans Want to Leave Edirne Province? A Letter to Emanuelidi Efendi, Member of the Chamber of Deputies from Izmir]. Edirne: Edirne Sanai'i Mektebi Matbaası, 1330 [March 1914–March 1915].
Seymour, Charles, ed. *The Intimate Papers of Colonel House.* 2 vols. London, 1926.
Shanafelt, Gary. *The Secret Enemy: Austria-Hungary and the German Alliance, 1914–1918.* New York, 1985.
Siegmund-Schultze, Friedrich. *Friedenskirche, Kaffeeklappe und die ökumenische Vision: Texte 1910–1969,* edited by Wolfgang Grünberg. Munich, 1990.
Simmel, Georg. *Soziologie: Untersuchungen über die Formen der Vergesellschaftung.* Frankfurt, 1992.
Sked, Alan. *The Decline and Fall of the Habsburg Monarchy, 1815–1918.* 2nd ed. Harlow, England, 2001.
Snyder, Jack. "Civil-Military Relations and the Cult of the Offensive, 1914 and 1984," *International Security* 9, 1 (1984), 108–46.
Snyder, Jack. *The Ideology of the Offensive: Military Decision Making and the Disasters of 1914.* Ithaca, NY, 1984.
Sondhaus, Lawrence. *Franz Conrad von Hötzendorf: Architect of the Apocalypse.* Boston, 2000.
Sowards, Steven W. *Austria's Policy of Macedonian Reform.* Boulder, CO, 1989.
Städtische Sparkasse, Freiburg. *Rechenschafts-Bericht für das Jahr 1914.* Freiburg, 1915.
Standage, Tom. *The Victorian Internet: The Remarkable Story of the Telegraph and the Nineteenth Century's On-Line Pioneers.* New York, 1998.
Stead, W. T. *The Americanisation of the World.* London, 1902.
Steiner, Zara S. *Britain and the Origins of the First World War.* Basingstoke and London, 1995 (first edition 1977).
Stengel, Baron Karl von. *Weltstaat und Friedensproblem.* Berlin, 1909.
Stevenson, David. "The Militarization of European Diplomacy before 1914", *International Security* 22, 1 (1997), 125–61.

Stevenson, David. "War by Timetable? The Railway Race before 1914," *Past & Present*, 162 (1999), 179–80.
Stevenson, David. *Armaments and the Coming of War: Europe, 1904–1914.* Oxford, 1996.
Stevenson, Richard L. *The Rise and Fall of Detente: Relaxations of Tension in US-Soviet Relations, 1953–1984.* London, 1985.
Stewart, Frank Henderson. *Honor.* Chicago, 1994.
Stockdale, Melissa K. "'My Death for the Motherland Is Happiness': Women, Patriotism, and Soldiering in Russia's Great War, 1914–1917," *American Historical Review* 109, 1 (2004).
Stoddard, John L. *John L. Stoddard's Lectures.* 10 vols. Chicago, 1897.
Storz, Dieter. *Kriegsbild und Rüstung vor 1914: Europäische Landstreitkräfte vor dem Ersten Weltkrieg.* Herford, 1992.
Strachan, Hew. *The First World War. Volume I: To Arms.* Oxford, 2001.
Sträter, Udo. *Sonthom, Bayly, Dyke und Hall. Studien zur Rezeption der englischen Erbauungsliteratur in Deutschland im 17. Jahrhundert,* Tübingen, 1987.
Şükrü Hanioğlu, M. *Preparation for a Revolution: The Young Turks, 1902–1908.* New York, 2001.
Sumida, Jon T. *In Defence of Naval Supremacy: Finance, Technology, and British Naval Policy 1889–1914.* London, 1989.
Takashi, Ito, ed., *Taisho shoki Yamagata Aritomo danwa hikki* [Record of Yamagata Aritomo's Conversations in Early Taisho]. Tokyo, 1981.
Taylor, A. J. P. *The Struggle for Mastery in Europe, 1848–1918.* Oxford and New York, 1954.
Taylor, A.J.P. *War by Timetable: How the First World War Began.* London, 1969.
Taylor, Seth. *Left-Wing Nietzscheans: The Politics of German Expressionism, 1910–1920.* New York, 1990.
Thompson, John A. *Woodrow Wilson: Profiles in Power.* London, 2002.
Tirpitz, Alfred v. *My Memoirs.* London, 1919.
Tirpitz, Alfred v. *Politische Dokumente,* vol. I, *Der Aufbau der deutschen Weltmacht.* Stuttgart and Berlin, 1924.
Tirpitz, Alfred von Tirpitz. *Politische Dokumente: Deutsche Ohnmachtspolitik im Weltkriege.* Hamburg and Berlin, 1926.
Tobisch, Manfred. *Das Deutschlandbild der Diplomatie Österreich-Ungarns von 1908–1914.* Frankfurt am Main, Berlin, Bern, 1994.
Tolstoy, Leo. "Christianity and Patriotism," in *Writings on Civil Disobedience and Nonviolence.* Philadelphia, 1987.
Leo Tolstoy, "Patriotism, or Peace?," in *Writings on Civil Disobedinece and Nonviolence.* Philadelphia, 1987.
Tolstoy, Leo. *Anna Karenina,* translated by Richard Pevear and Larissa Volokhonsky. New York, 2000.
Toprak, Zafer. *Milli İktisat-Milli Burjuvazi: Türkiye'de Ekonomi ve Toplum (1908–1950).* Türkiye Araştırmaları, no. 14. Ankara, 1995.
Trebilcock, Clive. *The Industrialization of the Continental Powers 1780–1914.* London, 1981.
Treitschke, Heinrich von. *Politics.* New York, 1916.
Trommler, Frank and Joseph McVeigh, eds. *America and the Germans: An Assessment of a Three-Hundred Year History,* vol. 2. Philadelphia, 1985.
Trotha, A. von. *Volkstum und Staatsführung: Briefe und Aufzeichnungen aus den Jahren 1915–1920.* Berlin, 1928.
Troy, Nancy. *Modernism and the Decorative Arts in France: Art Nouveau to Le Corbusier.* New Haven, CT, London, 1991.
Tsuneo, Izu. "Oshu taisenkan" [Perspective on the Great European War], *Nihon oyobi Nihonjin* (15 October 1914).
Tunstall, Jr. Graydon A., *Planning for War Against Russia and Serbia: Austro-Hungarian and German Military Strategies, 1871–1914.* New York, 1993.

Turk, Gayle. "The Case of Dr. Karl Muck: Anti-German Hysteria and Enemy Alien Internment During World War I." Undergraduate thesis, Harvard University, 1994.
Ullrich, Volker. *Kriegsalltag.* Cologne, 1982.
Ullrich, Volker. "Das deutsche Kalkül in der Julikrise 1914 und die Frage der englischen Neutralität," *Geschichte in Wissenschaft und Unterricht* 34 (1983).
Ungern-Sternberg, Wolfgang von. *Der Aufruf "An die Kulturwelt": Das Manifest der 93 und die Anfänge der Kulturpropaganda im Ersten Weltkrieg.* Stuttgart, 1996.
Vagts, Alfred. *Deutschland und die Vereinigten Staaten in der Weltpolitik.* 2 vols. New York, 1935.
Veer, Peter van der and Hartmut Lehmann, eds. *Nation and Religion. Perspectives on Europe and Asia.* Princeton, NJ 1999.
Verhey, Jeffrey. *The Spirit of 1914: Militarism, Myth, and Mobilization in Germany.* Cambridge, 2000.
Vermes, Gabor. *István Tisza: The Liberal Vision and Conservative Statecraft of a Magyar Nationalist.* New York, 1985.
Verosta, Stephan. *Kollektivaktionen der Mächte des Europäischen Konzerts (1886–1914).* Vienna, 1988.
Vogel, Jakob. "Military, Folklore, Eigensinn: Folkloric Militarism in Germany and France, 1871–1914," *Central European History* 33, 4 (2000), 487–504.
Wahlde, Peter von. "Military Thought in Imperial Russia." PhD diss., Indiana University, 1966.
Walzer, Michael. *Just and Unjust Wars: A Moral Argument with Historical Illustrations.* New York, 1977.
Watt, D. C. "The British Reactions to the Assassination at Sarajevo," *European Studies Review* 1 (1970).
Wawro, Geoffrey. "The Habsburg Flucht nach vorne in 1866: Domestic Political Origins of the Austro-Prussian War," *The International History Review* 17, 2 (May 1995), 221–48.
Weber, Eugen. *The Nationalist Revival in France, 1905–1914.* Berkeley, 1968.
Weber, Max. *Economy and Society: An Outline of Interpretive Sociology*, vol. 2, edited by Guenther Roth and Claus Wittich. Berkeley, 1978.
Weber, Max. *Zur Politik im Weltkrieg: Schriften und Reden 1914–1918.* Tübingen, 1988.
Webster, Charles K. *The Art and Practice of Diplomacy.* New York, 1961.
Wegner, Bernd, ed. *Wie Kriege enden: Wege zum Frieden von der Antike bis zur Gegenwart.* Paderborn, 2002.
Wehler, Hans-Ulrich. *Bismarck und der Imperialismus.* Cologne, 1969.
Weinberg, Barbara H., Doreen Bolger, and David Park Curry, eds. *American Impressionism and Realism: The Painting of Modern Life, 1885–1995.* New York, 1994.
Weiss, John, ed. *The Origins of Modern Consciousness.* Detroit, 1965.
Wernecke, Klaus. *Der Wille zur Weltgeltung: Aussenpolitik und Öffentlichkeit im Kaiserreich am Vorabend des Ersten Weltkrieges.* Düsseldorf, 1970.
Westlake, John. *International Law*, vol. 1, *Peace.* 2nd edition. Cambridge, 1910.
Westlake, John. *The Collected Papers of John Westlake on Public International Law*, Part 1, edited by Lassa Oppenheim, Cambridge, 1914.
Williamson, Jr., Samuel R. "Confrontation with Serbia: The Consequences of Vienna's Failure to Achieve Surprise in July 1914," *Mitteilungen des Österreichischen Staatsarchiv* 43 (1993).
Williamson, Jr., Samuel R. "Influence, Power, and the Policy Process: The Case of Franz Ferdinand, 1906–1914," *The Historical Journal* 17 (1974), 17–34.
Williamson, Jr., Samuel R. *Austria-Hungary and the Origins of the First World War.* Basingstoke and New York, 1991, 1993.
Williamson, Jr., Samuel R. and Russ Van Wyk. *July 1914: Soldiers, Statesmen, and the Coming of the Great War: A Brief Documentary History.* Boston, 2003.
Willis, Irene. *England's Holy War.* New York, 1928.
Wilsberg, Klaus. *"Terrible ami - aimable ennemi": Kooperation und Konflikt in den deutsch-französischen Beziehungen 1911–1914.* Bonn, 1998.
Witkop, Philipp. "Der deutsche Unterricht," in *Der Weltkrieg im Unterricht.* Gotha, 1915.
Witkop, Philipp, ed. *Kriegsbriefe gefallener Studenten.* Munich, 1928.

Wohl, Robert. *The Generation of 1914*. Cambridge, 1979.
Woodrow Wilson Papers, Volume XXX. Princeton, NJ 1966.
World Alliance of Churches for Promoting International Friendship. "The Churches and International Friendship," Report of Conference Held at Constance, 1914. London and New York, [n.d.].
Wortman, Richard. *Scenarios of Power: Myth and Ceremony in Russian Monarchy*. 2 vols. Studies of the Harriman Institute. Princeton, NJ, 1995.
Wulsin Family Papers, Series I, Box 24, Folder 1, Cincinnati Historical Society.
Wysocki, Josef. *150 Jahre Sparkasse Freiburg*. Freiburg, 1976.
Yoshitake, Oka. *Yamagata Aritomo: Meiji Nihon no shocho* [Yamagata Aritomo: Symbol of Meiji Japan]. Tokyo, 1958.
Young, Louise. *Japan's Total Empire: Manchuria and the Culture of Wartime Imperialism*. Berkeley, 1997.
Young, Robert J. *Marketing Marianne: French Propaganda in America, 1900–1940*. New Brunswick, NJ, 2004.
Zentner, Kurt. *Kaiserliche Zeiten: Wilhelm II. und seine Ära in Bildern und Dokumenten*. Munich, 1964.
Ziemann, Benjamin. *Front und Heimat: Ländliche Kriegserfahrung im südlichen Bayern 1914–1923*. Essen, 1997.
Zorn, Philipp. *Das Deutsche Reich und die internationale Schiedsgerichtsbarkeit*. Berlin, 1911.
Zuber, Terence. *Inventing the Schlieffen Plan: German War Planning, 1871–1914*. Oxford, 2002.
Zukin, Kuro (pseudo.), "Kono toki" [At this Time], *Chuo koron* (Fall 1914).
Zweig, Stefan. *Die Welt von Gestern: Erinnerungen eines Europäers*. Frankfurt, 1992.

INDEX

A
Aberdeen, George Gordon, 4th Earl of, 49
Abrams, Ray, 267
Adler, Victor, 174
Aerenthal, Alois, 36–7, 39
Afflerbach, Holger, 2,5, 6, 39,145
Aksakal, Mustafa, 8, 10
Albert, King of Belgium, 311
Albertini, Luigi, 1,165
Alexander II, 28
Allen, Woody, 271, 280
Amourel, General, 108
Applegate, Celia, 276
Ardagh, John, 103
Arago, Admiral, 108
Aritomo, Yamagata, 306, 308, 311
Arndt, Ernst Moritz, 242
Armold, Thomas, 242
Asquith, Herbert, 105, 163, 235
Axenfeld, Karl, 261

B
Baker, J. Allen, 263–4
Balfour, Arthur James, 105
Ballin, Albert, 164
Baudelaire, Charles, 273
Baumgart, Winfried, 44
Baykut, Cami, 296
Bebel, August, 173
Becker, Jean-Jacques, 2, 174, 201, 203–4
Beckmann, Max, 202, 276
Beernaert, Auguste, 101
Beethoven, Ludwig von, 276, 279, 326
Behnen, Michael, 36–7
Belinski, Leon, 68–70
Bennet, Arnold, 325
Benson, Frank, 273
Berchtold, Leopold, 62, 64–5, 67–72, 174, 190
Berndt, Otto, 155
Bernhardi, Friedrich von, 194, 306
Bertrab, Karl Hermann von, 80–1

Bethmann Hollweg, Theobold von, 53, 55, 70, 78, 81–7, 120, 122–26, 138, 140, 142, 166, 174, 188, 191, 261, 279
Bieberstein, Adolf Freiherr Marschall von, 113
Bille, 100
Bismarck, Otto von, 28, 30, 37–8, 116, 311
Bloch, Ivan, 305
Blücher, Gebhard Leberecht von, 242
Blumhardt, Christoph Friedrich, 267
Böcklin, Arnold, 276
Bolivar, Simon, 321
Bonaparte, Napoleon, 21–22, 39, 216, 239, 242, 276, 295, 305
Bourgeois, Leon, 100, 107, 109
Brooke, Rupert, 236
Bryan, William Jennings, 325
Bülow, Bernhard von, 76, 120, 126
Bundy, McGerorge, 140
Burián, Istvan, 62, 64
Burgess, John W., 327
Bush, George W., 64

C
Cadart, 273
Calvin, John, 258, 267
Canning, George, 49
Capelle, Eduard von, 80, 82, 124
Carnegie, Andrew, 109, 263–5, 267, 305
Carter, Jimmy, xii, 3, 11
Cartwright, Fairfax, 189
Cary, Joyce, 163
Castlereagh, Robert Stewart, 2. Marquess of Londonderry and Viscount, 46
Cavour, Camillo, 21, 28
Chamberlain, Joseph, 275
Charykov, 36
Chickering, Roger, 6, 200
Churchill, Randolf, 275
Churchill, Winston, 113–14, 125–26, 136, 280
Clausewitz, Carl von, 239–40

Conrad von Hötzendorf, Franz Graf, 5, 20, 64, 67–70, 141, 150–51, 153–57, 167
Cooper, John Milton, 320, 324, 332
Cooper, Sandi, 220
Corinth, Lovis, 276
Crozier, 103
Curzon, George Nathaniel, 275
Custance, Reginald, 118

D

Daikichiro, Tagawa, 311
Damvosch, Leopold, 277–78
Daniels, Emil, 187, 192
Deissmann, Adolf, 266, 268
Delcassé, Théophile, 29
Dickinson, Frederick, 8
Dill, Ludwig, 276
Dryander, Ernst von, 264
Dülffer, Jost, 4, 7, 9, 144, 220
Dupuis, Charles, 52
Durand-Ruel, Paul, 273
Durnovo, Petr, 223–24

E

Edward, VII, 119
Elliot, Charles W., 326–27, 332
Emmel, Joseph, 206
Emura, Asada, 307
Endicott, Mary, 275
Endres, Fritz, 162
Engels, Friedrich, 173
Epkenhans, Michael, 5, 9
Euken, Rudolf, 203

F

Falkenhayn, Erich von, 78, 80, 83–4, 87–8, 142, 163, 168–69
Farrar, Lancelot, 151
Ferguson, Niall, 138
Fisher, Sir John Arbuthnot, 103, 105, 114, 118
Forgách von Ghymes und Gocs, Graf Johann, 191
Förster, Stig, 152
Franz Ferdinand, xiii, 22, 54, 64, 65–8, 72, 79, 80, 140, 155–56, 288, 297
Franz Joesph, 52, 55, 61–2, 64–6, 68–9, 71, 87, 186, 235
Frederick the Great, 167
Frevert, Ute, 7, 9, 233
Fried, Alfred, 191
Fries, Karl, 260
Freud, Sigmund 204
Fry, Edward, 109

G

Gadski, Johanna, 279
Gakuin, Aoyama, 307
Galster, Karl, 107
Galsworthy, John, 325
Gambart, Ernest, 273
Gambetta, Léon, 242
Ganz, Rudolph, 277
Geinitz, Christian, 204–5, 208
George V, 84–6, 88
George, David Lloyd, 75, 77, 123, 163, 172, 237, 245
Genji, Shibukawa, 314
Gienow-Hecht, Jessica C. E., 7, 8, 10
Gilinsky, 99, 101
Giolitti, Giovanni, 165, 167
Glackens, William, 273
Gladstone, William, 38
Gneisenau, August Graf Neidhardt von, 242
Godowski, Leopold, 279
Goethe, Johann Wolfgang von, 326
Goltz, Colman von der, 296
Goluchowski, Agenor, 30
Goschen, Edward, 120, 122
Grey, Sir Edward, 52, 83,85–6, 105–9, 123–26, 135, 140, 184, 189–90, 236–37, 330–31
Grigorovich, I. K., 139
Gunji, Muko, 309

H

Haffner, Sebastian, 161, 169
Hakki, Hafiz, 293, 295–96
Haldane, Richard Burdon, 105, 124, 185, 188
Hamilton, Richard, 1
Hanzan, Ishikawa, 313
Harbutt, Frazer J., 9, 320
Harbutt, Frazer J., 320
Hardie, Keir, 236
Hardinge, Charles, 122
Harnack, Adolf von, 261, 264, 268
Haupt, Georges, 174
Hauptmann, Gerhard, 326
Hayes, C. J. H., 268
Heim, Karl, 264
Heinrich, Prince of Prussia, 84–6
Herwig, Holger, 1
Hess, Rudolf, 84
Hilmi, Şehbenderzade Ahmed, 294–95
Hirobumi, Ito, 311
Hirondo, Tonuzu, 308, 309
Hitler, Adolf, xiv, 268
Hobsbawm, Eric, 6, 164, 171, 184
Hobson, Rolf, 96
Hoffmann, Stanley, 45

Hohenlohe, Gottfried, 68
Holstein, Friedrich von, 106
Hopman, Albert, 169
House, Edward, 79, 164
Hoyos, Alexander, 67, 69–70, 163
Humbert, Charles, 137
Hus, Johann, 265

I
Iemitsu, Tokugama, 311
Ieyasu, Tokugawa, 311
Ihsan, Ali, 293
Ingenohl, Friedrich von, 82
Isaac, Jules, 174
Izvolski, Aleksandr Petrovich, 34, 36–9, 108

J
Jagow, Gottlieb von, 78, 138, 187, 191
Jaurès, Jean, 162
Jerome, Jennie, 275
Joll, James, I, 164, 170, 174
Jordan, David Starr, 326, 332
Joseph, Karl Franz, 67

K
Kailer, Karl, 70
Kakunari, Uma, 314
Kanjo, Tani, 304, 306
Kant, Emmanuel, 53, 326
Kaoru, Inoue, 312
Karabekir, Kazim, 293
Karnebeek, von, 100
Kautsky, Karl, 76
Kazan, Kayahara, 306
Keizo, Yamaguchi, 306, 307
Kennan, George, xiii, 213
Kennedy, John F., xiv
Kennedy, Paul, 126
Kessler, Harry, 244
Kiderlen-Wächter, Alfred von, 166–67, 188
Kießling, Friedrich, 6, 10
Kikou, Wada, 313
Kinglake, Alexander, 52
Kipling, Rudyard, 325
Kissinger, Henry, 22
Klemperer, Victor, 183
Köpke, Friedrich, 153
Koselleck, Reinhard, 174
Koskenniemi, Martti, 53
Kuniaki, Koiso, 316
Krivoshein, A. V., 224
Krobatin, Alex, 64, 68, 71
Kronenbitter, Günther, 5
Kruse, Wolfgang, 209

Külmann, Richard von, 166
Kutter, Hermann, 264

L
Lambert, Nicholas, 119
Lawrence, T. J., 52
Lee of Fareham, Viscount Arthur, 119
Lehmann, Hartmut, 7–9
Leiter, Mary, 275
Lenbach, Franz von, 276
Lenin, Vladimir, 174
Leo XIII, 30
Leslie, John, 64
Lichnowsky, Karl Max, 55, 83–4, 86, 88, 138
Liverpool, Robert Jenkinson, 2nd Earl of, 46
Lorimer, James, 52
Luck, Gary, xiii
Luther, Martin, 258, 267
Luxemburg, Rosa, 206
Lyncker, Moriz Freiherr von, 80, 82, 163

M
MacDonald, Ramsay, 236
Mahan, Alfred Thayer, 100, 102, 107, 114, 117
Maklavkov, Vasilii, 225
Mann, Heinrich, 183
Mann, Thomas, 183
Manzo, Watanab, 313
Martynov, E. I., 215
Masao, Kanbe, 314
May, Ernest, 324, 330
McKinley, William, 321
McMaster, John Bach, 324
Medlicott, William Norton, 45
Meinecke, Friedrich, 202
Meinhof, Carl, 262
Menzel, Adolph, 276
Mérey, Kajetan von, 175
Metternich, Clemens Wenzel Lothar von, 46, 49
Michaelis, Georg, 261, 264
Miliukov, Pavel, 220
Mizutaro, Takogi, 305
Moltke, Helmuth von, 5, 64, 71, 78, 83, 87–8, 120, 137–38, 141–42, 149–53, 155–57, 163, 167–69, 241, 242
Mombauer, Annika, 151–52
Mommsen, Wolfgang Justin, 6, 164, 167, 170, 175
Moore, John Basset, 332
Motokawa, Gorai, 311
Mott, John R., 260–64
Mozart, Wolfgang, 277
Muck, Karl, 272, 278
Müller, Karl Alexander von, 83, 85, 87, 172

Müller, Sven Oliver, 209
Muraviev, Michail, 95–6, 98

N
Napoleon III, 28
Nauman, Victor, 67
Nelidow, 109
Nelson, Horatio, 87
Nesselrode, Karl Robert Graf von, 49
Nicholas II, xiv, 7, 39, 76, 83, 85–6, 186–87, 216, 219, 224–25
Nicolson, Arthur, 124, 187, 189
Nietzsche, Friedrich, 327
Nipperdey, Thomas, 200–01
Nixon, Richard, xiv
Nobel, Alfred (did not find)
Nunn, Sam, xiii

O
Oberhoffer, Emil, 272
Oldham, Joseph H., 262

P
Page, Walter, 88, 322
Palmerston, Henry John Temple Viscount, 49
Pansa, Alberto, 163, 165
Pasha, Enver, 288, 290–93, 299
Pasha, Said Halim, 288, 292–93
Pašić, Nikola, 72
Penn, William, 257
Persius, Lothar, 107
Peter the Great, 218
Pichon, Stephen, 107
Plenge, Johann, 203
Plessen, Hans von, 80
Poe, Edgar Allan, 273
Pohl, Hugo von, 83, 85
Poincaré, Raymond, 136, 139, 162, 311
Pollard, Sidney, 45
Pollio, Alberto, 150
Portuael, Den Beer, 99
Potiorek, Oscar, 69
Powell, Baden, 218
Powell, Colin, xiii
Princip, Gavrillo, 140
Prokofii, 222

R
Rade, Marin, 264
Raithel, Thomas, 204, 207–08
Recai, 295
Rechberg, Johann Bernhard Graf, 37
Redlich, Joseph, 171
Ren, Nakashoji, 311
Renoir, Jean, 240

Rhodes, Cecil, 275
Richert, Dominik, 162
Richter, Julius, 262
Riezler, Kurt, 166–67
Ritter, Gerhard, 152
Rohkrämer, Thomas, 168
Röhl, John, 4, 9, 75
Roon, Albrecht von, 143
Rosenberger, Bernhard, 171
Roosevelt, Theodore, 105, 107, 321
Rouse, Ruth, 261

S
Salomon, Ernst von, 1, 163
San Giuliano, Antonio di, 165
Sanborn, Joshua A., 7, 213
Sanders, Liman von, 139
Sauer, Emil, 277
Sazonov, Sergei, 224
Schaff, Philip, 259
Scharnhorst, Gerhard von, 242
Schellendorff, Günther Bronsurt von, 80
Schemua, Blasius, 155
Schiff, Jacob, 327
Schiller, Friedrich, 246
Schlieffen, Alfred von, 152–53, 168
Schön, Wilhelm Freiherr von, 189
Schönleber, Gustav, 276
Schroeder, Paul, 2, 3, 9
Schüching, Walther, 110
Schulz, Matthias, 3
Schwarzhoff, Karl Julius von Groß genannt von, 99–100
Sebiha, N., 298
Seigo, Nakano, 313
Selborne, Wiliam Waldegrove Palmer Earl of, 114
Seligman, E. R. A., 328
Shimada, 316
Siegmund-Schultze, Friedrich, 264–66
Simmel, George, 237
Smiley, Albert, 263
Snyder, Jack 141
Söderbloom, Nathan, 268
Spiecker, Albert, 266
Staal, Baron de, 99
Stead, William, 108, 321
Stengel, Karl von, 53
Stevenson, David, 5, 9, 130
Stolypin, Peter, 39, 217
Strauss, Johann, 277–78
Strumm, Wilhelm von, 78, 84
Stürgleh, Karl, 64, 68, 70

Sukhomlinov, Vladimir 139–40
Sumida, Jon, 119
Szápáry, Friedrich, 68, 187
Szilas, Julius Szilassy von, 165–66
Szögyény, Ladislaus, 69, 80

T
Taft, William Howard, 312, 321
Takaaki, Kato, 303, 312, 315
Takashi, Hara, 305
Tanczos, Gabriel, 156
Tani, Viscount, 315
Taube, Baron, 224
Thibaud, Jacques, 279
Thomas, Theodore, 277–78
Thomson, Gaston, 107
Tirpitz, Alfred von, 5, 78, 82, 84, 87, 113–14, 117–26, 134, 169
Tisza, István, 62, 64–5, 67–72, 140
Tocqueville, Alexis de, 321
Tolstoy, Leo, 221–23, 226–27
Torrey, Reuben Archer, 264
Treitschke, Heinrich von, 248–49, 327
Truman, Harry, xii
Trumpener, Ulrich, 291
Tschirschky, Heinrich von, 68, 70, 83–4, 193
Tsuneo, Izu, 316
Tuchman, Barbara, xiv
Twain, Mark, 275

V
Valentini, Rudolf von, 87
Vanderbilt, Consuelo, 275
Verhey, Jeffrey, 201, 204
Victoria, Queen, 47
Virgil, 96, 109
Vittorio, Emanuele III, 165

Viviani, Renè, 139, 162
Volbach, Felix, 277

W
Wagner, Richard, 271
Waldersee, Georg Graf von, 78, 138, 142, 150, 168
Wangenheim, Hans von, 293
Warneck, Johannes, 262
Weber, Max, 233–34, 237, 245–46
Wedel, Georg von 81, 82
Weiss, Joseph, 279
Wells, H. G., 325
Wenninger, Karl Ritter von, 87, 162
Westlake, John, 52
Wilamowitz-Moellendorff, Ulrich von, 203
Wilhelm II, Kaiser, 62, 64–5, 67–8, 70, 75–88, 106–107, 116–17, 119, 123–25, 135, 140, 142, 163, 173, 186–87, 189, 193, 195, 224, 235, 264, 276, 278, 309, 311, 315, 323
Williamson, Samuel, 4, 10, 150
Wilsberg, Klaus, 167
Wilson, Keith, 1
Wilson, Woodrow, xv, 77, 79, 88, 321–24, 331–32
Witkop, Philipp, 246
Witte, Sergius, 34
Wohl, Robert, 174

Y–Z
Young, Robert, 274
Zorn, Philipp, 53
Zuber, Terence, 152
Zumtobel, Reinhard, 206
Zweig, Stefan, 162, 167

www.ingramcontent.com/pod-product-compliance
Lightning Source LLC
Chambersburg PA
CBHW071953290426
44109CB00018B/2003